Jimi Hendrix
Experience The Music

Belmo and Steve Loveless

From the cover of the bootleg release JIMI HENDRIX

We acknowledge the financial support of the Government of Canada through
the Book Publishing Industry Development Program for our publishing activities.
Published by Collector's Guide Publishing Inc., Box 62034,
Burlington, Ontario, Canada, L7R 4K2
Printed and bound in Canada by Webcom Ltd of Toronto
Jimi Hendrix Experience The Music / Belmo & Steve Loveless
ISBN 1-896522-45-9

Jimi Hendrix Experience The Music

Belmo and Steve Loveless

1998

From the cover of the bootleg release RIOTS IN BERKELEY

Front Cover Art by Monika Danneman
Back Cover Art by George Soister
Cover Design by Steve Loveless
Book Design & Layout by Belmo

Table Of Contents

Art by Sara Gauthier
See page 179 for details

Acknowledgements

The authors would like to thank the following people for all their help in making this book possible: Noel Redding, Bob Walker (Hot Wacks Press), Ric Connors (C.G. Publishing), Uli Jon Roth, The Steve Miller Band (especially Steve Miller, Gerry Stickells, Norton Buffalo and Billy Peterson), Terri Belmer, Joe Satriani, Linda Schardine, Barb Krisko, Scott Hacker, Tom Conner, Don M. West, Pete Howard (ICE Magazine), Scott (Dog) Dailey, George Soister, Denise Loveless, Mike Parshall, Phillip Lieffers, Walter Seekamp, Chris Seekamp, Nick Fisher, Bill Modzel, Mike Erway, and Sara Gauthier. Excuse us while we kiss these guys!

Dedication

Belmo's dedication: For those friends and family members who
have gone before their time. I'll see you in the next world.

Steve's dedication: To my loving and patient wife, Denise, who has put up with listening
to a LOT of Jimi Hendrix recordings for the last 9 months. And to my friend and big brother,
John, who introduced me to the music of Jimi so many years ago. Thanks.

Special Thank You

To the Hendrix family and Experience Hendrix for their continuing efforts to bring the music
of Jimi Hendrix to the millions of fans who love Jimi's music.
We appreciate your efforts.

"Jimi" by artist Scott Dailey

Foreword
by
Uli J. Roth

No other single artist of the Sixties Generation has been more written about than Jimi Hendrix. Although he was only in the international limelight for a period of four years, there exists an enormous legacy of recorded music. The purpose of this volume is to publish in book form for the first time a 'comprehensive' guide to the material that has so far come to light with the help of an army of ardent collectors. This book is a true labour of love and is a great help for all serious collectors and researchers in sifting and cataloguing this veritable jungle of material from all kinds of sources.

I vividly remember Monika (Dannemann) telling me how upset Jimi had been when he first heard that certain informal and uninspired recordings (Curtis Knight) had been released without his consent. Jimi felt that the material in which he participated only casually would be an insult and a disappointment to his fans. It has to be remembered that at that time, in 1969, Jimi was only known to the wider public through his handful of official album releases. All of these were mindblowingly exciting and groundbreaking at the time. The majority of rock musicians back then considered Jimi as being peerless—in a league of his own. But although Jimi was a true genius, not every note he ever played live or recorded was of a standard that he considered worth releasing. His self-censorship even went as far as including the Band Of Gypsys release, because of certain minor shortcomings, despite the fact that this album contains much of the finest guitar playing of all time.

So it can be safely assumed that Jimi would have hated the majority of all those posthumous releases, many of which were a disgrace and not fit for publication in any form. It is amazing to see that Jimi's reputation has survived this plethora of inferior albums, particularly those that were rerecorded and tampered with after his death (when they should have been left alone) by people who were not qualified. It is, in fact, evidence of his greatness that Jimi's art and message survived all this. Most artists would feel horrified and embarrassed to have every outtake, rehearsal and live gig published at random. Jimi was no exception here. But the truth is that all the stuff is out there and much of it, particularly concerts, films, etc. are full of inspiration and excitement.

Furthermore, Jimi Hendrix is now a historic figure—one of the all time greats music has ever produced—and with such a person different standards must be applied. Some of his music, home tapes and demos are, in a way, similar to Beethoven's musical sketchbooks, in the sense that they provide us with specific insights into the creative thought processes of an artistic genius of the first order. Despite the fact that his creative period was only three to four years long, Jimi was so prolific—luckily for us—and his output so constant, that he was able to leave behind a powerful musical legacy.

This book is written for those who are fascinated by the world of Jimi Hendrix and want to explore the subject further.

Finally, I would like to thank the authors on behalf of the Monika Dannemann Foundation for using one of Monika's paintings for the cover.

Uli Jon Roth
July 1998

Forward

Uli Jon Roth

In 1973 Uli Jon Roth became the lead guitarist with the German band Scorpions. He was with the band for five years and played on and wrote the music for five internationally successful albums. During his tenure with that band, the Scorpions became Germany's No. 1 rock export and was the first German rock group to achieve international acclaim. In 1978 Jon Roth formed his own band called Electric Sun. His main musical influences at that time were Jimi Hendrix on one side and classical music on the other. As early as his days of the Scorpions he created and pioneered his own brand of true virtuoso guitar playing, constantly breaking new ground and thus established himself as one of the most influential guitarists of the last two decades. Among the scores of guitar players around the globe who have cited Roth as one of their major influences are such players as Eddie Van Halen, Yngwie Malmsteen, Steve Vai and Joe Satriani.

In 1991 Uli Jon Roth became the musical director for a highly successful German TV production, "A Different Side Of Jimi Hendrix", during which he performed selected Hendrix material with a variety of international performers, including: Jack Bruce, Simon Philips, Jule Neigel, Zeno and Randy Hansen. 1993 saw the TV performance of his first symphony by the Brussels Symphony Orchestra under the title of "Symphonic Rock For Europe", which Roth directed. There were about 90 performers on stage including a full classical choir, rock band, and no less than four first class rock tenors. In 1995 Roth appeared together with Klaus Meine performing at the "Jose Carreras" charity TV gala which was viewed by millions. They performed Roth's "Bridge To Heaven", an anthem based on Puccini's famous "Nessun Dorma" melody.

After a touring absence of thirteen years, Uli Jon Roth could finally be heard and seen on European stages again in the spring of 1998. Roth and his current band performed on the G3 Tour together with two other guitar masters—Joe Satriani and Michael Schenker.

Uli Jon Roth is currently working on "Requiem For An Angel", a deeply moving, large-scale symphonic piece, dedicated to the memory of his girlfriend of 20 years, Monika Dannemann, who died tragically in 1996.

* The authors wish to thank Uli Jon Roth for his wonderful foreword, for his help with this book, and for allowing us to use Monika Dannemann's painting, "Purple Haze," for the cover of our book.

Music is a religion for me.
There'll be music in the hereafter, too.
Jimi: Berlin 1969

Preface

Writing and compiling a book covering all the recordings of Jimi Hendrix was difficult at best. Accurate information on many of his studio recordings and various live jams was not easy to come by—and even once we had the information we were not always certain as to its accuracy. Still, we sifted through all the clues, stories, facts and suppositions until we thought we had a reasonable picture of what was The Truth.

There are many fine books available which have covered various aspects of Jimi's recording career and his live performances. However, none were ever organized in a manner we would have liked. We wanted to see a book that would be easy to reference and fun to look at. We knew we could do that, but one problem was deciding just what information to include in the book. We did not want to write another history of Jimi's life. And there was really no point in pontificating on Jimi's obvious influence on rock music, nor on his abilities, which we all know were far ahead of his time. So we agreed that a short summary would suffice—as would an abbreviated timeline. We have therefore saved precious paper by concentrating on the official and unofficial recordings and their contents.

Our purpose in writing this reference book was to provide fans of Jimi's music with accurate and detailed information about the recorded music of Jimi Hendrix. We have hopefully done it in such a way as to help both the casual fan and the longtime collector gain a more complete picture of Jimi's musical career. In the short span of his life, the amount of music written, recorded and performed by Jimi Hendrix was prodigious—as evidenced by the contents of this book. We knew there was a lot of information out there on Jimi's recordings, but even we were surprised at the amount. 'Mindboggling' would be a good way to express what we uncovered in our research.

So here you have the results of over 30 years worth of collecting and 12 months of research and writing. We have done our best to check the facts, but with any book of this magnitude some errors or omissions occur. So please feel free to write us with your documented corrections and/or suggestions for future revisions and updates. Enjoy the book.

We had a jam session at some club in England,
and that's how Mitch, Noel and I got together.
Noel comes down expecting to play guitar, you know,
he was trying for The Animals, I dug his hair style,
so I asked him to play bass.
Jimi: London 1969

The Noel Redding Interview
By Belmo

Noel Redding was the bass player in the Jimi Hendrix Experience from the inception of the band in October 1966 until June 29, 1969. During that time Noel was an integral part of the worldwide musical phenomenon led by Jimi Hendrix. Noel's intuitive playing brought a cohesiveness to the songs recorded in the studios and this same intuition united the performances on stage between Jimi and Mitch. Perhaps the only other group capable of such effortless execution was Cream.

At the age of only 20 Noel auditioned to be the bass player for a performer he had never heard of. And to top it off Noel was a guitarist (spending four years on the road with the Lonely Ones and the Loving Kind) and had no training as a bassist. Still, the position he had originally wanted to try out for (guitarist for the Eric Burdon Band) had been filled and he needed work. He decided to give it a go. And as fate would have it, Jimi and manager Chas Chandler liked what they saw and heard and Noel was in. Shortly thereafter Mitch Mitchell was hired as the drummer and the power trio was nearly ready to meet the world. The rest, as is often said, is history.

The following interview took place via Trans-Atlantic telephone on May 16, 1998. I called Noel at his home in Northern Ireland where he has lived for the past 26 years. I found Noel to be warm, witty and intelligent. His memories of those heady days with the Jimi Hendrix Experience are remarkably clear and unblurred by the passage of time. What follows are portions of our conversation.

BELMO: *Are you still involved with music?*
NOEL: Oh, yes! I was out playing last night.

BELMO: *What kind of music are you playing?*
NOEL: A little bit of everything. I have gone back to my roots. I play Eddie Cochran, Elvis, Buddy Holly, the Blues and that kind of stuff.

BELMO: *Are you doing any Fat Mattress material?*
NOEL: No. But I did a tour in Germany last October with Neil Landon the original singer. He came up and we did two Fat Mattress songs. This year I did two brief American tours and a U.K. tour. I also did a TV special and a charity show. And soon I am off to Russia. After that it is off to San Francisco, then England and then Ireland, Singapore and Australia.

BELMO: *Are you doing any recording?*
NOEL: I will be recording an album in October when I will have a month off. I will be recording at home which is a better way of doing it, because then you don't have to worry about the time or the money. We will record it in my house and everyone will stay here. On guitars will be Eric Bell and Eric Shinkerman of the original Spin Doctors . And the original drummer from Status Quo - John Cochran. And the drummer I played with since 1969, Les Amson, and a young lady named Amanda Lee. The album will be quite diverse. We will be doing "Rain" and "Cry Baby Cry" by the Beatles. And there will be a Dylan song. The album will be half covers and half originals.

BELMO: *You have been playing music for a long time, haven't you?*

NOEL: Thirty-six years. I was 20 when I joined the Jimi Hendrix Experience.

BELMO: *How did you come to be in The Experience?*

NOEL: I was in a London band called The Loving Kind. It was about six months before I joined The Experience and Eric Burdon came up on stage and sang a blues song with us. He was very impressed with the band. Chas *(Chas Chandler - The Animals manger and "discoverer "of Jimi Hendrix)* was there as well. That was around September 27 or 28, 1966. I went to audition on guitar for Eric Burdon and The Animals after the original Animals had broken up. I think they had actually already gotten someone on guitar by then. That's when Chas Chandler asked me if I could play bass. I said 'No, but I'll give it a go.' So I was playing with a drummer, a keyboard player and this American gentleman. There were no vocals at all. We just played three tunes. He said what key they were in. Afterwards he asked if I wanted to go down to the pub and I said 'Yes,' and we had a pint of bitter each. I asked him about the American music scene and had he asked if I had ever seen Sam Cooke. And he asked me about the music scene in England. Back then it was the Kinks, Small Faces, The Move and obviously The Beatles and The Rolling Stones. And then he said, 'Would you like to join my group?'. And that was it. That was Mr. Hendrix.

BELMO: *Had you ever seen or heard Jimi Hendrix before then?*

NOEL: No.

BELMO: *What did you think when you first heard him play guitar?*

NOEL: Well, he was wearing a strange overcoat. The kind people didn't wear in London in those days. And he had a pair of winklepickers on. Those were pointy-toed shoes. He didn't actually play lead guitar. He basically played rhythm guitar. He was sussing-out myself, the drummer and the keyboard player. The next day I had to go to Kent which was about 17 miles away, so I had to get Chas Chandler to give me 10 shilling so I could go back to London. When I got to London they said they would pay me 15 pounds a week. In those days that was a lot of money. And I thought 'alright.' And then there was this huge problem about trying to decide on a drummer. But Chas Chandler worked that one out. And then we started rehearsing. But the rehearsals weren't really rehearsals. We learned old stuff like "Land Of A 1000 Dances" because it was a new band. Within about two weeks we were on tour in France with Johnny Halliday. We started in Evreux, about 10 miles from Paris, then we played in Paris and went back to England where we played in all these clubs. That is when we noticed The Beatles and The Rolling Stones coming to all our shows. Rehearsals were non-existent.

BELMO: *Do you remember your first recording session as a member of the Experience?*

NOEL: We did "Hey Joe" and "Stone Free." For "Hey Joe" we actually went around to different studios, because Chas was producing us, until he thought the vibe was right. And we got it in about three different studios. Then we did "Stone Free" and that was our first recording. Then after working in all the little clubs in England we went to Munchen (that's Munich) and worked at the Big Apple Club for like five days. Then we came back to London and did a few more clubs. We did the TV show "Ready Steady Go," and "Hey Joe" was released in January and suddenly it was #7 on the charts - which was rather fast in those days for a band in Britain. We then went on tour with the Walker Brothers and we went to America.

BELMO: *When you went into the studio to record the songs, had you first been given demo tapes by Jimi to familiarize yourself with the music?*

NOEL: No. We learned the songs in the studio. With him and me being a guitar player, I just learned the idea and Jimi would say to Mitch 'we got a break here and a break here' and Chas would say, 'Let's give it a go.' And we'd give it a go with rhythm guitar, bass guitar and drums. And Chandler would normally say after the first take or so, 'We got it chaps.'

BELMO: *What influenced you as a guitarist?*

NOEL: The Shadows influenced me. James Burton and the guitarist from Booker T.. There was also a band called Johnny Kidd and The Pirates from the early Sixties in England whose guitar player was Mick Green. Also Steve Cropper.

BELMO: *Would you say your bass playing was a uniting force in the band's music?*

NOEL: I would say so, because James was a blues player and I was a rock player and Mitchell was a jazz player. I think basically we fused together. And having been a guitar player, when I was playing bass I was playing chords all the time. And you'll note that when we are doing live music Hendrix is only playing rhythm and I'm filling out all these chords on bass guitar and then he goes into his solos at which point I change the riff or whatever. It was a weird thing, actually.

BELMO: *Did this just happen naturally?*

NOEL: Yes, it did.

BELMO: *Why do you think power trios, such as The Experience, Cream and Grand Funk Railroad were so huge in the late Sixties?*

NOEL: When you got a three-piece band all the musicians have got to be bloody good. To play three-piece is rather hard. The thing is, I like to do it. I've done it for the last 36 years.

BELMO: *How did the band get from one gig to another?*

NOEL: Gerry Stickells drove the van. He was an old friend of mine. He was a mechanic and we used to go out and have a pint. I got him the job with The Experience. I told him to bluff his way in. So when they asked him if he had ever worked with bands before, he said he did. It was his van. Hendrix and Mitchell would sit in the front and I would get a blanket or a coat and lay on top of the equipment in the back.

BELMO: *What kind of equipment were you using then?*

NOEL: The first bass I used I borrowed off Chas. It was one of those big Epiphone-type things. Hendrix had a Strat. And we used Marshall amps.

BELMO: *Who set up your stage and equipment?*

NOEL: During the first French tour me and Chas were the road managers. We actually carried the gear from the airplane and the coats or whatever. And when it came time to set the gear up, Hendrix and Mitchell would disappear. We did it on the German tour also. But when we got our hit, I got Stickells in. That was in November 1966. Because when we played in Munchen we flew and he drove down with all the gear. He worked with the band until I left the band in June 1969. Gerry kept on working with James after that.

BELMO: *Did you share the on stage gear with other groups at the same venues?*

NOEL: We always suggested we should share gear because it saved a lot of lugging about. I still do it to this day.

BELMO: *Your schedule was quite gruelling. You would be in a city one day and another the next. And sometimes you would play two gigs in one city on the same day. How did you keep your sanity?*

NOEL: We took amphetamines. (*Laughs.*) In the 1968 American tour we did 56 cities in 54 days. I'll never do it again. They worked us like mad. We would be in L.A. then New York then Seattle. It was stupid. Bad planning.

BELMO: *Are those years a blur to you?*

NOEL: No, I know 99% of what went on. I kept a diary. I missed a couple of days which were a bit weird, but I got a very good recollection, thank God.

BELMO: *Let's talk about some of the concerts you performed. What do you remember about Monterey Pop?*

NOEL: Jimi was tripping. I can't be more specific, but he was elsewhere. For me I had never been to America before and I was only 21 years old. I sat beside Brian Jones on the plane coming over and Brian liked me and he put something in my drink. I don't remember getting to New York. And then the next day we went from New York to 'Frisco where I met all these heroes - Otis Redding, Booker T.. It freaked me out. I was really young. And the complete attention of young ladies also freaked me out. I can't say any more but we did quite well on the road.

BELMO: *Were you around when Jimi and Pete Townsend argued about who would go on last at Monterey?*

NOEL: There was no argument. I knew Moon pretty well. They said, 'Do you want to go on next?', and we said 'We don't care.' And they said, 'What if we go on after you?'. And we said, 'Whatever, we can go on after.' There was no argument. We blew them off the stage anyway.

BELMO: *Tell me about the "Lulu" TV show.*

NOEL: We played "Voodoo Child" first, then we went into "Hey Joe." And then halfways through the tune Hendrix went 'phht' (as we had no cues) and we stopped and James said, 'I'm sick of playing all this shit and we're going to play this for Jack Bruce, Eric Clapton and Ginger Baker. We went straight into "Sunshine Of Your Love"—an instrumental version. By this time the director (a guy called Stanley Dorfman) was waving his hands and saying 'Stop!'. He wanted to stop us because it was live. At the end of the tune we stopped and we went upstairs to the dressing room. I said to Hendrix, 'We are going to be banned from the fucking BBC.' Then we go for a pint after the show and the director comes over and says, 'That was brilliant, chaps!'

BELMO: *When you played the Hollywood Bowl you were especially concerned that some of the fans would jump into the water at the front of the stage and possibly get electrocuted.*

NOEL: That's right. I warned the fans. I am the only person who got film of it. They jumped in the water to get to the stage. The cops wouldn't go near them because they were afraid of the electricity. I was actually quite worried about it.

BELMO: *What was stage security like for the performers?*

NOEL: There was no security. We had no one. At the most we had three blokes working for us. And if anyone came up on stage we would kick them in the head or that sort of stuff.

BELMO: *It is amazing to me that here you were—the biggest act in the world and there was no one there to protect you.*

NOEL: No. Not at all. It was ridiculous.

BELMO: *Was there ever a time when you feared for your safety?*

NOEL: Not really. Maybe a couple of times. At Sanger Bowl in New York in 1968 we were there with Janis Joplin. There were 18,000 people there, and after we played, Hendrix and Mitchell left first. I took a different route through the audience—or crawled through the audience! So I made my way back to the dressing room area without getting torn apart. We got torn apart in Texas once. We got torn apart in the Gardens in New York. They stole my glasses. They stole our shirts and we were standing there in just our t-shirts. That's when I learned about letting the others leave the stage first.

BELMO: *What are your memories of the Winterland shows?*

NOEL: We were there for four days in 1968. It was grand. It was recorded as well. And I never got a penny off of it.

BELMO: *You didn't?*

NOEL: I don't get a cent from the Jimi Hendrix Experience. I don't get nothing. I do get paid for the two songs I wrote. But I have never received nothing from the Jimi Hendrix Experience.

BELMO: *You wrote "Little Miss Strange" on 'Electric Ladyland.' Was it hard for you to get your songs on the albums?*

NOEL: Hendrix didn't show up at the studio for three days, so I started recording my songs. The other song I did was "She's So Fine" which I had written for the 'Tops Of The Pops' television. I had played it for Chas and he liked it. So we recorded it. On "Midnight Lightning"—they put that out after Jimi passed away—there were a couple of tracks on that album which were my tunes but which they said Jimi had written. One was called "Midnight." Eddie Kramer even confirmed that.

BELMO: *You played an eight-string bass on several tracks. That was certainly innovative at that time.*

NOEL: Yeah, it was. It was hard to play. I played it on "Little Miss Lover," "Spanish Castle Magic" and "You Got Me Floating."

BELMO: *How did it happen that the Jimi Hendrix Experience opened for The Monkees?*

NOEL: In 1967, just after we did the Monterey thing, we worked at the Fillmore West where we were supporting the Jefferson Airplane the first night and the second night they were supporting us. And then we were in the hotel one night and Janis Joplin was with us (she was a good mate of ours), and there was a phone call to Chas from the other manager (Michael Jeffery). And Michael said to Chas, 'Guess what?' and Chas said, 'What?'. 'We got this great tour. You are going to open for the Monkees.'

BELMO: *You were on that tour for six weeks. Is it true you were fired from the tour?*

NOEL: No, we just left. We did about six dates with them. It started in Florida and we went up the east side of America and we went to New York. We played at Forest Hills. At that point the promoter (who was Dick Clark) and Chas Chandler had decided that it didn't fit and we were playing only three songs and we were dying a death . So they leaked it to the press that the Daughters of the American Revolution said our act was obscene. It got into the world wide press and said the band had left the tour.

BELMO: *I would like to ask you about some of the artists you knew and performed with with. What can you tell me about Brian Jones of the Rolling Stones?*

NOEL: Brian Jones I had met in Speakeasy Club in London. It was early 1967. We got on very well together. He was one of the people I had met. Jeff Beck was another. He is still my favorite guitar player. I got to meet Keith Moon who was a very good friend of mine. We met Georgie Fame, Pete Townsend, McCartney. I met Lennon a couple three times. In those days all the musicians would hang out. There were a couple of pubs where we would all go to. We would go to the Speakeasy and people would jam. But, now, today, it is a bit different. There are these guys who think they are stars and won't do that. It's crap.

BELMO: *Are the stories about the competition between Jimi and Eric Clapton true?*

NOEL: No, that is B.S.

BELMO: *There has been a rumor floating around for years that John Lennon sang on Jimi's version of "Day Tripper." Is that true? Or was it you on backing vocals?*

NOEL: It was me doing the harmonies.

BELMO: *In 1988 there was a story published in a British magazine that Chas Chandler had found a box of tapes containing 60 mostly unfinished Hendrix songs. It went on to report that you and Mitch Mitchell were recording overdubs onto this material. Is this story true?*

NOEL: Yes. As you know Chas died and now his widow owns those tapes. I had met her recently when I was doing a television show in England. So all of that is still being negotiated. I had signed a contract for that, so when and if it comes out I will legally get money off of it. The music was basically alternate outtakes—different versions. Sometimes there was like maybe a mistake or something at which point Mitch and I went into the studio with Chas and we cleaned it up. But then it got bootlegged somehow. But it hasn't officially come out yet.

BELMO: *Here is a listing of some of the songs which have been bootlegged. "Lover Man," "Freedom," "Dolly Dagger," "Ezy Rider," "Izabella," and "Room Full Of Mirrors." Are these from those sessions?*

NOEL: Yes, that's right.

BELMO: *Do you collect bootlegs yourself?*

NOEL: No.

BELMO: *Do you have an interest in that material?*

NOEL: No.

BELMO: *Do you have much of that kind of material yourself?*

NOEL: I got a little bit of a collection of that stuff, but I don't play it much.

BELMO: *There is a bootleg album cover that shows the three of you with two blonde women who are topless. What is the story behind that photo?*

NOEL: That was taken in Maui in 1969. It was the last time we went to Hawaii. There were these two birds who took all their clothes off.

BELMO: *Do you keep up with all the new Hendrix releases which have been coming out?*

NOEL: I just got the new CD which has the BBC tapes. I phone MCA and they send me copies. I don't get any fucking checks, but I do get free copies.

BELMO: *When you think back of your days with the Jimi Hendrix Experience, are you nostalgic or are you bitter about the money problems...?*

NOEL: I survived and I'm not bitter about the money. It was an honor to play with Jimi, and now when I am on stage the appreciation from the audience still freaks me out a bit. People are bringing me albums to sign. When all I ever wanted to do was to be a professional musician.

BELMO: *I read somewhere that you guys were real tricksters when you were on the road touring. For instance, you once hid a hotel ashtray in Gerry Stickells suitcase and he got in trouble for that.*

NOEL: That's right. He was arrested.

BELMO: *What other things went on?*

NOEL: Mitch used to have these bouncing shoes with springs on them. He would put them on and bounce through the hotel. We would sometimes take stink bombs and release them in someone's hotel room and then leave. Or we would put the stink bombs under another drummer's bass pedal, so when he used it the bomb would go off there on the stage and there would be nothing they could do about it. We had a lot of fun.

BELMO: *Did you get along pretty well with Jimi and Mitch?*

NOEL: It was grand. We all got along well.

BELMO: *Noel, thank you very much for talking with me today.*

NOEL: My pleasure, mate.

Jimi & Noel: 1967

> *I listen to everything that's written. It keeps my interest.*
> *From rock to The Beatles to Muddy Waters to Elmore James*
> *which is a blues guitarist and singer.*
> Jimi: London 1967

Steve Miller Remembers Jimi

By Belmo

In April 1998 Steve Miller and I were chatting backstage after his concert at the Nutter Arena on the campus of Wright State University in Dayton, Ohio. Steve and his band were currently on the road with their "Space Cowboy 1998 Tour" in celebration of 30 years of the Steve Miller Band. Our conversation began (naturally enough) with talk of Paul McCartney's most recent album, "Flaming Pie," and the songs Steve co-wrote with Paul for the album. Steve asked me how my Beatles books were doing and he inquired what I was working on next. I told him about the Hendrix book (which you are now holding in your hand) and soon Steve was recounting stories of his associations with Jimi in the Sixties and his impressions of Jimi as a performer and artist. Steve also gives us some insight into Jimi's affairs the last few months of Jimi's troubled life. What follows are excerpts from our conversation.

BELMO: *What did you think of Jimi when you first saw him play at Monterey?*

STEVE MILLER: I thought he looked like Eartha Kit with a guitar. He was great. He was so cool and was so exciting and so much fun. It was a big power trio and Cream had just been through . Everybody was excited about big power trios. Jimi came in and he was great. When that trio worked, they were great.

I saw lots of his gigs at Winterland, San Francisco. I saw him lots of different times. We did Monterey Pop Festival with him and at some of those fairgrounds in California. They were really exciting and it was really cool to see Jimi play. Jimi was my favorite player. Whenever he was playing I wanted to go there and watch. And learn. And just watch him. And I had always thought that if he had lived he would have been like Duke Ellington. If he had gotten through all of his drug problems. The rock and roll world was so small and so screwed up then. They were so many people who were sick and strung out on drugs. People were dying and really messed up. Managers were messed up and agents were messed up. Nobody was getting taken care of. It was sad. But I always thought that he had the same kind of talent Duke Ellington had. He was that big of a musical talent. It was a shame that he got so screwed up—so lost in that goofy world where he didn't know how to take care of his money. Didn't know how to take care of himself. Such huge stardom so fast and all that stuff that happened to him.

BELMO: *What did you think of his blues playing?*

STEVE MILLER: I loved it. That is what I loved about him. He was a great blues player. "Red House" is my favorite Jimi Hendrix tune. He was doing what I do, in that he was taking blues and he was jamming it into rock and roll. He was putting it into British pop too. So all his stuff was blues based. He was doing a lot of Muddy Waters. And a lot of that Delta stuff is his guitar style. He brought it into the rock and roll world. He really opened it up.

You've seen the films of him playing. It is a magical thing to watch him work out. I learned a lot from him. I feel we missed a lot of really great music when he died so young. Twenty-seven years old. It was tragic. He seemed so old then. It seemed like he had been around forever. He was a 1,000 years old.

Jimi was an originator. I've had the opportunity to see a lot of really great originators. Les Paul was one. I worked with T-Bone Walker a lot. I jammed with Jimi. I played with Muddy Waters and Howlin' Wolf. All of those people are musical giants and Jimi was definitely in that league with Muddy Waters, Howlin' Wolf, Les Paul and T-Bone Walker—and that is a BIG statement. There was a lot of great work from that group of people.

BELMO: *What are some other stories you can tell us?*

STEVE MILLER: We were jamming in a club in LA and I was invited to go over and jam with Jimi. And so I went over and there were just a few people there. It was the one time that I got to hang with him, you know, where we weren't doing a gig and it wasn't business. And he told me a story about when he worked with Little Richard. Little Richard would fine people if he thought they were trying to look better than him. And he would fine him (Jimi) if he was out of tune. And he would fine him on the stage. He really worked him over and I thought that was funny.

Several times I saw him at the club *(The Speakeasy)* in London where everyone would hang out. We used to see him there a lot and played a lot of gigs with him. And then before he died, the last gig I did with him was at Temple University. It was cold. It was probably late spring. *(The date was May 16 - Belmo)* He was really sick. He looked like he was really strung out. He had a bunch of Mafia thugs were working with him. And when he came to the gig in Temple, he was pretty much wacked out in the back of the limousine along with Mitch Mitchell his drummer. Billy Cox was playing bass with him. His brother would come out and parade around and people thought that he was Jimi. He would tease the audience and stuff.

The thugs who were handling Jimi wouldn't let him play until he got $85,000 in cash. They made the promoter get the money in cash. Thirty thousand people had been there for 12 hours and it was late at night, dark, and cold and we had just finished playing. And he was on next. The Grateful Dead played, then we played, then Jimi. Whenever I used to see him play he would let me come out and sit on the stage. And I used to sit and watch him play. I would be just ten feet from him. And so I figured I would do that again. I went out there and then this guy came up and told me to get off the stage. I said 'Hey, man, I just finished playing a set and this is my equipment right here. Relax.' The guy pulled a gun on me and said, 'I told you to get off the stage'. At that point when Jimi came out and he walked by me, he smelled so bad it almost made you sick. They *(Jimi and Mitch)* had just shot up a whole lot of methedrine and he was completely wigged out. He and Mitch Mitchell both looked like they both weighed about 75 pounds. Mitch Mitchell was so skinny. It was tragic. It was a real life and death situation. They were both in really bad shape. They came out on the stage and they couldn't play for 20 minutes. They just made noise. They couldn't play "Johnny B. Goode". They couldn't get their band together. They made noise for 20 minutes and then finally they started coming down from the speed that they had just injected. I went out and watched them and I remember it was really sad because there was this young girl and her mother, and her mother was going 'Oh, yeah, he is really sexy. He is so cute'. But to me I was looking at him and I felt that I needed to take him home with me and save his life. I couldn't. There wasn't anything I could do. There were these guys around him who were bad—like thugs. Guys in suits with guns. And that was the last time I saw him.

About Steve Miller

Steve Miller's first album, "Children Of The Future", was released in 1968 and soon garnered a huge underground following. Thereafter his albums (20 thus far) and his singles would sell in the millions to a worldwide audience. His music is a staple of 'classic rock' radio stations. Who hasn't heard "Gangster Of Love", "Space Cowboy","Fly Like An Eagle", "Dance, Dance, Dance", "Wild Mountain Honey", "Jungle Love", "Abracadabra", "The Joker", "Jet Airliner"...?! Additionally, Steve is highly respected as a blues guitarist among his peers as well as a songwriter. In 1987 Steve received a star on the Hollywood Walk of Fame celebrating the 20th anniversary of his recording career (all with Capitol Records). Most recently Paul McCartney and Steve collaborated on several songs for Paul's "Flaming Pie" album released in 1997. Many considered the album Paul's best effort since "Band On The Run". Paul and Steve's first collaborative effort was in 1969 on "My Dark Hour" (released on Steve's album, "Brave New World").

Perhaps the best way to enjoy Steve's music is at the Steve Miller Band concerts which are known for their superb sound, note-perfect harmonies and the impeccable musicianship of his band. His concerts

draw several generations of fans and are guaranteed to be highly enjoyable events. And Jimi Hendrix fans will find it interesting to note that Steve's tour manager is none other than Gerry Stickells who was Jimi's road manger. It is truly a small world in the rock music business.

* Photo of Steve Miller by Belmo 1992

A Conversation With Joe Satriani

By Belmo

The following conversation took place August 5, 1998.

BELMO: *How old were you when you first heard Jimi's music?*

SATRIANI: I heard Jimi the month they released the single off 'Are You Experienced?'. I heard it on the radio and I asked my older siblings 'What is that amazing music?'. I was extremely young at the time—maybe 10 or 11 years old. They were so surprised at the music back then. It was very counterculture. Not like today when they use it to sell tacos. My family encouraged me to seek out music that I liked. I had already started taking drum lessons and I was really into music, but at that age it was more a fascination with the music and not a life choice.

I do remember the moment I heard "The Wind Cries Mary" coming over the radio and I thought it was the most amazing song I had ever heard. It was one of those experiences in life where you'll never forget where you are. It is a simple thing looking back on it, but for some reason when it is happening it completely seems to change your reality. I felt forever changed. Like I had moved to another level. I remember asking my older sisters 'Who is this guy?' and 'Where can I find his records?'. Soon they were bringing his records home and I was listening to his music constantly.

Finding out that he had died, one day, it is literally one of those stories that you remember exactly where you were. I remember distinctly finding out that he had died. I had on my football equipment and a kid told me Jimi had died. And I just turned around and walked in to the coach's office and said 'I'm quitting. I'm gonna play guitar.' Hearing Jimi was dead was a very tragic moment. It changed my life.

BELMO: *You must have been about 14 then?*

SATRIANI: Yes. You know, I stuck with the guitar and played every day. Hendrix's music was always sacred to me and for years I wouldn't even play it because I didn't want to defile it. But I secretly studied it and what I got from it in my own music was the spirit, the imagination, the invention—and without trying to copy it. I promised myself that I would not be like these white guitar players trying to play like Hendrix.

I was approached to do recordings on several of those records that have come out with musicians like Sting doing Hendrix songs, but I hate all those albums. All the artists who participate are great on the work they do on their own. But when I hear these records it makes me recoil. I came close once. Eddie Kramer almost got me to that point when I said I would do it if Noel and Mitch would agree. I would do it with them. In order for me to feel right—spiritually—about this, I'll do it with the guys who did it (or at least two thirds of that music). Otherwise, if it is just me and some trendy musicians, then forget it. Maybe someday I'll do a Hendrix cover on my own records and be able to treat it with the proper respect. I've heard a lot of versions of Jimi's music, but all it does is show the disparity of talent between the players. How much Jimi had and how much less everyone else has.

BELMO: *Do you collect Hendrix bootlegs?*

SATRIANI: I used to. I was an active collector, but after a while I got so overwhelmed with all the Hendrix material that was coming out and [the record companies] were releasing stuff that wasn't even good enough to be called bootlegs. So now I collect bootlegs of my own material. I think that at some point musicians realize that the only people who buy bootlegs are people who own all of the stuff that was legally issued. So it is not the issue that it used to be. Many bands now allow people to tape their live shows. It helps create familiarity with what it is you are trying to show people.

BELMO: *When you listen to "Voodoo Child" you sense an almost religious connection between Jimi and the song.*

SATRIANI: Jimi was connected to the source of that creativity. Like with any artist there is just no way to fathom why Beethoven or Mozart (for example) did it the way they did it. They can be analyzed and imitated, but there is no way anybody can come up with the next tune they would have written. It is very difficult because when you listen to "Purple Haze" it has very little to do with "Voodoo Child". Or "Burning Of The Midnight Lamp". What has that got to do with "1983"? Every time we would hear a new Hendrix record we would go like 'Wow!'. There were just not enough hours in the day for him. Or a year. Or his life. He was incredibly prolific during a time when rock was really like the Wild West. Factor in all those things that were going on around him then, and that he was able to make his mark, is pretty incredible.

BELMO: *What do you think is the legacy of Jimi's music?*

SATRIANI: Great artists perform a service by bridging the gap. We know what Bach did, what Beethoven did, what Mozart did. We know that they spent part of their lives perfecting what came before them. Then something happened when they put it all together and said 'This is the new stuff'. Then a whole generation of players followed that. They were the leaders of their generation. Jimi was one of those people. Maybe the premier electric guitar player of the mid-century to take us to the future. Nothing had really developed until Hendrix. There was a big difference between the guitar playing of the late 1800's and the Be Bop style where the music was about notes. This is where Jimi came in. The social structure was changing and music was not all about notes. Music Concrete had popped out of France and people are beginning to notice that the sound is also the message. Not just the sound created from the instruments of old but of the world. Sounds created from the world around us can be emulated by anything we can do it with. This is the avant garde.

And then there is this explosion of hillbilly music lead by Elvis Presley. Just think of it. You got a whole group of people growing up in the United States who are a new social force—teenagers—and you have these forces coming from all around and Jimi Hendrix is smack dab in the middle of it. He's the right age to be of that generation. He's getting hit with Coltrane and Miles Davis and Muddy Waters and John Lee Hooker. And he's getting hit with Stockhausen and Elvis Presley and soul music and Little Richard and Chuck Berry. It is all this stuff that is about to meet. And I think it meets in him. He didn't know it. I don't think any of these pivotal players know it. They are like the comet going through space—flying around and asking why is everyone looking at me?

I think that what he brought together was the sound of the world using the instrument not only to play the notes (and I do believe that to Jimi the notes were the important thing as was the sound), and he wasn't just agreeing. He was doing something about it. He had people who were one step ahead of him—like The Beatles who were into this thing. The 'Revolver' record was probably the first real rock record ever where there were songs not just written about love, but about about some odd subject like "Tomorrow Never Knows"—maybe the first real rock song. The sound of it, the structure, the lyrical content were pointing the way to a new style of music. Jimi had the musicianship and the improvisation. He added what was happening in avant garde in Europe and America as well as in Asia. It was the sound he was making. To hell with the notes. You put that together and you get those three Hendrix records. I can't think of music today that has that richness to it and the innocence and a worldliness at the same time. That is genius. Jimi had that genius.

BELMO: *Do you still play Hendrix records?*

SATRIANI: Absolutely. I played 'Band Of Gypsys' yesterday. I think that "Machine Gun" is a work of art. It is a special recording. The performance on it is unparalleled by any guitar player I have ever heard. Ever! It is so perfect. It is so inspired. It is so fresh. Innocence and genius at the same time.

BELMO: *When the newer, younger fan is listening to the music of Jimi Hendrix, what would you advise them to be listening for?*

SATRIANI: I've always told people to try and let the music into their hearts and discover what is special about it. Because you can tell people what is so special about this or about that, but they have to discover it for themselves. When I heard it for the first time it was by accident and I immediately fell in love with it. It changed my whole view of music and the world and who I was and what I was going to do for the rest of my life.

Joe Satriani

Joe Satriani first came to the notice of the masses in 1987 with the release of 'Surfing With The Alien'. His virtuoso guitar playing became a thing of legend and the album immediately went Gold. For a time he taught guitar to aspiring musicians. A few were to make their marks in the business as well - Steve Vai, Larry Lalonde of Primus and Kirk Hammett of Metallica. His recent album, 'Crystal Planet' is being hailed as a rock masterpiece. In the spring of 1998 Joe teamed up with Eric Johnson and Steve Vai and toured as G3 to a legion of grateful fans.

I formed this group with some other guys,
but they drowned me out. I didn't know why at first,
but after three months I realized
I'd have to get an electric guitar.
Jimi: Frankfurt 1967

JIMI HENDRIX: A BRIEF HISTORY

By Steve Loveless

If you ask the average person if they know what groups Jimi Hendrix played in, the response may be 'The Jimi Hendrix Experience', 'The Band Of Gypsys', or that he was a solo act. In reality Jimi played in no less than 11 groups during his brief career of just over 10 years. This book won't go into intimate details about Jimi's history; however, let's run down a brief history of Jimi's group associations. Like many musicians he was always eager to play with just about anyone if the opportunity arose. Jimi frequently jammed or sat in with dozens of other groups and performers. On many of the 'package' tours that Jimi was involved in during his early years, he filled in numerous times for acts on the bill when the need arose.

Al Hendrix (Jimmy's father) bought young Jimmy a ukulele in mid-1958. Later in that year Jimi decided to buy a used acoustic guitar from a friend of his father's. In the fall of 1959, Al bought Jimi his first electric guitar. Soon after he joined his first 'regular' band called The Rocking Kings. The band lasted until the middle of 1960 with the core lineup of Jimmy on a tuned down 6 string guitar for bass (and later on guitar), Webb Lofton on saxophone, and Lester Exkano on drums. Other band members that came and went during that time were Walter Harris on saxophone, James Woodberry on vocals and piano, Ulysses Heath on guitar, and Robert Green on piano.

By mid-1960 The Rocking Kings had dwindled to just Jimmy, Lofton and Exkano. The Rocking Kings' 'manager', James Thomas, joined the group along with his brother Perry Thomas on piano and Rolland Green on bass. They also changed the name of the group to The Tom Cats. The Tom Cats had a number of successful gigs—most which were at the regional Air Force, Army and Naval bases. Early in 1961 The Tom Cats lineup dropped Exkano and Lofton and picked up Richard Gayswood and Bill Rinnik. This was the lineup until Jimmy decided to enlist, on May 31, 1961, for a three year stint in the Army. In November he met Billy Cox at Fort Campbell, Kentucky. Jimmy and Billy immediately hit it off and began playing together with other friends at some local gigs (including the Pink Poodle Club in Tennessee). January of 1962 saw Jimmy and Billy with drummer Gary Ferguson form the group The King Kasuals. The group grew by four or five members by the summer of 1962. When Jimmy broke his ankle during a parachute jump and was discharged from the Army on July 2, he dropped out of the group.

Billy Cox had to wait until September to get his discharge, after which he and Jimmy moved to Tennessee, then to Indiana and finally back to Tennessee where Jimmy met Larry Lee. Jimmy and Billy continued playing as The King Kasuals after adding Leonard Moses on guitar, Harry Batchelor on vocals, Buford Majors on sax and Harold Nesbit on drums. Also around this time Jimmy, Billy, and Larry Lee joined Bob Fisher & The Barnevilles backing up Curtis Mayfield & The Impressions, as well as The Marvellettes for a few weeks. Jimmy and Billy also backed other R&B and blues artists when the opportunities arose.

By December 1962 Jimmy made his way to Vancouver for a rest where he stayed with his grandmother, Nora Hendrix. He played for the winter with a local band called The Vancouvers before deciding to go back East sometime in the first several months of 1963. After meeting 'Gorgeous' George Odell in Nashville, Jimmy teamed up with him and got involved with a couple of package tours traveling throughout the United States. Jimmy also occasionally backed many other performers—including The Supremes, Jackie Wilson, and Sam Cooke. During one of the tours he met Little Richard and occasionally played with Richard's band, The Upsetters. By the end of 1963 Jimmy had made some of his first recordings with Lonnie Youngblood.

At the start of 1964 Jimmy moved to New York City and by March had joined The Isley Brothers. He played, toured and recorded with the Isleys until around November when he decided to quit while in Nashville. For the rest of the year Jimmy again joined up with a package tour featuring Sam Cooke.

In January 1965 Jimmy met up with Little Richard again and was hired into the band as the guitar player. Little Richard made some recordings in February with Jimmy in the band. Also in February Jimmy, The Upsetters and two New York State singers ('Buddy & Stacey') are videotaped performing "Shotgun" in a Dallas, Texas, TV studio. The performance was broadcast on the Nashville show 'Night Train'. During this time Jimmy auditioned for Ike and Tina Turner, playing a few shows, but returned to Little Richard's band before quitting in June or July. On August 5, 1965, Jimmy recorded a single with the Isley Brothers at Atlantic Studios in New York. He then joined Curtis Knight and The Squires for the balance of the year—performing and recording with the group. Jimmy even recorded a single with Jayne Mansfield (the famous and voluptuous sex kitten of the Sixties) sometime in the latter part of the year. He also signed a three-year contract with Ed Chalpin. This contract would later cause him some serious legal problems.

Jimmy left the Isleys in January 1966 and joined the King Curtis band—performing and recording intermittently through mid-May. For a few weeks Jimmy teamed up with Carl Holmes & The Commanders until finally forming his first band (Jimmy James and The Blue Flames) around late June or early July. His band was sometimes known as The Rainflowers; and it was during this time that Jimmy hired Randy California (later of Spirit) to also play guitar. He also hired a drummer (name unknown) and another man named Randy to play bass. Other Rainflowers members would come and go, but it was on August 5, 1966 at the Cafe Wha' in Greenwich Village that Chas Chandler saw Jimmy James and The Blue Flames perform. A month and a half later Chas and Jimi flew to London where Jimi met Noel Redding at Noel's audition on September 9. On October 6th Mitch Mitchell joined the group and the Jimi Hendrix Experience was born. The band rehearsed for "about four hours" (as Jimi said in an interview) and played their first gig at The Novelty in Evreux France. The Experience remained together until June 29, 1969, when Noel Redding quit the band after the show at The Denver Pop Festival at Mile High Stadium in Denver, Colorado.

Because of obligations in the near future (some TV performances as well as the upcoming Woodstock Festival on August 18th), Jimi needed to get a new group together. Mitch Mitchell decided to stay with Jimi and old friends Juma Sultan and Jerry Velez (both percussionists), and old army buddies Billy Cox (bass) and Larry Lee (rhythm guitar) ultimately joined with Jimi to form the Gypsy Sun and Rainbows Band. The only performance this group gave was at Woodstock. The line up was short-lived and was disbanded by Jimi in October 1969. Thereafter, Jimi immediately formed The Band of Gypsys with Billy Cox on bass and Buddy Miles on drums. One of Jimi's concepts for the band of Gypsys (as well as The Gypsy Sun and Rainbow Band) was of an evolutionary band that could change and grow with its personnel and not have to be a 'regular' group. The Band of Gypsys debut was at the famous New Years Eve shows at the Fillmore East in New York City. However, once again this was a short-lived group as their last performance at Madison Square Garden on January 28, 1970 was a disaster. Jimi's manager, Michael Jeffery, fired Buddy Miles after the show and the Band of Gypsys was no more.

Jeffery tried to convince Jimi, Mitch and Noel to reform the Experience. The three even did a press conference announcing the reformation. But after a week or two Jimi simply couldn't come to terms with playing with Noel again. Jimi gave some thought to having Billy Cox and Jack Casady (of the Jefferson Airplane) join with him in forming a new band. Finally, he convinced a very reluctant Billy Cox to reform with Mitch and himself; thereafter, the three of them recorded some new songs and then embarked on a summer tour which became known as 'The Cry of Love Tour.' This was to be Jimi's final band lineup. Some venues billed the band as 'The Experience' or 'The Jimi Hendrix Experience', but many were billed only as 'Jimi Hendrix'. Jimi would simply introduce the band by member and did not refer to the group by name. Most fans and collectors refer to this final line up as the 'Cry Of Love Band'.

> *Music is gonna be here, regardless if it's rock or*
> *whatever, you know, and it's gonna influence a*
> *whole lotta people's minds now, because that's*
> *part of their church now.*
> Jimi: London 1970

Discography: An Explanation

This discography is organized in a simple and logical format for easy access to the data. Knowing that fellow collectors of Jimi's music desire detailed information of what recordings are available and where to locate them, we have divided the book into segments.

First, the terminology used in the discography is explained so that the reader will understand the difference between a pirated disc and one which is counterfeit, for example. This is followed by a listing of the OFFICIAL RELEASES. We begin with the SINGLES (45's and EP's) in chronological order. The major emphasis here on the American, British, German and French releases. Next up are the VINYL ALBUMS—again in chronological order. Reissues (such as 'numbered vinyl') of some of the titles are listed at the end of the descriptions of the original releases. We have made no attempt at listing the now obsolete 8-track tapes or cassettes. Nor have we attempted listing all the compilations (eg: "Looney Tunes And Merry Melodies" on Reprise Records) which contain a common song or two by Jimi nor have we listed the many tribute albums which contain no original performances by Jimi. The COMPACT DISCS are not listed chronologically as many of the same CDs were released in several different countries but in different years. Our emphasis here was on the American, British, German, French and Japanese releases.

There are some releases out of the mainstream which we placed in the RARE & MISCELLANEOUS category. These include acetate singles, 'public service' records, interview discs, and promo singles. The next segment features a sampling of the recordings Jimi had done WITH OTHER ARTISTS and the recordings he produced for them. Many of these fall into the 'semi-legal' category as the ownership of some of the recordings have often been called into question. Additionally, Jimi is often touted as being the headline performer on these recordings, when in actual fact he never even appeared on many of the titles listed by the manufacturers. We sorted out this mess for you the best we could.

A major portion of the discography is devoted to the BOOTLEGS of Jimi's recordings. These we have listed alphabetically for easy reference. Bootleggers frequently give songs fabricated titles to sometimes fool the unwary buyer into thinking new material is on their release. For the most part we have listed the song titles as they appear on the bootleg followed by the correct song title in parenthesis. For the numerous unnamed jams we generally listed the titles fabricated by the bootleggers followed by the title we are using to identify it in the indexes. In some cases we used the bootleggers' titles, as the titles have stuck over the years. In our comment section for the bootlegs we gave a brief description of the material as to source, sound quality and location. We have also included total timings for CD's if we know them. Individual song timings are occasionally listed but should be taken with a grain of salt. Using song running times to differentiate between versions from one disc to another is meaningless because so many discs are mastered at incorrect speeds. It is not unusual for the exact same recording to vary in time by over minute. For our hobby, acquiring a CD player with pitch control can be very helpful.

We also debated putting country of origin and release dates for releases—especially bootlegs. For legitimate commercial releases, country of origin and dates on the packaging are reasonably reliable. After all, they don't have much to hide. Bootlegs, on the other hand, frequently and intentionally print misleading information on packages to throw off everyone from the RIAA to the customs agents. For this reason we have not put in the release dates or country of origin because *who really knows anyway?* Please note that the authors neither condemn nor condone the practice of bootlegging. It is simply a fact of life or a necessary evil—depending on one's point of view. Bootlegs were—are—and will be.

Discography: An Explanation

This Flyer
is for that
MAN who
walked into
A pad at Woodstock
raised his AXE
and talked
To the people
Around him,
And they talked
Together.

The very first Jimi Hendrix bootleg was "This Flyer" released in early 1970 by parties unknown. This disc contained several poorly edited jams from the Mike Ephron Tapes. It was an inauspicious beginning. There were many bootlegs manufactured through the years (especially during the Seventies) which were of little or no value to the collector. The sound quality on many were just plain horrid—either because the vinyl pressings were inferior, or because the original source tapes were totally lacking in fidelity. But with the advent of the compact disc and improved recording technology, bootlegs made a gigantic leap forward in the late Eighties and on into the Nineties. By the latter part of the Eighties the quality of the outtakes and live shows also seemed to improve. Suddenly, amazing soundboard recordings, studio outtakes, demos and alternate mixes surfaced—many of which had never been documented by anyone before. It was as if a treasure chest had been discovered and fans of Jimi's music were rewarded with some wonderful musical gems.

Following the titles of some of the bootlegs are asterisks (*) indicating that these are worthwhile discs for your collection. (* indicates a disc with some unique or collectable material; ** is a disc most collectors will want to own; and *** is a MUST HAVE.) Also, some titles are followed by 'IN' which indicates the songs on these titles can be found in the SONG INDEX at the back of the book.

The information we've included on the CD-R titles produced by the Major Tom label came from the English book "From The Benjamin Franklin Studios". Major Tom saw limited distribution in the U.K.; however, some of the material is of such importance that we felt it necessary to include the data even though we were unable to locate any of these discs ourselves. (We'd love to have copies, so send them our way!) With the advent of the computer age it is now possible to make compact discs right in your home. These are called CD-Rs. These 'homemade bootlegs' can be made from any source: video, cassette, vinyl or compact disc. The list of CD-Rs grows by the hundreds each month. A few of these (such as those on Major Tom) do have some rare material on them and, as such, they deserve mention at least for documentation purposes.

Surprisingly, the number of FILMS of and about Jimi Hendrix is quite small. We have listed those known to exist both commercially and in the hands of private collectors. The chronological listing in the AUDIO/VIDEO ARCHIVES section begins with Jimi performing with Buddy & Stacey and The Upsetters on "Night Train" in February 1965. It ends with Jimi's last jam with Eric Burdon at Ronnie Scott's Club in London on September 16,1970. In these listings we have included dates, locations, songs performed, performers, length of the film and whether the film is black & white or color. Noel Redding filmed hours of home movies during his time with the Experience and it is hoped that these will someday see the light. It is a project he is considering for future release.

Jimi's taped television, radio and live performances (where known) are listed chronologically in the AUDIO/VIDEO ARCHIVES section and these include location, source, timings, and song listings. And where these recordings were preserved on vinyl or CD, we noted sample titles (legit and bootleg) in bold text. This segment also provides the best way to see the set lists for a certain concert or club date. Following that is a listing of all the dates played by Jimi. It is hard to imagine anyone touring and making public appearances at such a grueling pace and still retain some form of sanity. Undoubtably, the schedule lead to the use of illicit drugs (and more than a few wild nights with willing female fans) as a way of relieving the pressures of touring as well as the boredom.

The DISCOGRAPHY is divided into two parts: "Commercial Releases" and "Bootleg Releases". These are listed alphabetically for easy reference. Unless the words "A", "An" and "The" were used as proper nouns in the titles (such as: "A Session"), these were dropped for alphabetical purposes.

The SONG INDEX at the end of the book provides the reader with a quick and easy way of finding the songs or albums which are of special interest. This segment might certainly be the most valuable portion of the book, as it identifies thousands of songs by dates, takes, locations, album listings and more!

One final word before getting to the good stuff. A lot of you know all about the existence and availability of bootleg recordings. Some readers probably do not. Before getting excited about all this really cool unreleased music, if you don't already own the commercial releases, go buy all of them. This means 'Are You Experienced', 'Axis: Bold As Love', 'Electric Ladyland', 'Band Of Gypsys', The First Rays Of The New Rising Sun', ' South Saturn Delta' and the new 'BBC Sessions' CD's. Make sure you get the Hendrix family 'Experience Hendrix' pressings. They are the definitive and the best sounding versions available. Picking up the official 'Monterey Pop Festival' disc and Ryko's 'Live At Winterland' would be a good idea too. Then and only then can you fully appreciate and understand the importance and indispensable aspect of some of the bootleg recordings.

For this book various line-ups will be referred to as follows:

CK&S = Curtis Knight & The Squires

LR = Little Richard

LY = Lonnie Youngblood

JHE = The Jimi Hendrix Experience (Jimi, Mitch Mitchell, Noel Redding)

BOG = Band Of Gypsys (Jimi, Billy Cox, Buddy Miles)

GSRB = Gypsy Sun And Rainbow Band (Jimi, Mitch Mitchell, Juma Sultan, Jerry Velez, Billy Cox, & Larry Lee)

COL = Cry Of Love Band (Jimi, Mitch Mitchell, Billy Cox)

SOLO = Jimi alone or on all instruments.

JIMI = Jimi with musicians other than any of the above.

CAFE = The lineup that jammed with Jimi at the Cafe Au Go Go on March 17, 1968, in New York City (Jimi, Elvin Bishop, Buddy Miles, Harvey Brooks, Paul Butterfield, Herbie Rich, James Tatum, & Phillip Wilson)

GEN = The lineup that jammed with Jimi in the early part of April, 1969 at The Generation Club in New York City. (B.B. King, Buzzy Feiten, Paul Butterfield, Elvin Bishop, Don Martin, Al Kooper, Phillip Wilson, & a guy named Stuart - not to be confused with the Generation Club jam dated April 7, 1968)

SCENE = The lineup that jammed with Jimi at The Scene club in New York City sometime in March of 1968. (Jimi, Jim Morrison, members of The McCoys & possibly others)

Terminology

ACETATE: A one-sided disc which is heavier than commercially pressed records. Distribution is usually restricted to the artists, producers, management and publishing sectors of the industry. Oftentimes the acetate features a pre-final mix of the record and is therefore highly sought after by collectors.

ALTERNATE MIX: Refers to a differently mixed and commercially released version of an existing commercial release.

BOOTLEG: Bootlegs or underground recordings include unreleased material, such as demonstration and rehearsal tapes, studio outtakes and alternate takes, TV/radio performances, live performances and concerts.

COMPOSING TAPE: A recording that is of an unfinished song in the creative process of being composed.

COUNTERFEIT: Unauthorized recordings that attempt to completely reproduce an officially released album, including the music, album artwork and label graphics.

CR: This denotes a commercially released recording.

DEMO: A demonstration disc or tape used by artists, producers, music publishers and record companies for a variety of purposes. Usually consists of a rough version of a song yet to be formerly recorded and produced.

FORMAT: How the title was released - LP (vinyl), CD (compact disc), CD-R (a compact disc made on home equipment), EP (extended play), 45 (vinyl single).

LABEL: The name of the company which is printed on the label or disc. In the case of a bootleg, the name on the disc may not necessarily be the same company manufacturing the disc. For example, it may say "Swingin' Pig" on the label, but the bootleggers may be using that name as a cover to throw off the authorities or to give their product legitimacy.

MATRIX #: This is the identifying code (usually in the form of numbers and /or letters) printed on the cover or disc by the manufacturer to identify the disc or its sequential place in a catalog. In the case of bootlegs, different bootlegs will have the same matrix numbers.

OFFICIAL RELEASE: A track released on a video tape, laser disc or a source other that vinyl or compact disc. Not to confused with a "commercial release".

OUTFAKE: An 'outtake' created by the bootleggers with the purpose of passing off a re-mixed legitimate take as an alternate take.

OUTTAKE: Refers to a finished track that is usually left off a commercial release and relegated to the studio vaults. However, it is now common practice for record companies to add outtakes as 'bonus tracks' to album reissues and re-releases.

PIRATE DISC: Unauthorized recordings that reproduce legitimately released music with no attempt made to reproduce the legitimate album cover artwork or label.

SOURCE: Signifies if the music was from a recording studio, television or radio broadcasts, home recordings, audience concert tapes, soundboard concert tapes, alternate mixes, or legitimate cover versions. Mono or stereo is listed when known — though that is not always clear cut with some recordings (especially on the bootlegs where the recordings have been remixed by the bootleggers.)

SOUND QUALITY: We used our own 'ear' when rating the recordings, but generally they are as follows: 'poor' (unlistenable), 'fair' (barely listenable), 'good' (average quality), 'very good' (above average), 'excellent' (as good as any legitimate release) and 'superb' (better than the commercially released version).

TITLE: The actual title as printed on the front cover or spine. Generally the words 'A', 'An' and 'The' are dropped (or placed at the end of the title) for the purpose of alphabetizing.

UNUSED MIX: A different and unreleased mix of a commercially released recording. Found only on a bootleg release.

* Please note that all the photographs and album artwork are from the personal collections of the authors and are presented here for historical documentation only.

*You have the whole planned-out LP, and all of a sudden
they'll make 'Crosstown Traffic', for instance, a single,
and that's coming out of a whole other set.
It's almost like a sin for them to take off something
in the middle of all that and make that a single
and represent <u>US</u> at the particular time.*
Jimi: New York 1970

The Official Releases
The Singles

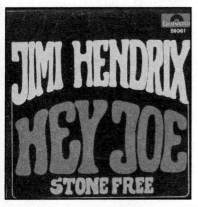

HEY JOE / STONE FREE
(Polydor 56139 - English) First release Dec 66 & (Polydor 59061 - German) 1966

HEY JOE / STONE FREE
(Polydor - DP 1673 - Japanese) 1967 & (Polydor - Italy & Sweden) 1967

HEY JOE / STONE FREE / 51ST ANNIVERSARY/ PURPLE HAZE
(Barclay - French) 1967 & (Polydor - Spanish) 1967

HEY JOE / ALL ALONG THE WATCHTOWER
(Polydor - German) 1967

PURPLE HAZE / 51ST ANNIVERSARY
(Track 604001 - English) Mar 67 & (Polydor 59072 - German) 1967 & (Polydor - Italy & Norway) 1967

THE WIND CRIES MARY / HIGHWAY CHILE
(Track 604004 - English) May 67 & (Polydor 59078 - German) 1967 & (Polydor - Sweden & Spain) 1967

HEY JOE / 51ST ANNIVERSARY
(Reprise 0572 - USA) May 67

PURPLE HAZE / THE WIND CRIES MARY
(Reprise 0597 - USA) Jun 67

THE BURNING OF THE MIDNIGHT LAMP / THE STARS THAT PLAY WITH LAUGHING SAM'S DICE
(Track 604007 - English) Aug 67 & (Polydor 59117 - German) 1967 & (Polydor - Denmark) 1967

FOXY LADY / HEY JOE
(Reprise 0641 - USA) Nov 67

UP FROM THE SKIES / ONE RAINY WISH
(Reprise 0665 - USA) Feb 68 & (Barclay 060959 - French)1968 & (Polydor 2310 268 - English) 1968 & (Polydor 59184 - German) 1968

ALL ALONG THE WATCHTOWER / THE BURNING OF THE MIDNIGHT LAMP
(Reprise 0767 - USA) Oct 68

ALL ALONG THE WATCHTOWER / CAN YOU SEE ME
(Polydor 59240 - German) 1968 & (Polydor DP-1605 - Japanese) 1968

ALL ALONG THE WATCHTOWER / LONG HOT SUMMER NIGHT
(Track 604025 - English) Oct 68 & (Barclay 060 993 - French) 1968

CROSSTOWN TRAFFIC / GYPSY EYES
(Reprise 0792 - USA) Nov 68 & (Track 604029 - English) 1968 & (Polydor 59 256 - German) 1968 & (Barclay 061 038 - French) 1968

FOXY LADY / SPANISH CASTLE MAGIC
(Polydor DP-1585 - Japanese) 1968

PURPLE HAZE / FIRE / UP FROM THE SKIES / HEY JOE
(Polydor - Mexico) EP 1968

THE WIND CRIES MARY / FIRE / UP FROM THE SKIES / HIGHWAY CHILE
(Polydor - Mexico) EP 1968

THE WIND CRIES MARY / LITTLE WING
(Polydor 1118 - USA) The authors have no other information on this disc.

STONE FREE / IF 6 WAS 9
(Reprise 0853 - USA) Sep 69

FIRE / THE BURNING OF THE MIDNIGHT LAMP
(Track 604033 - English) Nov 69 & (Polydor 59375 - German)

STEPPING STONE / IZABELLA
(Reprise 0905 - USA) Apr 70 (withdrawn)

VOODOO CHILE(SLIGHT RETURN) / HEY JOE / ALL ALONG THE WATCHTOWER
(Track 2095 001 - English) EP Oct 70

RED HOUSE / THE WIND CRIES MARY / PURPLE HAZE
(Polydor - Holland)

FREEDOM / ANGEL
(Reprise 1000 - USA) Mar 71 & (Polydor DP 1804 - Japanese) 1971

GYPSY EYES / PURPLE HAZE
(Polydor - German) 1971

GYPSY EYES / REMEMBER / PURPLE HAZE / STONE FREE
(Track 2094 010 - English) Oct 71 Maxi single

DOLLY DAGGER / STAR SPANGLED BANNER
(Reprise 1044 - USA) Oct 71

JOHNNY B. GOODE / LITTLE WING
(Polydor 2001-277 - English) Jan 72 & (Polydor 2001 277 - German) 1972 & (Polydor DP 1858 - Japanese) 1972

WATERFALL / 51ST ANNIVERSARY
(Barclay 61.389 - French) 1972

JIMI HENDRIX STORY VOL. 1
(Barclay Records, 61.358 - French) 1972
  Hey Joe / Stone Free

JIMI HENDRIX STORY VOL. 2
(Barclay Records, 61.359 - French) 1972
  Purple Haze / Highway Child

JIMI HENDRIX STORY VOL. 3
(Barclay Records, 61.360 - French) 1972
  The Wind Cries Mary / Red House

ALL ALONG THE WATCHTOWER
(Japan 1968)

ALL ALONG THE WATCHTOWER
(Germany 1968)

UP FROM THE SKIES
(Germany 1968)

6 SINGLES PACK
(Germany 1980)

BURNING OF THE MIDNIGHT LAMP
(Germany 1967)

51ST ANNIVERSARY
(Germany 1967)

JIMI HENDRIX STORY VOL. 4
(Barclay Records, 61.361 L - French) 1972
  Crosstown Traffic / Gypsy Eyes

JIMI HENDRIX STORY VOL. 5
(Barclay Records, 61.362 L - French) 1972
  Changes / Message To Love

JIMI HENDRIX STORY VOL. 6
(Barclay Records, 61.381 L - French) 1972
  Voodoo Child / All Along The Watchtower

JIMI HENDRIX STORY VOL. 7
(Barclay Records, 61.389 L - French) 1972
  Waterfall (inedit) / 51st Anniversary

JIMI HENDRIX STORY VOL. 8
(Barclay Records, 61.396 L - French) 1972
  1983...(A Merman I Should Turn To Be) / Come One (Part One)

JIMI HENDRIX STORY VOL. 9
(Barclay Records, 61.428 L - French) 1972
  Ezy Rider / Drifting

JIMI HENDRIX STORY VOL. 10
(Barclay Records, 61.487 L- French) 1972
  Izabella / Star Spangled Banner

JIMI HENDRIX STORY VOL. 11
(Barclay Records, 61.550 L - French) 1972
  Johnny B. Goode / Blue Suede Shoes

JIMI HENDRIX STORY VOL. 12
(Barclay Records, 61.660 - French) 1972
  Tax Free / Stepping Stone

HEAR MY TRAIN A'COMIN' / ROCK ME, BABY
(Reprise K 14286 - English) Aug 73

6 SINGLES PACK
(Special Limited Edition): (Polydor 260 8001- German) 1980
  Hey Joe / Stone Free, Purple Haze / 51st Anniversary, The Wind Cries Mary / Highway Chile, Burning Of The Midnight Lamp / The Stars That Play With Laughing Sam's Dice, All Along The Watchtower / Long Hot Summer Night, Voodoo Chile / Gloria

FIRE / ARE YOU EXPERIENCED
(CBS Records - England) 1982

ALL ALONG THE WATCHTOWER / CROSSTOWN TRAFFIC
(Reprise 0742 - USA) 1983

DAY TRIPPER / DRIVIN' SOUTH / HEAR MY TRAIN A COMIN'
(Rykodisc RCD31-008 - USA) CD 1988

PURPLE HAZE / 51ST ANNIVERSARY / ALL ALONG THE WATCHTOWER / HEY JOE
(Polydor PZCD 33 - English) CD 1988

GLORIA
(Polydor 887 585-2 - German) 1988 & (Polydor - Japanese) 1988

CROSSTOWN TRAFFIC
(Polydor PZCD 71 - English) CD 1990

ARE YOU EXPERIENCED?
(France 1967)

CROSSTOWN TRAFFIC
(Germany 1969)

THE WIND CRIES MARY
(France 1967)

THE WIND CRIES MARY
(Germany 1967)

HEY JOE
(Italy 1975)

CROSSTOWN TRAFFIC / VOODOO CHILE / ALL ALONG THE WATCHTOWER / HAVE YOU EVER BEEN (TO ELECTRIC LADYLAND)
(Wrangler - England) CD 1990

ALL ALONG THE WATCHTOWER / CROSSTOWN TRAFFIC
(Polydor 879-583-2 - French) 1991

BERLIN 69
(If 6 Was 9 C.D.) 7" 1991
  Berlin interview: January 23, 1969

JIMI HENDRIX 1970
(If 6 Was 9 C.D.) 7" 1991
  Interview with John Burke: January 4, 1970

CROSSTOWN TRAFFIC
(Polydor POL 940) CD 1991
  'Cornerstone' material

VOODOO CHILE
(Polydor) 12" 1991
  'Cornerstone' material

THE BURNING OF THE MIDNIGHT LAMP / MAY THIS BE LOVE / HIGHWAY CHILE / HEY JOE / PURPLE HAZE / THE WIND CRIES MARY
(Barclay - French) CD 1992

THE WIND CRIES MARY / FIRE
(Polydor - German) 1992

FROM THE ALBUM JIMI HENDRIX: FIRST RAYS OF THE NEW RISING SUN
(Experience Hendrix/MCA MCD-11636 - English) 1997
  Dolly Dagger / Night Bird Flying / Astro Man

DOLLY DAGGER / NIGHT BIRD FLYING
(Experience Hendrix/MCA MCA7P-55336 - USA) 1997

CAN YOU PLEASE CRAWL OUT YOUR WINDOW? / THE BURNING OF THE MIDNIGHT LAMP
(Experience Hendrix/MCA MCA13188/MCA7P-55454 - USA) 1998
  Best Buy promo single from the 'BBC Sessions' album.

The Vinyl Albums

ARE YOU EXPERIENCED?

(Track 612 001 - English) 05 Dec 67 & (Polydor 825 416-2 - English) 1967 & (Polydor 184 085 & 825 416-2 & 2428 301 - German) 1967 & (Polydor 2459 390 - German) 1968 & (Barclay 820 143 - French) 1968

ARE YOU EXPERIENCED /
AXIS: BOLD AS LOVE
(Polydor 2683 031 - ENGLAND 1973)

Foxy Lady	Manic Depression
Red House	Can You See Me?
Love Or Confusion	I Don't Live Today
May This Be Love	Fire
3rd Stone From The Sun	Remember
Are You Experienced?	

Comments: Jimi's manager, Chas Chandler, cemented a recording deal with Track Records in England in October 1966 and drummer Mitch Mitchell and bassist Noel Redding were brought in to back Jimi on tour and in the studio. Work began on the JHE album on October 23, 1966, at Olympic Studios and was concluded on April 3, 1967. Recordings were also made at CBS, DeLane Lea, Pye and Regent studios. The album was released in Europe in May 1967 to high acclaim and reached #2. In August the album was released in the U.S. on Reprise Records with a slightly different song lineup. It would hit #5 on the U.S. charts. Jimi first used his wah-wah effect on 'I Don't Live Today' and backwards guitar on 'Are You Experienced?'.

ARE YOU EXPERIENCED?

(Reprise RS 6261 - USA & Canada) Aug 67

Purple Haze / Manic Depression / Hey Joe / Love Or Confusion / May This Be Love / I Don't Live Today / The Wind Cries Mary / Fire / Third Stone From The Sun / Foxy Lady / Are You Experienced?

ARE YOU EXPERIENCED?

(Experience Hendrix 622-903V - USA) 1997 Numbered vinyl

ARE YOU EXPERIENCED?

(Experience Hendrix 622-903EV - English) 1997 Numbered vinyl

AXIS: BOLD AS LOVE

(Track 613003 - English) 01/12/67 & (Reprise RS 6281 - USA) 1967 & (Track 2407 011 - English) 1967 & (Polydor 184110 - German) 1967 & (Polydor 2343 097 & 2486 029 - Holland) 1967 & (Barclay 0820 167 - French) 1967 & (Polydor SMP-1398 - Japanese) 1968 & (Reprise REP M5 6281 - USA) 1968 & (Karussell 2499 006 - French) & (Polydor 813 572-2 - German) & (Polydor P33P 25023 - Japanese)

EXP	Up From The Skies	Spanish Castle Magic
Wait Until Tomorrow	Ain't No Telling	Little Wing
If Six Was Nine	You've Got Me Floating	Castles Made Of Sand
She's So Fine	One Rainy Wish	Little Miss Lover
Bold As Love		

Comments: After the highly successful first album and tour, the Jimi Hendrix Experience returned to Olympic Studios to record their follow up album. The recordings took place between May 4, 1967, and October 30, 1967. The European release was December 1, 1967, and in the Americas in January 1968. The album would reach #5 on the British charts and #3 on the American charts. Spanish Castle (by the way) was a club in Seattle where Jimi played in the early Sixties.

AXIS: BOLD AS LOVE

(Experience Hendrix 622-901V - USA) 1997 Numbered vinyl

AXIS: BOLD AS LOVE

(Experience Hendrix 622-901EV - English) 1997 Numbered vinyl

SMASH HITS
(Track 613004 - English) Apr 68 & (Polydor 2310 268 - English) 1968 & (Polydor 825 255-2 - German) 1968 & (Polydor 2491 539 - Holland) 1968 & (Polydor 613004 - Australia) 1968 & (Polydor MP-1413 - Japanese) 1968 & (Reprise MS 2025 - USA) 1969 & (Reprise MSK-2276 - USA)

Purple Haze / Fire / The Wind Cries Mary / Can You See Me / 51st Anniversary / Hey Joe / Stone Free / The Stars That Play With Laughing Sam's Dice / Manic Depression / Highway Chile / The Burning Of The Midnight Lamp / Foxy Lady

Comments: The first of several greatest hits packages, this album brought together some obscure singles and album tracks. It did extremely well, rising as high as #4 in the U.K. and #6 in the U.S.

ELECTRIC LADYLAND
(Reprise 2RS 6307 - USA) 2LP Oct 68 & (Track 613 008/9 - English) 2LP 1968 & (Polydor 823 359-2 - German) & (Polydor P58P25001 - Japanese) & (Polydor MPX-9955-6 - Japanese)

And The Gods Made Love	Have You Ever Been (To Electric Ladyland)
Crosstown Traffic	Voodoo Chile
Little Miss Strange	Long Hot Summer Night
Come On (Part I)	Gypsy Eyes
Burning Of The Midnight Lamp	Rainy Day, Dream Away
1983...(A Merman I Should Turn To Be)	Moon, Turn The Tides...Gently Gently Away
Still Raining, Still Dreaming	House Burning Down
All Along The Watchtower	Voodoo Child (slight return)

Comments: This was the first and the last album produced by Jimi Hendrix in the studio. It was released in October 1968 and would go on to reach #1 in the U.S.A. and #6 in England. Jimi experimented with many new recording techniques as well as guitar sounds - many which went unappreciated at the time. Said Jimi, "There's a 3D sound on there that's been used that you can't appreciate because, like, they didn't know how to cut it properly. They thought it was out of phase". This album is now recognized as being as influential as The Beatles' "Sergeant Pepper Lonely Hearts Club Band" album. As for the record cover in England featuring numerous nude beauties, Jimi was not all at pleased as he was not advised or informed of the cover ahead of time. Said Jimi, "People have been asking me about the English cover and I don't know anything about it. I didn't know it was going to be used". The nude cover is now a rock music collectable. Recorded at Olympic, Record Plant, Mayfair and Bell Sound studios.

ELECTRIC LADYLAND
(Experience Hendrix 622-902V - USA) 1997 Numbered vinyl

ELECTRIC LADYLAND
(Experience Hendrix 622-902EV - English) 1997 Numbered vinyl

ELECTRIC JIMI HENDRIX
(Track 2856 002 - English) Nov 68 (withdrawn)

Still Raining, Still Dreaming / House Burning Down / All Along The Watchtower / Voodoo Child (slight return) / Little Miss Strange / Long Hot Summer Night / Come On (PartI) / Gypsy Eyes / The Burning Of The Midnight Lamp

Comments: Intended as a stripped down version of ELECTRIC LADYLAND, but this idea was quickly withdrawn because of Jimi's objections.

SMASH HITS
(Reprise MS 2025 - USA) Jul 69

Red House / Purple Haze / Fire / The Wind Cries Mary / Can You See Me / Hey Joe / Stone Free / Manic Depression / Foxy Lady / Crosstown Traffic / All Along The Watchtower / Remember

Comments: The original release of this album included a color poster of Jimi, Mitch and Noel dressed up like cowboys and riding on the backs of horses. The photo was taken at a March 29, 1969, photo session on a Hollywood movie lot used for filming westerns.

BAND OF GYPSYS
(Capitol STAO-472 - USA) Apr 70 & (Capitol STAO-472 - India) 1970 & (Track 2406 002 - English) 1970 & (Polydor 2480 005 - German) 1970 & (Polydor 2491 507 - Holland) 1970 & (Barclay 0920 221 - French) 1970 & (Polydor 2406 002 & Polydor 3194 008 - Australia) 1970 & (Polydor MPA-7006 - Japanese) & (Reprise CRX 5195 - Canada) 1985

Who Knows	Machine Gun	Changes
Power Of Soul	Message To Love	We Gotta Live Together

Comments: Jimi's need to forge new ground both musically and professionally lead him to disband The Experience and to form the Band Of Gypsys. This new group reunited him with long-time friends - bassist Billy Cox and drummer Buddy Miles. Though there was no studio album from the group, two albums of live material (recorded during four shows at the Fillmore East on December 31, 1969, and January 1, 1970) would be released (the second posthumously). The original album reached #5 in the U.S. and #6 in the U.K. This album was the one owed to PPX/Capitol when they released Jimi to Reprise Records. There were three different covers for BAND OF GYPSYS: Track's original release featured the 'Dolls' version and the second version had a shot of Jimi from the Isle Of Wight. The Capitol version shows the band on stage at the Fillmore. Experience Hendrix promises an upgrade release. First two songs from January 1, 1970 (first show) and rest are from January 1, 1970 (second show)

BAND OF GYPSYS
(Experience Hendrix 622-904V - USA) 1997 Numbered vinyl

BAND OF GYPSYS
(Experience Hendrix 622-904EV- English) 1997 Numbered vinyl

BAND OF GYPSYS 2
(Capitol SJ-12416 - USA) 10/86 & (Capitol/EMI 1A 064-26 1174 1 - Holland) 1986
First Pressing:

Getting My Heart Back Together Again (1)	Foxy Lady (2)
Stop (2)	Voodoo Child (slight return) (3)
Stone Free (4)	Ezy Rider (5)

Comments: Second Pressing: The above songs plus Hey Joe / Hey Baby (The Land Of The New Rising Sun) / Lover Man - all from Berkeley, May 30, 1970, 2nd show.
It may say 'Band Of Gypsys' on the album, but in actual fact only three tracks are them. The other songs are from various other venues. The sound quality is noticeably inferior on this release. Song sources: (1) Band Of Gypsys, Fillmore East, December 31, 1969 (first show)/ (2)BOG, Fillmore East, January 1, 1970 (first show)/ (3) Second Atlanta Pop Festival, July 4, 1970 (Jimi, Mitch Mitchell, Billy Cox)/ (4) Berkeley, May 30, 1970 (second show)/ (5) Berkeley, May 30, 1970 (first show)

WOODSTOCK
(Cotillion SD 3500 - USA) Jun 70 & (Atlantic K60001 - English) 1970 & (Mobile Fidelity 4-816-1/2 - USA) 1988 & (Atlantic SD 500-2 - USA) 1989 & (Atlantic SD500-2 - English) 1989
Star Spangled Banner / Purple Haze / Instrumental Solo
Comments: Jimi was accorded one side of the soundtrack album for the highly successful movie soundtrack of the Woodstock Music and Art Fair Festival held the previous year in Bethel, New York. Jimi performed with his group called 'The Gypsy Sun & Rainbow Band' or 'The Sky Band' in the early morning of August 19, 1969. Most of the entire performance would be released on JIMI HENDRIX: WOODSTOCK in 1994 on compact disc.

HISTORIC PERFORMANCES RECORDED AT THE MONTEREY INTERNATIONAL POP FESTIVAL
(Reprise MS 2029 - USA) Sep 70 & (Atlantic 40 430 - French)
Like A Rolling Stone / Rock Me, Baby / Can You See Me / Wild Thing
Comments: Jimi Hendrix shared the billing on this album with Otis Redding. Each had one side of the record devoted to a selection of their performances at Monterey recorded on June 18, 1967. The album would reach #16 in the U.S.

THE CRY OF LOVE
(Reprise MS 2034 - USA) Mar 71 & (Track 2408 101 - English) & (Polydor 2480 027 - German) & (Barclay 080 433 - French) & (Polydor 2459 397 & 829 926-2 - German) & (Polydor P33P 25011 & MPF-1079 - Japanese) & (Polydor 847 242-2 - Australia) 1988

Freedom	Drifting	Ezy Ryder
Night Bird Flying	My Friend	Straight Ahead

MONTEREY (Jimi & Otis Redding)

CRY OF LOVE

IN THE WEST

RAINBOW BRIDGE

MIDNIGHT LIGHTNING

THE JIMI HENDRIX CONCERTS

Astro Man   Angel   In From The Storm
Belly Button Window*
Comments: This was the first of many posthumous albums released to a public ravenous for new
Hendrix music. Some of the songs on this album and on RAINBOW BRIDGE were originally intended
by Jimi to be part of a double album entitled FIRST RAYS OF THE NEW RISING SUN. THE CRY OF
LOVE would reach #2 in the U.K. and #3 in the U.S.. *"Belly Button Window" is said to be the last stu-
dio recording by Jimi. Eddie Kramer was the engineer.

WOODSTOCK TWO
(Cotillion SD 2400 - USA) Apr 71 & (Atlantic K60002 - English) & (Mobile Fidelity 4-816-3/4 - USA) 1989 & (Atlantic 781
981-2 - German) 1989
Jam Back At The House / Izabella / Getting My Heart Back Together Again
Comments: Part two of the Woodstock soundtrack again featured some of Jimi's performances at the
festival which took place in 1969.

EXPERIENCE
(Ember 5057 - English) Aug 71 & (Ariola 85 087TT - German) & (Sonet SLPS 1526 - Sweden) & (Entertainment
International SLDEI 782 - French)
Sunshine Of Your Love / Room Full Of Mirrors / Bleeding Heart (C# Blues) / Smashing Of Amps
Comments: This concert was filmed for theatrical release as EXPERIENCE, but it never found its way
to movie houses. Live at Royal Albert Hall from February 24, 1969.

THE FIRST GREAT ROCK FESTIVALS OF THE SEVENTIES: ISLE OF WIGHT / ATLANTA
POP FESTIVAL
(Columbia G3X 30805 - USA) Sep 71 & (CBS 66311 - English) 2LP
Message to Love / Midnight Lightnin' / Foxy Lady
Comments: The rest of the 2LP set was filled out with performances by some of the other artists attend-
ing the Festivals.

RAINBOW BRIDGE
(Reprise MS 2040 - USA) Oct 71 & (Reprise K44159 - English) & (Reprise REP 54004 - German) & (Reprise 54004 -
French) & (Reprise P-8167R - Japanese)
Dolly Dagger   Earth Blues
Pali Gap   Room Full Of Mirrors
Star Spangled Banner   Look Over Yonder
Getting My Heart Back Together Again*   Hey Baby (The Land Of The New Rising Sun)
Comments: This was the soundtrack to the movie documenting Jimi's performances in Maui, Hawaii,
on July 30, 1970. Only one* of these songs is an actual live recording performed by Jimi, Mitch and
Billy. *Berkeley, May 30, 1970 (first show).

ISLE OF WIGHT
(Polydor 2302 016 - English) Nov 71 & (Polydor 2310 139 & MC 3100 140 - German) & (Barclay 80 462 - French) & (Polydor
2310 151 - Spain) & (Polydor MP-2217 - Japanese) & (Polydor 2310 139 & 3100140 - Australia)
Midnight Lightnin'   Foxy Lady   Lover Man
Freedom   All Along The Watchtower   In From The Storm
Comments: The soundtrack of Jimi's appearance (incomplete) at the Isle Of Wight Pop Festival on
August 30, 1970, only made it as high as #17 in the United Kingdom. It certainly was not one of Jimi's
best performances. Billy Cox played bass and Mitch Mitchell handled the drumming duties. Also avail-
able as LIVE AT THE ISLE OF WIGHT (Polydor 847 236-1) LP 1991.

HENDRIX IN THE WEST
(Polydor 2302 018 - English) Jan 72 & (Reprise MS 2049 - USA) 1972 & (Polydor 2310 161 - German) 1972 & (Barclay 80
448 - French) 1972 & (Polydor 831 312-2 - German) & (Polydor P33P 25004 - Japanese)
Johnny B. Goode (1)   Lover Man (2)
Blue Suede Shoes (3)   Voodoo Child (slight return) (4)
God Save The Queen (5)   Sergeant Pepper's Lonely Hearts Club Band (5)
Little Wing (4)   Red House (6)
Comments: At the time of its release, this album was well-received for the diversity and quality of the
tracks. A very nice overview of some of Jimi's better live performances.
Song sources: (1) Berkeley (May 30, 1970,first show) / (2) Berkeley (May 30, 1970, second show) /

(3) Berkeley (May 30, 1970) rehearsals / (4) Royal Albert Hall (February 24, 1969) / (5) Isle Of Wight (August 30, 1970) / (6) San Diego (May 24, 1969)

MORE EXPERIENCE
(Ember NR 5061 - English) Mar 72 & (Sonet SLPS 1535 - Sweden) & (Entertainment International LDM 30.148 - French) & (Kaleidoscope KAL 19026 - French)

Little Wing / Voodoo Child (slight return) / Fire / Room Full Of Mirrors / Bleeding Heart / Purple Haze / Wild Thing

Comments: Live At Royal Albert Hall , February 24, 1969 (see above)

I DON'T LIVE TODAY: JIMI HENDRIX - HIS GREATEST HITS
(Polydor 22675-008) LP

WAR HEROES
(Polydor 2302 020 - English) Oct 72 & (Polydor 2310208 - German) 1972 & (Barclay 80467 - French) 1972 & (Reprise MS 2103 - USA) 1972

Bleeding Heart	Tax Free	Peter Gunn
Catastrophe	Stepping Stone	Midnight
Highway Chile	3 Little Bears	Beginning
Izabella		

Comments: Another posthumous collection of unreleased songs from the Hendrix archives. (The US version is minus 'Highway Chile' and has an edited - profanity deleted! - '3 Little Bears').

SOUNDTRACK RECORDINGS FROM THE FILM : JIMI HENDRIX
(Reprise K 64017 - English) Jun 73 & (Reprise 2RS 6481 - USA) 1973 & (Reprise REP 64 107 - German) 2LP 1973 & (Reprise 2RX 6481 - Canada) 1973 & (Reprise P-6315-6R - Japanese) 1973

Machine Gun (1) / Rock Me Baby (2) / Interview with Jimi / Purple Haze (3) / Interview with Jimi / Wild Thing (2) / Johnny B. Goode (3) / Interview with Jimi / Hey Joe (2) / Like A Rolling Stone (2) / Getting My Heart Back Together Again (4) / Interview with Jimi / Red House (1) / Star Spangled Banner (5) / Machine Gun (6) / In From The Storm (1)

Comments: A collection of live cuts from various sources: (3) Berkeley, (5)Woodstock, (2) Monterey Pop, (1) Isle Of Wight, (6) Fillmore East, (4) Royal Albert Hall and a number of interviews from different times in Jimi's career.

MUSIQUE ORIGINALE DU FILM JIMI PLAYS BERKELEY
(Barclay 80.555 - French) 1973

Johnny B. Goode / Purple Haze / Star Spangled Banner / Little Wing / Voodoo Child (slight return) / Machine Gun / I Don't Live Today / Lover Man

Comments: Studio tracks and live performances from several different concerts. Only "Johnny B. Goode" and "Lover Man" are from the Berkeley Concert.

LOOSE ENDS
(Polydor 2310 301 - English) Feb 74 & (Polydor 2310 301 - German) 1974 & (Barclay 80 491 - French) 1974 & (Polydor MPF-1083 - Japanese) 1974 & (Polydor 2310 301 - Italy) 1974

Coming Down Hard On Me Baby	Blue Suede Shoes
Jam 292	Drifter's Escape
Burning Desire	I'm Your Hootchie Coochie Man
Electric Ladyland	The Stars That Play With Laughing Sam's Dice

Comments: As the title suggests, some odds and ends of studio recordings which had been sitting in the vaults for a few years. Again, this was another of the posthumously released titles of dubious worth and quality.

CRASH LANDING
(Reprise MS 2204 - USA) Mar 75 & (Polydor 2310 398 - English) 1975 & (Polydor 827 932-2 - English) & (Polydor P33P 25024 - Japanese)

Message To Love	Somewhere
Crash Landing	Coming Down Hard On Me Baby
Peace In Mississippi	With The Power
Stone Free	M.L.K. (Martin Luther King)

Comments: The first of several controversial releases produced by Alan Douglas. Controversial because

Douglas went in and wiped all but Jimi's performances from the tapes and then added new instrumentation to the songs. Purists were none to pleased with Douglas for making such a radical alteration to Jimi's music. The results were mixed and critics were split in their opinions as to the artistic success of the new productions.

MIDNIGHT LIGHTNIN'
(Reprise MS 2229 - USA) Nov 75 & (Polydor 2310 415 - English) 1975 & (Polydor 825 166-2 - German) & (Polydor P33P 25025 - Japanese)

Trashman (aka Midnight)	Midnight Lightnin'
Getting My Heart Back Together Again	Gypsy Boy (New Rising Sun)
Blue Suede Shoes	Izabella
Machine Gun	Once I Had A Woman
Beginning	

Comments: Another album remixed by Douglas and considered to be the worst album released with Jimi's name on it. The 'Douglas Method' had few supporters after this horrendous release. A few critics called Douglas 'a leech of the worst kind' and 'a man without morals' for assuming he could rework the music of Hendrix. We'd have to agree.

RARE TRACKS
(Polydor 2482 274 - English) Apr 76 & (Polydor MPF 1009 - Japanese)
Dolly Dagger (from Isle of Wight)

THE ESSENTIAL JIMI HENDRIX
(Reprise 2RS 2245 - USA) Jul 78 & (Polydor MPZ 8109/10 - Japanese) 2LP 1978 & (Polydor 2612 034 & 2335-134/5 - English) 1978
Are You Experienced / Third Stone From The Sun / Purple Haze / Little Wing / If Six Was Nine / Bold As Love / Little Miss Lover / Castles Made Of Sand / Gypsy Eyes / The Burning Of The Midnight Lamp / Voodoo Child (slight return) / Have You Ever Been (To Electric Ladyland) / Still Raining, Still Dreaming / House Burning Down / All Along The Watchtower / Room Full Of Mirrors / Izabella / Freedom / Dolly Dagger / Stepping Stone / Drifting / Ezy Ryder & Gloria (as a one-sided single with the Polydor set)

JIMI HENDRIX
(Polydor 2625038 - German) 12LP box set / Maxi 12" single (1978)
Are You Experienced? / Axis: Bold As Love / Electric Ladyland (2 LP) / Band Of Gypsys / Isle Of Wight / Cry Of Love / In The West / War Heroes / Loose Ends / Midnight Lightning / Crash Landing Maxi 12" Single: Gloria (8'47") / Hey Joe (3'22")

THE ESSENTIAL JIMI HENDRIX VOLUME TWO
(Reprise 2RS 2293 & HS 2293 - USA) Jul 79 & (Polydor 2311 014 - English) 1979
Hey Joe / Fire / Foxy Lady / The Wind Cries Mary / I Don't Live Today / Crosstown Traffic / Wild Thing / Machine Gun / Star Spangled Banner & Gloria (as a one-sided single with the Reprise set).
Comments: "Gloria" was an unreleased studio track from TTG Studios, October 29, 1968.

NINE TO THE UNIVERSE
(Reprise HS 2299 - USA) Mar 80 & (Polydor 2344 155 - English) 1980 & (Polydor KI 8007 - Japanese) 1980 & as 'Message From Nine To The Universe' (WEA 38.023 - Brazil)
Message From Nine To The Universe / Jimi-Jimmy Jam / Young-Hendrix / Easy Blues / Drone Blues
Comments: Basically, a jam album which I doubt Jimi would have wanted released. These jams came from studio sessions recorded in 1969 and 1970. At the time these jams had no titles. See the Song Index for more detailed information on these tracks.

THE JIMI HENDRIX CONCERTS
(Reprise 2306-1 - USA) Aug 82 & (CBS 88592 - English) 1982 & (CBS 88592 - Holland) 1982 & (38MM-0204/5 - Japanese) 1982 & (Frituna FRIX-178 - Sweden) 2LP 1989
Fire (1) / I Don't Live Today (3) / Red House (4) / Stone Free (2) / Are You Experienced (1) / Little Wing (1) / Voodoo Child (slight return) (1) / Bleeding Heart (2) / Hey Joe (2) / Wild Thing (1) / Getting My Heart Back Together Again (1)
Comments: Another collection of some of Jimi's live performances from different times in his career. Song sources: (1) Winterland (Oct 68)/ (2)Royal Albert Hall (Feb 69)/ (3) San Diego (May 69)/ (4) Randall's Island (Jul 70)

LIVE
(Polydor 2302 114 - Holland) 1982 & (Polydor 3100 638 - Holland) 1982
  Contains a compilation of common live performances.

THE SINGLES ALBUM
(Polydor PODV 6 - English) 2LP Feb 83 & (Polydor 2625 047 - Holland) 2LP 1983
  Hey Joe / Stone Free / Purple Haze / 51st Anniversary / The Wind Cries Mary / Highway Chile / The Burning Of The Midnight Lamp / The Stars That Play With Laughing Sam's Dice / All Along The Watchtower / Long Hot Summer Night / Crosstown Traffic / Flying / Gypsy Eyes / Remember / Johnny B. Goode / Little Wing / Foxy Lady / Manic Depression / 3rd Stone From The Sun / Gloria

KISS THE SKY
(Reprise 25119 - USA) Oct 84 & (Polydor 823 704-1 - English) 1984 & (Reprise 9 25119-2 - USA) & (Polydor 823 704-2 - German)

Are You Experienced? (1)	I Don't Live Today (1)	Voodoo Child (slight return) (2)
Stepping Stone (2)	Castles Made Of Sand	Killing Floor (2)
Purple Haze	Red House	Crosstown Traffic
Third Stone From The Sun	All Along The Watchtower	

Comments: An assortment of studio and live tracks compiled to no one's benefit.
Song sources: (1) San Diego, May 24, 1969 / (2) Monterey, June 18, 1967.

JIMI PLAYS MONTEREY
(Reprise 25358-1 - USA) Feb 86 & (Polydor 827 990-1 - German) 1986 & (Reprise 9 25385-2 USA) 1986 & (Reprise 92 53584 - Canada) 1986

Killin' Floor	Foxy Lady	Like A Rolling Stone
Rock Me, Baby	Hey Joe	Can You See Me
The Wind Cries Mary	Purple Haze	Wild Thing

Comments: This is the complete performance (and in the correct running order) of the Jimi Hendrix Experience at the Monterey International Pop Festival which took place June 18, 1967. Jimi would become an instant rock star after his performance on this night - setting his guitar on fire and smashing it to bits would aid in this achievement. For many, this was Jimi's greatest stage moment and one which is etched in the psyche of all rock music fans. Also appearing on stage that day were Buffalo Springfield, The Blues Project, The Mamas & The Papas, The Grateful Dead and The Who.

JOHNNY B. GOODE
(Capitol MLP 15022 - USA) Jun 86 & (Capitol/EMI FA 3160 - English) Mini LP.
  All Along The Watchtower (1) / The Star Spangled Banner (1) / Machine Gun (2) / Voodoo Child (slight return)-part (2) / Johnny B. Goode (1).
  Comments: Recorded live (1) 2nd Atlanta Pop Festival (Jul 70) / (2) Berkeley (May 70).

LIVE AT WINTERLAND
(Rykodisc 0038 - USA) 2LP May 87 & (Polydor 833-004-1 - German) 2LP (three sides with one side blank)1987 & (Rykodisc 847 238-2 - Australia) 1987 & (Rykodisc 833 004-1 - English) 1987
  Prologue / Fire / Manic Depression / Sunshine Of Your Love / Spanish Castle Magic / Red House / Killin' Floor / Tax Free / Foxy Lady / Hey Joe / Purple Haze / Wild Thing / Epilogue
  Comments: A collection of live performances from Winterland in San Francisco and recorded on October 11, 1968 and October 12, 1968.

RADIO ONE
(Ryko Analogue RALP 0078-2 - USA) 2LP Nov 88 & (Castle Communications CCSLP - English) 2LP

Stone Free (1)	Radio One (2)
Day Tripper (2)	Killin' Floor (3)
Love Or Confusion (1)	Drivin' South (4)
Catfish Blues (4)	Wait Until Tomorrow (5)
Getting My Heart Back Together Again (5)	Hound Dog (4)
Fire (3)	I'm Your Hoochie Coochie Man (6)
Purple Haze (3)	Spanish Castle Magic (5)
Hey Joe (1)	Foxy Lady (1)
The Burning Of The Midnight Lamp (4)	

SOUNDTRACK RECORDINGS

THE SINGLES ALBUM

CRASH LANDING

LOOSE ENDS

WAR HEROES

FROM NINE TO THE UNIVERSE

Comments: A much-anticipated and highly successful release of some of Jimi's performances on the BBC. Jimi performed a total of 30 songs on the BBC - all of which can be found on JIMI HENDRIX EXPERIENCE: THE BBC SESSIONS.

Song sources: (1) 'Saturday Club' February 13, 1967 / (2) 'Top Gear' December 24, 1967 / (3) 'Saturday Club' March 28, 1967 / (4) 'Top Gear' October 6, 1967 / (5) 'Top Gear' December 15, 1967 / (6) 'Rythmn And Blues' October 17, 1967

LIVE & UNRELEASED
(Castle Communications HBLP 100 - French & English) 5LP Nov 89.

I Don't Live Today / Remember / Stone Free / Cherokee Mist / Star Spangled Banner / Bleeding Heart / Testify Pt. I / Drivin' South / I'm A Man / Like A Rolling Stone / Little One / Red House / Hey Joe / Instrumental / The Wind Cries Mary / Love Or Confusion / Foxy Lady / Third Stone From The Sun / Killin' Floor / Wild Thing / Tax Free / May This Be Love / Mr. Bad Luck / Look Over Yonder / The Burning Of The Midnight Lamp / You've Got Me Floating / Spanish Castle Magic / Bold As Love / One Rainy Wish / Little Wing / Drivin' South / The Things I Used To Do / All Along The Watchtower / Drifter's Escape / Cherokee Mist / Voodoo Chile / Voodoo Child (slight return) / ...And The Gods Made Love / 1983...A Merman I Should Turn To Be / Have You Ever Been (To Electric Ladyland) / Voodoo Chile / Rainy Day, Dream Away / Come On (Pt. 1) / Fire / Manic Depression / Astro Man / The Stars That Play With Laughing Sam's Dice / Machine Gun / Stepping Stone / Room Full Of Mirrors / Angel / Rainy Day Shuffle / Valleys Of Neptune / Drifting / Send My Love To Linda (2) / South Saturn Delta / God Save The Queen / Dolly Dagger / Can I Whisper In Your Ear / Night Bird Flying / Getting My Heart Back Together Again

Comments: Six-hour radio show. Interviews and mostly incomplete versions of the songs listed above. First aired in the U.S. during September 1988. Enjoyable.

CORNERSTONE 1967-1970
(Polydor 847 231-1 - English) LP 1990

Hey Joe / Foxy Lady / Purple Haze / The Wind Cries Mary / Have You Ever Been To (Electric Ladyland) / Crosstown Traffic / All Along The Watchtower / Voodoo Chile (slight return) / Star Spangled Banner / Stepping Stone / Room Full Of Mirrors / Ezy Rider / Freedom / Drifting / In From The Storm / Angel / Fire (live) / Stone Free (live)

Comments: Compilation of previously released material.

FIRST RAYS OF THE NEW RISING SUN
(Experience Hendrix 622-900V - USA) 1997 Numbered vinyl

See the CD entry for track information.

FIRST RAYS OF THE NEW RISING SUN
(Experience Hendrix 622-900EV - English) 1997 Numbered vinyl

SOUTH SATURN DELTA
(Experience Hendrix 622-905V - USA) 1998 Numbered vinyl

See the CD entry for track information.

SOUTH SATURN DELTA
(Experience Hendrix 622-905EV - English) 1998 Numbered vinyl

THE JIMI HENDRIX EXPERIENCE: BBC SESSIONS
(Experience Hendrix 622-909V - USA) 3 LP 1998

See the CD entry for track information.

THE JIMI HENDRIX EXPERIENCE: BBC SESSIONS
(Experience Hendrix 622-909EV - English) 3LP 1998

The Compact Discs

ARE YOU EXPERIENCED?

(Polydor 825 416-2 - German) & (Polydor 521 036-2 - English) & (Polydor P0CP-2019 - Japanese) 1991 & (MCA Records MCAD 10893 - USA) 1993 & (MCA Records MCASD10893 - Canada) 1993 & (Experience Hendrix MCAD-11602 - USA) 1997 & (Experience Hendrix/MCA MCA-11602 - English) 1997 & (Experience Hendrix/MCA MVCE-24027 - Japanese) 1997

Foxy Lady / Manic Depression / Red House / Can You See Me? / Love Or Confusion / I Don't Live Today / May This Be Love / Fire / 3rd Stone From The Sun / Remember / Are You Experienced?

AXIS: BOLD AS LOVE

(Polydor P0CP-2020 - Japanese) 1991 & (MCA MCAD-10894 - USA) 1993 & (MCA MCASD10894 - Canada) 1993 & (Experience Hendrix MCAD-11601 - USA) 1997 & (Experience Hendrix/MCA MCA-11601 - English) 1997 & (Experience Hendrix/MCA MVXE-24028 - Japanese) 1997

ELECTRIC LADYLAND

(Reprise 6307-2 - USA 2CD) 1990 & (Reprise CRJC-6307 - Canada) 1990 & (Polydor 823 359-2 -German 2CD) 1990 & (Polydor P58P 25001/2 - Japanese 2CD) 1990 & (Polydor P0CP-2021 - Japanese) 1991 & (Reprise 6307-2 - USA 1CD) & (Polydor 847 233-2 English 2CD) & (MCA MCAD-10895 - USA) 1993 & (MCA MCASD10895 - Canada) 1993 & (Experience Hendrix MCAD-11600 - USA)1997 & (Experience Hendrix/MCA MCA-11600 - English) 1997 & (Experience Hendrix/MCA MVCE-24029 - Japanese) 1997

SMASH HITS

(Reprise 2276-2 - USA) Nov 89 & (Reprise CD 2276 - Canada) 1989 & (Polydor 825 255-2 - German)

Purple Haze / Fire / The Wind Cries Mary / Can You See Me / Hey Joe / Stone Free / Manic Depression / Foxy Lady / Crosstown Traffic / All Along The Watchtower / Red House / Remember / 51st Anniversary / Highway Chile

WOODSTOCK

(Mobile Fidelity Sound Lab 4-816-1/2 - USA) & (Atlantic SD 500-2 - USA & English) & (MCA MCAD 11063 - USA) 1994 & (MCA MCASD11063 - Canada) 1994

WOODSTOCK 2

(Mobile Fidelity Sound Lab 4-816-3/4 - USA) & (Atlantic 781 981-2 - German)

JIMI PLAYS MONTEREY

(Reprise CD 25358 - Canada) 1986 & (Polydor P0CP-2026 - Japan) 1991

THE CRY OF LOVE

(Polydor P0CP-2023 - Japanese) 1991

THE LAST EXPERIENCE

(Bescol CD-42 - German/Italy?) Live at Royal Albert Hall / Feb. 24, 1969

Little Wing / Voodoo Child (slight return) / Room Full Of Mirrors (incomplete) / Fire / Purple Haze / Wild Thing / Bleeding Heart (incomplete) / The Sunshine Of Your Love / Room Full Of Mirrors / Bleeding Heart / Smashing Of Amps

ISLE OF WIGHT

(Polydor 831 313-2 - Netherlands) 1988 & (Polydor 831 313-2 - German) 1990 & (Polydor P0CP-2028 - Japanese) 1991

SMASH HITS

WOODSTOCK

BAND OF GYPSYS

LIVE AT WINTERLAND

KISS THE SKY

RADIO ONE

HENDRIX IN THE WEST
(Polydor 831 312-2 - German) 1990 & (Polydor P33P 25004 - Japanese) 1990

WAR HEROES
(Polydor P0CP-2024 - Japanese) 1991 & (Polydor 847 262-2 - German) 1993

THE ULTIMATE EXPERIENCE
(MCA MCAD 10829 - USA) 1992 & (MCA MCASD10829 - Canada) 1992 & (Polydor 517 235-2 - English) 1992

LOOSE ENDS
(Polydor 837 574-2 - German)

CRASH LANDING
(Polydor P0CP-2025 - Japanese) 1991

THE ESSENTIAL JIMI HENDRIX VOLUMES ONE AND TWO
(Reprise 26035-2 - USA) 11/89 2CD
Are You Experienced / Third Stone From The Sun / Purple Haze / Hey Joe / Fire / Foxy Lady / The Wind Cries Mary / Little Wing / If 6 Was 9 / Bold As Love / Little Miss Lover / Castles Made Of Sand / The Burning Of The Midnight Lamp / Voodoo Child (slight return) / Crosstown Traffic / Still Raining, Still Dreaming / Have You Ever Been (To Electric Ladyland) / All Along The Watchtower / House Burning Down / Room Full Of Mirrors / Izabella / Freedom / Dolly Dagger / Stepping Stone / Star Spangled Banner / Gloria

THE JIMI HENDRIX CONCERTS
(Media Motion Media CD 1 - English) 1989 & (Polydor P33P 25038 - Japanese) 1989 & (Reprise 9 2306-2 - USA) 1989 & (Castle Communications CCSCD 235 - French & English) 1989
Fire / Foxy Lady / I Don't Live Today / Red House / Stone Free / Are You Experienced / Little Wing / Voodoo Child (slight return) / Bleeding Heart / Hey Joe / Wild Thing / Getting My Heart Back Together Again

THE SINGLES ALBUM
(Polydor 827 369-2 - German) 2CD

KISS THE SKY
(Polydor P0CP-2029 - Japanese) 1991

LIVE AT WINTERLAND
(Polydor P0CP-2027 - Japanese) 1991 & (Rykodisc RCD 20038 - USA) 1987

RADIO ONE
(Rykodisc RCD 20078 - USA) 1989 & (Castle Communications CCSCD 212 - English) 1989

DAY TRIPPER
(Rykodisc RCD31-008 - USA) CD single 1988
Day Tripper / Drivin' South / Getting My Heart Back Together Again

PURPLE HAZE
(Polydor PZCD 33 - English) CD single 1988
Purple Haze / 51st Anniversary / All Along The Watchtower / Hey Joe

GLORIA
(Polydor 887 585-2 - German) CD single 1988
Gloria / Hey Joe / Voodoo Child (slight return) / Purple Haze

CROSSTOWN TRAFFIC
(Polydor PZCD 71 - English) 1988
Crosstown Traffic / Voodoo Child (slight return) / All Along The Watchtower / Have You Ever Been (To Electric Ladyland)

THE PEEL SESSION: THE JIMI HENDRIX EXPERIENCE
(Strange Fruit Records SFPSCD065 - England) EP 1988
Radio One Theme (1'27") / Day Tripper (3'18") / Wait Until Tomorrow (2'55") / Hear My Train A Comin' (4'52") / Spanish Castle Magic (3'06")
Comments: These songs are from the BBC sessions.

LIVE & UNRELEASED: THE RADIO SHOW
(Castle Communications HBCD 100 - English) 3CD 1989

LIFELINES
(Reprise 9 26435-2) CD 1991
Comments: Repackaging of "Live & Unreleased". Features three discs of rarities and one disc of Jimi live at the L.A. Forum on April 26, 1969.

BETWEEN THE LINES
(Reprise PRO CD-4541) CD 1991.
Comments: Sampler for "Lifelines".

SESSIONS
(Polydor 847 232-2) CD Box Set 1991
Are You Experienced?/ Axis: Bold As Love/ Electric Ladyland/ Cry Of Love

STAGES '67-'70
(Reprise PRO CD-5194 - USA) Promo CD 1991

STAGES
(Reprise 9 26732-2 - USA) 4CD Box Set 1991 & (Reprise CD 26732 - Canada) 1992 & (Polydor 511 763-2 - English) 1992 & (Polydor P0CP-2161/4 - Japanese) 1992
Stockholm 67 / Paris 68 / San Diego 69 / Atlanta 70
Stockholm (September 5, 1967): Sgt. Pepper / Fire / The Wind Cries Mary / Foxy Lady / Hey Joe / I Don't Live Today / Burning Of The Midnight Lamp / Purple Haze.
Paris (January 29, 1968): Killin' Floor / Catfish Blues / Foxy Lady / Red House / Drivin' South / The Wind Cries Mary / Fire / Little Wing / Purple Haze.
San Diego (May 24, 1969): Fire / Hey Joe / Spanish Castle Magic / Sunshine Of Your Love / Red House / I Don't Live Today / Purple Haze / Voodoo Child (slight return).
Atlanta (July 4, 1970): Fire / Lover Man / Spanish Castle Magic / Foxy Lady / Purple Haze / Hear My Train A Comin' / Stone Free / Star Spangled Banner / Straight Ahead / Room Full Of Mirrors / Voodoo Child (slight return).

FOOTLIGHTS
(Polydor 847 235-2 - German) CD Box Set 1991
Monterey / Live At The Isle Of Wight / Band Of Gypsys / Winterland

JOHNNY B. GOODE
(Capitol 432018-2) CD 1991
Comments: The soundtrack to the video. For more details refer to the Video Section of this book.

RARITIES ON CD VOL. 1 & VOL. 2
(On The Radio) CD 1991
Comments: Compilations of common material.

JIMI PLAYS BERKELEY
(BMG 791168 - UK) CD Single 1991
Comments: A 3-track CD single which was packaged with "Jimi Plays Berkeley" video.

ALL ALONG THE WATCHTOWER
Polydor 879 583-2 - French) CD Single 1991
Comments: A 3-track CD single released only in France.

THE WIND CRIES MARY
(Polydor 863 917-2 - German) CD Single 1992
Comments: A 4-track CD single released only in Germany.

LIVE AT WINTERLAND + 3
(Rykodisc RCD 20038/3+ - USA) CD 1992

CALLING LONG DISTANCE
(UniVibes UV-1001 - Ireland) CD 1992
The Burning Of The Midnight Lamp (Sept. 11, 1967, Stockholm) / Little Miss Lover (alternate take) / Foxy Lady (Nov. 10, 1967, Vitus Studio, Holland) / Catfish Blues (aka Experiencing The Blues) (Nov.

10, 1967, Vitus Studio, Holland) / Oh Man Is This Me Or What? (BBC interview, Dec. 15, 1967) / Purple Haze (March 19, 1968, Ottawa) / Fire (May 18, 1968, Miami, 2nd show) / Hear My Train A Comin' (May 18, 1968, Miami, 2nd show) / Spanish Castle Magic (Oct. 18, 1968, Winterland, 2nd show) / Slow Walking Talk (Oct. 25, 1968, unreleased studio)/Hendrix/Cox Jam / Hey Baby (New Rising Sun) (Sept. 3, 1970, Copenhagen) / Red House (Sept. 3, 1970, Copenhagen)

Comments: A disc of live cuts and outtakes made available only to subscribers of the Irish Hendrix fan club newsletter. This disc was bootlegged under the same title.

EXPERIENCE AT THE ROYAL ALBERT HALL
(J!MCO Records JICK-89100 - Japan) CD 1993

LIVE FOREVER
Guts & Grace/ Cohiba (697 124 004-2 - USA) CD 1993

Message To Love (May 30th, 1970, Berkeley - 1st show) / Fire (May 30th, 1970, Berkeley - 1st show) / I Don't Live Today (May 30, 1970, Berkeley - 2nd show)

The only official release containing these live performances. Rest of the disc filled out with live performances by other artists.

EXP OVER SWEDEN
(UniVibes UV-1002 - Ireland) CD 1994

Killin' Floor / Foxy Lady / Experiencing The Blues (aka Catfish Blues) / Hey Joe / Fire / The Wind Cries Mary / Purple Haze / Can You See Me*

Comments: A disc of Jimi live (September 4, 1967 & * May 24, 1967) in Sweden sent to subscribers of the Irish fan club newsletter for a small cost.

JIMI HENDRIX: BLUES
(MCA MCAD-11060 - USA) 1994 & (MCA MCASD11060 - Canada) 1994 & (Polydor 521 037-2 - English) 1994 & (Polydor 521 037-2 - French) 1994 & (Polydor 521 037-4 - English) 1994

1) Hear My Train A Comin'(acoustic)   2) Born Under A Bad Sign
3) Red House   4) Catfish Blues
5) Voodoo Chile Blues   6) Mannish Boy
7) Once I Had A Woman   8) Bleeding Heart
9) Jelly 292   10) Electric Church Red House
11) Hear My Train A Comin'

Comments: An excellent collection of 'blues' songs recorded during different times in Jimi's career. Unfortunately, many of the tracks are heavily edited or even composites of several takes.
Song sources: 1)December 19, 1967 (Bruce Fleming's photo studio) / 2) December 15, 1969 (Record Plant) / 3) December 13, 1966 (JHE at CBS Studios, London) / 4) November 10, 1967 (JHE Vitus Studios) / 5) May 2, 1968 (Record Plant / 6) April 22, 1969 (Record Plant) / 7) January 23, 1970 (Record Plant) / 8) March 18, 1969 (Record Plant) / 9) May 14, 1969 (Record Plant) / 10) October 29, 1968 (Hollywood's TTG Studios / 11) May 30, 1970 (Live at Berkeley)

JIMI HENDRIX: WOODSTOCK
(MCA Records MCAD-11063 - USA) 1994

Introduction / Fire / Izabella / Hear My Train A'Comin' (Get My Heart Back Together) / Red House / Jam Back At The House (Beginnings) / Voodoo Child (slight return) / Stepping Stone / The Star Spangled Banner / Purple Haze / Woodstock Improvisation / Villanova Junction / Farewell

Comments: This is not Jimi's complete performance at Woodstock. To get the complete show you will need to seek out the bootleggers' versions.

JIMI IN DENMARK
(UniVibes UV-1003 - Ireland) CD 1995

Experiencing The Blues (Jan. 7, 1968 - 2nd show) / Tax Free (Jan. 10, 1969 - 1st show) / Interview (Jan. 10, 1969) / Fire (Jan. 10, 1969 - 2nd show) / Voodoo Chile (slight return) (Jan. 10, 1969 - 2nd show) / Foxy Lady (Jan. 10, 1969 - 2nd show) / Spanish Castle Magic(Jan. 10, 1969 - 2nd show) / Freedom (Sept. 3, 1970)

Comments: Another disc available to UniVibe subscribers. This disc is a sampling of Jimi live in Denmark during several different performances.

EXP OVER SWEDEN

VOODOO SOUP

Live disc from LIFELINES

Cover art from STAGES

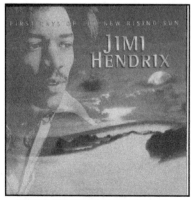

FIRST RAYS OF THE NEW RISING SUN

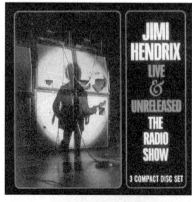

LIVE & UNRELEASED

JIMI BY HIMSELF: THE HOME RECORDINGS
(BSP-VC1) CD 1995

1983...A Merman I Should Turn To Be / Angel / Cherokee Jam / Hear My Train A Comin' / Gypsy Eyes
Comments: This is the compact disc released with the illustrated "Voodoo Child" book. For information on the tracks, refer to the Song Index. A recommended purchase for the music, although the cartoonish artwork in the book has little merit.

VOODOO SOUP
(MCA Records MCAD-11236 - USA) 1995 & (MCA MCASD11236 - Canada) 1995

The New Rising Sun / Belly Button Window / Stepping Stone / Freedom / Angel / Room Full O Mirrors / Midnight / Night Bird Flying / Drifting / Ezy Rider / Pali Gap / Message To Love / Peace Ii Mississippi / In From The Storm
Comments: This was MCA Records' attempt at compiling the tracks for the never-finished Hendrix concept album, THE FIRST RAYS OF THE NEW RISING SUN. It met with some success, still the quality just wasn't there. It would be left to Experience Hendrix (the new company run by the Hendrix family) to release the definitive version in 1997. However, this CD is the only place to get the hauntingly beautiful opening track - "The New Rising Sun".

BAND OF GYPSYS
(Polydor P0CP-2022 - Japanese) 1991 &(Capitol CDP 0777 7 96414 20 - USA) 1995 & (Experience Hendrix/MCASD 11607 - Canada) 1997 & (Experience Hendrix/MCA MCA-11607 - English) 1997 & (Experience Hendrix/MCA MVCE-24030 - Japanese) 1997 & (Capitol/Experience Hendrix 72434-93446-2-4 - USA) CD 1998

THE JIMI HENDRIX STORY
(Arcade ARC359 - French) 1996 Box Set

SOUTH SATURN DELTA
(Experience Hendrix/ MCA MCAD-11684 - USA) 1997 & (Experience Hendrix/ MCA MCA-11684 - English) 1997

1) Look Over Yonder	2) Little Wing
3) Here He Comes (Lover Man)	4) South Saturn Delta
5) Power Of Soul	6) Message To The Universe (Message To Love)
7) Tax Free	8) All Along The Watchtower
9) The Stars That Play With Laughing Sam's Dice	10) Midnight
11) Sweet Angel (Angel)	12) Bleeding Heart
13) Pali Gap	14) Drifter's Escape
15) Midnight Lightning	

Comments: Superb release from Experience Hendrix featuring studio outtakes and unreleased tracks.
Song sources (in order): October 27, 1968 (TTG Studios) / October 14, 1967 (demo) / October 29, 1968 (TTG Studios) / May 2/June 14, 1968 (Record Plant) / January 21- February 3, 1970 (Record Plant) / August 28, 1969 (Hit Factory) / January 26 & 28, 1968 (Olympic Studios) / January 21 & 26, 1968 (Olympic Studios) / July 19, 1967 (Mayfair Studios) / April 1 & 3, 1969 (Olmstead Studios) / November 13, 1967 (Olympic Studios) / March 24- June 1970 (Record Plant/Electric Lady Studios) / July 1, 1970 (Electric Lady Studios) / June/July/August 1970 (Electric Lady Studios) / March 23, 1970 (Record Plant)

FIRST RAYS OF THE NEW RISING SUN
(Experience Hendrix/MCA MCAD-11599 - USA) 1997 (Experience Hendrix/MCA MCA-11599 - English) 1997 & (Experience Hendrix/MCA MVCE-24031 - Japanese) 1997

Freedom	Izabella	Night Bird Flying
Angel	Room Full Of Mirrors	Dolly Dagger
Ezy Rider/Drifting	Beginnings	Stepping Stone
My Friend	Straight Ahead	Hey Baby (New Rising Sun)
Earth Blues	Astro Man	In From The Storm

Comments: Compiled under the direct supervision of the Hendrix family, this album was the first official attempt to gather together ALL the songs which Jimi had hoped to be his fourth studio release. The songs were recorded between March 1968 through August 1970. Many had appeared on WAR HEROES, CRY OF LOVE and RAINBOW BRIDGE but as different mixes or incomplete in form. This album is a wonderful example of what can be done with love and understanding and the master tapes. Refer to the Song Index for more information.

EXPERIENCE HENDRIX: THE BEST OF JIMI HENDRIX
(Experience Hendrix/MCA TTVCD2930 - English) 1997 & (Experience Hendrix/MCA MCD 11671 - Europe) 1997

Purple Haze / Fire / The Wind Cries Mary / Hey Joe / All Along The Watchtower / Stone Free / Crosstown Traffic / Manic Depression / Little Wing / If 6 Was 9 / Foxy Lady / Bold As Love / Castles Made Of Sand / Red House / Voodoo Child (slight return) / Freedom / Night Bird Flying / Angel / Dolly Dagger / Star Spangled Banner

THE JIMI HENDRIX EXPERIENCE: LIVE AT THE OAKLAND COLISEUM
(Dagger Records - DBRD 2-11743 - USA) 2CD 3/98

Disc 1: Fire / Hey Joe / Spanish Castle Magic / Hear My Train A Comin' / Sunshine Of Your Love / Tax Free / Red House

Disc 2: Foxey Lady / Star Spangled Banner / Purple Haze / Voodoo Child (slight return)

Comments: Authorized by Experience Hendrix. Excellent mono audience recording from April 27, 1969. The first of Dagger Records' 'official bootlegs' to be released. From a previously unknown tape. The highlight of this set is the 18-minute version of "Voodoo Child (slight return)" which will blow you away.

THE JIMI HENDRIX EXPERIENCE: BBC SESSIONS
(Experience Hendrix/MCA - MCAD2-11742 - USA) 2CD 1998

Disc 1: Foxey Lady / Alexis Korner Introduction / Can You Please Crawl Out Your Window? / Rhythm And Blues World Service / (I'm Your) Hoochie Coochie Man / Traveling With The Experience / Driving South / Fire / Little Miss Lover / Introducing The Experience / The Burning Of The Midnight Lamp / Catfish Blues / Stone Free / Love Or Confusion / Hey Joe / Hound Dog / Driving South / Hear My Train A Comin'

Disc 2: Purple Haze / Killing Floor / Radio One / Wait Until Tomorrow / Day Tripper / Spanish Castle Magic / Jammin' / I Was Made To Love Her / Foxey Lady / A Brand New Sound / Hey Joe / Manic Depression / Driving South / Hear My Train A Comin' / A Happening For Lulu / Voodoo Child (slight return) / Lulu Introduction / Hey Joe / Sunshine Of Your Love

Comments: Destined to be included in the 'must have' status for collectors this gather all of the BBC radio and television tracks available. The quality is superb with a wider and less compressed sound than before. A few unfortunate decisions were made however. Two minutes were cut from the end of "I Was Made To Love Her" ("Ain't Too Proud To Beg" in the index) and Alexis Korner's final guitar note is missing from "Can You Please Crawl Out Your Window". These are reasonably minor by comparison with the scope of the release overall but it does mean having to track down some bootleg somewhere to get 2 minutes worth of music that wouldn't have hurt anybody to have included in the first place.

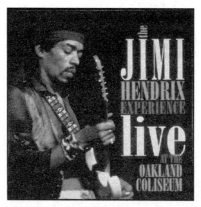

LIVE AT THE OAKLAND COLISEUM

Rare & Miscellaneous Recordings

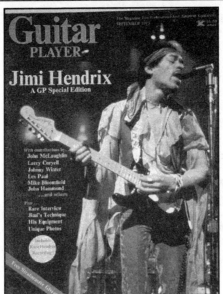

LITTLE MISS LOVER
(Emidisc - English)
> Acetate single (one-sided) pressed in late 1967

THE STARS THAT PLAY WITH LAUGHING SAM'S DICE
(Mayfair Recording Studio Inc. - USA)
> Acetate single (one-sided) pressed in 1967

THE IN SOUND
(United States Army USA-IS 67)
> A public service LP pressed in late 1967. Contains an interview with Jimi from Los Angeles recorded in 1967.

DREAM / DANCE
(Emidisc - English)
> Acetate single pressed in early 1968.

THE IN SOUND
(United States Army USA-IS51)
> A public service LP pressed in early 1968. Contains an interview with Jimi from Los Angeles recorded in 1967.

THE BURNING OF THE MIDNIGHT LAMP / HOUSE BURNING DOWN
(Bell Sound Studios Inc. - USA)
> Acetate single pressed in mid 1968.

ROLLING STONE FLEXI-DISC
(Rolling Stone) September 1973/ English

POSTER PRESS FLEXI-DISC
(Poster Press) Summer 1974/ German

...AND A HAPPY NEW YEAR
(Reprise PRO 595 - USA) 12/74 & (Reprise PRO-A 840 - USA) 12/79 Released as a promo single only.
> The Little Drummer Boy / Silent Night / Auld Lang Syne

GUITAR PLAYER FLEXI-DISC
(Guitar Player) September 1975/ USA

JIMI HENDRIX
(BBC LP 37480 - English) LP 1976 Interviews aired on BBC Radio Feb. 1976

From three different interviews: Jimi with Keith Altham at Hotel Cumberland, London, September 11, 1970 (the last recorded interview with Jimi)/Jimi with Klas Burling in Stockholm, Sweden, May 25, 1967/Jimi with Lennart Wretlind in Stockholm, January 9, 1969.

THE INTERVIEW
(Rhino Records RNDF 254 - USA)

Picture interview LP mid-Eighties & (CID Productions CID 006 - English) CD. The interview was done by Meatball Fulton at Jimi's flat in London in December 1967. Re-released in 1994 as THE INTERVIEW (CD Card CCD 4082).

RED HOUSE: VARIATIONS ON A THEME
(Hal Leonard HL00660040 - USA) CD 11/89.

Six live versions of Red House from the following venues:
1) Berkeley, May 30, 1970, first show
2) TTG Studios, October 29, 1968
3) L.A. Forum, April 26, 1969
4) Randall's Island, July 17, 1970
5) Royal Albert Hall, February 24, 1969
6) Winterland, October 10, 1968.

Available only in music stores.

FUZZ, FEEDBACK & WAH-WAH
(Hal Leonard HL00660036 - USA) CD Nov 89.

Contains only small portions of 42 songs. Available only in music stores.

WHAMMY BAR & FINGER GREASE
(Hal Leonard HL 00660038 - USA) CD Nov 89.

Contains only small portions of 40 songs. Available only in music stores.

FENDER SAMPLER
(Experience Hendrix/MCA MCA5P-4079 - USA) 1989

HENDRIX SPEAKS
(Rhino R2-70771 - USA)

Picture interview CD 1990 (Meatball Fulton from 1967-69 & Nancy Carter from 1969).

JIMI HENDRIX 1967
(If 6 Was 9 CD) CD 1991

Swedish interviews with Klas Burling.

JIMI HENDRIX 1970
(Merman - 1983) CD 1991

John Burke interview February 4, 1970.

INTROSPECTIVE
(Baktaback CINT 5006) CD 1991

Same as 'Jimi Hendrix 1970' and Scene Club from March 1968.

THE BEST + REST OF
(Action Replay CDAR 1022) CD 1991

Scene Club March 1968.

OCTAVIA & UNIVIBE
(Hal Leonard - HL00660275 - USA) 1993

RHYTHM
(Hal Leonard - HL00660281 - USA) 1993

CLASSIC ROCK COLLECTION, VOL. 1
(Rock Compact Disc - RCD1 - English) 1993

CROSSTOWN CONVERSATION
(CBAK 4082) 1994
  Picture interview CD

JIMI HENDRIX
(Sound and Media SAM006) 1995
  Picture interview CD & mini-booklet

IF SIX WERE NINE
(Laser Light 12824 - USA) CD 1997
  Interview disc featuring some brief Jimi interviews and
  audio history of Jimi as told by various friends and family
  members. Parts previously broadcast on the Westwood One
  Radio programs. Nothing remarkable here.

*I played with this little rhythm and blues group
named Curtis Knight & The Squires.
And I made a few records and
arranged a few songs for him.*
Jimi: Stockholm 1967

Hendrix With Others

Jimi performed and recorded with a great many artists, both early in his career and later on as his fame grew. The early recordings with Lonnie Youngblood reflected Youngblood's style and not Jimi's. The same can be said for the Curtis Knight, Isley Brothers and Little Richard records. Jimi was a session man for these recordings and his input was mainly limited to guitar playing and not to singing. Also be aware that many of the lead guitar parts and guitar solos were not Jimi's but the headliners. Only after Jimi became famous did the recording companies splash the name—JIMI HENDRIX—across the albums' cover art. So while Jimi is on some of these recordings, these are not true Hendrix releases.

Note that only the songs with Jimi's involvement are listed. Some of the original versions of the songs have been altered or edited by the record companies and are indicated by Roman numerals following the song titles. When possible we have listed the correct song titles and not the titles created by the record companies. This was often done by a few unscrupulous persons to make it appear that some of the songs were new to disc when in actuality the record companies were only recycling old titles.

Lonnie Youngblood

It was in the winter of 1963 that Jimi was hired to play guitar on some of Lonnie Youngblood's recording sessions. At the time, Youngblood was a well-known saxophonist in the Philadelphia area and Jimi was happy for the opportunity to play and record on Youngblood's records. If you listen closely you can hear Jimi's unique style of playing soul, the blues and rhythm & blues on these songs. These were Jimi's first recordings. Listed below is just a sampling of titles containing this material. Please note that we do not list the songs that Jimi had no involvement with.

ABTONE SESSIONS
(Jimco JICK-89273) CD
Goodbye, Bessie Mae / Soul Food.
  Also available as FREE SPIRIT (Thunderbolt CDTB 094) CD & EARLY JIMI HENDRIX LIVE (Fortune 3179) LP. Recorded in the studio in 1963.

CHEROKEE
(Dog 'N' Roll DNR 001 - Italy) CD 1993

Comments: The song listing is not known; however, what sets this apart is that it came packaged in a deluxe full-color tin.

COLLECTION
(The Collection COL017) LP

Soul Food / Let Me / Go Go Go Shoes / Sweet Thang.

Nine songs from February 24, 1969, are also included.

EARLY DAZE
(Hallmark Records 304182 - English) CD 1997

Go Go Shoes / Go Go Place / Soul Food (That's A What I Like) / Under The Table I / Under The Table II / Goodbye, Bessie Mae / Wipe The Sweat I / Wipe The Sweat II / Wipe The Sweat III

EARLY YEARS (THE)
(Charly Records CDCD 1189 - English) CD 1994

Go Go Shoes / Go Go Place / Soul Food (That's A What I Like) / Under The Table I / Under The Table II / Goodbye, Bessie Mae / Wipe The Sweat I / Wipe The Sweat II / Wipe The Sweat III

Comments: This is probably your best bet if you want a representative collection of this period.

FOR REAL
(DJMMD 8011 - English) 2LP Nov 75

Go Go Shoes / Wipe The Sweat IV / Under The Table Part IV / Wipe The Sweat V / Under The Table V / Goodbye, Bessie Mae / Sweet Thang / Groovemaker / Fox

GANGSTER OF LOVE
(Arc TOP 124) LP

Let Me Go / Soul Food / Voices

Also available as EXPERIENCES (Pulsar PULS 004) CD.

GO GO SHOES / GO GO PLACE
(Fairmount Records F-1002 -USA) Single 1963

GROOVE MAKER
(Dressed To Kill DTKBOX*!) 3CD 1998

Disc 1: *Little Richard and Jimi Hendrix*

Whole Lotta Shakin' Goin' On / Goodnight Irene / Keep A Knockin' / Going Home Tomorrow / Belle Stars / Long Tall Sally / Lawdy Miss Clawdy / Why Don't You Love Me / Lucille / Hound Dog / Money Honey / Funky Dish Rag

Disc 2: *Classic Sessions 1966*

Red House (Scene Club) / Sweet Thing / Blues Blues* / Groove Maker / Peoples Peoples* / She's A Fox (aka Fox) / Woah Eeh* / Gonna Take The Lot* / Lime Lime*

Disc 3: *Lonnie Youngblood Featuring Jimi Hendrix*

Go Go Shoes / Go Go Place / Soul Food (That's What I Like) / Under The Table I / Under The Table II / Goodbye, Bessie Mae / Two In One Goes / Wipe The Sweat I / Wipe The Sweat II / Wipe the Sweat III

Comments: Common material from several sources and songs (*) with no Jimi involvement. NO JIMI on Disc 1! Disc 2 is with Youngblood. Avoid this one.

HENDRIX
(Royal Collection RC 83113) LP

Contains the Scene Club jams from March 1968 and Go Go Shoes / Sweet Thang. Available on MASTERPIECES (Pulsar PULS 008), VOICE IN THE WIND (Trace 0401022) and VOLUME 1 / VOLUME 2 (WisePack LECDD 603). VOLUME 1 is available as a single called GOOD FEELING (Object OR0149). VOLUME 2 is a copy of WOKE UP AND FOUND MY SELF DEAD on Red Lightning.

JIMI HENDRIX
(Bellaphon 288 07 161) LP

She's A Fox (aka 'Fox')

JIMI HENDRIX IN CONCERT
(Springboard SPB-4031 - USA) LP 1980's
Under The Table III (partial) / Sweet Thang / Bleeding Heart / Tomorrow Never Knows (partial) / Outside Woman Blues / Sunshine Of Your Love
Comments: The last four songs are from the Scene Club 1968.

NIGHTLIFE
(Thunderbird CDTB 075) CD
Jimi plays on the Scene Club jams only. Incorrectly states that Jimi plays on the Lonnie Youngblood songs.

ORIGINAL JIMI HENDRIX ROOTS OF HENDRIX
(Musidisc 30 CV 1315 - French) LP 1980's
Wipe The Sweat I / Wipe The Sweat II / Goodbye, Bessie Mae / Soul Food (That's A What I Like) / Under The Table II (partial) / Under The Table III

RARE HENDRIX
(Enterprise ENTF 3000 - English) LP 07/72 & (Trip TLP-9500 - USA) & (Joker Records CSM 3535 - Italian)
Go Go Shoes / Go Go Place

SOUL FOOD (THAT'S WHAT I LIKE) / GOODBYE, BESSIE MAE
(Fairmount Records F-1022 - USA) Single 1964

THE GENIUS OF JIMI HENDRIX
(Trip TLP-9523 -USA) LP 09/74
Sweet Thang / Groovemaker / Fox (aka: She's A Fox)
Comments: These songs can also be found on JIMI HENDRIX - SUPERSTAK (TSX-3509) on Trip's 2LP 'budget' release.

THE LEGEND
(Sm'art Art WZ 98015 - Germany) CD 1995
Comments: Song listing not known; however, comes in a full-color tin.

TWO GREAT EXPERIENCES TOGETHER
(Maple Records LPM 6004 - USA) LP 03/71 & (Joker SM 3536 - Italian)
Wipe The Sweat I / Wipe The Sweat II / Wipe The Sweat III / Goodbye, Bessie Mae / Soul Food (That's A What I Like) / Under The Table I / Under The Table II / Under The Table III

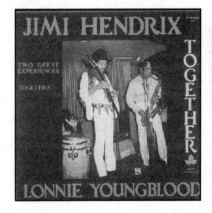

WHIPPER
(Pilz 44 7430-2 - Germany) CD 1994
Comments: Song listing not known; however, comes in a full-color tin. For some collectors that is reason enough to purchase this release.

The Isley Brothers

The Isley Brothers were in need of a guitarist and as luck would have it, a friend had seen Jimi perform at the Palm Cafe in New York and was immediately sold on him. Shortly thereafter Jimi auditioned for the Isleys and was hired to tour and record with the band. Their first recording with Jimi on lead guitar was "Testify" on their own T-Neck label. Jimi did some additional recordings with them a bit later as noted below.

TESTIFY (PART 1) / TESTIFY (PART 2)
(T-Neck 45-501 - USA) Single 1964 & (Atlantic 45-2263 - USA) 1964

THE LAST GIRL / LOOKING FOR LOVE
(T-Neck 45-2263 - USA) Single 1964 & (Atlantic AT 4010 - English) 1964

MOVE OVER AND LET ME DANCE / HAVE YOU EVER BEEN DISAPPOINTED?
(Atlantic 45-2303 - USA) Single 1965

IN THE BEGINNING
(T-Neck TNS 3007 - USA) LP 1971 & (Polydor 2310 105 - German) &
(Brunswick 2911 508 - German)

> Move Over Let Me Dance Part 1 / Have You Ever Been
> Disappointed?, Part 1 & Part 2 / Testify, Part 1 / Testify, Part
> 2 / Move Over Let Me Dance, Part 2 / The Last Girl /
> Looking For Love

THE ISLEY BROTHERS - THE COMPLETE UA SESSIONS
(United Artists CDP-7- 952032)

> The liner notes state that Jimi played on some of these
> tracks; however, that is not so. The recordings took place
> before Jimi performed with them.

THE ISLEY BROTHERS STORY VOL. 1: ROCKIN' SOUL 1959-68
(Rhino R2 70908) USA 1991

> Testify Part I and II / The Last Girl / Move Over Let Me Dance.

Little Richard & The Upsetters

Jimi played with Little Richard off and on during 1965 and played guitar on only a couple of Little Richard recordings. However, when you look in the record bins you might be fooled into thinking Jimi played on many more. This was not true. There were (and are) a few unscrupulous people in the record business who have no qualms about lying to the record buying public. Caveat emptor!

I DON'T KNOW WHAT YOU'VE GOT BUT IT'S GOT ME (PART 1) / I DON'T KNOW WHAT YOU'VE GOT BUT IT'S GOT ME (PART 2)
(Vee Jay Records VJ-698 - USA) Single 1965
> **Comments:** Jimi on tremelo.

LITTLE RICHARD IS BACK
(Vee Jay VJ-698 - USA) 1964
> **Comments:** NO Jimi.

MR. BIG
(Joy 195 - English) LP 1971
> I Don't Know What You've Got But It's Got Me Part I / Dancin' All Around The World

THE COLLECTION
(Castle Communications CCSLP227 - French) LP 1989 & (Castle Communications CCSCD227 - French) CD
> I Don't Know What You've Got But It's Got Me / Dancin' All Around The World

ROCK 'N' ROLL SPECIAL
(PMC CD 926 - German)
    I Don't Know What You've Got But It's Got Me (Part 1 & 2) / Dancin' All Around The World

RIP IT UP
(Chameleon Records D2-74797 - USA) CD 1989
    I Don't Know What You've Got But It's Got Me (Part 1 & 2)

LITTLE RICHARD AND JIMI HENDRIX
(Classic Rock CDCD 1108)
    Jimi does not appear on this 'official' European release.

LITTLE RICHARD - LONG TALL SALLY
(Trace 0401312)
    Dancin' All Around The World (listed incorrectly as "All Around The World").

Rosa Lee Brooks

MY DIARY / UTEE
(Revis Records 1013 - USA) Single 1965
    Jimi played tremelo on "My Diary" and guitar on "Utee". These were recorded in early 1965 in Los Angeles at the instigation of friend Arthur Lee (composer of "My Diary") and leader of the group Love.

King Curtis

Jimi played only briefly with King Curtis (noted sax session man) in early 1966 and played guitar on just the three songs listed below. Jimi soon went 'solo' to seek his fortune.

HELP ME (PART I) / HELP ME (PART II)
(Atco Records 45-6402 - USA) Single 1966

BLAST OFF/ PATA PATA
(Atlantic 45-2468 - USA) Single 1967.
    Jimi plays guitar on "Blast Off" only.

Jayne Mansfield

AS THE CLOUDS DRIFT BY / SUEY
(London HL 10147 - English) Single July 1967.
    Jimi plays guitar on "Suey" only; although Chalpin says Jimi played on both songs. Recorded late 1965 at Studio 76 Inc in NYC. Producer Ed Chalpin was apparently responsible for Jimi getting this session gig with the blonde bombshell. These songs are available on the CD TOO HOT TO HANDLE.

Curtis Knight & The Squires

The saga of Jimi's association with Curtis Knight and Ed Chalpin is one of naivete, deception, and misrepresentation. In October 1965 Jimi signed a contract with Chalpin's record company (PPX Enterprises). When Curtis Knight introduced Jimi to Chalpin, Jimi knew nothing of contracts and was an easy mark for the shrewd Chalpin (who knew a good thing when he saw it - and that good thing was Jimi). The contract Jimi signed practically indentured him to Chalpin for three years and with a financial arrangement that was meant to keep Jimi in the poor house. The 1% royalty Jimi signed off on was a disgrace. This contract would later haunt Jimi and force him in 1967 to make a number of substandard recordings with Knight (known now as the PPX Recordings) to fulfill his obligations to Chalpin. Before these sessions, however, Jimi did studio work with Curtis Knight and toured briefly with them in late 1965 and early 1966. Their gig of December 26, 1965, at George's Club 20 in Hackensack, New Jersey, and another at an unknown venue (late 1965 or early 1966) were recorded for posterity, and whole and parts of these shows would turn up on bootlegs and quasi-legal albums in the following years. Many songs were credited to Jimi and Curtis Knight, but a good share were faked, edited, altered and/or falsely identified. The songs listed below will help clear up some of that mess; however, we freely admit that the picture of Jimi's true involvement on these is far from clear. (Note: the Roman numerals following the song titles indicate edited or altered mixes of the original recordings.)

Live Songs:
Let The Good Times Roll (aka Come On-Part 1 & Hard Night) / Twist & Shout / Bo Diddley / Drivin' South / I'm A Man (2 versions) / Killin' Floor (2 versions) / California Night (aka Mr. Pitiful) / Ain't That Peculiar? / What'd I Say / Bright Lights, Big City / Get Out Of My Life Woman / I'll Be Doggone / (I Can't Get No) Satisfaction / Sugar Pie, Honey Bunch (I Can't Help Myself) / Land Of A Thousand Dances / You Got Me Running (aka Not This Time) / Money / Let's Go, Let's Go, Let's Go (aka Running Slow) / You Got What It Takes (aka Some Boys Say) / Sweet Little Angel / Walkin' The Dog / Wooly Bully / Bleeding Heart / Mercy Mercy (aka Have Mercy Baby) / Something You Got / Just A Little Bit / Stand By Me / Hold On To What You Got / Day Tripper / Hang On Sloopy / I Got You (I Feel Good) / One Night With You / Shotgun (Note: all these songs were originally recorded in mono.)

Studio 1965 Songs:
How Would You Feel / Welcome Home / Hornet's Nest (aka Level) / Knock Yourself Out / You Don't Want Me / Gotta Have A New Dress / Don't Accuse Me / Fool For You Baby (aka Fool About You) / Simon Says / Strange Things / No Such Animal (Part 1 & 2) / Last Night / There Is Something On Your Mind

Studio 1967 Songs:
Hush Now (aka Wah Wah) / Flashing (edited from Day Tripper) / Ballad Of Jimi (aka My Best Friend) / No Business / Future Trip (edited from Day Tripper) / Happy Birthday / Gloomy Monday / Day Tripper I / Odd Ball / Love Love / Get That Feeling (aka Second Time Around) / U.F.O.

THE AUTHENTIC PPX STUDIO RECORDINGS
VOL. 1: Get That Feeling
(CBH Records SPV-085-44222) CD 1996 German
   Get That Feeling / How Would You Feel? / Hush Now / No Business / Simon Says / Gotta Have A New Dress / Strange Things / Welcome Home

VOL. 2: Flashing
(CBH Records SPV-085-44212) CD 1996 German
   Love Love / Day Tripper / Gloomy Monday / Fool For Your Baby / Don't Accuse Me / Hornets Nest / Flashing / Oddball / Happy Birthday

VOL. 3: Ballad Of Jimi
(CBH Records SPV-085-44682) CD 1996 German
   UFO / You Don't Want Me (instr) / Better Times Ahead / Future Trip / Wah Wah (instr) / Everybody Knew But Me / Mercy Lady Day / If You Gonna Make A Fool Of Somebody / My Best Friend (instr) / The Ballad of Jimi / Second Time Around

VOL. 4: Live At George's Club
(CBH Records SPV-085-44692) CD 1996 German
   Drivin' South (Instr) / Ain't That Peculiar / I'll Be Doggone / I've Got A Sweet Little Angel / Bright Lights Big City / Get Out Of My Life Woman / Last Night(instr) / Sugar Pie, Honey Pie / What'd I Say / Shotgun

VOL. 5: Something On Your Mind
(CBH Records SPV-085-44892) CD 1997 German
   California Night (Live) / Level (instr) / I Feel Good / Let It Alone (live) / Knock Yourself Out (instr) / Something On Your Mind(live) / I Should've Quit You (live) / Hard Night (live instr) / I'm A Man (live) / Instrumental

VOL. 6: On The Killing Floor
(CBH Records SPV-085-44902) CD 1997 German
   On The Killing Floor (live) / Money (live) / Nobody Loves Me (live) / Love/ You Got Me Running (live) / Mr Pitiful (live) / Torture Me Honey (instr) / Sleepy Fate (instr) / Satisfaction (live)
   Comments: A very good collection of the Curtis Knight material recorded for PPX. If you are able to find this set, it will be expensive. Also, some of the songs have no Jimi involvement. The sound quali-

ty is very good as is the packaging.

BALLAD OF JIMI / GLOOMY MONDAY
(Decca DL 25 430 - German) Single Oct 70 & (London HLZ 10321 - English)

EARLY JIMI HENDRIX
(Stateside 5C 054-91962 - Holland) LP 1970's
Drivin' South / I'm A Man I / Killin' Floor / California Night I / Ain't That Peculiar? / What'd I Say I / Bright Lights, Big City I

EARLY JIMI HENDRIX PART 2
(Stateside 5C 052-92031 - Holland) LP 1970's
Last Night I / Get Out Of My Life Woman / I'll Be Doggone / (I Can't Get No) Satisfaction / Sugar Pie, Honey Bunch (I Can't Help Myself) I / Land Of A Thousand Dances / California Night I / U.F.O. I

FLASHING: JIMI HENDRIX PLAYS CURTIS KNIGHT SINGS
(Capitol ST 2894 - USA) LP 1968
Gloomy Monday I / Fool For You Baby / Day Tripper I / Odd Ball I / Love Love I / Hornet's Nest II / Happy Birthday I / Flashing II / Don't Accuse Me I

GET THAT FEELING
(Capitol ST 2856 - USA) LP Dec 67 & (London SH 8349 - English) 1967 & (London LDY 379256 - Holland) 1968 & (Quality SV 1812 - Canada) 1968 & (Birchmount BM567 - Canada) 1968
Ballad Of Jimi I / No Business I / Future Trip / Gotta Have A New Dress / Hornet's Nest II / Don't Accuse Me I / Hush Now II / Flashing II / Knock Yourself Out II / Happy Birthday I

GET THAT FEELING/ DAY TRIPPER
(Quality SV-1822-2 - Canada) Vinyl single 1969

GUITAR GIANTS VOL. I
(Babylon DB 80020 - German) 2LP 1980's
California Night II / California Night III / Get That Feeling III / Wooly Bully / Bleeding Heart I / Killin' Floor II / Welcome Home II / Sugar Pie, Honey Bunch (I Can't Help Myself) II / Get Out Of My Life Woman / Ain't That Peculiar / Bleeding Heart II / Fool For You Baby / Killin' Floor I / Land Of A Thousand Dances / Twist & Shout / Knock Yourself Out II / Let The Good Times Roll

GUITAR GIANTS VOL. II
(Babylon DB 80021 - German) 2LP 1980's
Last Night II / You Got What It Takes III / I'm A Man II / Don't Accuse Me II / Hush Now II / Odd Ball I / No Business II / Ballad Of Jimi II / Strange Things I / You Got Me Running I / Walkin' The Dog I / Flashing I / Hush Now V / No Business I / U.F.O. I / Love Love I / Hornet's Nest II / Ballad Of Jimi IV / How Would You Feel?

HISTORIC HENDRIX
(Pair Records SPCD2 - USA) CD 1986
Get That Feeling I / How Would You Feel? / Hush Now IV / No Business I / Simon Says I / Gotta Have A New Dress / Strange Things I / Welcome Home II / Love Love I / Day Tripper I / Gloomy Monday I / Fool For You Baby / Happy Birthday I / Don't Accuse Me II / Hornet's Nest I / Flashing I / Odd Ball I

HORNETS NEST / KNOCK YOURSELF OUT
(RSVP 1124 - USA) Single 1966

HOW WOULD YOU FEEL? / WELCOME HOME
(RSVP 1120 - USA) Single 1966

HUSH NOW / FLASHING
(London HL 10160 - English) Single Oct 67
Comments: During an interview in 1969 Jimi remarked, "When I played it, I discovered that it had been recorded with a jam session I did in New York. We had only been practicing in the studio. I had no idea it was being recorded. On one side of the disc is 'Hush Now'...I only play the guitar, the singer's voice has been superimposed. On the other—'Flashing'—all I do is play a couple of notes. Man, was I shocked when I heard it."

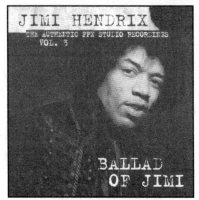

PPX RECORDINGS VOL. 3

PPX RECORDINGS VOL. 4

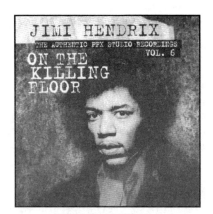

PPX RECORDINGS VOL. 6

GET THAT FEELING

LAST NIGHT

HUSH NOW/ FLASHING

HUSH NOW
(Astan 201021 - German) LP 1981
> Love Love IV / Hornet's Nest III / Gloomy Monday II / Hush Now II / No Business I / U.F.O. I / Simon Says I / Day Tripper I

IN THE BEGINNING
(Ember NR 5068 - English) LP 1973
> You Got Me Running I / Money / Let's Go, Let's Go, Let's Go I / You Got What It Takes I / Sweet Little Angel I / Walkin' The Dog I / There Is Something On Your Mind / Let The Good Times Roll

IN THE BEGINNING
(Everest CBR 1031 - English) 2LP 1980's
> Sugar Pie, Honey Bunch (I Can't Help Myself) II / Day Tripper / Mr. Pitiful / Stand By Me / Bright Lights, Big City I / (I Can't Get No) Satisfaction / You Got What It Takes I / Land Of A Thousand Dances / I'm A Man I / Hold (On To) What You've Got / Twist & Shout / What'd I Say II / Woolly Bully / Walkin' The Dog I / Hang On Sloopy
>
> Comments: This set is fairly decent and is probably the one to seek out for the Curtis Knight material.

JIMI HENDRIX INSTRUMENTAL
(Music For Pleasure 2M 046/94370 - French) LP 1980's
> Strange Things II / Hush Now VI / Hornet's Nest II / No Business II / Hush Now V / Ballad Of Jimi II / Love Love III

JIMI HENDRIX THE COLLECTION
(Object Enterprises OR 0071 - French) CD 1990

JIMMY JAMES AND HIS BLUE FLAMES
(Blue Flames 5205) Single
> Bright Lights, Big City / I'm A Man / No Such Animal Pt. 1 / No Such Animal Pt. 2

LAST NIGHT
(Astan 201016 - German) LP 1981
> Let's Go, Let's Go, Let's Go II / Sweet Little Angel II / You Go What It Takes II / Walkin' The Dog II / Bright Lights, Big City II / Sweet Little Angel III / Money / You Go Me Running I / Hang On Sloopy / Last Night I

LEGENDS OF ROCK (THE)
(Strand 6.28530 DP - German) 2LP 1980's
> U.F.O. II / Get That Feeling I / Drivin' South / How Would You Feel? / Ballad Of Jimi II / Gloomy Monday I / I'm A Man I / Hush Now IV / California Night I / Land Of A Thousand Dances / Love Love III / Get Out Of My Life Woman / Don't Accuse Me I

LOOKING BACK WITH JIMI HENDRIX
(Ember EMB 3428 - English) LP 1975
> Ballad Of Jimi IV / Don't Accuse Me II / Hang On Sloopy / Twist & Shout / Bo Diddley / Hush Now V / Knock Yourself Out II / No Business I / Gotta Have A New Dress / Flashing II

MR. PITIFUL
(Astan 201019 - German) LP 1981
> Wooly Bully / Bleeding Heart I / Mercy Mercy / Something You Got / Just A Little Bit / Stand By Me / Hold (On To) What You Got / Killin' Floor II / California Night I

MY BEST FRIEND
(Astan 201017 - German) LP 1981
> Day Tripper II / No Business II / Ballad Of Jimi II / Get That Feeling I / Happy Birthday I / Hush Now II / Odd Ball I

NO SUCH ANIMAL PART 1 / NO SUCH ANIMAL PART 2
(RCA 2033 - English) Single Feb 71 & (Audio Fidelity Records AF 167 - USA) & (Bellaphon BF 18019 - German) & (Audio Fidelity AF 45.003H - Holland) & (Audio Fidelity Records AF 11.002 - French)

ROCK LEGENDS
(Rock Legends Of America RWJH-07) EP

No Such Animal Pt. 1 / No Such Animal Pt. 2 / Soul Food / Goodbye, Bessie Mae / Go Go Shoes I / Go Go Shoes II / My Diary / Utee

SECOND TIME AROUND
(Astan 201018 - German) LP 1981

Hush Now V / Love Love III / Let The Good Times Roll / Get That Feeling II / Happy Birthday II

16 GREATEST CLASSICS
(Bigtime 2615252 - German) CD 1989

Strange Things I / Welcome Home II / Day Tripper I / Simon Says I / Fool For You Baby / Don't Accuse Me II / Flashing I / Odd Ball I / Hornet's Nest I / Happy Birthday I

STRANGE THINGS
(Success 2171CD) CD

Flashing I / Hornet's Nest I / Don't Accuse Me II / Simon Says I / Day Tripper I / Welcome Home II / Strange Things I / Odd Ball I / Soul Food (That's A What I Like) / Tomorrow Never Knows (part) / Instrumental 4 / Monday Morning Blues

Comments: The first nine tracks are of Jimi with the Squires. "Soul Food" is with Lonnie Youngblood and the last two tracks are jams with Mike Ephron. "Tomorrow Never Knows" is from the Scene Club March 1968.

THE GREAT JIMI HENDRIX IN NEW YORK
(London 379 008 XNU - Holland) 2LP Dec 68

Get That Feeling I / Hush Now III / Welcome Home II / Simon Says I / Simon Says II / Love Love II / U.F.O. I / Hush Now IV / Strange Things I / Odd Ball II / Future Trip / Flashing II / Ballad Of Jimi I / Love Love I / Gloomy Monday I / Hush Now II / Day Tripper I

THE PSYCHEDELIC VOODOO CHILD
(Remember RMB 75003) LP

Comments: A catchy title; however, only thirteen of the twenty songs have Jimi playing on them (with the Squires). Also includes "Soul Food" with Lonnie Youngblood.

WELCOME HOME
(Astan 201020 - German) LP 1981

You Got Me Running II / What'd I Say? II / Bleeding Heart II / Sugar Pie, Honey Bunch (I Can't Help Myself) I / Get Out Of My Life Woman / Ain't That Peculiar / Welcome Home II / I'll Be Doggone / Drivin' South

WHAT'D I SAY?
(Music For Pleasure MFP 5278 - USA) LP 1972

Drivin' South / California Night I / Killin' Floor I / What'd I Say? / I'll Be Doggone / Bright Lights, Big City I

ṀcGough & ṀcGear

MCGOUGH & MCGEAR
(EMI Parlophone PCS 7047 - English) LP 04/68 & (Parlophone PCS 7332 - English) LP 1989 & (EMI CDP 7 91877 2 - English) CD 1989

So Much / Ex Art Student

Comments: Jimi plays lead guitar on these two songs produced by Paul McCartney (Mike McGear is Paul's brother). Other performers on this album were Noel Redding, Mitch Mitchell, Jack Bruce, Paul McCartney and Dave Mason.

Fat Mattress

FAT MATTRESS
(Polydor 583 056 - English) LP Aug 69 & (Atco SD 33-309 - USA) LP Oct 69 & CD
How Can I Live?
Comments: Jimi plays some percussion only on the one song from friend Noel Redding's album. Mitch Mitchell also performs on this album.

Robert Wyatt

SLOW WALKING TALK/ SLOW WALKING TALK
(Mastering Lab - USA) Acetate single 1968
Comments: Jimi played bass - using Noel Redding's right-handed instrument. One take! It is the same song on both sides of the acetate.

Eire Apparent

ROCK 'N" ROLL BAND / YES I NEED SOMEONE
(Buddah Records 201039 - English) Single Mar 69 & (Buddah Records 2011-117 - USA)
Comments: Jimi played guitar on both songs.

SUNRISE
(Buddah Records 203 021 - English) LP May 69 & (Buddah Records BDS 5031) LP 1969 & (Repetoire RR 4174-WZ - German) 1991 & (One Way Records OW 27734 - Canada) 1993
Yes I Need Someone* / Rock 'N' Roll Band* / The Clown* / Mr. Guy Fawkes* / Someone Is Sure To (Want You)* / Morning Glory* / Magic Carpet* / Captive In The Sun* / Got To Get Away / 1026 .
Comments: The U.S. version replaces "Rock 'N' Roll Band" with "Let Me Stay". *Jimi on lead guitar.

Timothy Leary

YOU CAN BE ANYONE THIS TIME AROUND
(Douglas 1 - USA) LP Apr 70 & (Rykodisc RCD 10249) CD 1992
Live And Let Live
Comments: Jimi plays bass on this one song only. Stephen Stills plays lead guitar. Recorded in May 1969. Timothy Leary's dead and on the outside looking in.

Lightnin' Rod

DORIELLA DU FONTAINE / DORIELLA DU FONTAINE
(Celluloid CART 232 - USA) 12-inch single Jul 84 & (Carrere Records 332 - English) 12-inch single & (Restless 72663-2 USA) 1992
Comments: Jimi plays guitar and bass on both tracks. Recorded in November 1969 and produced by Alan Douglas.

Doriella Du Fontaine

Stephen Stills

STEPHEN STILLS
(Atlantic 2401 004 - English) LP Nov 70 & (Atlantic SD 7202) LP Nov 70 & (Atlantic 940 058 - French) LP & (Atlantic 7202-2 - USA) CD
Old Times Good Times
Comments: Jimi on lead guitar. This was the first take. There are said to be hours of jamming with Jimi and Stephen on tape in Stephen's possession. When do we get to hear this?

Love

FALSE START
(Blue Thumb BTS 22 - USA) LP Dec 70
Slick Dick / Ride That Vibration / The Everlasting First
Comments: Jimi may not have played guitar on "Slick Dick" or "Ride That Vibration." This is an excellent album if you can find it.

THE EVERLASTING FIRST/ KEEP ON SHINING
(Harvest HAR 5030 - English) Single Nov 70 & (Blue Thumb 7116 - USA) Single & (Blue Thumb 5C 006-92 011 - Holland) Single.
Comments: Jimi did not play on "Keep On Shining".

Buddy Miles Express

EXPRESSWAY TO YOUR SKULL
(Mercury 20137 SMLC - English) LP Jan 69 & (Mercury SR-61196 - USA) 1969
Comments: Jimi just wrote the introductory liner notes which appeared on the inside cover of the LP.

ELECTRIC CHURCH
(Mercury 20163SMCL - English) LP 1969 & (Mercury SR-61222 - USA) LP
Comments: Jimi did not play on this record; however, he did produce "Miss Lady", "69 Freedom Special", "Destructive Love" and "My Chant".

THE BEST OF BUDDY MILES
(Mercury Records 314 510 310-2 -USA) CD 1997
Comments: Includes "Miss Lady" and an unedited and previously unreleased version of "69 Freedom Special".

Cat Mother And The All Right Newsboys

THE STREET GIVETH...AND THE STREET TAKETH AWAY
(Polydor 24-4001 - USA) LP Jun 69 & (Polydor 184 300 - English) LP & CD (Polydor 537616-2 - USA 1997)
Comments: Jimi produced the songs for the album. He did not perform on any of the tracks although it is rumored he may have played rhythm guitar on "Track In 'A' (Nebraska Nights)."

CAN YOU DANCE TO IT? / MARIE
(Polydor PD2-14007 - USA) Vinyl single 1969

Ghetto Fighters

GHETTO FIGHTERS
(unreleased) 1970

Comments: Produced by Jimi and the Ghetto Fighters (Arthur & Albert Allen). Engineered by Eddie Kramer. This album has yet to see the light of day and probably won't given the state of the music business today.

Some cat went to a private practice session with
a tiny tape recorder and made a pirate LP.
The quality must be terrible.
Jimi: London 1969

The Bootlegs

Picture disc from A SESSION (Jimi & Traffic)

500,000 HALOS   IN ***
NO LABEL (exp 500000/HTX 01) CD (66:25)

Drifter's Escape (2:14) / Stone Free (13:17) / Villanova Junction Blues (4:18) / Bolero (6:14) / Getting My Heart Back Together Again (8:21) / Message To The Universe (Message To Love)(7:55) / Hendrix-Young Jam (Fuzzy Guitar Jam)(19:55) / Belly Button Window (4:05)

Comments: Excellent stereo recordings. Rumor has it that some of this material was at one time considered for the official BLUES release, but for some reason it never occurred. Lots of rarities here and several titles which are available here in their longest form yet. This disc has the first complete release of the opening song for the Woodstock show "Message To Love". Highly recommended.

1968 A.D.   IN *
WHOOPY CAT (WKP-0012) CD (72:36)

Rainy Day Shuffle / Rainy Day Dream Away / Gypsy Eyes / Gypsy Eyes / Gypsy Eyes / Come On (Part One) / Come On (Part One) / Three Little Bears / Tax Free / Ezy Rider (instrumental) / House Burning Down / House Burning Down / Burning Of The Midnight Lamp / Foxy Lady / Fire / Hear My Train A Comin' / Purple Haze

Comments: A nice collection of mostly common outtakes and demos. Most of the Whoopy Cat releases are good additions to your collection, although some of the studio material can be found in better sound on some newer releases.

1968 A.D. PART TWO   IN *
WHOOPY CAT (WKP-0013) CD (74:59)

1983..A Merman I Should Turn To Be / Angel / Cherokee Mist / Hear My Train A Comin' / Voodoo Chile-Cherokee Mist - Gypsy Eyes / Long Hot Summer Night / Long Hot Summer Night / Have You

Ever Been To Electric Ladyland / All Along The Watchtower / Voodoo Chile / Rainy Day Jam Out Take / Rainy Day Jam Out Take / 1983..A Merman I Should Turn To Be / Have You Ever Been To Electric Ladyland / Little Miss Strange / Somewhere / 1983..A Merman I Should Turn To Be

Comments: Tracks 1-8 are from the home composing demo tape from early 1968. Most of this tape was issued on a CD that came with the book "Voodoo Child: The Illustrated Legend Of Jimi Hendrix" in better sound and in sort of a two track stereo mix. Tracks 9-16 are alternate studio versions. Track 16 is the CR in poor quality. A good but not necessary CD.

A BAND OF GYPSYS: GYPSY BLUES
OCTAVIA (OCT 9505) CD-R

Jam Session / Jam Session / Message To Love / Message To Love / Message To Love / Message To Love / Ezy Rider / Ezy Rider / Ezy Rider / Jam Session

Comments: Probably made in somebody's basement - so good luck ever trying to find one. Too bad as the Ezy Rider material is unavailable elsewhere except on another equally obscure CD-R.

A MAN OF OUR TIME
NAPOLEON (NLP 11018) LP

Side 1: Highway Chile / Stone Free / Hound Dog / Foxy Lady
Side 2: Foxy Lady / Little Miss Lover / Experiencing The Blues / Sunshine Of Your Love
Comments: Material common to CD boots. All of this material has been commercially released now.

...AND A HAPPY NEW YEAR
REPRISE (fake) Vinyl single

Little Drummer Boy / Silent Night/ Auld Lang Syne
Comments: Pirated copy of the legitimate promo single. These tracks are very commonly booted.

AT THE ISLE OF WIGHT
QWSD-9603 CD

God Save The Queen / Sergeant Pepper's Lonely Hearts Club Band / Spanish Castle Magic / All Along The Watchtower / Voodoo Chile (slight return) / Machine Gun / Freedom / Red House / Dolly Dagger / In From The Storm

Comments: These tracks all come from the Isle Of Wight soundboard film and is rendered obsolete by the legitimate release.

A SESSION IN *
OH BOY (1-9027) CD (60:26)

Jam Thing / Guitar Thing (Lonely Avenue Part 1) / Session Thing

Comments: The players on tracks 1 & 3 are Jimi, Steve Winwood on organ, Chris Wood on flute or sax, Jim Capaldi on drums and some report that Jack Casady from Jefferson Airplane is on bass. Track 2 is a jam with Buddy Miles. A portion of the last jam is included on NOT JUST A VOODOO CHILE (Pilot HJCD071) which also includes a commercially released version of "Peace In Mississippi," "Come On Part One" and 14:32 of someone (NOT Jimi) on acoustic guitar. The sound quality on all three jams is excellent. All three tracks appear on other releases, but this is worthwhile to pick up if you don't already have them.

ACOUSTIC JAMS IN *
SPINX (SX CD 001) CD (CD1 59:12, CD2 53:55)

CD1: Long Summer Night 1&2 / 1983... / Angel / Cherokee Mist / Astro Man / Money / Voodoo Child / Come On / Hear My Train / Voodoo Child / Gypsy Eyes 1 & 2 / Beginnings
CD2: Little Miss Strange / Three Little Bears / Inst. / Gypsy Eyes / 1983... / Drifting / Look Over Yonder / Send My Love To You / Drifting / Belly Button Window / Freedom / Valley Of Neptune / Cherokee Mist / Acoustic Jam
Comments: The sound is very good to excellent. This is a European disc. The cover sticker states that this is a 'Double Sided' CD. However, when you take off the shrink wrap and open the case you will find two CDs glued together. This disc WILL JAM most CD players. Re-released as two separate discs. This has most of the home acoustic composing tape from early 1968 and material that's not common but has been booted elsewhere.

ALIVE
TRADE MARK OF QUALITY (TMQ 72003 & TMQ 7509) 2LP

Side 1: Spanish Castle Magic / Foxy Lady / Lover Man / Hear My Train A Comin'

Side 2: Room Full Of Mirrors / Hey Baby (New Rising Sun) / Villanova Junction / Freedom/ Message To Love

Side 3: Ezy Rider / Machine Gun / Star Spangled Banner / Purple Haze

Side 4: Voodoo Chile (slight return) / Lightning

Comments: Fair audience tape recorded April 25, 1970, at the Los Angeles Forum, L.A., California. Also on LIVE AT THE LOS ANGELES FORUM (Rubber Dubber 900 2) & (K & S 013) & (POD), ENJOY JIMI HENDRIX (Rubber Dubber 70 001), LIVE AT THE FORUM (King Kong) & (Munia M1622) & (Contraband), and ALIVE (Box Top Records 70413/6).

AMERICAN DREAM
WORLD PRODUCTIONS OF COMPACT MUSIC (WPOCM 0589 D 023 2) CD

Tax Free (9:31) / Purple Haze (4:10) / Wild Thing (6:45) / Earth Blues (4:08) / Hey Joe (4:04) / Hey Baby (6:07) / Lover Man (2:50) / Hound Dog (4:26)

Comments: These recordings are very good to excellent soundboard. Tracks 1-3 are from Ottawa, Canada, March 19, 1968. Tracks 4-8 are from Berkeley, May 30, 1970 (second show). European CD. Both of these shows are available complete on other CD's.

ANTHOLOGY IN
BOX 9 (3 CD)

CD1: Foxy Lady / I Don't Live Today / Red House / Spanish Castle Magic / Star Spangled Banner / The Wind Cries Mary / The Burning Of The Midnight Lamp / Fire

CD2: Purple Haze / Voodoo Chile (slight return) / Sunshine Of Your Love / Experiencing The Blues / Killin' Floor / Can You Please Crawl Out Your Window / Hey Joe

CD3: Tax Free / Sergeant Pepper's Lonely Hearts Club Band / Drivin' South / Little Wing / Little Miss Lover / Wild Thing / Bleeding Heart / Room Full Of Mirrors

Comments: A collection of live soundboard tracks from the LA Forum, Royal Albert Hall & Stockholm. All of these shows can be found complete on other CD's.

APARTMENT JAM 70 IN ***
SPICY ESSENCE CD

Jam 1 (Country Blues) / Jam 2 / Room Full Of Mirrors / Astro Man - Valleys Of Neptune / Jam 3 / Jam 4 / Jam 5 (Country Blues-the same as Jam 1)

Comments: These jams between Jimi and an unknown guitarist were probably recorded at Jimi's New York apartment sometime in late 1969. This was originally released as a very obscure acetate pressing. The first 4 tracks are also on the old vinyl boot TWO SIDES OF THE SAME GENIUS (Amazing Kornyphone TAKRL H-6770). All of this material was include on the Major Tom release SESSION 4. All of these releases are hard to find.

ATLANTA IN **
JMH 009/02 2CD

Disc 1: Fire / Lover Man / Spanish Castle Magic / Red House / Room Full Of Mirrors / Hear My Train A Comin' / Message To Love / All Along The Watchtower / Freedom/ Foxy Lady / Purple Haze / Hey Joe

Disc 2: Voodoo Child (slight return) / Stone Free / Star Spangled Banner / Straight Ahead / Hey Baby (New Rising Sun) / Lord I Sing The Blues / Dance / Nightbird Flying / Lonely Avenue Jam (part1) / My Friend / 1983...A Merman I Should Turn To Be / Drivin' South - Everything's Gonna Be Alright / Jams 1 & 2

Comments: The complete show from the 2nd International Pop Festival in Atlanta, GA, on July 4, 1970. Patched together from a couple of sources, it's nice to get the whole show on one release. Disc 2 is filled out some harder to find jams in complete form ('Drivin' South / Everything's Gonna Be Alright' along with the 2 loose jams that followed the McLaughlin sessions).

ATLANTA SPECIAL IN **
THE GENUINE PIG (TCP - CD - 121) CD (60:16)

Message To Love (4:46) / Blue Suede Shoes (4:08) / Machine Gun (6:20) / All Along The Watchtower

(3:45) / Freedom (3:52) / Foxy Lady (4:09) / Purple Haze (3:55) / Hey Joe (4:11) / Voodoo Chile (6:49) / Stone Free - Star Spangled Banner (8:15) / Straight Ahead - Hey Lady (8:07)

Comments: The first three tracks are from the Berkeley soundcheck, May 30, 1970. The rest are from the Atlanta Pop Festival, July 4, 1970. Not the complete show. Also on ATLANTA (Toasted TRW 1946). European CD. Excellent soundboard. A nice companion to the commercial STAGES Atlanta show.

AULD LANG SYNE   IN ***
JH (69-100-03) 2CD (CD1 45:26, CD2 43:44)

CD1: Theme 2001 / Auld Lang Syne / Who Knows / I'm A Man (Stepping Stone) / Burning Desire / Fire / Ezy Ryder / Machine Gun

CD2: Crash Landing/ Stone Free/ Them Changes/ Message To Love/ Stop

Comments: Recorded at the Fillmore East, New York, December 31, 1969. A longer part of the 2nd show than is booted on single disc titles. Very good to excellent soundboard. European CD. Deluxe black & white cover.

BACK TO BERLIN!   IN ***
MIDNIGHT BEAT (MB CD 049) CD (56:41)

Straight Ahead / Spanish Castle Magic / Sunshine Of Your Love / Hey Baby (Land Of The New Rising Sun) / Message To Love / Machine Gun, The Breeze And I / Purple Haze / Red House / Foxy Lady / Ezy Rider / Hey Joe

Comments: Recorded at The Deutschland Halle, Berlin, Germany, September 4, 1970. Excellent audience tape. The show originally ended with the start of "Power Of Soul" which Jimi aborts, and then he begins playing "Lover Ma'" when the tape runs out. Both of these are left off this disc.

BALL AND CHAIN   IN ***
HONEYBED RECORDS (HBR-024/Jimi 009) CD (72:58)

Honeybed / Three Little Bears / South Saturn Delta - Jam / Piano Roll 1 / Piano Roll 2 / Piano Roll 3 / Everything's Gonna Be Allright / Messenger / Message To Love / Power Of Soul / Electric Church Jam / Hear My Freedom

Comments: An excellent sounding CD with lots of new material at the time of its release. Essential material for the collector and highly recommended. Most of this material also showed up on the BLACK GOLD box set.

BALTIMORE CIVIC CENTER, JUNE 13, 1970   IN *
STARQUAKE (SQ 09) CD (72:00)

Pass It On / Lover Man / Machine Gun / Ezy Rider / Red House / Message Of Love / Hey Joe / Freedom / Hear My Train A Comin' / Room Full Of Mirrors / Foxy Lady / Purple Haze / Star Spangled Banner / Voodoo Child (slight return) - 'Keep On Groovin'

Comments: Recorded live at the Baltimore Civic Center, June 13, 1970. Poor to good audience tape of the complete show. Japanese CD. Recommended only because it's the only release of the complete show.

BAND OF GOLD
MAJOR TOM (MT 087) 5 CD-Rs

Disc 1: Power Of Soul / Lover Man / Hear My Train A Comin' / Them Changes / Izabella / Machine Gun / Stop / Ezy Rider / Bleeding Heart / Earth Blues / Burning Desire (These are all from December 31, 1969 - first show).

Disc 2: Auld Land Syne / Who Knows / Stepping Stone / Burning Desire / Fire/ Ezy Rider / Machine Gun

Disc 3: Power Of Soul / Stone Free - Sunshine Of Your Love - Outside Woman Blues - Cherokee Mist / Them Changes / Message To Love / Stop / Foxy Lady / Voodoo Child (slight return) / Purple Haze (Discs two and three are from the second show recorded December 31, 1969).

Disc 4: Who Knows / Machine Gun / Them Changes / Power Of Soul / Stepping Stone / Foxy Lady / Stop / Earth Blues (Taken from the first show recorded January 1, 1970).

Disc 5: Stone Free / Them Changes / Power Of Soul / Message To Love / Earth Blues / Machine Gun / Voodoo Child (slight return) / We Gotta Live Together / Wild Thing / Hey Joe / Purple Haze (These are from the second show of January 1, 1970).

Comments: These are all of the complete shows from The Band Of Gypsys from 12/31/69 and 1/1/70.

Reportedly the stereo master has recently surfaced for these shows. The authors have not been able to acquire even a tape copy of this (can anybody out there help?), so we do not know if this disc is from a stereo, mono, single or multiple source. Nor do we have any idea as to the sound quality; but I'd say if you happened across a copy of this, BUY IT. Experience Hendrix LLC has promised a new release of more BOG performances in 1999 and I would be amazed (but certainly delighted) if it were all four shows complete and in sequence.

BAND OF GYPSIES: HAPPY NEW YEAR, JIMI   IN
SILVER SHADOW (CD 9103) CD (75:14)
Intro: Bill Graham / Auld Lang Syne / Who Knows / Stepping Stone / Burning Desire / Fire / Ezy Ryder / Machine Gun / Power Of Soul / Stone Free / Sunshine Of Your Love / Them Changes
Comments: Only part of the second show recorded live at the Fillmore East, NYC, December 31, 1969. Look for AULD LANG SYNE instead.

BAND OF GYPSYS REHEARSALS (THE)   IN ***
WHOOPY CAT (WKP-0003) CD (71:46)
Ezy Rider / Power of Soul / Changes / Lover Man / Message To Love / Earth Blues Today / Ezy Ryder / Message To Love / Who Knows (two takes) / Message To Love(2)
Comments: Probably recorded at Baggies on December 31, 1969. A very good disc to get a good representation of the newly formed BOG's rehearsals for the legendary Fillmore East shows on New Years Eve and New Years Day. This disc has the best single collection of the most representative selection of these recordings. Other releases with some of these sessions on them are NOTES IN COLOURS (JHR 001/002), BAND OF GYPSIES VOL 3 (BM 063-2) and THE THINGS I USED TO DO (Golden Memories GM 890738). The Major Tom CD-R'S SESSIONS 1 & SESSIONS 2 appear to be dedicated to gathering all of the known BOG rehearsals, including some material that is unique to those releases.

BAND OF GYPSYS - THE ULTIMATE   IN **
JMH 010/3 3 CD
Disc 1: Bill Graham Intro / Auld Lang Syne / Who Knows / Stepping Stone / Burning Desire / Fire / Ezy Rider / Machine Gun / Power Of Soul / Stone Free - Sunshine Of Your Love / Them Changes / Message To Love
Disc 2: Stop / Little Drummer Boy - Silent Night / Burning Desire / Hoochie Koochie Man / Blue Suede Shoes / Message To Love / Ezy Rider / Power Of Soul / Them Changes / Lover Man / Who Knows / Message To Love / Crash Landing
Disc 3: Who Knows / Stepping Stone / Foxy Lady / Power Of Soul / Earth Blues / Machine Gun / Voodoo Child (slight return) / We Gotta Live Together / Gypsy Boogie Jam / Mannish Boy (2)
Comments: A nice chunk of Band Of Gypsys performances and rehearsals spread over three CD's. The 2nd show from 12/31/69 is on disc one and the first track on disc two. The rest of disc two and the last two tracks on disc three are from the rehearsals at Baggies. The remainder of disc three is a mix of both shows from 1/1/70. Overall sound is very good.

BAND OF GYPSYS VOL. 3   IN ***
BEECH MARTIN (BM 063/2) CD (CD1 76:07, CD2 62:51)
CD 1: Message To Love / Ezy Rider / Power of Soul / Changes / Lover Man / Who Knows / Message of Love / Keep on Groovin' / Izabella - Machine Gun / Stepping Stone I / Stepping Stone II / Izabella (Instrumental) / Crash Landing / Little Drummer Boy / Silent Night / Auld Lang Syne / Burning Desire / Hoochie Coochie Man / Interview (January 9, 1969)
CD 2: Power of Soul (no vocal) / Lover Man / Hear My Train A Comin' / Changes / Machine Gun / Happy New Year (Auld Lang Syne)
Comments: On CD #1 tracks 1-7 are Band of Gypsys rehearsals from Baggies, December 1969. 8 is a studio jam. 9 is an early studio version. 10-11 are copies of rare CR's. 12 is from the same session as track 9. 13 is is the original version. 14-16 are from the CR's.
CD #2 was recorded on December 31st, 1969, at the Fillmore East, NYC, and is a mono soundboard tape. Tracks 1-5 are from the first show and "Happy New Year" is from the second. Very good to excellent soundboard.

500,000 HALOS

1968 A.D.

1968 A.D. PART TWO

ACOUSTIC JAMS

ATLANTA

AULD LANG SYNE

BERKELEY CONCERT
AUDIFON (AF 008) LP
Side 1: Fire / Johnny B. Goode / Hear My Train A Comin' / Foxy Lady / Machine Gun
Side 2: Freedom / Red House / Message To Love / Ezy Ryder / Voodoo Chile (slight return)
Comments: Recorded at the Berkeley Community Center, May 30, 1970. First Show. Obsolete.

BERKELEY CONCERTS (THE)   IN **
WHOOPY CAT (WKP-0008) 2 CD (CD1 63:49, CD2 74:23)
Fire / Johnny B.Goode / Hear My Train A Comin' / Foxy Lady / Machine Gun / Freedom / Red House / Message To Love / Ezy Rider / Star Spangled Banner / Voodoo Chile (slight return) / Straight Ahead / Hey Baby (Land Of The New Rising Sun) / Lover Man / Stone Free / I Don't Live Today / Machine Gun / Foxy Lady / Star Spangled Banner / Purple Haze / Voodoo Chile (slight return)/ Midnight Lightning
Comments: Excellent soundboard tape recorded at Berkeley, May 30, 1970. The first show is missing "Star Spangled Banner" and "Purple Haze" while the second show is missing "Hey Joe". RIOTS IN BERKELEY (Beech Martin BM 038) has the full second show. Recommended as a good release to get the majority of both shows in one place, but frustrating for the couple of missing tracks.

BERKELEY SOUNDCHECKS   IN ***
WHOOPY CAT (WKP-0008) CD & RED ROBIN (ROB-1002) CD (64:58)
Message To Love / Blue Suede Shoes (2) / Hey Baby (Land Of The New Rising Sun) / Ezy Ryder / Earth Blues / Room Full Of Mirrors / Villanova Junction / Midnight Lightning / Freedom / Power Of Soul / Machine Gun / Ezy Ryder / Hey Joe / Purple Haze / Message To Love / Freedom / Hey Baby (Land Of The New Rising Sun)
Comments: The first 12 songs are from the afternoon soundcheck at Berkeley (May 30, 1970), the next three from the Isle Of Wight Festival and the last three from Atlanta.

BEST OF JIMI HENDRIX
FIGA RECORDS (52648 / S2666) LP
Side 1: Side 2 of ROYAL ALBERT HALL
Side 2: Foxy Lady / Purple Haze / Instrumental / Can You See Me / Voodoo Chile
Comments: Useless

BEST OF JIMI HENDRIX LIVE IN CONCERT
I.C.R. 7 LP
Side 1: Side 2 of ROYAL ALBERT HALL
Side 2: Easy Rider / Getting My Heart Back To You / Wild Thing / Like A Rolling Stone
Comments: Useless

BEST OF THE BOOTLEGS   IN
MS 666 CD
Astro Man Jam (studio jam with Cox & Mitchell recorded June 24, 1970) / Calling All Devil's Children (TTG Studio outtake , October 21, 1968) / 1983...A Merman I Should Turn To Be (demo) / Angel (demo) / God Save The Queen (NOT Jimi) / Cherokee Mist (Record Plant outtake, May 2, 1968) / Electric Church Red House (TTG Studio outtake, October 29, 1968) / Mr. Bad Luck ('Look Over Yonder' outtake, Olympic Studios, May 4, 1967) / All Along The Watchtower (Olympic Studios outtake, January 21, 1968) / Jungle Jam - Beginning (Hit Factory jam, September 1969) / Drivin' South - Sgt. Pepper / Heavy Jam
Comments: Sound quality is only fair to good here. Pass this one by as all these tracks appear elsewhere and in much better quality.

BIGGEST SQUARE IN THE BUILDING (THE)   IN *
UNKNOWN LABEL CD (68:47)
Are You Experienced / Let Me Stand Next To Your Fire / The Wind Cries Mary / Tax Free / Foxy Lady / Hey Joe / Spanish Castle Magic / Red House / Purple Haze / Wild Thing
Comments: Recorded live at the State Fair Music Hall, Texas, February 16, 1968. Very good audience tape of a complete and unedited recording with what sounds like stereo separation! Reasonably well-balanced with guitar, drums, vocals and bass; although the bass is a bit boomy and the tape runs too slow. Pop this into your CD player with pitch control and you have a thoroughly listenable disc.

BLACK DEVIL
GREAT DANE RECORDS (GDR CD 9104) CD

Killin' Floor / Catfish Blues / Foxy Lady / Red House / Drivin' South / The Wind Cries Mary / Fire / Little Wing / Purple Haze

Comments: Recorded live at the Olympia, Paris, January 29, 1968. Excellent mono. European CD. Time 50:38. Made obsolete by the STAGES release.

BLACK GOLD IN ***
MIDNIGHT BEAT (MBCD 058/59/60/61/62) 5CD BOX SET

CD 1: I Was Made To Love Her - Ain't Too Proud To Beg (Parts 1 & 2)* (8:35) / Voodoo Chile (slight return) (Takes 1-15)** (32:43) / Long Hot Summer Night (Parts 1 & 2)(Jimi solo) (4:23) / 1983...(A Merman I Should Turn To Be) (Jimi solo)(4:00) / Moon Turn The Tides...Gently Gently Away (Jimi Solo) (3:28) / Angel (Jimi Solo)(3:22) / Cherokee Mist (Jimi Solo)(3:12) / Getting My Heart Back Together Again (Jimi Solo)(1:21) / Voodoo Chile (Jimi Solo)(6:07) / Gypsy Eyes (Jimi Solo)(5:53) / Gypsy Eyes (Jimi Solo)(4:14)

Comments: *Jimi & Stevie Wonder, BBC sessions, 1967. **Studio sessions 1968. The rest of the tracks were recorded at Jimi's hotel room at the Drake Hotel in April 1968.

CD 2: South Saturn Delta (acoustic, June 14, 1968) (3:29) / Rainy Day, Dream Away (overdub session, take 1) (0:56) / Rainy Day, Dream Away (overdub session, take 2)(2:19) / Rainy Day, Dream Away (overdub session, take 3)(10:21) / Third Stone From The Sun - Villanova Junction Blues (instr.)(5:47) / Jam Back At The House (aka: Beginnings) (5:57) / Bleeding Heart (3:48) / Pride Of Man (take 1)(1:28) / Pride Of Man (take 2)(2:18) / Midnight - Valleys Of Neptune Rising (aka: Bolero) (takes 1-7)(14:51) / Sending My Love To Linda (May 69 w/ Stephen Stills)(takes 1-3)(11:06)

CD 3: Had To Cry Today (jam with Lee Michaels) (16:30) / Paper Aeroplanes (rehearsals - 17 takes)(26:41) / Blue Suede Shoes (jam)(11:36) / Izabella (August 29, 1969, overdub session, take 2)(3:50) / Izabella (two takes)(4:41) / Honey Bed (takes 1-4)(7:52)

CD 4: Mannish Boy (rehearsals - takes 1-7)(39:55) / Closer To The Truth (aka: Room Full Of Mirrors) (22:06)

CD 5: Voodoo Chile (The Blues Session - takes 1-5)(36:44) / Instrumental Jam: Stepping Stone - Sending My Love To Linda - Freedom - Here Comes The Sun - Cherokee Mist - All Devil's Children)(23:48) / Three Little Bears (Jimi solo)*(10:05) / Gypsy Eyes (Jimi solo)*(2:38) / 1983...(A Merman I Should Turn To Be)*(4:27) / Untitled Instrumental (0:44)

Comments: *These are from an acoustic session recorded at the Record Plant on April 20, 1968. A very nice set to have with a number of bits and pieces available only here.

BLACK STRINGS IN
CDM (G-53 258) CD

Angel / Wait Until Tomorrow / Manic Depression / Little Wing / Can You Please Crawl Out Your Window / Stone Free / One Rainy Wish / Experiencing The Blues / Drivin' South / Burning Of The Midnight Lamp / Send My Love To Linda / The Things I Used To Do

Comments: Mostly live and BBC material that is available commercially now.

BLUES
TOASTED (2S912) 2LP

Side 1: A copy of Side 2 of SMASHING AMPS (TMOQ 71028)
Side 2: A copy of Side 1 of SMASHING AMPS (TMOQ 71028)
Side 3: A copy of Side 2 of SKY HIGH (Sky Dog Records)
Side 4: A copy of Side 1 of SKY HIGH (Sky Dog Records)
Comments: Very good to excellent stereo. Deluxe color front cover.

BLUES AT MIDNIGHT IN ***
MIDNIGHT BEAT (MBCD 037) CD (77:25)

Little Wing (9:19) / Everything's Gonna Be Allright (8:47) / Three Little Bears Part 1 (Jam) (15:54) / Three Little Bears Part 2 (6:19) / Instrumental Jam (8:45) / Stormy Monday (8:24) / Blues In C (19:49)*

Comments: The complete (but resequenced) show recorded live at The Cafe Au Go Go, Greenwich Village, New York, March 17, 1968. Track 7 is from The Generation Club, New York, April 1968. Very good to excellent soundboard except: *Good to very good. European CD. Deluxe color cover. Picture

CD. Some song fade-in at beginning and fade-out at end. See THE KING'S JAM for the complete Generation Club show. A highly recommended show with some nice jamming.

BORN ON THE FOURTH OF JULY
EGG (004) CD-R
Star Spangled Banner (8 versions)
Comments: Nothing remarkable here on this homemade compact disc. Merely a collection of the legit version and numerous live performances.

BROADCASTS
TRADEMARK OF QUALITY (TMQ 1841) LP
Side 1: Purple Haze (1) / Wild Thing (1) / Voodoo Chile (slight return) (2) / Hey Joe (2) / Sunshine Of Your Love (2)
Side 2: Drivin' South (3) / Experiencing The Blues (3) / Hound Dog (3) / Little Miss Lover (3) / Love Or Confusion (4) / Foxy Lady (4) / Hey Joe (4) / Stone Free (4)
Comments: An odds and ends collection of performances from several different sources. These have been bootlegged numerous times and on numerous labels: BROADCASTS (Trademark Of Quality/Ruthless Rhymes) / BROADCASTS (Trademark of Quality TMOQ 71019) missing 'Stone Free' / LIVE EXPERIENCE 1967-68 (Voodoo Chile) / LIVE EXPERIENCE (Berkeley LEHH) & (Product of Distinction POD 0584-001) / GOODBYE JIMI (Kustom 005) & (Goodbye 723) & (Box Top Rec. - colored vinyl). (1) March 15, 1968, Atwood Hall, Worcester, Massachusetts / (2) Jan. 4, 1969, "Happening For Lulu", BBC TV, London / (3) Oct. 6, 1967, BBC Radio, London / (4) Feb. 13, 1967, BBC Radio, London

BROADCASTS IN
LUNA (LU 9204) CD (70:35)
Voodoo Chile (slight return) / Hey Joe / Sunshine Of Your Love / Purple Haze / Wild Thing / Like A Rolling Stone / Hoochie Coochie Man / Hey Joe / Foxy Lady / Red House / Hear My Train A Comin' / Red House
Comments: A collection of various live material.

BROADCASTS / MAUI, HAWAII
TRADE MARK OF QUALITY (TMOQ 7501) 2LP
Comments: Budget double album of two single LPs.

BURNING AT FRANKFURT IN *
MIDNIGHT BEAT (MB CD 040) CD (63:44)
Come On Part 1 (6:40) / Fire (4:15) / Red House (12:34) / I Don't Live Today (10:03) / Little Wing (3:52) / Foxy Lady (5:32) / Sunshine Of Your Love (11:41) / Hey Joe (4:32) / Purple Haze (4:30)
Comments: Recorded live at The Jahrhunderthalle, Frankfurt, Germany, January 17, 1969. European picture CD. The complete show from a good audience tape but a bit shrill sounding. Recommended because it's the only release of this concert and is for the completist.

CAFE AU GO-GO JAM SESSION IN ***
KOINE (K880802) CD
Everything's Going To Be Allright (6:24) / Stormy Monday (7:39) / Three Little Bears Jam (14:47) / Jam 1 (5:48) / Jam 2 (8:02) / Little Wing Jam (8:40)
Comments: Recorded on March 17th, 1968, at the Cafe Au Go Go, NYC. Very good mono soundboard. Vocals are low. European CD. Deluxe color cover. With Paul Butterfield, Elvin Bishop, Harvey Brooks, Herbie Rich & Buddy Miles. The complete show and in the correct sequence. The one to find.

CALLING LONG DISTANCE IN ***
DYNAMITE STUDIO (DS930055) CD (75:05)
The Burning Of The Midnight Lamp (Sept. 11, 1967, Stockholm) / Little Miss Lover (alternate take) / Foxy Lady (Nov. 10, 1967, Vitus Studio, Holland) / Catfish Blues (aka Experiencing The Blues) (Nov. 10, 1967, Vitus Studio, Holland) / Oh Man Is This Me Or What? (BBC interview, Dec. 15, 1967) / Purple Haze (March 19, 1968, Ottawa) / Fire (May 18, 1968, Miami, 2nd show) / Hear My Train A Comin' (May 18, 1968, Miami, 2nd show) / Spanish Castle Magic (Oct. 18, 1968, Winterland, 2nd show) / Slow Walking Talk (Oct. 25, 1968, unreleased studio) / Hendrix/Cox Jam / Hey Baby (New Rising Sun) (Sept. 3, 1970, Copenhagen) / Red House (Sept. 3, 1970, Copenhagen)

BALL & CHAIN

BAND OF GYPSYS 3

BAND OF GYPSYS REHEARSALS

THE BERKELEY CONCERTS

BEST OF THE BOOTLEGS

BIGGEST SQUARE...

Comments: This was originally released by Univibes as a CD for their subscribers and in the index is considered a commercial release although it is a bit on the 'grey' side. Also available on OH MAN, IS THIS ME OR WHAT (Cool Daddy) CD.

CAN YOU HERE ME ROCK IN *

HEMERO 01 2LP

Side 1: Foxy Lady, Hey Joe, Stone Free, Fire, Purple Haze (Star Club, Hamburg, Germany, March 17, 1967) / Spanish Castle Magic (Stockholm, Sweden, January 9, 1969)

Side 2: Purple Haze (Beat Club, London 1967) / Manic Depression (Winterland, October 12, 1968) / Foxy Lady (outtake, Royal Albert Hall, February 24, 1969) / Hear My Train A Comin' (rehearsal, Woodstock, August 18, 1969)

Side 3: Stone Free / Fire / Red House / Message To Love / Lover Man

Side 4: All Along The Watchtower / Ezy Rider / Star Spangled Banner / Purple Haze / Voodoo Chile (Slight Return)

Comments: Side 3 & Side 4 are from Downing Stadium, New York, July 17, 1970. Very good stereo. 'Here' should have been spelled 'Hear', of course! Pretty much obsolete except for the hard to find Ronnie Scott's Club material.

CAN YOU PLEASE CRAWL OUT YOUR WINDOW? IN *

(RUTHLESS RHYMES JIMI 1) / (SLIPPED DISC JIMI 1) / (Dragonfly 5) / (LXXXIV SERIES #56 - red vinyl) LP

Side 1: Interview: Alexis Korner / Auld Lang Syne / Interview: Alan Douglas / Little Drummer Boy - Silent Night* / Alexis Korner / Mother Earth (Ronnie Scott's Club with Eric Burdon Band) / Interview: Alexis Korner & Paul McCartney / Interview: Alexis Korner

Side 2: The Burning Of The Midnight Lamp / Interview: Alexis Korner / Can You Please Crawl Out Your Window / Interview: Alexis Korner / Drivin' South / Tobacco Road (Ronnie Scott's Club with Eric Burdon Band)

Comments: From the 1976 BBC "Insight" radio broadcast. Excellent stereo except [*] which is good mono. Pretty much obsolete except for the hard to find Ronnie Scott's Club material.

CANADIAN CLUB IN *

WORLD PRODUCTION OF COMPACT MUSIC (WPOCM CD 0888D006 - 2) CD

Foxy Lady / Fire / Killin' Floor / Red House / Spanish Castle Magic / Hey Joe / Purple Haze / In The Midnight Hour (Ain't Too Proud To Beg)

Comments: Recorded live at Ottawa, Canada, March 19, 1968. Very good mono from the soundboard. Some surface noise and the sound levels vary. Commonly booted. An acceptable release, but Firepower's SUPERCONCERT 1968 is the one I prefer. "Ain't To Proud To Beg" is available commercially, although in edited form.

CAT'S SQUIRREL IN *

CSO (01 / 2) 2CD (CD1 65:26, CD2 61:33)

CD 1: Voodoo Chile (slight return) / Foxy Lady / Red House / Sunshine Of Your Love / I Don't Live Today / Hear My Train A Comin'

CD 2: Spanish Castle Magic / Purple Haze / The Star Spangled Banner / Sgt. Pepper's Lonely Hearts Club Band / Fire / Hey Joe / Catfish Blues / The Wind Cries Mary / Purple Haze / Spanish Castle Magic / Wild Thing

Comments: CD 1: Recorded live at Lorensberg Circus, Gothenberg, Sweden, January 8, 1969. CD 2: Tracks 4-11 were recorded live at Tivolis Koncersal, Copenhagen , January 7, 1968. Poor audience recording.

CHEROKEE MIST IN **

TRIANGLE (PYCD 070) CD (65:49)

Country Blues - Astro Man - Solo Improvisation (The most complete version available of this jam) / Calling All Devil's Children / Valleys Of Neptune / Cherokee Mist / Ships Passing In The Night / Easy Blues / Little Drummer Boy / The Queen (David Henderson) / Drone Blues / Guitar Improvisation (Instrumental Improvisation) / Stepping Stone / Send My Love To Linda (Heaven Has No Sorrow) - Most complete version available.

Comments: A very nice overall collection of studio material plus the best source for the "Country Blues" jam as well as "Heaven Has No Sorrow". Recommended.

COLLECTION
GRAFFITI (GRCD 13) CD

Spanish Castle Magic / Star Spangled Banner / Purple Haze / Voodoo Child (slight return) / Sunshine Of Your Love / Foxy Lady / I Don't Live Today / Red House

Comments: Recorded live at The Forum in Los Angeles, April 26, 1969. This has been booted many times.

COME ON STOCKHOLM 1970 IN **
JH (001 / 002) 2CD (CD1 - 45:48, CD2 - 45:39)

CD1: Here Comes Your Lover Man / Catfish Blues / Race With The Devil / Ezy Ryder / Red House / Come On / Room Full Of Mirrors / Hey Baby (The Land Of The New Rising Sun) / Drum Solo

CD2: Message To Love / Machine Gun / Voodoo Child (slight return) / In From The Storm / Purple Haze / Foxy Lady, Star Spangled Banner

Comments: Recorded live at the Stora Scenen, Grona Lund, Stockholm, Sweden, August 31, 1970. A good audience recording worth adding to your collection. Recommended.

COMPLETE BBC SESSION AND... (THE)
THE LAST BOOTLEG RECORDS (LBR 036 / 2) 2CD

CD 1: Radio One Theme (1:57) / Catfish Blues (5:23) / Interview At BBC 1967 during "Hey Joe" session (1:54) / Hey Joe (4:03)/ Foxy Lady (2:47) / Stone Free (3:30) / Love Or Confusion (2:54) / Look Over Yonder (Mr. Bad Luck) (2:58) / Purple Haze (3:03) / Killin' Floor (2:29) / Fire (2:41) / The Wind Cries Mary (3:06) / Wild Thing (1:54) / Ma Pouppee Qui Fait No (3:42) / The Burning Of The Midnight Lamp (3:44) / Jam # 1 With Stevie Wonder (3:24) / Jam #2 With Stevie Wonder (5:06) / Little Miss Lover (2:57) / Drivin' South (4:47) / Experience The Blues (5:29) / Hound Dog (2:44) / All Along The Watchtower (3:46)

CD 2: Can You Please Crawl Out Your Window (3:34) / Hoochie Koochie Man (5:35) / Spanish Castle Magic (3:22) / Day Tripper (3:22) / Sgt. Pepper's Lonely Hearts Club Band (1:58) / Getting My Heart Back Together (4:57) / Wait Until Tomorrow (2:55) / Hey Joe (demo) (2:59) / Purple Haze (unreleased demo) (2:46) / Red House (various takes) (10:55) / I Don't Live Today (various takes)(16:19) / Fire (instrumental) (2:36) / The Wind Cries Mary (instrumental) (3:41) / Gloria (9:03)/ Hound Dog (acoustic) (2:29)

Comments: All tracks are excellent soundboard. CD1: BBC Studios during 1967 sessions (except Tracks 8 and 13). CD2: Recorded live at the BBC Studios during the1967 sessions (except tracks 5, 14, and 15). European CD. Picture CDs. Rendered obsolete by the legitimate release THE JIMI HENDRIX EXPERIENCE: BBC SESSIONS with the exception of the unedited "Ain't Too Proud To Beg" and "Can You Please Crawl Out Your Window". The studio material on Disc 2 is copied from the OUT OF THE STUDIO: DEMOS FROM 1967 disc.

COMPLETER IN **
WHOOPY CAT (WKP-0018-19) 2CD (CD1 74:01, CD2 72:31)

CD1: Bold As Love / She's So Fine / The Stars That Play With Laughing Sam's Dice / Little Miss Lover / Dream / Dance / Ain't Too Proud To Beg / Peace In Mississippi / Izabella / Izabella / Izabella / Machine Gun / Midnight Lightning / Country Blues / Cherokee Mist - In From The Storm - Valleys Of Neptune / Izabella - Machine Gun

CD2: Lord I Sing The Blues For You And Me / Easy Blues / Dance / Beginning / Straight Ahead / Astro Man Jam / Freedom - Ezy Rider - Highway Of Broken Hearts - Seven Dollars In My Pocket - Highway Of Desire - Midnight Lightning / Night Bird Flying - Ships Passing In The Jungle / Drivin' South - Sergeant Pepper's Lonely Hearts Club Band

Comments: A fine sounding mixed bag of miscellaneous jams, unused mixes and alternate versions of studio material. Much of this material can be found elsewhere but this is a nice package if you can find it.

COPENHAGEN '70 IN ***
WHOOPY CAT (WKP-0044/0045) 2CD (CD1 69:45, CD2 40:30)

CD 1: Stone Free / Foxy Lady / Message To Love / Hey Baby (New Rising Sun) / All Along The Watchtower / Machine Gun / Spanish Castle Magic / Ezy Rider / Freedom / Red House / In From The

Storm/ Purple Haze

CD 2: Voodoo Chile (slight return) - Calling All Devil's Children - Outside Woman Blues - Sunshine Of Your Love / Hey Joe / Fire / Power Of Soul / Send My Love To Linda - Live And Let Live (2 versions) / Power Of Soul

Comments: A very good and complete audience recording live at K. B. Hallen, Copenhagen, Denmark, September 3, 1970. The last three songs are studio outtakes including several takes of "Power Of Soul" unavailable elsewhere. Highly recommended.

CROSSTOWN TRAFFIC IN **

LABEL UNKNOWN CD (63:48)

Dear Mr. Fantasy / Rock Me Baby / Foxy Lady / I Don't Live Today / Hey Joe / Fire / Red House / Purple Haze / Wild Thing

Comments: Recorded live at the Moody Coliseum, Southern Methodist University, Dallas, Texas, August 3,1968. Very good complete and unedited audience recording. Recommended just for the rare performance of "Dear Mr. Fantasy".

DANTE'S INFERNO IN **

PINK POODLE (POO 002) CD (74:41)

The Stars That Play With Laughing Sam's Dice / You Make Me Feel / Hey Joe / Help Me (Part 1) / Red House / Interview (Flip Wilson on the "Tonight Show" - July 10, 1969) / Lover Man / Lover Man / Ain't Gonna Be No Next Time (Curtis Knight) / Message From Nine To The Universe

Comments A mixed bag of studio and live of varying sound quality and one of two sources to find the complete "Message From Nine To The Universe". The other is MIXDOWN MASTERS.

DAVENPORT, IOWA '68

CREATIVE ARTISTRY (26K10 / 55K10) 2LP

Side 1: Are You Experienced

Side 2: Lover Man / Foxy Lady / Red House Intro

Side 3: Red House

Side 4: I Don't Live Today / Fire

Comments: Recorded on August 11, 1968 at the Col Ballroom, Davenport, Iowa. Very good stereo.

DE LANE LEA DEMOS AND OLYMPIC OUTS IN

GOLD STANDARD CD-R (70:36)

Purple Haze / Red House / Ma-Pouppee-Qui-Fait-No / I Don't Live Today (takes 1-4) / The Wind Cries Mary / Takin' Care Of No Business / Gypsy Blood / Lover Man / Little One / Room Full Of Mirrors / Mr. Bad Luck (Look Over Yonder) / Sunshine Of Your Love / Shame Shame Shame / Cat Talkin' To Me

Comments: Excellent stereo from soundboard. European CD-R with a deluxe color cover. Pretty much a copy of the OUT OF THE STUDIO CD and parts of STUDIO HAZE.

DEMOS 1968 IN ***

WORLD PRODUCTION OF COMPACT MUSIC (WPOCM 071) CD (39:45)

Purple Haze / Red House / La Pouppee Qui Fait Non (instrumental) / I Don't Live Today / I Don't Live Today / I Don't Live Today / I Don't Live Today / I Don't Live Today / Fire / The Wind Cries Mary

Comments: An excellent collection of studio outtakes and backing tracks. Also available as OUT OF THE STUDIO: DEMOS FROM 1967 (3HCD 931022). See also OUT OF THE STUDIO 1 & 2. A bit on the short side but highly recommended and absolutely essential.

DIAMONDS IN THE DUST IN ***

MIDNIGHT BEAT (MBCD 022/23) 2CD (CD174:27, 76:33)

CD 1: Jungle Jam - Beginning - Drivin' South - Sergeant Pecker's Lonely Hearts Club Band / Cherokee Mist / Cherokee Mist - In From The Storm / Dance / Everything's Gonna Be Alright / Jam Session / Jam Session / Freedom Jam - Ezy Rider - Highway Of Broken Hearts - Seven Dollars In My Pocket - Highway Of Desire - Midnight Lightning

CD 2: Send My Love To Linda / Send My Love To Linda / Send My Love To Linda / Lord I Sing The Blues For Me And You / Studio Catastrophe / Villanova Junction - Ships Passing In The Night (fake) / Li'l Dog O'Mine - Heaven Has No Sorrow - Valleys Of Neptune / Jam Session / Jam Session / Ships Passing In The Night

Comments: Excellent quality studio jams and rehearsals. Still the only place to find the complete unedited "Freedom / Ezy Rider Jam". Highly recommended.

DON'T MISS HIM THIS TIME (THE COMPLETE SHOW)   IN **
TRIANGLE (PYCD 096) CD

Let Me Stand Next To Your Fire (3:37) / Hey Joe (4:54) / Spanish Castle Magic, Drum Solo (9:06) / Sunshine Of Your Love, Spanish Castle Magic (2:54) / Red House (14:13) / I Don't Live Today (7:28) / Foxy Lady (6:09) / Purple Haze (5:49) / Voodoo Child (10:36).

Comments: Recorded live at the International Sport Arena, San Diego, May 24,1969. Excellent soundboard. European CD. Necessary because somebody at Reprise thought it was a good idea to leave "Foxy Lady" off of the STAGES set so we have to rely on the bootleggers for the complete show.

DRIVING SOUTH WITH THE J.H.E.
LABEL UNKNOWN LP

Side 1: Killin' Floor / Catfish Blues / Foxy Lady / Red House
Side 2: Drivin' South / Tune Up Song / The Wind Cries Mary / Fire / Little Wing / Purple Haze
Comments: Recorded live at L'Olympia, Paris, January 29,1968. Excellent soundboard. European bootleg with a black & green insert cover. Only 10 copies made on black vinyl.

DRONE BLUES   IN
GREAT DANE RECORDS (GDR CD SAT 2) CD (72:50)

Drone Blues / Lord I Sing The Blues For Me And You / Traffic Jam / Once I Had A Woman / B.B. King Jam / Country Blues / Everything's Gonna Be All Right / Further On Up The Road

Comments: Various live recordings and studio outtakes from 1967 and 1969. Sound is mostly very good to excellent. European CD. Time 72:50. Originally came issued with a nice magazine; however you need to read Italian.

EARTH TONES   IN ***
WHOOPY CAT (WKP-0041) CD (75:50)

Mannish Boy / Mannish Boy / Izabella / Izabella / Jam Session / Power Of Soul / Power Of Soul / Power Of Soul

Comments: This is one of those great 'fly on the wall' type discs with long segments of studio run throughs with breakdowns, false starts and some bits of studio chat. Much of this has been copied elsewhere but this is the most complete way to find it.

ELECTRIC ANNIVERSARY JIMI   IN *
MIDNIGHT BEAT (MB CD 024) CD (78:19)

Pride Of Man (Valleys Of Neptune Jam) (3:43) / World Traveler (8:06) / It's Too Bad (10:44) / Cherokee Mist (5:38) / You Make Me Feel (4:30) / Jungle Jam (5:58) / All Devil's Children (4:17) / Little Drummer Boy, Silent Night (4:53) / Auld Lang Syne (with background choir) (2:30) / Instrumental Jams: Sending My Love To Linda, Live And Let Live, Valleys Of Neptune Arising (9:43) / Message From Nine To The Universe (incomplete) (15:51)

Comments: Picture CD. Very good to excellent sound. Recommended as a good collection of studio material though it is not uncommon material.

ELECTRIC BIRTHDAY JIMMY
EBJ 01 LP

Side 1: Lonely Avenue (Valley Of Neptune) / World Traveler / It's Too Bad
Side 2: Strato Strut (Message From Nine To The Universe) / Cherokee Mist / Guitar Improvisation / Midnight Lightning
Comments: Common outtakes from the Record Plant in NYC 1969. Excellent stereo.

ELECTRIC CHURCH MUSIC - PART ONE
GUITAR HERO (71056) LP

Side 1: Fire (3:50) / Tax Free (12:00) / Spanish Castle Magic (7:30) / Interview (00:15)
Side 2: Red House (14:30) / I Don't Live Today (7:50) / Jimi speaks (1:00)
Comments: Recorded live at Falkoner Koncertet, Copenhagen, January 10, 1969. Very good & excellent stereo. European bootleg with a yellow & black insert cover. Only six made on black vinyl.

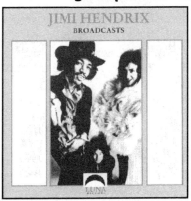

BROADCASTS

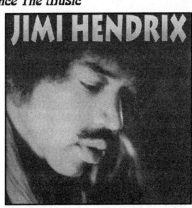

BURNING AT FRANKFURT

CALLING LONG DISTANCE
(Cover art of Univibe release)

CAT'S SQUIRREL

COME ON STOCKHOLM 1970

COMPLETER

ELECTRIC GUITARLAND
THE EASY RIDER YEARS CD

Voodoo Child (slight return) / Fire / Foxy Lady / Hey Joe / Purple Haze / Little Wing / The Wind Cries Mary / Red House / Burning Of The Midnight Lamp / Wild Thing / Sunshine Of Your Love / Sergeant Pepper's Lonely Hearts Club Band / Experiencing The Blues / Spanish Castle Magic / Like A Rolling Stone / Can You See Me / Tax Free

Comments: A really mixed bag of live soundboard material from the 1967 Monterey Festival, Vitus studio, 1968 Paris, & 1969 Stockholm and L.A. Forum shows. Useless unless you like these sort of packages.

ELECTRIC GYPSYS IN
PILOT (HJCD 070) CD

Mannish Boy / Jam Session / Astro Man Jam / Ezy Rider Jam / Izabella / Stepping Stone / Valleys Of Neptune

Comments: Very good sound. Some of the "Mannish Boy" session, some incomplete jams, and copies of some rare CRs. Not necessary.

ELECTRIC GYPSY IN
40176 / 15 CD (71:45)

1983 - A Merman I Should Turn To Be / America The Beautiful (Fake) / Cherokee Mist / Astro Man / Red House / Look Over Yonder / Midnight Sun (Fake) / House Burning Down / The Stars That Play With Laughing Sam's Dice / Can You Please Crawl Out Your Window / The Stars That Play With Laughing Sam's Dice / Purple Haze / Voodoo Chile / Lover Man / Shame, Shame, Shame

Comments: European CD. A compilation of common live, studio, and fake tracks. Don't bother.

ELECTRIC HENDRIX 1 IN
PYRAMID (PY CD 030) CD (59:56)

Power Of Soul / Peace In Mississippi / Captain Coconut (Jam - Cherokee Mist) / Crash Landing / Instrumental (Lord I Sing The Blues For Me And You) / Lover Man / Stone Free / Ezy Rider Instrumental Jam (Dance) / Valleys Of Neptune / Drifter's Escape / Midnight (by the Rainbow Bridge Band)

Comments: Good to very good quality unused mixes, studio jams and outtakes. All of this is available elsewhere more complete or in better sound.

ELECTRIC HENDRIX 2 IN
PYRAMID (PY CD 031) CD (56:03)

Somewhere / Come Down Hard On Me Baby / Come Down Hard On Me Baby / Peace In Mississippi / Mannish Boy (Stepping Stone) / Highway Of Broken Hearts - Seven Dollars In My Pocket - Highway Of Desire - Midnight Lightning / Once I Had A Woman / Ezy Rider (instrumental)

Comments: Good to very good quality unused mixes, studio jams and outtakes. All of this is available elsewhere more complete or in better sound.

ELECTRIC JIMI IN **
JAGUARONDI (JAG CD 001) CD

CD1: Tax Free / Foxy Lady / I Don't Live Today / Red House
CD2: Spanish Castle Magic / Star Spangled Banner / Voodoo Child / Mitch Mitchell drum solo / Sunshine Of Your Love / Voodoo Child

Comments: A CD release of the LP (See next listing). Excellent stereo recording from the LA Forum, April 26, 1969. European CD. Time CD1 40:38, CD2 38:30. Parts of this show have been commercially released but not the full show.

ELECTRIC JIMI
JAGUARONDI (JAG 001/2) 2LP

Side 1: Tax Free / Foxy Lady
Side 2: I Don't Live Today / Red House / Spanish Castle Magic
Side 3: Star Spangled Banner / Purple Haze
Side 4: Voodoo Chile (slight return) / The Sunshine Of Your Love

Comments: Recorded live on April 26, 1969, Los Angeles Forum, L.A., California. Also on SPANISH CASTLE MAGIC (Toasted TRW 1952) 2LP & LIVE AT THE LOS ANGELES FORUM (Zipper LA4M 42669) &

LIVE IN L.A. FORUM (Electrecord ELE 03858) 1LP - edited. See the previous entry.

ELECTRIC LADY JAMS
SURE NICE SHOES RECORDS (H3600) LP
Side 1: Drivin' South - Everythings Gonna Be Alright
Side 2: Drone Blues / Jimi-Jimmy Jam
Comments: Excellent mono. Same as LET'S DROP SOME LUDES AND VOMIT WITH JIMI (vinyl release).

ELECTRIC LADYLAND OUTTAKES IN
INVASION UNLIMITED (IU9417-1) CD (76:54)
Have You Ever Been (To Electric Ladyland) / All Along The Watchtower / Little One / Come On (Part One) / Voodoo Chile (slight return) / Room Full Of Mirrors / Gypsy Eyes / Gypsy Eyes / House Burning Down / Ezy Rider (instrumental) / Cat Talkin' To Me / Taking Care Of Business / Angel / 1983..A Merman I Should Turn To Be / 1983..A Merman I Should Turn To Be / Valleys Of Neptune / Cherokee Mist - In From The Storm / Freedom
Comments: Very good sound. A hodge podge of studio material that's not really in the context that the title suggests. Lots of Chandler tapes material and other commonly booted stuff.

ELECTRONIC CHURCH MUSIC IN
PYRAMID (PY CD 23) CD
Intro (:43) / Killin' Floor (6:50) / Spanish Castle Magic (7:57) / Fire (3:10) / Hey Joe (3:54) / Red House (11:56) / Sunshine Of Your Love (3:54)
Comments: Recorded live at Konserthusetr, Stockholm, Sweden, January 9, 1969. Excellent stereo. European CD. Deluxe black & white cover with purple type. A copy of the first show. Get ON THE KILLING FLOOR instead.

ENJOY JIMI HENDRIX
RUBBER DUBBER (70 001) LP
Comments: Recorded live on April 25, 1970, at the L. A. Forum. Also available as LIVE AT THE FORUM with Side 2 & Side 4 reversed. One of those classic old boots that is now eclipsed by CD releases. The cover graphic is still a classic.

EVERY WAY TO PARADISE IN *
TINTAGEL (TIBX 0021 / 22 / 23 / 24) 4CD
CD 1: Earth Blues (4:23) / Mr Bad Luck (Look Over Yonder) (3:04) / Room Full Of Mirrors (3:05) / Electric Indians (Drone Blues) (8:56) / Voodoo Blues (It's Too Bad) (4:51) / Cactus (Valleys of Neptune) (3:22) / Drivin' South Jam (Drivin' South / Everythings Gonna Be Alright / Jams) (45:26)
CD 2: America The Beautiful (Fake) (4:50) / Cherokee Mist (6:42) / Valleys Of Neptune (Session Thing)(31:16) / Martin Luther King (Jam / Cherokee Mist) (5:49) / Home Acoustic Jam (Fake) (14:33) / Gypsy Sunset (Lonely Avenue Part 2) (2:59) / Valleys Of Neptune (5:44)
CD 3: Where Some (Somewhere) (4:16) / Seven Dollars In My Pocket (Highway Of Broken Hearts Medley) (14:24) / Instrumental Jam (Ezy Rider instrumental jam) (5:04) / Calling All Devil's Children (7:37) / Easy Blues (7:45) / Little Drummer Boy - Silent Night (2:27) / Danny Boy (God Save The Queen - and it's fake anyway) (5:08) / Tomorrow Never Knows (Three Little Bears) (21:57)
CD4: The Things I Used To Do (6:51) / Untitled Jam (Easy Blues)(3:43) / Ain't Too Proud To Beg (incomplete) (4:53) / Shame, Shame, Shame (1:56) / Jungle Jam (4:39) / Jazz Jimi Jazz (Calling All Devil's Children)(6:16) / Midnight (Fake) / Little One (take 1)(Version #2) (6:00) / Little One (take 2) (Version #1)(7:07) / Demo Outtake - with Robert Wyatt (1983...A Merman I should Turn To Be)(4:14) / Gloomy Monday (with Curtis Knight) (takes 1 & 2) (3:18)
Comments: Mostly very good to excellent sound. Some just good. Many of the titles are incorrect. The correct titles are in parenthesis. A few fake tracks and a number of incomplete versions don't make this a completely desirable box set. One bright spot is the complete "Drivin' South / Everythings Gonna Be Alright / Jam" available only here and on ATLANTA (JMH 009/2). European CD. Box set. Each case has deluxe color cover. Picture CDs. 24 page book.

EXPERIENCE IN
I.C.R. 10 LP
Comments: Pirate of Ember release of same title. Recorded live at the Royal Albert Hall, February 24,

1969. Also available as ROYAL ALBERT HALL.

EXPERIENCE 2   IN
MORE M.T.T. 10.21 LP
Wild Thing / Can You See Me / Like A Rolling Stone / Tax Free / Izabella / Beginning / Rock Me Baby / Spanish Castle Magic / Experiencing The Blues
Comments: Everything here has been on CR's except the complete "Tax Free" (April 26, 1969, live at The Forum in Los Angeles) as found on this disc.

EXPERIENCE ORIGINAL SOUND TRACK
JHE 1 / 2 LP
Side 1: C Blues / Smashing Amps
Side 2: Sunshine Of Your Love / Room Full Of Mirrors
Comments: Mostly useless.

EXPERIENCE THE VOODOO SESSIONS   IN ***
VC 2568 CD (73:48)
The Slight Return Session: Yours Truly (guitar, vocal) / Bob Dylan's Grandmother (bass) / Queen Bee (drums) (Record Plant May 3, 1968) / The Blues Session: Yours Truly (guitar, vocal) / Pooneil (bass) / Queen Bee (drums) / Mr. Fantasy (organ) (Record Plant May 2, 1968)
Comments: European CD. An excellent sounding disc that provides all of the available sessions for Voodoo Chile (slight return) (also found on BLACK GOLD) and "Voodoo Chile". An outstanding disc and highly recommended. Of course, since its release bits and pieces have shown up on other releases, but this is the only place to get it all on one disc.

EYES AND IMAGINATION   IN
TSD 18970 CD (61:57)
Backward Experiment / Freedom / Lover Man / Jungle Beginning / Bleeding Heart / Bleeding Heart / Earth Blues / Astro Man Jam / Ezy Rider / Room Full Of Mirrors / Captain Coconut (Jam / Cherokee Mist) / Valleys Of Neptune Arising / Once I Had A Woman / Dolly Dagger
Comments: European CD. Primarily common tracks and unused mixes.

51ST ANNIVERSARY (THE STORY OF LIFE...)   IN **
JMH RECORDS (001-008) 8CD Box Set (CD1 77:11, CD2 57:31, CD3 62:39, CD4 72:22, CD5 79:01, CD6 77:42, CD7 77:36, CD8 75:19)
CD 1: Collage (3:53) / Hey Joe (2:56) / Jimi Interview (1:54) / How Would You Feel (Curtis Knight and Jimi) 2:55) / Love Or Confusion (2:49) / Sgt. Pepper's Lonely Hearts Club Band (1:56) / All Along The Watchtower (3:45) / Little Wing (3:01) / Electric Church Red House (6:43) / Spanish Castle Magic (3:06) / Hear My Train A Comin' (4:32) / Rock'N'Roll Band (with Eire Apparent 3:22) / Stepping Stone (4:08) / Gloria (8:44)/ My Diary (with Rosa Lee Brooks (2:20) / Utee (with Rosa Lee Brooks 2:00) / The Burning Of The Midnight Lamp (4:31) / Little Miss Lover (2:19) / Foxy Lady (3:18) / Catfish Blues (7:46) / Slow Walkin' Talk (3:00)
CD 2: Traffic Jam - Hey Baby Jam (Jam Thing - 5:28 & 14:46), Jazz Jam (FAKE 5:31) / Moonlight Jam (FAKE 4:50) / Studio Catastrophe (1:58), Valley Of Neptune (Take 2) (5:50) / Rainy Day Super Jam (Rainy Day Shuffle - 5:22) / Nervous Breakdown (Marshall Attack Jam - 3:52) / Captain Coconut And Cherokee Mist Jam MLK (Jam / Cherokee Mist - 6:27), Crash Landing (4:29)
CD 3: #7 Man (Stepping Stone - 7:32) / Voodoo Chile (20:45) / Somewhere Over The Rainbow (Somewhere - 3:37) / Red House (7:30) / Angel (3:23) / 1983...A Merman I Should Turn To Be (4:00) / First Jam (Drivin' South) / Everything's Gonna Be Alright - 15:49)
CD4: 7 Dollars In My Pocket (Highway Of Broken Hearts Medley - 15:09) / Devil Jam (Hollywood Jam - 9:31) / Lover Man (4:58) / Midnight Lightning (4:35) / Further On Up The Road (1:54) / The Things I Used To Do (7:09) / Once I Had A Woman (5:36) / Machine Gun (8:25) / Lord I Sing The Blues For Me And You (4:15) / Country Blues (6:33) / Stop (4:41)
CD5: Midnight Lightning (6:31) / Lower Alcatraz (Midnight Lightning-3:41) / There Goes Ezy Rider - 7 Dollars In My Pocket - Highway Of Broken Hearts Medley - 11:38 - Yes, this **is** repeated a second time only in a shorter edit) / Heavy Rider Jam (Ezy Rider Jam- 9 :29) / Easy Blues (7:47) / Gypsy Boy (3:15) / Peace In Mississippi (4:26) / Bluesiana Jam (Blue Window Jam - 17:03) / BB King Slow Instrumental Jam (Introduction By B. B. King & Blues Jam No 2 Part 2 - 19:46)

COPENHAGEN '70

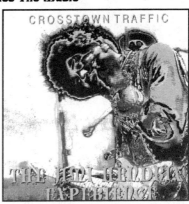

CROSSTOWN TRAFFIC

DANTE'S INFERNO

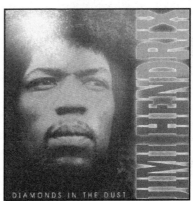

DIAMONDS IN THE DUST

DRONE BLUES

EARTH TONES

CD6: Two Guitars Jam (FAKE - 10:19) / San Francisco Bay Blues (FAKE - 8:12) / Gypsy Eyes (4:24) / Cherokee Mist (7:11) / The Street Things (produced by Jimi for The Buddy Miles Express - 5:12) / In From The Storm (3:42) / Freedom (3:29) / Somewhere Over The Rainbow II (Somewhere - 3:37) / Belly Button Window (4:48) / Captain Coconut II, Cherokee Mist (Jam / Cherokee Mist - 6:17 - Yep, another repeated track) / Rider Blues (for the **third** time it's Highway Of Broken Hearts Medley - 11:38) / Electric Ladyland (4:33)/ Jazzy Jamming (South Saturn Delta-4:55)

CD7: She's So Fine (2:47) / Axis Bold As Love (3:32) / EXP (1:56) / Up From The Skies (2:56) / Love Jam (Jazz Jimi Jazz - 13:09) / Electric Ladyland (6:19) / Pass It On (Straight Ahead - 7:30) / Hey Baby (New Rising Sun) (6:06) / Stone Free (4:08) / Hey Joe (4:53) / Freedom (5:12) / Red House (7:55) / Ezy Rider (6:37) / New Rising Sun Theme (Hey Baby - New Rising Sun) / Midnight Lightning - 4:51)

CD8: Fire (3:45) / Getting My Heart Back Together Again (Hear My Train A Comin' - 7:02) / Spanish Castle Magic (9:44) / Purple Haze (7:20) / Tax Free (14:21) / Message To Love (4:00) / Red House (5:14) / Voodoo Chile (slight return) (5:36) / Machine Gun (10:55) / Hey Baby (7:19)

Comments: The quality varies throughout the set but is mostly very good. A lot of rarities gathered in one spot even though a couple of tracks are repeated multiple times and there are several fake tracks with no involvement from Jimi. Many song titles are incorrect. The correct titles are in parenthesis. A nice set if you can find it. European CD. This set comes in a large box with an extensive book (in Italian) and a video (PAL system).

FILLMORE CONCERTS (THE) IN **
WHOOPY CAT (WKP - 0006 / 7) 2CD (CD1 66:51, CD2 56:27)

CD 1: Power Of Soul / Lover Man / Hear My Train A Comin' / Them Changes / Machine Gun / Auld Lang Syne / Who Knows / Steppin' Stone / Burning Desire / Fire / Ezy Ryder

CD 2: Machine Gun / Power Of Soul / Stone Free / Them Changes / Message To Love / Stop

Comments: Recorded live at the Fillmore East, NYC, December 31, 1969. Very good soundboard. The shows are incomplete but it's a reasonable way to get a fair sampling of these legendary shows. Worth finding.

FIRE IN
THE SWINGING PIG (TSP 018) LP (47:19)

Side 1: Sergeant Pepper's Lonely Hearts Club Band / The Wind Cries Mary / Foxy Lady / Fire / Hey Joe / I Don't Live Today

Side 2: The Burning Of The Midnight Lamp / Purple Haze / Foxy Lady / Purple Haze / Experiencing The Blues

Comments: September 5, 1967. Radiohuset, Stockholm, Sweden / November 10, 1967. Vitus Studios, Bussum, Holland

Also available on CD from The Swingin' Pig as **FIRE** (TSP-CD-018). Made obsolete by commercial releases.

FIRST NIGHT AT THE ROYAL ALBERT HALL IN ***
MIDNIGHT BEAT (MB CD 047/48) 2CD (CD1 55:37, CD2 51:39)

CD 1: Hey Joe / Hound Dog 1 / Hound Dog 2 / Hound Dog 3 / Voodoo Chile (slight return) / Lonesome Train / Tax Free / Let Me Stand Next To Your Fire / Getting My Heart Back Together Again / Foxy Lady

CD 2: Red House / Sunshine Of Your Love / Spanish Castle Magic - Message To Love / Star Spangled Banner - Purple Haze / Introductions / Voodoo Chile (slight return)

Comments: CD 1: Tracks 1-6 were recorded February 24, 1969, at the Royal Albert Hall in London. These are from a soundboard recording and are quite good. Tracks 7-10 and all the tracks from Disc Two are from a fair audience recording from February 18, 1969, at the Royal Albert Hall. Recommended because this is the only place to get the complete soundcheck on CD and the first time the February 18 show has been available anywhere.

FIRST RAYS: THE SESSIONS IN **
WHOOPY CAT (WKP-0002) CD (71:11)

Freedom / Freedom / Freedom / Drifting / Drifting / Drifting / Ezy Rider / Ezy Rider / Angel / Dolly Dagger / Earth Blues / Room Full Of Mirrors / Bleeding Heart / Izabella / Message To Love / Power Of Soul / Lover Man / Valleys Of Neptune / Gypsy Boy

Comments: Very good to excellent quality CD of alternate takes and unused mixes the the commercial versions. Overall a nice collection of rare tracks.

FIRST RAYS OF THE NEW RISING SUN (THE) IN
LIVING LEGEND (LLRCD 023) CD (64:09)

Angel (3:11) / Voodoo Chile (6:53) / Cherokee Mist (2:19) / Things I Used To Do (3:54) / Like A Rolling Stone (3:06) / I'm A Man (3:04) / First Rays Of The New Rising Sun (0:59) / Little Wing (2:20) / Look Over Yonder (2:55) / One Rainy Wish (3:29) / Manic Depression (4:45) / Are You Experienced (9:53) / Red House (12:50) / Machine Gun (5:30) / Send My Love To Linda (1:27)

Comments: A collection of material lifted from the broadcast of the "Live And Unreleased" radio show.

FIRST RAYS OF THE NEW RISING SUN (THE) IN **
TRIANGLE PYCD 084-2 2CD (CD1 72:07, CD2 76:15)

CD 1: Izabella / Machine Gun / I'm A Man - So I'm Trying To Be (Stepping Stone) / Lord I Can See The Blues (Lord I Sing The Blues) / I'm A Man - So I'm Trying To Be (Stepping Stone) / Beginnings / Valleys Of Neptune

CD 2: Send My Love To Linda / Ships Passing In The Night / Heaven Has No Sorrow / Valleys Of Neptune / Alcatrazz (Midnight Lightning) / Night Bird Flying / Live And Let Live (Bolero) / Highway Of Desire - 7 Dollars In My Pocket (Highway of Broken Hearts Medley) / Midnight Lightning / Angel / Look Over Yonder / Astro Man Jam / 1983...A Merman I Should Turn To Be

Comments: A very nice double package with some long rehearsals and studio jams that are essential for your collection. This "Izabella" session tape is only available complete here and on the Golden Memories THINGS I USED TO DO. Recommended.

FIRST TIME IN CANADA
BUNNY MUSIC (INM0192) 2LP

Side 1: Intro - Killin' Floor* / Tax Free* / Fire* / Red House*
Side 2: Foxy Lady* / Hey Joe* / Spanish Castle Magic* / Purple Haze*
Side 3: Hound Dog** / Hey Joe^
Side 4: Purple Haze^ / Hear My Train A Comin'***
Comments: * Capital Theater, Ottawa, Canada, March 19, 1968 (second show - soundboard) / ** "Backstage at RAH!", February 18, 1969 / ^ Marquee Club, London, March 2, 1967 / *** Bruce Fleming Studio, London, December 19, 1967. Also available on CANADIAN CLUB (World Productions of Compact Music WPOCM 0888 D 006-2), PURPLE SONGS (Lost Rose LR CD 16) and SUPERCONCERT 1968 (Fire Power FP03).

FLAMES IN
MISSING IN ACTION (M.I.A. ACT 11) CD (76:55)

Catfish (7:40) / 1983 (4:10) / Somewhere Over The Rainbow (3:42) / Can You Please Crawl Out Your Window (3:25) / Gloomy Monday (2:32) / Ain't Too Proud To Beg (4:35) / Electric Ladyland (3:44) / Lonely Avenue (3:44) / World Traveler (6:48) / It's Too Bad (9:16) / Strato Strut (4:20) / Cherokee Mist (7:10) / Farther On Up The Road (1:34) / Down In Mississippi (4:15) / Midnight Lightning (3:51) / Silent Night (3:20) / Candle Waltz (1:40)

Comments: European CD. Not much here that you can't find with better sound on other boots or on commercial releases.

FLAMING GUITAR
ROCK CALENDAR RECORDS (RC 2108) CD

Hear My Train A Comin' / Fire / Spanish Castle Magic / Red House / I Don't Live Today / Foxy Lady / Purple Haze / Voodoo Chile (slight return) / Room Full of Mirrors / Sunshine of Your Love

Comments: Recorded live at San Jose Pop Festival, May 25, 1969. European CD. A good audience recording with the guitar being way up front, the bass and drums barely audible and the vocals sounding a bit thin and distant. This release cuts Jimi's show intro and tuning (about 2 minutes) which is complete on the Midnight Beat release HISTORIC CONCERT VOL. 2. Get that one instead.

FOXY HENDRIX
HEN 5000 2LP

Sides 1-2: Copy of WINK OF AN EYE (79-108/109)
Sides 3-4: Copy of LIVE IN STOCKHOLM (Fruit End C10168)
Comments: Very good to excellent mono.

FOXY LADY / PURPLE HAZE
Vinyl single
Comments: Pressed on red lacquer and made to appear to be an acetate. From the BBC.

FREAK OUT BLUES   IN**
GH 001 CD (74:57)
Intro By Jimi (0:03) / Midnight Lightning (4:02) / Voodoo Chile (8:57) / Rainy Day 'try out' (Rainy Day outtakes)(1:33) / Red House (6:55) / Bleeding Heart (3:39) / Blue Window Jam (8:23) / Villanova Junction Blues (Lonely Avenue Jam Part 2)(3:55) / Funky Blues Jam (Strato Strut)(1:46) / Once I Had A Woman (5:17) / Police Blues (Blue Suede Shoes)(11:13) / Country Blues (6:40) / Freedom Jam (Freedom / Ezy Rider...Jam) (8:27) / Acoustic Medley (3:23)
Comments: Good to very good sound. European CD. This has a few things on it that are harder to find - like the complete "Blue Suede Shoes" jam. Recommended.

FREAK OUT JAM   IN **
GH 002 CD (76:01)
Interview / Bright Lights Big City / World Traveller / It's Too Bad / Message To Love / Things I Used To Do (Instrumental) / Things I Used To Do (vocal) / Cherokee Mist - In From The Storm - Valleys Of Neptune / Bolero (Jam With Horns And Piano) / Hear My Train A Comin' / Drivin' South / Jam Session (Hollywood Jam) / Mushy Name (Ezy Rider) / Drifter's Escape / Midnight Lightning / Midnight Lightning Rap (Jam H290) / Hound Dog
Comments: A nice companion piece to FREAK OUT BLUES that features a number of Jimi's studio jams - some common, some not. Recommended.

FREE CONCERT   IN *
MIDNIGHT BEAT (MBCD 013) CD (71:34)
Lover Man / Experiencing The Blues / Ezy Rider / Come On / Room Full Of Mirrors / Hey Baby (New Rising Sun) / Message To Love / Machine Gun / Voodoo Chile (slight return) / In From The Storm / Purple Haze / Foxy Lady
Comments: Good to very good audience recording from Stora Scenen, Tivoli Garden, Stockholm, Sweden, August 31, 1970. The biggest frustration is the exclusion of "Red House" that should come after "Ezy Rider". It does exist on tape and there's no reason for it to be left off.

FROM THE OUTSKIRTS OF INFINITY
MAJOR TOM (MT 002) CD-R
Jam #1 in E / Earth Blues Jam / Things I Used To Do (1-4) / Calling All Devil's Children / Jam with Drum Loop / Rainy Day Practice Session / Rainy Day Dream Away - Still Raining Still Dreaming
Comments: The first six tracks were recorded at the Record Plant on May 15, 1969. These jams with Jimi included Stephen Stills, Dallas Taylor and Johnny Winter. "Jam With Drum Loop" has Jimi jamming with Steve Winwood over a drum machine. The "Rainy Day" sessions are from June 1968.

FUCKIN' HIS GUITAR FOR DENMARK   IN
POLYMORE J.H.Co. LP
Side 1: Sergeant Pepper's Lonely Hearts Club Band / Fire / Hey Joe / Experiencing The Blues
Side 2: The Wind Cries Mary / Purple Haze / Spanish Castle Magic / Wild Thing
Comments: Recorded January 7, 1968, at the Tivolis Konsertsal, Copenhagen, Denmark. Excellent stereo. Crackles. One of the more interesting Jimi titles.

GET THE EXPERIENCE!
INVASION UNLIMITED (IU9424-1) CD
Hey Joe (outfake) / Purple Haze / The Wind Cries Mary / Fire / Red House / I Don't Live Today / La Pouppee Qui Fait Non / Are You Experienced / She's So Fine / The Stars That Play With Laughing Sam's Dice / Wait Until Tomorrow (not Jimi) / Wait Until Tomorrow / One Rainy Wish / Ain't No Telling / Bold As Love / Spanish Castle Magic / You Got Me Floating / Send My Love To Linda / Dance / Dream
Comments: Besides having an outfake and an outright fake track, this was assembled from previous releases. Get it only if you have to.

GIMME JIMI
TRADEMARK OF QUALITY (JH 549) LP
Side 1: Red House / Message To Love / Ezy Rider
Side 2: Foxy Lady / Machine Gun / Freedom
Comments: Live show from Berkeley Community Center, Berkeley, California, May 30, 1970 (first show). Incomplete & obsolete.

GIMMIE THE GLAD EYE
DTD 003 2CD
CD 1: Stone Free (2:26) / Hey Joe (3:56) / Purple Haze (3:09) / Catfish (7:54) / Foxy Lady (3:19) / Purple Haze (5:06) / Voodoo Chile (3:34) / Hey Joe (2:38) / Sunshine Of Your Love (1:17) / Angel (3:08) / Like A Rolling Stone (3:06)
CD 2: Fire (3:30) / Hear My Train A Comin' (5:44) / Red House (7:03) / Stone Free (6:34) / Are You Experienced, Stone Free (7:13) / Sunshine Of Your Love (5:31) / Foxy Lady (4:37) / Like A Rolling Stone (5:10) / Voodoo Chile (3:48) / Purple Haze (3:48)
Comments: From various live sources 1967-69. Very good to excellent stereo. European CD.

GOLD COLLECTION
DIGITAL (DEJA2) CD
Foxy Lady / I Don't Live Today / Red House / Spanish Castle Magic / Star Spangled Banner / The Wind Cries Mary / The Burning Of The Midnight Lamp / Fire / Purple Haze / Voodoo Chile (slight return) / Sunshine Of Your Love / Experiencing The Blues / Killin' Floor / Can You Please Crawl Out Your Window / Hey Joe
Comments: Various live tracks from Los Angeles, 1969, and Stockholm, Sweden.

GOLDEN AGE
FREMUS (CDFR 0434) CD
Hey Joe / Lover Man / Mastermind / Flamenco Solo / Purple Haze / Gypsy Woman / Foxy Lady / Fire / Izabella / Star Spangled Banner
Comments: Recorded live at the Woodstock Festival. An incomplete selection best avoided by the discerning collector.

GONE BUT NOT FORGOTTEN
TEDDY BEAR RECORDS (TB 21) CD
Tax Free (9:51) / Killin' Floor (5:17) / Fire (2:51) / Red House (9:41) / Foxy Lady (4:50) / Hey Joe (5:28) / Spanish Castle Magic (4:05) / Purple Haze (6:38)
Comments: Recorded live at the Capitol Theatre, Ottawa, Canada, March 19, 1968. Second show. Good to very good sound. European CD. Picture CD.

GOOD DIE YOUNG (THE)
WHITE KNIGHT (WK22) 2LP
Side 1: I Don't Live Today (LA Forum, April 26, 1969, excellent stereo) / Pass It On (Berkeley, May 5, 1970, poor mono) / The Wind Cries Mary (Stockholm, May 24, 1970, excellent stereo)
Side 2: On The Killin' Floor (Monterey, June 16, 1967, fair mono) / Lover Man (Royal Albert Hall, February 24, 1969, excellent stereo) / Stone Free (Royal Albert Hall, February 24, 1969, excellent stereo) / All Along The Watchtower (Atlanta Pop, April 7, 1970, very good stereo)
Side 3: Fire (Randalls Island, June 17,1970, very good mono)/ Spanish Castle Magic (Stockholm, September 1, 1969, poor mono)/ Freedom (Isle of Wight, August 8, 1970, excellent stereo)/ Cherokee Suite (outtake, February 3,1968, excellent stereo)
Side 4: Are You Experienced (Singer Bowl, July 8, 1968, very good mono) / Come On Pt. 1 (Stockholm, July 31, 1970, good stereo) / Stop (Fillmore East, December 31, 1968, fair mono)

GOOD KARMA   IN
TRADE MARK OF QUALITY (TMQ 71060) LP
Side 1: Fire / Johnny B. Goode / Hear My Train A Comin'
Side 2: Foxy Lady / Machine Gun / Freedom
Comments: Recorded May 30, 1970, Berkeley Community Center, Berkeley, California. First show. Fair mono. Also available as GOOD KARMA 1 (Berkeley 2022) & (Trade Mark Of Quality TMQ 71060) & (Box Top Records - colored vinyl). This and GOOD KARMA 2 were the first outing for the soundboards from this

ELECTRIC ANNIVERSARY JIMI

ELECTRIC GYPSY

ELECTRIC LADYLAND OUTTAKES

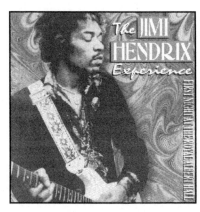

FIRST NIGHT AT THE
ROYAL ALBERT HALL

ENJOY JIMI HENDRIX

EXPERIENCE

now oft-bootlegged show.

GOOD KARMA 2 IN
TRADE MARK OF QUALITY (TMQ 71079) LP & (BERKELEY 2023) LP
Side 1: Red House / Message To Love / Ezy Rider
Side 2: Star Spangled Banner / Purple Haze / Voodoo Chile (slight return)
Comments: Recorded May 30, 1970, Berkeley Community Center, Berkeley, California. First show. Fair mono. Also on GOOD KARMA 2 (Box Top Records - colored vinyl).

GOOD VIBES IN
RUTHLESS RHYMES (1850) 2LP
Side 1: Interview / Hey Joe / Interview / Hound Dog
Side 2: Interview / Voodoo Chile (slight return) / Interview / Hear My Train A Comin' / Interview
Comments: Recorded live on February 24, 1969. Rehearsals from the Royal Albert Hall, London, England. The interviews were recorded in March 1969 with Jay Harvey of KDAY Radio in the Hollywood Palladium. Very good mono - some crackles. Also on GOOD VIBES (Trademark Of Quality TMQ 71042) & (Vicki Vinyl 1142) & (Boxtop Records) & (Mushroom Vol. 7/1850) & (POD) and as HE WAS A FRIEND OF YOURS (Out To Lunch 1). Made obsolete by FIRST NIGHT AT THE ROYAL ALBERT HALL on Midnight Beat.

GOODBYE JIMI
WCF 723 LP
Side 1: Purple Haze, Wild Thing (Worchester, Mass., March 15, 1968) / Voodoo Chile, Hey Joe, Sunshine Of Your Love (Lulu Show January 4, 1968) / Drivin' South (Top Gear Show 1967)
Side 2: Experiencing The Blues (Top Gear 1967) / Hound Dog (Top Gear 1967) / Little Miss Lover (Top Gear 1967) / Love Or Confusion (Saturday Club 1967) / Foxy Lady (Saturday Club 1967) / Hey Joe (BBC Saturday Club) / Stone Free (Saturday Club)
Comments: Good mono. Also on Kustom Records (005) - poor mono & as BROADCASTS (TMOQ 71019) & as LIVE EXPERIENCE on BERKELEY (LE - HH).

GREATEST HITS LIVE IN
CHARTBUSTERS CHER-089-A CD
Hey Joe / The Wind Cries Mary / Purple Haze / The Burning Of The Midnight Lamp / Fire / I Don't Live Today / Foxy Lady / Little Wing / Manic Depression / All Along The Watchtower / Stone Free / Sgt. Pepper / Are You Experienced / Like A Rolling Stone / Sgt. Pepper / Star Spangled Banner / Wild Thing / Freedom / Voodoo Child (slight return)
Comments: A pretty much useless package of, well, just what it sounds like. Most of this live material is available commercially or has been bootlegged numerous times.

GUEST EXPERIENCE
WESTWOOD ONE RARITIES ON CD VOL. 77 CD
So Much / Ex Art Student / Rock N Roll Band / Yes I Need Someone / The Clown / Morning Glory / Mr. Guy Fawkes / Doriella Du Fontaine / Old Times Good Times / The Everlasting First / Slow Walkin' Talk / Captive In The Sun/ Let Me Stay/ Someone Is Sure To (Want You)/ Live And Let Live
Comments: Westwood One Radio Special featuring Jimi on other people's records. See entries in the "Jimi With Others" section of this book for more details.

GUITAR HERO IN
DOCUMENT DR 013 CD (53:16)
Side 1: Radio One Theme (1:37) / Experiencing The Blues (5:23) / Can You Crawl Out Your Window (3:31) / I'm Your Hoochie Coochie Man (5:24) / Drivin' South (5:24) / Spanish Castle Magic (3:03) / Day Tripper (3:11)
Side 2: Wait Until Tomorrow (2:52) / Stone Free (3:20) / Foxy Lady (2:53) / Little Miss Lover (2:52) / The Burning Of The Midnight Lamp (3:37) / Hound Dog (2:39) / Hey Joe (3:54) / Getting My Heart Back Together Again (4:27)
Comments: From an FM re-broadcast of the BBC recordings. Excellent mono. Source: London Top Gear, October 17, 1967 and October 26, 1967. Swedish bootleg. Repressed by K&S (011). Also available on GUITAR HERO (Stoned 3) and PRIMAL KEYS (Impossible Record Works 1-02). Obsolete

GUITARS AND AMPS
WORLD PRODUCTION OF COMPACT MUSIC (WPOCM CD 0888D005 - 2)CD

Killin' Floor / Catfish / Foxy Lady / Red House / Drivin' South / Fire / Little Wing / Purple Haze

Comments: Recorded live at the Olympia Theatre, Paris, January 29, 1968. Good to very good sound. Some surface noise.

GUITAR WIZZARD
DOCUMENT (DR 1305) CD Single

Hound Dog / Foxy Lady

GYPSY CHARM IN
MUM (MUCD 018) CD

Drifter's Escape / Dolly Dagger / Somewhere / Stepping Stone / Dance / Cherokee Mist / Sunshine Of Your Love / Red House (3 versions) / I Don't Live Today (2 versions) / Little Drummer Boy / Earth Blues / Look Over Yonder / La Pouppee Qui Fait Non / Drifting / Valleys Of Neptune / Purple Haze / Foxy Lady

Comments: Excellent sound. Another reissue from Mum Records - known for recycling common Hendrix bootlegs.

GYPSY HAZE IN *
LORDS OF ARCHIVE RECORDS (L.A.R. 6) CD (63:23)

Message Of Love / Ezy Rider, Paper Airplanes (false start) / Paper Airplanes / Earth Blues / Them Changes (take 1) / Them Changes (take 2) / Lover Man (take 1) / Lover Man (take 2) / Paper Airplanes / Lover Man / Hear My Train / Them Changes / Little Drummer Boy

Comments: The first 7 tracks are rehearsals from Baggies prior to the Fillmore shows followed by four tracks from the first show at the Fillmore East, NYC, December 31, 1969. The final track is copied from the promo single. Mostly excellent soundboard. Some hiss. European CD.

GYPSY ON CLOUD NINE
JESTER PRODUCTIONS 2LP

Side 1: Further Up The Road / Astro Man / The Things We Used To Do

Side 2: Once I Had A Woman / Ezy Rider (incomplete) / Message To Love

Side 3: Captain Coconut (Jam / Cherokee Mist) / Jam (Ezy Rider Jam) / Peace In Mississippi

Side 4: Little Drummer Boy / Izabella - Machine Gun / Blue Suede Shoes Part 2 (Midnight Lightning)

Comments: Studio jams from the Record Plant 1969. Excellent stereo. Song listings on labels wrong.

GYPSY SUN AND RAINBOWS IN
MANIC DEPRESSION (MDCD 05/06) 2CD

Hear My Train A Comin' / Spanish Castle Magic / Red House / Mastermind / Lover Man / Foxy Lady / Jamming At My House (Beginnings) / Izabella / Gypsy Woman / Fire / Voodoo Chile / Star Spangled Banner / Purple Haze / Flamenco Solo / Villanova Junction Blues / Hey Joe / Woodstock Interview / Rehearsals At Liberty House, Woodstock 14 Aug 69 / Lover Man / Lover Man / Hear My Train A Comin' / Spanish Castle Magic

Comments: Recorded live at the Woodstock Festival, Bethel, New York, August 18 , 1969. Good to very good stereo. 8 page book. This is the complete show minus the opening song "Message To Love" (See 500,000 HALOS) plus four rehearsals at Jimi's house in Shokan, NY, prior to the show.

GYPSY SUNS, MOONS AND RAINBOWS IN
SIDEWALK MUSIC (JHX 8868) CD (55:02)

Crash Landing / Midnight Lightning / Machine Gun / Farther On Up The Road / Astro Man / Country Blues / Lord I Sing The Blues (For Me And You) / Message To Love / Stone Free / Instrumental Jam(Rock And Roll Jam) / Izabella

Comments: Alternate studio versions that are found on many other releases. Excellent stereo from tape. European CD. Deluxe insert. 55 minutes. Re-issued as MOONS AND RAINBOWS (Insect IST 48).

HAPPY NEW YEAR, JIMI
COPS AND ROBBERS (JTYM 01) LP

Side 1: Power Of Soul / Lover Man / Machine Gun

Side 2: Bleeding Heart / Earth Blues / Burning Desire

Comments: Recorded live on December 31, 1969, Fillmore East, NYC. Only part of the first show soundboard.

HAVE MERCY ON ME BABY! IN ***
MIDNIGHT BEAT (MB CD 038) CD (70:31)

Killin' Floor (1:19) / Have Mercy (4:06) / Can You See Me (4:28) / Like A Rolling Stone (8:36) / Rock Me Baby (3:15) / Catfish Blues (9:01) / Stone Free (3:31) / Hey Joe (4:16) / Wild Thing (8:10) / I Don't Live Today (8:16) / Hear My Train A Comin' (8:56) / Spanish Castle Magic (6:31)

Comments: Tracks 1-9 recorded live at The Flamingo Club, London, February 4 , 1967. Tracks 10-12 are from The Philharmonic Hall, New York, November 28, 1968. Poor to good audience tapes. Picture CD. Jimi introduces his new band as 'The Experience'. Recommended for the historical aspect. The Flamingo Club tracks only were also issued on LIVE AT THE FLAMINGO CLUB, LONDON 2.4.67 (No Label).

HE WAS A FRIEND OF YOURS
OUT TO LUNCH PRODUCTION 1 LP

Side 1: Hey Joe (uncut) / Hound Dog

Side 2: Hound Dog (cont.) / Voodoo Chile / Lonesome Town

HEAR MY FREEDOM IN ***
KOBRA RECORDS (KRCR 10) CD

Hear My Freedom / Izabella/(3:45) / Instrumental Jam with Larry Young (Fuzzy Guitar Jam)(19:39) / Sending My Love To Linda, Live And Let Live (11:15) / Ezy Rider Jam (Ezy Rider Jam / Cherokee Mist)(19:14) / Rainy Day Dream Away Still Raining Still Dreaming (7:55) / Voodoo Child (slight return) - takes 10-12 (3:47)

Comments: Excellent soundboard. This features some of the longest available versions of otherwise common jams ("Fuzzy Guitar Jam" & "Ezy Rider Jam / Cherokee Mist"). Highly Recommended. European CD.

HELL'S SESSIONS
BELLA GODIVA (Rec BGR 001) LP

Side 1: Rainbow Jam (Drivin' South) / Electric Indians (Drone Blues) / Voodoo Blues (It's Too Bad - incomplete)

Side 2: Pali Gap Revisited (Jimi / Jimmy Jam - incomplete) / Tunnel Of Love (Young / Hendrix - incomplete)

Comments: Recorded between August 9 & 12, 1968, at the Electric Ladyland Studios in NYC.

HENDRIX: BUSTED IN TORONTO! IN
VENUE (VE100502) CD (67:36)

Fire / Hear My Train A Comin' / Spanish Castle Magic - 3rd Stone From The Sun - Little Miss Lover / Red House / Foxy Lady / Room Full Of Mirrors - Crash Landing - Midnight Lightning - Gypsy Eyes / Purple Haze / Voodoo Chile (slight return)

Comments: Recorded live at the Maple Leaf Gardens, Toronto, Canada, May 3, 1969. Good to very good audience recording of a complete show. The guitar and vocals are pretty up front while the bass and drums are a bit low and the sound as a whole has a lot of echo. This show was also released as part of the I DON'T LIVE TODAY box set.

HENDRIX, CLAPTON, MAYALL & BRUCE
CONTRABAND (CBM 4) LP

Side 1: Strangers That Play, Highway Chile (Hendrix) / Hear Me Calling (Bruce) / Camels & Elephants (Baker)

Side 2: No Reply, I'm No Stranger, Sonny Boy Blow, Stand Back Bark (Mayall & Clapton)

Comments: First two cuts live and the rest studio. Also on Munia (MBR 707). Excellent stereo. Another of those semi-ripoff releases that put out tracks by famous artists before they were really good.

HENDRIX IN WORDS AND MUSIC IN
OUTLAW RECORDS OTR 1100030 2 CD

Disc 1: Meatball Fulton Interview / Purple Haze / Meatball Fulton / Gangster Of Love (no Jimi) / Bleeding Heart / Meatball Fulton / Wild Thing / Nancy Carter Interview / From This Day On (no Jimi)

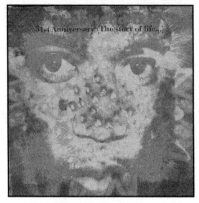

51ST ANNIVERSARY

FIRST RAYS OF THE NEW RISING SUN

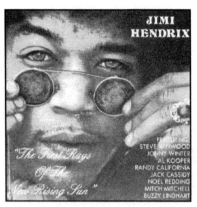

FIRST RAYS: THE SESSIONS

FREAK OUT BLUES

FREAK OUT JAM

FREE CONCERT

/ Nancy Carter / Win Your Love (no Jimi) / Voice In The Wind (no Jimi)

Disc 2: Manic Depression / Killin' Floor / Red House / Fire / Little Wing / Hey Joe / Purple Haze / Wild Thing

Comments: A bunch of interviews with people other than Jimi mixed in with live material from the Royal Albert Hall and Winterland shows. Avoid.

HENDRIX LIVE IN HAWAII
HEN RECORDS (37 - WCF) LP

Side 1: Some Slow Thing (7:16) / Boogie It All Together (9:04) / Guitar Improvisation (6:31)

Side 2: Get On Home Boogie (8:30) / Stevie's Walk (11.42)

Comments: Titles wrong. Good mono. Also available as RAINBOW BRIDGE on Shalom which is better quality.

HEY JOE
ON STAGE (ON PD 2316) LP

Side 1: Voodoo Chile (slight return) / Foxy Lady / Hey Joe / Purple Haze / Wild Thing

Side 2: Sergeant Pepper's Lonely Hearts Club Band / Spanish Castle Magic / Like A Rolling Stone / Can You See Me

Comments: A compilation of common live cuts from Monterey and Stockholm.

HEY JOE IN
CROCODILE BEAT (CB 53039) CD

Like A Rolling Stone / Voodoo Child (slight return) / Purple Haze / Sunshine Of Your Love / Red House / Gypsy Eyes / Hey Joe / Foxy Lady / Wild Thing / Experiencing The Blues / Sgt. Pepper

Comments: A compilation of live cuts from Monterey, Stockholm, L.A., Paris and one studio track. Don't bother.

HIGH, LIVE 'N' DIRTY
NUTMEG (NUT-1001) LP

Side 1: F.H.I.T.A. / No!No! / In The Morning

Side 2: Jimi's Blues / Peoples, Peoples

Comments: This is one of those 'quasi-legal' releases of material pressed by several different companies hoping to cash in on the Hendrix name. This material was recorded at The Scene in NYC probably sometime in March (sixth?) of 1968. Present on this night were Jim Morrison (obviously very drunk), some members of The McCoys and maybe Buddy Miles. The actual titles of the songs (not including Jim Morrison's shouted obscenities) are: "Tomorrow Never Knows", "Outside Woman Blues" / "Sunshine Of Your Love", "Red House", "I'm Gonna Leave This Town" / "Everything's Gonna Be Allright", "Bleeding Heart". Also available as WOKE UP THIS MORNING AND FOUND MYSELF DEAD (Red Lightnin' RL0015) LP and CD, TOMORROW NEVER KNOWS (Happy Bird B/90166) LP.

HISTORIC CONCERT IN
MIDNIGHT BEAT (MB CD 017) CD (53:58)

Intro, Are You Experienced / Fire / Red House / I Don't Live Today / Foxy Lady / Like A Rolling Stone / Purple Haze / The Star Spangled Banner / Hey Joe / Wild Thing

Comments: Recorded live at the New York Rock Festival, Singer Bowl, Flushing Meadow Park, Queens, New York, August 23, 1968. Poor recording from a particularly noisy audience. The balance is heavier on guitar and vocals and a bit thin on bass and drums. For the collector who needs every show out there. This is the concert Noel Redding speaks of in the interview at the beginning of this book. Picture CD.

HISTORIC CONCERT VOL. 2 - HIGH TIMES AT SAN JOSE POP IN
MIDNIGHT BEAT (MB CD 050) CD (68:55)

Intro, Hear My Train A Comin' / Fire, Drum Solo / Spanish Castle Magic / Red House / I Don't Live Today / Foxy Lady / Purple Haze / Voodoo Chile (slight return) / Villanova Junction Blues / Message To Love / Room Full Of Mirrors / Sunshine Of Your Love

Comments: Recorded live at the San Jose Pop Festival, Santa Clara, Country Fairground, San Jose, CA, May 25, 1969. A good audience recording with the guitar being way up front, the bass and drums audible and the vocals sounding a bit thin and distant. This is the better release of this show (as opposed to FLAMING GUITAR).

HISTORIC PERFORMANCES IN
AQUARIUS (AQ 67-JH-080) CD

Intro by B.B. King (1) / Instrumental 1 (Blues jam No. 2 Part 2) (1) / Instrumental 2 (Blues Jam No. 3) (1) / Instrumental 3 (It's My Own Fault) (1) / I Don't Live Today (2) / Red House (2) / Foxy Lady (2) / Voodoo Chile (slight return) (3) / Hey Joe (3) / Sunshine of Your Love (3)

Comments: (1) April 15, 1968 at the Generation Club, NYC (very good soundboard) / (2)February 24th, 1969 at The Royal Albert Hall (very good soundboard) / (3) January 4th, 1969 on the Lulu Show.

HOME AT WOODSTOCK
CSD 1564 LP

Side 1: Jam

Side 2: Jam / Jam / Madagascar

Comments: For more detailed information refer to THIS FLYER and JIMI HENDRIX AT HIS BEST VOL. 1.

HOOCHIE COOCHIE MAN
TOASTED (TRW 1953) 2LP

Side 1: Inst. (recorded at Jimi's NYC apartment early 1968) / I'm A Man (Club 20, Hackensack, NJ, December 26, 1964) / Like A Rolling Stone (after hours jam with Al Kooper & Buzzy Linhart at Steve Paul's Scene) / Red House (Paris Olympia, first public gig of the JHE)

Side 2: Hoochie Coochie Man (BBC 1967) / Foxy Lady (alternate studio version) / Lover Man (outtake) / Look Over Yonder (outtake) / One Rainy Wish (alternate mix) / Drivin' South (BBC 1967) / Things I Used To Do (studio jam with Johnny Winter 1968) / Drifter's Escape (unreleased version December 1968)

Side 3: Cherokee Mist (unreleased) / Voodoo Chile (slight return - alternate take) / 1983 (A Merman I Should Be - alternate version) / Room Full Of Mirrors (unreleased version November 1968) / Angel (demo recorded at JH's NYC apartment late 1968) / Valleys Of Neptune (recorded for the never released 'First Rays Of The New Rising Sun' double LP) / Send My Love To Linda (unfinished song from one of Jimi's last sessions)

Side 4: South Saturn Delta (another track intended for 'First Rays Of The New Rising Sun') / Dolly Dagger (Isle Of White, August 30, 1970) / Hey Joe, Hey Baby, Lover Man (Berkeley Community Centre, May 30, 1970)

Comments: TMOQ labels. Excellent stereo.

HOVERING IN WINTERLAND
TUFF BITES (TB.95.1015) CD

Like A Rolling Stone / Spanish Castle Magic / Lover Man / Hey Joe / Fire / Foxy Lady / Purple Haze / Little Wing / Everything's Gonna Be Alright

Comments: Tracks 1 -7 recorded live at Winterland, San Francisco, October 11, 1968 (second show). The last two songs are from the Cafe Au Go Go, NYC, March 17, 1968.

I DON'T LIVE TODAY IN
ACL 007 3 CD

Disc 1: The Wind Cries Mary / I Don't Live Today (3) / La Pouppee Qui Fait Non / Taking Care Of Business / One Rainy Wish / Have You Ever Been (To Electric Ladyland) / South Saturn Delta (parts 1 & 2) / Rainy Day Shuffle - Rainy Day, Dream Away / Cat Talking To Me (2) / Room Full Of Mirrors / Sunshine Of Your Love / Jam / Ships Passing In The Night / Highway Of Broken Hearts Medley

Disc 2: Valleys Of Neptune / Machine Gun / Stepping Stone (2) / Lonely Avenue Jam Part 1 / Midnight Lightning (2) / Come Down Hard On Me Baby / Drifter's Escape / Belly Button Window / Bolero

Disc 3: Fire / Hear My Train A Comin'/ Spanish Castle Magic - Third Stone From The Sun - Little Miss Lover / Red House / Foxy Lady / Room Full Of Mirrors - Midnight Lightning - Gypsy Eyes / Purple Haze / Voodoo Child (slight return)

Comments: The first two discs are a mixed bag of studio jams, Chandler Tapes material, unused mixes and alternate mixes in very good to excellent sound. The third disc is the audience tape of the Maple Leaf Gardens show from Toronto, Canada, on May 3, 1969.

I DON'T LIVE TODAY, MAYBE TOMORROW IN ***
LIVING LEGEND (LLRCD 030) CD

Tax Free (16:22) / Spanish Castle Magic (11:38) / Star Spangled Banner (2:32) / Purple Haze (5:40) / Red House (11:06) / Foxy Lady (6:23) / I Don't Live Today (6:37) / Voodoo Chile (slight return)(17:52) / Sunshine Of Your Love

Comments: Recorded live at the LA Forum, April 26, 1969. Soundboard - excellent stereo. Songs here are in the correct running order for a nice change of pace. Legitimately released as part of the LIFE-LINES box set minus "Foxy Lady" which was on CONCERTS - unfortunately in a very different mix. Also available on ELECTRIC JIMI (Jaguarondi 001/2), LIVE AT LOS ANGELES FORUM (Armando Cucio Editore), LOS ANGELES 1969 (WPOCM 067), LIVE IN L.A. FORUM (Black Panther BPCD 050) and numerous others.

IN CONCERT IN
STARLIFE (ST 3612) 3 CD

Disc 1: Intro / Killin' Floor / Spanish Castle Magic / Fire / Hey Joe / Red House / Sunshine Of Your Love / Experiencing The Blues / Foxy Lady / Red House / Drivin' South / Fire / Little Wing / Purple Haze

Disc 2: Purple Haze / Killin' Floor / The Burning Of The Midnight Lamp / Hound Dog / Experiencing The Blues / Little Miss Lover / Radio One / Ain't Too Proud To Beg / Can You Please Crawl Out Your Window / I'm Your Hoochie Coochie Man / Drivin' South / Spanish Castle Magic / Wait Until Tomorrow / Stone Free / Day Tripper / Hear My Train A Comin'

Disc 3: Red House / I'm Gonna Leave This Town - Everything's Gonna Be Alright / Bleeding Heart / Morrison's Lament - Tomorrow Never Knows - Uranus Rock - Outside Woman Blues - Sunshine Of Your Love

Comments: Disc one serves up the ever-popular January 9, 1969, Stockholm first show and the January 29, 1968, Paris Musicorama second show (sans the opener-"Killin' Floor"). Disc two is a mixed bag of obsolete BBC material. Disc three is a copy of WOKE UP THIS MORNING AND FOUND MYSELF DEAD. Pass on this one.

IN EXPERIENCE
Comments: Mike Ephron jam sessions and some Woodstock tracks.

IN EUROPE 67/68/69 IN
VULTURE (CD 009/2) 2CD

CD 1: Sergeant Pepper's Lonely Hearts Club Band / Hey Joe / I Don't Live Today / The Wind Cries Mary / Foxy Lady / Fire / The Burning Of The Midnight Lamp / Purple Haze / Experiencing The Blues / Foxy Lady / Red House / Drivin' South / The Wind Cries Mary / Fire / Little Wing / Purple Haze / Can You Please Crawl Out Your Window

CD 2: Killin' Floor / I Don't Live Today / Spanish Castle Magic / Hey Joe / Voodoo Chile (slight return) / Sunshine Of Your Love / Red House / Fire / Purple Haze / Star Spangled Banner / Little Miss Lover

Comments: This starts with the 8 tracks from the September 5, 1967, broadcast from Stockholm. Next up are 8 of the 9 ("Killin' Floor" is missing) songs from the January 29, 1968, Paris Olympia second show. Last are one track from the January 9, 1969, Stockholm, first show and all of the second show. There are also two BBC tracks. The 1967 & 1968 shows and the BBC tracks have all been commercially released. The 1969 Stockholm show can't justify this set as it is a common show to find.

IN FROM THE STORM IN **
SILVER RARITIES (SIRA 109/110) 2CD (CD170:30, CD2 72:09)

CD 1: Spanish Castle Magic / Lover Man / Hey Baby (New Rising Sun) / In From The Storm / Message To Love / Foxy Lady / Hear My Train A Comin' / Voodoo Chile (slight return) / Fire / Purple Haze / Dolly Dagger - Earth Blues / Ezy Rider / Red House

CD 2: Freedom / Beginning - Straight Ahead / Hey Baby (New Rising Sun) / Stone Free / Hey Joe / Stepping Stone / Lord I Sing The Blues For You And Me / Lover Man

Comments: Tracks 1 - 10 recorded live in Maui, Hawaii, June 30, 1970 (first show). Tracks 11 - 18 are from the second show. The last three tracks are the familiar studio outtakes. The entire set is is from a mediocre soundboard tape and is mastered too fast. Not an easy listen but the shows are complete. Not one of the COL's best performances in my book.

IN MEMORIAM: LIVE IN SWEDEN
MIDNIGHT BEAT (MB CD 138/39/40) 2CD & CD-ROM Box Set (CD1 56:48, 69:20)

CD 1: Killin' Floor (7:49) / Spanish Castle Magic (7:31) / Fire (2:57) / Hey Joe (5:13) / Voodoo Child (slight return) (13:43) / Red House (11:06) / Sunshine Of Your Love (8:09)

CD 2: I Don't Live Today (11:43) / Spanish Castle Magic (6:11) / Hey Joe (7:21) / Voodoo Child (slight return) (9:52) / Sunshine Of Your Love (12:05) / Red House (12:08) / Let Me Stand Next To Your Fire (2:49) / Purple Haze (4:00) / Star Spangled Banner (3:18)

CD 3: Killin' Floor (7:16) / Spanish Castle Magic (7:39) / Fire (3:03) / Hey Joe (3:53) / Voodoo Child (slight return) (14:00) / Red House (11:37) / Sunshine Of Your Love (8:06)

Comments: CD 1: Recorded live at the Konserthuset, Stockholm, Sweden, January 9, 1969 (first show). CD 2: The second show from January 9, 1969. CD 3: This unique disc brings bootlegging into the 21st century with its interactive CD-Rom and a b&w movie of the first show from Stockholm on January 9, 1969. The sound quality is excellent, though not as crisp and dynamic as the Swinging Pig release. The movie is low-end and is only about 3" x 3" on the screen. Still, it is really cool.

INCIDENT AT RAINBOW BRIDGE
Unknown label LP
Side 1: Intro. Jam / Red House / Villanova Blues
Side 2: Hear My Baby Calling / Incident At Rainbow Bridge
Comments: Very good audience recording of selections from both shows at Maui on July 30, 1970.

INCIDENT AT RAINBOW BRIDGE / ISLE OF WIGHT FESTIVAL   IN ***
TRIANGLE (PYCD 060-2) 2CD
CD 1: Dolly Dagger / Villanova Junction / Ezy Rider / Red House / Freedom / Beginning / Straight Ahead / Hey Baby (New Rising Sun) / Voodoo Chile (slight return) / Fire / Little One / Little One
CD 2: Intro / The Queen / Sergeant Pepper's Lonely Hearts Club Band / Spanish Castle Magic / Machine Gun / Red House / Hey Baby (New Rising Sun) / Hey Joe / Purple Haze / Voodoo Chile (slight return) / In From The Storm
Comments: Disc one is the first 8 tracks from the second show and 2 tracks from the first show at Maui from 30 Jul 70. Disc 2 is a selection of material from the 30 Aug 70 show at the Isle Of Wight Festival. The ONLY truly redeeming part of this set is that it is the only place to find the complete and unedited version of "Machine Gun"- including Jimi's intro to the song. The CD WIGHT has the complete song without the intro. All other releases commercial or otherwise are incomplete. Highly recommended for just one track!

INSIDE THE RAINBOW
BLUE (SX501) 2LP
Side 1: Killin' Floor / Spanish Castle Magic / Foxy Lady / Room Full Of Mirrors
Side 2: All Along The Watchtower / Hey Joe / Hey Baby (New Rising Sun) / Message To Love
Side 3: Spanish Castle Magic / Hey Baby (New Rising Sun) / Ezy Rider
Side 4: Hey Joe / Purple Haze / Voodoo Chile (slight return)
Comments: These are common live tracks lifted from LAST BRITISH CONCERT and WINK OF AN EYE.

ISLAND MAN   IN **
SILVER RARITIES (SIRA 39/40) 2CD (CD1 70:25, CD2 49:59)
CD 1: Intro and tune up / God Save the Queen - Sgt.Pepper's Lonely Hearts Club Band - Spanish Castle Magic / All Along The Watchtower / Machine Gun / Lover Man / Freedom / Red House / Dolly Dagger / Midnight Lightning
CD 2: Foxy Lady / Message to Love / Hey Baby (Land of the New Rising Sun) / Ezy Rider / Hey Joe / Voodoo Chile / In From the Storm.
Comments: Recorded live on August 31st, 1970, Isle of Wight. Very good soundboard from a composite of sources including an incomplete "Machine Gun". See INCIDENT AT RAINBOW BRIDGE / ISLE OF WIGHT FESTIVAL for the most complete version. See also RACE WITH THE DEVIL for the whole show from a single source but with an incomplete "Machine Gun". WIGHT has the complete "Machine Gun" sans intro but again is compiled from a variety of sources. For my money this is another of the shows that us fans should DEMAND be released complete (and that means NO EDITS - PERIOD). Most of it has been released commercially all chopped up and edited to death in little bits and pieces that only suggest the musical beauty and the artistic integrity and inspiration of this performance. I think it's one of Jimi's best ever and a darn long one clocking in at around 110 minutes—almost twice as long

GOOD KARMA 1

GOOD VIBES

GUITAR HERO

GYPSY ON CLOUD NINE

GYPSY CHARM

HENDRIX: BUSTED IN TORONTO

as an average performance. Throw in that it was the last professionally recorded (and filmed) performance before his death 19 days later.... it's actually unbelievable that we can't go to the corner CD store and buy it.

ISLE OF WIGHT
SPACE LP
Side 1: Foxy Lady / improv. - Hey Baby - drum solo / Ezy Rider
Side 2: Voodoo Chile / drum solo - In From The Storm / rap
Comments: Good mono. European bootleg.

ISLE OF WIGHT VOL. 1
LS 3843 LP
Side 1: Intro by Jeff Dexter / Lover Man / Freedom
Side 2: Red House / Machine Gun
Comments: Recorded on August 30, 1970 at the Isle Of Wight Festival, East Afton Farm, England. Reissue of JIMI HENDRIX LIVE ISLE OF WIGHT 30-8-70.

ISLE OF WIGHT VOL. 2
LS 3844 LP
Side 1: Foxy Lady / Hey Baby (New Rising Sun) / Ezy Rider
Side 2: Voodoo Chile (slight return) / In From The Storm
Comments: Same info as above. Source: From Polydor LP ISLE OF WIGHT. Reissue of JIMI HENDRIX LIVE ISLE OF WIGHT 30-8-70 VOL. 2.

ISLE OF WIGHT, VOLUMES 1 & 2
VIOLET SYSTEMS PRODUCTIONS (Hamburg, Germany) 2LP
Side 1: Intro by Jeff Dexter / Lover Man / Freedom / Red House
Side 2: Machine Gun / Foxy Lady
Side 3: Hey Baby (New Rising Sun) / Ezy Rider
Side 4: Voodoo Chile (slight return) / In From The Storm / Star Spangled Banner
Comments: Same recording information as above. Good mono. Two double album sets. Includes "Star Spangled Banner" & a long version Of "Hey Baby". Album 1 - blue cover. Album 2 - red cover.

IT NEVER TAKES AN END IN ***
SWINGING PIG (TGP-CD- 118) CD (60:08)
Earth vs Space - Gypsy Eyes - Red House - Machine Gun - Things That I Used To Do / The Train Keeps A Rollin' - Earth Blues / Hear My Train A Comin' - Voodoo Chile - Baby, Let The Good Times Roll - Express Horns Jam / We Gotta Live Together - I Feel So Good
Comments: Recorded at Devonshire Downs, June 22nd, 1969, at The Newport Pop Festival. Excellent stereo. Jimi decided to jam with the Buddy Miles Express two days after the Experience's show at the same venue doing some truly great guitar work. "The Things I Used To Do" and "We Gotta Live Together - I Feel So Good" are incomplete, which is too bad as the first really gets cooking. The CD lists everything under just four indexes because most of the songs are extended medley / jams. A very interesting show and highly recommended.

IT'S ONLY A PAPER MOON IN
LUNA RECORDS (9420) CD (69:20)
Here Comes Your Lover Man (4:08) / Let Me Stand Next To Your Fire (3:19) / Foxy Lady (5:06) / Red House (15:12) / Hey Jude (7:05) / Sunshine Of Your Love, Getting My Heart Back Together Again (9:19) / Can You Please Crawl Out Your Window (5:28) / Purple Haze (6:10) / Are You Experienced (8:52) / I Don't Live Today (7:05)
Comments: Tracks 1-8 from an excellent mono soundboard tape from the Fillmore East, NYC, March 10, 1968. The start of track 1 is cut slightly. Track 9 is an excellent audience recording from Col Ballroom, Davenport, Iowa, August 11, 1968 (See DAVENPORT IOWA, 68). Track 10 from San Jose Pop Festival, Santa Clara, CA, May 25,1969. Good to very good audience recording (See HISTORIC CONCERT VOL. 2). Also available as ONE NIGHT STAND (HEP CAT 1001/SCORPIO) CD.

JAM
BERKELEY (2029) LP

Side 1: Red House / I'm Gonna Leave This Town - Everything's Gonna Be Alright / Bleeding Heart
Side 2: Tomorrow Never Knows / Outside Woman Blues - Sunshine Of Your Love
Comments: Recorded March 1968 at The Scene Club, New York City, New York. Features Jim Morrison drunk on his ass during the jam session. Bootlegged numerous times. Also on SKY HIGH (Trade Mark Of Quality TMQ 73031) & (Kustom SPJH 1) & (Sky Dog sgsh 2017378) & BLUES (Toasted 2S912): Sides three & four.

JAM THE NIGHT
TRADEMARK OF QUALITY (TMQ71116) LP
Side 1: The Dufontaine Rap / Instrumental Jam / Purple Haze / Wild Thing
Side 2: Power To Love / Midnight Lightning / Foxy Lady
Comments: Recorded live at the Isle Of Wight 1970 & The Empire, November 18, 1967. Excellent stereo. Sheet with song listing inside. Only 500 made.

JAMES MARSHALL: MIDNIGHT LIGHTNING
MARSHALL (JMH1-2) 2LP
Side 1: Crash Landing / Midnight Lightning / Izabella - Machine Gun
Side 2: Further On Up The Road / Astro Man Jam
Side 3: Country Blues / Lord I Sing The Blues / Message To Love
Side 4: Stone Free / Rock And Roll Jam / Izabella

JEWEL BOX IN
HOME RECORDS (HR-5824-3) CD (71:37)
Love Or Confusion / Spanish Castle Magic / Hear My Train A Comin' / Voodoo Chile (slight return) / Burning Desire / Hoochie Coochie / Stop / Johnny B. Goode / Freedom / Midnight / Beginning / Rock And Roll Band / Earth Blues / Pali Gap / Hey Baby (New Rising Sun)
Comments: Virtually everything on this disc has been released commercially. Don't bother. Also on INHERITANCE (Ex-ellent EX 52530) and RARITIES ON COMPACT DISC VOL. 3 (On The Radio).

JIMI: A MUSICAL LEGACY IN ***
(The Definitive Collection Of Unreleased Rarities 1963 -1970)
KISS THE STONE (KTS BX 010) 4CD Box Set (CD1 71:00, CD2 74:08, CD376:00, CD4 75:38)
CD 1: Goodbye, Bessie Mae / Soul Food (That's What I Like) (Jimi's first recording, Philadelphia, September 1963) / My Diary, Utee (Jimi on Lee Brooks single, Los Angeles, January 1964) / Testify (Isley Brothers single, New York City, March 1964) / Whole Lotta Shakin', Hound Dog (No Jimi, just Little Richard, Los Angeles, July 1965) / I'm A Man, Strange Things, How Would You Feel? (with Curtis Knight and The Squires, New York City, October 1965) / Free Spirit, House Of The Rising Sun (No Jimi, just Curtis Knight, George's Club Hackensack, New Jersey, January 1966) / Hey Joe (vocal reference tape, De Lane Studios, London, October 23, 1966) / Red House (original take, London, December 13, 1966) / I Don't Live Today (alternate take), Purple Haze (monitor mix), Fire (alternate take), The Wind Cries Mary (instrumental), Are You Experienced? (backward take) (London, February 1967) / Purple Haze (acetate London, February 1967)
CD 2: Room Full Of Mirrors, Shame Shame Shame (early attempts, London, May 4, 1967) / Catfish Blues (Vitus Studios, Holland, September 10, 1967) / She's So Fine, Axis: Bold As Love (Olympic Studios, London, September 1967) / EXP, Up From The Skies (outtakes, September 1967) / Little One (take 1, Olympic Studios, London, October 5 , 1967) / Love Or Confusion (London, February 13, 1967) / Gloria (TTG Studios, London, October 2, 1967) / Burning Of The Midnight Lamp, Sergeant Pepper's Lonely Hearts Club Band (Stockholm, September 5, 1967) / Like A Rolling Stone (Saville Theatre, London, August 27, 1967) / The Stars That Play With Laughing Sam's Dice (unreleased take, New York, July 18, 1967) / Dream, Dance (Olympic Studios, London, December 20, 1967) / Electric Ladyland (alternate take, London, October 25, 1967) / Ain't Too Proud To Beg Jam (recorded for BBC's 'Top Gear', London, October 6, 1967) / Getting My Heart Back Together Again (BBC outtake, London, December 15, 1967) / Castles Made Of Sand (reversed original with what would become the backwards guitar track, London, October 1967)
CD 3: All Along The Watchtower (alternate take, Olympic Studios, London, January 28, 1968) / 1983...(A Merman I Should Turn To Be) (home demo, London, February 1968) / Somewhere (Sound Centre Studios, New York City, March 1968) / Morrison's Lament - Tomorrow Never Knows (jam with Jim Morrison, The Scene, New York City, March 1968) / Wild Thing (Atwood Hall, Clark University,

Worcester, Mass., March 15, 1968) / Angel (reference tape), Gypsy Eyes (outtake), Cherokee Mist (outtake) (New York City, April and October 1968) / God Save The Queen (No Jimi, just David Henderson) / Three Little Bears (The Record Plant, New York City, May 2, 1968) / Voodoo Child (home recording, New York City, May 1968) / Traffic Jam (a jam with 3 members of Traffic and Jack Casady, London, June 1968) / Duelling Guitars (Jimi and Beck? or Stills? summer 1968) / Spanish Castle Magic (Winterland, San Francisco, October 11, 1968)

CD4: Jimi Comments, Voodoo Child, Hey Joe - Sunshine Of Your Love (Lulu's BBC TV show, London, January 4, 1969) / Jimi - Jimmy Jam (jam with John McLaughlin, New York City, March 25, 1969) / Ships Passing In The Night (embryonic version of 'Night Bird Flying', New York City, April 14, 1969) / Message To Love, Lord I Sing The Blues (rehearsal for Woodstock, Shokan, New York, August 1969) / Little Drummer Boy, Silent Night, Taps, Auld Lange Syne (The Record Plant, New York City, December 1969) / Earth Blues (Baggies, New York City, December 20, 1969) / Gypsy Boy, Alcatraz, Captain Coconut II - Cherokee Mist, Bleeding Heart (unreleased tracks, The Record Plant, New York City, early 1970) / Killin' Floor, Voodoo Child (Love And Peace Festival, Fehmarn, Germany, September 6, 1970. Jimi's last concert appearance)

Comments: Another excellent collection from the people who gave you The Beatles ARTIFACTS box sets. Four picture CDs in a really nifty digi-book with a full color (if not a little bit difficult to read) book containing material sources, photos and interview transcripts. In spite of a few fake tracks this recommended set gathers a huge chunk of the best of bootlegged material (both live and studio) and presents it in a rough chronology. The overall sound quality is very good to excellent. A nice collection for beginners to the world of Hendrix rarities.

JIMI AT THE BEEB
JIMI 5-0 CD

Hey Joe (4:01) / Foxy Lady (2:45) / Stone Free (3:26) / Love Or Confusion (2:55) / Purple Haze (3:04) / Killin' Floor (2:27) / Fire (2:33) / The Wind Cries Mary (3:05) / Wild Thing (1:51) / Burning Of The Midnight Lamp (3:41) / Jam #1 (3:20) / Jam #2 (5:02) / Little Miss Lover (2:55) / Drivin' South (4:48) / Experiencing The Blues (5:27) / Hound Dog (2:43) / All Along The Watchtower (3:57) / Can You Please Crawl Out Your Window (3:25) / Spanish Castle Magic (3:12) / Day Tripper (3:14) / Getting My Heart Back Together (4:57) / Wait Until Tomorrow (3:04)

Comments: From the London BBC sessions of February 13, 1967 and October 6, 1967. Excellent stereo. Made obsolete by the CR BBC SESSIONS.

JIMI HENDRIX
Vinyl single

Side 1: Spanish Castle Magic
Side 2: Fire / Hey Joe

Comments: Excellent mono. From Stockholm, January 9, 1969 (second show). 33-1/3 rpm. Black & white picture sleeve. Also available as a black & white picture disc.

JIMI HENDRIX
BLUE FLAMES RECS. (5205)

Vinyl single
Side 1: Bright Lights Big City (3:16) / I'm A Man (4:25) (Excellent stereo)
Side 2: No Such Animal 1 (2:27) / No Such Animal 2 (2:36) (Excellent mono)

Comments: Brown picture sleeve. Same as JIMMY JAMES AND HIS BLUE FLAMES.

JIMI HENDRIX
IN STEP RECORD (SLSJH 106AA) - Vinyl single

Side 1: Red House Part 1
Side 2: Red House Part 2

Comments: NY Pop Festival 1970. Deluxe black & white cover sleeve. Artists name on label 'Paul Adams'. Same as RED HOUSE.

JIMI HENDRIX
QCS 1447 LP

Side 1: Message Nine To The Universe (Band of Gypsys with Devon Wilson on vocals)
Side 2: Cherokee Mist (with Mitch Mitchell) / Messenger (with Buddy Miles) / Strato Strut (Band of

HENDRIX IN WORDS & MUSIC

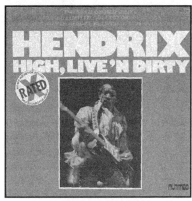

HIGH, LIVE 'N DIRTY

HISTORIC CONCERT 2
(HIGH TIMES IN SAN JOSE)

IN MEMORIAM: LIVE IN SWEDEN

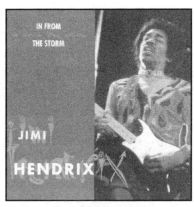

IN FROM THE STORM

Gypsys)
Comments: Outtakes from the Record Plant, NYC 1969. Excellent mono.

JIMI HENDRIX
EXPO (EXPO 18) CD
Red House (10:35) / Voodoo Chile (slight return) (7:20) / Little Wing (3:10) / Wild Thing (1:21) / Bleeding Heart (3:23) / Night Life* (6:11) / Fire (3:39) / Room Full Of Mirrors (2:55) / Psycho* (2:39) / Hot Trigger* (3:58) / Free Spirit* (5:40) / Groove Maker* (2:21) / Voice In The Wind* (2:46) / Suspicious* (3:54) / She's A Fox (2:45) / Two And One Goes* (2:32)
Comments: A collection of odds and ends - some (*) which have no Jimi involvement whatsoever. "Red House" was recorded at the Scene Club, NYC, March 7, 1968. The remainder of the tracks are from Jimi's performance at the Royal Albert Hall, London, February 24, 1969. This is one release best avoided by the discriminating collector as there is nothing new here and a lot of non-Jimi material. Excellent to fair mono/stereo.

JIMI HENDRIX
VC 6970 LP
Side 1: Voodoo Chile / Purple Haze / 3rd Stone From The Sun
Side 2: Star Spangled Banner
Comments: This record actually is a pirate of THE EXPERIENCE BAND from West Germany. Excellent stereo.

JIMI HENDRIX   IN
IMTRAT 40-90355 CD
Are You Experienced / Voodoo Child (slight return) / Red House / Foxy Lady / Like A Rolling Stone / Sunshine Of Your Love / Hey Joe / Star Spangled Banner / Purple Haze / Little Wing / Fire
Comments: A selection of Winterland performances. Get the Whoopy Cat sets instead.

JIMI HENDRIX   IN
FLUTE FLCD 2008
Spanish Castle Magic / Red House / Experiencing The Blues / Wild Thing / Burning Of The Midnight Lamp / Sunshine Of Your Love / Drivin' South / Fire / Purple Haze / Room Full Of Mirrors / Can You Please Crawl Out Your Window / Little Miss Lover
Comments: Another boring CD of various common live material and a couple of BBC tracks.

JIMI HENDRIX & JACK BRUCE   IN ***
MAJOR TOM (MT 045) CD-R
Jam 1 / Jam 2 / Everything Is Going To Be Alright / Sunshine Of Your Love / Jam 3 / Jam 4 / Jam 5 / Jam 6 / Midnight Lightning
Comments: Recorded at TTG Studios on or about October 17, 1968. Jamming with Jimi were Jack Bruce, Buddy Miles and Jim McCarty. This material has not appeared elsewhere and given the total obscurity and unavailability of this label, seems destined to remain so.

JIMI HENDRIX AT HIS BEST VOLUME 1
SAGA (6313) LP and JOKER (SM 3271) LP
Side 1: She Went To Bed With My Guitar (Stepping Stone) / Free Thunder (Instrumental 1) / Cave Man Bells (Instrumental 2)
Side 2: Strokin' A Lady On Each Hip (Villanova Junction) / Baby Chicken Strut (Instrumental 4)
Comments: Jams recorded at Jimi's rented house on Tavor Hollow Road, New York, probably in September 1969. These songs come from the so-called "Ephron Tapes" as Mike Ephron (who played keyboards on these jams) supposedly owned the tapes and was said to have been given permission by Jimi to release the music with the profits going to the Black Panthers. This seems highly unlikely. Also present for the recordings were Jerry Velez on percussion and Juma Sultan on flute and percussion. You would think after seeing that this material was recorded at Jimi's prime that it would be some great jamming. NOT SO! This is some of the worst meandering and playing ever released. Well, maybe some of The Beatles "Get Back" rehearsals are worse, but not by much. Apart from purely historical interest by virtue of it's existence, this is garbage and should **NEVER** have been released. This is one of the 'quasi-legal' albums released in the early Seventies. Some of this material and the songs on the next two volumes can be found on THIS FLYER, JIMI HENDRIX (Pantonic Pan), JIMI HENDRIX '64 among others. Note

that incorrect song titles were given to the tracks. Correct titles in parenthesis.

JIMI HENDRIX AT HIS BEST VOLUME 2
SAGA (6314) LP and JOKER (SM 3272) LP
Side 1: Down Man Blues (Instrumental 4) / Feels Good (Flying - Here I Go) / Fried Cola (Instrumental 5)
Side 2: Monday Morning Blues / Jimi Is Tender Too (Key To The Highway) / Madagascar (Instrumental 6)
Comments: See previous entry for recording information.

JIMI HENDRIX AT HIS BEST VOLUME 3
SAGA (6315) LP and JOKER (SM 3273) LP
Side 1: Young Jim (Instrumental 7 / Gypsy Boy - New Rising Sun) / Lift Off (Instrumental 8)
Side 2: Swift's Wing (Instrumental 9) / Giraffe (Earth Blues)
Comments: See previous entries for recording information.

JIMI HENDRIX EXPERIENCE   IN
ROCKSTARS IN CONCERT (6127092) CD
Hey Joe / Foxy Lady / Purple Haze / Little Wing / Killin' Floor / Voodoo Child (slight return) / Wild Thing / Fire / The Wind Cries Mary / Red House / The Burning Of The Midnight Lamp / Star Spangled Banner / Can You See Me / Spanish Castle Magic
Comments: Another CD collection of common and commercially released live material.

JIMI HENDRIX EXPERIENCE (THE)
UFO (201018) LP
Side 1: Killin' Floor / Catfish Blues / Foxy Lady
Side 2: Red House (Noel Redding plays guitar & Hendrix plays bass) / Drivin' South / Purple Haze
Comments: Recorded live at the Paris Olympia, January 29, 1968. Very good stereo.

JIMI HENDRIX JAMMING WITH FRIENDS
KOINE (V880802) LP
Side 1: Everything's Going To Be Alright / Three Little Bears / Swing Jimi Jam
Side 2: Stormy Monday / Funky Jam / Little Wing
Comments: Recorded March 17, 1968. Jam session at the Cafe Au Go Go, New York City. Present were Buddy Miles, Elvin Bishop, Paul Butterfield, Harvey Brooks and Herbie Rich.

JIMI HENDRIX LIVE
CDDV (2041) CD
Foxy Lady / Hey Joe / The Wind Cries Mary / Burning Of The Midnight Lamp / Red House / Fire / Little Wing / Voodoo Chile (slight return) / Killin' Floor / Sunshine Of Your Love / Sgt. Pepper's Lonely Hearts Club Band / Purple Haze / Star Spangled Banner
Comments: Assorted live cuts from Stockholm 1967 & 1969, except tracks 5-7 recorded in Paris 1968. Tracks 8-10 recorded in L. A. 1969. European CD. Time 51:08.

JIMI HENDRIX STORY
JOKER (3271 - 3273) 3LP
Side 1: She Went To Bed With My Guitar / Free Thunder / Cave Man Bells
Side 2: Strokin A Lady On Each Hip / Baby Chicken Strut
Side 3: Down Mean Blues / Feels Good / Fried Cola
Side 4: Monday Morning Blues / Jim Is Tender Too / Madagascar
Side 5: Young Jim / Lift Off
Side 6: Swift's Wing / Spiked With Heady Dreams / Giraffe
Comments: Titles wrong. Pirate of European imports. Very good stereo. From the Mike Ephron tapes. A copy of JIMI HENDRIX AT HIS BEST VOL. 1-3.

JIMI HENDRIX VOL. 2 / A MAN OF OUR TIME   IN
NAPOLEON (NPL 11018) LP
Side 1: Highway Chile (studio) / No Reply (Mayall & Clapton) / Stone Free (JHE) / Camels & Elephants (Ginger Baker) / Hound Dog (JHE) / Foxy Lady (JHE)
Side 2: Purple Haze (JHE) / Hear Me Calling Your Name (Bruce) / Little Miss Lover (JHE) /

Experiencing The Blues (JHE) / Sonny Boy Blow (Mayall & Clapton) / Sunshine Of Your Love (JHE)

Comments: Italian bootleg with deluxe blue cover. Appears to be a compilation of BROADCASTS (TMOQ 71019) and HENDRIX, CLAPTON, MAYALL AND BRUCE (CBM4).

JIMI IN DENMARK   IN **
DYNAMITE STUDIOS (DS95J356) CD (75:05)

Catfish Blues (9:24) / Tax Free (11:49) / Master James And Co. (Interview) (23:32) / Fire (4:01) / Voodoo Child (slight return) (7:24) / Foxy Lady (4:54) / Spanish Castle Magic (9:31) / Freedom (4:02)

Comments: Excellent audience recordings from several shows in Denmark. This is a copy of the official CD available through Univibes.

JIMI - INSIDE THE RAINBOW
BLUE RECORDS (SX501) 2LP

Sides 1-2: A copy of WINK OF AN EYE (79-108/109)

Sides 3-4: A copy of LAST BRITISH CONCERT (79-036)

Comments: Sides 1-2: good mono. Sides 3-4: excellent stereo.

JIMI PLAYS BERKELEY   IN *
JMH (005 / 2) 2CD

CD 1: REHEARSAL: Blue Suede Shoes (4:30) / Power Of Soul (2:50) / Machine Gun (7:30) / Message Of Love (5:37) / Room Full Of Mirrors (1:50) / Freedom (4:35) / FIRST SHOW: Johnny B Goode (4:45) / Hear My Train A Coming (12:09) / Freedom (5:24) / Red House (7:58) / Ezy Rider (6:36)

CD 2: SECOND SHOW: Pass It On (8:30) / Hey Baby (New Rising Sun) (5:40) / Lover Man (3:00) / Stone Free (4:32) / Hey Joe (5:15) / I Don't Live Today (5:32) / Machine Gun (11:23) / Foxy Lady (6:31) / The Star Spangled Banner (Traditional) (2:29) / Purple Haze (4:00) / Voodoo Child (10:16) / Rehearsal Jam (Ezy Rider Jam)(9:08)

Comments: Recorded live at the Berkeley Community Center, May 30, 1970 (Memorial Day). Excellent soundboard. The soundcheck material is only part of the complete soundcheck. The full soundcheck is on THE BERKELEY SOUNDCHECKS on Whoopy Cat and re-released on Red Robin. The First show material is incomplete while the Second show on disc two is complete. Picture CDs.

JIMMY JAMES AND HIS BLUE FLAMES
BLUE FLAMES (5205) Vinyl single

Side A: Bright Lights, Big City / I'm A Man

Side B: No Such Animal (Part 1) / No Such Animal (Part 2)

JOHN LENNON - DAY TRIPPER JAM
CONTRABAND (CBM 4242) LP

Day Tripper

Comments: This track was recorded December 15, 1967 in London. It has been a persistent rumor that John Lennon had performed on "Day Tripper". That claim is entirely without merit. Noel Redding confirmed in an interview with the authors that Lennon was not present for the taping and that it was Noel who sang background vocals.

KING OF GYPSIES   IN
ROCKYSSIMO (RK 001) CD

Suspicious (not Jimi) / Voodoo Chile (slight return) / Purple Haze / Something You Got / Red House / She's So Fine (not Jimi) / Fire / Wild Thing / Sunshine Of Your Love / Bleeding Heart / Room Full Of Mirrors / Star Spangled Banner

Comments: A mostly useless collection of a couple of fake tracks, a George's club track and the rest from the Royal Albert Hall show from 24 Feb 69.

KING & WONDER SESSIONS   IN
OH BOY (1-9170) CD

Tommy Vance Intro / Ain't Too Proud To Beg (incomplete) / Little Miss Lover / Drivin' South (Catfish Blues / Rolling And Tumbling) / Experiencing The Blues / Burning Of The Midnight Lamp / Hound Dog / Like A Rolling Stone / Blues Jam No.1 Part 1 (Jam Session)

Comments: Obsolete BBC material with the last two tracks from the Generation Club Show.

KING'S JAM (THE) IN ***
KLONDYKE (KR 26) CD (64:32)

Like A Rolling Stone / Blues Jam #1 (Part 1) / Blues Jam #1 (Part 2) / B.B. King introduces the band / Blues Jam #2 (Part 1) / Blues Jam #2 (Part 2) / Blues Jam #3 / It's My Own Fault

Comments: This is as complete of a release from the jam session with B. B. King at the Generation Club, NYC, April 1968, as has been released. Also present were Elvin Bishop (guitar & vocals), Paul Butterfield (harmonica), Al Kooper (organ), Buzzy Feiten (bass), Don Martin (guitar), Phillip Wilson (drums) and Stewart (piano). Also available as BLUES JAM (Alegra CD 9036).

KISS THE SKIES IN *
MUM (MUCD 024) CD

Freedom / Crash Landing / Three Little Bears / Bleeding Heart / My Friend / Ships Passing In The Night / Straight Ahead / I Don't Live Today / Stepping Stone (2 versions) / Beginnings / Bolero (aka: Live And Let Die) / 1983...A Merman I Should Turn To Be / Freedom - Ezy Rider - Highway Of Broken Hearts - Seven Dollars In My Pocket / Purple Haze

Comments: Mum Records are known for their reissues of previously booted material. Expect nothing new here; still, the MUM releases are nice collections.

KRALINGEN ISLE OF WIGHT
WESTCOAST RECORDS (WCR 001-S) LP

God Save The Queen / Sergeant Pepper's Lonely Hearts Club Band / Spanish Castle

Comments: This is a 'various artist' release from the early Seventies. These three Hendrix cuts are from the Isle Of Wight Festival.

LADYLAND IN FLAMES IN
MARSHALL RECORDS (L 30640) 2LP

Side 1: Valleys Of Neptune (Lonely Avenue) / World Traveler / It's Too Bad

Side 2: Message From Nine To the Universe (Strato Strut) / Cherokee Mist / Lonely Avenue Jam Part 1 (Guitar Improv) / Midnight Lightning

Side 3: Angel / Cherokee Mist / Lonely Avenue Jam Part 1 (Electric Ladyland) / Midnight Lightning / Farther On Up The Road / Instrumental Improvisation

Side 4: Earth Blues / Look Over Yonder (Mr. Bad Luck) / Little Miss Strange (Instrumental Jam) / Somewhere Over The Rainbow / 1983...A Merman I Should Turn To Be / Peace In Mississippi

Comments: An obsolete collection of incomplete studio material.

LAST AMERICAN CONCERT
JUPITER (444) LP

Side 1: Interview (2:10) / Hey Babe, In From The Storm (5:35) / Hear My Train A Comin' (5:25) / Voodoo Child (5:20) / Maui Sunset (2:40)

Side 2: Foxy Lady (4:45) / Red House (6:45) / Easy Rider (4:30) / Purple Haze (4:30)

Comments: Recorded live in Maui, Hawaii, July 30, 1970. Excellent mono.

LAST AMERICAN CONCERT
21465 LP

Comments: A color picture disc copy of LAST AMERICAN CONCERT (JUPITER 444). Excellent mono.

LAST AMERICAN CONCERT VOL. 1
THE SWINGING PIG (TSP 062) LP

Side 1: Lover Man / Hey Baby (New Rising Sun) / In From The Storm / Message To Love / Foxy Lady

Side 2: Hear My Train A Comin' / Voodoo Chile (slight return) / Fire / Purple Haze

Comments: Recorded July 30, 1970, in Maui, Hawaii. First show. Also on VOODOO CHILE (Oil Well RSC 014 CD). See CD entry.

LAST AMERICAN CONCERT VOL. 1 IN **
THE SWINGIN' PIG (TSP CD 062) CD (46:32)

Lover Man / Hey Baby / In From The Storm / Message To Love / Foxy Lady / Hear My Train A Comin' / Voodoo Chile (slight return) / Fire / Purple Haze

Comments: Recorded live at Haleakala Crater, Maui, Hawaii, July 30, 1970. Most of the first show minus the opening song ("Spanish Castle Magic"). Excellent stereo soundboard. Recommended.

ISLAND MAN

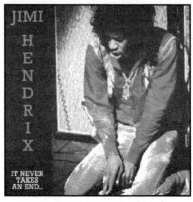

IT NEVER TAKES AN END

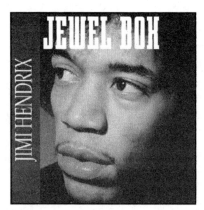

JEWEL BOX

JAMES MARSHALL: MIDNIGHT LIGHTNING

JIMI: A MUSICAL LEGACY

JIMI HENDRIX

LAST AMERICAN CONCERT VOL. 2
THE SWINGING PIG (TSP 072) LP
Side 1: Dolly Dagger / Villanova Junction / Ezy Rider / Red House
Side 2: Freedom / Beginning / Straight Ahead / Hey Baby (New Rising Sun)
Comments: Recorded July 30, 1970, in Maui, Hawaii. Second show.

LAST AMERICAN CONCERT VOL. 2   IN **
THE SWINGIN' PIG (TSP - CD - 072) CD (38:27)
Dolly Dagger (missing the first few seconds) / Villanova Junction (Instrumental) / Ezy Rider / Red House / Freedom / Beginnings (Jam Back At The House) / Straight Ahead (Not listed on CD) / Hey Baby(Land Of The New Rising Sun)
Comments: Recorded live at the Haleakala Crater, Maui, Hawaii , July 30, 1970 (Second show). Excellent stereo soundboard of the first part of the show. Missing are "Stone Free" and "Hey Joe".

LAST AMERICAN CONCERT: ALIVE AND FLOWING FROM THE CRATER OF THE SUN   IN
JUPITER (444) LP
Side 1: Interview (March 1969 / KDAY Radio - Hollywood Palladium) / Hey Baby (New Rising Sun) / In From The Storm / Hear My Train A Comin' / Voodoo Chile (slight return)
Side 2: Hey Baby (New Rising Sun) / Foxy Lady / Red House / Ezy Rider / Purple Haze
Comments: Another compilation of live tracks from the two Maui shows, July 30, 1970. Also available as UNKNOWN, WELLKNOWN (Raven JH 6146) but without the interview.

LAST BRITISH CONCERT
79 - 036 LP
Side 1: Spanish Castle Magic / Hey Baby / Ezy Rider
Side 2: Hey Joe / Purple Haze / Voodoo Chile (slight return)
Comments: Recorded live at the Isle of Wight, August 30, 1970. Incomplete. Excellent stereo.

LAST BRITISH CONCERT / LAST AMERICAN
POSTAGE RECORDS 2LP
Sides 1-2: Copy of LAST BRITISH CONCERT (79-036)
Sides 3-4: Copy of LAST AMERICAN CONCERT (Jupiter 444)
Comments: Sides 1-2 Excellent stereo. Sides 3-4 Excellent mono.

LEGENDARY STARCLUB TAPES   IN
THE EARLY YEARS (02 - CD - 3309) CD (46:50)
Intro / Foxy Lady / Hey Joe / Stone Free / Fire / Purple Haze / I Don't Live Today / Spanish Castle Magic / Voodoo Chile
Comments: Very good mono. Tracks 1-5 are from Hamburg, Germany, March 18th, 1967. Tracks 6-9 are from Stockholm, January 9th, 1969. European CD. The best place to find the Hamburg material is on TOMORROW...OR JUST THE END OF TIME (Batz).

LET'S DROP SOME LUDES AND VOMIT WITH JIMI - RECORD PLANT JAMS VOL. 2   IN **
MIDNIGHT BEAT (MB CD 026) CD (77:09)
Drivin' South, Everything's Gonna Be Alright (23:54) / Drone Blues (Night Bird Flying) (5:55) / Easy Blues (7:52) / Drone Blues (Strato Strut) (8:51) / I'm A Man - instrumental (Jungle) (6:25) / I'm A Man - with vocals (Stepping Stone) (15:20) / Instrumental Jam (Hollywood Jam) (9:00)
Comments: Excellent quality sound. European CD with a reasonably tasteless title. A nice collection of studio jams with some less commonly booted tracks. The "Driving South / Everythings Gonna Be Alright" is almost complete - missing about 2 minutes from the start but with the two jams at the end. "Night Bird Flying" and "Jungle" are less common as well.

LIFETIME OF EXPERIENCE (A)
SLEEPY DRAGON (DRA 5510) 2LP
Side 1: Stone Free / Improv and Drum Solo / Are You Experienced / Stone Free Reprise / Sunshine of Your Love
Side 2: Hear My Train A Comin' / Red House
Side 3: Foxy Lady / Like A Rolling Stone / Voodoo Chile (slight return)
Side 4: Drum Solo / Purple Haze / Newport Jazz / Paul's Blues

Comments: Record live at the Newport Jazz Festival, June 20, 1969. Last two cuts are from the Cafe Au Go Go, NYC, March 17, 1968. Good to excellent mono recordings.

LISTEN TO THIS ERIC   IN ***
JH (003/004) 2CD

CD 1: Lover Man / Stone Free / Hear My Train A Comin' / I Don't Live Today / Red House / Foxy Lady
CD 2: Sunshine Of Your Love / Bleeding Heart / Fire/ Little Wing / Voodoo Child (slight return) / Room Full Of Mirrors / Purple Haze / Wild Thing / Star Spangled Banner
Comments: Recorded live at the Royal Albert Hall on February 24, 1969. From an excellent stereo soundboard tape. Features sepia tone picture CDs with yellow text. CD1 - 53:19 / CD2 - 51:58.

LITTLE WING   IN
OIL WELL (RSC 036) CD (50:15)

Fire / Are You Experienced / Little Wing / Voodoo Chile (slight return) / Wild Thing / Like A Rolling Stone / Hear My Train A Comin'
Comments: Excellent stereo soundboard lifted from commercial releases. The only redeeming value in this at all is that tracks 2, 4 & 6 are the track s from the "bonus" CD-3 from the hard to find commercial LIVE AT WINTERLAND +3 box set.

LIVE   IN
DV MORE (CDDV 2041) CD

Foxy Lady / Hey Joe / The Wind Cries Mary / The Burning Of The Midnight Lamp / Red House / Fire / Little Wing / Voodoo Child (slight return) / Killin' Floor / Sunshine Of Your Love / Sgt. Pepper / Purple Haze / Star Spangled Banner
Comments: Another compilation of common live material that can be easily found more complete on other releases.

LIVE
BLACK GOLD (BG 2022 / 3) 2LP

Comments: Copy of GOOD KARMA (TMOQ 71060) & GOOD KARMA 2 (TMOQ 71079). Fair mono. Deluxe black & white cover.

LIVE AT FLAMINGO CLUB, LONDON
MY PHOENIX (ZA 25) CD

Killin' Floor (fades in) / Have Mercy Baby / Can You See Me / Like A Rolling Stone / Rock Me Baby / Catfish Blues / Stone Free / Hey Joe / Wild Thing
Comments: Recorded live at The Flamingo Club, London 2-4, 1967. Poor to good audience recording. Japanese CD. Deluxe black & white cover. Purple background with yellow type. Time 42:03.

LIVE AT MONTEREY POP FESTIVAL 1967
DOCUMENT RECORDS (DR 021) CD

Can You See Me (3:23) / Hey Joe (4:10) / Purple Haze (3:28) / The Wind Cries Mary (3:21) / Killin' Floor (3:06) / Foxy Lady (3:07) / Like A Rolling Stone (6:55) / Rock Me Baby (3:18) / Wild Thing (9:19)
Comments: Excellent stereo recording. European CD copy of the commercial release. Time 40:08.

LIVE AT OLYMPIA THEATRE
BLACK PANTHER (BPCD 017) CD

Comments: Excellent mono. European CD. Re-issue of GUITARS AND AMPS (WPOCM CD 088D005 - 2). Time 45:32. Made obsolete by the CR.

LIVE AT RANDALL'S ISLAND 7-17-70   IN **
MOON TREE RECORDS (PH 1692) LP

Side 1: Stone Free / Fire/ Message To Love / Lover Man / Foxy Lady
Side 2: Ezy Rider / Star Spangled Banner / Purple Haze / Voodoo Chile
Comments: Recorded live at the New York Pop Festival, Randall's Island, New York, July 17, 1970. Excellent stereo. Color wraparound cover. Also on CAN YOU HERE ME ROCK (Hemero 01): Sides three & four, both CD releases of Imtrat's LIVE USA and on MESSAGE OF LOVE (PYCD 043). All releases are missing "Red House" which was CR on CONCERTS and VARIATIONS ON A THEME and "All Along The Watchtower" which has never turned up anywhere. Easier to find on CD.

LIVE AT THE FORUM 1970 IN **
WHOOPY CAT (WKP-0021/22) 2CD (CD1 73:35, CD2 71:07)

CD 1: Spanish Castle Magic / Foxy Lady / Lover Man / Hear My Train A Comin' / Message To Love / Ezy Rider / Machine Gun / Room Full Of Mirrors / Hey Baby (New Rising Sun) / Villanova Junction / Freedom / Star Spangled Banner / Purple Haze

CD 2: Voodoo Chile (slight return) / Lightning / Who Knows / Earth Blues / Freedom / Message To Love / Hey Baby (New Rising Sun) / Straight Ahead / Red House

Comments: A selection of live tracks from several concerts: Los Angeles Forum, April 25,1970 (good audience recording-complete show from the "far tape") / Baltimore Civic Center, June 13, 1970 (good audience recording of 2 songs) / Vejlby Risskov Hallen, Arhus, Sweden, September 2, 1970 (very good audience recording of the 3 songs performed this night) / Madison Square Garden, January 28, 1970 (poor to good audience recording of the disastrous show that spelled the end of the Band Of Gypsys). Recommended because of the historical significance of these shows - not the recording quality. The complete 13 Jun 70 show is available on BALTIMORE CIVIC CENTER (Starquake SQ-09).

LIVE AT THE FORUM
MUNIA (REC. 28 - WCF) 2LP

Side 1: Spanish Castle Magic (5:11) / Foxy Lady (4:00) / Getting Your Brothers Shoes Together (2:40) / Getting My Heart Back Together Again (4:24)

Side 2: The Star Spangled Banner - Purple Haze (11:30) / Voodoo Child (7:56)

Side 3: Room Full Of Mirrors (20:22)

Side 4: Message To Love (4:30) / Easy Rider (2:53) / Machine Gun (9:58)

Comments: Recorded live at LA Forum on April 25, 1970. Poor to good mono from the "near tape". Also available as HENDRIX LIVE (TMOQ 7509 & 72003); LIVE AT THE LA FORUM (CBM 28/29) and 'SCUSE ME WHILE I KISS THE SKY. Also released as LIVE IN LA APRIL 1970 on four 33 rpm 7" discs.

LIVE AT THE HOLLYWOOD BOWL IN **
TRADE MARK OF QUALITY (2LP) & RSR INTERNATIONAL 251 (2LP)

Side 1: Are You Experienced? / Voodoo Chile (slight return)

Side 2: Red House / Fire / Hey Joe

Side 3: I Don't Live Today / Little Wing / Star Spangled Banner / Purple Haze

Side 4: Sergeant Pepper's Lonely Hearts Club Band / The Wind Cries Mary / Foxy Lady / Sunshine Of Your Love / Burning Of The Midnight Lamp

Comments: Sides 1-3 recorded live on September 14, 1968, at the Hollywood Bowl. Side 4 recorded at Stockholm, Sweden. 1967 & 1969. Good to very good stereo. This is the only release ever of the Hollywood Bowl material.

LIVE AT THE PHILHARMONIC HALL
LABEL UNKNOWN LP

Side 1: I Don't Live Today / Waiting For That Train

Side 2: Spanish Castle Magic / Lover Man I, Lover Man II ("Tonight Show", 10 July 69. Very good mono)

Comments: Recorded live at the Philharmonic Hall, NYC, November 28, 1968. Fair mono audience recording.

LIVE FROM MONTEREY
STARLIGHT RECORDS (SL 87007) LP

Side 1: Killin' Floor / Like A Rolling Stone / Foxy Lady / Rock Me Baby / Can You See Me

Side 2: Hey Joe / Purple Haze / The Wind Cries Mary / Wild Thing / Auld Lang Syne (cv) / Little Drummer Boy - Silent Night (cv)

Comments: Recorded on June 18, 1967 at the Monterey Pop Festival, Monterey, California. Complete show but songs are incorrectly sequenced. Also on MONTEREY POP FESTIVAL (Document DR 0212-026).

LIVE FROM OTTAWA
STARLIGHT RECORDS (SL 87010) LP

Side 1: Foxy Lady / Fire / Killin' Floor / Red House / Spanish Castle Magic

Side 2: Hey Joe / Tax Free / Purple Haze

JIMI IN DENMARK

KING & WONDER SESSIONS

KISS THE SKIES

LADYLAND IN FLAMES

LAST AMERICAN CONCERT VOL. 1

LAST AMERICAN CONCERT VOL. 2

Comments: Recorded March 19, 1968, at the Capitol Theater, Ottawa, Canada. Also available on MAGIC FINGERS (Towne RG 2001). Very good mono.

LIVE IN ATLANTA

TOASTED RECORDS (TRW 1946) 2LP

Side 1: Fire / Lover Man / Spanish Castle Music / Red House

Side 2: Room Full Of Mirrors / Hear My Train A Comin' / Message To Love

Side 3: All Along The Watchtower / Purple Haze / Hey Joe / Voodoo Chile

Side 4: Stone Free / Star Spangled Banner / Hey Baby

Comments: Recorded live at the Atlanta Pop Festival, July 4, 1970. Very good mono.

LIVE IN CONCERT 1967   IN

LIVING LEGEND RECORDS (LLR CD 001) CD (47:06)

Hey Joe / Voodoo Chile / Experience The Blues / Can You Please Crawl Out Your Window / Hoochie Coochie Man / Drivin' South / Spanish Castle Magic / Day Tripper / Wait Until Tomorrow / Stone Free / Foxy Lady / Little Miss Lover / Burning Of The Midnight Lamp / Hound Dog

Comments: Various live tracks from Stockholm 1967 & London BBC 1967 which are available commercially. One of the earliest CD boot releases.

LIVE IN COPENHAGEN 1968 / 70   IN *

THE SWINGIN' PIG (TSP-CD-220-2) 2CD (CD1 46:38, CD2 36:17)

CD 1: Catfish Blues (aka: Experiencing The Blues) / Tax Free / Fire / Voodoo Chile (slight return) / Foxy Lady / Spanish Castle Magic

CD 2: Freedom / Red House / In From The Storm / Purple Haze / Voodoo Chile (slight return) - Calling All Devil's Children - Outside Woman Blues - Sunshine Of Your Love

Comments: CD 1: This is a copy of the Univibes CD LIVE IN DENMARK. CD 2: Recorded live at the K.B. Hallen, Copenhagen, September 3, 1970. Excellent audience recordings.

LIVE IN LONDON 1967   IN

BLACK PANTHER (BPCD 016) CD

Hey Joe (1) / Foxy Lady (1) / Love or Confusion (1) / Purple Haze (2) / Killin' Floor (21) / The Burning of the Midnight Lamp (3) / Hound Dog (3) / Experiencing The Blues (3) / Little Miss Lover (3) / Radio One (3) / Ain't Too Proud To Beg (4) / Can You Please Crawl Out Your Window (5) / Hoochie Coochie Man (5) / Drivin' South (5) / Spanish Castle Magic (6) / Wait Until Tomorrow (6) / Stone Free (1) / Day Tripper (6) / Hear My Train A'Comin' (6)

Comments: The songs are from the following BBC Radio broadcasts: (1) Saturday Club, February 13th, 1967 / (2) Saturday Club, March 28th, 1967 / (3) Top Gear, October 6th, 1967 / (4) BBC Studios, October 6th, 1967, featuring Stevie Wonder on Drums / (5) Rhythm and Blues Show, October 17th, 1967 / (6) Top Gear, December 15th, 1967. Sound quality is excellent mono. At the time of its release this was the best sounding and most complete collection of Jimi's BBC performances available. See also GUITAR HERO (Document DR 013 CD), LIVE IN CONCERT (Living Legend LLR-CD 001). Re-issue of LONDON 1967 (Koine K 881104). Time 66:25. Obsolete with the exception of the unedited "Ain't Too Proud To Beg" (but missing the opening jam) and "Can You Please Crawl Out Your Window".

LIVE IN LA, APRIL 1970

BREAD AND CIRCUS (4 EP vinyl set)

EP 1: Spanish Castle Magic / Foxy Lady / Hear My Train A Comin'

EP 2: Room Full Of Mirrors / Hey Baby (New Rising Sun) / Villanova Junction / Freedom

EP 3: Message To Love / Ezy Rider / Machine Gun

EP 4: Star Spangled Banner / Purple Haze / Voodoo Chile (slight return) / Midnight Lightning

Comments: These songs were recorded at the Los Angeles Forum on April 25, 1970. Missing is "Lover Man" after "Foxy Lady". Also available as 2LP sets (including "Lover Man") on LIVE AT THE LOS ANGELES FORUM (K&S RECORDS 013) 150 pressed on multi-colored vinyl. Original TMOQ plates. And on LIVE AT THE LOS ANGELES FORUM (Rubber Dubber 900 2), ENJOY JIMI HENDRIX (Rubber Dubber 70 001), LIVE AT THE FORUM, LOS ANGELES (Contraband/King Kong/Munia) / ALIVE (Trade Mark Of Quality TMQ 72003) / A PORTRAIT OF JIMI and numerous others.

LIVE IN LOS ANGELES FORUM CA., U.S.A.
BLACK PANTHER (BPCD 050) CD

Tax Free / Star Spangled Banner / Purple Haze / Spanish Castle Magic / Red House / Instrumental - Foxy Lady / I Don't Live Today

Comments: Recorded live at The Forum, LA, April 26, 1969. Excellent mono. Time 69:05. Available on vinyl as APRIL 26, 1969, LIVE IN L. A. FORUM, CA., U.S.A. (Electrecord ELE 03858) and LIVE AT THE LOS ANGELES FORUM - APRIL 26, 1969 (Zipper LA4M42669). This show was CR as part of the LIFE-LINES box set but with "Tax Free" in edited form.

LIVE IN NEW YORK
BLACK PANTHER (BPCD 018) CD

Comments: European CD. Very good mono. Re-issue of CAFE AU GO GO (Koine' K880802). Time 51:22.

LIVE IN OTTAWA, CANADA 3/19/68
JHE (L 10C) LP

Side 1: Tax Free (10:07) / Fire (2:47) / Red House (9:16)

Side 2: Foxy Lady (4:31) / Hey Joe (4:44) / Spanish Castle Magic / Purple Haze

Comments: Recorded live in Ottawa. Excellent mono.

LIVE IN PARIS   IN
THE SWINGIN' PIG (TSP CD 016) CD (50:39)

Killin' Floor / Catfish Blues / Foxy Lady / Red House / Drivin' South / The Wind Cries Mary / Fire / Little Wing / Purple Haze

Comments: Recorded live at Olympia, Paris, January 29, 1968. Second show. Excellent stereo soundboard. Also available as LIVE IN PARIS (The Swinging Pig TSP-016) LP, LIVE AT THE OLYMPIA THEATRE (JH 68 P) LP, DRIVING SOUTH WITH THE JIMI HENDRIX EXPERIENCE (Tan Studio) LP. Made obsolete by the CR on STAGES.

LIVE IN SAN DIEGO
BLACK PANTHER (BPCD 049) CD

Foxy Lady / Purple Haze / Voodoo Chile / Fire / Hey Joe / Spanish Castle Magic / I Don't Live Today

Comments: Recorded live at San Diego, March 1969. Excellent mono. Time 45:51. CR on STAGES.

LIVE IN STOCKHOLM
FRUIT END (C10168) LP

Comments: Original from which PIPE DREAM was made. Excellent stereo. European bootleg. See next entry for recording information.

LIVE IN STOCKHOLM
DOCUMENT (DR 003) CD (47:06)

Sgt. Pepper's Lonely Hearts Club Band (1:44) / Hey Joe (4:03) / I Don't Live Today (4:16) / The Wind Cries May (3:30) / Foxy Lady (3:32) / Fire (3:02) / Burning Of The Midnight Lamp (3:53 - first public performance) / Purple Haze (5:03) / Sunshine Of Your Love (7:36) / Voodoo Child - slight return (10:09)

Comments: Swedish radio recordings from Radiohus Studio, September 5, 1967, unless noted. Excellent stereo. Made obsolete by the CR on STAGES. A very early boot CD release.

LIVE USA   **
IMTRAT (900.036) CD

Stone Free / Fire / Message To Love / Lover Man / Foxy Lady / Ezy Rider / Star Spangled Banner / Purple Haze / Voodoo Chile (slight return) / Tax Free / I Don't Live Today

Comments: Tracks 1-8 recorded live at the New York Pop Festival, Randall's Island, July 17, 1970. All releases are missing "Red House" which was CR on CONCERTS and VARIATIONS ON A THEME and "All Along The Watchtower" which has never turned up anywhere.

LIVE USA   IN **
IMTRAT (902.001) 2 CD

CD 1: Stone Free / Fire/ Message To Love / Lover Man / Foxy Lady / Ezy Rider / Star Spangled Banner / Purple Haze / Voodoo Chile (slight return) / Tax Free / I Don't Live Today

CD 2: Wild Thing / Spanish Castle Magic / Red House / Tax Free / Foxy Lady / Hey Joe / Hound Dog / Everything's Gonna Be All Right / Funky Jam

Comments: Tracks 1-8 recorded live at the New York Pop Festival, Randall's Island, July 17, 1970. All releases are missing "Red House" which was CR on CONCERTS and VARIATIONS ON A THEME and "All Along The Watchtower" which has never turned up anywhere. The remainder of the tracks are various songs commonly booted.

LIVE! IN
BLACK (B-05) CD
Little Wing / Purple Haze / Earth VS Space - Midnight Lightning - Gypsy Eyes - Machine Gun / God Save The Queen / Sergeant Pepper's Lonely Hearts Club Band / Spanish Castle Magic / The Wind Cries Mary / Foxy Lady / Freedom / Dolly Dagger / Voodoo Chile (slight return) / Hey Joe / Fire
Comments: Basically a sampler on live shows. Nice to listen to as a greatest hits live sort of thing but that's the extent of it.

LIVE WITHDRAWN (THE)
BABY CAPONE (BC 077) CD
Are You Experienced (13:28) / Voodoo Chile (Slight Return) (5:45) / Like A Rolling Stone (11:48) / Spanish Castle Magic (9:42) / Villanova Junction Blues, Fire (3:11) / Guitar Improvisation (4:47) / Villanova Junction Blues (2:54) / Freedom (5:09) / Red House (7:48) / Ezy Rider (7:01) / Hey Baby (New Rising Sun) (4:47)
Comments: Tracks 1-4 recorded live at Winterland, San Francisco, October 10, 11 and 12, 1968. Tracks 5-7 are from the Woodstock Festival, August 18, 1969. Tracks 8-10 are from the first concert, Berkeley Community Center, May 30, 1970. Track 11 is from the first show at Haleakala Crater, Maui, Hawaii, July 30, 1970. Excellent stereo soundboard. European CD. Picture CD.

LIVING REELS VOL. 1 IN
JMH (011) CD
Castle Made Of Sand (3:04) / Spanish Castle Magic (2:51) / South Saturn Delta I (4:58) / Wait Until Tomorrow (3:31) / Ain't No Telling (1:57) / One Rainy Wish (4:00) / She's So Fine (2:42) / Axis: Bold As Love (3:39) / Up From The Skies (3:02) / Jam #I (Jazz Jimi Jam)(5:13) / Little Wing - Outfake (2:31) / Unknown (Playing Over James Brown)(3:38) / Axis: Bold As Love II (3:34) / EXP (1:56) / Up From The Skies II (2:57) / Jam #II (Jam Jimi Jazz)(13:11) / Sitar Song (Little One)(3:19) / Hey Joe - Outfake (3:29) / I Don't Live Today - Outfake (2:21) / Fire - Outfake (2:42) / Foxy Lady - Outfake (3:11)
Comments: Excellent stereo soundboard. European CD. A compilation of outfakes, questionable tracks, Sotheby's tracks and other common stuff.

LIVING REELS VOL. II IN
JMH (012 / 2) 2CD
CD 1: Tax Free (5:10) / Three Little Bears (5:06) / Gypsy Eyes (4:28) / Cherokee Mist (7:09) / Rock 'N' Roll Jam (1:56) / Little Wing (9:46) / Rock Me Baby (Everything's Gonna Be Alright)(7:11) / Voodoo Chile Session (27:10) / Look Over Yonder (2:35) / Rainy Day Jam (Rainy Day Shuffle)(5:34)
CD 2: Somewhere I (3:42) / Peace In Mississippi #1 (5:41) / Jimi And Mitch Jam (Lonely Avenue Part 1)(5:40) / Somewhere II (3:40) / My Friend (4:22) / 1983 (A Mermaid I Should Turn To Be) (3:57) / Electrical Ladyland (6:31) / Are You Experienced (17:46), Voodoo Chile (slight return) (7:33) / Red House (11:00) / Fire (Miami Pop Festival, May 18, 1968 - 2:54)
Comments: Excellent stereo soundboard. European CD. A second volume of commonly booted material lifted from other releases. At least this one doesn't have any outfakes.

LOADED GUITAR IN *
STARLIGHT RECORDS (SL 87013) LP
Side 1: Hear My Train A Comin' (Dick Cavett 1967) / Isabella (Dick Cavett 1969) / Machine Gun (Dick Cavett 1969) / Purple Haze (Dutch TV) / Hey Joe (Beat Club) / Purple Haze (Beat Club) / Sgt. Pepper's Lonely Hearts Club Band (Dutch TV)
Side 2: Foxy Lady (Dutch TV) / Hey Joe (Ready Steady Go) / Sunshine Of Your Love (Ready Steady Go) / Hear My Train A Comin' (Dutch TV) / I Don't Live Today (Stockholm 1967) / The Wind Cries Mary (Stockholm 1967) / Fire (Stockholm 1967) / The Burning Of The Midnight Lamp (Stockholm 1967)
Comments: A nice reissue collection mostly of TV performances with a couple of radio tracks thrown in. A good place to get this material on vinyl.

LONDON 1967
K881104 CD

Hey Joe (4:00) [1] / Foxy Lady (2:48) [1] / Love Or Confusion (2:36) [1] / Purple Haze (3:05) [2] / Killin' Floor (2:30) [2] / Burning Of The Midnight Lamp (3:40) [3] / Hound Dog (2:38) [3] / Experiencing The Blues (5:12) [3] / Little Miss Lover (2:47) [3] / Radio One Theme (1:04) [3] / Ain't Too Proud To Beg (4:35 - Stevie Wonder on drums) [3] / Can You Please Crawl Out Your Window (3:25) [4] / I'm Your Hootchie Kootchie Man (5:11 - John Lee Hooker on guitar) [4] / Drivin' South (5:10) [4] / Spanish Castle Magic (2:55) [5] / Wait Until Tomorrow (2:46) [5] / Stone Free (3:14) [5] / Day Tripper (3:05) [5] / Getting My Heart Back Together Again (4:14) [5]

Comments: Excellent sound. BBC recordings from: [1] February 13. [2] March 28. [3] October 6. [4] October 17. [5] December. European CD.

LORD I CAN SEE THE BLUES
HUMPHREY (EC1333) LP

Side 1: Lord I Sing The Blues For You And Me / Country Blues / Mannish Boy
Side 2: Jam/ Easy Blues / Experiencing The Blues / Straight Ahead
Comments: Common jam sessions. Also available as MANNISH BOY (Contraband CBM 88).

LORD OF THE STRINGS (THE)
RSR / INTERNATIONAL (RSR 213) 2LP

Side 1: Hear My Train A Comin' / Spanish Castle Magic / Red House
Side 2: Master Mind / Lover Man / Foxy Lady / Jam Back At The House / Izabella
Side 3: Gypsy Woman / Fire/ Voodoo Chile / Star Spangled Banner
Side 4: Star Spangled Banner (cont.) / Purple Haze / A Minor Jam / Hey Joe
Comments: Complete Woodstock performance, August 18, 1969, from soundboard. Excellent stereo. At the time this was the first and best pressing of the complete performance on vinyl. Also available on Rock Solid (213A-D) and on Box Top. Also rereleased with deluxe color cover (1000 copies). All from original plates.

THE LOST CONCERT SERIES is a series of 10 CDs with hard to find shows from audience tapes. These are all burned on blank CD-Rs and I wouldn't be surprised to know that there were only a handful of each title made. Unless someone else reissues them in larger quantities, neither you nor I will find one.

LOST CONCERTS VOL. 1: CLEVELAND 1968 *
CD-R No Label

Fire / I Don't Live Today / Red House / Foxy Lady / Spanish Castle Magic / Manic Depression / Purple Haze / Wild Thing / Jam

Comments: A fair to good recording live from the audience at the Public Music Hall, Cleveland, Ohio, March 26, 1968. The "Jam" is from the Generation Club, NYC, April 7, 1968, with Roy Buchanan. Recommended for audience recording completist.

LOST CONCERTS VOL. 2: DAVENPORT, IOWA *
CD-R No Label

Are You Experienced / Lover Man / Foxy Lady / Red House / I Don't Live Today / Fire / Foxy Lady / Little Wing / Red House / Fire

Comments: Tracks 1-6 are from Davenport, Iowa, August 11, 1968. Tracks 7-10 are from The Coliseum, Spokane, Washington, September 8, 1968. Fair to good audience recording. Recommended for audience recording completist.

LOST CONCERTS VOL. 3: BERLIN 1970 *
CD-R No label

Straight Ahead / Spanish Castle Magic / Sunshine Of Your Love / Hey Baby (New Rising Sun) / Message To Love / Machine Gun / Purple Haze / Red House / Foxy Lady / Ezy Rider / Hey Joe / Power Of Soul / Lover Man

Comments: Recorded live at the Deutschlandhalle, Berlin, West Germany, September 4, 1970. Fair to good audience recording. Recommended for audience recording completist.

LOST CONCERTS VOL. 4: DETROIT 1968 *
CD-R No label

LET'S DROP SOME LUDES...

LITTLE WING

LIVE AT THE FORUM 1970

LIVE IN PARIS

LIVE IN STOCKHOLM

LOST IN SWEDEN

Fire / I Don't Live Today / Sunshine Of Your Love / Red House / Foxy Lady / Hey Joe / Purple Haze
Comments: Recorded live at the Cobo Hall, Detroit, Michigan, November 30, 1968. Fair to good audience recording. Recommended for audience recording completist.

LOST CONCERTS VOL. 5: SWEDEN 1967 *
CD-R No label

Foxy Lady / Rock Me Baby / Hey Joe / Can You See Me / Purple Haze / Wild Thing / Rock Me Baby / Experiencing The Blues / Hey Joe / Purple Haze / Manic Depression
Comments: Tracks 1-6 were recorded at Stora Scenen, Tivoli Garden, Stockholm, Sweden, May 24, 1967. Tracks 7-10 are from the September 4, 1967, shows in Stockholm. "Manic Depression" is from the television broadcast for "Late Line-Up". Fair to good audience recording. Recommended for audience recording completist.

LOST CONCERTS VOL. 6: PHOENIX 1968 *
CD-R No label

Are You Experienced / Come On (Part 1) / Little Wing / Voodoo Chile (slight return) / Fire / Spanish Castle Magic / Foxy Lady / Like A Rolling Stone / Sunshine Of Your Love / Hey Joe / Star Spangled Banner / Purple Haze / Summertime Blues
Comments: Tracks 1-12 were recorded live at Memorial Coliseum, Phoenix, Arizona, September 4, 1968. "Summertime Blues" is from the Saville Theatre, London, England, August 27, 1967. Fair to good audience recording. Recommended for audience recording completist.

LOST CONCERTS VOL. 7: BLACKPOOL 1967 *
CD-R No label

Sergeant Pepper's Lonely Hearts Club Band / Fire / Hey Joe / The Wind Cries Mary / Purple Haze / Wild Thing / Tax Free / Foxy Lady / Like A Rolling Stone / Killin' Floor / Red House
Comments: Tracks 1-6 were recorded live at the Opera House, Blackpool, England, November 25, 1967. Tracks 7-11 are from Hunter College, New York, March 2, 1968. Fair to good audience recording. Recommended for audience recording completist.

LOST CONCERTS VOL. 8: HOUSTON 1968 *
CD-R No Label

Red House / I Don't Live Today / Spanish Castle Magic / Fire - Sunshine Of Your Love / Voodoo Chile (slight return) / Purple Haze / Manic Depression / Tony Glover interview / Fire / Are You Experienced / Voodoo Chile (slight return) / Red House / Foxy Lady / Little Wing / Spanish Castle Magic / Sunshine Of Your Love / Star Spangled Banner / Purple Haze
Comments: Tracks 1-11 were recorded live at the Sam Houston Coliseum, Houston, Texas, August 4, 1968. Tracks 12-18 are from Minneapolis Auditorium, Minneapolis, Minnesota, November 2, 1968. Fair to good audience recording. Recommended for audience recording completist.

LOST CONCERTS VOL. 9: BOSTON 1970 *
CD-R No Label

Stone Free / Lover Man / Red House / Freedom / Foxy Lady / Purple Haze / Star Spangled Banner / All Along The Watchtower / Message To Love / Fire / Spanish Castle Magic / Voodoo Chile (slight return)
Comments: Recorded live at the Boston Gardens, Boston, Massachusetts, June 27, 1970. Fair to good audience recording. Recommended for audience recording completist.

LOST CONCERTS VOL. 10: COLUMBIA 1968 *
CD-R No Label

Are You Experienced / Rock Me Baby / Foxy Lady / Hey Joe / Fire / I Don't Live Today / Purple Haze / Wild Thing - Star Spangled Banner
Comments: Recorded live at the Merriweather Post Pavilion, Columbia, Washington, August 16, 1968. Fair to good audience recording. Recommended for audience recording completist.

LOST EXPERIENCE (THE) IN
JHCD 203 CD

Spanish Castle Magic / Little One / Little One / Wait Until Tomorrow / Jazz Jimi Jazz / Have You Ever Been (To Electric Ladyland) / Drivin' South - Sergeant Pepper's Lonely Hearts Club Band / Heavy Jam / TTG Instrumental - Experience Jam (Marshall Attack Jam) / 1983...A Merman I Should Turn To Be /

Rainy Day Shuffle

Comments: Mostly material from the Sotheby's Tapes with a few tracks that are available commercially.

LOST IN SWEDEN IN ***
WHOOPY CAT (WKP-0046/47) 2 CD (CD1 61:49, CD2 78:23)

CD 1: Foxy Lady / The Burning Of The Midnight Lamp / Fire / Experiencing The Blues / Hey Joe / Purple Haze / Foxy Lady / Rock Me Baby / Hey Joe / Can You See Me / Purple Haze / Wild Thing

CD 2: Sgt. Pepper / EXP / Up From The Skies / Spanish Castle Magic / Foxy Lady / Little Wing / Fire / Experiencing The Blues / The Wind Cries Mary / Purple Haze / Sgt. Pepper / Rock Me Baby / Experiencing The Blues / Hey Joe / Purple Haze

Comments: Disc One: Tracks 1-6 were recorded live at Stora Scenen, Stockholm, September 11, 1967. Tracks 7-12 were recorded live at the Stora Scenen, May 24, 1967. Disc Two: Tracks 1-10 were recorded live at Stora Salen, Stockholm, January 8, 1968. Tracks11-15 were recorded live at Stora Scenen, Stockholm, September 4, 1967. All shows are good to very good audience tapes of complete shows. The 8 Jan 68 show features a rare live performance of "EXP", and even though this is the most challenging show on the release to listen to because lots of flaws on the tape, it is a great show and performance. This is the best place to get all of this material gathered onto one release.

LOST WINTERLAND TAPES IN
STARQUAKE SQ (05-1-2) 2 CD (65:20 - 75:57)

CD 1: Foxy Lady / Manic Depression / Sunshine Of Your Love / Little Wing / Spanish Castle Magic / Red House / Voodoo Chile / The Star Spangled Banner / Purple Haze

CD 2: Foxy Lady / Like A Rolling Stone / The Star Spangled Banner / Purple Haze / Tax Free / Lover Man / Blue Window Jam*

Comments: CD 1: Winterland, 2nd show, October 12 , 1968. CD 2: Tracks 1-4 Winterland, 1st show, October 10, 1968. CD 2: Tracks 5 - 6 Winterland, 2nd show, October 10,1968. * With the Buddy Miles Express, March 15 , 1969. Very good mono soundboard compilation. Japanese CD.

LOVE AND PEACE IN **
MIDNIGHT BEAT (MBCD 015) CD (67:27)

Killin' Floor / Spanish Castle Magic / All Along The Watchtower / Hey Joe / Hey Baby (New Rising Sun) / Message To Love / Foxy Lady / Red House / Ezy Rider / Freedom / Room Full Of Mirrors / Purple Haze / Voodoo Chile (slight return)

Comments: Recorded live at the Love And Peace Festival, Isle Of Fehmarn, September 6, 1970. This is from the so-called 'windy' tape because you can hear the sound of the wind blowing across the microphone. Jimi's last stage performance. Not the greatest performance but historically significant.

LOVER MAN
ON STAGE (CD 12065) CD

Stone Free / Star Spangled Banner / Straight Ahead / Room Full Of Mirrors / Lover Man / Spanish Castle Magic / Foxy Lady / Purple Haze / Hear My Train A Comin' / Fire / Voodoo Chile (slight return)

Comments: Bootleg taken from STAGES of the Atlanta show. The sequence of the tracks have been altered as well.

MAGIC FINGERS
TOWNE RECORDS (RG 2001) 2LP

Side 1: Foxy Lady (5:01) / Fire (4:05) / Killin' Floor (6:14)

Side 2: Red House (9:36) / Spanish Castle Magic (5:12) / Hey Joe (5:16)

Side 3: Instrumental (10:30) / Purple Haze (7:00)

Side 4: I Don't Live Today (4:47) (LA Forum April 26 '69, very good stereo) / In The Midnight Hour; Jam (5:00) (London 1967 with Stevie Wonder on drums, very good stereo) / Dolly Dagger (7:25) (studio mixing session at Electric Lady, excellent stereo)

Comments: Sides 1-3 were recorded live in Ottawa, March 1968. Very good mono.

MAGIC HAND IN *
MUM (MUCD 012) CD

Purple Haze / Lover Man / Message To Love / Crash Landing / Red House / Izabella / Angel / Angel (band demo) / Stepping Stone (Trying To Be) / Fire / The Wind Cries Mary / Machine Gun / Bleeding

Heart / Foxy Lady / Little Wing / Astro Man Jam

Comments: An odds and ends collection of studio outtakes available elsewhere but necessary to a good collection. Worth getting if you don't have this material.

MASTERS MASTERS (THE) IN
ROCKIN' RECORDS (JH - 01) CD (60:40)

Jimi Hendrix - John McLaughlin jam / Look Over Yonder / Seven Dollars In My Pocket Blues (Highway Of Broken Hearts Medley) / Jungle Jam / Devil's Jam (Calling All Devil's Children) / All Along The Watchtower (original tracks) / Red House - Electric Church Jam / Midnight / Axis: Bold As Love (original tracks) / Jazz Jimi Jazz / Electric Ladyland / Crash Landing

Comments: A classic of it's time, this was the first taste of much of this material. All of it is now available in better quality or more complete on other releases. Excellent stereo. Deluxe color cardboard envelope.

MAUI, HAWAII
TRADE MARK OF QUALITY (TMOQ 71018) LP

Side 1: Hey Baby (New Rising Sun) / Red House / Beginning / Straight Ahead

Side 2: Hear My Train A Comin' / Villanova Junction - Ezy Rider

Comments: Recorded live at Maui, Hawaii, July 30, 1970. A selection of songs from both the shows. Other titles are: INCIDENT AT RAINBOW BRIDGE (Dragon) / MAUI, HAWAII (Trade Mark Of Quality JH 106) / LIVE IN HAWAII 1970 (HEN 37-WCF), LIVE IN HAWAII 1970 (Trademark Of Quality) / SOMEWHERE OVER THE RAINBOW (Product Of Distinction POD 0784-002) / MAGICAL GARDEN / RAINBOW BRIDGE (Shalom 3123) & (Contraband CBM3123) - missing the first track. Mostly good mono.

MCLAUGHLIN SESSIONS IN *
HML (CD 9409) CD (59:53)

Live At The Burwood (Young/Hendrix) / World Traveller / My Brothers Dead (It's Too Bad) / Tribute to Donna (Message From Nine To The Universe) / Tarnia (Drivin' South - Everything's Gonna Be Alright) / Doin' Gern (Drone Blues) / You Wouldn't Understand (Valleys Of Neptune) / Uncommon Ground (Jimi-Jimmy Jam) Tarot Mistress (Young / Hendrix)

Comments: A collection of jam sessions with really goofy made up titles. John McLaughlin is even on a couple of them. Some really essential material. Unfortunately much of it is in edited form.

MESSAGE OF LOVE IN ***
TRIANGLE (CD 043) CD (44:56)

Stone Free / Fire / Message To Love / Lover Man / Foxy Lady / Ezy Rider / The Star Spangled Banner / Purple Haze / Voodoo Chile (slight return) / Outro: stage announcements

Comments: Recorded live at Downing Stadium, Randall's Island, NY, July 17, 1970. Very good-excellent stereo soundboard. Also available on Imtrats CD releases of LIVE USA. All releases are missing "Red House" which was CR on CONCERTS and VARIATIONS ON A THEME and "All Along The Watchtower" which has never turned up anywhere. European CD. Time 44.46.

MIDNIGHT LIGHTNING
MARSHALL RECORDS LP

Side 1: Crash Landing / Midnight Lightning / Machine Gun / Further On Up The Road / Astro Man

Side 2: Astro Man cont. / Lord, I See The Blues (For Me & You) / Message To Love / Stone Free / Instrumental Jam / Izabella

Comments: Common outtakes from 1968. Excellent stereo.

MIDNIGHT MAGIC
WAGGLE RECORDS (1936) 2LP

Side 1: Foxy Lady / Purple Haze / Voodoo Chile

Side 2: Fire/ Hey Joe / Spanish Castle Magic / I Don't Live Today

Side 3: Midnight Outtake / Electric Church Blues / Red House / Jimi & John McLaughlin Jam / Midnight Lightning Solo

Side 4: Drivin' South / Sgt. Pepper / Radio Commercials

Comments: Sides 1-2 recorded live at San Diego 1969. Sides 3-4 outtakes. Excellent stereo. TMOQ labels.

LOVE AND PEACE

THE MASTERS MASTERS

MAUI, HAWAII

MCLAUGHLIN SESSIONS

MESSAGE OF LOVE

MIDNIGHT MAGIC

MIDNIGHT SHINES DOWN IN *
BLUE KANGAROO (BK-04) CD

Crash Landing / Midnight Lightning / Izabella - Machine Gun / Further On Up The Road / Astro Man Jam / Country Blues / Lord I Sing The Blues For Me And You / Message To Love / Stone Free / Rock And Roll Jam / Izabella / Have You Ever Been (To Electric Ladyland) / All Along The Watchtower / Calling All Devil's Children

Comments: A fine disc of excellent quality but common studio material.

MIDNIGHT SUN IN
THE THIRD EYE (NK 007) CD

Midnight Sun / Can't Find My Baby / I Can't Find It Without You / Walk Right In, Always See Your Face / Skin/ Stay Away / Only You / See Myself In You / Slowtime Blues (Things I Used To Do) / Country Blues / All Along The Watchtower 1 / All Along The Watchtower 2 / Jam (Jam Thing)

Comments: Tracks 1 - 8 are from the unreleased 1970 Love album, BLACK BEAUTY, and has no Jimi involvement. Tracks 9 & 10 are unreleased studio songs from 1970. Tracks 11 & 12 are alternate takes from 1968 featuring Dave Mason. Track 13 is an alternate studio version with Chris Wood from 1968. Mostly excellent stereo.

MIXDOWN MASTER TAPES VOL. 1-3 IN ***
DANDELION (DL 005/06/07) 3CD (CD1 66:31, CD275:38, CD3 74:19)

CD 1: S.T.P. WITH L.S.D. / Can You Please Crawl Out Your Window / Calling All Devil's Children / Hear My Freedom / Machine Gun / Star Spangled Banner / Freedom Jam / Message From Nine To The Universe

CD 2: Jazz Jimi Jazz / Cat Talkin' To Me / Rainy Day Dream Away / Moon Turn The Tides Gently Gently Away / Heaven Has No Sorrow / Valleys Of Neptune / 3 Little Bears / Bleeding Heart / Bleeding Heart / Cherokee Mist

CD 3: Dance / Lord I Sing The Blues / Midnight Lightning / Country Blues / Villanova Junction / Gypsy Boy / Valleys Of Neptune / 3 Little Bears / Ezy Rider - Cherokee Mist

Comments: Excellent quality throughout. Absolutely essential material with some being the most complete available. Buy or Die.

MOONS AND RAINBOWS
INSECT (IST 48) CD (55:02)

Crash Landing / Midnight Lightning / Machine Gun / Farther Up The Road / Astro Man / Country Blues / Message To Love / Stone Free / Instrumental Jam / Izabella

Comments: Alternate studio versions in excellent quality. European CD. A copy of GYPSY SUNS, MOONS AND RAINBOWS (Sidewalk JHX 8868).

MORE ELECTRICITY FROM NEWPORT IN **
LUNA (LU 9201) CD (72:09)

Stone Free - Drum Solo / Are Your Experienced - Stone Free / Sunshine of Your Love / Fire / Hear My Train A Comin' / Red House / Foxy Lady / Like A Rolling Stone / Voodoo Chile (slight return) - Drum Solo / Purple Haze / Interview / Hear My Train A Comin'

Comments: Tracks 1-10 are the complete show recorded June 20th, 1969, at The Newport Pop Festival. A good soundboard with minimal stereo separation. The mix sounds a bit muffled with a slant towards the vocals and a bit light on the bass and drums. Tracks 11-12 are from July 1969 "Dick Cavett Show". Also available on WIZARDS VISION (World Productions Of Compact Music WPOCM 0789 D 026-2) but without the Cavett tracks.

MULTICOLOURED BLUES IN **
LUNA (LU 9317) 2CD (CD1 78:50, CD2 75:31)

CD 1: Earth Blues (4:04) / Dolly Dagger (3:49) / Room Full Of Mirrors (3:03) / Stepping Stone (4:18) / Bleeding Heart (3:09) / Drifter's Escape (3:00) / Midnight (Tax Free)(4:54) / 3 Little Bears (4:57) / Jam Back At The House (Beginnings)(5:27) / Freedom (3:28) / Lover Man (2:43) / My Friend (4:31) / Astro Man (11:14) / Straight Ahead (3:48) / 1983...A Merman I Shall Turn To Be (4:26) / Maui Sunset (Villanova Junction)(11:50)

CD 2: Slow Time (Valleys Of Neptune)(4:29) / Freedom (4:14) / Drifting (4:06) / Angel (4:11) / Belly Button Window (5:11) / Nightbird Flying (3:30) / Pride Of Man (Drifting 2 versions and Cherokee Mist

- In From The Storm - Valleys Of Neptune medley) (15:44) / Ezy Rider (3:57) / Instrumental, Winter Blues (Hollywood Jam) (9:19) / Instrumental (Last Thursday Morning) (3:18) / Crash Landing (4:26) / Message To Love (3:27) / Instrumental, Ezy Rider Rev. (Ezy Rider Jam)(9:31)

Comments: Very good-excellent sound. Some hiss and surface noise. Lots of worthwhile outtakes and unused mixes if you don't already have them. One exclusive track is some jamming at Jimi's Shokan house with the GSRB under the title "Maui Sunset" on Disc One. Recommended.

MUSIC FOR FANS
MUSIC OF DISTINCTION (MOD 1003) LP

Side 1: Message From Nine To The Universe / Cherokee Mist

Side 2: Drone Blues / Strato Strut

Comments: Copy of JIMI HENDRIX (QCS 1447). Excellent mono.

MUSICORAMA
PYRAMID (CD 042) CD

Intro (0:44) / Killin' Floor (4:14) / Catfish Blues (7:49) / Foxy Lady(4:50) / Red House (5:52) / Drivin' South (instrumental) (8:14) / The Wind Cries Mary (4:35) / Fire (2:46) / Little Wing (5:02) / Purple Haze (6:07)

Comments: Recorded live at Olympia, Paris, January 29, 1968. Excellent stereo. Made obsolete by the CR on STAGES.

NEVER FADE
PHOENIX (44775) 2LP

Sides 1-2: Rerelease of PRIMAL KEYS (Impossible Recordworks 1- 02)

Sides 3-4: Rerelease of PIPE DREAM (TAKRL 1959)

NOT JUST A VOODOO CHILE   IN
PILOT RECORDS (HJCD071) CD

Beyond The Valleys Of Neptune (Session Thing) / Martin Luther King (Jam / Cherokee Mist) / Come On / Home Acoustic Jam (fake - not Jimi)

Comments: The sound quality on the jams is excellent. "Come On" is an alternate mix from a rare French single.

NOTES IN COLOURS   IN **
JHR (001/002) 2CD

CD 1: Izabella / Ezy Rider / Room Full Of Mirrors / Who Knows / Message To Love / Message To Love / God Save The Queen (David Henderson) / Had To Cry Today / Drifting / Drifting / Jam Session / Angel / Drifting / Angel / Belly Button Window / Angel / Dolly Dagger

CD 2: Bleeding Heart / Earth Blues / Gypsy Boy / Astro Man Jam / Bold As Love / Dream / Dance / Little Miss Lover / Little One / Little One / Castles Made Of Sand / Spanish Castle Magic / One Rainy Wish / Spanish Castle Magic / Ain't No Telling / Jazz Jimi Jazz

Comments: A nice collection of outtakes, alternate versions, unused mixes and a "Drifting" session that is nice to get. Even with a fake track (David Henderson must be most most widely bootlegged unknown person on earth), this set is recommended.

OFFICIAL BOOTLEG ALBUM (THE)   IN *
YELLOW DOG (YD 051) CD (72:09)

Drivin' South (3:21) / Catfish Blues (5:29) / Wait Till Tomorrow (2:57) / Burning Of The Midnight Lamp (3:58) / Sgt. Pepper's Lonely Hearts Club Band (1:41) / Hound Dog (2:43) / Electric Church, Red House (7:25) / Are You Experienced? (6:18) / Look Over Yonder (2:30) / Earth Blues (4:13) / The Wind Cries Mary (4:17) / Little Wing (3:34) / 1983... (A Merman I Should Turn To Be) (7:39) / Angel (3:20) / God Save The Queen (5:06) / Cherokee Mist (7:08)

Comments: Common outtakes and jams. Very good to excellent sound from a label you can generally trust at least for audio quality. An easy place to get this material if you don't already have it.

OH, ATLANTA   IN ***
TENDOLAR (TDR 009) CD (74:04)

Fire / Lover Man / Spanish Castle Magic / Red House / Room Full Of Mirrors / Hear My Train A Comin' / Message To Love / All Along The Watchtower / Freedom / Foxy Lady / Purple Haze / Hey Joe

/ Voodoo Chile / Stone Free / Star Spangled Banner

Comments: This is an excellent stereo soundboard recording from the Atlanta Pop Festival from Atlanta GA., July 4, 1970. This is as much as has been available before from a single stereo source and in the correct sequence. Highly recommended. I hope the last two songs from the show turn up soon from the same source.

OLYMPIA (THE)
JH (68 P) LP
Side 1: Killin' Floor / Catfish Blues / Foxy Lady / Red House / The Wind Cries Mary
Side 2: Drivin' South / Fire / Little Wing / Purple Haze
Comments: Recorded live at the Olympia Theatre, Paris, January 29, 1968. Excellent stereo. European bootleg. Deluxe yellow & black cover. Picture label.

OLYMPIC GOLD VOL. 1   IN ***
BLIMP LABEL PRESENTS (BL-006) CD (62:56)
I Don't Live Today (1-5) / Red House (1-4) / Purple Haze / No, No, No, No, No (La Pouppee Qui Fait Non) / Fire / The Wind Cries Mary / Can You See Me? (1-4) / 51st Anniversary (1-3) / Fire (#1-5)
Comments: This is fabulous! Fantastic outtakes, many for the first time ever and in beautiful sound. This and OLYMPIC GOLD VOL. 2 are absolute must haves. Don't even think of not owning these. This material destined is to be recycled until the end of time, so it should be easy to find.

OLYMPIC GOLD VOL. 2   IN ***
BLIMP LABEL PRESENTS (BL-007) CD (62:56)
51st Anniversary / Can You See Me? / Manic Depression / Hey Joe / Instrumental (no Jimi involvement) / Hey Joe (2-4) / Red House / Remember (1-6) / Manic Depression (1-2)
Comments: See comments for VOLUME 1.

ON A PUBLIC SAXOPHONE
HILLSIDE RECORDS (54RH003) CD
Utee / My Diary / Can You Please Crawl Out Your Window / Little Miss Lover / Experiencing The Blues / Fire / Hear My Train A Comin' / Spanish Castle Magic / Electric Lady Jam / Burning Of The Midnight Lamp / Like A Rolling Stone / I Don't Know What You Got (But It's Got Me)
Comments: Common outtakes and live tracks. Also available as RARITIES (Genuine Pig TGP-CD-091). Jimi would often introduce himself at concerts as the cat playing the 'public saxophone.'

ON THE KILLING FLOOR
THE SWINGING PIG (TSP-012-3) 3LP
Side 1: Killin' Floor / Spanish Castle Magic / Fire / Hey Joe / Voodoo Chile (slight return)
Side 2: Red House / Sunshine Of Your Love
Side 3: I Don't Live Today / Spanish Castle Magic
Side 4: Hey Joe / Voodoo Chile (slight return)
Side 5: Sunshine Of Your Love / Red House
Side 6: Fire / Purple Haze / Star Spangled Banner
Comments: Recorded January 9, 1969, in Stockholm, Sweden, at Kornserrthuset and features both shows.

ON THE KILLING FLOOR   IN ***
THE SWINGIN' PIG (TSP CD 012 - 2) 2CD (CD1 56:48, CD2 69:20)
CD 1: Killin' Floor / Spanish Castle Magic / Fire / Hey Joe / Voodoo Chile (slight return) / Red House / Sunshine Of Your Love / I Don't Live Today
CD 2: Spanish Castle Magic / Hey Joe / Voodoo Chile (slight return) / Sunshine Of Your Love / Red House / Fire / Purple Haze / Star Spangled Banner
Comments: Recorded live at the Konserthuset, January 9, 1969, Stockholm, Sweden. CD 1: First Show / CD 2: Second Show. <u>Perfect</u> stereo. This set is the ultimate Jimi Hendrix bootleg. This is what bootlegging was invented for. Find this original set at all costs. The Midnight Beat box IN MEMORIAM: LIVE IN SWEDEN is an acceptable substitute, but I think the sound and dynamics on this set are better. Buy or die.

ONCE UPON A TIME IN

WALL OF SOUND (WS-CD 011) CD (52:02)

The Wind Cries Mary / Fire / Little Wing / Purple Haze / Can You See Me / Hey Joe / Foxy Lady / Tax Free / Red House / Wild Thing

Comments: Various live tracks from Monterey, Ottawa and Paris. Get the full shows instead.

ONE NIGHT AT THE ARENA IN **

VENUE (VE 00501) CD (59:32)

Lover Man / I Don't Live Today / Red House / Hear My Train A Comin' / Spanish Castle Magic / Sunshine Of Your Love / Foxy Lady / Purple Haze / Star Spangled Banner / Voodoo Chile (slight return)

Comments: Recorded live at The Arena, Providence, Rhode Island, May 17, 1969. A reasonably listenable audience recording of the full show. If anything, the bass is a bit boomy and the vocals a bit echoey.

OST - RAINBOW BRIDGE AND MORE

LABEL UNKNOWN CD

Dolly Dagger / Earth Blues / Pali Gap / Room Full Of Mirrors / Star Spangled Banner / Look Over Yonder / Hear My Train A Comin' / Hey Baby (New Rising Sun) / Izabella / Stepping Stone / Little Drummer Boy - Silent Night - Auld Lang Syne / Like A Rolling Stone / Jazz Jimi Jazz

Comments: A copy of the album on CD lifted from vinyl and filled out with stuff you probably already have. I guess people buy this kind of stuff 'cause they can't stand not having an album on CD. I know I did.

OUT OF THE STUDIO 1 & 2 IN ***

DEE LANE LEA (560-1/2) 2CD

CD 1: I Don't Live Today (5) / Red House (4) / Purple Haze / La Pouppee Qui Fait Non / Fire / The Wind Cries Mary / Can You See Me (4) / 51st Anniversary (3) / Fire (5) / 51st Anniversary / Can You See Me

CD 2: Manic Depression / Hey Joe (4) / Hey Joe (3) / Red House / Remember (6) / Manic Depression (2)

Comments: A superb collection of alternate studio versions (mostly backing tracks) - many of which are available here for the first time. Mostly excellent soundboard. Certainly a must for all collectors. See DEMOS 1968. CD1 - 69:20 / CD2 - 47:29.

OUTTAKES & STUDIO SESSIONS

GENUINE PIG (TGP-CD-088) CD

Takin' Care Of Business / Cryin' Blue Rain / Lover Man / There Ain't Nothin' Wrong / Room Full oF Mirrors / Look Over Yonder / Sunshine Of Your Love / Shame, Shame, Shame / Cat Talkin' To To Me / Freedom / Lover Man / Untitled Instrumental / Untitled Instrumental / Dolly Dagger / Bleeding Heart / Earth Blues / Ezy Ryder / Izabella / Ezy Ryder / Room Full Of Mirrors / Come On (Part 1)

Comments: A copy (and not a very good one) of STUDIO HAZE with "Come On (Part 1)" added at the end.

PAPER AIRPLANES IN **

MIDNIGHT BEAT (MB CD 025) CD (78:00)

Message To Love / Somewhere (Take 1) / Somewhere (Take 2) / Crash Landing (Take 1) / Crash Landing (Take 2) / Crash Landing (Take 3) / Come Down Hard On Me Baby (Take 1) / Come Down Hard On Me Baby (Take 2) / Peace In Mississippi (Take 1) / Peace In Mississippi (Take 2) / Peace In Mississippi (Take 3) / Peace In Mississippi (Take 4) / Power Of Soul / Stone Free / Jam - Cherokee Mist / Lord I Sing The Blues For Me And You / Lover Man

Comments: This is a very nice sounding disc with multiple unused mixes of and original versions of songs later butchered by Alan Douglas. Recommended.

PARIS IS JAMESTOWN

INSTANT ANALYSIS (L 28266) LP

Side 1: Foxy Lady / The Wind Cries Mary / Rock Me Baby / Red House / Purple Haze

Side 2: Hey Joe / Purple Haze / Foxy Lady / Love Or Confusion / Killin' Floor / Burning The Midnight Lamp / Hound Dog / Day Tripper

Comments: Tracks 1-5 recorded October 9, 1967, Paris. The rest are from BBC sessions. Excellent stereo. Also available as PARIS 67 (Instant Analysis).

MIXDOWN MASTER TAPES 1-3

MOONS AND RAINBOWS

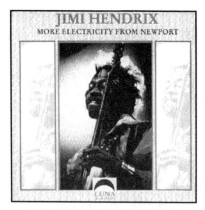

MORE ELECTRICITY FROM NEWPORT

MULTICOLOURED BLUES

THE OFFICIAL BOOTLEG ALBUM

OLYMPIC GOLD VOL. 1

PARIS 66 / 67   IN *
WHOOPY CAT (WKP - 0012) CD (68:26)

Killin' Floor (1:11) / Hey Joe (2:50) / Foxy Lady (3:54) / The Wind Cries Mary (3:23) / Rock Me Baby (3:41) / Red House (6:01) / Purple Haze (5:11) / Wild Thing (5:37) / Have Mercy (3:15) / EXP (2:14) / Up From The Skies(4:37) / Little Wing (4:06) / I Don't Live Today (8:19) / Can You Please Crawl Out Your Window? (3:11)

Comments: Tracks 1-2 are in good quality from the soundboard recorded live at L'Olympia, Paris, October 18, 1966. What is on this disc is from a 1992 French radio rebroadcast (with voiceover) of part of the show which is the first recorded live performance of The Experience. The full 10 minute segment was recorded but has yet to surface. Tracks 3-8 are in very good quality from the soundboard at the L'Olympia in Paris, October 9, 1967. This show is also on Pyramid RFT CD 004 THE WILD MAN OF POP PLAYS VOL. 2. Track 9 is from good but slightly muffled sounding audience recording at the Flamingo Club, London, February 4, 1967. This song plus the rest of the show are on Midnight Beat's HAVE MERCY ON ME BABY! (MBCD 038). Tracks 10-13 recorded live at Konserthuset, Stockholm, Sweden January 8, 1968, which is just a selection of tracks from the whole show released on Whoopy Cat's LOST IN SWEDEN. Track 14 is from a very good audience tape from the Fillmore East, NYC, May 10, 1968. The complete show is available as IT'S ONLY A PAPER MOON (Luna LU9420) and ONE NIGHT STAND (Hep Cat 1001). Overall a nice selection of material but with much of it available as complete shows on other releases. You should find those if you can.

PEACE MUD & TEARS
NOLABEL LP

Side A: Come On (Part 1) / Jam - Cherokee Mist / 1983...A Merman I Should Turn To Be / One Rainy Wish

Side B: Look Over Yonder / Room Full Of Mirrors / Izabella / Stepping Stone / Valleys Of Neptune

PHILHARMONIC PLUS   IN
BULLDOG RECORDS (BRCD1901) CD 71:27.

I Don't Live Today / Getting My Heart Back Together / Spanish Castle Magic / Interview / Lover Man / Hey Joe / Hound Dog / Voodoo Chile / Getting My Heart Back Together / Dolly Dagger

Comments: Tracks 1-3 are from the the good audience tape from Philharmonic Hall, NYC, November 28, 1968. Tracks 4-5 are from the "Tonight Show," July 19, 1969. Tracks 6-9 are the afternoon rehearsals from Royal Albert Hall, February 24 , 1969. Track 10 is a breakdown mix with Eddie Kramer from the radio show. Sound is good to very good. Not much here that you can't find easier or better elsewhere.

PIPE DREAM
AMAZING KORNYPHONE (TAKRL 1959) LP

Side 1: Sgt. Pepper's Lonely Hearts Club Band (1:57) / Hey Joe (3:37) / I Don't Live Today (4:01) / The Wind Cries May (3:22) / Foxy Lady (3:06) / Fire (3:09)

Side 2: Burning Of The Midnight Lamp (3:37) (first public performance) / Purple Haze (4:59) / Sunshine Of Your Love (9:40) / Voodoo Child (slight return)(6:35) (recorded live at Konsterhus, Stockholm January 9, 1969)

Comments: Swedish radio recordings from Radiohus Studio, September 5, 1967 unless otherwise noted. Good stereo. Cover says Amsterdam '68 . Also on the bootlegs LIVE IN STOCKHOLM (Wizardo WRMB 333) & (Fruit End 10168) and FOXY HENDRIX (HEN 5000) and NEVER FADE (Phoenix 44775): Sides three & four.

PLEIADES RISING
This is simply a 4LP collection which includes BROADCASTS, GIMME JIMI, GOOD VIBES and MAUI, HAWAII.

POCAHONTAS
Another repackaging in a 2LP set which includes BROADCASTS and GOOD VIBES.

POWER OF SOUL   IN
STARQUAKE (SQ - 10) CD 70:46

Power Of Soul / Lover Man / Hear My Train A Comin' / Them Changes / Izabella, Machine Gun / Stop

/ Ezy Ryder / Bleeding Heart / Earth Blues / Burning Desire
Comments: The complete first show of the BOG at the Fillmore East, December 31, 1969. Good audience tape. Japanese CD.

PRIMAL KEYS IN
IMPOSSIBLE RECORDWORKS (1 - 02) LP
Comments: Copy of GUITAR HERO with a black & white deluxe cover. All obsolete material.

PURPLE HAZE / HIGHWAY CHILE
NAPOLEON (NP 1018) Vinyl single
Comments: "Purple Haze" from Atwood Hall in Massachusetts (March 15, 1968). "Highway Chile" is from the commercial release.

PURPLE HAZE
ON STAGE (12010) CD
The Wind Cries Mary (3:40) / Burning Of The Midnight Lamp (4:00) / Foxy Lady (3:18) / Voodoo Chile (7:25) / Killin' Floor (5:08) / Sgt. Pepper's Lonely Hearts Club Band (1:53) / Hey Joe (4:30) / Sunshine Of Your Love (4:18) / Little Wing (3:30) / Fire (2:39) / Red House (4:18) / Purple Haze (4:03) / Star Spangled Banner (3:05)
Comments: Stockholm 1967 /1969. Tracks 9, 10, 11 in Paris 1968 and Track 8 in Los Angeles 1969. Also available as FOXY LADY (ALEGRA CD 9008) CD.

PURPLE HAZE IN WOODSTOCK
ITM (960004) CD
Announcement (0:33) / Hear My Train A Comin' (9:29) / Spanish Castle Magic (8:47) / Lover Man (4:47) / Fire (3:14) / Voodoo Chile (14:55) / Star Spangled Banner (3:53) / Purple Haze (5:14) / Hey Joe (4:53)
Comments: Recorded live at Woodstock, New York, August 8, 1969. Excellent stereo soundboard. European CD. Disc reads 'Albert Collins - Alive And Cool' (ITM 960003) but it's Hendrix.

PURPLE SONGS **
LOST ROSE (LR CD 16) CD
Tax Free (9:51) / Killin' Floor (5:17) / Fire (2:51) / Red House (9:41) / Foxy Lady (4:50) / Hey Joe (5:28) / Spanish Castle Magic (4:00) / Purple Haze (6:38)
Comments: Recorded live at the Capital Theatre, Ottawa, Canada, March 19, 1968. Very good soundboard that is easy to find released under many titles and belongs in every collection. European CD.

RAINBOW BRIDGE
CONTRABAND (CBM 3213) LP
Comments: Same as HENDRIX LIVE IN HAWAII.

RAINBOW BRIDGE 2 IN *
JMH (003/2) 2CD
CD 1: Rainbow Band: It's A Beautiful Day (1:53) / Chuck Wein Introduction (2:19) / Jimi Hendrix - Cry Of Love Band: Spanish Castle Magic (4:43) / Lover Man (2:34) / Hey Baby (4:36) / In From The Storm (5:00) / Message To Love (4:49) / Foxy Lady (4:45) / Hear My Train A Comin' (9:08) / Voodoo Chile (slight return) (7:16) / Fire (3:51) / Purple Haze (4:17) / Dolly Dagger (5:09) / Villanova Junction Blues (5:27) / Ezy Rider (4:55)
CD 2: Red House (6:45) / Freedom (4:21) / Jam Back The House (6:59) / Land Of The Rising Sun (4:46) / Dolly Dagger (Isle Of Wight 1970) (5:34) / Hey Baby (Isle Of Wight 1970) (7:17) / Hear My Train A Comin' (Berkeley 1970) (11:11) / Message To Love (Fillmore 1969) (4:32) / Ezy Rider (Fillmore 1969) (4:54) / Room Full Of Mirrors (B.O.G. 1969) (3:03) / Stepping Stone (B.O.G. 1969) (4:09) / Earth Blues (B.O.G. 1969) (4:20) / Hey Baby (C.O.L.B. 1970) (6:00)
Comments: The complete first show and part of the second recorded live at the Haleakala Crater, Maui, Hawaii, July 30, 1970, unless otherwise noted. Excellent soundboard. European CD. Picture CDs.

RARE MASTERS SERIES, VOLUME 3
THE GENUINE PIG (TGP-CD-134) CD
Spanish Castle Magic (3:37) / Lover Man (2:31) / Hey Baby (Land Of The New Rising Sun) (9:04) / Message Of Love (4:06) / Foxy Lady (4:17) / Hear My Train A Comin' (8:36) / Voodoo Chile (7:11) /

Fire (3:32) / Purple Haze (4:16) / Dolly Dagger (10:36) / Ezy Rider (4:48) / Red House (6:32) / Freedom (4:14)

Comments: Recorded live in Maui, July 30, 1970. Complete first show. Excellent soundboard. Includes a booklet with five photographs and a reproduction of the show's poster.

RARITIES ON COMPACT DISC: VOL. 1 IN *
ON THE RADIO CD

Izabella / Stepping Stone / Angel / Day Tripper / Little Drummer Boy - Silent Night - Auld Lang Syne / 51st Anniversary / The Stars That Play With Laughing Sam's Dice / Fire / Gloria / My Diary / Utee / Have You Ever Been (To Electric Ladyland) / Come On (Part 1) / All Along The Watchtower / Drifter's Escape / Sergeant Pepper's Lonely Hearts Club Band / Sunshine Of Your Love / Come Down Hard On Me Baby / Blue Suede Shoes / Hound Dog

Comments: Sourced mostly from commercially released material that is otherwise unavailable on CD, some from rare singles and the like.

RECORD PLANT JAMS IN
PILOT (HJCD69) CD

Valleys Of Neptune / Cherokee Mist / Drivin' South - Everything's Gonna Be Alright Jam / Jimi - Jimmy Jam

Comments: The desirable track here is the long version of "Drivin' South...Jam".

RECORDED LIVE IN EUROPE 1967 IN
BULLDOG RECORDS (BGLP 023) LP and CD (BGCD 023)

Side 1: Sgt. Pepper's Lonely Hearts Club Band / Hey Joe / I Don't Live Today / The Wind Cries Mary / Foxy Lady / Fire / The Burning Of The Midnight Lamp / Purple Haze

Side 2: Killin' Floor / Experiencing The Blues / Foxy Lady / Red House / The Wind Cries Mary / Drivin' South / Fire

Comments: Side One recorded live September 5, 1967. Radiohuset, Stockholm, Sweden . Side Two recorded live January 29, 1968. L'Olympia, Paris, France. A typical Bulldog mixed bag of common material.

RECORDED LIVE PARIS OLYMPIA JANUARY 29, 1968
UFO (201018) LP

Side 1: Killin' Floor / Catfish Blues / Foxy Lady

Side 2: Red House / Drivin' South / Purple Haze

Comments: From January 29, 1968, Paris. Second Show. Very good stereo.

RED HOUSE
LABEL UNKNOWN Vinyl Single

Red House (Pt. 1) / Red House (Pt. 2)

Comments: Recorded on Randall Island, New York, July 17, 1970. Song is edited to fit the single format.

REDSKIN JAMMIN' IN
JH 01/2 2CD

CD 1: Cherokee Mist / Redskin Jammin'(Jimi / Jimmy Jam) / Bad Feelings (World Traveller) / It's Too Bad / Sky Jam (Strato Strut) / Coast To Coast (Drivin' South - Everythings Gonna Be Alright / Bridge To Nowhere (Drone Blues) / Ezy Rider / Message To Love

CD 2: Lover Man / Stratoblaster (Peace In Mississippi) / Midnight Sun (Marshall Attack Jam) / Mars Is My Hometown (Jam - Cherokee Mist) / Soul Power (Ezy Rider Jam / Java Jam (Peace In Mississippi) / Little Drummer Boy / Heavy Weather (Calling All Devils Children) / Wild Thing / Freedom / Stone Free / Hey Joe / I Don't Live Today

Comments: A serious mixed bag of material. First, the disc was available in a standard jewel case or in a very elaborate package for a lot more $$. Second, almost every track is given a really goofy fake title - probably to trick collectors into thinking there is new material. Third, it has edits of material easily available elsewhere, and it "doctors" a studio track as well as common live material to give the impression that it is new material. Pretty low budget overall. The only redeeming parts of this disc is the longest available version of "Jimi / Jimmy Jam" to appear anywhere and a complete "Drivin' South / Everythings Gonna Be Alright" (but without the 2 jams that should follow). Buy at your own risk.

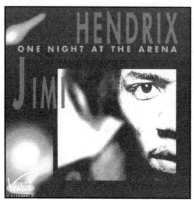

ONE NIGHT AT THE ARENA

OUT OF THE STUDIO

PAPER AIRPLANES

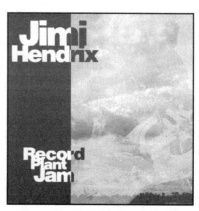

RECORD PLANT JAM

REDSKIN JAMMIN'

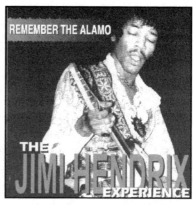

REMEMBER THE ALAMO

REMEMBER THE ALAMO IN *
NO LABEL CD (55:54)

Sgt. Pepper's Lonely Hearts Club Band / Can You Please Crawl Out Of Your Window / The Wind Cries Mary / Let Me Stand Next To Your Fire / Cat Fish Blues / Foxy Lady / Hey Joe / Purple Haze / Wild Thing

Comments: Recorded live at the Will Rogers Auditorium, Fort Worth, Texas, February 17, 1968. Very good audience tape. Complete and unedited recording.

RIOTS IN BERKELEY IN ***
BEECH MARTIN (BM 038) CD

Pass It On (Straight Ahead) / Hey Baby (New Rising Sun) / Lover Man / Stone Free / Hey Joe / I Don't Live Today / Machine Gun / Foxy Lady / The Star Spangled Banner / Purple Haze / Voodoo Chile (slight return) / Blue Suede Shoes / Ezy Rider

Comments: Recorded live at the Berkeley Community Centre, May 30, 1970. The complete second show. "Blue Suede Shoes" is a rehearsal. "Ezy Rider" is from the first show. Excellent stereo soundboard. European CD. A nice disc to get as it has "Hey Joe" where it belongs. This was deleted from the Whoopy Cat package THE BERKELEY CONCERTS.

ROCK LEGENDS
ROCK LEGENDS OF AMERICA (RWJH-07) EP

Side A: No Such Animal (Part 1) / No Such Animal (Part 2) / Soul Food / Goodbye, Bessie Mae

Side B: Go Go Shoes / Go Go Place / My Diary / Utee

ROMAN COLISEUM (THE)
STARQUAKE (SQ-11) CD (69:21)

Lover Man / Come On (Part 1) / Red House / Fire / Spanish Castle Magic / Hear My Train A Comin' / I Don't Love Today / Voodoo Chile (slight return) / Purple Haze

Comments: Recorded live at the Madison Square Garden, May 18, 1969. Poor audience recording. Japanese CD.

ROYAL ALBERT HALL
BERKELEY (2288) LP

Side 1: Sunshine Of Your Love (6:45) / Outside Woman Blues / Sunshine Of Your Love (Medley) / Room Full Of Mirrors (8:12)

Side 2: Blues In C (8:27) / People People People / Star Spangled Banner

Comments: Recorded live on February 24, 1969, at the Royal Albert Hall, London. Excellent stereo. Also on EXPERIENCE (Immaculate Conception CBMR-10), LIVE AT THE ALBERT HALL (Kustom SPJH 1) & (Jimi 2288), SMASHING AMPS (Dragonfly 5) & (Slipped Disc) & (Ruthless Rhymes) & (Duck).

ROYAL ALBERT HALL IN ***
BLIMP LABEL (008/9) 2CD

CD 1: Lover Man / Stone Free, drum solo / Hear My Train A Comin' / I Don't Live Today / Red House / Foxy Lady

CD 2: Sunshine Of Your Love / Bleeding Heart / Fire / Little Wing / Voodoo Child (slight return) / Room Full Of Mirrors / Purple Haze / Wild Thing / The Star Spangled Banner

Comments: The complete live stereo recording from the Royal Albert Hall on February 24, 1969. Excellent soundboard. CD1 - 53:20 / CD2 - 52:00.

SCREAMING EAGLE IN **
PINK POODLE (POO 001) CD

Rainy Day, Dream Away - Still Raining Still Dreaming / Crosstown Traffic / Woodstock (no Jimi) / Drivin' South - Sergeant Pepper's Lonely Hearts Club Band / Stone Free / Mocking Bird / Voodoo Chile (slight return) / Jazz Jimi Jazz / Are You Experienced / Instrumental Jam (Larry Young Instrumental Jam) / Suey / Burning Of The Midnight Lamp / Shotgun

Comments: A very desirable piece due to versions of several tracks unavailable elsewhere ("Rainy Day...", "Stone Free", "Mockingbird", "Voodoo Chile...", "Larry Young Instrumental Jam", "Suey" and "Shotgun"). Unfortunately, a very hard piece to find.

'SCUSE ME WHILE I KISS THE SKY'
RUBBER DUBBER (9022 2334 - 7) LP
> **Comments:** Same as LIVE AT THE FORUM. Also available on Hen Records.

'SCUSE ME WHILE I KISS THE SKY   IN **
SONIC ZOOM (SZ1001) CD
> Are You Experienced / Fire / Wind Cries Mary, Tax Free, Drum Solo / Foxy Lady / Hey Joe / Spanish
> Castle Magic / Improvisation / Purple Haze / Wild Thing / Star Spangled Banner / Hey Joe / Guitar
> Improvisation / Purple Haze / Wild Thing
> **Comments:** Tracks 1-11 recorded live at the Memorial Auditorium, Dallas, Texas, February 16, 1968.
> Tracks 12-15 are from Will Rogers Auditorium, Fort Worth, Texas, February 17, 1968. Good-very good
> audience recording. A great package to find both of the 1968 Texas shows.

SESSIONS 1
MAJOR TOM (MT 153) CD-R
> Message To Love (9 takes) / Ezy Rider (4 takes) / Power Of Soul / Earth Blues
> **Comments:** The Band Of Gypsys rehearsals from December 1969 at Baggies.

SESSIONS 2
MAJOR TOM (MT 154) CD-R
> Them Changes (2 takes) / Lover Man (2 takes) / Who Knows (1-7 with 7 being incomplete) / Message
> To Love (2 takes) / Bolero (2 takes) / Come Down Hard On Me Baby / Midnight Lightning / Bolero (7
> takes) / Send My Love To Linda - Live And Let Live (3 takes)
> **Comments:** More Band Of Gypsys rehearsals recorded at Baggies in December '69.

SESSIONS 3
MAJOR TOM (MT 155) CD-R
> Hear My Train A Comin' / Villanova Junction / Message From Nine To The Universe / Izabella (2 takes)
> / Night Bird Flying / Freedom / Straight Ahead / Astro Man / ...And The Gods Made Love / Jam Session
> / Sunshine Of Your Love / Jam Session
> **Comments:** A varied assortment of common rarities.

SESSIONS 4
MAJOR TOM (MT 156) CD-R
> Country Blues / Jam Session - Parts 1-3) / Izabella / The Rumble / Astro Man - Valleys Of Neptune /
> Jam Session / Power Of Soul / Jam Session / Room Full Of Mirrors
> **Comments:** These jams were most likely recorded in 1969 at Jimi's New York apartment.

SESSIONS 5
MAJOR TOM (MT 157) CD-R
> Stepping Stone / Free Thunder / Cave Man Bells / Strokin' A Lady On Each Hip / Baby Chicken Strut
> / Down Mean Blues / Feels Good / Fried Cola
> **Comments:** The source of this disc and SESSIONS 6 is the Mike Ephron session tapes from September
> 1969. These featured Jimi on guitar, Mike Ephron on piano, Jerry Velez on percussion and Juma Sultan
> on flute and percussion. See also THIS FLYER and JIMI AT HIS BEST.

SESSIONS 6
MAJOR TOM (MT 158) CD-R
> Monday Morning Blues / Jimi Is Tender Too / Madagascar / Young Jim / Lift Off / Swift's Wing / Spike
> With Heady Dreams / Giraffe
> **Comments:** See previous listing for recording information.

SESSIONS 7
MAJOR TOM (MT 159) CD-R
> Valleys Of Neptune - Hound Dog - Stoop Down Baby / Things I Used To Do / Midnight Train / Earth
> Blues / Jam Session / Rainbow Bridge Movie Promo / Blue Suede Shoes (Berkeley soundcheck) / Hey
> Baby (Berkeley soundcheck) / Earth Blues (Berkeley soundcheck) / If Six Was Nine / House Burning
> Down / Drifter's Escape / Earth Blues / Message To Love (8 takes)
> **Comments:** An assortment of live tracks and studio outtakes.

SESSIONS 8
MAJOR TOM (MT 160) CD-R

Freedom / Lover Man (2 takes) / Midnight Lightning / Bleeding Heart / Tax Free / Drifter's Escape - Come Down Hard On Me Baby - Midnight Lightning - In From The Storm - Night Bird Flying / Studio Catastrophe / Ezy Rider (outfake) / Dance On The Desert - Acoustic Medley / Beginning / Dance

Comments: Various outtakes, alternate mixes and jams.

SESSIONS 9
MAJOR TOM (MT 161) CD-R

Lover Man / Room Full Of Mirrors / Villanova Junction Blues / Midnight Lightning / Jimi - Jimmy Jam / Belly Button Window / Interview with John Burke / Stars That Play With Laughing Sam's Dice (outfake) / Them Changes (outfake) / Mannish Boy - Dooji Wooji Jam (put together by the bootlegger) / Send My Love To Linda - Live And Let Live / Message To Love / Angel / Izabella / Dolly Dagger

Comments: Another collection of outtakes, outfakes and jams.

SESSIONS 10
MAJOR TOM (MT 162) CD-R

Bright Lights, Big City / Foxy Lady / Hey Joe / Stone Free / Fire / Purple Haze / Gypsy Boy (New Rising Sun) / Drifting (2 takes) / Jam Session / Angel (2 takes) / Stone Free / Hey Joe / Purple Haze

Comments: More outtakes, radio broadcasts and jams.

SHINE ON EARTH, SHINE ON   IN *
SIDEWALK MUSIC (89010) 2CD

CD 1: Little Wing / Everything's Gonna Be Allright/ Tomorrow Never Knows

CD 2: Somewhere Over The Rainbow / Power Of Soul / Stone Free / Crash Landing / Drone Blues / Once I Had A Woman / Freedom / Stepping Stone

Comments: Double European CD. Disc one has most of the Cafe Au Go Go show from June 17, 1968, NYC. Disc two cuts are various outtakes, unused mixes and a couple of live tracks. Disc two has some necessary material, but the Cafe Au Go Go show is available more complete and in the right sequence on CAFE A GO GO - JAM SESSION or LIVE IN NEW YORK.

SHOKAN SUNRISE   IN ***
UNKNOWN LABEL CD

Izabella / Instrumental (Shokan Jam #1) / Beginnings, If 6 Was 9 / Shokan Sunrise (Shokan jam #2) / Izabella / Flute Instrumental (No Jimi here) / Jimi's March (The Dance) / African Instrumental (The Sundance) / Message Of Love / Beginnings / Jimi's March (Live Version)

Comments: Recorded at house that Jimi rented at Shokan, New York, August 1969. This is where the rehearsals for the newly formed Gypsy Sun And Rainbow Band took place for the upcoming performance at the Woodstock Festival. The sound quality is mediocre with a lot of hiss. The material is historically significant if not terribly inspired playing. The last track is from an audience tape from the performance at the Tinker Street Cinema on August 14, 1969. Listening to this combined with the Mike Ephron jams from roughly the same time frame you wonder what kind of mind set Jimi was in and where the energy for the legendary Woodstock performance came from.

SKY HIGH
SKY DOG RECORDS LP

Side 1: People People People / Sunshine Of Your Love

Side 2: Red House / I'm Gonna Leave This Town

Comments: Record Plant Studio, NYC 1970. Excellent stereo. European bootleg. Deluxe black & white cover. Jimi Hendrix, Johnny Winter (lead guitars) / Jimi Hendrix, Jim Morrison (vocals) / Mitch Mitchell, Jim Morrison (drums) / Noel Redding (bass). Also available as JAM (Berkeley 2029) & SKY HIGH (TMOQ 73031) & Kustom SP JH1.

SMASHING AMPS   IN
TRADE MARK OF QUALITY (TM OQ 71028) & (TMOQ 1813) LP

Side 1: Sunshine Of Your Love / Room Full Of Mirrors / Smashing Amps

Side 2: Bleeding Heart / Purple Haze, Waitin' For That Train, Wild Thing ("Hear My Music Talking" film soundtrack)

RIOTS IN BERKELEY

SHINE ON EARTH, SHINE ON

SHOKAN SUNRISE

SMASHING AMPS

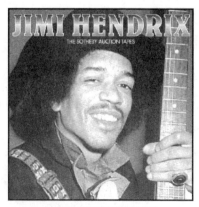

SOTHEBY AUCTION TAPES

STONE FREE

Comments: Same as on EXPERIENCE (Ember Records) unless otherwise noted. Very good mono. Mediocre material from the Royal Albert Hall show 24 Feb 69.

SOTHEBY AUCTION TAPES IN *
MIDNIGHT BEAT (MBCD 010) CD

Spanish Castle Magic / Have You Ever Been (To Electric Ladyland) / Wait Until Tomorrow / South Saturn Delta / Ain't No Telling / Little One (2) / One Rainy Wish / Castles Made Of Sand / Ain't No Telling / She's So Fine / Up From The Skies / Bold As Love / Burning Of The Midnight Lamp / Dream / Dance / Little Miss Lover / Can You Please Crawl Out Your Window / Little Miss Lover / May This Be Love

Comments: An acceptable package of some of the real Sothebys Auction Tapes padded out with other material that was not really part of those tapes. All essential material and this is a good way to pick it up.

A brief history of the Sothebys Auction Tapes: Jimi's former girlfriend, Kathy Etchingham, put eight reels of tape up for auction at Sothebys in London on December 22, 1981. These tapes were of Jimi's performances at some of the BBC sessions, assorted jams and "Axis: Bold As Love" rough mixes. The tapes sold for 1500 Pounds to American Bob Terry. Bob Terry reported the following songs were on the tapes: Radio One / Spanish Castle Magic / Day Tripper / Get Myself Together (Hear My Train A Comin') / Golden Rose (One Rainy Wish) / Call Out My Window (Can You Please Crawl Out Your Window) / Wait Until Tomorrow / Castles Made Of Sand / Little One (2 versions with Brian Jones) / See You Tomorrow (Ain't No Telling) / two instrumentals (Jazz Jimi Jazz & South Saturn Delta) / fucking around (Have You Ever Been To Electric Ladyland) / Playing Over James Brown / Bold As Love / Up From Skies (2 versions) / EXP. Other songs have been booted as Sothebys Tapes, but are from other sources.

SOTHEBY'S REELS IN
GOLD STANDARD (TOM-800) CD

EXP / Up From The Skies / Spanish Castle Magic / Wait Until Tomorrow / Ain't No Telling (2) / Little Wing (fake mix) / If Six Was Nine (fake mix) / You Got Me Floating / Castles Made Of Sand / She's So Fine / One Rainy Wish / Little Miss Lover / Bold As Love / 1983...A Merman I Should Turn To Be / Jam Session / Jam - Cherokee Mist / Ezy Rider Jam / Somewhere

Comments: Some of the real Sothebys Auction Tapes padded out with other material that was not really part of those tapes. This release is marred by a couple of outfakes and mastering way off speed.

SOTHEBY'S PRIVATE REELS IN *
JHR (003 / 004) 2CD

CD 1: Castles Made Of Sand #1 (2:48) / Spanish Castle Magic #1 (2:50) / Jam #1 (South Saturn Delta) (4:48) / Electric Ladyland #1 (5:04) / Wait Until Tomorrow #1 (3:24) / Ain't No Telling #1 (1:54) / Instrumental #1 (Little One)(3:35) / Instrumental #2 (Little One)(3:36) / All Along The Watchtower (3:48) / One Rainy Wish #1 (3:52) / She's So Fine (2:37) / Axis Bold As Love (3:31) / EXP (1:55) / Up From The Skies (2:55) / Calling All Devil's Children (Jazz Jimi Jazz)(12:52) / Electric Ladyland #2 (6:17)

CD 2: Jam #2 (South Saturn Delta)(4:30) / Electric Ladyland #3 (4:37) / Wait Until Tomorrow #2 (3:15) / Ain't No Telling #2 (1:46) / Instrumental #3 (Little One)(3:23) / Instrumental #4 (Little One)(3:25) / Castles Made Of Sand #2 (2:40) / Spanish Castle Magic #2 (2:40) / Jam #3 (12:26) / Electric Ladyland #4 (5:28) / One Rainy Wish #2 (3:40) / May This Be Love (3:16) / Fire (2:50) / Are You Experienced? (4:22) / Foxy Lady (3:27) / I Don't Live Today (4:02) / Radio One Jingle (1:07)

Comments: Boy this is a weird release and a 50% rip off. Disc one is pretty much all of the the actual Sotheby Auction Tapes. All of the material on disc two (with the exception of five tracks which are outfakes) are copies of the exact same tracks from disc one. Recommended only because the Sotheby's material is well collected here, not because it's any kind of a value.

SPANISH CASTLE MAGIC / FIRE / HEY JOE
UNKNOWN LABEL EP

Comments: From Konserthuset, Stockholm, (second show), January 9, 1969. Available as a picture disc and on black vinyl.

SPANISH CASTLE MAGIC
TOASTED (TRW 1952) 2LP
Side 1: Tax Free / Star Spangled Banner / Purple Haze
Side 2: Spanish Castle Magic / Red House
Side 3: Inst. / Foxy Lady / I Don't Live Today
Side 4: Voodoo Chile (slight return) / Sunshine of Your Love / Voodoo Chile (cont.)
Comments: Recorded live at the LA Forum, April 26, 1969. Excellent stereo. TMOQ labels.

SPICY ESSENCE - APARTMENT JAM 70
UNKNOWN LABEL CD
Jam I / Jam II / Room Full Of Mirrors / Astro Man - Valleys of Neptune / Jam III / Jam IV / Jam V
Comments: Recorded at Jimi's New York apartment (with Taj Mahal?) 1970. Good to very good sound.
European CD. Time 49:16.

STAR PORTRAIT
KEN (712/3) 2LP
Side 1: Voodoo Chile / Hey Joe / First Trial Of Star Spangled Banner
Side 2: Red House / Hey Joe / Who Knows / Purple Haze
Side 3: Cry One Stage / Only One Guitar / Born In Slums
Side 4: Old Man Curtis / Cross Electric Town
Comments: Obviously, the track titles for the songs on sides three and four were made up by the boot-
leggers. We do not know the correct titles for some of the cuts.

STAR SPANGLED BLUES (THE)
NEUTRAL ZONE (NZCD 89011) CD
Like A Rolling Stone (1) / Lover Man (1) / Hey Joe (1) / Fire (1) / Foxy Lady (1) / Purple Haze (1) /
Blue Suede Shoes (2) / Foxy Lady (3) / Blown Amp Blues (3) / Star Spangled Banner (3)
Comments: Record live at (1) Winterland, October 11th, 1968 (Second show with Herbie Rich from
Buddy Miles Band on organ - not on "Purple Haze") / (2) May 30th, 1970, Berkeley soundcheck / (3)
Winterland, October 12th, 1968 (First show). Excellent soundboard. Incomplete shows.

STAR SPANGLED BLUES IN
WAGGLE RECORDS (1935) 2LP
Side 1: Like A Rolling Stone / Rock Me Baby / Hey Joe
Side 2: Fire / Foxy Lady / Purple Haze / Blue Suede Shoes*
Side 3: Foxy Lady / Blown Amp Blues / Star Spangled Banner
Side 4: Ezy Rider / Hey Joe / Hey Baby / Lover Man
Comments: See above for recording information. Side 4: Berkeley Community Centre, May 30, 1970.
Excellent stereo. TMOQ labels.

STEREO EXPERIENCE
FIGA 1 LP
Comments: Same as EXPERIENCE (Ember Records).

STILL REIGNING, STILL ROCKING
GIANT (GSR 002) 2LP Box Set
Comments: This box set includes: PARIS IS SIR JAMESTOWN and LIVE FROM OTTAWA, postcard,
sticker, computer disc quiz, magazine and ad reprints for fanzines - "J.I.M.I." and "Univibes."

STONE FREE IN
SILVER RARITIES (SIRA 58 / 59) 2CD
CD 1: Lover Man / Stone Free / Gettin' My Heart Back Together Again / I Don't Live Today / Red house
/ Foxy Lady
CD 2: Sunshine Of Your Love / Slow Blues In C Sharp / Fire / Little Wing / Voodoo Chile / Jam / Purple
Haze / Wild Thing / Star Spangled Banner
Comments: Recorded live at the Royal Albert Hall, February 24, 1969. Complete performance. Good-
very good mono soundboard from more than one source with a bit of hiss. European CD. This is anoth-
er one of those shows that really deserves a complete official release. A very good show with a good
song line-up. A stereo soundboard has recently surfaced as ROYAL ALBERT HALL 1969 (Blimp 008/9) and

LISTEN TO THIS ERIC making this release obsolete. This show was also filmed and parts of it are available on bootleg video.

STUDIO EXPERIENCE IN
SODIUM HAZE MUSIC (SH 009) CD

Jam 1 (Drifting) / Jam 2 (Drifting) / Look Over Yonder / Send My Love To You (Send My Love To Linda) / Drifting / Belly Button Window / Freedom / Valley Of Neptune / Long Hot Summer Night / 1983/ Angel / Voodoo Chile / Come On / Gypsy Eyes

Comments: A very good sounding disc of recycled material mostly from the acoustic home composing tape from early 1968 with some studio outtakes.

STUDIO HAZE IN ***
INA6 (93-19171) CD

Takin' Care Of Business / Cryin, Blue Rain (Gypsy Blood) / Lover Man / There Ain't Nothin' Wrong (Little One) / Room Full Of Mirrors / Look Over Yonder / Sunshine Of Your Love / Shame, Shame, Shame / Cat Talkin' To Me / Freedom / Lover Man / Untitled Instrumental #1 (Valleys Of Neptune) / Untitled Instrumental #2 (Freedom) / Dolly Dagger / Bleeding Heart / Earth Blues / Ezy Ryder / Izabella / Ezy Ryder / Room Full Of Mirrors

Comments: A very important and first time release of some of the Chandler Tapes material along with a number of unused alternate mixes of other songs. Highly recommended. Very good to excellent with some hiss and a few incorrect titles. European CD. Time 72:42. Also released as INFLAME (JHCD 071) and OUTTAKES AND STUDIO SESSIONS (Genuine Pig TGP-CD-088), but avoid this one as the sound quality is inferior to the original release - and on vinyl as STUDIO HAZE (Nando-01), but edited. All of this has also been hacked up and released piecemeal on many other discs.

A brief history of the Chandler Tapes: It was reported in a British music magazine ("Sounds") in 1988 that Chas Chandler uncovered in a storage space three boxes of tapes containing over 60 songs by Hendrix. These included working tracks, jams, alternate versions and many of the original multi-tracks of those songs. It was also reported that Mitch Mitchell and Noel Redding were called in to add overdubs to a number of these tracks. This has been confirmed by Belmo in his interview with Noel. The tapes are now in the possession of Chandler's widow and negotiations are underway to have them released. Happily, we can listen to some of the original 'lost songs' on this bootleg until these tracks are finally released officially.

STUDIO RECORDINGS 1967 - 68
KISS THE SKY (00016) CD

Purple Haze (experimental mix) / Red House (four takes) / La Pouppee Qui Fait No (cover version) / I Don't Live Today (four takes) / Fire (instrumental) / The Wind Cries Mary (instrumental) / Takin' Care Of Business (complete with horns) / Cryin' Blue Rain (slow blues) / Lover Man (alternative version) / There Ain't Nothing Wrong (Noel Redding vocal) / Room Full Of Mirrors (alternative version) / Look Over Yonder (alternative version) / Sunshine Of Your Love (studio version) / Shame Shame Shame (alternative version) / Cat Talkin' To Me (Mitch Mitchell vocals)

Comments: Studio outtakes. Tracks 1-6 from 1967. Tracks 7-15 from 1968. Excellent soundboard. European CD. Time 70:36. Also available as STUDIO RECORDINGS 1967-68 (Cuma) and DE LANE LEA DEMOS AND OLYMPIC OUTS (Cuma).

SUPERCONCERT 1968 IN **
FIRE POWER (FP-03) CD

Killin' Floor / Tax Free / Fire / Red House / Foxy Lady / Hey Joe / Spanish Castle Magic / Purple Haze / Wild Thing

Comments: Recorded live at the Capitol Theatre, Ottawa, Canada, March 19, 1968. This is the second show and is from the soundboard tape. This is a widely bootlegged show with this disc providing the most complete version of it. "Wild Thing" is cut off on the tape (the tape probably ran out before the end of the show) and only the intro survived - which is not included on all other releases.

SWEET ANGEL IN
WORLD PRODUCTION (WPOCD CD 0589 D022-2) CD

Stone Free (2:26) / Hey Joe (3:56) / Purple Haze (3:09) / Catfish (7:54) / Foxy Lady (3:19) / Purple Haze (5:06) / Voodoo Chile (3:34) / Hey Joe (2:38) / Sunshine Of Your Love (1:17) / Angel (3:08) / Like

STUDIO HAZE

SUPERCONCERT 1968

SYMPHONY OF EXPERIENCE

TALENT & FEELING VOL. 2

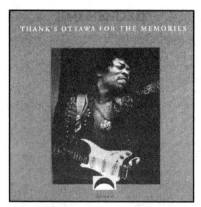

THANKS OTTAWA FOR THE MEMORIES

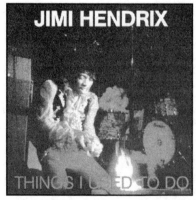

THINGS I USED TO DO

A Rolling Stone(3:06)
Comments: Tracks 1-3 are from the Bremen Beat Club, May 18, 1967. Tracks 4-6 live in Bussum, Vitus Studios, November 10, 1967. Tracks 7-9 are from the "Lulu Show," January 4, 1968. Tracks 10-11 are from rehearsals in NYC, December 1968. Tracks 1-3 are very good stereo. Tracks 4-6 are very good mono. Tracks 7-9 are good stereo. Tracks 10-11 are excellent stereo. Time 41:06.

SYMPHONY OF EXPERIENCE IN
THIRD STONE DISCS (TSD-24966) CD
Hey Joe / Purple Haze / Are You Experienced / She's So Fine / Little Miss Lover / Drivin' South / Instrumental Jam, Ain't Too Proud To Beg / Can You Please Crawl Out your Window? / Drivin' South / Wait Until Tomorrow / Castles Made Of Sand / Spanish Castle Magic / Bold As Love / Getting My Heart Back Together Again / Dream / Dance / Drivin' South, Sergeant Pepper's Lonely Hearts Club Band / All Along The Watchtower / Little One / Little One
Comments: A good sounding disc of studio outtakes, BBC material and a couple of fake tracks. The only different stuff here (and it's pretty marginal) are the backwards recordings of "Are You Experienced?" and "Castles Made Of Sand" so you can hear the backwards guitar solos played forward. The version of "Ain't Too Proud To Beg" is complete.

TALENT & FEELING VOL. 1 IN
EXTREMELY RARE (EXR 17) CD
Ezy Rider / Message To Love / Things I Used To Do / Lover Man / Midnight Lightning / Night Bird Flying - Ships Passing In The Night / Lover Man / Peace In Mississippi / Lord I Sing The Blues For Me And You / Lover Man / Jam Session (Jam With Horns And Piano) / Peace In Mississippi / Little Drummer Boy
Comments: A very good to excellent disc of material slightly less common than on Volume 2 on the same label.

TALENT & FEELING VOL. 2 IN
EXTREMELY RARE (EXR 22) CD
Trying To Be (Stepping Stone) / Crash Landing / Drifter's Escape / Power Of Soul / Highway Of Broken Hearts Medley / Captain Coconut (Jam - Cherokee Mist) / Crash Landing / Somewhere Over The Rainbow (Somewhere) / Lover Man / Message To Love / Cherokee Mist / Instrumental Jam (Hollywood Jam)
Comments: A very good to excellent sounding disc with miscellaneous studio jams, outtakes and unused mixes. As usual the "Highway Of Broken Hearts Medley" and "Jam - Cherokee Mist" jam are incomplete. This was released a year prior to VOLUME 1 on the same label.

T'ANKS FOR THE MAMARIES
TRADEMARK OF QUALITY/AMAZING KORNYPHONE (BOZO 1) LP
Little Drummer Boy - Silent Night - Auld Lang Syne
Comments: This record is a 'various artists' bootleg and includes tracks by other groups as well.

TEN YEARS AFTER
RECORD MAN/WEIRD SOUNDS (RM 911) LP
Side 1: Purple Haze / Wild Thing / Voodoo Chile / Hey Joe / Sunshine Of Your Love / Drivin' South
Side 2: Day Tripper / Experiencing The Blues / Hound Dog / Little Miss Lover / Lover Or Confusion / Foxy Lady / Stone Free
Comments: Various BBC cuts. See BROADCASTS for recording information. Very good mono with some crackles.

THANKS OTTAWA FOR THE MEMORIES IN *
LUNA RECORDS (LU 9319) CD
Intro, Killin' Floor / Tax Free / Fire / Red House / Foxy Lady / Hey Joe / Spanish Castle Magic / Purple Haze / Hound Dog (acoustic)* / Hey Joe* / Purple Haze* / Hear My Train A Comin' (acoustic)**
Comments: Recorded live in Ottawa, Canada, March 19, 1968 and is missing the "Wild Thing" intro after "Purple Haze". * Marquee Club TV broadcast. ** Outtake from Bruce Fleming's photo studio without the false start.

THEIR LEGENDS LIVE ON
JAAR (83425) Vinyl single
  Day Tripper (BBC) / Claudine (The Rolling Stones)

THINGS I USED TO DO (THE)   IN
GOLDEN MEMORIES (GM 890738) CD
  The Things I Used To Do / Three Little Bears / Gypsy Eyes / Who Knows / Who Knows / Message To
  Love / Message To Love / Izabella / I Don't Live today
  Comments: Very good-excellent stereo & mono. European CD. Common studio outtakes, unused
  mixes, and rehearsals.

THIS FLYER
(No label) LP
  Side 1: Jam
  Side 2: Jam / Jam / Madagascar
  Comments: This was the very first Jimi Hendrix bootleg. 4000 copies were pressed - 3000 sold in the
  U.S. and 1000 in England. The material is from the truly awful Mike Ephron Tapes. The jams are also
  known as "Gypsy Boy/ New Rising Sun", "Free Thunder", "Swift Wing","Down Mean Blues", "Fried
  Cola", "Feels Good", "Monday Morning Blues", "Lift Off" and "Madagascar". Most of these are hor-
  ribly edited. See also HOME AT WOODSTOCK, IN EXPERIENCE, and JIMI HENDRIX AT HIS BEST
  VOL. 1-3.

THIS GUITAR ON FIRE
BLACK SUN MUSIC (BSM 001) CD
  Hear My Train A Comin' (9:30) / Fire (6:12) / Spanish Castle Magic (5:20) / Red House (11:39) / I
  Don't Live Today (6:43) / Foxy Lady (3:23) / Purple Haze (3:43) / Voodoo Chile (15:30) / Room Full
  Of Mirrors (2:24) / Sunshine Of Your Love (4:33)
  Comments: Recorded live at the San Jose Pop Festival, March 15, 1969. Good audience tape. European
  CD. Also available as FLAMING GUITAR (Rock Calendar RC 2108) and best on HISTORIC CONCERT VOL
  2 (Midnight Beat MBCD 050)

THIS ONE'S FOR YOU   IN
VMI EZY RYDERS LP
  Side 1: Lover Man / Jam With Horns And Piano / Peace In Mississippi / Little Drummer Boy (Auld
  Lang Syne) / Jam? (Calling All Devil's Children and Jungle)
  Side 2: Ezy Rider / Message To Love / The Things We Used To Do / Lover Man / Jam and Keep On
  Groovin' (Midnight Lightning)
  Comments: I like the sub-title on the label: "Peace In Miss-A-Hippie". Clever huh? Excellent stereo.
  Deluxe color cover - folder type cover. Song listings on labels are incorrect. Ordinary stuff.

TOMORROW...OR JUST THE END OF TIME   IN **
BATZ (0028) CD
  Tomorrow or Just The End Of Time (aka Stone Free) / Love Or Confusion / Foxy Lady / Hey Joe /
  Purple Haze / Hey Joe / Purple Haze / Foxy Lady* / Hey Joe* / Stone Free* / Fire* / Purple Haze* /
  Killing Floor / Fire / Purple Haze
  Comments: The first four and last three tracks are from the commercial BBC release ('Saturday Club,
  Feb. 13, 1967, & Saturday Club March 28, 1967). Tracks five and six are from Jimi's appearance on
  'Beat Club' (March 2, 1967). Unfortunately, these are mismastered as one channel only. The reason for
  buying this disc is for the 'Twenclub' recordings (*) from Hamburg (March 18, 1967). The sound qual-
  ity is excellent.

TTG STUDIOS ???   IN
WHO AM I? (WAI 015) CD
  I'm A Man / Drifter's Escape (Help Me In My Weakness) / Instrumental (Lord I Sing The Blues) / Lover
  Man / Freedom [Outfake] / Drifting / Instrumental #2 (Little Miss Strange) / I See Fingers...
  (Somewhere) / Calling All Devil's Children (My Friend) / Organ Jazz Solo (Rainy Day Shuffle) / Let
  The Sun Take A Holiday - Rainy Day Rain All Day (Rainy Day Shuffle - Rainy Day Dream Away) /
  Gypsy Eyes / Three Little Bears / Tax Free / Instrumental (Ezy Rider Instrumental Jam) / Instrumental
  (Rock And Roll Jam) / Valley Of Neptune (take1) / (1983...A Merman I should Turn To Be) / Valley Of

Neptune (take 2) (1983...A Merman I should Turn To Be)

Comments: Studio outtakes from 1968-70. Poor to good sound here and nothing you can't find better on other releases.

TURN 'ER ON
APEJH-818169 LP

Side 1: In From The Storm / Johnny B. Goode / Hey Joe / Purple Haze / Machine Gun

Side 2: Hear My Train A Comin' / Wild Thing / Like A Rolling Stone / Red House

TV SESSIONS
MAJOR TOM (MT 035) CD-R

Shotgun / Hey Joe / Manic Depression / Foxy Lady / Hey Joe / Wild Thing / Interview: Dick Cavett / Hear My Train A Comin' / Introduction: Dick Cavett / Izabella / Machine Gun / Interview: Dick Cavett / Purple Haze / Purple Haze / Purple Haze / The Burning Of The Midnight Lamp / The Wind Cries Mary

Comments: A collection of Jimi's television appearances.

TWO DAYS AT NEWPORT   IN **
JMH (007 / 2) 2CD

CD 1: Stone Free (4:05) / Drum Solo (2:00) / Are You Experienced (6:25) / Stone Free (1:50) / Sunshine Of Your Love (6:00) / Fire (3:10) / Hear My Train A Comin (14:00) / Like A Rolling Stone (5:04) / Voodoo Child (Slight Return) (5:15) / Drum Solo (2:52) / Purple Haze (3:51) / Red House (7:10) / Foxy Lady (4:30)

CD 2: Power Of Soul, Jam Improvisation (2:20) / Hear My Train A Comin' (9:39) / Voodoo Child (slight return), Rock 'N' Roll Jam (10:42) / Come On (4:59) / Star Spangled Banner (5:31) / We Gotta Live Together (18:31) / The Things We Used To Do (2:43) / Keep On Movin' (Midnight Lightning) (11:45)* / The Sweet Things (Destructive Love, Jimi only produced this track) (5:17)*

Comments: Recorded live at the Newport Pop Festival. CD1 June 20, CD2 June 22, 1969 with Buddy Miles Express. *Record Plant Studios, November 14, 1969, with Buddy Miles Express. Excellent soundboard. A very good place to get both of these shows as one package.

TWO SIDES OF THE SAME GENIUS   IN
AMAZING KORNYPHONE (TAKRL H-6770) LP

Side 1: The Wind Cries Mary / Foxy Lady / Fire / Sgt. Pepper's Lonely Hearts Club Band / Hey Joe / I Don't Live Today / The Burning Of The Midnight Lamp / Purple Haze

Side 2: Astro Man - Valleys Of Neptune / Power Of Soul / Room Full Of Mirrors / Country Blues

Comments: Side one recorded live September 5, 1967. Radiohuset, Stockholm, Sweden. Side 2 from Sept. 1969 (?) or January 1970 at Jimi's New York apartment.

ULTIMATE BBC COLLECTION 1967 (THE)
CLASSICAL (CL 006) CD

Hey Joe (4:01) / Foxy Lady (2:45) / Stone Free (3:26) / Love Or Confusion (2:55) / Purple Haze (3:04) / Killin' Floor (2:27) / Fire (2:33) / The Wind Cries Mary (3:05) / Wild Thing (1:51) / Burning Of The Midnight Lamp (3:41) / Jam #1 (3:20) / Jam #2 (5:02) / Little Miss Lover (2:55) / Drivin' South (4:48) / Experiencing The Blues (5:27) / Hound Dog (2:43) / All Along The Watchtower (3:57) / Can You Please Crawl Out Your Window (3:25) / Spanish Castle Magic (3:12) / Day Tripper (3:14) / Getting My Heart Back Together (4:57) / Wait Until Tomorrow (3:04)

Comments: Recorded for the BBC 1967. Excellent soundboard. European CD. Made obsolete by the CR with the exception of the unedited "Ain't Too Proud To Beg" and "Can You Please Crawl Out Your Window".

ULTIMATE LIVE COLLECTION!
THE BEAT GOES ON (BGO BX 9307-4) 5CD Box Set

CD 1: Hear My Train A Comin' / Killin' Floor / Hey Joe / Are You Experienced / Like A Rolling Stone / Lover Man / Hey Joe / Fire

CD 2: Foxy Lady / Little Wing / Star Spangled Banner / Purple Haze / Earth Versus Space - Midnight Lightning - Gypsy Eyes - Machine Gun / Power Of Soul / Lover Man / Hear My Train A Comin' / Them Changes / Hey Joe / Purple Haze / Wild Thing

CD 3: Message To Love / Hear My Train A Comin' / Red House / Beginning / Izabella / Fire / Voodoo Chile (slight return) - Stepping Stone

THIS GUITAR'S ON FIRE

THIS ONE'S FOR YOU

TOMORROW...OR JUST THE END OF TIME

TTG STUDIOS ???

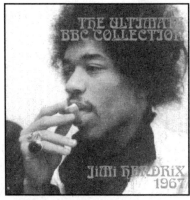

THE ULTIMATE BBC COLLECTION

UNSURPASSED STUDIO TAKES

CD 4: Star Spangled Banner / Purple Haze / Villanova Junction / Hey Joe

CD 5: Fire / Johnny B. Goode / Hear My Train A Comin' / Foxy Lady / Machine Gun / Red House / Message To Love / Ezy Rider / Voodoo Chile (slight return)

Comments: A very good sounding "best of" collection of material from Winterland, Fillmore East, Woodstock and Berkeley. Nice but I prefer finding the complete shows on other releases.

ULTRA RARE TRAX
GENUINE PIG (TGP-CD-090) CD

Intro By Jimi (0:03) / Midnight Lightning (4:02) / Voodoo Chile (8:57) / Rainy Day Try Out (1:33) / Red House (6:55) / Bleeding Heart (3:39) / Blue Window Jam (8:23) / Villanova Junction Blues (Lonely Avenue Jam Part 2) (3:55) / Funky Blues Jam (Strato Strut)(1:46) / Once I Had A Woman (5:17) / Police Blues (Blue Suede Shoes)(11:13) / Country Blues (6:40) / Freedom Jam (Freedom Ezy Rider...Jam (8:27) / Acoustic Medley (3:23)

Comments: Good to very good sound. A direct copy of FREAKOUT BLUES.

UNFORGETABLE EXPERIENCE IN
UNKNOWN LABEL LP

Side 1: I Don't Live Today (1) (5:14) / Hey Joe (2) (3:33) / Purple Haze (2) (2:52) / The Wind Cries Mary (3) (3:19) / Foxy Lady (4) (5:28)

Side 2: Red House (4) (11:25) / Hear My Train A Comin' (4) (9:40)

Comments: (1) Soundboard recording, April 26, 1969. (2) Marquee Club, March 2 , 1967. (3) Stockholm, April 24,1967. (4) Soundboard recording from Royal Albert Hall, February 24, 1969. Excellent stereo.

UNKNOWN WELLKNOWN
JH 6146 LP

Side 1: Star Spangled Banner - Purple Haze - Instrumental Solo (Woodstock)

Side 2: Hear My Train A Comin' (London 1967) / Day Tripper (Top Gear 1967) / Hound Dog (Royal Albert Hall rehearsal Feb 24 , 1969)

Comments: A copy of LAST AMERICAN CONCERT. Excellent mono.

UNSURPASSED STUDIO TAKES IN **
YELLOW DOG (YD 050) CD

Hey Joe (3:06) / Lover Man (3:11) / All Along The Watchtower (3:59) / Three Little Bears (12:37) / Indian Song (Cherokee Mist) (7:09) / Trying To Be (Stepping Stone) (7:21) / Crosstown Traffic (2:28) / Message To Love (7:43) / Crash Landing (4:25) / Somewhere Over The Rainbow (3:23) / Double Guitars (Bleeding Heart)(3:23) / Astro Man Jam (11:26)

Comments: An excellent stereo disc of studio outtakes and jams every collection needs. Experienced collectors probably have all of this material but for new collectors this is a fairly easy disc to find.

UP AGAINST THE BERLIN WALL IN
MIDNIGHT BEAT (MBCD 046) CD

Fire / Hey Joe / Spanish Castle Magic / Foxy Lady / Red House / Come On (Part 1) / Sunshine Of Your Love / Purple Haze

Comments: A typical audience tape with up front guitar and vocals, bass and drums less audible. Recorded live at the Sportpalast in Berlin, West Germany, January 23, 1969. Nice to have for completists but not really necessary for casual collectors.

VALLEY OF NEPTUNE IN
PC 28355 CD

Hey Joe / Red House / Voodoo Chile (slight return) / Machine Gun / The Wind Cries Mary / Foxy / Fire / Experiencing The Blues / Like A Rolling Stone / Purple Haze / Killin' Floor / Hear My Train A Comin' / Stop / Sunshine Of Your Love

Comments: Excellent sounding CD of live material from soundboards. Most of this is available commercially. Pass on it.

VARIOUS ARTISTS: ISLE OF WIGHT
WESTCOAST (WCR 001-S) LP

God Save The Queen / Sergeant Pepper's Lonely Hearts Club Band / Spanish Castle Magic

Comments: The first three songs by Jimi are from the August 30, 1970, Isle of Wight Festival.

VERY BEST (THE)
IREC/RETRO MILLENIUM (MILCD-03) CD

Purple Haze / Voodoo Chile (slight return) / Sunshine Of Your Love / Experiencing The Blues / Killin' Floor / Can You Please Crawl Out Your Window / Hey Joe / The Burning Of The Midnight Lamp / Fire / Tax Free / Sergeant Pepper's Lonely Hearts Club Band / Drivin' South / Little Wing / Little Miss Lover / Wild Thing / Spanish Castle Magic / Star Spangled Banner / The Wind Cries Mary / Foxy Lady

Comments: An odds and ends collection of songs from the BBC, Paris, Stockholm and Los Angeles 1969.

VOICE OF EXPERIENCE IN
RHINOZEROUS (RHP 789) CD

Room Full Of Mirrors / Gloria / Come Down Hard On Me Baby / Like A Rolling Stone / One Rainy Wish / Come On (Part 1) / Bleeding Heart / Freedom / Further On Up The Road / Astro Man Jam / Blue Suede Shoes / Little One (2) / Angel

Comments: Excellent sounding disc of common and commercially released material.

VOLUME 2: A MAN OF OUR TIME
NAPOLEON (NLP 11018) LP

Side 1: Highway Chile (cv) / Stone Free / Hound Dog / Foxy Lady / Purple Haze

Side 2: Little Miss Lover / Experiencing The Blues / Sunshine Of Your Love

Comments: "Highway Chile" is from SMASH HITS. See BROADCASTS for recording information on remainder.

VOODOO BLUES IN
SMURF 2CD

CD 1: Voodoo Chile (slight return) / Come On (Part1) / Gypsy Eyes / Long Hot Summer Night (2) / 1983...A Merman I Should Turn To Be / Voodoo Chile - Cherokee Mist - Gypsy Eyes

CD 2: Angel / 1983...A Merman I Should Turn To Be / One Rainy Wish / Earth Blues / Look Over Yonder / Room Full Of Mirrors / Drone Blues / It's Too Bad (Voodoo Blues)

Comments: Yet another release with the early 1968 home composing tape filled out with common studio outtakes. Much of this disc was lifted from the CR LIFELINES.

VOODOO IN LADYLAND IN
MUM (MUCD 006) CD

Hey Joe / Crosstown Traffic / Voodoo Chile (slight return) / House Burning Down / All Along The Watchtower / Room Full Of Mirrors (2 versions) / Tax Free / Come On (Part 1) / Gypsy Eyes / Little One / Taking Care Of No Business / Like A Rolling Stone / Ezy Ryder / Cat Talkin' To Me / Freedom / Calling All Devil's Children / (Have You Ever Been To) Electric Ladyland / 1983...(A Merman I Should Turn To Be)

Comments: Another nice sounding odds and ends collection of previously booted material from MUM Records.

VOODOO SESSIONS IN ***
VC 2568 CD

Voodoo Chile (slight return): Takes 1-20 / Voodoo Chile: Takes 1-5 & 8

Comments: An excellent sounding that provides all of the available sessions for "Voodoo Chile (slight return)" (also found on BLACK GOLD) and "Voodoo Chile". An outstanding disc and highly recommended. Of course, since its release, bits and pieces have shown up on other releases, but this is the only place to get it all on one disc.

WARM HELLO OF THE SUN (THE) IN *
UNKNOWN LABEL 2CD

CD 1: Spanish Castle Magic / Killin' Floor / Getting My Heart Back Together Again / Message To Love / Hey Baby, The Land Of The New Rising Sun / In From The Storm

CD 2: Hey Joe / Foxy Lady / Red House / Room Full Of Mirrors / Straight Ahead / Purple Haze / Voodoo Chile (slight return)

Comments: Recorded live at the Stora Scenen, Liseberg, Goteborg, Sweden, September 1, 1970. Good audience tape. Japanese CD. Time CD 1: 45:52, CD 2: 46:02. Recommended because it's the only place to get this complete show.

WELCOME TO THE ELECTRIC CIRCUS IN **
MIDNIGHT BEAT (MB CD 016) CD

Fire / Foxy Lady / Tax Free / Spanish Castle Magic / Red House / Sunshine Of Your Love / I Don't Live Today, Star Spangled Banner / Purple Haze

Comments: Recorded live at the Falkoner Centret, Copenhagen, Denmark, January 10, 1969. Good-very good audience recording of the complete show. Picture CD. This is a very good show and a nice performance as well.

WELCOME TO THE ELECTRIC CIRCUS VOL. 2 IN *
MIDNIGHT BEAT (MB CD 018) CD

Freedom / Message To Love / Land Of The Rising Sun, Drum Solo / Hey Baby / All Along The Watchtower / Ezy Rider / Red House / In From The Storm / Purple Haze / Voodoo Chile (slight return) / Hey Joe / Fire

Comments: Tracks 1-3 are live from Vejiby Risskov Hallen, Arhus, Denmark, September 2, 1970. Tracks 4-12 are live from The KB Hallen, Copenhagen, Denmark, September 3, 1970. Good audience recordings. Picture CD. The K.B. Hallen show is unfortunately incomplete missing five songs from that evening's lineup. Recommended for it's ease of acquisition of the material it does offer.

WIGHT IN ***
JMH (006 / 2) 2CD

CD 1: The Queen (Traditional) (2:40) / Sgt. Pepper's Lonely Hearts Club Band (1:50) / Spanish Castle Magic (4:38) / All Along The Watchtower (5:00) / Machine Gun (22:11) / Lover Man (3:10) / Freedom (4:24) / Red House (11:33) / Dolly Dagger (6:00) / Midnight Lightning (6:50)

CD 2: Foxy Lady (9:07) / Message To Love (6:10) / Hey Baby (New Sun Rising) (7:24) / Ezy Rider (3:59) / Hey Joe (3:25) / Purple Haze (8:23) / Voodoo Child (7:43) / In From the Storm (6:12) / Bonus Outtakes: Trying To Be A Jam (7:39) / Lover Man (5:15) / Message To Love (3:29) / Freedom (4:07)

Comments: Recorded live at The Isle Of Wight Pop Festival (East Afton Farm), August 30, 1970. Complete and excellent soundboard from a variety of sources. This is one of the only releases that features the complete version of "Machine Gun". European CD. Picture CDs. Recommended.

WILD MAN OF POP PLAYS, VOL. 1 IN **
PYRAMID (RFT CD 003) CD Time: 49:02

Sgt. Pepper's Lonely Hearts Club Band / The Wind Cries Mary / Foxy Lady / Fire / Hey Joe / I Don't Live Today / Burning Of The Midnight Lamp / Purple Haze / Introduced By An Unknown Lady / Stone Free / Hey Joe / Purple Haze / The Wind Cries Mary / Purple Haze

Comments: Tracks 1-8 are live at 'The Radiohuset', Stockholm, Sweden, September 5, 1967. Tracks 9-12 are live in Germany 1967 at 'Beat Beat Beat' TV show, May 18, 1967. Tracks 13-14 are from the Swedish TV show 'Popside', May 24, 1967. Excellent mono. Along with Volume 2, this is a recommended package of several early broadcast performances by The Experience. Also available on Black Panther (BP-068) CD and on vinyl from Pyramid.

WILD MAN OF POP PLAYS, VOL. 2 IN **
PYRAMID (RFT CD 004) CD Time: 67:44

Introduced By Rosalie Peters / Catfish Blues / Foxy Lady / Purple Haze / Purple Haze / Wild Thing / Introduced By Alexis Korner / Hear My Train A'Comin' / Foxy Lady / The Wind Cries Mary / Rock Me Baby / Red House / Purple Haze / Wild Thing

Comments: Tracks 1-4 are live in Holland, recorded at the Vitus Studio, Bussum, November 10, 1967, for the Dutch TV show HOEPLA. Tracks 5-6 are live at the 'Opera House', Blackpool, England, November 25, 1967. Tracks 7-8 were recorded at the Bruce Fleming Photo Studio, London, England, December 19, 1967. Tracks 9-14 were recorded at L'Olympia, Paris, France, October 9, 1967. Tracks 5-6 are very good mono - rest excellent mono. Along with Volume 2, this is a recommended package of several early broadcast performances by The Experience. This includes Jimi's false start so we get to hear "My Train A Coming" with Alexis Korner's voiceover intro not found on most other releases. The false start without voiceover is only available on the video "A Film About Jimi Hendrix". Also available on Black Panther (BP-071) CD and on vinyl from Pyramid.

VOODOO IN LADYLAND

THE VOODOO SESSIONS

WELCOME TO THE ELECTRIC CIRCUS

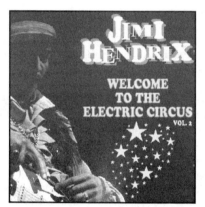

WELCOME TO THE ELECTRIC VOL. 2

WILD MAN OF POP PLAYS, VOL. 1

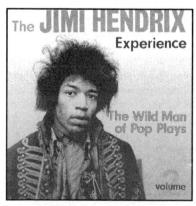

WILD MAN OF POP PLAYS, VOL. 2

WINK OF AN EYE
79-108/109 LP
Side 1: Killin' Floor / Spanish Castle Magic / Foxy Lady / Room Full Of Mirrors
Side 2: All Along The Watchtower / Hey Joe / Land Of The New Rising Sun / Message To Love
Comments: Recorded live at the Isle of Fehmarn, September 6, 1970. Jimi's last concert. Also available as WINK OF AN EYE (HEN 5000 C/D) & (Loma M-105) LP. Very good mono. Title taken from Jimi's last poem.

WINK OF AN EYE (THE) IN **
WHOOPY CAT (WKP 0033/34) 2CD Time CD 1: 75:14, CD 2: 77:24.
CD 1: Tax Free / Getting My Heart Back Together / Fire / Spanish Castle Magic / Red House / Foxy Lady / Star Spangled Banner / Purple Haze / Spanish Castle Magic
CD 2: Killin' Floor / Spanish Castle Magic / All Along The Watchtower / Hey Joe / Land Of The Rising Sun / Message To Love / Foxy Lady / Red House / Ezy Rider / Freedom / Roomful Of Mirrors / Purple Haze / Voodoo Child (slight return)
Comments: CD1 tracks 1-8 were recorded live at the Denver Pop Festival, Mile High Stadium, June 29 1969. CD1 track 9 is from Madison Square Garden, May 18, 1969. CD2 is from the Love And Peace Festival, Isle Of Fehmarn, September 6, 1970. Poor to good sound quality audience tapes. The last concert by The Experience and the last concert by Jimi prior to his death together in the same package. Recommended mostly for the historical importance of these tapes not because of great performances of sound quality.

WINTERLAND VOL. 1 IN ***
WHOOPY CAT (WKP-0025/26) 2CD Time CD 1: 58:44 CD2 69:55
CD 1: Are You Experienced / Voodoo Child (slight return) / Red House / Foxy Lady / Like A Rolling Stone / Star Spangled Banner / Purple Haze
CD 2: Tax Free / Lover Man / Sunshine Of Your Love / Killin' Floor / Hey Joe / Star Spangled Banner / Purple Haze
Comments: Recorded live at Winterland, San Francisco, October 10, 1968. Disc One is from the first show and Disc Two from the second show. This along with volumes 2 and 3 are from very good to excellent mono soundboard tapes. The tapes suffer from occasional dropouts or edits and a bit of hiss but not so much as to dull the thrill from listening to these performances. This is a mature and not yet burned out Experience giving their all at a marathon 3 day / 2 shows a day venue at a classic San Francisco theatre. Fabulous material and fabulous performances with a few guest artists (Herbie Rich, Virgil Gonsales, and Jack Casady) which were all mixed out of commercial releases. You can almost get a contact buzz listening to these discs. Highly recommended. Although bits and pieces have been commercially released over the years, we can only hope that the complete stereo tapes get released someday.

WINTERLAND VOL. 2
Whoopy Cat (WKP-0027/28) 2CD Time: CD1 72:11 CD2 67:54
CD 1: Are You Experienced / Voodoo Chile (slight return) / Red House / Sergeant Pepper's Lonely Hearts Club Band / Fire / The Wind Cries Mary / Foxy Lady / I Don't Live Today / Hey Joe / Can You Please Crawl Out Your Window / Manic Depression / Like A Rolling Stone / Purple Haze
CD 2: Tax Free / Spanish Castle Magic / Like A Rolling Stone / Lover Man / Hey Joe / Fire / Foxy Lady / Purple Haze
Comments: CD 1: First three songs recorded live at Winterland, San Francisco, October 11, 1968 (First show). Rest from Opera House, Chicago, February 25, 1968. CD 2: Winterland, San Francisco, October 11, 1968 (Second show). See comments for Volume 1. Only the first three tracks from the first show are available because of tape equipment problems during the performance.

WINTERLAND VOL. 3 IN ***
WHOOPY CAT (WKP-0029/30) 2CD Time: CD1 63:04 CD2 68:47
CD 1: Fire / Lover Man / Like A Rolling Stone / Foxy Lady / Jam / Tax Free / Hey Joe / Purple Haze / Wild Thing
CD 2: Foxy Lady / Manic Depression / Sunshine Of Your Love / Little Wing / Spanish Castle Magic / Red House / Voodoo Child (slight return) / This Is America / Purple Haze

Comments: Recorded live at the Winterland, San Francisco, October 12, 1968. Disc One is from the first show and Disc Two is from the second show. See comments for Volume 1.

WINTERLAND DAYS (THE)   IN ***
MANIC DEPRESSION (MDCD 001) 2CD Time CD 1: 59:07 CD 2: 66:29

CD 1: Voodoo Child / Red House / Sunshine Of Your Love / Hear My Train A Comin' / Hey Joe / Star Spangled Banner, Purple Haze

CD 2: Are You Experienced / Spanish Castle Magic / Fire / Foxy Lady / Lover Man / Like A Rolling Stone / Redding - Mitchell Jam & Tax Free / Little Wing

Comments: Recorded live at the Winterland, San Francisco. CD 1: October 10. CD 2: tracks 1-4 October 11. **CD 2:** tracks 5-8 October 12. Very good-excellent mono. Soundboard. European CD. Also available as a 3LP set from same company. Basically a "best of" collection from the Winterland shows. Highly recommended if you just don't think you need all six shows.

WIZARD'S VISION
WORLD PRODUCTION (WPOCM 0789D026 - 2) CD

Fire (3:30) / Hear My Train A Comin' (5:44) / Red House (7:03) / Stone Free (6:34) / Are You Experienced, Stone Free Again (7:13) / Sunshine Of Your Love (5:31) / Foxy Lady (4:37) / Like A Rolling Stone (5:10) / Voodoo Chile (8:01) / Purple Haze (3:48)

Comments: Recorded live at the Newport Pop Festival, June 20, 1969.

WOKE UP THIS MORNING AND FOUND MYSELF DEAD
RED LIGHTNING (RL 0015) LP

Side 1: Red House / Woke Up This Morning / Bleeding Heart

Side 2: Morrison's Lament / Tomorrow Never Knows / Uranus Rock / Outside Woman Blues / Sunshine Of Your Love

Comments: Recorded live at 'The Scene' Club, New York, 1968. Excellent mono. Picture disc. See HIGH, LIVE 'N' DIRTY for actual track titles and information.

WOKE UP THIS MORNING AND FOUND MYSELF DEAD   IN *
RED LIGHTING (RL CD 0068) CD Time 53:47

Red House / Wake Up This Morning & You Find Yourself Dead / Bleeding Heart / Morrison's Lament / Tomorrow Never Knows / Uranus Rock / Outside Woman Blues / Sunshine Of Your Love

Comments: An excellent stereo soundboard recorded live at The Scene Club in New York City sometime in March 1968 with Jim Morrison, members of The McCoys & Buddy Miles. It's really too bad that Jim Morrison had to be such an ass - shouting profanities during this club jam - because there is some enjoyable music going on here. Recommended as a historical recording. Referred as CR in the Song Index as it can be considered a 'semi-legal' release. Toss a coin.

WOODSTOCK MONDAY, AUGUST 18, 1969, 8:AM   IN ***
JMH (008/2) 2CD

CD 1: Introduction (2:10) / Message To Love (4:00) / Hear My Train A Comin'(9:15) / Red House (5:40) / Call Me Mastermind (3:27) / Lover Man (5:37) / Foxy Lady (4:17) / Jam Back At The House (8:24) / Izabella (5:10) / Gypsy Woman (5:26) / Fire (3:53)

CD 2: Voodoo Chile - Stepping Stone (12:19) / Star Spangled Banner (3:41) / Purple Haze (3:25) / Guitar Improvisation (4:58) / Villanova Junction Blues (3:04) / Hey Joe (4:50) / Woodstock Interview (1:51) / Lover Man (5:10)* / Lover Man (5:27)* / Hear My Train A Comin' (8:28)* / Spanish Castle Magic (4:52)* / Hear My Train A Comin' (2:33)** / Machine Gun** (2:35) / Izabella (3:24)**

Comments: The title says it all. This is the best sounding and most complete of all the Woodstock bootlegs. This is another show we should all be buying legitimately if the powers that be could just remove their heads from that dark hole... * Liberty House, Shokan, New York, August 14, 1969 - Gypsy Sun And Rainbows Session. ** 'Dick Cavett Show', ABC Studios, NYC September 9, 1969. Excellent stereo soundboard. CD2 tracks 8-11 Good-very good sound. Tracks 12-14 Very good-excellent line recording from TV. Picture CDs.

WOODSTOCK NATION   IN *
WHITE BIRD RECORDS (WBR 89090 1 / 2) 2CD Time CD 1: 54:56, CD 2: 53:06

CD 1: Intro / Hear My Train A Comin' / Spanish Castle Magic / Red House / Mastermind / Lover Man

WINTERLAND VOL. 1

WINTERLAND VOL. 2

WINTERLAND VOL. 3

WINTERLAND DAYS

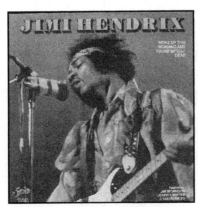

WOKE UP THIS MORNING AND...

WOODSTOCK NATION

/ Foxy Lady / Jamming Back At House (Beginnings)

CD 2: Izabella / Gypsy Woman / Fire / Medley: Voodoo Chile (slight return), Star Spangled Banner, Purple Haze, Instrumental Solo / Hey Joe (Encore)

Comments: Recorded live at the Woodstock Festival, Bethel, New York, August 18, 1969. Excellent stereo soundboard. Mastered at too fast a speed so what might have been an excellent release is marred. This release is missing the opening song "Message To Love" found on the previous listing as well as on 500,000 HALOS. European CD.

WOODSTOCK REHEARSALS 1969 (THE)   IN **

MIDNIGHT BEAT (MB CD 039) CD Time: 73:55

Lover Man (4:19) / Hear My Train A Comin' (8:33) / Spanish Castle Magic (4:47) / Izabella (4:31) / Message Of Love (5:31) / Instrumental Jam I (The Dance)(11:38) / Instrumental Jam I (Sundance) (2:23) / Jam Back At The House 1 (Beginnings) (6:18)/ Instrumental Jam III (Shokan Jam #1) (4:37)/ Jam Back At The House II (Beginnings) (4:23) / Jam Back At The House III (Beginnings) (5:37) / If Six Was Nine (1:29) / Sun Dance (Sundance)(5:43) / Free Form Blues (Shokan Jam #2)(6:16)

Comments: Good to very good line recordings from Jimi's house at Traver Hollow in Shokan, New York on or about August 14, 1969. Tracks 13-14 are good line recordings live from the Tinker Street Cinema in Woodstock, New York on August 10, 1969. Tracks 13-14 are poor to good. Picture CD. Recommended to put in perspective Jimi's problem of putting together a new band after the breakup of The Experience at the end of June and rehearsing the Gypsy Suns And Rainbow Band prior to his Woodstock commitment in the middle of August. Much of this material was also on SHOKAN SUNRISE, but is easier to find on the Midnight Beat label.

WOW!

UNKNOWN LABEL LP

Side 1: Like A Rolling Stone / Rock Me Baby / Can You See Me / Wild Thing

Side 2: Red House / Star Spangled Banner / Purple Haze / Instrumental Solo

Comments: The four tracks on Side 1 are from MONTEREY (Reprise), "Red House" is from SMASH HITS (Reprise) & the other cuts on Side 2 are from WOODSTOCK LP.

YOU CAN'T USE MY NAME   IN *

ROCK FOLDERS (Q9020-PRO) LP

Side 1: Cat Fish Blues (Experiencing The Blues) / You Can't Use My Name (Jimi & Ed Chalpin chat) / Gloomy Monday (takes 1&2) / Untitled Instrumental (Little Miss Strange)

Side 2: Dolly Dagger / Freedom / Stone Free / Hey Joe / Maui Sunset (Hey Baby - New Rising Sun) (complete with the segue into "Midnight Lightning")

Comments: Side 1 includes Holland 1967, PPX Studio 1967 & Electric Ladyland Studio 1967/68. Side 2 is live in Maui 1970 from the second show. Excellent stereo in a gatefold sleeve. Recommended just for the studio chat with Ed Chalpin. This is where Jimi tells Ed that he doesn't want his name anywhere on the record - thus, the 'You can't use my name' reference. Chalpin, being the honorable person that he was, goes ahead and uses Jimi's name even after promising Jimi that he wouldn't.

YOU CAN'T USE MY NAME

The Essential Bootlegs

The following titles are those bootlegs which we deem to be the most essential to the collector of rare Hendrix recordings. For the rarest music with the best sound available, you can't go wrong with these choices. The list is divided into two categories: "Live Recordings" and "Studio Outtakes". The bootlegs are listed alphabetically for easy reference. Do whatever it takes to find these releases.

LIVE RECORDINGS

Apartment Jam 70
Back To Berlin!
Band Of Gypsys Vol. 3
Blues At Midnight
Copenhagen '70
Have Mercy On Me Baby!
Incident At Rainbow Bridge / Isle Of Wight Festival
King's Jam
Message Of Love
On The Killing Floor
Royal Albert Hall
Wight
Winterland Days

Atlanta
Band Of Gypsys Rehearsals
Berkeley Soundchecks
Cafe Au Go Go Jam Session
First Night At The Royal Albert Hall
I Don't Live Today, Maybe Tomorrow
It Never Takes An End
Listen To This Eric
Oh, Atlanta
Riots In Berkeley
Tomorrow...Or Just The End Of Time
Winterland Vol. 1 & Vol. 3
Woodstock Monday, August 18, 1969

STUDIO OUTTAKES

500,000 Halos
Ball And Chain
Calling Long Distance
Diamonds In The Dust
Experience The Voodoo Sessions
Jimi: A Musical Legacy
Mixdown Master Tapes Vol. 1 - 3
Out Of The Studio 1 & 2
Studio Haze

Auld Lang Syne
Black Gold
Demos 1968
Earth Tones
Hear My Freedom
Jimi Hendrix & Jack Bruce
Olympic Gold Vol. 1 - 2
Shokan Sunrise
Voodoo Sessions

THANKS FOR THE MAMMARIES
(the cover of an unreleased bootleg)

Here Comes Black Gold!
Or
The Unreleased Jimi Hendrix Rarities

While a good share of Jimi's studio outtakes, jams, home recordings and live performances have been released, both officially and unofficially, there are still a few rarities that have yet to see any type of general release. Some of these rarities have recently found their way onto a few obscure CD-Rs; however, the music on these discs will undoubtably remain unavailable to most collectors.

What follows is a listing of the live recordings (mostly audience tapes) and studio outtakes, home recordings, etc. which we can hope to someday see released. Certainly not all of the unreleased songs are listed here as there is just no way of knowing what is in the hands of collectors, friends (Noel, Mitch or Kathy Etchingham, for example) and family members. There is assuredly a great amount of material still in the vaults of the record companies, but access to those musical treasures have not been accorded to these authors. Tapes of live recordings are generally of poor quality due to the state of the technology at the time. Still, we are often surprised by an excellent recording ('Live At The Oakland Coliseum') which had been unknown up to that point. Hopefully, a few more of these will appear in the future.

We suggest you utilize these listings as a gauge to measure the amount of material awaiting discovery. We like to think of these as our 'wish list'. Happy hunting.

The Studio Rarities

(These include studio outtakes, home recordings, jams and unreleased tracks.)

All Along The Watchtower: January, 21, 1968 (basic version with Dave Mason and Mitch Mitchell)

Black Gold Suite: A 'works in progress' by Jimi begun in the spring of 1970 at his apartment in New York. The tapes are of Jimi solo on guitar. The following songs are on the tapes: Suddenly November Morning / Drifting / Captain Midnite / Local Commotion / Here Comes Black Gold / Stepping Stone / Little Red Velvet Room / The Jungle Is Waiting / Send My Love To Joan Of Arc / God Bless The Day / Black Gold / Machine Gun / Here Comes Black Gold / Astro Man (Parts 1 & 2) / I've Got A Place To Go. Mitch Mitchell is said to have the tapes in his possession.

Bleeding Heart: Spring 1969 (complete version of the jam with Billy Cox and Buddy Miles—edited version on the commercial release 'Blues'.)

Bleeding Heart: December 18, 1969 (complete recording with Juma Sultan)

Bleeding Heart: March 24, 1970 (complete alternate mix recorded with Juma)

Bold As Love: October 29, 1967 (alternate mix)

Bolero: February 1, 1970 (jam session in Jimi's NY apartment with Mitch Mitchell)

Bolero: July 14, 1970 (complete jam session with Billy Cox and others)

Burning Desire: November 14, 1969 (jam with Buddy Miles)

Burning Of The Midnight Lamp (The): July 1967 (from acetate with a different mix)

Calling All Devils Children: October 21, 1968 (extended version with Lee Michaels)

Calling All Devils Children: 1968 (complete jam session with players unknown)

Chandler Tapes: These are 15 songs that were recorded by Jimi, but were left unfinished. Some have found their way to bootlegs. For more information see 'Studio Haze' in the bootleg section.

Come Down Hard On Me Baby: July 14, 1970 (instrumental rehearsal)

Drifting: Early 1970 (overdub and mixing tape of the "Drifting" session)

Drinking Wine: September 23, 1969 (unreleased song with Cox, Mitchell & Juma)

Driving South: March 25, 1969 (alternate mix recorded with McLaughlin & Buddy Miles & Dave Holland)

Driving South: May 15, 1969 (jam session with Johnny Winter, Dallas Taylor & Stephen Stills)

Earth Blues: May 22, 1969 (alternate take with the Band Of Gypsys & Devon Wilson)

Earth Blues: December 1969 (alternate take with the Band Of Gypsys)

Electric Church Jam: October 21, 1968 (complete jam with Lee Michaels & Buddy Miles)

Everything's Gonna Be Alright: October 1968 (jam with Mitchell and Michaels)

Faye Tape: This tape was put up for sale in 1995 at Sotheby's Auction House. It purportedly contains about 30 minutes of Jimi detailing his feelings through words and music about his relationship with his girlfriend Faye Pridgeon. It did not sell and thus remains an enigma.

Feel So Good: 1969 (part of a jam session medley recorded in Newport)

Freedom: February 1, 1970 (jam with Mitch Mitchell in Jimi's NY apartment)

Freedom: Summer 1970 (overdub and mixing session by Jimi)

Go My Own Way: April 3, 1967 (unreleased Experience song)

Hallaluya: May 15, 1969 (unreleased jam with Stephen Stills, Johnny Winter & Dallas Taylor)

Inside Out: June 11, 1968 (jam session with Jack Bruce, Buddy Miles & Jim McCarty - tape is said to have been lost)

Izabella: October 18, 1968 (unreleased instrumental version)

Jack Bruce Jam: October 17, 1968 (jam session with Jack Bruce, Buddy Miles & Jim McCarty)

Jams With Piano: October 1968 (probably with Mitch Mitchell & Lee Michaels - about 20 minutes of jamming focused on the piano)

John McLaughlin Jam: March 25, 1969 (jam sessions with McLaughlin, Buddy Miles & Dave Holland - portions have been bootlegged of this 6 hour session)

Larry Young Jam: May 1969 (all but "Fuzzy Guitar Jam" have been booted)

Last Thursday Morning: July 20, 1970 (unreleased instrumental with Mitchell & Cox - may have been released under another title)

Lee Michaels Jam: October 21, 1968 (includes two jams - one untitled & the other is "Hear My Freedom" with Buddy Miles)

Little Little Girl: May 1968 (not Jimi, but Noel Redding)

Lona Blues: June 11, 1968 (jam with Miles, Bruce & McCarty - may have been released under another title)

Lullaby For The Summer: April 1969 (early version of "Earth Blues")

Machine Gun: August 29, 1969 (alternate take featuring Larry Lee)

Machine Gun: June 15, 1970 (features Jimi on unused solo for song's intro)

Mannish Boy: April 22, 1969 (recording session with Devon Wilson, Billy Cox & others)

Mannish Boy / Izabella / You Make Me Feel: August 1969 (session tape)

Mastermind: August 30, 1969 (unreleased studio recording by Larry Lee)

Message To Love: August 1968 (unreleased studio take)

Message To Love: December 1969 (studio sessions with the Band Of Gypsys)

Messenger: October 20, 1968 (unreleased instrumental - numerous takes)

Messing Around: June 16, 1970 (unreleased jam with Cox, Mitchell & Juma)

Midnight Lightning: July 14, 1970 (instrumental version with Cox, Mitch & Juma)

Mitch Mitchell Jams: February 1, 1970 (recorded at Jimi's New York apartment - most of these jams are unreleased, with over 30 minutes known to exist on tape)

My Friend: March 23, 1970 (Noel Redding song with Jimi on guitar)

Night Bird Flying: August 1970 (alternate instrumental mix with Cox, Mitch & Juma)

Paul Caruso Rag Session: Spring 1968 (recorded at Jimi's NY apartment and consisting of conversation and bits of "All Along The Watchtower" and "Bright Lights, Big City")

Power Of Soul: September 24, 1969 (jam session with Buddy Miles)

Power Of Soul: January 16, 1970 (Band Of Gypsys jam session)

Rainy Day Sessions: June 1968 (jam sessions and rehearsals - portions have been bootlegged)

Room Full Of Mirrors Poetry Recital: 1969 (Jimi recites poetry over Eric Burdon's "Closer To The Truth" song)

Shokan House Jams: August 1969 (numerous jams were recorded at Jimi's house in Woodstock - portions have been booted though most still remain unreleased)

South Saturn Delta / Three Little Bears / Jam: May 2, 1968 (studio jam session with Mitch Mitchell)

Stephen Stills / Dallas Taylor Jams: May 1969 (only portions of the entire session have been bootlegged - some of the titles are "Dooji Wooji Jam", "Send My Love To Linda / Live And Let Live")

Sotheby's Tapes: An assortment of songs and working tapes sold at auction. Some have found their way onto bootlegs. See 'The Sotheby's Tapes' in the bootleg section for more information on the tracks.

Sundance: August 1969 (complete version—10:20—with Billy Cox, Mitch Mitchell, Juma Sultan, Jerry Velez & Larry Lee)

Sundance: August 1969 (same as above, but an alternate mix - 8:20)

Tax Free: January 1968 (alternate mix)

Them Changes: November 1969 (studio outtake with Band Of Gypsys)

Thing I Used To Do Jam: May 1969 (with Johnny Winter, Stephen Stills & Dallas Taylor—only portions have been booted)

Valleys Of Neptune: June 26, 1970 (complete session rehearsals)

Valleys Of Neptune: June 26, 1970 (alternate mix)

Valleys Of Neptune: June 26, 1970 (alternate instrumental version)

Villanova Junction: August 1969 (32 minute jam recorded at Jimi's Shokan House)

Voodoo Child (slight return): May 3, 1968 (session rehearsals with 20 takes)

We Gotta Live Together / Feel So Good: June 22, 1969 (jam session with Buddy Miles & others at Newport, Devonshire Downs)

Winter Blues: May 6, 1969 (jam session at the Record Plant)

The Live Recordings

(Live performances, club jams, and concerts*)

I Got You (I Feel Good): October 1965 with Curtis Knight & The Squires at the Queen's Inn, New York.

George's Club, NY: December 26, 1965, with Curtis Knight. The complete original mono recordings. For more information see the 'Hendrix With Others' section.

Blaises Club*, London: December 21, 1966, five songs with the JHE.

Hey Joe: December 29, 1966, with The Breakaways on "Top Of The Pops".

Purple Haze: March 30, 1967, on "Top Of The Pops". Two versions.

Purple Haze: May 4, 1967, on "Top Of The Pops".

The Wind Cries Mary: May 10, 1967, on "Top Of The Pops".

Hey Joe / Wild Thing: May 11, 1967, on "Music Hall Of France", Paris TV.

Wild Thing: May 21, 1967, on "Beat Forum", Copenhagen, Denmark.

The Burning Of The Midnight Lamp: August 24, 1967, on "Tops Of The Pops".

Saville Theatre*, London: August 27, 1967. 30 minutes.

Dans In*, Stockholm, Sweden: September 4, 1967. 52 minutes.

Blackpool*, England: November 25, 1967.

Winterland*, California: February 3, 1968. Second show. 57 minutes.

Hunter College*, New York: March 2, 1968. Second show. 25 minutes.

Washington, D.C.*: March 10, 1968. First show. 36 minutes.

Cleveland*, Ohio: March 26, 1968. 58 minutes.

Montreal*, Canada: April 2, 1968. 46 minutes.

Generation Club, NYC: April 7, 1968. Jam with Roy Buchanan.

Generation Club, NYC: April 1968. Jams with B.B. King, Elvin Bishop, Paul Butterfield, Al Kooper, Buzzy Feiten, Don Martin & others. 120 minutes.

Palasport*, Italy: May 26, 1968. 45 minutes.

Sam Houston Coliseum*, Houston: August 4, 1968. 35 minutes.

Columbia*, Maryland: August 16, 1968. 46 minutes.

Phoenix*, Arizona: September 4, 1968. 62 minutes.

Spokane*, Washington: September 8, 1968. 21 minutes.

Portland*, Oregon: September 9, 1968. 65 minutes.

Minneapolis*, Minnesota: November 2, 1968. 30 minutes.

Boston*, Massachusetts: November 16, 1968. 42 minutes.

Providence*, Rhode Island: November 27, 1968. 100 minutes.

Detroit*, Michigan: November 30, 1968. 34 minutes.

Chicago*, Illinois: December 1, 1968. 68 minutes.

Hamburg*, Germany: January 11, 1969. 66 minutes.
Munster*, Germany: January 14, 1969. 49 minutes.
Nuremburg*, Germany: January 16, 1969. 57 minutes.
Stuttgart*, Germany: January 19, 1969. 29 minutes.
Vienna*, Austria: January 22, 1969. Both shows. 81 minutes.
"Pop Expo", Hollywood: March 30, 1969. Jams with Delaney & Bonnie. 10 minutes
Philadelphia*, Pennsylvania: April 12, 1969. 60 minutes.
Memphis*, Tennessee: April 18, 1969. 57 minutes.
Dallas*, Texas: April 20, 1969. 56 minutes.
Indianapolis*, Indiana: May 11, 1969. 64 minutes.
Baltimore*, Maryland: May 16, 1969. 57 minutes.
Newport Jams: June 22, 1969, at Devonshire Downs, "Newport '69". About 90 minutes of various jams with Buddy Miles and others. Portions have been booted.
Tinker Street Cinema Jam: August 10, 1969. 40 minutes of jamming with Juma Sultan & Jerry Velez.
Woodstock Festival*: August 18, 1969. Surprisingly, the complete and totally unedited performance has never been pressed.
United Block Assoc. Benefit: September 5, 1969. "Voodoo Child (slight return)" & "Machine Gun". 25 minutes.
Fillmore East*, New York: December 31, 1969 & January 1, 1970. Soundboard tapes of all the shows exist. These are the complete shows.
Sacramento*, California: April 26, 1970. 50 minutes.
Milwaukee*, Wisconsin: May 1, 1970. 60 minutes.
Madison*, Wisconsin: May 2, 1970. 80 minutes.
St. Paul*, Minnesota: May 3, 1970. 74 minutes.
Norman*, Oklahoma: May 8, 1970. Second show. 65 minutes.
Fort Worth*, Texas: May 9, 1970. 74 minutes.
San Antonio*, Texas: May 10, 1970. 65 minutes.
Evansville*, Indiana: June 10, 1970. 67 minutes.
San Bernardino*, California: June 20, 1970. 43 minutes.
Boston*, Massachusetts: June 27, 1970. 57 minutes.
Seattle*, Washington: July 26, 1970. 77 minutes.
"Isle Of Wight"*, England: August 30, 1970. 100+ minutes. Soundboard!
Berlin*, West Germany: September 4, 1970. 60 minutes.

You know, you put in your favourite star and all of a sudden this music and the audio, I mean the visual scene comes on.
Jimi: London 1970

The Official Hendrix Film Archives

A FILM ABOUT JIMI HENDRIX: *(Warner Home Video - 1973)* 102 minutes. Documentary with interviews and various live footage from Jimi's career. This is the only source for the breakdown of "Hear My Train A Coming" from the Bruce Fleming Studio.

ALIVE ON LIVE: *(Japanese Laserdisc)* 42 minutes of just Jimi's bits as included in the film "Rainbow Bridge".

AT LAST THE BEGINNING...THE MAKING OF ELECTRIC LADYLAND: *(Rhino Video—1998)* 60 minutes. An excellent documentary on the making of Jimi's landmark album, "Electric Ladyland." Includes footage from Noel Redding's personal 8mm archives.

BEAT CLUB: GUITAR HEROES: *(Japanese Laserdisc)*
CLASSIC ALBUMS - ELECTRIC LADYLAND: *(Eagle Rock - 1998)* English version of the Rhino video.
EXPERIENCE (aka SEE MY MUSIC TALKING): *(BMG Video & Palace Video—1987 & Warner/Reprise Video)* 33 minutes. Interviews/two live cuts from Blackpool, November 25, 1967, and acoustic version of "Getting My Heart Back Together Again" from December 19, 1967. Also available through Douglas Music (Japanese) on video or laser disc.
JIMI HENDRIX AT THE ATLANTA POP FESTIVAL: *(BMG Video & BMG Japanese Laserdisc—1992)* Parts of the performance from the 2nd Atlanta Pop Festival, July 4, 1970.
JIMI HENDRIX AT THE ISLE OF WIGHT: *(Rhino Home Video—1996 & CBS/Sony Video & BMG Video & BMG Japanese Laserdisc—1990)* 56 minutes. Parts of the performance from September 18, 1970.
JIMI HENDRIX AT WOODSTOCK: *(BMG Video—1992 & BMG Japanese Laserdisc—1992)* 57 minutes. Parts of Jimi's performance at Woodstock.
JIMI HENDRIX CONCERT: *(Media Home Entertainment— USA—1978 & Video Tape Network—Canada—1978)* 27 minutes. Odds and ends of live cuts from various sources.
JIMI PLAYS BERKELEY: *(BMG Video & Palace Video—1971 & Japanese Laserdisc 1990 & Warner/Reprise & Westron Video)* 55 minutes. Rehearsals and live cuts from both Berkeley shows of May 30, 1970.
JIMI PLAYS MONTEREY: *(BMG Video—1986 & Virgin Music Video—1987 & HBO Home Video—1987 & Rhino Video—1997 & BMG Japanese Laserdisc—1986)* 50 minutes. Nearly complete Monterey concert and two cuts from London, December 22, 1967.
JIMI PLAYS THE GREAT ROCK FESTIVALS: *(BMG Video—1994 & BMG Japanese Laser Disc—1994)*
JOHNNY B. GOODE: *(Virgin Music Video—1985 & Sony—1985)* 26 minutes. Live cuts from Atlanta Pop and Berkeley plus promotional films.
MESSAGE TO LOVE: *(PNE Video & Sony Video)* 120 minutes. The Isle of Wight Festival is documented with performances by many of the artists attending the festival. Still no complete video of Jimi's performance at the festival.
ON THE ROAD—THE ULTIMATE EXPERIENCE LIVE!: *(Douglas Music Video & Douglas Music Laser Disc - 1994)* 60 minutes. "Purple Haze" from Blackpool plus various live tracks from Woodstock, Berkeley, Maui & Atlanta.
PSYCHOMANIA: *(Magnum Music Group)*
RAINBOW BRIDGE: *(Video Tape Network—Canada 1978 & Rhino Home Video—1997 & Japanese Laser Disc—1995 & Sirius Publishing Music CD—1997)* 125 minutes. An incomplete and horribly edited version of the concert in Maui from July 30, 1970.
ROCK AND ROLL GREATEST YEARS 1967 VOL. 1 & 2: *(The Video Collection - English)*
ROCK AND ROLL GREATEST YEARS 1970: *(The Video Collection—English)*
STRANGE BREW: *(Activision Laser Disc)*
SUPERSTARS IN CONCERT: *(Telstar Video—1989)* 104 minutes. 11 minutes of odds & ends of Jimi's performances.
25 YEARS OF THE MARQUEE: *(BBC Video)*
WOODSTOCK & WOODSTOCK 2: *(Warner Home Video & MCA Home Video & MCA Laser Disc & Universal Home Video—Japanese)* Some of Jimi's performances at Woodstock.
WOODSTOCK (25TH ANNIVERSARY EDITION): *(Warner Home Video—1994 & Warner Laser Disc—1994)*
WOODSTOCK: THE LOST PERFORMANCES: *(Warner Home Video—1996 & Warner Laser Disc—1996)*

The Unreleased Jimi Hendrix Films

ATLANTA: The complete concert of the '2nd Atlanta Pop Festival' performed on July 4, 1970.

BERKELEY: A film by Peter Pilafian of both the complete concerts from May 30, 1970.

THE LAST EXPERIENCE: A film by Jerry Goldstein & Steve Gold. The complete concert from the Royal Albert Hall, February 24, 1969. A California company called Event Media offered an incomplete version of this concert for sale (in 1998) as a mono video and as a 2-cassette stereo audio tape.

RANDALL'S ISLAND: The complete concert of 'The New York Pop Festival', Downing Stadium, July 17, 1970.

WAKE AT GENERATION: A film by D.A. Pennebaker. This was the concert performed in memory of the recently assassinated Martin Luther King. Recorded at the Generation Club, NYC, April 7, 1968. Features the six-minute jam of Jimi with Roy Buchanan and others. A bootleg of this video is floating around among collectors.

WINTER FESTIVAL FOR PEACE: A film by Michael Jeffery. Contains footage of The Band Of Gypsys' final concert at Madison Square Garden, NYC, January 28, 1970.

* Plus all of Noel Redding's home movies shot on silent 8MM movie film. Portions of these films have been aired on various television specials and video compilations.

> *We call our music Electric Church Music*
> *'cos it's like a religion to us.*
> Jimi: London 1969

Jimi Hendrix:
Audio / Video Archives

Audio tapes of Jimi's live performances and interviews are quite numerous. Some are from audience tapes and others are soundboard. A few come from television performances or even from studio sessions (certainly the rarest and the most desirable for collectors). Many have found their way onto commercial releases, quasi-legal albums and bootlegs; however, a number of tapes are only circulating among collectors. Hopefully more of these tapes will reach all of us so we, too, can enjoy them. A few of these have recently been pressed as limited quantity CD-Rs by such folks as Major Tom. And, of course, all of the BBC performances are now on disc. The listings we have included here are only those known to us, but not necessarily in our possession. Titles of some (but certainly not all) official and bootleg releases are given to help in your search for these recordings. The listing below is also useful as a reference for set lists of some of Jimi's concerts.

Video of Jimi is even rarer as he lived before the advent of camcorders. However, a few folks in the audience filmed bits and pieces of performances on the now antiquated 8mm film. There were a number of television shows taped and a small number of concerts were professionally filmed. So there are some tapes of these floating around amongst collectors, and these we have listed chronologically for you. The best and the rarest of the 8mm films are those shot by Noel Redding and he has promised to release them in their entirety someday.

1965

February: "Night Train" (Nashville's Channel 5 TV show) Dallas, Texas
    Song: Shotgun
    Audio: With Buddy & Stacey and The Upsetters (soundboard tape—3 minutes)
    Bootleg: SCREAMING EAGLE (Pink Poodle)

Video: B&W—3 minutes.

October: Queen's Inn, Queens Boulevard, New York, NY
Song: I Got You (I Feel Good)
Audio: With Curtis Knight & The Squires (soundboard tape—3 minutes)

December 26: George's Club 20, Hackensack, NJ
Songs: Shotgun / One Night With You
Audio: With Curtis Knight & The Squires (soundboard tape—6 minutes)

1966

October 18: "Musicorama", L'Olympia, Paris, France
Songs: Killin' Floor / Hey Joe / Wild Thing
Audio: With Mitch Mitchell, Noel Redding, Chas Chandler and Johnny Halliday
Bootleg: PARIS 1966/67 (missing "Wild Thing")
Video: B&W—30 seconds. Also includes footage of Jimi smoking backstage.

December 21: Blaises, Queensgate, London
Songs: Rock Me Baby / Third Stone From The Sun / Like A Rolling Stone / Hey Joe / Wild Thing
Audio: JHE (audience recording)

December 29: "Top Of The Pops", BBC Lime Grove Studios, London, England
Song: Hey Joe
Audio: With The Breakaways on backing vocals (original broadcast—3 minutes) / rebroadcast on February 2, 1967.

1967

January 31: Saville Theatre, London, England
Song: Hey Joe
Video: JHE on "Superstars In Concert" film (color - 3 minutes - lip sync). Rebroadcast on "Drop In", Swedish TV (B&W—3 minutes—lip sync)

February 4: Flamingo Club, London, England
Songs: Killin' Floor / Have Mercy Baby / Can You See Me / Like A Rolling Stone / Rock Me Baby / Catfish Blues / Stone Free / Hey Joe / Wild Thing / Day Tripper
Audio: JHE (audience recording—46 minutes)
Bootlegs: HAVE MERCY ON ME BABY (MB038) / LIVE AT THE FLAMINGO CLUB (My Phoenix ZA25)

February 13: "Saturday Club", BBC Broadcasting House, London, England
Songs: Foxy Lady / Stone Free / Hey Joe / Love Or Confusion / Foxy Lady
Audio: JHE / BBC acetate (5 minutes) Includes an interview with Jimi by Brian Matthews. Originally broadcast on "BBC Light", February 18, 1967 (15 minutes).
              "Love Or Confusion" can be found on the bootleg JEWEL BOX (Home Records HR592403). All of the tracks are now on the CR BBC SESSIONS.

March 2: "Beat Club", Marquee, London, England
Songs: Hey Joe I / Purple Haze I / Hey Joe II / Purple Haze II
Audio: JHE with introductions by Dave Lee Travis.
Bootlegs: First two songs are on THANKS OTTAWA FOR THE MEMORIES (Luna LU 9319 - CD) & TOMORROW...OR JUST THE END OF TIME (Batz) & FIRST TIME IN CANADA (Bunny Music BM 0192) 'Hey Joe II' is on LOADED GUITAR (Starlight SL 87013).
Video: B&W—14 minutes & color—7 minutes

March 7: "Tienerklanken" TV show, Brussels, Belgium
Songs: Hey Joe / Stone Free
Video: JHE (B&W—7 minutes—lip sync)

March 18: "Twenclub", Radio House, Hamburg, Germany
- **Songs:** Foxy Lady / Hey Joe / Stone Free / Fire / Purple Haze
- **Audio:** JHE / Includes on-stage interviews with Jimi and Noel by Jochem Rathmann. Rebroadcast on "Hamburg Swings", BBC Light, July 1, 1967 (25 minutes) and on German radio NDR-FM, Nov. 28, 1992 (20 minutes)
- **Bootleg:** TOMORROW...OR JUST THE END OF TIME (Batz) & THE LEGENDARY STAR CLUB TAPES (Early Years 02-CD-3309).

March 28: "Saturday Club", BBC Broadcasting House, London, England
- **Songs:** Killin' Floor / Fire / Purple Haze
- **Audio:** JHE / From the original BBC transcription disc first broadcast on "BBC Light", April 1, 1967 (9 minutes).
These are now available on the CR BBC SESSIONS. The last track is on Ryko's RADIO ONE.

March 30: "Top Of The Pops", BBC Lime Grove Studios, London, England
- **Songs:** Purple Haze I / Purple Haze II
- **Audio:** JHE / From the original broadcast on "Top Of The Pops" BBC TV, April 6, 1967 (4 minutes)
- **Bootleg:** LOADED GUITAR
- **Video:** JHE (B& W—4 minutes) & rebroadcast on German TV (B&W—2 minutes).

April 17: "Late Night Line Up", BBC TV Studio, Kingsway, London, England
- **Song:** Manic Depression
- **Audio:** JHE / From the original broadcast.
- **Bootleg:** THE LOST CONCERTS VOL. 5 SWEDEN 1967 (CD-R)
- **Video:** JHE (B&W—3 minutes) & rebroadcast on "Jimi Hendrix—Laughing Dice", "Def II", September 5, 1990, BBC 2 (30 seconds)

May 4: "Top Of The Pops", BBC Lime Grove Studios, London, England
- **Song:** Purple Haze
- **Audio:** JHE / From the original broadcast (4 minutes)

May 10: "Top Of The Pops", BBC Lime Grove Studios, London, England
- **Song:** The Wind Cries Mary
- **Audio:** JHE / From the original broadcast (3 minutes)
- **Video:** Originally broadcast on May 18, 1967 (B&W—silent—4 minutes).

May 11: "Music Hall Of France", French TV, Paris, France
- **Songs:** Hey Joe / Wild Thing
- **Video:** JHE (B&W—8 minutes)

May 17: Hotel Intercontinental, Frankfurt, Germany
JHE: Interview with Jimi, Mitch and Noel by Hans Carl Schmidt, German radio (17 minutes)

May 18: "Beat Beat Beat", German TV, Stadthalle, Offenbach, Germany
- **Songs:** Stone Free / Hey Joe / Purple Haze
- **Audio:** JHE / From the original broadcast (10 minutes)
- **Bootleg:** WILD MAN OF POP PLAYS VOL. 1 (Pyramid 003 - CD), SWEET ANGEL & GIMME THE GLAD EYE.
- **Video:** B&W—9 minutes and B&W—11 minutes

May 19: Konserthallen, Liseberg, Liseberg Nöjespark, Gothenburg, Sweden
- **Video:** JHE (color—3 minutes—silent 8mm)

May 21: Falkoner Centret, Copenhagen, Denmark
- **Song:** Wild Thing
- **Audio:** JHE / Includes interview by Carsten Grolin and originally broadcast on "Beat Forum", Danish Radio, June 2, 1967 (5 minutes)

May 24: Stora Scenen, Grona Lund, Stockholm, Sweden
- **Songs:** Foxy Lady / Rock Me Baby / Hey Joe / Can You See Me / Purple Haze / Wild Thing
- **Audio:** JHE / Audience recording (28 minutes)
- **Bootleg:** LOST IN SWEDEN (Whoopy Cat WKP 0046/47 - CD)
- **Video:** Color—silent 8mm—1 minute.

May 24: "Popside", Swedish TV, Stockholm, Sweden
- **Songs:** The Wind Cries Mary/ Purple Haze
- **Audio:** JHE / Soundboard (8 minutes)
- **Bootleg:** WILD MAN OF POP PLAYS VOL. 1 (Pyramid 003 - CD)
- **Video:** B&W—8 minutes

May 25: "Pop 67 Special", Stockholm, Sweden
- **Audio:** JHE / Interview by Klas Burling (11 min. 28 sec)

June 18: "Monterey International Pop Festival", Monterey, CA
- **Songs:** Killin' Floor / Foxy Lady / Like A Rolling Stone / Rock Me Baby / Hey Joe / Can You See Me / The Wind Cries Mary / Purple Haze / Wild Thing
- **Audio:** JHE / Soundboard recording of entire show by Eric Weinbang for Wally Heider Recording (45 minutes). Available officially and on numerous bootlegs.
- **Video:** "Keep On Rocking" film (color—3 minutes—one camera) & (color—20 minutes—five cameras). This was officially released on video.

July 20: Salvation Club, Greenwich Village, NYC
- **Video:** JHE / color—silent 16mm—10 minutes

August 17: Rudolf Valentino's mansion, Watts, Los Angeles, CA
- **Video:** JHE / Color—40 minutes—silent. Camera follows Jimi in and around the mansion.

August 24: "Top Of The Pops", BBC Lime Grove Studios, London, England
- **Song:** The Burning Of The Midnight Lamp
- **Audio:** JHE / Broadcast on September 7, 1967 (5 minutes)

August 27: Saville Theatre, London, England
- **Songs:** Summertime Blues / Fire / The Wind Cries Mary / Foxy Lady / Catfish Blues / I Don't Live Today / Red House / Hey Joe / Purple Haze
- **Audio:** JHE / Audience recording (29 minutes)
- **Bootleg:** THE LOST CONCERTS VOL. 6 PHOENIX 1968

September 4: Stora Scenen, Grona Lund, Stockholm, Sweden
- **Songs:** Sgt. Pepper's Lonely Hearts Club Band / Rock Me Baby / Catfish Blues / Hey Joe / Purple Haze
- **Audio:** JHE / Audience recording (29 minutes)
- **Bootleg:** LOST IN SWEDEN (Whoopy Cat WKP 0046/47 - CD)
- **Video:** JHE / Color—silent 8mm—2 minutes

September 4: Dans In, Grona Lund, Stockholm, Sweden
- **Songs:** Killin' Floor / Foxy Lady / Catfish Blues / Hey Joe / Fire / The Wind Cries Mary / Purple Haze
- **Audio:** JHE / Audience recording (52 minutes)
- **Bootlegs:** THE LOST CONCERTS VOL. 5 SWEDEN 1967 and EXP OVER SWEDEN

September 5: "Tonarskvall", Radiohuset, Stockholm, Sweden
- **Songs:** Sgt. Pepper's Lonely Hearts Club Band / Fire / The Wind Cries Mary / Foxy Lady / Hey Joe / I Don't Live Today / The Burning Of The Midnight Lamp / Purple Haze
- **Audio:** JHE / Originally broadcast on "Pop 67", September 6, 1967,with interview by Klas Burling (31 minutes). Officially released on the STAGES box set and numerous bootlegs.

September 11: Radiohuset, Stockholm, Sweden
Audio: JHE / Interview originally broadcast on "Pop 67", October 9, 1967 (5 minutes). Hosted by Leif H. Andersson.

September 11: Stora Scenen, Grona Lund, Stockholm, Sweden
Songs: Foxy Lady / The Burning Of The Midnight Lamp / Fire / Catfish Blues / Hey Joe / Purple Haze
Audio: JHE / Audience recording (35 minutes)
Bootleg: LOST IN SWEDEN (Whoopy Cat WKP 0046/0047 - CD)
Video: JHE / Color—silent 8mm—3 minutes

October 6: "Top Gear", Playhouse Theatre BBC, London, England
Songs: Jam - Ain't Too Proud To Beg / Little Miss Lover / Catfish Blues / The Burning Of The Midnight Lamp / Drivin' South / Hound Dog
Audio: JHE / Originally broadcast on BBC Radio One, October 15, 1967 (20 minutes). Stevie Wonder on drums. Short interview.
Bootlegs: "The Burning Of The Midnight Lamp" is on LIVE EXPERIENCE 67-68. "Little Miss Lover" is on the 3 CD ANTHOLOGY set. "Jam - Ain't Too Proud To Beg" is on BLACK GOLD (Midnight Beat MBCD 058-062). All tracks are now available on the CR BBC SESSIONS.

October 9: "Musicorama", l'Olympia, Paris, France
Songs: Hey Joe / Foxy Lady / The Wind Cries Mary / Rock Me Baby / Red House / Purple Haze / Wild Thing
Audio: JHE / Soundboard recording (36 minutes)
Bootlegs: Songs 2-7 are on WILDMAN OF POP PLAYS VOL. 2 (Pyramid CD 004) and PARIS 66/67 (Whoopy Cat WKP-012 - CD).
Video: From "Superstars In Concert" film (40 minutes)

October 10: "Dim Dam Dom", French TV, Paris, France
Songs: The Burning Of The Midnight Lamp / Hey Joe
Video: JHE / Originally broadcast on French TV, November 12, 1967 (color—7 minutes—lip sync).

October 11: Montparnasse, Paris, France
Songs: The Burning Of The Midnight Lamp / The Wind Cries Mary
Video: JHE / Hanging around at the market (B&W—3 minutes—lip sync) & visiting a building site (B&W—3 minutes—lip sync).

October 12: "Musicorama", TV studio, Paris, France
Songs: The Wind Cries Mary / The Burning Of The Midnight Lamp
Video: Jimi miming with a violin (B&W—8 minutes)

October 17: "Rhythm And Blues", Playhouse Theatre BBC, London, England
Songs: Signature tune / Can You Please Crawl Out Your Window / I'm Your Hoochie Coochie Man / Drivin' South
Audio: JHE / Originally broadcast on November 13, 1967. Introductions by Alexis Korner and with Alexis on slide guitar on "I'm Your Hoochie Coochie Man" (15 minutes)
Bootleg: "I'm Your Hoochie Coochie Man" is on ANTHOLOGY (Box 9). The entire set is on the commercial release BBC SESSIONS.

October 18: Leicester Square, London, England
Video: Jimi among the guests at the premiere of Richard Lester's film, "How I Won The War" (starring John Lennon). A brief 10 seconds and in living color.

November 10: Vitus Studio, Bussum, Holland
Songs: Foxy Lady / Catfish Blues - Cat's Squirrel / Purple Haze I / Purple Haze II (false start)
Audio: JHE / Originally broadcast on "Hoepla", Dutch TV, November 23, 1967 (8 minutes) & soundboard recording (25 minutes) with intro by Rosalie Peters.
Bootleg: WILDMAN OF POP PLAYS VOL. 2 (Whoopy Cat)

Video: Silent 8mm—color—3 minutes

November 25: Opera House, Blackpool, Lancashire, England
  Songs: Sgt. Pepper's Lonely Hearts Club Band / Fire / Hey Joe / The Wind Cries Mary / Purple Haze / Wild Thing
  Audio: JHE / Audience recording (11 minutes)
  Bootleg: "The Wind Cries Mary", "Purple Haze" and "Wild Thing" are on THE LOST CONCERTS VOL. 6 (Blank label CD-R). 'Purple Haze' and 'Wild Thing' are on THE WILD MAN OF POP PLAYS VOL. 2.
  Video: JHE / Color (8 minutes). Shows JHE performing "Purple Haze" & "Wild Thing".

December ?: Jimi's Apartment, Upper Berkeley Street, London, England
  Audio: Jimi is interviewed by Meatball Fulton (22 minutes)

December 15: "Top Gear", Playhouse Theatre BBC, London , England
  Songs: Radio One Jingle / Spanish Castle Magic* / Day Tripper* / Hear My Train A Comin' I / Hear My Train A Comin' II / Wait Until Tomorrow - I Want To Tell You*
  Audio: JHE / *Originally broadcast on BBC Radio One, December 24, 1967 (15 minutes) with intro by Brian Matthew. And with a short interview by Tony Hall about Jimi's wah-wah pedal (6 minutes). Also both versions of "Hear My Train A Comin'" and with complete introductions by Jimi (10 minutes).
  Bootleg: "Spanish Castle Magic" is on JEWEL BOX (Home Records HR5924-3). All tracks are now available on the CR BBC SESSIONS.

December 19: Bruce Fleming Photo Studio, London, England
  Song: Hear My Train A Comin' / interview
  Video: Jimi solo/ Color—10 minutes

December 22: "Christmas On Earth Continued", Olympia, London, England
  Songs: Sgt. Pepper's Lonely Hearts Club Band / Foxy Lady / Wild Thing
  Audio: JHE / Soundboard tape
  Bootleg: "Sgt. Pepper" and "Foxy Lady" are on LOADED GUITAR.
  Video: Color—10 minutes

1968

January 7: Tivolis Koncertsal, Copenhagen, Denmark (first show)
  Songs: Sgt. Pepper's Lonely Hearts Club Band / Fire / Hey Joe / Catfish Blues - Cat's Squirrel / The Wind Cries Mary / Purple Haze / Spanish Castle Magic / Wild Thing
  Audio: JHE / Audience recording (42 minutes)
  Bootleg: CAT'S SQUIRREL (CS 001/2 - CD).

January 8: "Pop 68 Special", Stockholm, Sweden
  Audio: Jimi interviewed by Lief Andersson (4'28").

January 8: Konserthuset, Stockholm, Sweden (first show)
  Songs: Sgt. Pepper's Lonely Hearts Club Band / EXP / Up From The Skies / Spanish Castle Magic / Foxy Lady / Little Wing / Fire / Catfish Blues - Cat's Squirrel / The Wind Cries Mary / Purple Haze
  Audio: JHE / Audience recording (51 minutes)
  Bootleg: LOST IN SWEDEN (Whoopy Cat WKP-0046/47)

January 29: l'Olympia, Paris, France—SECOND SHOW
  Songs: Killin' Floor / Catfish Blues / Foxy Lady / Red House / Drivin' South / The Wind Cries Mary / Fire / Little Wing / Purple Haze
  Audio: JHE / Soundboard recording (51 minutes). Noel on guitar on "Red House". This performance is officially available on the STAGES box set and on numerous bootlegs.

January 30: Pan Am Building, NYC
  Audio: Various interviews from "The British Are Coming" press reception (25 minutes).

February 2?: Winterland Arena, San Francisco, CA
  Song: Can You Please Crawl Out Your Window (soundcheck)
  Audio: JHE / Soundboard recording (3 minutes).

February 3: Winterland Arena, San Francisco, CA
  Songs: FIRST SHOW: Sgt. Pepper's Lonely Hearts Club Band / Fire / Hey Joe / Foxy Lady / The Wind Cries Mary / Killin' Floor / Little Wing / Purple Haze
       SECOND SHOW: Rock Me Baby / Red House / Foxy Lady / Like A Rolling Stone / Purple Haze
  Audio: JHE / Audience recording (57 minutes)

February 5/6/10/14: San Francisco; Tempe, AZ; Tucson, AZ.; Los Angeles; Denver, CO; Houston, TX
  Noel Redding's home movies (silent—8mm—color) from Los Angeles, San Francisco, Tempe and Tucson. Originally broadcast on "South Bank Documentary", October 1, 1989. Approximately 3 1/2 minutes total time. These include some scenes on the road, Jimi with a girl in a parking lot, Mitch arriving at the Denver airport, Jimi and friends in a car, Jimi at a motel and a swimming pool, and Gerry Stickells giving airplane tickets to Jimi and friends.

February 16: State Fair Music Hall, Dallas, TX
  Songs: Are You Experienced / Fire / The Wind Cries Mary / Tax Free / Foxy Lady / Hey Joe / Spanish Castle Magic / Red House / Purple Haze / Wild Thing
  Audio: JHE / Stereo audience recording (60 minutes)
  Bootleg: THE BIGGEST SQUARE IN THE BUILDING

February 17: Will Rogers Auditorium, Fort Worth, TX
  Songs: Sgt. Pepper's Lonely Hearts Club Band / Can You Please Crawl Out Your Window / The Wind Cries Mary / Fire / Catfish Blues / Foxy Lady / Outside Woman Blues / Sunshine Of Your Love / Hey Joe / Purple Haze / Wild Thing - Taps
  Audio: JHE / Stereo audience recording (60 minutes)
  Bootleg: REMEMBER THE ALAMO

February 25: Civic Opera House, Chicago, IL
  Songs: Sgt. Pepper's Lonely Hearts Club Band / Fire / The Wind Cries Mary / Foxy Lady / I Don't Live Today / Hey Joe / Can You Please Crawl Out Your Window / Manic Depression / Like A Rolling Stone / Purple Haze
  Audio: JHE / Audience recording (32 minutes)
  Bootleg: WINTERLAND VOL. 2 (Whoopy Cat WKP 27/28 - CD)

March 2: Hunter College, New York, NY—SECOND SHOW
  Songs: Tax Free / Foxy Lady / Like A Rolling Stone / Killin' Floor / Red House
  Audio: JHE / Audience recording (25 minutes)
  Bootleg: THE LOST CONCERTS VOL. 6 (Blank label CD-R)

March 10: International Ballroom, Washington Hilton Hotel, Washington , DC—FIRST SHOW
  Songs: Killin' Floor / Foxy Lady / The Wind Cries Mary / Fire / Red House / I Don't Live Today / Purple Haze / Wild Thing
  Audio: JHE / Audience recording (36 minutes)
  Bootleg: STIMMEN DER WELT 2 (Major Tom MT 025) CD-R.

March 15: Atwood Hall, Clark University, Worcester, MA
  Songs: Foxy Lady / Purple Haze / Wild Thing
  Audio: JHE / Soundboard recording of "Purple Haze" & "Wild Thing" (12 minutes)
  Bootlegs: LIVE EXPERIENCE 1967-68 (Voodoo Chile), BROADCASTS (TMOQ 1841), BROADCASTS (Luna LU 9024 - CD), GOODBYE JIMI (Kustom 005) and others. There is also a one minute bit of interview made backstage by Tony Palmer.

Video: JHE / Some footage from both shows plus short interviews with Jimi and Mitch by Tony Palmer (color—90 minutes).

March 17: Cafe Au Go Go, Greenwich Village, NYC

Songs: Jams I-III / Jam (Little Wing - Everything's Gonna Be Alright) / Stormy Monday Jam (Three Little Bears) / Jam

Audio: Jimi with Paul Butterfield (harmonica), Elvin Bishop (guitar), Harvey Brooks (bass), Herbie Rich (organ), Buddy Miles (drums), Phillip Wilson (drums) and James Tatum (sax). Soundboard recording (stereo—90 minutes)

Bootlegs: Last four songs on BLUES AT MIDNIGHT, CAFE AU GO GO JAM SESSION (Koine K8802802), J.H. LIVE IN NEW YORK (Black Panther BPCD018) and SHINE ON EARTH, SHINE ON (Sidewalk SW 89010/11).

March 19: "Superconcert", Capitol Theatre, Ottawa, Ontario, Canada—SECOND SHOW

Songs: Killin' Floor / Tax Free / Fire / Red House / Foxy Lady / Hey Joe / Spanish Castle Magic / Purple Haze / Wild Thing

Audio: JHE / Soundboard recording (60 minutes)

Bootlegs: SUPERCONCERT 1968 (Firepower FP-03), THANKS, OTTAWA, FOR THE MEMORIES (Luna LU9319) and PURPLE SONGS (Lost Rose LR 16).

March 26: Public Music Hall, Cleveland, OH—SECOND SHOW

Songs: Sgt. Pepper's Lonely Hearts Club Band / Fire / I Don't Live Today / Red House / Foxy Lady / Spanish Castle Magic / Manic Depression / Purple Haze / Wild Thing - Taps

Audio: JHE / Audience recording (58 minutes)

Bootleg: THE LOST CONCERTS VOL. 1 (BLANK LABEL CD-R) contains the first nine songs.

Video: JHE / About five minutes of color concert footage.

April 2: Paul Sauve Arena, Montreal, Quebec, Canada

Songs: Killin' Floor / Hey Joe / Fire / The Wind Cries Mary / Foxy Lady I Don't Live Today / Manic Depression / Purple Haze / Wild Thing - Taps

Audio: JHE / Audience recording (46 minutes)

April 7: Generation Club, 52 West 8th Street, NYC

Song: Jam

Audio: Jimi with Roy Buchanan

Bootleg: THE LOST CONCERTS VOL. 1 (Blank label CD-R)

Video: Jimi / From the "Wake At Generation" film by D.A. Pennebaker (color—5 minutes) with Roy Buchanan on guitar and Jimi watching Buddy Guy's performance.

April 15?: Generation Club, 52 West 8th Street, NYC

Songs: Jams I, II / Like A Rolling Stone / San-Ho-Zay / Jams III, IV (It's My Own Fault)

Audio: Jimi with B.B. King (guitar and vocals), Elvin Bishop (guitar and vocals), Paul Butterfield (harmonica), Al Kooper (organ), Buzzy Feiten (bass), Don Martin (guitar), Phillip Wilson (drums) and Stewart (piano). Jimi plays on only a few of these songs and jams. Source: Private recording from reels (120 minutes).

Bootlegs: THE KING'S JAM (Klondyke KR 26 - CD)

April ?: The Record Plant, NYC

Audio: Jimi is interviewed by Michael Rosenbaum (5 min. 12 sec.)

May 10: Fillmore East, NYC

Songs: Lover Man / Fire / Foxy Lady / Red House / Hey Joe / Sunshine Of Your Love / Hear My Train A Comin' / Can You Please Crawl Out Your Window / Purple Haze / Wild Thing

Audio: JHE / Audience recording (60 minutes)

Bootlegs: IT'S ONLY A PAPER MOON (Luna LU 9420 - CD) & ONE NIGHT STAND (Hep Cat 1001/Scorpio).

May 18: "Underground Pop Festival", Gulf Stream Race Track, Hallendale, FL

Songs: Foxy Lady / Hear My Train A Comin' / Fire / Purple Haze

Audio: JHE / Stereo soundboard recording (21 minutes)

Bootlegs: All four songs on 1968 AD (Whoopy Cat WKP-0001) and "Hear My Train A Comin'" & "Fire" are on the 51ST ANNIVERSARY box set (JMH 001/8).

Video: JHE / From ABC News TV, September 18, 1970 (B&W—4 minutes)—with offstage footage.

May 24: Malpensa airport, Milano, Italy
Video: JHE / Noel Redding's home movie (color—silent 8mm—30 seconds) of JHE departure to Rome, Italy. From the "South Bank Documentary", October 1, 1989.

May 26: Palasport, Bologna, Italy
Songs: Fire / Hey Joe / Stone Free / Red House / Tax Free - Come On (Part I) / Mary Had A Little Lamb / Purple Haze / Foxy Lady
Audio: JHE / Audience recording (45 minutes)

May 27: Malpensa airport, Milano, Italy
Video: JHE / Noel Redding's home movie (color—silent 8mm—30 seconds) of JHE departure to London. From the "South Bank Documentary", October 1, 1989.

May 30: "Beat Monster Concert", Hallenstadion, Zurich, Switzerland
Songs: Voodoo Child (slight return) / Stone Free / I Don't Live Today / Red House / Hey Joe / Foxy Lady / Manic Depression / Fire / Purple Haze
Audio: JHE / Audience recording (54 minutes)
Bootleg: The complete show is on MONSTER (SJ-0001) CD-R.
Video: "Hits A Go-Go", Swiss TV (B&W—2 minutes)

May 31: "Beat Monster Concert", Hallenstadion, Zurich, Switzerland
Songs: Voodoo Child (slight return) / Stone Free / I Don't Live Today / Red House / Hey Joe / Foxy Lady / Manic Depression / Fire / Purple Haze
Video: JHE / Silent 8mm—color—3 minutes & 2 minutes.

June 5: "It Must Be Dusty!", ATV, Elstree Studios, Borehamwood, England
Songs: Stone Free / Mocking Bird / Voodoo Child (slight return)
Audio: JHE / Soundboard recording (13 minutes). Includes a duet with Dusty Springfield on "Mocking Bird".
Bootleg: SCREAMING EAGLE (Pink Poodle POO 001)

August 3: Moody Coliseum, Southern Methodist University, Dallas, TX
Songs: Dear Mr. Fantasy / Rock Me Baby / Foxy Lady / I Don't Live Today / Hey Joe - I Feel Fine / Fire / Red House / Purple Haze - Taps / Wild Thing
Audio: JHE / Stereo audience recording (63 minutes)
Bootleg: CROSSTOWN TRAFFIC

August 4: Sam Houston Coliseum, Houston, TX
Songs: Red House / I Don't Live Today / Spanish Castle Magic / Fire / Voodoo Child (slight return) / Purple Haze / Manic Depression
Audio: JHE / Audience recording (35 minutes)
Bootleg: THE LOST CONCERTS VOL. 8 HOUSTON 1968 (Blank label CD-R)

August 10: Auditorium Theatre, Chicago, IL
Video: JHE / Silent 8mm—color—1 minute

August 11: Col Ballroom, Davenport, IA
Songs: Are You Experienced / Lover Man / Foxy Lady / Red House / I Don't Live Today / Fire
Audio: JHE / Audience recording (45 minutes). Mono with one song in stereo.
Bootlegs: DAVENPORT, IOWA (Creative Artistry - 2LP) and THE LOST CONCERTS VOL. 2 (Blank label CD-R)

August 16: Merriweather Post Pavilion, Columbia, MD
Songs: Are You Experienced / Rock Me Baby / Foxy Lady / Hey Joe / Fire / I Don't Live Today / Purple Haze / Wild Thing - Star Spangled Banner - Taps

Audio: JHE / Audience recording (46 minutes)
Bootleg: THE LOST CONCERTS VOL. 10 COLUMBIA 1968 (Blank label CDR)

August 23: "The New York Rock Festival", Singer Bowl, Flushing Meadows Park, Queens, NYC
Songs: Are You Experienced / Fire / Red House / I Don't Live Today / Like A Rolling Stone / Foxy Lady / Purple Haze / Hey Joe / Wild Thing - Star Spangled Banner
Audio: JHE / Audience recording (57 minutes)
Bootleg: HISTORIC CONCERT (Midnight Beat MBCD 017)
Video: JHE / Silent 16mm (dubbed sound—color—20 minutes) "Are You Experience?", "Fire", "Hey Joe" & "Wild Thing".

September 4: Memorial Coliseum, Phoenix, AZ
Songs: Are You Experienced / Come On (Part I) / Little Wing / Voodoo Child (slight return) / Fire / Spanish Castle Magic / Foxy Lady / Like A Rolling Stone / Sunshine Of Your Love / Hey Joe / Star Spangled Banner / Purple Haze
Audio: JHE / Audience recording (62 minutes)
Bootleg: THE LOST CONCERTS VOL. 6 PHOENIX 1968

September 7: CBC TV, Pacific Coliseum, Vancouver, Canada
Audio: JHE / A backstage interview with the band (2 min. 40 sec.)
Video: Backstage interviews with Jimi, Mitch and Noel (B&W—6 minutes) from CBC TV by Terry David Mulligan.

September 8: Coliseum, Spokane, WA
Songs: Foxy Lady / Little Wing / Red House/ Fire
Audio: JHE / Audience recording (21 minutes)
Bootleg: THE LOST CONCERTS (Blank label CD-R)

September 9: Memorial Coliseum, Portland, OR
Songs: Are You Experienced / Fire / Hey Joe / Foxy Lady / Voodoo Child (slight return) / Little Wing / Spanish Castle Magic / Red House / Star Spangled Banner / Purple Haze
Audio: JHE / Audience recording (65 minutes)

September 14: Hollywood Bowl, Los Angeles, CA
Songs: Are You Experienced / Voodoo Child (slight return) / Red House / Foxy Lady / Fire / Hey Joe / Sunshine Of Your Love / I Don't Live Today / Little Wing (false start) / Star Spangled Banner / Purple Haze
Audio: JHE / Audience recording (72 minutes)
Bootleg: LIVE AT THE HOLLYWOOD BOWL
Video: Silent 8mm—color—5 minutes

October 10: Winterland Arena, San Francisco, CA
Songs: FIRST SHOW: Are You Experienced/ Voodoo Child (slight return)/ Red House/ Foxy Lady/ Like A Rolling Stone/ Star Spangled Banner/ Purple Haze-Outside Woman Blues
SECOND SHOW: Tax Free/ Lover Man/ Sunshine Of Your Love/ Hear My Train A Comin'/ Killin' Floor/ Hey Joe/ Star Spangled Banner/ Purple Haze
Audio: JHE / FIRST SHOW: Stereo soundboard (65 minutes)
Audio: JHE / SECOND SHOW: Stereo soundboard (74 minutes) with Jack Casady on bass on last four songs.
Bootleg: WINTERLAND VOL.1 (Whoopy Cat WKP-0025/26)

October 11: Winterland Arena, San Francisco, CA
Songs: FIRST SHOW: Are You Experienced / Voodoo Child (slight return) / Red House / Foxy Lady / Star Spangled Banner / Purple Haze
SECOND SHOW: Tax Free / Spanish Castle Magic / Like A Rolling Stone / Lover Man / Hey Joe / Fire / Foxy Lady / Purple Haze
Audio: JHE / FIRST SHOW: Stereo soundboard (44 minutes). Virgil Gonsales (flute) on "Are You Experienced".

Audio: JHE / SECOND SHOW: Stereo soundboard (75 minutes). Herbie Rich (organ) on "Like A Rolling Stone", "Lover Man", "Hey Joe", "Fire", "Foxy Lady". Also as an audience recording of both shows (106 minutes).

Bootlegs: Select songs can be found spread out on a number of different bootlegs such as WINTERLAND VOL. 2 (Whoopy Cat WKP-0027/28), WINTERLAND DAYS, THE STAR SPANGLED BLUES (Neutral Zone NZCD 89011), LITTLE WING (Oil Well RSC 036 CD), BROADCASTS (Luna CD).

October 12: Winterland Arena, San Francisco, CA
Songs: FIRST SHOW: Fire / Lover Man / Like A Rolling Stone / Foxy Lady / Noel Redding - Mitch Mitchell jam / Tax Free / Hey Joe / Purple Haze / Wild Thing
SECOND SHOW: Foxy Lady / Manic Depression / Sunshine Of Your Love / Little Wing / Spanish Castle Magic / Red House / Voodoo Child (slight return) / Star Spangled Banner / Purple Haze
Audio: JHE / Stereo soundboard recording (FIRST SHOW—66 minutes / SECOND SHOW—71 minutes)
Bootleg: WINTERLAND VOL. 3 (Woopy Cat WKP-0029/30) and spread out on several other titles.

October 29: TTG Studios, Hollywood, CA
Video: JHE / Color—9 minutes. Footage of the recording session.

October 30: Laurel Canyon, CA
Video: JHE / Silent 8mm—color—5 minutes. JHE driving cars and footage around a house. And the "All Along The Watchtower" promo clip (includes footage from the previous day—color—4 minutes).

November 2: Minneapolis Auditorium, Minneapolis, MN
Songs: Fire / Are You Experienced / Voodoo Child (slight return) / Red House / Foxy Lady / Little Wing / Spanish Castle Magic / Sunshine Of Your Love / Star Spangled Banner / Purple Haze
Audio: JHE / Audience recording (35 minutes) includes a back-stage interview by Tony Glover.
Bootleg: THE LOST CONCERTS VOL. 1 HOUSTON 1968 (Blank label CDR)

November 16: Boston Garden, Boston, MA
Songs: Fire / Spanish Castle Magic / Voodoo Child (slight return) / Red House / Foxy Lady / Purple Haze
Audio: JHE / Audience recording (42 minutes)

November 27: Rhode Island Arena, Providence, RI
Songs: Sgt. Pepper's Lonely Hearts Club Band / Fire / Hey Joe / I Don't Live Today / Voodoo Child (slight return) / Red House / Sunshine Of Your Love / Spanish Castle Magic / Foxy Lady / Star Spangled Banner / Purple Haze
Audio: JHE / Audience recording (100 minutes)

November 28: "An Electric Thanksgiving", Philharmonic Hall, New York, NY
Songs: FIRST SHOW: Fire / I Don't Live Today / Hear My Train A Comin' / Spanish Castle Magic / Foxy Lady / Red House / Sunshine Of Your Love / Purple Haze
Audio: JHE / Audience recording (75 minutes)
Bootleg: PHILHARMONIC HALL and PHILHARMONIC PLUS (BRCD 1901)
According to Mitch Mitchell the entire show was filmed and recorded; however, no soundboard tapes have come to light.

November 30: Cobo Hall, Detroit, MI
Songs: Fire / Spanish Castle Magic / I Don't Live Today / Sunshine Of Your Love / Voodoo Child (slight return) / Red House / Foxy Lady / Hey Joe / Purple Haze
Audio: JHE / Stereo audience recording (34 minutes) of first six songs only. Mono audience recording (48 minutes) "Fire", "I Don't Live Today", "Sunshine Of Your Love","Red House", "Foxy Lady", "Hey Joe", "Purple Haze".
Bootleg: THE LOST CONCERTS VOL. 4 (Blank label CD-R) & PANIC IN DETROIT (Major Tom MT 112) CD-R contains the mono audience recording.

December 1: Coliseum, Chicago, IL
Songs: Killin' Floor / I Don't Live Today / Spanish Castle Magic / Foxy Lady / Red House / Sunshine Of Your Love / Voodoo Child (slight return) / Fire/ Purple Haze
Audio: JHE / Audience recording (68 minutes)

1969

January 4: "Happening For Lulu", BBC Television Centre, London, England
Songs: Voodoo Child (slight return) / Hey Joe / Sunshine Of Your Love
Audio: JHE / Soundboard recording
Bootleg: BROADCASTS (Luna LU 9024) & CR BBC SESSIONS
Video: B&W—9 minutes.

January 7: Jimi's Apartment, 25 Brook St., London, England
Audio: Jimi and band are interviewed for "Through The Eyes Of Tomorrow" for CBC TV, Canada.
Video: Jimi / Interview with Jimi by Hugh Curry ("Through The Eyes Of Tomorrow", CBC TV, Toronto, Canada—B&W—10 minutes)

January 8: Lorensbergs Cirkus, Gothenburg, Sweden
Songs: SECOND SHOW: Voodoo Child (slight return) / Foxy Lady / Red House / Sunshine Of Your Love / I Don't Live Today / Third Stone From The Sun / Hear My Train A Comin' / Spanish Castle Magic / drum solo / Purple Haze / Star Spangled Banner
Audio: JHE / Audience recording (83 minutes)
Bootleg: CATS SQUIRREL (CS 001/2) CD
Video: Silent 8mm—color—2 minutes

January 9: Konserthuset, Stockholm, Sweden
Songs: FIRST SHOW: Killin' Floor / Spanish Castle Magic / Fire / Hey Joe / Voodoo Child (slight return) / Red House / Sunshine Of Your Love
SECOND SHOW: I Don't Live Today / Spanish Castle Magic / Hey Joe / Reveille / Voodoo Child (slight return) / Sunshine Of Your Love / Red House / Fire / Purple Haze / Star Spangled Banner
Audio: JHE / FIRST SHOW: Soundboard recording (56 minutes)
Audio: JHE / SECOND SHOW: Soundboard recording (69 minutes)
Audio: Jimi / Interview by Lennart Wreitlind ("Pop 69 Special"—January 12, 1969—10 minutes—Swedish radio)
Bootlegs: ON THE KILLING FLOOR (The Swinging Pig TSP-012/3) CD. Contains both shows. Also on LIVE IN SWEDEN (Midnight Beat MBCD 138/39/40) Box set with CD-Rom.
Video: B&W—56 minutes. Video on LIVE IN SWEDEN (Midnight Beat MBCD 138/39/40) CD-Rom.

January 10: Falkoner Teatret, Falkoner Centret, Copenhagen, Denmark
Songs: FIRST SHOW: Fire / Foxy Lady / Tax Free / Spanish Castle Magic / Red House / Sunshine Of Your Love / I Don't Live Today - Third Stone From The Sun / Purple Haze
SECOND SHOW: Fire / Voodoo Child (slight return) / Foxy Lady / Spanish Castle Magic / Hear My Train A Comin'
Audio: JHE / FIRST SHOW: Audience recording (68 minutes)
Audio: JHE / SECOND SHOW: Audience recording (25 minutes)
Bootlegs: WELCOME TO THE ELECTRIC CIRCUS (Midnight Beat MBCD 016). FIRST SHOW: JIMI IN DENMARK (Dynamite Studios DS95J356). Univibes (Fan Club Release) has an interview with Jimi by Niels Olaf Gudme on CD (23 minutes).

January 11: Musikhalle, Hamburg, Germany
Songs: FIRST SHOW: Are You Experienced / Johnny B. Goode / Spanish Castle Magic / Hear My Train A Comin' / Fire / I Don't Live Today - Third Stone From The Sun / Red House / Sunshine Of Your Love / Voodoo Child (slight return)
Audio: JHE / Audience recording (66 minutes)
Bootleg: LIVE IN HAMBURG 1969 (Major Tom MT 030) CD-R

January 13: "Beat Club", Studio Du Monde, Cologne, Germany
    Audio: Jimi is interviewed during an autograph session (2 minutes).
    Video: B&W—2 minutes—with German voice-over.

January 14: Halle Münsterland, Münster, Germany
    Songs: Red House / Fire / Foxy Lady / All Along The Watchtower / Hey Joe / Voodoo Child (slight
                return) - Gypsy Eyes / Purple Haze
    Audio: JHE / Audience recording (49 minutes)
    Bootleg: LIVE IN MUNSTER 1969 (Major Tom MT 031) CD-R

January 16: Meistersingerhalle, Nuremberg, Germany
    Songs: FIRST SHOW: Come On (Part I) / I Don't Live Today / Hey Joe / Fire / Red House / Foxy
                Lady / Purple Haze / Voodoo Child (slight return)
    Audio: JHE / Audience recording (57 minutes)
    Bootleg: LIVE IN NURNBERG 1969 (Major Tom MT 032) CD-R

January 17: Jahrhunderthalle, Frankfurt, Germany
    Songs: SECOND SHOW: Come On (Part I) / Fire / Red House / I Don't Live Today / Reveille /
                Little Wing / Foxy Lady / Hear My Train A Comin' / Sunshine Of Your Love / Hey Joe /
                Purple Haze / Voodoo Child (slight return)
    Audio: JHE / Audience recording (66 minutes) "Hear My Train A Comin'" is incomplete.
    Bootlegs: BURNING AT FRANKFURT (Midnight Beat MBCD 040) & LIVE IN FRANKFURT 1969 (Major Tom
                MT 043) CD-R.

January 19: Liederhalle, Stuttgart, Germany
    Songs: FIRST SHOW: Come On (Part I) / Foxy Lady / Red House / Sunshine Of Your Love /
                Star Spangled Banner / Purple Haze
    Audio: JHE / Audience recording (29 minutes)
    Bootleg: LIVE IN STUTTGART 1969 (Major Tom MT 033) CD-R

January 22: "Stimmen der Welt", Konzerthaus, Vienna, Austria
    Songs: FIRST SHOW: Come On (Part I) / Hey Joe / Fire / Hear My Train A Comin' / Spanish
                Castle Magic / Foxy Lady / Stone Free / Purple Haze
                SECOND SHOW: Are You Experienced / Fire / Lover Man / Sunshine Of Your Love - Cat's
                Squirrel / Spanish Castle Magic
    Audio: JHE / Audience recording (81 minutes)
    Bootlegs: STIMMEN DER WELT 1 & 2 (Major Tom MT 025 & 025) CD-Rs.

January 23: Sport Palast, Berlin, Germany
    Songs: Fire / Hey Joe / Spanish Castle Magic / Foxy Lady / Red House / Come On (Part I) / Sunshine
                Of Your Love / Purple Haze
    Audio: JHE / Includes backstage chat and a few notes of "Fire" and some film soundtrack ("Last
                Experience") and an audience recording of the concert (44 minutes)
    Bootleg: UP AGAINST THE BERLIN WALL (Midnight Beat MBCD 046)
    Video: JHE / At the airport, driving through Berlin and arriving at Hotel Kempinski. Color—5 min-
                utes—from "Last Experience" film.

February 13: London, England
    Video: Footage of Jimi at the launch party for Mary Hopkin's new album (B&W—5 minutes).

February 14: Seymour Hall, London, England
    Video: Jimi receives Disc Award for Top Musician from Maurice Gibb ("Movietone News"—B&W—
                15 seconds).

February 18: Royal Albert Hall, London, England
    Songs: Tax Free / Fire / Hear My Train A Comin' / Foxy Lady / Red House / Sunshine Of Your Love
                / Spanish Castle Magic / Message To Love / Star Spangled Banner / Purple Haze / Voodoo
                Child (slight return)

Audio: JHE / Audience recording (90 minutes)
Bootleg: FIRST NIGHT AT THE ROYAL ALBERT HALL (Midnight Beat MBCD 047/048).

February 24: Royal Albert Hall, London, England
Songs: SOUNDCHECK: Hey Joe / Hound Dog I, II, III, IV, V / Voodoo Child (slight return) I, II / Hear My Train A Comin'
Audio: JHE / Soundboard recording (30 minutes)
Bootlegs: GOOD VIBES (Ruthless Rhymes 1850), FIRST NIGHT AT THE ROYAL ALBERT HALL (Midnight Beat), PHILHARMONIC PLUS (BRCD 1901).

February 24: Royal Albert Hall, London, England
Songs: Lover Man / Stone Free / Hear My Train A Comin' / I Don't Live Today / Red House / Foxy Lady / Sunshine Of Your Love / Bleeding Heart / Fire / Little Wing / Voodoo Child (slight return) / Room Full Of Mirrors / Purple Haze / Wild Thing / Smashing The Amps
Audio: JHE / Stereo soundboard (102 minutes) with Kwasi "Rocky" Dzidzournu, Chris Wood and Dave Mason on "Room Full Of Mirrors". Recording by Glyn Johns.
Bootlegs: LISTEN TO THIS ERIC (Batz) and on numerous other bootlegs but not complete. Also on CONCERTS (Reprise Records) and HENDRIX IN THE WEST (Reprise Records), but again only a few of the songs.
Video: From "Last Experience" film (color—105 minutes)

February or March?: 25 Brook Street, London, England
Songs: Hound Dog (Two Old Maids)
Audio: Jimi solo / From "Last Experience" film (5 minutes)
Bootleg: FREAKOUT JAM
Video: Jimi solo / From "Last Experience" film (color—5 minutes) includes interview.

March 30: "Pop Expo, Teenage Fair", Hollywood Palladium, Hollywood, CA
Songs: Jams / Room Full Of Mirrors
Audio: Jimi / Audience recording (10 minutes) with Delaney and Bonnie and a back-stage interview with Jimi by Jay Harvey for KDAY Radio.

April 12: Spectrum Arena, Philadelphia, PA
Songs: Red House / Foxy Lady / I Don't Live Today / Hear My Train A Comin' / Stone Free / Star Spangled Banner / Purple Haze / Voodoo Child (slight return)
Audio: JHE / Audience recording (60 minutes)
Bootleg: PHILADELPHIA PA (Major Tom MT 199) CD-R.

April 18: North Hall, Ellis Auditorium Amphitheatre, Memphis, TN
Songs: SECOND SHOW: Fire / I Don't Live Today / Hear My Train A Comin' / Sunshine Of Your Love / Stone Free / Foxy Lady / Star Spangled Banner / Purple Haze / Voodoo Child (slight return)
Audio: JHE / Audience recording (57 minutes)
Bootleg: LONG DISTANCE INFORMATION (Major Tom MT 131) CD-R.

April 20: Memorial Auditorium, Dallas, TX
Songs: Stone Free / Hear My Train A Comin' / Foxy Lady / I Don't Live Today / Fire / Red House / Star Spangled Banner / Purple Haze / Voodoo Child (slight return)
Audio: JHE / Audience recording (56 minutes)
Bootleg: DALLAS (Major Tom MT 198) CD-R.

April 26: Los Angeles Forum, Los Angeles, CA
Songs: Tax Free / Foxy Lady / Red House / Spanish Castle Magic / Star Spangled Banner / Purple Haze / I Don't Live Today / Voodoo Child (slight return) / Sunshine Of Your Love
Audio: JHE / Stereo soundboard recording by Abe Jacob for Wally Heider Recording (83 minutes) and includes an introduction by Jimmy Rabbit.
Bootlegs: Entire show on ANTHOLOGY (Box 9), but songs not in proper running order and on I DON'T LIVE TODAY, MAYBE TOMORROW (Living Legend LLRCD 030). Parts of the concert are on

numerous other bootlegs and on the LIFELINES box set.

Video: JHE / Silent 8mm—B&W—4 minutes

April 27: Oakland Coliseum, Oakland, CA

Songs: Fire / Hey Joe / Spanish Castle Magic / Hear My Train A Comin' / Sunshine Of Your Love / Red House / Foxy Lady / Star Spangled Banner / Purple Haze / Voodoo Child (slight return)

Audio: JHE / Audience recording (85 minutes).

Mono recording officially released by Experience Hendrix in 1998 on LIVE AT THE OAKLAND COLISEUM.

May 3: Maple Leaf Gardens, Toronto, Ontario, Canada

Songs: Fire / Hear My Train A Comin' / Spanish Castle Magic / Third Stone From The Sun / drum solo / Little Miss Lover / Red House / Foxy Lady / Room Full Of Mirrors / Crash Landing - Keep On Groovin' - Gypsy Eyes / Purple Haze / Voodoo Child (slight return)

Audio: JHE / Audience recording (70 minutes)

Bootleg: BUSTED IN TORONTO (Venue) and LIVE AT THE MAPLE LEAF GARDENS (ACL 007) and as a disc included on I DON'T LIVE TODAY box set.

Video: Silent 8mm—color—4 minutes

May 11: Fieldhouse, State Fairgrounds Coliseum, Indianapolis, IN

Songs: Come On (Part I) / Hey Joe / Stone Free / Hear My Train A Comin' / Fire / Red House / Foxy Lady / Voodoo Child (slight return)

Audio: JHE / Audience recording (64 minutes)

Bootleg: AT THE COLLISEUM (Major Tom MT 132) CD-R.

May 16: Civic Center, Baltimore, MD

Songs: Lover Man / Hear My Train A Comin' / Fire / Red House / I Don't Live Today / Foxy Lady / Purple Haze / Spanish Castle Magic / Voodoo Child (slight return)

Audio: JHE / Audience recording (57 minutes)

Video: JHE / Silent 8mm—color—5 minutes

May 17: Rhode Island Arena, Providence, RI

Songs: Lover Man / I Don't Live Today / Red House / Hear My Train A Comin' / Spanish Castle Magic / Sunshine Of Your Love / Foxy Lady / Purple Haze / Voodoo Child (slight return)

Audio: JHE / Audience recording (67 minutes)

Bootleg: ONE NIGHT AT THE ARENA (Venue VE 100501)

May 18: Madison Square Garden, NYC

Songs: Lover Man / Come On (Part I) / Red House / Fire / drum solo / Spanish Castle Magic / Villanova Junction / Hear My Train A Comin' / I Don't Live Today / Voodoo Child (slight return) / Purple Haze

Audio: JHE / Audience recording (70 minutes)

Bootleg: THE ROMAN COLISEUM (Starquake SQ11)

Video: Silent 16mm—color—9 minutes

May 24: International Sports Arena, San Diego, CA

Songs: Fire / Hey Joe / Spanish Castle Magic / Sunshine Of Your Love / Red House / I Don't Live Today / Foxy Lady / Purple Haze / Voodoo Child (slight return)

Audio: JHE / Stereo soundboard recording (63 minutes) by Abe Jacob for Wally Heider Recording. All the songs except "Foxy Lady" are on the STAGES box set.

May 25: "San Jose Pop Festival", Santa Clara, CA

Songs: Hear My Train A Comin' / Fire / drum solo / Spanish Castle Magic / Red House / I Don't Live Today / Foxy Lady / Purple Haze / Voodoo Child (slight return) - Message To Love - Room Full Of Mirrors - Sunshine Of Your Love

Audio: JHE / Audience recording (66 minutes)

Bootlegs: HISTORIC CONCERT VOL. 2 (Midnight Beat MBCD 017) and FLAMING GUITAR (Rock Calendar Records RC 2108).

Video: Silent 16mm—color—3 minutes

June 15: Beverly Rodeo Hyatt House, Beverly Hills, CA
     Audio: Jimi is interviewed by Nancy Carter (26 min. 30 sec.).

June 19: Old City Hall Court House, Toronto, Ontario, Canada
     Video: JHE / Silent 8mm—color—3 minutes

June 20: "Newport '69 Pop Festival", San Fernando Valley State College, Devonshire Downs, CA
     Songs: Stone Free / drum solo / Third Stone From The Sun / Are You Experienced / Stone Free / Sunshine Of Your Love / Fire / Hear My Train A Comin' / Red House / Foxy Lady / Like A Rolling Stone / Voodoo Child (slight return) / drum solo / Purple Haze
     Audio: JHE / Soundboard recording (64 minutes—from roll 5 and 6—64 minutes),
     Bootlegs: MORE ELECTRICITY FROM NEWPORT (Luna LU9201) and WIZARD'S VISIONS (WPOCM 0789).

June 22: "Newport '69 Pop Festival", San Fernando Valley State College, Devonshire Downs, CA
     Songs: Earth Versus Space (Keep On Groovin')', Gypsy Eyes, Machine Gun / The Things That I Used To Do / The Sky Is Crying / We Gotta Live Together / Feeling So Good / Power Of Soul - The Train Kept A Rollin' - Earth Blues / Hear My Train A Comin' / Voodoo Child (slight return) / Come On (Part I) - jam
     Audio: Jimi with Buddy Miles (drums and vocals), Eric Burdon and Sunshine (vocals),Tracy Nelson (background vocals), Brad Campbell (bass), Cornelius Flowers (sax), Terry Clements (sax), and Lee Oskar (harmonica). Soundboard recording (85 minutes) from rolls 14, 15, and 16 of the film of the festival.
     Bootleg: IT NEVER TAKES AN END (The Genuine Pig TGP-CD-118)
     Video: Jimi / 16mm—color—85 minutes. With Buddy Miles, Eric Burdon and others.

June 29: Denver Pop Festival, Mile High Stadium, Denver, CO
     Songs: Tax Free - Tomorrow Never Knows / Hear My Train A Comin' / Fire / Spanish Castle Magic / Red House / Foxy Lady / Star Spangled Banner / Purple Haze
     Audio: JHE / Audience recording (65 minutes). This was the last performance of the original Experience.
     Bootleg: THE WINK OF AN EYE (Whoopy Cat WKP-0033)
     Video: Silent 8mm—color—2 minutes. Last concert with the original Experience.

July 7: "Dick Cavett Show", ABC TV Studios, West 57th Street, NYC
     Song: Hear My Train A Comin'
     Audio: Jimi with Cox and Mitchell
     Bootleg: WOODSTOCK MONDAY AUGUST 1969 - 8 A.M.
     Video: Jimi with Billy Cox and Mitch Mitchell (color—15 minutes) and includes a short interview.

July 10: "Tonight Show", NBC TV, NYC
     Songs: Lover Man I / Lover Man II
     Audio: Jimi with Billy Cox and Ed Shaughnessy (9 minutes) and includes an interview by Flip Wilson. Johnny Carson evidently didn't want to sully himself by being present for Jimi's performance. Too bad, Johnny, you really missed out.
     Bootlegs: DANTE'S INFERNO (Pink Poodle POO 002) and the first track and interview on PHILHARMONIC PLUS (BRCD 1901).
     Video: Jimi with Billy Cox and Ed Shaughnessy (color—9 minutes) and an interview by Flip Wilson.

August 10: Tinker Street Cinema, Woodstock, NY
     Songs: The Dance / Sundance / Earth Blues / Star Spangled Banner
     Audio: Jimi with the Gypsy Sons and Rainbows from an audience recording (39 minutes) of the rehearsals.
     Bootleg: THE WOODSTOCK REHEARSALS (Midnight Beat MBCD 038). "The Dance" and "Sundance" only.

August 18: "Woodstock Music And Art Fair", Bethel, NY
   Songs: Message To The Universe / Hear My Train A Comin' / Spanish Castle Magic / Red House / Master Mind / Lover Man / Foxy Lady / Beginning (a.k.a. Jam Back At The House) / Izabella / Gypsy Woman / Fire / Voodoo Child (slight return) - Stepping Stone / Star Spangled Banner / Purple Haze / Villanova Junction / Hey Joe
   Audio: Jimi with the Gypsy Sun and Rainbow Band. Most of this performance has been legitimately released on compact disc and complete on WOODSTOCK MONDAY 8 A.M..
   Video: Jimi with the Gypsy Sun and Rainbow Band. Most of this performance has been legitimately released on video.

September 3: Frank's Restaurant, Harlem, NYC
   Audio: Jimi's press conference for the "United Block Association Benefit" (7 minutes).
   Video: Jimi at the press conference (color—five minutes).

September 5: "United Block Association Benefit", 139th Street near Lennox Avenue, Harlem, NYC
   Songs: Voodoo Child (slight return) / Machine Gun
   Audio: Jimi / Audience recording (25 minutes) yet to be bootlegged. Where is this?

September 8: "Dick Cavett Show", ABC TV Studios, West 57th Street, NYC
   Songs: Izabella / Machine Gun
   Video: Jimi with Billy Cox and Mitch Mitchell (color—25 minutes). Broadcast on VH1 in 1997.

November 27: Madison Square Garden, NYC
   Video: Jimi / Backstage scenes with the Rolling Stones (silent 16mm—color—7 minutes).

December 12?: Jimi's Apartment, 59 West 12th St., Greenwich Village, NYC
   Audio: Susan Clark interviewed Jimi for the book, "Superstars—In Their Own Words" (70 minutes).

December 31: Fillmore East, NYC
   Songs: FIRST SHOW: Power Of Soul / Lover Man / Hear My Train A Comin' / Them Changes / Izabella / Machine Gun / Stop / Ezy Ryder / Bleeding Heart / Earth Blues / Burning Desire
                SECOND SHOW: Auld Lang Syne / Who Knows / Stepping Stone / Burning Desire / Fire / Ezy Ryder / Machine Gun - Taps / Power Of Soul / Stone Free - March from the Nutcracker Suite / drum solo / Outside Woman Blues - Cherokee Mist - Sunshine Of Your Love / Them Changes / Message To Love / Stop / Foxy Lady / Voodoo Child (slight return) / Purple Haze
   Audio: Band Of Gypsys / Stereo soundboard recording (25 minutes—first four songs of FIRST SHOW) by Eddie Kramer for Wally Heider Recording. Audience recording (69 minutes—first 11 songs of FIRST SHOW). Soundboard recording (90 minutes—first 12 songs of SECOND SHOW) by Kramer. Audience recording (102 minutes—SECOND SHOW).
   Bootlegs: POWER OF SOUL (Starquake SQ 10) FIRST SHOW / AULD LANG SYNE (JH-69-100-03/4) SECOND SHOW. Portions are on many other boots and legitimate releases.
   Video: Band Of Gypsys / 16mm—color—15 minutes. Filmed by Amalie R. Rothschild

1970

January 1: Fillmore East, NYC
   Songs: FIRST SHOW: Who Knows / Machine Gun / Them Changes / Power Of Soul / Stepping Stone / Foxy Lady / Stop / Earth Blues
                SECOND SHOW: Stone Free - Little Drummer Boy / Earth Blues / Machine Gun / Voodoo Child (slight return) / We Gotta Live Together - Sing A Simple Song / Wild Thing / Hey Joe / Purple Haze
   Audio: Band Of Gypsys / Stereo soundboard (65 minutes—incomplete) by Eddie Kramer for Wally Heider Recording.
   Bootlegs: Portions appear on several different bootlegs (eg: THE ULTIMATE LIVE COLLECTION). None are complete shows.
   Video: Band Of Gypsys / B&W—53 minutes. Video of first show by Jan Blom and portions of the first show video taped by Woody Vasulk (B&W—29 minutes).

January 28: "Winter Festival For Peace", Madison Square Garden, NYC
 Songs: Who Knows / Earth Blues
 Audio: Band Of Gypsys / From the film (15 minutes—color) and from an audience recording (17 minutes).
 Bootleg: LIVE AT THE FORUM 1970 (Whoopy Cat WKP-21/22) Last performance of Band Of Gypsys.
 Video: 16mm—color—1 minute

February 4: "Rolling Stone" interview conducted by John Burks at Mike Jeffrey's NYC apartment
 Audio: Jimi's interview is published in the March 19, 1970, issue of "Rolling Stone".

April 25: Los Angeles Forum, Los Angeles, CA
 Songs: Spanish Castle Magic / Foxy Lady / Lover Man / Hear My Train A Comin' / Message To Love / Ezy Ryder / Machine Gun / Room Full Of Mirrors / Hey Baby (The Land Of The New Rising Sun) / Villanova Junction / drum solo / Freedom / Star Spangled Banner / Purple Haze / Voodoo Child (slight return) - Keep On Groovin'
 Audio: JHE (with Mitch Mitchell and Billy Cox) / Audience recording (the so-called 'near tape'—85 minutes). And from an audience recording (the 'far tape'—86 minutes).
 Bootlegs: **LA FORUM** (Rubber Dubber) / This is the 'near tape' and also on 'SCUSE ME WHILE I KISS THE SKY (Luna LU 9421). The 'far tape' is bootlegged on LIVE AT THE FORUM 1970 (Whoopy Cat WKP-21/22).

April 26: "Cal Expo", State Fairgrounds, Sacramento, CA
 Songs: Lover Man / Spanish Castle Magic / Freedom / Machine Gun / Foxy Lady / Room Full Of Mirrors / Ezy Ryder / Purple Haze / Star Spangled Banner / Voodoo Child (slight return)
 Audio: JHE / Audience recording (50 minutes)
 Bootleg: CAL EXPO (Major Tom MT 106) CD-R.

May 1: Milwaukee Auditorium, Milwaukee, WI
 Songs: Spanish Castle Magic - The Breeze And I / Lover Man / Hear My Train A Comin' / Ezy Ryder / Freedom / Message To Love / Foxy Lady / Star Spangled Banner / Purple Haze / Voodoo Child (slight return)
 Audio: JHE / Audience recording (60 minutes)
 Bootleg: STRONG BREW (Major Tom MT 107) CD-R.

May 2: Dane County Memorial Coliseum, Madison, WI
 Songs: Fire / Room Full Of Mirrors / Hear My Train A Comin' / Lover Man / Red House / Message To Love / Ezy Ryder / Machine Gun / Star Spangled Banner / Foxy Lady / Voodoo Child (slight return) / Purple Haze
 Audio: JHE / Audience recording (80 minutes)
 Bootleg: WISCONSIN MEMORIAL (Major Tom MT 108) CD-R.

May 3: St. Paul Civic Center, St. Paul, MN
 Songs: Fire / Room Full Of Mirrors / Lover Man / Hear My Train A Comin' / Ezy Ryder / Machine Gun / Freedom / Foxy Lady / Red House / Star Spangled Banner / Purple Haze / Voodoo Child (slight return) - Cat's Squirrel
 Audio: JHE / Audience recording (74 minutes)

May 8: University Of Oklahoma Field House, Norman, OK
 Songs: SECOND SHOW: Fire / drum solo / Spanish Castle Magic / Machine Gun / Lover Man / Foxy Lady / Hear My Train A Comin' / Message To Love / Red House / Star Spangled Banner / Purple Haze / Voodoo Child (slight return)
 Audio: JHE / Audience recording (65 minutes)
 Bootleg: UNIVERSITY OF OKLAHOMA (Major Tom MT 109) CD-R.

May 9: Will Rogers Coliseum, Fort Worth, TX
 Songs: Fire / Lover Man / Hear My Train A Comin' / Foxy Lady / Room Full Of Mirrors / Red House / Freedom / Ezy Ryder / Machine Gun / Star Spangled Banner / Purple Haze / Voodoo Child (slight return)

Audio: JHE / Audience recording (74 minutes)

May 10: San Antonio Hemisphere Arena, San Antonio, TX
Songs: Fire / Foxy Lady / Machine Gun / Freedom / Red House / Message To Love / Hear My Train A Comin' / Ezy Ryder / Room Full Of Mirrors / Star Spangled Banner / Purple Haze / Voodoo Child (slight return)
Audio: JHE / Audience recording (65 minutes)
Bootleg: SAN ANTONIO (Major Tom MT 110) CD-R.

May 16: Temple University Stadium, Philadelphia, PA
Songs: Sgt. Pepper's Lonely Hearts Club Band / Johnny B. Goode / Machine Gun / Lover Man / Foxy Lady / Red House / Freedom / Fire/ Hear My Train A Comin' - Keep On Groovin' / Purple Haze / Voodoo Child (slight return)
Audio: JHE / Audience recording (57 minutes)
Bootleg: WORSHIP (Major Tom MT 111) CD-R.
Video: JHE / Silent 8mm—color—3 minutes

May 30: Berkeley Community Theatre, Berkeley, CA
Songs: SOUNDCHECK: Message To Love / Blue Suede Shoes / Hey Baby (The Land Of The New Rising Sun) / Ezy Ryder / Earth Blues / Room Full Of Mirrors / Villanova Junction / Keep On Groovin' / Freedom / Power Of Soul (intro only) / Machine Gun
Audio: JHE / Stereo soundboard recording (40 minutes—incomplete, missing "Ezy Ryder") by Abe Jacob for Wally Heider Recording.
Bootleg: THE BERKELEY SOUNDCHECK (Whoopy Cat WKP-008). "Blue Suede Shoes" is on the official HENDRIX IN THE WEST.

May 30: Berkeley Community Theatre, Berkeley, CA
Songs: FIRST SHOW: Fire / Johnny B. Goode / Hear My Train A Comin' / Foxy Lady / Machine Gun / Freedom / Red House / Message To Love / Ezy Ryder / Star Spangled Banner / Purple Haze / Voodoo Child (slight return)
SECOND SHOW: Pass It On / Hey Baby (The Land Of The New Rising Sun) / Lover Man / Stone Free / Hey Joe / I Don't Live Today / Machine Gun / Foxy Lady / Star Spangled Banner / Purple Haze / Voodoo Child (slight return) - Keep On Groovin'
Audio: JHE / Stereo soundboard recording (75 minutes) FIRST SHOW (The first nine songs and "Voodoo Child (slight return)". And a complete audience recording (87 minutes) of entire show. Stereo soundboard recording (60 minutes) SECOND SHOW (missing "Hey Joe"). And a complete audience recording (62 minutes) of the entire show.
Bootlegs: **THE BERKELEY CONCERTS** (Whoopy Cat WKP-004/5) contains the soundboard recordings. Numerous other bootlegs contain portions of the two shows.
Video: SECOND SHOW / Silent 8mm—color—2 minutes. Both shows and the soundcheck were filmed for an official release but was never made available.

June 10: Roberts Municipal Stadium, Evansville, IN
Songs: Spanish Castle Magic / Fire / Lover Man / Red House / Foxy Lady / Machine Gun / Message To Love / Freedom / Hear My Train A Comin' / Star Spangled Banner / Purple Haze / Voodoo Child (slight return) - Keep On Groovin'
Audio: JHE / Audience recording(67 minutes)

June 13: Civic Center Baltimore, MD
Songs: Pass It On / Lover Man / Machine Gun / Ezy Ryder / Red House / Message To Love / Hey Joe / Freedom/ Hear My Train A Comin' / Room Full Of Mirrors / Foxy Lady / Purple Haze / Star Spangled Banner / Voodoo Child (slight return) - Keep On Groovin'
Audio: JHE / Stereo audience recording (73 minutes)
Bootleg: BALTIMORE CIVIC CENTER (Starquake SQ-09)
Video: JHE / Silent 8mm—color—4 minutes

June 20: Swing Auditorium, San Bernardino, CA
Songs: All Along The Watchtower / Room Full Of Mirrors / Machine Gun / Message To Love / Hear

My Train A Comin' / Foxy Lady / Hey Joe / Purple Haze / Voodoo Child (slight return) - Keep On Groovin'

Audio: JHE / Audience recording (43 minutes)

June 27: Boston Garden, Boston, MA
Songs: Stone Free / Lover Man / Red House / Freedom / Foxy Lady / Purple Haze / Star Spangled Banner / All Along The Watchtower / Message To Love / Fire / Spanish Castle Magic / Voodoo Child (slight return)
Audio: JHE / Audience recording (57 minutes) which is on the CD-R THE LOST CONCERTS VOL. 9 BOSTON 1970 and stereo audience recording (50 minutes) which is missing "Freedom".

July 4: "Second Atlanta International Pop Festival", Gainesville, GA
Songs: Fire / Lover Man / Spanish Castle Magic - The Breeze And I / Red House / Room Full Of Mirrors / Hear My Train A Comin' / Message To Love / All Along The Watchtower / Freedom / Foxy Lady / Purple Haze / Hey Joe / Voodoo Child (slight return) / Stone Free / Star Spangled Banner / Straight Ahead / Hey Baby (The Land Of The New Rising Sun)
Audio: JHE / Stereo soundboard (40 minutes) and a stereo audience recording (85 minutes). Most of this show is on the official Reprise release STAGES. There are a number of bootlegs which contain the other portions of this performance.
Video: Only parts of this performance were officially released on video.

July 17: "New York Pop", Downing Stadium, Randall's Island, New York, NY
Songs: Stone Free / Fire / Red House / Message To Love / Lover Man / All Along The Watchtower / Foxy Lady / Ezy Ryder / Star Spangled Banner - An English Country Garden / Purple Haze / Voodoo Child (slight return)
Audio: JHE / Stereo soundboard recording (45 minutes) which is missing "Red House" & "All Along The Watchtower". And there is an audience recording (55 minutes) of entire show.
Bootlegs: The stereo soundboard recording is available on MESSAGE OF LOVE (Pyramid PYCD 043). CAN YOU HERE ME ROCK (Keri Hemero 01) contains the audience tape but is incorrectly sequenced.
Audio: JHE / From "The Day The Music Died" film (color—7 minutes) Songs: "Foxy Lady'"& "Star Spangled Banner'.
Bootlegs: MESSAGE OF LOVE (Pyramid PYCD 043) contains all but "Red House" which is on the official Reprise CONCERTS.
Video: The show was filmed in its entirety but was never officially released.

July 25: International Sports Arena, San Diego, CA
Video: JHE / Silent 8mm—color—3 minutes

July 26: Sicks Stadium, Seattle, WA
Songs: Fire / Message To Love / drum solo / Lover Man / Freedom / Red House / Foxy Lady / Machine Gun / Star Spangled Banner / Purple Haze / Hear My Train A Comin' - Keep On Groovin' / Voodoo Child (slight return) / Hey Baby (The Land Of The New Rising Sun)
Audio: JHE / Audience recording (77 minutes)
Video: JHE / Silent 8mm—color—3 minutes

July 30: "Rainbow Bridge Vibratory Colour-Sound Experiment", Haleakala Crater, Maui, HI
Songs: FIRST SHOW: Spanish Castle Magic / Lover Man / Hey Baby (The Land Of The New Rising Sun) / In From The Storm / Message To Love / Foxy Lady / Hear My Train A Comin' / Voodoo Child (slight return) / drum solo / Fire / Purple Haze
SECOND SHOW: Dolly Dagger / Villanova Junction / Ezy Ryder / Red House / Freedom / Beginning / Straight Ahead / Hey Baby (The Land Of The New Rising Sun) (intro only) / Keep On Groovin' / Race With The Devil / drum solo / Stone Free - Hey Joe
Audio: JHE / Soundboard recording (105 minutes). The drums were overdubbed by Mitch at Electric Lady Studios.
Bootlegs: IN FROM THE STORM (Silver Rarities 109/110) features the entire concert but is mastered too fast. LAST AMERICAN CONCERT VOL. 1 (The Swinging Pig TSP-062) has all but "Spanish Castle

Magic" from the FIRST SHOW and LAST AMERICAN CONCERT VOL. 2 (The Swinging Pig TSP-072) has all but the last two songs from the SECOND SHOW.

Video: Portions of this show have been commercially released on video.

August 1: Honolulu International Center Arena, Honolulu, HI
  Video: JHE / Silent 8mm—color—5 minutes

August 30: "Isle Of Wight Festival", East Afton Farm, Isle Of Wight, England
  Songs: God Save The Queen / drum solo / Sgt. Pepper's Lonely Hearts Club Band / Spanish Castle Magic / All Along The Watchtower / Machine Gun - Race With The Devil / Lover Man / Freedom / Red House / Dolly Dagger / Keep On Groovin' / Foxy Lady / Message To Love / Hey Baby (The Land Of The New Rising Sun) / Ezy Ryder / Hey Joe / Purple Haze / Voodoo Child (slight return) / drum solo / In From The Storm
  Audio: JHE / A portion of this show has been legitimately released on ISLE OF WIGHT (Polydor).
  Video: Some of this performance is commercially available on the Rhino video.

August 31: Stora Scenen, Grona Lund, Stockholm, Sweden
  Songs: Lover Man / Catfish Blues / Midnight Lightnin' / Ezy Ryder / Red House / Come On (Part 1) / Room Full Of Mirrors / Hey Baby (The Land Of The New Rising Sun) / Message To Love / Machine Gun / Voodoo Child (slight return) / In From The Storm / Purple Haze / Foxy Lady
  Audio: JHE / Audience tape (107 minutes) and a five minute interview backstage with Klas Burling.
  Bootlegs: COME ON STOCKHOLM 1970 & FREE CONCERT (Midnight Beat MBCD 013)
  Video: Only 15 minutes of this show was taped (B&W film by Dave van Dijk and Eric Seagal)

September 1: Stora Scenen, Liseburg, Gothenburg, Sweden
  Songs: Spanish Castle Magic / Killin' Floor / Getting My Heart Back Together Again / Message To Love / Hey Baby (Land Of The New Rising Sun) / In From The Storm / Hey Joe / Foxy Lady / Red House / Room Full Of Mirrors / Straight Ahead / Purple Haze / Voodoo Child (slight return)
  Audio: JHE / Audience tape (92 minutes)
  Bootleg: THE WARM HELLO OF THE SUN

September 2: Vejlby Risskov Hallen, Arhus, Denmark
  Songs: Freedom / Message To Love / Hey Baby (The Land Of The New Rising Sun)
  Audio: JHE / Audience tape (25 minutes). Jimi left the stage after performing these songs because of illness / exhaustion.
  Bootleg: LIVE AT THE FORUM 1970 (WHOOPY CAT WKP-0021/22)
  Video: JHE / Color—8mm—4 minutes

September 3: K.B. Hallen, Copenhagen
  Songs: Stone Free / Foxy Lady / Message To Love / Hey Baby (The Land Of The New Rising Sun) / All Along The Watchtower / Machine Gun / Spanish Castle Magic / Ezy Ryder / Freedom / Red House / In From The Storm / Purple Haze / Voodoo Child (slight return) / Hey Joe / Fire
  Audio: JHE / Audience tape (90 minutes)
  Bootleg: WELCOME TO THE ELECTRIC CIRCUS VOL. 2 (Midnight Beat MBCD 018) and COPENHAGEN '70 (Whoopy Cat WKP-0044/0045).
  Video: Color—8mm—3 minutes

September 4: "Super Concert '70", Deutschlandhalle, Berlin, West Germany
  Songs: Straight Ahead / Spanish Castle Magic / Sunshine Of Your Love / Hey Baby (The Land Of The New Rising Sun) / Message To Love / Machine Gun / Purple Haze / Red House / Foxy Lady / Ezy Ryder / Hey Joe / Power Of Soul / Lover Man
  Audio: JHE / Audience recording (60 minutes) and a backstage interview by Sgt. Keith Roberts & Chris Bromberg for the Air Force News (15 minutes).
  Bootleg: THE LOST CONCERTS VOL. 3 BERLIN 1970 (Blank label CD-R) and LIVE IN BERLIN 1970 (Major Tom MT 034) CD-R.

September 6: "Love And Peace Festival", Isle Of Fehmarn, Germany

  Songs: Killin' Floor / Spanish Castle Magic / All Along The Watchtower / Hey Joe / Hey Baby (The Land Of The New Rising Sun) / Message To Love / Foxy Lady / Red House / Ezy Ryder / Freedom / Room Full Of Mirrors / Purple Haze / Voodoo Child (slight return)

  Audio: JHE / Audience recording (the 'windy' tape—77 minutes) & audience recording (the 'stage' tape—75 minutes).

  Bootlegs: THE WINK OF AN EYE (Whoopy Cat WKP-0033/0034) THE STAGE TAPE. LOVE AND PEACE (Midnight Beat MBCD 015) THE WINDY TAPE.

  Video: Film of Jimi in car and walking onto the stage (color—2 minutes). Originally broadcast on "Popgrusical". Jimi shown on and off the stage (B&W—3 minutes) and rebroadcast in 1994 on "Jimi Hendrix auf Fehmarn: Das Letzte Konzert" (The Last Concert). There is also an 8mm film (silent—color—4 minutes).

September 11: Cumberland Hotel, London, England

  Audio: Jimi was interviewed by BBC's Keith Altham (BBC transcription disc—30 minutes). Available on JIMI HENDRIX (BBC LP 37480).

September 16: Ronnie Scott's Club, London, England

  Songs: Paint It Black / Blackbird / Spill The Wine / Mystery Train / Mother Earth / Tobacco Road

  Audio: Jimi jammed with Eric Burdon & War on "Mother Earth" and "Tobacco Road". Audience recording (40 minutes). This is the last recording of Jimi Hendrix.

  Bootleg: CAN YOU PLEASE CRAWL OUT YOUR WINDOW (Ruthless Rhymes JIMI 1) which includes "Mother Earth" and "Tobacco Road".

> *All I can really remember is like, getting out of the Army and*
> *then try to get something together, and*
> *then I was playing in different groups all over the States.*
> Jimi: London 1969

Jimi Hendrix: The Early Years 1959-1966

1959:
At age 17 Jimmy (with The Velvetones?) performs for the first time in public at the Washington National Guard Armory, Kent, Washington.

1959 / 1960:
Jimmy next joins The Rocking Kings where they perform at numerous local halls and school dances.

1960 / 1961:
Jimmy becomes a member of The Tom Cats and perform at local clubs and military bases.

1961 / 1962:
In November 1961 he meets Billy Cox at Fort Campbell and they eventually start a group called The King Kasuals (Jimmy on guitar, Billy on bass and Gary Ferguson on drums). This line-up changes numerous times over the following months.

1963:
Jimmy joins with Gorgeous George and tours with him. Jimmy also did some backing work for a number of soul performers (including Little Richard & The Upsetters, Sam Cooke, The Supremes). Philadelphia, Pennsylvania: Jimmy records with Lonnie Youngblood.

1964:
March - Jimmy joins the Isley Brothers on tour and for recording sessions.

1965:
January - Jimmy joins the Little Richard tour but occasionally plays with Ike & Tina Turner.

October - Jimmy joins Curtis Knight & The Squires with whom he tours and records with. He also toured with Joey Dee and the Starlighters during this period.

1966:

January - Jimmy joins the King Curtis group with whom he tours with for about 6 months and also records with them.

May 13 - Jimmy plays with Curtis Knight & The Squires at the Cheetah in NYC. After this last gig with them Jimmy joins Carl Holmes & The Commanders for a month.

June - Jimmy forms his own band which he calls 'Jimmy James And The Blue Flames'.

July - The Animal's manager, Chas Chandler, sees Jimmy and his group perform at the Cafe Wha? and would later persuade him to hop a plane to London.

August - Jimmy would play a few more gigs in NYC before flying to London in September where he would change his name from Jimmy to 'Jimi'.

Art by Sara Gauthier

* This 22" X 32" poster print from a pencil drawing by Sara Gauthier can be purchased by sending a $25 money order (United States only) to Saraart, Box 913, Indian River, MI, 49749. Allow three weeks for delivery. Sorry, no foreign orders.

Touring is outasight. It's really good, you know, we're getting through to a lot of people that we normally wouldn't have if we wasn't on tour.
Jimi: Minneapolis 1968

Jimi Ḥendrix Øn Tour 1966-1970

Club dates, jams, concerts, radio / television shows

*From September 24, 1966 to September 18, 1970,
Jimi Hendrix performed at 525 official concerts.*

September, 1966
24 - Scotch Of St. James, London (Jimi's first public jam in England)
27 - Scotch Of St. James, London (Jimi jams with The VIPs)
29 - Blaises, London (Jimi jams with The Brian Auger Trinity)

October, 1966
 1 - The Polytechnic, London (Jimi jams with Cream)
 5 - Birdland, Les Cousins, London (Jimi jams with American blues performers)
 6 - Aberbach Publishing House, London (Jimi, Mitch Mitchell & Noel Redding's first rehearsal)
13 - Novelty, Evreux, France (first official public performance)
14 - Cinema Rio, Nancy, France (unconfirmed)
15 - Salle Des Fetes,Villerupt, France
16 - Louxumbourg, Grand Duchy Of Luxembourg
18 - L'Olympia, Paris
24 - Knuckles Club, Soho, London (Jimi jams with The Deep Feeling)
25 - Scotch of St. James, London (JHE's London debut)

November, 1966
 8 - Big Apple Club, Munich, West Germany (2 shows)
 9 - Big Apple Club, Munich, West Germany (2 shows)
10 - Big Apple Club, Munich, West Germany (2 shows)
11 - Big Apple Club, Munich, West Germany (2 shows) (first time Jimi smashes his guitar)
25 - Bag O'Nails, Soho, London (press concert)
26 - Ricky Tick, Hounslow, UK

December, 1966
10 - Ram Jam Club, Brixton, London
13 - "Ready Steady Go" TV show taped at Rediffusion Studios, Kingsway, UK
16 - Chislehurst Caves, Bromley, UK
21 - Blaises Club, Queensgate, London
22 - Guildhall, Southampton, UK (2 shows)
23 - Ricky Tick, Hounslow, UK
26 - Upper Cut Club, Forest Gate, London
29 - "Tops Of The Pops" TV show taped, BBC TV, London
31 - Hillside Social Club (Stan's/Toft's), Folkestone, UK

January, 1967
 4 - Bromel Club, Bromley Court Hotel, Bromley, UK (2 shows)

7 - New Century Hall, Manchester, UK
8 - Mojo A Go Go / Tollbar, Sheffield, UK
11 - Bag O'Nails, Sheffield, UK (2 shows)
12 - 7 1/2 Club, Mayfair, London
13 - 7 1/2 Club, Mayfair, London
14 - Beachcomber Club, Nottingham, UK
15 - Kirk Levington, Yorkshire, UK
16 - 7 1/2 Club, Mayfair, London
17 - 7 1/2 Club, Mayfair, London
18 - 7 1/2 Club, Mayfair, London & "Top Of The Pops" TV show taped
19 - Speakeasy, London
20 - Haverstock Hill Country Club, Hampstead, London
21 - Refectory, Golders Green, London
22 - The Astoria, Oldham, UK
24 - Marquee Club, London
25 - Oxford Cellar, Norwich, UK
27 - Chislehurst Caves, Bromley, UK
28 - Upper Cut Club, Forest Gate, London
29 - Saville Theatre, London (2 shows)
30 - "Pop North" show taped, Portland Place, London
31 - Saville Theatre, London ('Hey Joe' promo film taped)

February, 1967

1 - New Cellar Club, South Shields, UK
2 - "Top Of The Pops" TV show taped at the Imperial Club, Darlington, UK
3 - Ricky Tick Club, Hounslow, UK
4 - Ram Jam Club, Brixton, London & Flamingo Club,Wardour Street, London
6 - Star Hotel, Croydon, UK
8 - Bromel Club, Bromley, UK
9 - Locarno Club, Bristol, UK
10 - The Plaza, Newbury, UK
11 - Blue Moon, Cheltenham, UK
12 - Sinking Ship Clubland, Stockport, UK
13 - "Saturday Club" radio show taped
14 - The Civic Club, Grays, UK & Speakeasy, London (Jimi jams with The Pretty Things)
15 - Dorothy Ballroom, Cambridge, UK
17 - Ricky Tick, Windsor, UK
18 - University of York, Yorkshire, UK
19 - Blarney Club,Tottenham Court Road, London
20 - The Pavilion, Bath, UK
22 - Roundhouse, Chalk Farm, London
23 - The Pavilion, Worthing, UK
24 - University Of Leiceter, Leiceshire, UK
25 - Corn Exchange, Chelmsford,UK
26 - Cliffs Pavilion, Southend-on-Sea, UK (2 shows)

March, 1967

1 - Orchid Ballroom, Purley, UK
2 - "Beat Club" TV show taped, Marquee Club, London
4 - La Faculte de Droit d'Assas, Law Society Graduation Ball, Paris
5 - Twenty Club, Mouscron, Belgium & Twenty Club, Lens, Paris
6 - TV show taped in Brussels, Belgium
9 - Skyline Ballroom, Hull, UK
10 - Club A Go Go, Newcastle-upon-Tyne, UK (2 shows)
11 - International Club, Leeds, UK

12 - Gyro Club, Ilkley, UK (show stopped before JHE played - club overcrowded)
14 - "Fan Club" TV show taped in Amsterdam, Holland
17 - Star Club, Hamburg, West Germany
18 - Star Club, Hamburg, West Germany (2 shows)
19 - Star Club, Hamburg, West Germany (2 shows)
23 - Guildhall, Southampton, UK
25 - The Starlight Room, Gliderdrome, Boston, UK
26 - Tabernacle Club, Stockport, UK
27 - "Saturday Club" TV show taped, BBC TV
28 - Assembly Hall, Aylesbury, UK
30 - "Top Of The Pops" TV show taped in London
31 - Finsbury Park Astoria, London (2 shows) Official start of JHE UK Tour (Jimi sets his guitar on fire for the first time)

April, 1967

1 - Gaumont, Ipswich, UK (2 shows)
2 - Gaumont, Worcester, UK (2 shows)
5 - Odeon, Leeds, UK (2 shows)
6 - Odeon, Glasgow, Scotland (2 shows)
7 - ABC, Carlisle, UK (2 shows)
8 - ABC, Chesterfield, UK (2 shows)
9 - The Empire, Liverpool, UK (2 shows)
10 - "Monday Monday" radio show taped, The Playhouse, London
11 - Granada, Bedford, UK (2 shows)
12 - Gaumont, Southampton, UK (2 shows)
13 - Gaumont, Wolverhampton, UK (2 shows)
14 - Odeon, Bolton, UK (2 shows)
15 - Odeon, Blackpool, UK (2 shows)
16 - De Montfort Hall, Leicester, UK (2 shows)
17 - "Late Night Line Up" TV show taped, BBC TV, Kingsway, UK
18 - The Speakeasy, London (Jimi jams with Georgie Fame and Ben E. King)
19 - Odeon, Birmingham, UK (2 shows)
20 - ABC, Lincoln, UK (2 shows)
21 - City Hall, Newcastle-upon-Tyne, UK (2 shows)
22 - Odeon, Manchester, UK (2 shows)
23 - Gaumont, Stafford, UK (2 shows)
25 - Colston Hall, Bristol, UK (2 shows)
26 - Capitol, Cardiff, Wales (2 shows)
27 - ABC, Aldershot, UK (2 shows)
28 - Adelphi, Slough, Bucks, UK (2 shows) & UFO, London (Jimi jams with Tomorrow)
29 - Winter Gardens, Bournemouth, UK (2 shows)
30 - Granada, Tooting, London (2 shows) (last date of first JHE UK tour)

May, 1967

4 - "Top Of The Pops" TV show taped, BBC-TV
6 - Imperial Ballroom, Nelson, UK
7 - Saville Theatre, London (2 shows)
10 - "Tops Of The Pops" TV show taped, BBC-TV
11 - "Music Hall Of France" TV show taped, Paris
12 - Bluesville 67 Club, Manor House, London
13 - Imperial College, Kensington, London
14 - Belle Vue, Manchester, UK
15 - Neu Welte, Berlin, West Germany (2 shows)
16 - Big Apple, Munich, West Germany (2 shows)

18 - "Beat Beat Beat" TV show taped, Offenback Stadthalle, Frankfurt, Germany & K52 Club, Frankfurt (Jimi jams with Mitch Mitchell, Sandie Shaw, Dave Dee and Beaky)
19 - Liseberg, Gothenburg, Sweden (2 shows)
20 - Mariebergsskogen, Karlstaad, Sweden (2 shows)
21 - Falkoner Centret, Copenhagen, Denmark
22 - Kulttuuritalo" TV show taped, Helsinki, Finland
23 - Klubb Bongo, Malmo, Sweden (2 shows)
24 - "Popside" TV show taped, Stockholm, & Grona Lund (Stora Scenen & Dans In), Stockholm, Sweden
27 - Star Palace, Kiel, West Germany (2 shows)
28 - Jaguar Club, Herford, West Germany
29 - Tulip Bulb Auction Hall, Spalding, UK
31 - The Speakeasy, London (Jimi jams with Eric Clapton, Jack Bruce, Graeme Edge & Jose Feliciano)

June, 1967
4 - Saville Theatre, London (2 shows)
18 - Monterey International Pop Festival, Monterey, California (Jimi emerges as a superstar)
20 - Fillmore West, San Francisco (2 shows)
21 - Fillmore West, San Francisco (2 shows)
22 - Fillmore West, San Francisco (2 shows)
23 - Fillmore West, San Francisco (2 shows)
24 - Fillmore West, San Francisco (2 shows)
25 - Afternoon - Golden Gate Park, San Francisco (free concert) Evening - Fillmore West, San Francisco (2 shows)
27 - Stephen Stills' home, Malibu, California (Jimi hangs and jams for 14 hours with Stills, Buddy Miles, Bruce Palmer & Hugh Masekela)

July, 1967
1 - Earl Warren Showgrounds, Santa Barbara, California
2 - Whiskey A Go Go, Los Angeles
3 - The Scene Club, NYC
4 - The Scene Club, NYC
5 - Rheingold Festival, Central Park, NYC
8 - Jacksonville Coliseum, Jacksonville, Florida (w/ Monkees)
9 - Miami Beach Convention Hall, Miami (w/ Monkees)
11 - Charlotte Coliseum, Charlotte, North Carolina (w/ Monkees)
12 - Greensboro Coliseum, Greensboro, North Carolina (w/ Monkees)
13 - Forest Hills Stadium, Forest Hills, New York (w/ Monkees)
14 - Forest Hills Stadium, Forest Hills, New York (w/ Monkees)
15 - Forest Hills Stadium, Forest Hills, New York (w/ Monkees)
16 - Forest Hills Stadium, Forest Hills, New York (w/ Monkees) - The last JHE show with The Monkees.
18 - Gaslight Club, Greenwich Village, New York
19 - Gaslight Club, Greenwich Village, New York
20 - Salvation Club, NYC
21 - Cafe A Go Go, NYC
22 - Cafe A Go Go, NYC (2 shows)
23 - Cafe A Go Go, NYC (2 shows)
25 - The Generation, NYC (Jimi jams with Al Kooper, B.B. King & Ted Nugent)
26 - The Gaslight, Greenwich Village, NYC (Jimi jams with John Hammond Jr.)

August, 1967
3 - Salvation Club, NYC
4 - Salvation Club, NYC
5 - Salvation Club, NYC
7 - Salvation Club, NYC

8 - Salvation Club, NYC
9 - Ambassador Theater, Washington, DC (2 shows)
10 - Ambassador Theater, Washington, DC (2 shows)
11 - Ambassador Theater, Washington, DC (2 shows)
12 - Ambassador Theater, Washington, DC (2 shows)
13 - Ambassador Theater, Washington, DC (2 shows)
15 - Fifth Dimension Club, Ann Arbor, Michigan (2 shows)
18 - Hollywood Bowl, Los Angeles (2 shows)
19 - Earl Warren Showgrounds, Santa Barbara, California
22 - "Simon Dee Show" TV show taped, BBC TV
24 - "Top Of The Pops" TV show taped, BBC TV
27 - Saville Theatre, London & The Speakeasy (Jimi jams with Fairport Convention)
29 - Nottingham Blues Festival, Nottingham, UK

September, 1967
3 - Liseburg, Gothenburg, Sweden (2 shows)
4 - Stora Scenen & Dans In, Grona Lund, Stockholm, Sweden
5 - Radiohaus, Stockholm, Sweden (live broadcast)
6 - Varsteras Idrottshallen, Varsteras, Sweden (2 shows)
7 - Club Filips, Stockholm (Jimi jams with Bo Hansson & Janne Karlsson) & En Till Club, Stockholm (Jimi jams with Noel Redding - Jimi on bass & Noel on lead guitar)
8 - Popladen, Hogbo, Sweden (2 shows)
9 - Mariebergsskogen, Karlstaad, Sweden (2 shows)
10 - Stora Salen, Lund, Sweden (2 shows)
11 - Stora Scenen & Dans In, Grona Lund, Stockholm, Sweden
12 - Lisebergs, Gothenburg, Sweden (2 shows)
15 - Manor House, London (Jimi jams with Eric Burdon & The New Animals)
25 - "Guitar-In", Royal Festival Hall, London

October, 1967
6 - "Top Gear" radio show taped (jams with Stevie Wonder)
7 - Wellington Club, Dereham, UK
8 - Saville Theatre, London (2 shows)
9 - L'Olympia, Paris
10 - "Dim Dam Dom 68" TV show taped in Paris
13 - "Good Evening" TV show with Jonathan King (taped) at ATV, London
15 - Starlight Ballroom, Crawley, UK
17 - "BBC World Service Rhythm And Blues" radio show taped in London
22 - Pier Pavilion, Hastings, UK
24 - Marquee Club, London
28 - California Ballroom, Dunstable, UK

November, 1967
8 - Manchester University, Manchester, UK
10 - "Day TV" show taped, Bussem, Holland & Ahoy Hal, Rotterdam, Holland
11 - Sussex University, Brighton, UK
14 - Royal Albert Hall, London (opening date for second UK tour)
15 - Winter Gardens, Bournemouth, UK (2 shows)
17 - City Hall, Sheffield, UK (2 shows)
18 - Empire Theatre, Liverpool, UK (2 shows)
19 - Coventry Theatre, Coventry, UK (2 shows)
22 - Guild Hall, Portsmouth, UK (2 shows)
23 - Sophia Gardens Pavilion, Cardiff, Wales (2 shows)
24 - Colston Hall, Bristol, UK (2 shows)
25 - Opera House, Blackpool, UK (2 shows)
26 - Palace Theatre, Manchester, UK (2 shows)

27 - Whitla Hall, Queen's College, Belfast, Northern Ireland (2 shows)

December, 1967
1 - Town Hall, Chatham, UK (2 shows)
2 - The Dome, Brighton, UK (2 shows)
3 - Theatre Royal, Nottingham, UK (2 shows)
4 - City Hall, Newcastle-upon-Tyne, UK (2 shows)
5 - Green's Playhouse, Glasgow, Scotland (2 shows)
8 - Elstree, ATV Studios, London, "Good Evening" TV show with Jonathon King is taped
12 - The Speakeasy, London (Jimi jams with the Fairport Convention)
15 - The Playhouse BBC Theatre, London, "Top Gear" radio show taped
16 - Shepherd's Bush, London, "Top Of The Pops" TV show taped, BBC TV
22 - "Christmas On Earth Continued", Olympia, London (2 sets) & The Speakeasy (Jimi jams with Eric Burdon, Harry Hughes & Dave Mason between sets)
31 - The Speakeasy, London (Jimi plays a 30-minute version of 'Auld Lang Syne' at the New Year's Eve party)

January, 1968
2 - The Railway Hotel, Hampstead (Jimi jams with John Mayall & Al Sykes)
4 - Lorensburg Cirkus, Gothenburg, Sweden (2 shows)
5 - Jernvallen Sports Hall, Sandvikan, Sweden
7 - Tivolis Koncerthall, Copenhagen, Denmark (2 shows)
8 - Stora Salen, Konserthuset, Stockholm, Sweden (2 shows)
22 - The Speakeasy, London (Jimi jams with Sam Gopal's Dream)
29 - L'Olympia, Paris (2 shows)

February, 1968
1 - Fillmore West, San Francisco (2 shows)
2 - Winterland, San Francisco (2 shows)
3 - Winterland, San Francisco (2 shows)
4 - Winterland, San Francisco (2 shows)
5 - Arizona State University,Tempe, Arizona
6 - VIP Club,Tucson, Arizona
8 - Sacramento State College, Sacramento, California
9 - Convention Center, Anaheim, California (2 shows)
10 - Shrine Auditorium, Los Angeles & Jimi jams with David Crosby, Buddy Miles & Harvey Brooks
11 - Robertson Gym, Santa Barbara, California
12 - Center Arena, Seattle, Washington
13 - Ackerman Ballroom, UCLA, Los Angeles
14 - Regis College, Denver, Colorado
15 - Municipal Auditorium, San Antonio, Texas
16 - State Fair Music Hall, Dallas, Texas
17 - Will Rogers Auditorium, Ft. Worth, Texas (after the show Jimi jams with Billy Gibbons)
18 - Music Hall, Houston, Texas (2 shows)
21 - Electric Factory, Philadelphia (2 shows)
22 - Electric Factory, Philadelphia (2 shows)
23 - Masonic Temple, Detroit, Michigan
24 - C.N.E. Coliseum, Toronto, Canada & later JHE jams with Robbie Robertson & The Hawkes
25 - Civic Opera House, Chicago (2 shows)
27 - The Factory, Madison, Wisconsin (2 shows)
28 - The Scene, Milwaukee, Wisconsin (2 shows)
29 - The Scene, Milwaukee, Wisconsin (2 shows)

March, 1968
2 - Hunter College, NYC (2 shows)
3 - Veteran's Memorial Auditorium, Columbus, OH

4 - The Scene Club, NYC (Jimi jams with Eric Clapton)
6 - The Scene Club, NYC (Jimi jams with The Hollies)
8 - Brown University, Providence, Rhode Island
9 - Stony Brook, N.Y.U., Long Island, New York
10 - International Ball Room, Washington, D.C. (2 shows)
13 - The Scene Club, NYC (Jimi jams with a drunk Jim Morrison and members of The McCoys)
15 - Atwood Hall, Clark University, Worcester, MA (2 shows)
16 - Lewiston Armory, Lewiston, Maine
17 - Cafe A Go Go, NYC (Jimi jams with Paul Butterfield, Elvin Bishop & Harvey Brooks)
19 - Capitol Theatre, Ottawa, Canada (2 shows)
21 - Community War Memorial, Rochester, NY
22 - Bushnell Memorial Hall, Hartford, Connecticut
23 - Memorial Auditorium, Buffalo, NY
24 - IMA Auditorium, Flint, Michigan
25 - Otto's Grotto, Cleveland (Jimi jams with Good Earth)
26 - Music Hall, Cleveland, Ohio (2 shows)
27 - The Fairgrounds, Muncie, Indiana
28 - Xavier University, Cincinnati, Ohio (2 shows)
29 - The Cheetah Club, Chicago (Jimi jams with The Paul Butterfield Blues Band)
30 - Fieldhouse, Toledo University, Toledo, Ohio
31 - The Arena, Philadelphia, Pennsylvania

April, 1968

2 - Paul Suave Arena, Montreal, Quebec, Canada
4 - Civic Dome, Virginia Beach, Virginia (2 shows)
5 - Symphony Hall, Newark, New Jersey & Generation, NYC (Jimi jams with Buddy Guy)
6 - White Plains Convention Center, White Plains, New York
7 - Generation, NYC (Jimi jams with Roy Buchanan)
19 - Troy Armory, Troy, New York

May, 1968

3 - The Town Hall, NYC (Jimi jams with Mitch Mitchell and Joe Tex and his band)
10 - Fillmore East, NYC (2 shows)
18 - Miami Pop Festival, Hallendale, Florida (2 shows)
20 - The Wreck Bar, The Castaways Hotel, Miami, Florida (Jimi jams with Frank Zappa, Noel Redding, Jimmy Carl Black and Arthur Brown)
23 - Piper Club, Milan, Italy
24 - Brancaccio Theatre, Rome (2 shows) & Titial Club, Rome (JHE jam with The Folks)
25 - Brancaccio Theatre, Rome (2 shows)
26 - Palasport, Bologna, Italy (2 shows)
30 - Beat Monsters Concert, Hallenstadion, Zurich, Switzerland
31 - Beat Monsters Concert, Hallenstadion, Zurich, Switzerland & earlier in the day Jimi jammed with Steve Winwood, Dave Mason, Chris Wood and others at The Hallenstadion.

June, 1968

5 - "Dusty Springfield" TV show taped, London
8 - The Fillmore East, NYC (Jimi jams with The Electric Flag)
13 - Reality House Rehab Center, NYC (Jimi jams with Jeff Beck)
15 - The Scene Club, NYC (Jimi jams with Eric Clapton & Jeff Beck)
16 - The Daytop Music Festival, Staten Island, New York (Jimi jams with Jeff Beck) and again in the evening at The Scene Club with Jeff Beck.
22 - The Scene Club, NYC (Jimi jams with Larry Coryell)

July, 1968

6 - Woburn Music Festival, Woburn Abbey, UK
15 - Sgt. Pepper's Club, Palma, Majorca, Spain

Rare Jimi Hendrix poster promoting their May 10, 1968
appearance at the Fillmore East

18 - Sgt. Pepper's Club, Palma (JHE jam with Neil Landon & Jim Leverton)
30 - Independence Hall, Baton Rouge, Louisiana (2 shows)
31 - Municipal Auditorium, Shreveport, Louisiana

August, 1968

1 - City Park Stadium, New Orleans, Louisiana
2 - Municipal Auditorium, San Antonio, Texas (2 shows)
3 - Southern Methodist University, Dallas, Texas
4 - Sam Houston Coliseum, Houston, Texas
10 - Auditorium Theater, Chicago, Illinois (2 shows)
11 - Colonial Ballroom, Davenport, Iowa
16 - Merriweather Post Pavilion, Columbia, Maryland
17 - Municipal Auditorium, Atlanta, Georgia (2 shows)
18 - Curtis Hixon Hall, Tampa, Florida
20 - The Mosque, Richmond, Virginia (2 shows)
21 - Civic Dome, Virginia Beach, Virginia (2 shows)
23 - The New York Rock Festival,Singer Bowl, Flushing Meadow, New York
24 - Bushnell Memorial Hall, Hartford, Connecticut
25 - Carousel Theater, Framingham, Massachusetts (2 shows)
26 - Kennedy Stadium, Bridgeport, Connecticut
30 - Langoon Opera House, Salt Lake City, Utah

September, 1968
1 - Red Rocks Park, Denver, Colorado
3 - Balboa Stadium, San Diego, California
4 - Memorial Coliseum, Phoenix, Arizona
5 - Swing Auditorium, San Bernadino, California
6 - Center Coliseum, Seattle, Washington
7 - Pacific Coliseum, Vancouver, Canada
8 - Coliseum, Spokane, Washington
9 - Memorial Coliseum, Portland, Oregon
13 - Oakland Coliseum, Oakland, California
14 - Hollywood Bowl, Los Angeles
15 - Memorial Auditorium, Sacramento, California
18 - Whisky A Go Go, Los Angeles (JHE jam with Buddy Miles, Eric Burdon & Graham Bond)

October, 1968
5 - International Center, Honolulu, Hawaii
10 - Winterland, San Francisco (2 shows)
11 - Winterland, San Francisco (2 shows)
12 - Winterland, San Francisco (2 shows)
19 - Whisky A Go Go, Los Angeles (Jimi jams with Lee Michaels)
26 - Civic Auditorium, Bakersfield, California

November, 1968
1 - Municipal Auditorium, Kansas City, Missouri
2 - Auditorium, Minneapolis, Minnesota
3 - Kiel Auditorium, St. Louis, Missouri
11 - The Scene Club, NYC (Jimi jams with Fleetwood Mac)
15 - Cincinnati Gardens, Cincinnati, Ohio
16 - Boston Gardens, Boston, Massachusetts
17 - Yale University, New Haven, Connecticut
22 - Jacksonville Coliseum, Jacksonville, Florida
23 - Curtis Hixon Hall, Tampa, Florida
24 - Convention Hall, Miami Beach, Florida
27 - Rhode Island Auditorium, Providence, Rhode Island
28 - Philharmonic Hall, NYC (2 shows)
30 - Cobo Arena, Detroit, Michigan

December, 1968
1 - Coliseum, Chicago, Illinois

January, 1969
4 - "Lulu Show" taped, BBC TV, London
8 - Lorensberg Cirkus, Gothenburg, Sweden (2 shows)
9 - Konserthuset, Stockholm, Sweden (2 shows)
10 - Falkoner Centret, Copenhagen, Denmark (2 shows)
11 - Musikhalle, Hamburg, West Germany (2 shows)
12 - Rheinhalle, Dusseldorf, West Germany (2 shows)
13 - Sporthalle, Koln, West Germany & later Jimi and Noel jam at a small club
14 - Halle Munsterland, Munster, West Germany
15 - Deutsches Museum, Munich, West Germany (2 shows)
16 - Meistersingerhalle, Nurnburg, West Germany (2 shows)
17 - Jahrhunderthalle, Frankfurt, West Germany (2 shows)
19 - Liederhalle, Stuttgart, West Germany (2 shows)
21 - Wacken Halle 16, Strasbourg, France
22 - Konzerthaus, Vienna, Austria (2 shows)
23 - Sportpalast, West Berlin, West Germany

February, 1969

18 - Royal Albert Hall, London
23 - The Speakeasy, London (Jimi jams with Dave Mason and Jim Capaldi)
24 - Royal Albert Hall, London

March, 1969

6 - The Speakeasy, London (Jimi jams with Billy Preston)
8 - Ronnie Scott's Club, London (Jimi jams with Roland Kirk)
10 - The Speakeasy, London (Jimi jams with The Gods)
30 - The Hollywood Palladium, Los Angeles (Jimi jams on stage with Delaney & Bonnie)

April, 1969

11 - Dorton Arena, Raleigh, North Carolina
12 - Spectrum, Philadelphia, Pennsylvania
18 - Ellis Auditorium, Memphis, Tennessee (2 shows)
19 - Sam Houston Coliseum, Houston, Texas
20 - Memorial Auditorium, Dallas, Texas
26 - The Forum, Los Angeles
27 - Oakland Coliseum, Oakland, California

May, 1969

2 - Cobo Hall, Detroit, Michigan
3 - Maple Leaf Gardens, Toronto, Canada
4 - Memorial Auditorium, Syracuse, New York
7 - Memorial Auditorium, Tuscaloosa, Alabama
9 - Coliseum, Charlotte, North Carolina
10 - Civic Center, Charleston, West Virginia
11 - State Fair, Grand Coliseum, Indianapolis, Indiana
13 - The Scene Club, NYC (Jimi jams with Stephen Stills & Johnny Winter)
16 - Civic Center, Baltimore, Maryland
17 - Rhode Island Auditorium, Providence, Rhode Island
18 - Madison Square Garden, NYC
23 - Seattle Coliseum, Seattle, Washington
24 - Sports Arena, San Diego, California
25 - Santa Clara Pop Festival, San Jose, California
30 - Waikiki Shell, Honolulu, Hawaii (cancelled after 30 minutes - rescheduled for the 31st)
31 - Waikiki Shell, Honolulu, Hawaii

June, 1969

1 - Waikiki Shell, Honolulu, Hawaii
20 - Newport Pop Festival, Devonshire Downs, California
22 - Newport Pop Festival (Jimi jams with Eric Burdon, Buddy Miles & Mother Earth)
29 - Denver Pop Festival, Mile High Stadium, Denver, Colorado (last concert of JHE with Noel Redding)

July, 1969

10 - Jimi appears on the "Johnny Carson Tonight Show" (hosted by Flip Wilson) where he is interviewed and performs 'Lover Man'. Later in the month Jimi is interviewed on the "Dick Cavett Show" and performs 'Getting My Heart Back Together'.

August, 1969

10 - Tinker Street Cinema, Woodstock (Jimi jams with Juma, Jerry Velez and others)
18 - Woodstock Music and Art Fair, Bethel, New York (performs as 'Gypsy Sons & Rainbows')

September, 1969

5 - Street Festival, Harlem, NYC (Jimi and Mitch Mitchell)
9 - Ungano's, NYC (Jimi jams with Mountain)
10 - Salvation Club, NYC (Gypsy Sons And Rainbow)

19 - Boiceville House, New York (Jimi jams with Mike Euphron & Juma Sultan)

November, 1969
27 - Madison Square Garden, NYC (Jimi jams backstage with Mick Taylor after the Stones concert)

December, 1969
31 - Fillmore East, NYC (Band Of Gypsys debut) (2 shows) & The Cafe A Go Go (Jimi jams with The James Cotton Blues Band)

January, 1970
  1 - Fillmore East, NYC (2 shows) w/ Band Of Gypsys
21 - Jimi and Taj Mahal jam at Jimi's NYC apartment
28 - Madison Square Garden, NYC (2 shows). Last concert with Band Of Gypsys

February, 1970
  1 - Jimi and Mitch Mitchell Jam at Jimi's NYC apartment

March, 1970
18 - The Speakeasy, NYC (Jimi jams with Stephen Stills)

April, 1970
25 - Los Angeles Forum, Los Angeles ('Cry Of Love" tour with Mitch Mitchell & Billy Cox begins)
26 - State Fairground, Sacramento, California

May, 1970
  1 - Milwaukee Auditorium, Milwaukee, Wisconsin
  2 - Dane County Coliseum, Madison, Wisconsin
  3 - St. Paul Civic Center, St. Paul, Minnesota
  4 - Village Gate, New York (Timothy Leary Benefit)
  8 - University of Oklahoma, Norman, Oklahoma (2 shows)
  9 - Will Rogers Auditorium, Fort Worth, Texas
10 - Hemisphere Arena, San Antonio, Texas
16 - Temple University Stadium, Philadelphia, Pennsylvania
30 - Berkeley Community Theater, Berkeley, California (2 shows)

June, 1970
  5 - Memorial Auditorium, Dallas, Texas
  6 - Sam Houston Coliseum, Houston, Texas
  7 - Assembly Center Arena, Tulsa, Oklahoma
  9 - Mid-South Coliseum, Memphis, Tennessee
10 - Roberts Municipal Stadium, Evansville, Indiana
13 - Baltimore Civic Center, Baltimore, Maryland
19 - Civic Auditorium, Albequerque, New Mexico (2 shows)
20 - Swing Auditorium, San Bernadino, California
21 - Ventura County Playgrounds, Ventura, California
23 - Mammoth Gardens, Denver, Colorado
27 - Boston Garden, Boston, Massachusetts

July, 1970
  4 - Second Atlanta International Pop Festival, Bryon, Georgia
  5 - Miami Jai Alai Fronton, Miami, Florida (2 shows)
17 - New York Pop Festival, Downing Stadium, Randalls Island, New York
25 - Sports Arena, San Diego, California
26 - Sicks Stadium, Seattle, Washington
30 - Rainbow Bridge Vibratory Color Sound Experiment, Haleakala Crater (Rainbow Ridge), Maui, Hawaii

August, 1970
  1 - Honolulu International Center, Oahu, Hawaii

30 - Isle of Wight Festival, East Afton Farm, Isle Of Wight, UK
31 - Stora Scene, Grona Lund, Stockholm, Sweden

September, 1970
  1 - Stora Scene, Liseburg, Gothenburg, Sweden
  2 - Vejlby-Risskov Hallen, Aarhus, Denmark (cancelled after 3 songs - Jimi tired)
  3 - K. B. Hallen, Copenhagen, Denmark
  4 - Super Concert '70, Deutschlandhalle, Berlin, West Germany
  6 - "Love And Peace Festival" at Isle Of Fehmarn, West Germany (the last concert of Jimi Hendrix)
16 - Ronnie Scott's, London - Jimi jams with Eric Burdon & War ("Mother Earth" & "Tobacco Road")
18 - Jimi Hendrix passes away.

...the story of life is quicker than the wink of an eye.
The story of love is hello and goodbye
until we meet again.
From Jimi's last poem "The Story Of Life"
written in London the day before he died.

Index To The Discography
Official Releases

Bootleg Releases

User's Guide To The Song Index

Song Title:

Songs titles are list alphabetically. Titles used are what we feel are the correct titles or the popular collectors titles (eg. "Heavy Jam") for a song. Occasionally we simply used one of the made-up titles for a song invented by the bootleggers. The title in parenthesis after the regular title indicates what that track is called on a particular release because many releases use made-up titles or have simply mistitled a song. Don't confuse this with the few titles that have a subtitle in parenthesis as part of the regular title [eg. "Voodoo Chile (slight return)" or "Hey Baby (New Rising Sun)"].

We have generally not broken down jams and medleys into their individual song components. Frequently a melody or a few lyrics of a song shows up for only a few bars in studio jams. Jimi frequently did medleys of several songs during live performances. Unless it is something we felt pertinent (like the melody of "Message To Love" that creeps up during "Spanish Castle Magic" at the 18 Feb 69 Royal Albert Hall show - which was the first time this appeared - even before any studio recordings were attempted) we did not list these medley components separately. Sometimes longer jams have been booted many times but broken into distinctive components (see "Highway Of Desire"), so we have attempted to list these and cross-refence them.

Date:

The dates given are, in the case of live performances, the concert date. For radio and TV recordings it is the date of the recording rather than the broadcast. Studio recording dates are for the basic version on which overdubs or mixing may have been done on several occasions afterwards.

Throughout the book, dates are given in standard American numerical date format (mm/dd/yy). In the Date column of the song index, however, dates are given in the alphanumeric format dd MMM yy, where the month is given as a standard 3-letter abbrieviation. For example, March 12th, 1969 would be given as 12 Mar 69. This format is felt to be the most quickly understood format when examining song index entries.

A double-question-mark (??) means that we are uncertain about a particular month, day, or year (depending on the placement.) Adjacent double-question-marks are always separated by a slash to ensure clarity. A single-question-mark (?) immediately following a month, day, or year denotes that there is some evidence for the value given, but that we are not completely convinced of its authenticity. (Example: ?? Mar 68 means this recording was possibly done in March and definitely in 1968, but we don't know what day.)

Comments:

While compiling and editing this database, it became apparent that there were many different ways to sort, identify and organize the various versions and performances of the same song title. We tried to do this in a way that we as collectors would find useful for sorting and cross-referencing. We had originally hoped to present the song index in several sorts, but space restrictions forces us to settle on one. Songs are listed in chronological order of recording dates as best as we know. This is interesting as it was not uncommon for Jimi to debut new songs live before attempting studio recordings. It also helps to chronical the studio recording history of songs.

Most all titles are given a CR or a BR status. CR means 'commercial release' (or 'commercially released'), while BR means 'bootleg release'. Each unique version of a recording is given a different BR or CR number. A commercial release is a CD, LP or single that is released by a legitimate record company that would pay royalties to the appropriate parties. A bootleg release is a non-official release that pays no royalties and are illegal to manufacture or distribute for financial gain. Occasionally you will see a reference to an 'official release'. This refers to a videotape of laserdisc release of a song unavailable commercially on CD or LP. You will notice that songs on many bootleg releases are given a CR status. This means that this version of that song is based on or is a variation of a commercially released basic recording or even the actual commercial release itself. This is common especially with live or broadcast songs. These were frequently bootlegged long before a CR which then makes these bootlegs obsolete. (The authors would like to see ALL bootlegs obsolete.) Even though a song is given an identical CR or BR status, the sound quality is likely to vary substantially from release to release as many different tape sources and generations would be used.

Mix numbers are assigned when there are different mixes made to the same exact recording. This can mean mono or stereo or an alternate or unused mix. Alternate mixes refer to other commercially released mixes or edits that vary from the original commercially released mix. The original first release of a CR is given 'CR 1' status and if there is both a mono and a stereo mix, the stereo is given 'mix 1' status. Unused mixes are different mixes of the basic CR but were unreleased until a bootlegger got hold of them.

Release:

This is the title of the CD, LP, 45, videotape or laserdisc followed by '(CR)' if it is a commercial release. The format, label and catalog number then follow.

Location / Venue:

This is the recording studio or concert venue where the song was recorded.

Band:

This is the abbreviation of the basic band lineup as described at the beginning of this book. (Eg: BOG = Band Of Gypsys)

Personnel:

These are the other musicians who appear or perform on a recording.

SONG TITLE	DATE	COMMENTS	RELEASE	LOCATION / VENUE	BAND	PERSONNEL
...And The Gods Made Love	29 Jun 68	CR 1.	Electric Ladyland (CR) CD MCACD-11600	Record Plant, New York, NY	Jimi	Mitch Mitchell / Drums
1983...A Merman I Should Turn To Be	13? Mar? 68	BR 1. Possibly the demo from 3 / 13 / 68. "Sessions " implies a very stripped version but this has overdubs & a full sound, plus the lyrics still need work. It's possible that overdubs were added prior to the 4 / 22 / 68 session that produced the CR 1.	Ladyland In Flames LP Marshall Records JIMI 1,2,3,4	Sound Center?, New York, NY	JHE	
1983...A Merman I Should Turn To Be	13? Mar? 68	BR 1. Possibly the demo from 3 / 13 / 68. "Sessions " implies a very stripped version but this has overdubs & a full sound, plus the lyrics still need work. It's possible that overdubs were added prior to the 4 / 22 / 68 session that produced the CR 1.	You Can't Use My Name L P Rock Folders 2, Q 9020	Sound Center?, New York, NY	JHE	
1983...A Merman I Should Turn To Be	13? Mar? 68	BR 1. Possibly the demo from 3 / 13 / 68. "Sessions " implies a very stripped version but this has overdubs & a full sound, plus the lyrics still need work. It's possible that overdubs were added prior to the 4 / 22 / 68 session that produced the CR 1.	1968 AD Part Two CD Whoopy Cat WKP 0013	Sound Center?, New York, NY	JHE	
1983...A Merman I Should Turn To Be (Valleys Of Neptune Take 1)	13? Mar? 68	BR 1. Possibly the demo from 3 / 13 / 68. "Sessions " implies a very stripped version but this has overdubs & a full sound, plus the lyrics still need work. It's possible that overdubs were added prior to the 4 / 22 / 68 session that produced the CR 1.	TTG Studios ???? CD WHOAMI WAI 015	Sound Center?, New York, NY	JHE	
1983...A Merman I Should Turn To Be	13? Mar? 68	BR 1. Possibly the demo from 3 / 13 / 68. "Sessions " implies a very stripped version but this has overdubs & a full sound, plus the lyrics still need work. It's possible that overdubs were added prior to the 4 / 22 / 68 session that produced the CR 1.	Multicolored Blues CD Luna LU 9317	Sound Center?, New York, NY	JHE	
1983...A Merman I Should Turn To Be	13? Mar? 68	BR 1. Possibly the demo from 3 / 13 / 68. "Sessions " implies a very stripped version but this has overdubs & a full sound, plus the lyrics still need work. It's possible that overdubs were added prior to the 4 / 22 / 68 session that produced the CR 1.	Voodoo Blues CD Smurf	Sound Center?, New York, NY	JHE	
1983...A Merman I Should Turn To Be	13? Mar? 68	BR 1. Possibly the demo from 3 / 13 / 68. "Sessions " implies a very stripped version but this has overdubs & a full sound, plus the lyrics still need work. It's possible that overdubs were added prior to the 4 / 22 / 68 session that produced the CR 1.	Flames CD Missing In Action ACT 1	Sound Center?, New York, NY	JHE	
1983...A Merman I Should Turn To Be	13? Mar? 68	BR 1. Possibly the demo from 3 / 13 / 68. "Sessions " implies a very stripped version but this has overdubs & a full sound, plus the lyrics still need work. It's possible that overdubs were added prior to the 4 / 22 / 68 session that produced the CR 1.	Electric Ladyland Outtakes CD Invasion Unlimited IU 9417-1	Sound Center?, New York, NY	JHE	
1983...A Merman I Should Turn To Be	13? Mar? 68	BR 1. Possibly the demo from 3 / 13 / 68. "Sessions " implies a very stripped version but this has overdubs & a full sound, plus the lyrics still need work. It's possible that overdubs were added prior to the 4 / 22 / 68 session that produced the CR 1.	Every Way To Paradise CD Tintangel TIBX 021 / 22 / 23 / 24	Sound Center?, New York, NY	JHE	
1983...A Merman I Should Turn To Be	13? Mar? 68	BR 1. Possibly the demo from 3 / 13 / 68. "Sessions " implies a very stripped version but this has overdubs & a full sound, plus the lyrics still need work. It's possible that overdubs were added prior to the 4 / 22 / 68 session that produced the CR 1.	Voodoo In Ladyland CD MUM MUCD 006	Sound Center?, New York, NY	JHE	

SONG TITLE	DATE	COMMENTS	RELEASE	LOCATION / VENUE	BAND	PERSONNEL
1983...A Merman I Should Turn To Be	13? Mar? 68	BR 1. Possibly the demo from 3 / 13 / 68. "Sessions " implies a very stripped version but this has overdubs & a full sound, plus the lyrics still need work. It's possible that overdubs were added prior to the 4 / 22 / 68 session that produced the CR 1.	Kiss The Skies CD Mum MUCD 024	Sound Center?, New York, NY	JHE	
1983...A Merman I Should Turn To Be	13? Mar? 68	BR 1. Possibly the demo from 3 / 13 / 68. "Sessions " implies a very stripped version but this has overdubs & a full sound, plus the lyrics still need work. It's possible that overdubs were added prior to the 4 / 22 / 68 session that produced the CR 1.	Sotheby's Reels, The CD Gold Standard TOM-800	Sound Center?, New York, NY	JHE	
1983...A Merman I Should Turn To Be	13? Mar? 68	BR 1. Possibly the demo from 3 / 13 / 68. "Sessions " implies a very stripped version but this has overdubs & a full sound, plus the lyrics still need work. It's possible that overdubs were added prior to the 4 / 22 / 68 session that produced the CR 1.	Atlanta CD JMH 009 / 02	Sound Center?, New York, NY	JHE	
1983...A Merman I Should Turn To Be	13? Mar? 68	BR 1. Possibly the demo from 3 / 13 / 68. "Sessions " implies a very stripped version but this has overdubs & a full sound, plus the lyrics still need work. It's possible that overdubs were added prior to the 4 / 22 / 68 session that produced the CR 1.	Atlanta CD JMH 009 / 02	Sound Center?, New York, NY	JHE	
1983...A Merman I Should Turn To Be	13? Mar? 68	BR 1. Possibly the demo from 3 / 13 / 68. "Sessions " implies a very stripped version but this has overdubs & a full sound, plus the lyrics still need work. It's possible that overdubs were added prior to the 4 / 22 / 68 session that produced the CR 1.	Living Reels Vol 2 CD JMH 012 / 2	Sound Center?, New York, NY	JHE	
1983...A Merman I Should Turn To Be	?? Mar 68	CR 2 mix 1. "Stereo" mix of this composing tape.	Jimi By Himself The Home Recordings (CR) BSP-VC1	New York Apartment	Solo	
1983...A Merman I Should Turn To Be	?? Mar 68	CR 2 mix 2. Mono mix of this composing tape. A 'Stereo' mix of this in better sound is on 'Jimi By Himself, The Home Recordings' CD.	Electric Gypsy CD Scorpio? 40176 / 15	New York Apartment	Solo	
1983...A Merman I Should Turn To Be	?? Mar 68	CR 2 mix 2. Mono mix of this composing tape. A 'Stereo' mix of this in better sound is on 'Jimi By Himself, The Home Recordings' CD.	Acoustic Jams CD Sphinx SX CD 001	New York Apartment	Solo	
1983...A Merman I Should Turn To Be	?? Mar 68	CR 2 mix 2. Mono mix of this composing tape. A 'Stereo' mix of this in better sound is on 'Jimi By Himself, The Home Recordings' CD.	1968 AD Part Two CD Whoopy Cat WKP 0013	New York Apartment	Solo	
1983...A Merman I Should Turn To Be	?? Mar 68	CR 2 mix 2. Mono mix of this composing tape. A 'Stereo' mix of this in better sound is on 'Jimi By Himself, The Home Recordings' CD.	Official Bootleg Album, The CD Yellow Dog YD 051	New York Apartment	Solo	
1983...A Merman I Should Turn To Be (Valleys Of Neptune Take 2)	?? Mar 68	CR 2 mix 2. Mono mix of this composing tape. A 'Stereo' mix of this in better sound is on 'Jimi By Himself, The Home Recordings' CD. Incomplete.	TTG Studios ???? CD WHOAMI WAI 015	New York Apartment	Solo	
1983...A Merman I Should Turn To Be	?? Mar 68	CR 2 mix 2. Mono mix of this composing tape. A 'Stereo' mix of this in better sound is on 'Jimi By Himself, The Home Recordings' CD.	51st Anniversary CD Future Disc JMH 001 / 8	New York Apartment	Solo	

Song	Date	Notes	Source	Location	Credit	Musicians
1983...A Merman I Should Turn To Be	?? Mar 68	CR 2 mix 2. Mono mix of this composing tape. A 'Stereo' mix of this in better sound is on 'Jimi By Himself, The Home Recordings' CD.	First Rays Of The New Rising Sun CD Triangle PYCD 084-2	New York Apartment	Solo	
1983...A Merman I Should Turn To Be	?? Mar 68	CR 2 mix 2. Mono mix of this composing tape. A 'Stereo' mix of this in better sound is on 'Jimi By Himself, The Home Recordings' CD.	Best Of The Bootlegs CD MS 666	New York Apartment	Solo	
1983...A Merman I Should Turn To Be	?? Mar 68	CR 2 mix 2. Mono mix of this composing tape. A 'Stereo' mix of this in better sound is on 'Jimi By Himself, The Home Recordings' CD.	Voodoo Blues CD Smurf	New York Apartment	Solo	
1983...A Merman I Should Turn To Be	?? Mar 68	CR 2 mix 2. Mono mix of this composing tape. A 'Stereo' mix of this in better sound is on 'Jimi By Himself, The Home Recordings' CD.	Studio Experience CD Sodium Haze SH 099	New York Apartment	Solo	
1983...A Merman I Should Turn To Be	?? Mar 68	CR 2 mix 2. Mono mix of this composing tape. A 'Stereo' mix of this in better sound is on 'Jimi By Himself, The Home Recordings' CD. Incomplete.	Electric Ladyland Outtakes CD Invasion Unlimited IU 9417-1	New York Apartment	Solo	
1983...A Merman I Should Turn To Be	?? Mar 68	CR 2 mix 2. Mono mix of this composing tape. A 'Stereo' mix of this in better sound is on 'Jimi By Himself, The Home Recordings' CD.	Jimi: A Musical Legacy CD KTS BX 010	New York Apartment	Solo	
1983...A Merman I Should Turn To Be	?? Mar 68	CR 2 mix 2. Mono mix of this composing tape. A 'Stereo' mix of this in better sound is on 'Jimi By Himself, The Home Recordings' CD.	Black Gold CD Midnight Beat MBCD 058-062	New York Apartment	Solo	
1983...A Merman I Should Turn To Be	?? Mar 68	BR 2. An instrumental run through from this mono composing tape possibly from the same session as the CR 2.	Acoustic Jams CD Sphinx SX CD 001	New York Apartment	Solo	
1983...A Merman I Should Turn To Be	?? Mar 68	BR 2. An instrumental run through from this mono composing tape possibly from the same session as the CR 2.	Black Gold CD Midnight Beat MBCD 058-062	New York Apartment	Solo	
1983...A Merman I Should Turn To Be	22 Apr 68	CR 1 mix 1.	Electric Ladyland (CR) CD MCACD-11600	Record Plant, New York, NY	Jimi	Jimi Hendrix / Percussion, Jimi Hendrix / Bass, Mitch Mitchell / Drums, Chris Wood / Flute
1983...A Merman I Should Turn To Be	23 Apr 68	CR 1 mix 2. This is an alternate mix as included on 'Lifelines'.	Lifelines (CR) CD Reprise 9 26435-2	Record Plant, New York, NY	Jimi	Jimi Hendrix / Percussion, Jimi Hendrix / Bass, Mitch Mitchell / Drums, Chris Wood / Flute
1983...A Merman I Should Turn To Be	23 Apr 68	CR 1 mix 2. This is an alternate mix as included on 'Lifelines'.	Lost Experience, The, CD JHCD203	Sound Center, New York, NY	Jimi	Jimi Hendrix / Percussion, Jimi Hendrix / Bass, Mitch Mitchell / Drums, Chris Wood / Flute
1983...A Merman I Should Turn To Be (Moon Turn The Tides...Gently Gently Away)	23 Apr 68	CR 1 mix 3. An alternate mix of CR 1. Officially released on "Lifelines".	Mixdown Master Tapes Volume 2 CD Dandelion DL 006	New York Apartment	Jimi	Jimi Hendrix / Percussion, Jimi Hendrix / Bass, Mitch Mitchell / Drums, Chris Wood / Flute

SONG TITLE	DATE	COMMENTS	RELEASE	LOCATION / VENUE	BAND	PERSONNEL
51st Anniversary	11 Jan 67	CR 1 mix 1. Mono mix only. An alternate mix with a stereo double vocal track is found on 'Olympic Gold Vol 2'.	Smash Hits (CR) CD Reprise 2276-2	Olympic Sound Studios, London, England	JHE	
51st Anniversary	11 Jan 67	CR 1 mix 1. Mono mix only. An alternate mix with a stereo double vocal track is found on 'Olympic Gold Vol 2'.	Rarities On Compact Disc CD On The Radio	Olympic Sound Studios, London, England	JHE	
51st Anniversary	11 Jan 67	CR 1 mix 1. Mono mix only. An alternate mix with a stereo double vocal track is found on 'Olympic Gold Vol 2'.	Are You Experienced? (CR) CD MCACD 11602	Olympic Sound Studios, London, England	JHE	
51st Anniversary	11 Jan 67	CR 1 mix 1. Mono mix only. An alternate mix with a stereo double vocal track is found on 'Olympic Gold Vol 2'.	The Singles Album (CR) CD Polydor 827 369-2	Olympic Sound Studios, London, England	JHE	
51st Anniversary	11 Jan 67	BR 1. Alternate instrumental studio take #1 that breaks down and continues with the next take.	Olympic Gold Vol 1 CD Blimp 0067	Olympic Sound Studios, London, England	JHE	
51st Anniversary	11 Jan 67	BR 2. Alternate instrumental studio take #2 that breaks down and continues with the next take.	Olympic Gold Vol 1 CD Blimp 0067	Olympic Sound Studios, London, England	JHE	
51st Anniversary	11 Jan 67	BR 3. Alternate instrumental studio take #3 that is complete.	Olympic Gold Vol 1 CD Blimp 0067	Olympic Sound Studios, London, England	JHE	
51st Anniversary	11 Jan 67	CR 1 mix 2. This is an unused mix that has a stereo double vocal track over the mono basic CR backing track.	Olympic Gold Vol 2 CD Blimp 007	Olympic Sound Studios, London, England	JHE	
Acoustic Medley	?? / ?? 70?	BR 1. Jimi on acoustic guitar. The medley includes a number of very brief phrases from "Midnight Lightning", "Power Of Soul" and 'Freedom' to name a few. Not very exciting overall.	Freak Out Blues CD GH 001	New York Apartment	Solo	
Ain't Gonna Be No Next Time	?? / ?? 65?	Curtis Knight sans Jimi.	Dante's Inferno CD Pink Poodle POO 002	New York, NY	No Jimi	
Ain't No Telling	26 Oct 67	CR1 mix 1 (stereo)	Axis: Bold As Love (CR) CD MCACD 11601	Olympic Sound Studios, London, England	JHE	
Ain't No Telling	26 Oct 67	CR 1 mix 2 (mono)	Notes In Colours CD JHR 001 / 002	Olympic Sound Studios, London, England	Jimi	
Ain't No Telling	26 Oct 67	CR 1 mix 2 (mono)	Axis: Bold As Love LP Track Records 612 003	Olympic Sound Studios, London, England	JHE	
Ain't No Telling	26 Oct 67	CR 1 mix 3. This is an alternate mix with a slight variation in that the guitar solo track stays in the right channel rather than	Axis: Bold As Love LP Track Records	Olympic Sound Studios, London,	JHE	

Song	Date	panning from right to left.	Release	Location	Personnel	Bass
Ain't No Telling	26 Oct 67	CR 1 mix 4. An unused stereo mix.	Sotheby Auction Tapes, The CD Midnight Beat MBCD 010	Olympic Sound Studios, London, England	JHE	
Ain't No Telling	26 Oct 67	CR 1 mix 4. An unused stereo mix.	Sotheby Auction Tapes, The CD Midnight Beat MBCD 010	New York Apartment	JHE	
Ain't No Telling	26 Oct 67	CR 1 mix 4. An unused stereo mix.	Sotheby's Private Reels CD JHR 003 / 004	Olympic Sound Studios, London, England	JHE	
Ain't No Telling	26 Oct 67	CR 1 mix 4. An unused stereo mix.	Sotheby's Private Reels CD JHR 003 / 004	Olympic Sound Studios, London, England	JHE	
Ain't No Telling	26 Oct 67	CR 1 mix 4. An unused stereo mix.	Sotheby's Reels, The CD Gold Standard TOM-800	Olympic Sound Studios, London, England	JHE	
Ain't No Telling	26 Oct 67	CR 1 mix 4. An unused stereo mix.	Living Reels Vol 1 CD JMH 011	Olympic Sound Studios, London, England	JHE	
Ain't No Telling	26 Oct 67	CR 1 mix 4. An unused stereo mix.	Get The Experience CD Invasion Unlimited IU 9424-1	Olympic Sound Studios, London, England	JHE	
Ain't No Telling	26 Oct 67	CR 1 mix 4. An unused stereo mix.	Sotheby's Reels, The CD Gold Standard TOM-800	Olympic Sound Studios, London, England	JHE	
Ain't Too Proud To Beg (Jammin' & I Was Made To Love Her)	06 Oct 67	CR 1 mix 1. With the opening jam but incomplete because the last 2 minutes are cut off.	BBC Sessions (CR) CD MCACD 2-11742	Top Gear, BBC Playhouse Theatre, London, England	Jimi	Noel Redding / Bass
Ain't Too Proud To Beg	06 Oct 67	CR 1 mix 2. BBC Performance. Complete and with the opening jam.	Symphony Of Experience CD Third Stone Discs TDS 24966	Top Gear, BBC Playhouse Theatre, London, England	Jimi	Noel Redding / Bass
Ain't Too Proud To Beg (Jam 1 & Jam 2)	06 Oct 67	CR 1 mix 2. BBC Performance. Complete and with the opening jam.	Ultimate BBC Collection CD Classical CL006	Top Gear, BBC Playhouse Theatre, London, England	Jimi	Noel Redding / Bass
Ain't Too Proud To Beg	06 Oct 67	CR 1 mix 2. BBC Performance. Complete and with the opening jam.	Live In London 1967 CD Koine Records K881104	Top Gear, BBC Playhouse Theatre, London, England	Jimi	Noel Redding / Bass
Ain't Too Proud To Beg	06 Oct 67	CR 1 mix 2. BBC Performance. Complete and with the opening jam.	Canadian Club CD WPOCM 0888 D 006-2	Top Gear, BBC Playhouse Theatre, London, England	Jimi	Noel Redding / Bass

SONG TITLE	DATE	COMMENTS	RELEASE	LOCATION / VENUE	BAND	PERSONNEL
Ain't Too Proud To Beg	06 Oct 67	CR 1 mix 2. BBC Performance. Complete and with the opening jam.	Completer, The CD Whoopy Cat WKP 0018 / 19	Top Gear, BBC Playhouse Theatre, London, England	Jimi	Noel Redding / Bass
Ain't Too Proud To Beg (Jam 1 & Jam 2)	06 Oct 67	CR 1 mix 2. BBC Performance. Complete and with the opening jam.	Complete BBC Session And.... The CD Last Bootleg Records LBR 036 / 2	Top Gear, BBC Playhouse Theatre, London, England	Jimi	Noel Redding / Bass
Ain't Too Proud To Beg	06 Oct 67	CR 1 mix 2. BBC Performance. Complete and with the opening jam.	Jimi: A Musical Legacy CD KTS BX 010	Top Gear, BBC Playhouse Theatre, London, England	Jimi	Noel Redding / Bass
Ain't Too Proud To Beg	06 Oct 67	CR 1 mix 2. BBC Performance. Complete and with the opening jam.	Black Gold CD Midnight Beat MBCD 058-062	Top Gear, BBC Playhouse Theatre, London, England	Jimi	Noel Redding / Bass
Ain't Too Proud To Beg (Stevie Wonder Jam)	06 Oct 67	CR 1 mix 3. BBC Performance. Complete but missing the opening jam.	Things I Used To Do CD The Early Years 02-CD-3334	Top Gear, BBC Playhouse Theatre, London, England	Jimi	Noel Redding / Bass
Ain't Too Proud To Beg	06 Oct 67	CR 1 mix 3. BBC Performance. Complete but missing the opening jam.	In Concert CD Starlife ST 3612	Top Gear, BBC Playhouse Theatre, London, England	Jimi	Noel Redding / Bass
Ain't Too Proud To Beg	06 Oct 67	CR 1 mix 3. BBC Performance. Complete but missing the opening jam.	Flames CD Missing In Action ACT 1	Top Gear, BBC Playhouse Theatre, London, England	Jimi	Noel Redding / Bass
Ain't Too Proud To Beg (Wonder Jam)	06 Oct 67	CR 1 mix 3. BBC Performance. Complete but missing the opening jam.	King And Wonder Sessions CD Oh Boy 1-9170	Top Gear, BBC Playhouse Theatre, London, England	Jimi	Noel Redding / Bass
Ain't Too Proud To Beg	06 Oct 67	CR 1 mix 3. BBC Performance. Complete but missing the opening jam.	Every Way To Paradise CD Tintangel TIBX 021 / 22 / 23 / 24	Top Gear, BBC Playhouse Theatre, London, England	Jimi	Noel Redding / Bass
All Along The Watchtower	21 Jan 68	CR 1 mix1 (stereo). Incomplete. Final overdubs were done in the US at the Record Plant.	Ultimate BBC Collection CD Classical CL006	Olympic Sound Studios, London, England	Jimi	Jimi Hendrix / Bass, Dave Mason / Acoustic Guitar, Mitch Mitchell / Drums, Brian Jones / Percussion
All Along The Watchtower	21 Jan 68	CR 1 mix1 (stereo). Final overdubs were done in the US at the Record Plant.	Red House CD The Entertainers CD294	Olympic Sound Studios, London, England	Jimi	Jimi Hendrix / Bass, Dave Mason / Acoustic Guitar, Mitch Mitchell / Drums, Brian Jones / Percussion
All Along The Watchtower	21 Jan 68	CR 1 mix1 (stereo). Final overdubs were done in the US at the Record Plant.	Complete BBC Session And.... The CD Last Bootleg Records LBR 036 / 2	Olympic Sound Studios, London, England	Jimi	Jimi Hendrix / Bass, Dave Mason / Acoustic Guitar, Mitch Mitchell / Drums, Brian Jones / Percussion
All Along The Watchtower	21 Jan 68	CR 1 mix1 (stereo). Final overdubs were done in the US at the	Electric Ladyland (CR)	Olympic Sound	Jimi	Jimi Hendrix / Bass, Dave

Title	Date	Notes	CD / Catalog	Studio	Producer	Personnel
		Record Plant.	CD MCACD-11600	Studios, London, England		Mason / Acoustic Guitar, Mitch Mitchell / Drums, Brian Jones / Percussion
All Along The Watchtower	21 Jan 68	CR 1 mix1 (stereo). Final overdubs were done in the US at the Record Plant.	The Singles Album (CR) CD Polydor 827 369-2	Olympic Sound Studios, London, England	Jimi	Jimi Hendrix / Bass, Dave Mason / Acoustic Guitar, Mitch Mitchell / Drums, Brian Jones / Percussion
All Along The Watchtower	21 Jan 68	CR 1 mix1 (stereo). Final overdubs were done in the US at the Record Plant.	Smash Hits (CR) CD Reprise 2276-2	Olympic Sound Studios, London, England	Jimi	Jimi Hendrix / Bass, Dave Mason / Acoustic Guitar, Mitch Mitchell / Drums, Brian Jones / Percussion
All Along The Watchtower	21 Jan 68	CR 1 mix1 (stereo). Final overdubs were done in the US at the Record Plant.	Midnight Sun CD Third Eye NK 007	Olympic Sound Studios, London, England	Jimi	Jimi Hendrix / Bass, Dave Mason / Acoustic Guitar, Mitch Mitchell / Drums, Brian Jones / Percussion
All Along The Watchtower	21 Jan 68	CR 1 mix 2 (mono). This on an Italian 45 and is a true mono mix.	Single: All Along The Watchtower / Can You See Me Polydor 59 240	Olympic Sound Studios, London, England	Jimi	Jimi Hendrix / Bass, Dave Mason / Acoustic Guitar, Mitch Mitchell / Drums, Brian Jones / Percussion
All Along The Watchtower	21 Jan 68	CR 1 mix 3 (mono). This on a US 45 where one channel of the stereo mix 1 was split to both channels.	Single: All Along The Watchtower / Crosstown Traffic Reprise GRE 0742	Olympic Sound Studios, London, England	Jimi	Jimi Hendrix / Bass, Dave Mason / Acoustic Guitar, Mitch Mitchell / Drums, Brian Jones / Percussion
All Along The Watchtower	21 Jan 68	CR 1 mix 4. Reverb was added to the right channel for the 'Legacy' LP. It almost sounds like a mono mix done as a fake stereo mix.	Legacy (CR) LP Polydor	Olympic Sound Studios, London, England	Jimi	Jimi Hendrix / Bass, Dave Mason / Acoustic Guitar, Mitch Mitchell / Drums, Brian Jones / Percussion
All Along The Watchtower	21 Jan 68	CR 1 mix 4. Reverb was added to the right channel for the 'Legacy' LP. It almost sounds like a mono mix done as a fake stereo mix.	Sotheby's Private Reels CD JHR 003 / 004	Olympic Sound Studios, London, England	Jimi	Jimi Hendrix / Bass, Dave Mason / Acoustic Guitar, Mitch Mitchell / Drums, Brian Jones / Percussion
All Along The Watchtower	21 Jan 68	CR 1 mix 5. An alternate mix of the CR prior to the Record Plant overdubs.	South Saturn Delta (CR) CD MCACD 11684	Olympic Sound Studios, London, England	Jimi	Jimi Hendrix / Bass, Dave Mason / Acoustic Guitar, Mitch Mitchell / Drums, Brian Jones / Percussion
All Along The Watchtower	21 Jan 68	CR 1 mix 6. An unused mix prior to the Record Plant overdubs and a bit different than mix #5 from 'South Saturn Delta'.	Master's Masters, The CD JH-01	Olympic Sound Studios, London, England	Jimi	Jimi Hendrix / Bass, Dave Mason / Acoustic Guitar, Mitch Mitchell / Drums, Brian Jones / Percussion
All Along The Watchtower	21 Jan 68	CR 1 mix 6. An unused mix prior to the Record Plant overdubs and a bit different than mix #5 from 'South Saturn Delta'.	Unsurpassed Studio Takes CD Yellow Dog YD 050	Olympic Sound Studios, London, England	Jimi	Jimi Hendrix / Bass, Dave Mason / Acoustic Guitar, Mitch Mitchell / Drums, Brian Jones / Percussion

SONG TITLE	DATE	COMMENTS	RELEASE	LOCATION / VENUE	BAND	PERSONNEL
All Along The Watchtower	21 Jan 68	CR 1 mix 6. An unused mix prior to the Record Plant overdubs and a bit different than mix #5 from 'South Saturn Delta'.	Symphony Of Experience CD Third Stone Discs TDS 24966	Olympic Sound Studios, London, England	Jimi	Jimi Hendrix / Bass, Dave Mason / Acoustic Guitar, Mitch Mitchell / Drums, Brian Jones / Percussion
All Along The Watchtower	21 Jan 68	CR 1 mix 6. An unused mix prior to the Record Plant overdubs and a bit different than mix #5 from 'South Saturn Delta'.	Best Of The Bootlegs CD MS 666	Olympic Sound Studios, London, England	Jimi	Jimi Hendrix / Bass, Dave Mason / Acoustic Guitar, Mitch Mitchell / Drums, Brian Jones / Percussion
All Along The Watchtower	21 Jan 68	CR 1 mix 6. An unused mix prior to the Record Plant overdubs and a bit different than mix #5 from 'South Saturn Delta'.	Midnight Shines Down CD Blue Kangaroo BK 04	Olympic Sound Studios, London, England	Jimi	Jimi Hendrix / Bass, Dave Mason / Acoustic Guitar, Mitch Mitchell / Drums, Brian Jones / Percussion
All Along The Watchtower	21 Jan 68	CR 1 mix 6. An unused mix prior to the Record Plant overdubs and a bit different than mix #5 from 'South Saturn Delta'.	Electric Ladyland Outtakes CD Invasion Unlimited IU 9417-1	Olympic Sound Studios, London, England	Jimi	Jimi Hendrix / Bass, Dave Mason / Acoustic Guitar, Mitch Mitchell / Drums, Brian Jones / Percussion
All Along The Watchtower	21 Jan 68	CR 1 mix 6. An unused mix prior to the Record Plant overdubs and a bit different than mix #5 from 'South Saturn Delta'.	Jimi: A Musical Legacy CD KTS BX 010	Olympic Sound Studios, London, England	Jimi	Jimi Hendrix / Bass, Dave Mason / Acoustic Guitar, Mitch Mitchell / Drums, Brian Jones / Percussion
All Along The Watchtower	21 Jan 68	CR 1 mix 6. An unused mix prior to the Record Plant overdubs and a bit different than mix #5 from 'South Saturn Delta'.	Voodoo In Ladyland CD MUM MUCD 006	Olympic Sound Studios, London, England	Jimi	Jimi Hendrix / Bass, Dave Mason / Acoustic Guitar, Mitch Mitchell / Drums, Brian Jones / Percussion
All Along The Watchtower	21 Jan 68	CR 1 mix 6. An unused mix prior to the Record Plant overdubs and a bit different than mix #5 from 'South Saturn Delta'.	Midnight Sun CD Third Eye NK 007	Olympic Sound Studios, London, England	Jimi	Jimi Hendrix / Bass, Dave Mason / Acoustic Guitar, Mitch Mitchell / Drums, Brian Jones / Percussion
All Along The Watchtower	21 Jan 68	Only 30 seconds (and under voiceover) of this version is available on "Lifelines". A few short bits from this session were released on the 'Classic albums - Electric Ladyland' videotape documentary.	Lifelines (CR) CD Reprise 9 26435-2	Olympic Sound Studios, London, England	Jimi	Jimi Hendrix / Bass, Dave Mason / Acoustic Guitar, Mitch Mitchell / Drums, Brian Jones / Percussion
All Along The Watchtower	04 Jul 70	CR 3. Complete live performance. Released incomplete on the 'Johnny B. Goode' CR.	Atlanta Special CD Genuine Pig TGP 121	2nd International Pop Festival, Atlanta, GA	COL	
All Along The Watchtower	04 Jul 70	CR 3. Complete live performance. Released incomplete on the 'Johnny B. Goode' CR.	At The Atlanta Pop Festival (CR) Laserdisc BMG BVLP 77 (74321-10987)	2nd International Pop Festival, Atlanta, GA	COL	
All Along The Watchtower	04 Jul 70	CR 3. Complete live performance. Released incomplete on the 'Johnny B. Goode' CR.	Atlanta CD JMH 009 / 02	2nd International Pop Festival, Atlanta, GA	COL	

Song	Date	Notes	Release	Location	Source	Personnel
All Along The Watchtower	04 Jul 70	CR 3. Complete live performance. Released incomplete on the 'Johnny B. Goode' CR.	Oh, Atlanta CD Tendolar TDR-009	2nd International Pop Festival, Atlanta, GA	COL	
All Along The Watchtower	04 Jul 70	CR 3. Live performance. Incomplete	Johnny B. Goode (CR) CD Capitol 430218-2	2nd International Pop Festival, Atlanta, GA	COL	
All Along The Watchtower	17 Jul 70	BR 1. Live performance.	Can You Here Me LP Hemero 01 / KERI	New York Pop-Downing Stadium, Randalls Island, NY	COL	
All Along The Watchtower	30 Aug 70	CR 2. Live Performance.	Island Man CD Silver Rarities SIRA 39 / 40	Isle Of Wight Festival, Isle Of Wight, England	COL	
All Along The Watchtower	30 Aug 70	CR 2. Live Performance.	At The Isle Of Wight (CR) Laserdisc CBS / Sony CLSM 791	Isle Of Wight Festival, Isle Of Wight, England	COL	
All Along The Watchtower	30 Aug 70	CR 2. Live Performance.	Isle Of Wight / Atlanta Pop Festival (CR) LP Columbia G3X 3085	Isle Of Wight Festival, Isle Of Wight, England	COL	
All Along The Watchtower	30 Aug 70	CR 2. Live Performance.	Rarities On Compact Disc CD On The Radio	Isle Of Wight Festival, Isle Of Wight, England	COL	
All Along The Watchtower	30 Aug 70	CR 2. Live Performance.	Greatest Hits Live CD Chartbusters CHER 089A	Isle Of Wight Festival, Isle Of Wight, England	COL	
All Along The Watchtower	30 Aug 70	CR 2. Live Performance.	Wight CD JMH 006 / 2	Isle Of Wight Festival, Isle Of Wight, England	COL	
All Along The Watchtower	03 Sep 70	BR 2. Live performance.	Welcome To The Electric Circus Vol 2 CD Midnight Beat 018	K.B. Hallen, Copenhagen, Denmark	COL	
All Along The Watchtower	03 Sep 70	BR 2. Live performance.	Copenhagen '70 CD Whoopy Cat WKP 044 / 45	K.B. Hallen, Copenhagen, Denmark	COL	
All Along The Watchtower	06 Sep 70	BR 3. Live performance.	Love & Peace CD Midnight Beat MBCD 015	Love And Peace Festival, Isle Of Fehrman, Germany	COL	
All Along The Watchtower	06 Sep 70	BR 3. Live performance.	Wink Of An Eye CD Whoopy Cat WKP 0033 / 34	Love And Peace Festival, Isle Of Fehrman, Germany	COL	
Angel (Little Wing)	14 Oct 67	CR 4. The earliest composing tape of this song.	South Saturn Delta (CR) CD MCACD 11684	Olympic Sound Studios, London, England	Jimi	Mitch Mitchell / Drums

SONG TITLE	DATE	COMMENTS	RELEASE	LOCATION / VENUE	BAND	PERSONNEL
Angel	13 Nov 67	CR 3. A second studio demo by Jimi.	South Saturn Delta (CR) CD MCACD 11684	Olympic Sound Studios, London, England	Solo	
Angel	?? Mar 68	CR 2 mix 1. "Stereo" mix of this composing tape.	Jimi By Himself The Home Recordings (CR) BSP-VC1	New York Apartment	Solo	
Angel	?? Mar 68	CR 2 mix 2. The mono mix from this composing tape.	First Rays Of The New Rising Sun CD Living Legend LLRCD 023	New York Apartment	Solo	
Angel	?? Mar 68	CR 2 mix 2. The mono mix from this composing tape.	Acoustic Jams CD Sphinx SX CD 001	New York Apartment	Solo	
Angel	?? Mar 68	CR 2 mix 2. The mono mix from this composing tape.	Ladyland In Flames LP Marshall Records JIMI 1,2,3,4	New York Apartment	Solo	
Angel	?? Mar 68	CR 2 mix 2. The mono mix from this composing tape.	Lifelines (CR) CD Reprise 9 26435-2	New York Apartment	Solo	
Angel	?? Mar 68	CR 2 mix 2. The mono mix from this composing tape.	1968 AD Part Two CD Whoopy Cat WKP 0013	New York Apartment	Solo	
Angel	?? Mar 68	CR 2 mix 2. The mono mix from this composing tape.	Official Bootleg Album, The CD Yellow Dog YD 051	New York Apartment	Solo	
Angel	?? Mar 68	CR 2 mix 2. The mono mix from this composing tape.	51st Anniversary CD Future Disc JMH 001 / 8	New York Apartment	Solo	
Angel	?? Mar 68	CR 2 mix 2. The mono mix from this composing tape.	First Rays Of The New Rising Sun CD Triangle PYCD 084-2	New York Apartment	Solo	
Angel	?? Mar 68	CR 2 mix 2. The mono mix from this composing tape.	Best Of The Bootlegs CD MS 666	New York Apartment	Solo	
Angel	?? Mar 68	CR 2 mix 2. The mono mix from this composing tape.	Sweet Angel CD Compact Music WPOCM 0589	New York Apartment	Solo	
Angel	?? Mar 68	CR 2 mix 2. The mono mix from this composing tape.	Voodoo Blues CD Smurf	New York Apartment	Solo	
Angel	?? Mar 68	CR 2 mix 2. The mono mix from this composing tape.	Studio Experience CD Sodium Haze SH 099	New York Apartment	Solo	
Angel	?? Mar 68	CR 2 mix 2. The mono mix from this composing tape.	Electric Ladyland Outtakes CD Invasion Unlimited IU 9417-1	New York Apartment	Solo	

Song	Date	Notes	Release	Location	Group	Musician
Angel	?? Mar 68	CR 2 mix 2. The mono mix from this composing tape.	Notes In Colours CD JHR 001 / 002	New York Apartment	Solo	
Angel	?? Mar 68	CR 2 mix 2. The mono mix from this composing tape.	Rarities On Compact Disc CD On The Radio	New York Apartment	Solo	
Angel	?? Mar 68	CR 2 mix 2. The mono mix from this composing tape.	Jimi: A Musical Legacy CD KTS BX 010	New York Apartment	Solo	
Angel	?? Mar 68	CR 2 mix 2. The mono mix from this composing tape.	Black Strings CD CDM G-53 258	New York Apartment	Solo	
Angel	?? Mar 68	CR 2 mix 2. The mono mix from this composing tape.	Black Gold CD Midnight Beat MBCD 058-062	New York Apartment	Solo	
Angel	?? Mar 68	CR 2 mix 2. The mono mix from this composing tape.	Magic Hand CD Mum MUCD 012	New York Apartment	Solo	
Angel	23 Jul 70	CR 1 mix 1	First Rays Of The New Rising Sun (CR) CD MCACD 11599	Electric Lady Studio, New York, NY	COL	
Angel	23 Jul 70	CR 1 mix 1	The Singles Album (CR) CD Polydor 827 369-2	Electric Lady Studio, New York, NY	COL	
Angel	23 Jul 70	CR 1 mix 2.	Voodoo Soup (CR) CD MCA 11206	Electric Lady Studio, New York, NY	COL	
Angel	23 Jul 70	CR1 mix 3. Unused mix with the percussion mixed forward.	Multicolored Blues CD Luna LU 9317	Electric Lady Studio, New York, NY	COL	
Angel	23 Jul 70	CR1 mix 3. Unused mix with the percussion mixed forward.	First Rays - The Sessions CD Whoopy Cat WKP 0002	Electric Lady Studio, New York, NY	COL	
Angel	23 Jul 70	CR1 mix 3. Unused mix with the percussion mixed forward.	Notes In Colours CD JHR 001 / 002	Electric Lady Studio, New York, NY	COL	
Angel	23 Jul 70	CR1 mix 3. Unused mix with the percussion mixed forward.	Magic Hand CD Mum MUCD 012	Electric Lady Studio, New York, NY	COL	
Angel	23 Jul 70	BR 1. A short bit of jamming of the "Angel" guitar riff between some takes of "Drifting" during the same session as the CR 1 of 'Angel'. See 'Drifting' BR 2.	Notes In Colours CD JHR 001 / 002	Electric Lady Studio, New York, NY	COL	
Angel	23 Jul 70	BR 2. Unused instrumental false start and full take.	Notes In Colours CD JHR 001 / 002	Electric Lady Studio, New York, NY	COL	
Are You Experienced?	03 Apr 67	CR 1 mix 1 (stereo)	Are You Experienced? (CR) CD MCACD 11602	Olympic Sound Studios, London, England	JHE	Jimi / Piano
Are You Experienced?	03 Apr 67	CR 1 mix 2 (mono)	Are You Experienced? (CR) LP Track 612 001	Olympic Sound Studios, London, England	JHE	Jimi / Piano

SONG TITLE	DATE	COMMENTS	RELEASE	LOCATION / VENUE	BAND	PERSONNEL
Are You Experienced?	03 Apr 67	CR 1 mix 3. Jimi's backwards guitar overdub reversed to play forward. This version plays through to the start of the song.	Symphony Of Experience CD Third Stone Discs TDS 24966	Olympic Sound Studios, London, England	JHE	Jimi / Piano
Are You Experienced?	03 Apr 67	CR 1 mix 3. Jimi's backwards guitar overdub reversed to play forward. This release has just the overdub part.	Screaming Eagle CD Pink Poodle POO 001	Olympic Sound Studios, London, England	JHE	Jimi / Piano
Are You Experienced?	03 Apr 67	CR 1 mix 3. Jimi's backwards guitar overdub reversed to play forward. This release has just the overdub part.	Get The Experience CD Invasion Unlimited IU 9424-1	Olympic Sound Studios, London, England	JHE	Jimi / Piano
Are You Experienced?	03 Apr 67	CR 1 mix 3. Jimi's backwards guitar overdub reversed to play forward. This version plays through to the start of the song.	Jimi: A Musical Legacy CD KTS BX 010	Olympic Sound Studios, London, England	JHE	Jimi / Piano
Are You Experienced?	16 Feb 68	BR 1. Live performance	Biggest Square In The Building, The CD Reverb Music 1993	State Fair Music Hall, Dallas, TX	JHE	
Are You Experienced?	16 Feb 68	BR 1. Live performance	Scuse Me While I Kiss The Sky CD Sonic Zoom SZ 1001	State Fair Music Hall, Dallas, TX	JHE	
Are You Experienced?	16 Feb 68	BR 1. Live performance	Scuse Me While I Kiss The Sky CD Sonic Zoom SZ 1001	State Fair Music Hall, Dallas, TX	JHE	
Are You Experienced?	11 Aug 68	BR 2. Live performance	It's Only A Paper Moon CD Luna 9420	Col Ballroom, Davenport, IA	JHE	
Are You Experienced?	11 Aug 68	BR 2. Live performance	Davenport, Iowa '68 LP Creative Artistry 26K10 / 55K10	Col Ballroom, Davenport, IA	JHE	
Are You Experienced?	11 Aug 68	BR 2. Live performance	One Night Stand CD Hep Cat 101	Col Ballroom, Davenport, IA	JHE	
Are You Experienced?	23 Aug 68	BR 3. Live performance	Historic Concert CD Midnight Beat MBCD 017	New York Rock Festival, Singer Bowl, Queens, NY	JHE	
Are You Experienced?	14 Sep 68	BR 4. Live performance	Live At The Hollywood Bowl LP RSR / International RSR 251	Hollywood Bowl, Los Angeles, CA	JHE	
Are You Experienced?	10 Oct 68	CR 2. Live performance.	First Rays Of The New Rising Sun CD Living Legend LLRCD 023	Winterland Theatre, San Francisco, CA 1st Show	JHE	
Are You Experienced?	10 Oct 68	CR 2. Live performance.	Concerts (CR) CD Reprise 9-22306-2	Winterland Theatre, San Francisco, CA 1st Show	JHE	

Song	Date	Note	Flute Note	Release	Location	Group	Musician
Are You Experienced?	10 Oct 68	CR 2. Live performance.		Winterland Vol 1 CD Whoopy Cat WKP 025 / 26	Winterland Theatre, San Francisco, CA 1st Show	JHE	
Are You Experienced?	10 Oct 68	CR 2. Live performance.		Jimi Hendrix CD Imtrat 40-90355	Winterland Theatre, San Francisco, CA 1st Show	JHE	
Are You Experienced?	10 Oct 68	CR 2. Live performance.		Greatest Hits Live CD Chartbusters CHER 089A	Winterland Theatre, San Francisco, CA 1st Show	JHE	
Are You Experienced?	11 Oct 68	CR 3 mix 1. Live performance with Virgil Gonzales' flute part mixed out.		Official Bootleg Album, The CD Yellow Dog YD 051	Winterland Theatre, San Francisco, CA 1st Show	JHE	
Are You Experienced?	11 Oct 68	CR 3 mix 1. Live performance with Virgil Gonzales' flute part mixed out.		Little Wing CD Oil Well RSC 036	Winterland Theatre, San Francisco, CA 1st Show	JHE	
Are You Experienced?	11 Oct 68	CR 3 mix 1. Live performance with Virgil Gonzales' flute part mixed out.		Ultimate Live Collection, The CD The Beat Goes On BGO BX 9307-4	Winterland Theatre, San Francisco, CA 1st Show	JHE	
Are You Experienced?	11 Oct 68	CR 3 mix 1. Live performance with Virgil Gonzales' flute part mixed out.		Live At Winterland +3 (CR) CD-3 Rykodisc 20038 / +3	Winterland Theatre, San Francisco, CA 1st Show	JHE	Virgil Gonzales / Flute (Mixed Out)
Are You Experienced?	11 Oct 68	CR 3 mix 2. Live performance with Virgil Gonzales' flute part intact.		Winterland Days, The CD Manic Depression 001	Winterland Theatre, San Francisco, CA 2nd Show	JHE	
Are You Experienced?	11 Oct 68	CR 3 mix 2. Live performance with Virgil Gonzales' flute part intact.		Winterland Vol 2 CD Whoopy Cat WKP 00279 / 28	Winterland Theatre, San Francisco, CA 2nd Show	JHE	
Are You Experienced?	11 Oct 68	CR 3 mix 2. Live performance with Virgil Gonzales' flute part intact.		Living Reels Vol 2 CD JMH 012 / 2	Winterland Theatre, San Francisco, CA 2nd Show	JHE	
Are You Experienced?	20 Jun 69	BR 5. Live performance		More Electricity From Newport CD Luna LU 9201	Newport Pop Festival, San Fernando State, Northridge, CA	JHE	
Are You Experienced?	20 Jun 69	BR 5. Live performance		A Lifetime Of Experience LP Sleepy Dragon 55 10	Newport Pop Festival, San Fernando State, Northridge, CA	JHE	
Are You Experienced?	07 Mar 67	An outtake of CR 1 mix 1.		Sotheby's Private Reels CD JHR 003 / 004	Olympic Sound Studios, London, England	JHE	Jimi / Piano

SONG TITLE	DATE	COMMENTS	RELEASE	LOCATION / VENUE	BAND	PERSONNEL
Astro Man	25 Jun 70	CR 1 mix 1.	First Rays Of The New Rising Sun (CR) CD MCACD 11599	Electric Lady Studio, New York, NY	COL	Juma Sultan / Percussion
Astro Man	25 Jun 70	CR 1 mix 1.	Cry Of Love, The (CR) CD Reprise 2034-2	Electric Lady Studio, New York, NY	COL	Juma Sultan / Percussion
Astro Man	25 Jun 70	CR 1 mix 2. An unused mix of the CR 1 featuring some additional guitar overdubs.	Sir James Marshall LP Jester Productions JP 106	Electric Lady Studio, New York, NY	COL	Juma Sultan / Percussion
Astro Man Jam	24 Jun 70	BR 1 mix 1. The longer version of the take 7 instrumental track recorded the day before the CR. In this version Jimi refers to the song as "Asshole Man". All of these versions are incomplete.	Notes In Colours CD JHR 001 / 002	Electric Lady Studio, New York, NY	COL	Juma Sultan / Percussion
Astro Man Jam	24 Jun 70	BR 1 mix 1. The longer version of the take 7 instrumental track recorded the day before the CR. In this version Jimi refers to the song as "Asshole Man". All of these versions are incomplete.	Completer, The CD Whoopy Cat WKP 0018 / 19	Electric Lady Studio, New York, NY	COL	Juma Sultan / Percussion
Astro Man Jam	24 Jun 70	BR 1 mix 2. The shorter version of the take 7 instrumental track recorded the day before the CR 1. In this version Jimi refers to the song as "Asshole Man". All of these versions are incomplete.	Electric Gypsy CD Scorpio? 40176 / 15	Electric Lady Studio, New York, NY	COL	Juma Sultan / Percussion
Astro Man Jam	24 Jun 70	BR 1 mix 2. The shorter version of the take 7 instrumental track recorded the day before the CR 1. In this version Jimi refers to the song as "Asshole Man". All of these versions are incomplete.	Unsurpassed Studio Takes CD Yellow Dog YD 050	Electric Lady Studio, New York, NY	COL	Juma Sultan / Percussion
Astro Man Jam	24 Jun 70	BR 1 mix 2. The shorter version of the take 7 instrumental track recorded the day before the CR 1. In this version Jimi refers to the song as "Asshole Man". All of these versions are incomplete.	Multicolored Blues CD Luna LU 9317	Electric Lady Studio, New York, NY	COL	Juma Sultan / Percussion
Astro Man Jam	24 Jun 70	BR 1 mix 2. The shorter version of the take 7 instrumental track recorded the day before the CR 1. In this version Jimi refers to the song as "Asshole Man". All of these versions are incomplete.	First Rays Of The New Rising Sun CD Triangle PYCD 084-2	Electric Lady Studio, New York, NY	COL	Juma Sultan / Percussion
Astro Man Jam	24 Jun 70	BR 1 mix 2. The shorter version of the take 7 instrumental track recorded the day before the CR 1. In this version Jimi refers to the song as "Asshole Man". All of these versions are incomplete.	Best Of The Bootlegs CD MS 666	Electric Lady Studio, New York, NY	COL	Juma Sultan / Percussion
Astro Man Jam	24 Jun 70	BR 1 mix 2. The shorter version of the take 7 instrumental track recorded the day before the CR 1. In this version Jimi refers to the song as "Asshole Man". All of these versions are incomplete.	Gypsy Suns, Moons And Rainbows CD Sidewalk JHX 8868	Electric Lady Studio, New York, NY	COL	Juma Sultan / Percussion
Astro Man Jam	24 Jun 70	BR 1 mix 2. The shorter version of the take 7 instrumental track	Voice Of Experience	Electric Lady Studio,	COL	Juma Sultan / Percussion

Song	Date	Release	Location	Source	Musician	Notes
Astro Man Jam		CD Rhin· zerous RHP 789	New York, NY		Juma Sultan / Percussion	recorded the day before the CR 1. In this version Jimi refers to the song as "Asshole Man". All of these versions are incomplete.
Astro Man Jam	24 Jun 70	Midnight Shines Down CD Blue Kangaroo BK 04	Electric Lady Studio, New York, NY	COL	Juma Sultan / Percussion	BR 1 mix 2. The shorter version of the take 7 instrumental track recorded the day before the CR 1. In this version Jimi refers to the song as "Asshole Man". All of these versions are incomplete.
Astro Man Jam	24 Jun 70	Electric Gypsy's CD Pilot HJCD 070	Electric Lady Studio, New York, NY	COL	Juma Sultan / Percussion	BR 1 mix 2. The shorter version of the take 7 instrumental track recorded the day before the CR 1. In this version Jimi refers to the song as "Asshole Man". All of these versions are incomplete.
Astro Man Jam	24 Jun 70	Mannish Boy LP Contraband CBM 88	Electric Lady Studio, New York, NY	COL		BR 1 mix 2. The shorter version of the take 7 instrumental track recorded the day before the CR 1. In this version Jimi refers to the song as "Asshole Man". All of these versions are incomplete.
Astro Man / Valleys Of Neptune	?? / Aug-Sep / 69	Acoustic Jams CD Sphinx SX CD 001	Shokan Or N Y C Apartment	Jimi		BR 2. An acoustic jam / medley made starting with "Astro Man" and working its way into "Valleys Of Neptune" with some improvising mixed in.
Astro Man / Valleys Of Neptune (They Call Me Extra Man)	?? / Aug-Sep / 69	Two Sides Of The Same Genius LP Amazing Kornyphone TAKRL H677	Shokan Or N Y C	Jimi	Unknown Guitarist	BR 2. An acoustic jam / medley made starting with "Astro Man" and working its way into "Valleys Of Neptune" with some improvising mixed in.
Astro Man / Valleys Of Neptune	?? / Aug-Sep / 69	Apartment Jam 70 CD Spicy Essence	Shokan Or N Y C Apartment	Jimi	Unknown Guitarist	BR 2. An acoustic jam / medley made starting with "Astro Man" and working its way into "Valleys Of Neptune" with some improvising mixed in.
Astro Man / Valleys Of Neptune (Gloomy Monday Takes 1 & 2)	?? / Aug-Sep / 69	Every Way To Paradise CD Tintangel TIBX 021 / 22 / 23 / 24	Shokan Or N Y C Apartment	Jimi	Unknown Guitarist	BR 2. An acoustic jam / medley made starting with "Astro Man" and working its way into "Valleys Of Neptune" with some improvising mixed in.
Auld Lang Syne	?? Dec 69	Band Of Gypsys Vol 3	Baggies, New York, NY	BOG		BR 1. Part of a medley that also includes "Silent Night" and "Little Drummer Boy".
Auld Lang Syne	?? Dec 69	Electric Anniversary Jimi CD Midnight Beat MBCD 024	Baggies, New York, NY	BOG		BR 1. Part of a medley that also includes "Silent Night" and "Little Drummer Boy".
Auld Lang Syne	?? Dec 69	Can You Please Crawl Out Your Window? LP Ruthless Rhymes Jimi1	Baggies, New York, NY	BOG		BR 1. Part of a medley that also includes "Silent Night" and "Little Drummer Boy".
Auld Lang Syne	31 Dec 69	Band Of Gypsys Vol 3	Fillmore East, New York, NY 2nd Show	BOG		BR 2. Live performance
Auld Lang Syne	31 Dec 69	This One's For You LP Veteran Music MF-243	Fillmore East, New York, NY 2nd Show	BOG		BR 2. Live performance
Auld Lang Syne	31 Dec 69	Auld Lang Syne CD JH 100 03	Fillmore East, New York, NY 2nd Show	BOG		BR 2. Live performance

SONG TITLE	DATE	COMMENTS	RELEASE	LOCATION / VENUE	BAND	PERSONNEL
Auld Lang Syne	31 Dec 69	BR 2. Live performance	Band Of Gypsys: Happy New Year CD Silver Shadow CD 9103	Fillmore East, New York, NY 2nd Show	BOG	
Auld Lang Syne	31 Dec 69	BR 2. Live performance	Fillmore Concerts, The CD Whoopy Cat WKP 0006 / 7	Fillmore East, New York, NY 2nd Show	COL	
Auld Lang Syne	31 Dec 69	BR 2. Live performance	Band Of Gold CD-R Major Tom MT 087	Fillmore East, New York, NY 2nd Show	BOG	
Auld Lang Syne	31 Dec 69	BR 2. Live performance	Band Of Gypsys- The Ultimate CD JMH 010/3	Fillmore East, New York, NY 2nd Show	BOG	
Backwards Guitar Experiment	19 Jan 70	BR 1. About a minutes worth of some guitar experimenting.	Eyes And Imagination CD Third Stone TSD 18970	Record Plant, New York, NY	Jimi	
Beginnings	?? Aug 69	BR 1. From the rehearsal at Jimi's Shokan house shortly before the legendary Woodstock performance.	Woodstock Rehearsals CD Midnight Beat MBCD 009	Shokan House, Woodstock, NY	GSRB	
Beginnings	?? Aug 69	BR 1. From the rehearsal at Jimi's Shokan house shortly before the legendary Woodstock performance.	Shokan Sunrise CD	Shokan House, Woodstock, NY	GSRB	
Beginnings	?? Aug 69	BR 2. A second take from the rehearsal at Jimi's Shokan house shortly before the legendary Woodstock performance. This continues with a take of "If Six Was Nine"	Woodstock Rehearsals CD Midnight Beat MBCD 009	Shokan House, Woodstock, NY	GSRB	
Beginnings	?? Aug 69	BR 2. A second take from the rehearsal at Jimi's Shokan house shortly before the legendary Woodstock performance. This continues with a take of "If Six Was Nine"	Shokan Sunrise CD	Shokan House, Woodstock, NY	GSRB	
Beginnings	18 Aug 69	BR 3. Live performance of the complete song.	Woodstock Nation CD Wild Bird 89090 1 / 2	Woodstock Music And Art Fair, Bethel, NY	GSRB	
Beginnings	18 Aug 69	BR 3. Live performance of the complete song.	At Woodstock (CR) Laserdisc BMG BVLP 86	Woodstock Music And Art Fair, Bethel, NY	GSRB	
Beginnings	18 Aug 69	BR 3. Live performance of the complete song.	Gypsy Sun And Rainbows CD Manic Depression MDCD 05 / 06	Woodstock Music And Art Fair, Bethel, NY	GSRB	
Beginnings	18 Aug 69	BR 3. Live performance of the complete song.	Woodstock Monday, August 18 1969, 8AM CD JMH 008	Woodstock Music And Art Fair, Bethel, NY	GSRB	
Beginnings	18 Aug 69	BR 3. Live performance of the complete song.	Ultimate Live Collection, The CD The Beat Goes On BGO BX 9307-4	Woodstock Music And Art Fair, Bethel, NY	GSRB	

Song	Date	Notes	Release	Location	Jimi	Midnight Lightning Line Up 1975
Beginnings	28 Aug 69	CR 2. Recorded by the GSRB, the original musicians were replaced in 1975.	Midnight Lightning (CR) LP Reprise MS 2229	Hit Factory, New York, NY		
Beginnings	18 Aug 69	CR 3 mix 1. Edited from the complete performance.	Experience II CD More MTT 1021	Woodstock Music And Art Fair, Bethel, NY	GSRB	
Beginnings	18 Aug 69	CR 3 mix 1. Edited from the complete performance.	Woodstock Two L P (CR) Cotillion SD 2400	Shokan House, Woodstock, NY	GSRB	
Beginnings	18 Aug 69	CR 3 mix 2. Edited from the complete performance.	Woodstock (CR) CD MCA 11063	Woodstock Music And Art Fair, Bethel, NY	GSRB	
Beginnings	01 Jul 70	CR 1 mix 1.	War Heroes (CR) CD Polydor 847-2622	Electric Lady Studio, New York, NY	COL	Juma Sultan / Percussion
Beginnings	01 Jul 70	CR 1 mix 2. The unedited take used for the CR 1.	Acoustic Jams CD Sphinx SX CD 001	Electric Lady Studio, New York, NY	COL	Juma Sultan / Percussion
Beginnings	01 Jul 70	CR 1 mix 2. The unedited take used for the CR 1.	Multicolored Blues CD Luna LU 9317	Electric Lady Studio, New York, NY	COL	Juma Sultan / Percussion
Beginnings	01 Jul 70	CR 1 mix 2. The unedited take used for the CR 1.	First Rays Of The New Rising Sun CD Triangle PYCD 084-2	Electric Lady Studio, New York, NY	COL	Juma Sultan / Percussion
Beginnings	01 Jul 70	CR 1 mix 2. The unedited take used for the CR 1.	Jewel Box CD Home HR-5824-3	Electric Lady Studio, New York, NY	COL	Juma Sultan / Percussion
Beginnings	01 Jul 70	CR 1 mix 2. The unedited take used for the CR 1.	Completer, The CD Whoopy Cat WKP 0018 / 19	Electric Lady Studio, New York, NY	COL	Juma Sultan / Percussion
Beginnings	01 Jul 70	CR 1 mix 2. The unedited take used for the CR 1.	Black Gold CD Midnight Beat MBCD 058-062	Electric Lady Studio, New York, NY	COL	Juma Sultan / Percussion
Beginnings	01 Jul 70	CR 1 mix 2. The unedited take used for the CR 1.	Kiss The Skies CD Mum MUCD 024	Electric Lady Studio, New York, NY	COL	Juma Sultan / Percussion
Beginnings	01 Jul 70	CR 1 mix 2. The unedited take used for the CR 1.	First Rays Of The New Rising Sun (CR) CD MCACD 11599	Electric Lady Studio, New York, NY	COL	Juma Sultan / Percussion
Beginnings	30 Jul 70	BR 4. Live performance of a medley with 'Straight Ahead'.	Maui, Hawaii LP JH 106 (Trademark Of Quality?)	Rainbow Bridge Vibratory Sound-Color Experiment, Maui, HI 2nd Show	COL	
Beginnings	30 Jul 70	BR 4. Live performance of a medley with 'Straight Ahead'.	Last American Concert Vol 2 CD The Swingin' Pig TSP-072	Rainbow Bridge Vibratory Sound-Color Experiment, Maui, HI 2nd Show	COL	

SONG TITLE	DATE	COMMENTS	RELEASE	LOCATION / VENUE	BAND	PERSONNEL
Beginnings	30 Jul 70	BR 4. Live performance of a medley with 'Straight Ahead'.	In From The Storm CD Silver Rarities SIRA 109 / 110	Rainbow Bridge Vibratory Sound-Color Experiment, Maui, HI 2nd Show	COL	
Beginnings	30 Jul 70	BR 5. Live performance of a medley with 'Straight Ahead'.	Rainbow Bridge 2 CD JMH 003 / 2	Rainbow Bridge Vibratory Sound-Color Experiment, Maui, HI 1st Show	COL	
Belly Button Window	23 Jul 70	BR 1. An instrumental studio track recorded a month before Jimi's solo CR version.	Acoustic Jams CD Sphinx SX CD 001	Electric Lady Studio, New York, NY	COL	
Belly Button Window	23 Jul 70	BR 1. An instrumental studio track recorded a month before Jimi's solo CR version.	Multicolored Blues CD Luna LU 9317	Electric Lady Studio, New York, NY	COL	
Belly Button Window	23 Jul 70	BR 1. An instrumental studio track recorded a month before Jimi's solo CR version.	Studio Experience CD Sodium Haze SH 099	Electric Lady Studio, New York, NY	COL	
Belly Button Window	23 Jul 70	BR 1. An instrumental studio track recorded a month before Jimi's solo CR version.	Notes In Colours CD JHR 001 / 002	Electric Lady Studio, New York, NY	COL	
Belly Button Window	23 Jul 70	BR 1. An instrumental studio track recorded a month before Jimi's solo CR version.	I Don't Live Today CD ACL 007	Electric Lady Studio, New York, NY	COL	
Belly Button Window	23 Jul 70	BR 1. An instrumental studio track recorded a month before Jimi's solo CR version.	51st Anniversary CD Future Disc JMH 001 / 8	Electric Lady Studio, New York, NY	COL	
Belly Button Window	22 Aug 70	CR 1 mix 1.	First Rays Of The New Rising Sun (CR) CD MCACD 11599	Electric Lady Studio, New York, NY	Solo	
Belly Button Window	22 Aug 70	CR 1 mix 1.	Cry Of Love, The (CR) CD Reprise 2034-2	Electric Lady Studio, New York, NY	Solo	
Belly Button Window	22 Aug 70	CR 1 mix 2.	Voodoo Soup (CR) CD MCA 11206	Electric Lady Studio, New York, NY	Solo	
Belly Button Window	22 Aug 70	BR 2. An unused composite of the CR 1 version and an Outtake from the same session. This was originally intended for the commercial "Blues" CD but ultimately rejected.	500,000 Halos CD EXP 500,000	Electric Lady Studio, New York, NY	Solo	
Bleeding Heart (Peoples People's)	?? Mar 68	CR 4. Live performance.	High Live And Dirty (CR) LP Nutmeg NUT 1001	Scene Club, New York, N Y	Scene	
Bleeding Heart	?? Mar 68	CR 4. Live performance.	In Concert CD Starlife ST 3612	Scene Club, New York, NY	Scene	
Bleeding Heart	?? Mar 68	CR 4. Live performance.	Woke Up This Morning And Found Myself Dead CR (CD) RLCD 0068	Scene Club, New York, NY	Scene	

Song	Date	Recording	Release	Location	Lineup	Musicians
Bleeding Heart	24 Feb 69	CR 3 mix 1. Live Performance.	Last Experience, The (CR) CD Bescol CD 42	Royal Albert Hall, London, England	JHE	
Bleeding Heart	24 Feb 69	CR 3 mix 1. Live Performance.	Smashing Amps LP Trademark Of Quality TMQ 1813	Royal Albert Hall, London, England	JHE	
Bleeding Heart	24 Feb 69	CR 3 mix 1. Live Performance.	Voice Of Experience CD Rhinozerous RHP 789	Royal Albert Hall, London, England	JHE	
Bleeding Heart	24 Feb 69	CR 3 mix 1. Live Performance.	King Of Gypsies CD Rockyssimo RK 001	Royal Albert Hall, London, England	JHE	
Bleeding Heart	24 Feb 69	CR 3 mix 1. Live Performance.	Hendrix In Words And Music CD Outlaw Records OTR 1100030	Royal Albert Hall, London, England	JHE	
Bleeding Heart	24 Feb 69	CR 3 mix 1. Live Performance.	Anthology CD Box 9	Royal Albert Hall, London, England	JHE	
Bleeding Heart	24 Feb 69	CR 3 mix 2. Live performance that is edited from CR 3 mix 1.	Last Experience, The (CR) CD Bescol CD 42	Royal Albert Hall, London, England	JHE	
Bleeding Heart	24 Feb 69	CR 3 mix 2. Live performance that is edited from CR 3 mix 1.	Stone Free CD Silver Rarities SIRA 58 / 59	Royal Albert Hall, London, England	JHE	
Bleeding Heart	24 Feb 69	CR 3 mix 3. Live performance. A slightly different edit than CR 3 mix 2.	Concerts (CR) CD Reprise 9-22306-2	Royal Albert Hall, London, England	JHE	
Bleeding Heart	24 Feb 69	CR 3 mix 4. Live Performance. Stereo	Royal Albert Hall CD Blimp 008 / 009 & Listen To This Eric CD JH 003 / 4	Royal Albert Hall, London, England	JHE	
Bleeding Heart	21 May 69	CR 1 mix 1.	Jimi Hendrix: Blues (CR) CD MCA MCAD-11060	Record Plant, New York, NY	BOG	
Bleeding Heart	31 Dec 69	BR 1. Live performance	Band Of Gypsys Happy New Year, Jimi LP Cops & Robbers JTYM 01	Fillmore East, New York, NY 2nd Show	BOG	
Bleeding Heart	31 Dec 69	BR 1. Live performance	Band Of Gold CD-R Major Tom MT 087	Fillmore East, New York, NY 1st Show	BOG	
Bleeding Heart	31 Dec 69	BR 1. Live performance	Power Of Soul CD SQ-10	Fillmore East, New York, NY 1st Show	BOG	
Bleeding Heart	24 Mar 70	CR 2 mix 1.	War Heroes (CR) CD Polydor 847-2622	Record Plant, New York, NY	COL	Juma Sultan / Percussion
Bleeding Heart	24 Mar 70	CR 2 mix 1.	South Saturn Delta (CR) CD MCACD 11684	Record Plant, New York, NY	COL	Juma Sultan / Percussion

SONG TITLE	DATE	COMMENTS	RELEASE	LOCATION / VENUE	BAND	PERSONNEL
Bleeding Heart (Peoples People's)	24 Mar 70	CR 1 mix 2. Unused mix.	Studio Haze CD INA 6	Record Plant, New York, NY	COL	Juma Sultan / Percussion
Bleeding Heart	24 Mar 70	CR 1 mix 2. Unused mix.	Freak Out Blues CD GH 001	Record Plant, New York, NY	COL	Juma Sultan / Percussion
Bleeding Heart	24 Mar 70	CR 1 mix 2. Unused mix.	Multicolored Blues CD Luna LU 9317	Record Plant, New York, NY	COL	Juma Sultan / Percussion
Bleeding Heart	24 Mar 70	CR 1 mix 2. Unused mix.	First Rays - The Sessions CD Whoopy Cat WKP 0002	Record Plant, New York, NY	COL	Juma Sultan / Percussion
Bleeding Heart	24 Mar 70	CR 1 mix 2. Unused mix.	Notes In Colours CD JHR 001 / 002	Record Plant, New York, NY	COL	Juma Sultan / Percussion
Bleeding Heart	24 Mar 70	CR 1 mix 2. Unused mix.	Kiss The Skies CD Mum MUCD 024	Record Plant, New York, NY	COL	Juma Sultan / Percussion
Bleeding Heart	24 Mar 70	CR 1 mix 2. Unused mix.	Jimi: A Musical Legacy CD KTS BX 010	Record Plant, New York, NY	COL	Juma Sultan / Percussion
Bleeding Heart	24 Mar 70	CR 1 mix 2. Unused mix.	Eyes And Imagination CD Third Stone TSD 18970	Record Plant, New York, NY	COL	Juma Sultan / Percussion
Bleeding Heart (Double Guitars)	24 Mar 70	CR 1 mix 3. Unused mix.	Unsurpassed Studio Takes CD Yellow Dog YD 050	Record Plant, New York, NY	COL	Juma Sultan / Percussion
Bleeding Heart (Dueling Guitars)	24 Mar 70	CR 1 mix 3. Unused mix.	Jimi: A Musical Legacy CD KTS BX 010	Record Plant, New York, NY	COL	Juma Sultan / Percussion
Bleeding Heart (Double Guitars)	24 Mar 70	CR 1 mix 3. Unused mix.	Magic Hand CD Mum MUCD 012	Record Plant, New York, NY	COL	Juma Sultan / Percussion
Bleeding Heart	24 Mar 70	CR 1 mix 3. Unused mix.	Eyes And Imagination CD Third Stone TSD 18970	Record Plant, New York, NY	COL	Juma Sultan / Percussion
Bleeding Heart	24 Mar 70	CR 1 mix 3. Unused mix.	Mixdown Master Tapes Volume 2 CD Dandelion DL 006	Record Plant, New York, NY	COL	Juma Sultan / Percussion
Bleeding Heart	24 Mar 70	CR 1 mix 4. Unused mix.	Black Gold CD Midnight Beat MBCD 058-062	Record Plant, New York, NY	COL	Juma Sultan / Percussion
Bleeding Heart Guitar Rehearsal	?? / ?? 70?	BR 1. About 30 seconds of jamming.	Mixdown Master Tapes Volume 2 CD Dandelion DL 006	Electric Lady?, New York, NY	Solo	
Blown Amp Blues (Jam)	12 Oct 68	BR 1. Live performance. A title given in reference to a Redding / Mitchell jam after Jimi's amp blows and they cover with some improvising.	Winterland Vol 3 CD Whoopy Cat WK P0029/ 30	Winterland Theatre, San Francisco, CA 1st Show	JHE	

Song	Date	Notes	Release	Venue	Group	
Blown Amp Blues	12 Oct 68	BR 1. Live performance. A title given in reference to a Redding / Mitchell jam after Jimi's amp blows and they cover with some improvising.	Star Spangled Blues CD Neutral Zone NZCD 89011	Winterland Theatre, San Francisco, CA 1st Show	JHE	
Blue Suede Shoes	23 Jan 70	CR 1 mix 1. This is mostly studio chat prior to the performance which fades shortly into it.	Loose Ends (CR) LP Polydor 837574-2	Record Plant, New York, NY	BOG	
Blue Suede Shoes	23 Jan 70	CR 1 mix 1. This is mostly studio chat prior to the performance which fades shortly into it.	Voice Of Experience CD Rhinozerous RHP 789	Record Plant, New York, NY	BOG	
Blue Suede Shoes	23 Jan 70	CR 1 mix 1. This is mostly studio chat prior to the performance which fades shortly into it.	Rarities On Compact Disc CD On The Radio	Record Plant, New York, NY	BOG	
Blue Suede Shoes	23 Jan 70	CR 1 mix 1. This is mostly studio chat prior to the performance which fades shortly into it.	Band Of Gypsys- The Ultimate CD JMH 010 / 3	Record Plant, New York, NY	BOG	
Blue Suede Shoes	23 Jan 70	CR 1 mix 2. This is the unreleased and longest available version. This is missing the studio chat.	Sir James Marshall LP Jester Productions JP 106	Record Plant, New York, NY	BOG	
Blue Suede Shoes (Police Blues)	23 Jan 70	CR 1 mix 2. This is the unreleased and longest available version. This is missing the studio chat.	Freak Out Blues CD GH 001	Record Plant, New York, NY	BOG	
Blue Suede Shoes	23 Jan 70	CR 1 mix 2. This is the unreleased and longest available version. This is missing the studio chat.	Black Gold CD Midnight Beat MBCD 058-062	Record Plant, New York, NY	BOG	
Blue Suede Shoes	23 Jan 70	CR 1 mix 2. This is the unreleased and longest available version. This is missing the studio chat. Incomplete.	Things I Used To Do CD The Early Years 02-CD-3334	Record Plant, New York, NY	BOG	
Blue Suede Shoes	23 Jan 70	CR 2. A real hatchet job of the long version with new musicians to make a 3 1 / 2 minute composite.	Midnight Lightning (CR) LP Reprise MS 2229	Record Plant, New York, NY	BOG	Midnight Lightning Line Up 1975
Blue Suede Shoes	30 May 70	CR 3. Live Performance from the soundcheck.	Riots In Berkeley CD Beech Marten BM 038	Berkeley Community Theater, Berkeley, CA Sound Check	COL	
Blue Suede Shoes	30 May 70	CR 3. Live Performance from the soundcheck.	Atlanta Special CD Genuine Pig TGP 121	Berkeley Community Theater, Berkeley, CA Sound Check	COL	
Blue Suede Shoes	30 May 70	CR 3. Live Performance from the soundcheck.	Hendrix In The West (CR) LP Polydor 2302018 A	Berkeley Community Theater, Berkeley, CA Sound Check	COL	
Blue Suede Shoes	30 May 70	CR 3. Live Performance from the soundcheck.	Star Spangled Blues CD Neutral Zone NZCD 89011	Berkeley Community Theater, Berkeley, CA Sound Check	COL	
Blue Suede Shoes	30 May 70	CR 3. Live Performance from the soundcheck. This is followed by another short take.	Berkeley Soundchecks, The CD Whoopy Cat WKP 0008	Berkeley Community Theater, Berkeley, CA Sound Check	COL	

SONG TITLE	DATE	COMMENTS	RELEASE	LOCATION / VENUE	BAND	PERSONNEL
Blue Suede Shoes	30 May 70	CR 3. Live Performance from the soundcheck. This is followed by another short take.	Jimi Plays Berkeley CD JMH 005 / 2	Berkeley Community Theater, Berkeley, CA Sound Check	COL	
Blue Window Jam	15 Mar 69	BR 1-2. Both the Buddy Miles Express only take and the next take when Jimi joins in.	Lost Winterland Tapes CD Starquake SQ 051-2	Mercury Sound Studios, New York, NY	Jimi	Buddy Miles Express
Blue Window Jam (Bluesiana Jam)+A301	15 Mar 69	BR 1-2. Both the Buddy Miles Express only take and the next take when Jimi joins in.	51st Anniversary CD Future Disc JMH 001 / 8	Mercury Sound Studios, New York, NY	Jimi	Buddy Miles Express
Blue Window Jam	15 Mar 69	BR 2. Just take 2 with Jimi joining the Buddy Miles Express.	Freak Out Blues CD GH 001	Mercury Sound Studios, New York, NY	Jimi	Buddy Miles Express
Blue Window Jam	15 Mar 69	BR 2. Just take 2 with Jimi joining the Buddy Miles Express.	Diamonds In The Dust CD Midnight Beat MBCD 022 / 23	Mercury Sound Studios, New York, NY	Jimi	Buddy Miles Express
Blues Jam No 1 Part 1	?? Apr 68	BR 1. Live performance.	King's Jam, The CD Klondyke KR 26	Generation Club, New York, NY	GEN	
Blues Jam No. 1 Part 1 B.B. King Blues Jam)	?? Apr 68	BR 1. Live performance.	Blues At Midnight CD Midnight Beat MBCD 037	Generation Club, New York, NY	GEN	
Blues Jam No. 1 Part 1 (King Session)	?? Apr 68	BR 1. Live performance.	King And Wonder Sessions CD Oh Boy 1-9170	Generation Club, New York, NY	GEN	
Blues Jam No. 1 Part 2	?? Apr 68	BR 1. Live performance.	King's Jam, The CD Klondyke KR 26	Generation Club, New York, NY	GEN	
Blues Jam No 2 Part 1	?? Apr 68	BR 1. Live performance.	King's Jam, The CD Klondyke KR 26	Generation Club, New York, NY	GEN	
Blues Jam No 2 Part 2 (Instrumental 1)	?? Apr 68	BR 1. Live performance.	Historic Performances CD Aquarius AQ 67-JH-080	Generation Club, New York, NY	GEN	
Blues Jam No. 2 Part 2	?? Apr 68	BR 1. Live performance.	King's Jam, The CD Klondyke KR 26	Generation Club, New York, NY	GEN	
Blues Jam No. 2 Part 2 (B.B. King Slow Instrumental Jam)	?? Apr 68	BR 1. Live performance.	51st Anniversary CD Future Disc JMH 001 / 8	Generation Club, New York, NY	GEN	
Blues Jam No. 3 Instrumental 2)	?? Apr 68	BR 1. Live performance. This is the complete version.	Historic Performances CD Aquarius AQ 67-JH-080	Generation Club, New York, NY	GEN	
Blues Jam No. 3		BR 1. Live performance. Incomplete.	King's Jam, The CD	Generation Club,	GEN	

Title	Date	Notes	Release	Location	Group
Bold As Love	29 Oct 67	CR 1 mix 1.	Notes In Colours CD JHR 001 / 002	Olympic Sound Studios, London, England	JHE
Bold As Love	29 Oct 67	CR 1 mix 1.	Axis: Bold As Love (CR) CD MCACD 11601	Olympic Sound Studios, London, England	JHE
Bold As Love	29 Oct 67	CR 1 mix 2 (mono)	Axis: Bold As Love (CR) LP Track6120 003	Olympic Sound Studios, London, England	JHE
Bold As Love	29 Oct 67	CR 1 mix 3. Unused mix without overdubs and a completely different vocal.	Master's Masters, The CD JH-01	Olympic Sound Studios, London, England	JHE
Bold As Love	29 Oct 67	CR 1 mix 3. Unused mix without overdubs and a completely different vocal.	Sotheby Auction Tapes, The CD Midnight Beat MBCD 010	Olympic Sound Studios, London, England	JHE
Bold As Love	29 Oct 67	CR 1 mix 3. Unused mix without overdubs and a completely different vocal.	51st Anniversary CD Future Disc JMH 001 / 8	Olympic Sound Studios, London, England	JHE
Bold As Love	29 Oct 67	CR 1 mix 3. Unused mix without overdubs and a completely different vocal.	Symphony Of Experience CD Third Stone Discs TDS 24966	Olympic Sound Studios, London, England	JHE
Bold As Love	29 Oct 67	CR 1 mix 3. Unused mix without overdubs and a completely different vocal.	Get The Experience CD Invasion Unlimited IU 9424-1	Olympic Sound Studios, London, England	JHE
Bold As Love	29 Oct 67	CR 1 mix 3. Unused mix without overdubs and a completely different vocal.	Notes In Colours CD JHR 001 / 002	Olympic Sound Studios, London, England	JHE
Bold As Love	29 Oct 67	CR 1 mix 3. Unused mix without overdubs and a completely different vocal.	Completer, The CD Whoopy Cat WKP 0018 / 19	Olympic Sound Studios, London, England	JHE
Bold As Love	29 Oct 67	CR 1 mix 3. Unused mix without overdubs and a completely different vocal.	Jimi: A Musical Legacy CD KTS BX 010	Olympic Sound Studios, London, England	JHE
Bold As Love	29 Oct 67	CR 1 mix 3. Unused mix without overdubs and a completely different vocal.	Sotheby's Reels, The CD Gold Standard TOM-800	Olympic Sound Studios, London, England	JHE
Bold As Love	29 Oct 67	CR 1 mix 3. Unused mix without overdubs and a completely different vocal.	Living Reels Vol 1 CD JMH 011	Olympic Sound Studios, London, England	JHE

SONG TITLE	DATE	COMMENTS	RELEASE	LOCATION / VENUE	BAND	PERSONNEL
Bold As Love	29 Oct 67	CR I mix 3. Unused mix. Repeated twice on this CD.	Sotheby's Private Reels CD JHR 003 / 004	Olympic Sound Studios, London, England	JHE	
Bolero (Live And Let Live)	01 Jul 70	BR 1. Instrumental run through.	First Rays Of The New Rising Sun CD Triangle PYCD 084-2	Electric Lady Studio, New York, NY	COL	Juma Sultan / Percussion
Bolero	01 Jul 70	BR 1. Instrumental run through.	500,000 Halos CD EXP 500,000	Electric Lady Studio, New York, NY	COL	Juma Sultan / Percussion
Bolero	01 Jul 70	BR 1. Instrumental run through.	I Don't Live Today CD ACL 007	Electric Lady Studio, New York, NY	COL	Juma Sultan / Percussion
Bolero (Live And Let Live)	01 Jul 70	BR 1. Instrumental run through.	Kiss The Skies CD Mum MUCD 024	Electric Lady Studio, New York, NY	COL	Juma Sultan / Percussion
Bolero (Pride Of Man)	14 Jul 70	BR 2. Studio rehearsal. This breaks down and continues with the next take.	Black Gold CD Midnight Beat MBCD 058-062	Electric Lady Studio, New York, NY	COL	Juma Sultan / Percussion
Bolero (Pride Of Man)	14 Jul 70	BR 3. This continues from the previous take and is followed by 'Come down Hard On Me Baby' and a version of 'Midnight Lightning'.	Black Gold CD Midnight Beat MBCD 058-062	Electric Lady Studio, New York, NY	COL	Juma Sultan / Percussion
Bolero (Midnight / Valleys Of Neptune 1)	14 Jul 70	BR 4. Following a version of "Midnight Lightning', there are several false starts and a complete take.	Black Gold CD Midnight Beat MBCD 058-062	Electric Lady Studio, New York, NY	COL	Juma Sultan / Percussion
Born Under A Bad Sign	15 Dec 69	CR 1.	Jimi Hendrix: Blues (CR) CD MCA MCAD-11060	Record Plant, New York, NY	BOG	
Bright Lights, Big City	?? / ?? 68	BR 1. An impromptu jam of this blues classic from one of Jimi's many apartment jams. sessions.	Freak Out Jam CD GH 002	New York Apartment	Jimi	Paul Caruso / Harmonica
Burning Desire	?? Dec 69	CR 1	Band Of Gypsys Vol 3	Record Plant Or Baggies, NY, NY	BOG	
Burning Desire	?? Dec 69	CR 1	Loose Ends (CR) LP Polydor 837574-2	Record Plant Or Baggies, NY, NY	BOG	
Burning Desire	?? Dec 69	CR 1	Jewel Box CD Home HR-5824-3	Record Plant Or Baggies, NY, NY	BOG	
Burning Desire	?? Dec 69	CR 1	Band Of Gypsys- The Ultimate CD JMH 010 / 3	Record Plant Or Baggies, NY, NY	BOG	
Burning Desire	31 Dec 69	BR 1. Live performance	Band Of Gypsys Happy New Year, Jimi LP Cops & Robbers JTYM 01	Fillmore East, New York, NY 2nd Show	BOG	
Burning Desire	31 Dec 69	BR 1. Live performance	Band Of Gold CD-R Major Tom MT 087	Fillmore East, New York, NY 1st Show	BOG	

Song	Date	Take	Notes	Release	Location	Band	Personnel
Burning Desire	31 Dec 69	BR 2. Live performance		Auld Lang Syne CD JH 100 03	Fillmore East, New York, NY 2nd Show	BOG	
Burning Desire	31 Dec 69	BR 2. Live performance		Band Of Gypsys: Happy New Year CD Silver Shadow CD 9103	Fillmore East, New York, NY 2nd Show	BOG	
Burning Desire	31 Dec 69	BR 2. Live performance		Fillmore Concerts, The CD Whoopy Cat WKP 0006 / 7	Fillmore East, New York, NY 2nd Show	COL	
Burning Desire	31 Dec 69	BR 2. Live performance		Band Of Gold CD-R Major Tom MT 087	Fillmore East, New York, NY 2nd Show	BOG	
Burning Desire	31 Dec 69	BR 2. Live performance		Power Of Soul CD SQ-10	Fillmore East, New York, NY 1st Show	BOG	
Burning Desire	31 Dec 69	BR 2. Live performance		Band Of Gypsys- The Ultimate CD JMH 010 / 3	Fillmore East, New York, NY 2nd Show	BOG	
Burning Of The Midnight Lamp	06 Jul 67	CR 1 mix 1 (stereo)		Red House CD The Entertainers CD294	Mayfair Studios, New York, NY	JHE	Sweet Inspirations / Backing Vocals, Jimi / Harpsichord
Burning Of The Midnight Lamp	06 Jul 67	CR 1 mix 1 (stereo)		Electric Ladyland (CR) CD MCACD-11600	Mayfair Studios, New York, NY	JHE	Sweet Inspirations / Backing Vocals, Jimi / Harpsichord
Burning Of The Midnight Lamp	06 Jul 67	CR 1 mix 1 (stereo)		The Singles Album (CR) CD Polydor 827 369-2	Mayfair Studios, New York, NY	JHE	Sweet Inspirations / Backing Vocals, Jimi / Harpsichord
Burning Of The Midnight Lamp	06 Jul 67	CR 1 mix 1 (stereo)		Legacy (CR) LP Polydor	Mayfair Studios, New York, NY	JHE	Sweet Inspirations / Backing Vocals, Jimi / Harpsichord
Burning Of The Midnight Lamp	06 Jul 67	CR 1 mix 2 (mono)		Single Burning Of The Midnight Lamp / STP With LSD Track 604 007	Mayfair Studios, New York, NY	JHE	Sweet Inspirations / Backing Vocals
Burning Of The Midnight Lamp	06 Jul 67	CR 1 mix 3. From a longer mixing session tape.		Sotheby Auction Tapes, The CD The Midnight Beat MBCD 010	Mayfair Studios, New York, NY	JHE	Sweet Inspirations / Backing Vocals, Jimi / Harpsichord
Burning Of The Midnight Lamp	06 Jul 67	CR 1 mix 4. From a longer mixing session tape. This is an almost complete version and the start of another which fades out.		1968 AD CD Whoopy Cat WKP 0001	Mayfair Studios, New York, NY	JHE	Sweet Inspirations / Backing Vocals, Jimi / Harpsichord
Burning Of The Midnight Lamp	06 Jul 67	CR 1 mix 5. From a longer mixing session tape.		Screaming Eagle CD Pink Poodle POO 001	Mayfair Studios, New York, NY	JHE	Sweet Inspirations / Backing Vocals, Jimi / Harpsichord
Burning Of The Midnight Lamp	05 Sep 67	CR 2. BBC performance.		Live In Stockholm 1967 CD Document DR 003	Studio 4, Radiohuset, Stockholm, Sweden	JHE	
Burning Of The Midnight Lamp	05 Sep 67	CR 2. BBC performance.		Wild Man Of Pop Plays Vol 1, The CD Pyramid RFTCD 003	Studio 4, Radiohuset, Stockholm, Sweden	JHE	

SONG TITLE	DATE	COMMENTS	RELEASE	LOCATION / VENUE	BAND	PERSONNEL
Burning Of The Midnight Lamp	05 Sep 67	CR 2. BBC performance.	Stages Stockholm 67 (CR) CD Reprise 9 27632-2	Studio 4, Radiohuset, Stockholm, Sweden	JHE	
Burning Of The Midnight Lamp	05 Sep 67	CR 2. BBC performance.	Official Bootleg Album, The CD Yellow Dog YD 051	Studio 4, Radiohuset, Stockholm, Sweden	JHE	
Burning Of The Midnight Lamp	05 Sep 67	CR 2. BBC performance.	Live At The Hollywood Bowl LP RSR / International RSR 251	Studio 4, Radiohuset, Stockholm, Sweden	JHE	
Burning Of The Midnight Lamp	05 Sep 67	CR 2. BBC performance.	Recorded Live In Europe CD Bulldog BGCD 023	Studio 4, Radiohuset, Stockholm, Sweden	JHE	
Burning Of The Midnight Lamp	05 Sep 67	CR 2. BBC performance.	Two Sides Of The Same Genius LP Amazing Kornyphone TAKRL H677	Studio 4, Radiohuset, Stockholm, Sweden	JHE	
Burning Of The Midnight Lamp	05 Sep 67	CR 2. BBC performance.	Fire CD The Entertainers CD297	Studio 4, Radiohuset, Stockholm, Sweden	JHE	
Burning Of The Midnight Lamp	05 Sep 67	CR 2. BBC performance.	In Europe 67 / 68 / 69 CD Vulture CD 009 / 2	Studio 4, Radiohuset, Stockholm, Sweden	JHE	
Burning Of The Midnight Lamp	05 Sep 67	CR 2. BBC performance.	Very Best, The CD Irec / Retro MILCD-03	Studio 4, Radiohuset, Stockholm, Sweden	JHE	
Burning Of The Midnight Lamp	05 Sep 67	CR 2. BBC performance.	Live CD DV More CDDV 2401	Studio 4, Radiohuset, Stockholm, Sweden	JHE	
Burning Of The Midnight Lamp	05 Sep 67	CR 2. BBC performance.	Jimi Hendrix Experience CD Rockstars In Concert 6127092	Studio 4, Radiohuset, Stockholm, Sweden	JHE	
Burning Of The Midnight Lamp	05 Sep 67	CR 2. BBC performance.	Jimi: A Musical Legacy CD KTS BX 010	Studio 4, Radiohuset, Stockholm, Sweden	JHE	
Burning Of The Midnight Lamp	05 Sep 67	CR 2. BBC performance.	Foxy Lady CD Alegra CD 9008	Studio 4, Radiohuset, Stockholm, Sweden	JHE	
Burning Of The Midnight Lamp	05 Sep 67	CR 2. BBC performance.	Jimi Hendrix CD Flute FLCD 2008	Studio 4, Radiohuset, Stockholm, Sweden	JHE	
Burning Of The Midnight Lamp	05 Sep 67	CR 2. BBC performance.	Loaded Guitar LP Starlight SL 87013	Studio 4, Radiohuset, Stockholm, Sweden	JHE	
Burning Of The Midnight Lamp	05 Sep 67	CR 2. BBC performance.	Greatest Hits Live CD Chartbusters CHER 089A	Studio 4, Radiohuset, Stockholm, Sweden	JHE	

Song	Date	Notes	Release	Location	Band
Burning Of The Midnight Lamp	05 Sep 67	CR 2 BBC performance.	Anthology CD Box 9	Studio 4, Radiohuset, Stockholm, Sweden	JHE
Burning Of The Midnight Lamp	06 Oct 67	CR 3. BBC performance	Guitar Hero CD Document DR 013	Top Gear, BBC Playhouse Theatre, London, England	JHE
Burning Of The Midnight Lamp	06 Oct 67	CR 3. BBC performance	Primal Keys LP Impossible Record Works	Top Gear, BBC Playhouse Theatre, London, England	JHE
Burning Of The Midnight Lamp	06 Oct 67	CR 3. BBC performance	Radio One (CR) CD Rykodisc RCD 20078	Top Gear, BBC Playhouse Theatre, London, England	JHE
Burning Of The Midnight Lamp	11 Sep 67	CR 4. Live performance.	51st Anniversary CD Future Disc JMH 001 / 8	Stora Scenen, Grona Lund, Stockholm, Sweden	JHE
Burning Of The Midnight Lamp	06 Oct 67	CR 3. BBC performance	Ultimate BBC Collection CD Classical CL006	Top Gear, BBC Playhouse Theatre, London, England	JHE
Burning Of The Midnight Lamp	06 Oct 67	CR 3. BBC performance	Live In London 1967 CD Koine Records K881104	Top Gear, BBC Playhouse Theatre, London, England	JHE
Burning Of The Midnight Lamp	06 Oct 67	CR 3. BBC performance	Live In Concert 1967 CD Living Legend LLR-CD 001	Top Gear, BBC Playhouse Theatre, London, England	JHE
Burning Of The Midnight Lamp	06 Oct 67	CR 3. BBC performance	Can You Please Crawl Out Your Window? LP Ruthless Rhymes Jimi1	Top Gear, BBC Playhouse Theatre, London, England	JHE
Burning Of The Midnight Lamp	06 Oct 67	CR 3. BBC performance	In Concert CD Starlife ST 3612	Top Gear, BBC Playhouse Theatre, London, England	JHE
Burning Of The Midnight Lamp	11 Sep 67	CR 4. Live performance.	Rarities CD The Genuine Pig TGP-CD-091	Stora Scenen, Grona Lund, Stockholm, Sweden	JHE
Burning Of The Midnight Lamp	06 Oct 67	CR 3. BBC performance	King And Wonder Sessions CD Oh Boy 1-9170	Top Gear, BBC Playhouse Theatre, London, England	JHE
Burning Of The Midnight Lamp	06 Oct 67	CR 3. BBC performance	Complete BBC Session And..., The CD Last Bootleg Records LBR 036 / 2	Top Gear, BBC Playhouse Theatre, London, England	JHE
Burning Of The Midnight Lamp	11 Sep 67	CR 4. Live performance.	Calling Long Distance (CR) CD Univibes & Booted On Dynamite DS930055	Stora Scenen, Grona Lund, Stockholm, Sweden	JHE

SONG TITLE	DATE	COMMENTS	RELEASE	LOCATION / VENUE	BAND	PERSONNEL
Burning Of The Midnight Lamp	06 Oct 67	CR 3. BBC performance	Black Strings CD CDM G-53 258	Top Gear, BBC Playhouse Theatre, London, England	JHE	
Burning Of The Midnight Lamp	11 Sep 67	CR 4. Live performance.	Lost In Sweden CD Whoopy Cat WKP 0046 / 0047	Stora Scenen, Grona Lund, Stockholm, Sweden	JHE	
Burning Of The Midnight Lamp	06 Oct 67	CR 3. BBC performance	BBC Sessions (CR) CD MCACD 2-11742	Top Gear, BBC Playhouse Theatre, London, England	JHE	
Calling All Devil's Children	21 Oct 68	BR 1 mix 1. The basic version without the "drug bust" overdub at the end but fades off the first 2 minutes.	This One's For You LP Veteran Music MF-243	T.T.G. Studios, Hollywood, CA	JHE	
Calling All Devil's Children (All Devil's Children)	21 Oct 68	BR 1 mix 1. The basic version without the "drug bust" overdub at the end but fades in cutting of the first 2 minutes.	Electric Anniversary Jimi CD Midnight Beat MBCD 024	T.T.G. Studios, Hollywood, CA	JHE	
Calling All Devil's Children (Heavy Weather)	21 Oct 68	BR 1 mix 1. The basic version without the "drug bust" overdub at the end but fades in cutting off the first 2 minutes.	Redskin' Jammin' CD JH 01 / 02	T.T.G. Studios, Hollywood, CA	JHE	
Calling All Devil's Children (Devil's Jam)	21 Oct 68	BR 1 mix 2. The complete take with the "drug bust" overdub added at the end of the song.	Master's Masters, The CD JH-01	T.T.G. Studios, Hollywood, CA	JHE	
Calling All Devil's Children	21 Oct 68	BR 1 mix 2. The complete take with the "drug bust" overdub added at the end of the song.	Best Of The Bootlegs CD MS 666	T.T.G. Studios, Hollywood, CA	JHE	Eric Barret & Others / Studio Noise
Calling All Devil's Children	21 Oct 68	BR 1 mix 2. The complete take with the "drug bust" overdub added at the end of the song.	Cherokee Mist CD Triangle PYCD 070	T.T.G. Studios, Hollywood, CA	JHE	Eric Barret & Others / Studio Noise
Calling All Devil's Children (Devil's Jam)	21 Oct 68	BR 1 mix 2. The complete take with the "drug bust" overdub added at the end of the song.	Midnight Shines Down CD Blue Kangaroo BK 04	T.T.G. Studios, Hollywood, CA	JHE	
Calling All Devil's Children (Jazz Jimi Jam)	21 Oct 68	BR 1 mix 2. The complete take with the "drug bust" overdub added at the end of the song.	Every Way To Paradise CD Tintangel TIBX 021 / 22 / 23 / 24	T.T.G. Studios, Hollywood, CA	JHE	Eric Barret & Others / Studio Noise
Calling All Devil's Children	21 Oct 68	BR 1 mix 2. The complete take with the "drug bust" overdub added at the end of the song.	Every Way To Paradise CD Tintangel TIBX 021 / 22 / 23 / 24	T.T.G. Studios, Hollywood, CA	JHE	
Calling All Devil's Children	21 Oct 68	BR 1 mix 2. The complete take with the "drug bust" overdub added at the end of the song.	Voodoo In Ladyland CD MUM MUCD 006	T.T.G. Studios, Hollywood, CA	JHE	Eric Barret & Others / Studio Noise
Calling All Devil's Children	21 Oct 68	BR 1 mix 3. This is another version along the lines of the 'Drug Bust' but with what sounds like Jimi making a speech with lots of crowd participation.	Mixdown Master Tapes Volume 1 CD Dandelion DL 005	T.T.G. Studios, Hollywood, CA	JHE	Others / Studio Noise
Calling All Devil's Children	?? / ?? 68-69	BR 2. Studio jam with Jimi on bass incorporating some of the riffs from "Calling All Devil's Children" throughout the jam.	Black Gold CD Midnight Beat MBCD 058-062	Record Plant?	Jimi	Unknown / Other Musicians

Song	Date	Notes	Release	Venue	Group
Can You Please Crawl Out Your Window?	17 Oct 67	CR 1. BBC performance.	Electric Gypsy CD Scorpio? 40176 / 15	Rhythm And Blues, BBC Playhouse Theatre, London, England	JHE
Can You Please Crawl Out Your Window?	17 Oct 67	CR 1. BBC performance.	Guitar Hero CD Document DR 013	Rhythm And Blues, BBC Playhouse Theatre, London, England	JHE
Can You Please Crawl Out Your Window?	17 Oct 67	CR 1. BBC performance.	Primal Keys LP Impossible Record Works	Rhythm And Blues, BBC Playhouse Theatre, London, England	JHE
Can You Please Crawl Out Your Window?	17 Oct 67	CR 1. BBC performance.	Sotheby Auction Tapes, The CD Midnight Beat MBCD 010	Rhythm And Blues, BBC Playhouse Theatre, London, England	JHE
Can You Please Crawl Out Your Window?	17 Oct 67	CR 1. BBC performance.	Symphony Of Experience CD Third Stone Discs TDS 24966	Rhythm And Blues, BBC Playhouse Theatre, London, England	JHE
Can You Please Crawl Out Your Window?	17 Oct 67	CR 1. BBC performance.	Ultimate BBC Collection CD Classical CL006	Rhythm And Blues, BBC Playhouse Theatre, London, England	JHE
Can You Please Crawl Out Your Window?	17 Oct 67	CR 1. BBC performance.	Live In London 1967 CD Koine Records K881104	Rhythm And Blues, BBC Playhouse Theatre, London, England	JHE
Can You Please Crawl Out Your Window?	17 Oct 67	CR 1. BBC performance.	Live In Concert 1967 CD Living Legend LLR-CD 001	Rhythm And Blues, BBC Playhouse Theatre, London, England	JHE
Can You Please Crawl Out Your Window?	17 Oct 67	CR 1. BBC performance.	Can You Please Crawl Out Your Window? LP Ruthless Rhymes Jimi1	Rhythm And Blues, BBC Playhouse Theatre, London, England	JHE
Can You Please Crawl Out Your Window?	17 Oct 67	CR 1. BBC performance.	In Europe 67 / 68 / 69 CD Vulture CD 009 / 2	Rhythm And Blues, BBC Playhouse Theatre, London, England	JHE
Can You Please Crawl Out Your Window?	17 Oct 67	CR 1. BBC performance.	Very Best, The CD Irec / Retro MILCD-03	Rhythm And Blues, BBC Playhouse Theatre, London, England	JHE

SONG TITLE	DATE	COMMENTS	RELEASE	LOCATION / VENUE	BAND	PERSONNEL
Can You Please Crawl Out Your Window?	17 Oct 67	CR 1. BBC performance.	In Concert CD Starlife ST 3612	Rhythm And Blues, BBC Playhouse Theatre, London, England	JHE	
Can You Please Crawl Out Your Window?	17 Oct 67	CR 1. BBC performance.	Rarities CD The Genuine Pig TGP-CD-091	Rhythm And Blues, BBC Playhouse Theatre, London, England	JHE	
Can You Please Crawl Out Your Window?	17 Oct 67	CR 1. BBC performance.	Flames CD Missing In Action ACT 1	Rhythm And Blues, BBC Playhouse Theatre, London, England	JHE	
Can You Please Crawl Out Your Window?	17 Oct 67	CR 1. BBC performance.	Complete BBC Session And..., The CD Last Bootleg Records LBR 036 / 2	Rhythm And Blues, BBC Playhouse Theatre, London, England	JHE	
Can You Please Crawl Out Your Window?	17 Oct 67	CR 1. BBC performance.	Black Strings CD CDM G-53 258	Rhythm And Blues, BBC Playhouse Theatre, London, England	JHE	
Can You Please Crawl Out Your Window?	17 Oct 67	CR 1. BBC performance.	BBC Sessions (CR) CD MCACD 2-11742	Rhythm And Blues, BBC Playhouse Theatre, London, England	JHE	
Can You Please Crawl Out Your Window?	17 Oct 67	CR 1. BBC performance.	Anthology CD Box 9	Rhythm And Blues, BBC Playhouse Theatre, London, England	JHE	
Can You Please Crawl Out Your Window?	17 Oct 67	CR 1. BBC performance. Incomplete.	Jimi Hendrix CD Flute FLCD 2008	Rhythm And Blues, BBC Playhouse Theatre, London, England	JHE	
Can You Please Crawl Out Your Window?	17 Feb 68	BR 1. Live performance	Remember The Alamo CD	Will Rogers Auditorium, Fort Worth, TX	JHE	
Can You Please Crawl Out Your Window?	25 Feb 68	BR 2. Live performance	Winterland Vol 2 CD Whoopy Cat WKP 00279 / 28	Civic Opera House, Chicago, IL	JHE	
Can You Please Crawl Out Your Window?	10 May 68	BR 3. Live performance	Live In Paris 66 / 67 CD Whoopy Cat WKP 0012	Fillmore East, New York, NY	JHE	

Song	Date	Take / Mix	Release	Location	Band
Can You Please Crawl Out Your Window?	10 May 68	BR 3. Live performance	It's Only A Paper Moon CD Luna 9420	Flamingo Club, London, England	JHE
Can You Please Crawl Out Your Window?	10 May 68	BR 3. Live performance	One Night Stand CD Hep Cat 101	Fillmore East, New York, NY	JHE
Can You Please Crawl Out Your Window?	10 May 68	BR 3. Live performance	Live At The Flamingo Club, London, 2-4-67 CD	Flamingo Club, London, England	JHE
Can You Please Crawl Out Your Window?	11 Oct 68	BR 4. Live performance	Mixdown Master Tapes Volume 1 CD Dandelion DL 005	Winterland Theatre, San Francisco, CA Sound Check	JHE
Can You See Me?	13 Dec 66	BR 1. Alternate session take #1 with an off mic guide vocal. this breaks downs and continues with the next take.	Olympic Gold Vol 1 CD Blimp 0067	CBS Studios, London, England	JHE
Can You See Me?	13 Dec 66	BR 2. Alternate session take #2 with an off mic guide vocal. this cuts before the end and continues with the next take.	Olympic Gold Vol 1 CD Blimp 0067	CBS Studios, London, England	JHE
Can You See Me?	13 Dec 66	BR 3. Alternate session take #3 with an off mic guide vocal. this breaks downs and continues with the next take.	Olympic Gold Vol 1 CD Blimp 0067	CBS Studios, London, England	JHE
Can You See Me?	13 Dec 66	CR 1 mix 1 (stereo)	Are You Experienced? (CR) CD MCACD 11602	CBS Studios, London, England	JHE
Can You See Me?	13 Dec 66	CR 1 mix 1 (stereo)	Smash Hits (CR) CD Reprise 2276-2	CBS Studios, London, England	JHE
Can You See Me?	13 Dec 66	CR 1 mix 1 (stereo)	Smash Hits (CR) CD Reprise 2276-2	CBS Studios, London, England	JHE
Can You See Me?	13 Dec 66	CR 1 mix 2 (mono)	Are You Experienced? (CR) LP Track 612 001	CBS Studios, London, England	JHE
Can You See Me?	13 Dec 66	CR 1 mix 3. Fake stereo mix made by adding reverb to the right channel.	Legacy (CR) LP Polydor	CBS Studios, London, England	JHE
Can You See Me?	13 Dec 66	CR 1 mix 4. This is the raw backing tracking track used for the CR. You can hear an off mic guide vocal.	Olympic Gold Vol 1 CD Blimp 0067	CBS Studios, London, England	JHE
Can You See Me?	13 Dec 66	CR 1 mix 5. This features a double tracked lead vocal and a guitar overdub.	Olympic Gold Vol 2 CD Blimp 007	CBS Studios, London, England	JHE
Can You See Me?	04 Feb 67	BR 4. Live performance.	Have Mercy On Me Baby CD Midnight Beat MBCD 038	Flamingo Club, London, England	JHE
Can You See Me?	24 May 67	BR 5. Live performance.	Lost In Sweden CD Whoopy Cat WKP 0046 / 0047	Stora Scenen, Grona Lund, Stockholm, Sweden	JHE

SONG TITLE	DATE	COMMENTS	RELEASE	LOCATION / VENUE	BAND	PERSONNEL
Can You See Me?	24 May 67	BR 5. Live performance.	EXP Over Sweden (CR) CD UniVibes 1002	Stora Scenen, Grona Lund, Stockholm, Sweden	JHE	
Can You See Me?	18 Jun 67	CR 2. Live performance.	Once Upon A Time CD Wall Of Sound WS CD011	Monterey International Pop Festival, Monterey, CA	JHE	
Can You See Me?	18 Jun 67	CR 2. Live performance.	Monterey Pop CD Evil 006 1 / 2	Monterey International Pop Festival, Monterey, CA	JHE	
Can You See Me?	18 Jun 67	CR 2. Live performance.	Jimi Hendrix Experience CD Rockstars In Concert 6127092	Monterey International Pop Festival, Monterey, CA	JHE	
Can You See Me?	18 Jun 67	CR 2. Live performance.	Experience II CD More MTT 1021	Monterey International Pop Festival, Monterey, CA	JHE	
Can You See Me?	18 Jun 67	CR 2. Live performance.	Jimi Plays Monterey (CR) CD Polydor 827990-2	Monterey International Pop Festival, Monterey, CA	JHE	
Can't Find My Baby	?? Mar 70 ?	This is a recording by the group "Love" for the unreleased 'Black Beauty' album. Jimi's involvement is highly unlikely.	Midnight Sun CD Third Eye NK 007	Olympic Sound Studios, London, England	Love	
Captain Coconut	COMPOSITE	CR 1. A composite of recordings from July-August 1970 from Electric Lady, January 23 1970 from The Record Plant & August-September 1969 from The Hit Factory.	Crash Landing (CR) LP Reprise MS 2204	Electric Lady, Hit Factory And The Record Plant, New York NY	Jimi	Crash Landing Line Up 1974
Castles Made Of Sand	29 Oct 67	CR 1 mix 1	Axis: Bold As Love (CR) CD MCACD 11601	Olympic Sound Studios, London, England	JHE	
Castles Made Of Sand	29 Oct 67	CR 1 mix 2. This mix has eliminated the cross channel vocal pans as well as some guitar parts.	Axis: Bold As Love LP Backtrack 2407 011	Olympic Sound Studios, London, England	JHE	
Castles Made Of Sand	29 Oct 67	CR 1 mix 3. Unused mix.	Sotheby Auction Tapes, The CD Midnight Beat MBCD 010	Olympic Sound Studios, London, England	JHE	
Castles Made Of Sand	29 Oct 67	CR 1 mix 3. Unused mix.	Sotheby's Private Reels CD JHR 003 / 004	Olympic Sound Studios, London, England	JHE	
Castles Made Of Sand	29 Oct 67	CR 1 mix 3. Unused mix.	Sotheby's Private Reels CD JHR 003 / 004	Olympic Sound Studios, London, England	JHE	

Song	Date	Notes	Release	Studio		Personnel
Castles Made Of Sand	29 Oct 67	CR 1 mix 3. Unused mix.	Notes In Colours CD JHR 001 / 002	Olympic Sound Studios, London, England	JHE	
Castles Made Of Sand	29 Oct 67	CR 1 mix 3. Unused mix.	Sotheby's Reels, The CD Gold Standard TOM-800	Olympic Sound Studios, London, England	JHE	
Castles Made Of Sand	29 Oct 67	CR 1 mix 3. Unused mix.	Living Reels Vol 1 CD JMH 011	Olympic Sound Studios, London, England	JHE	
Castles Made Of Sand	29 Oct 67	CR 1 mix 4. The CR played reversed so the backward overdubs are now forwards.	Symphony Of Experience CD Third Stone Discs TDS 24966	Olympic Sound Studios, London, England	JHE	
Castles Made Of Sand	29 Oct 67	CR 1 mix 4. The CR played reversed so the backward overdubs are now forwards.	Jimi: A Musical Legacy CD KTS BX 010	Olympic Sound Studios, London, England	JHE	
Cat Talking To Me	04 May 67	BR 1. From the Chandler Tapes reel with the 1988 overdubs.	Studio Haze CD INA 6	Olympic Sound Studios, London, England	JHE	Mitch Mitchell / Lead Vocal, Mitch Mitchell & Noel Redding / Overdubs In 1988
Cat Talking To Me	04 May 67	BR 1. From the Chandler Tapes reel with the 1988 overdubs.	DeLane Lea And Olympic Outs CD Gold Standard CD-R	Olympic Sound Studios, London, England	JHE	Mitch Mitchell / Lead Vocal, Mitch Mitchell & Noel Redding / Overdubs In 1988
Cat Talking To Me	04 May 67	BR 1. From the Chandler Tapes reel with the 1988 overdubs.	Electric Ladyland Outtakes CD Invasion Unlimited IU 9417-1	Olympic Sound Studios, London, England	JHE	Mitch Mitchell / Lead Vocal, Mitch Mitchell & Noel Redding / Overdubs In 1988
Cat Talking To Me	04 May 67	BR 1. From the Chandler Tapes reel with the 1988 overdubs.	I Don't Live Today CD ACL 007	Olympic Sound Studios, London, England	JHE	Mitch Mitchell / Lead Vocal, Mitch Mitchell & Noel Redding / Overdubs In 1988
Cat Talking To Me	04 May 67	BR 1. From the Chandler Tapes reel with the 1988 overdubs.	Voodoo In Ladyland CD MUM MUCD 006	Olympic Sound Studios, London, England	JHE	Mitch Mitchell / Lead Vocal, Mitch Mitchell & Noel Redding / Overdubs In 1988
Cat Talking To Me (Lonely Avenue Jam)	?? Jan 68	BR 2. A later version than the Chandler Tapes version. A portion of this was broadcast on the 'Live And Unreleased' radio show. This is the complete version.	Message From Nine To The Universe CD Oil Well 122	Olympic Sound Studios, London, England	JHE	Mitch Mitchell / Drums
Cat Talking To Me	?? Jan 68	BR 2. A later version than the Chandler Tapes version. A portion of this was broadcast on the 'Live And Unreleased' radio show. This is the complete version.	Mixdown Master Tapes Volume 2 CD Dandelion DL 005	Olympic Sound Studios, London, England	JHE	Mitch Mitchell / Lead Vocal
Cat Talking To Me	?? Jan 68	BR 2. A later version than the Chandler Tapes version. A portion of this was broadcast on the 'Live And Unreleased' radio show. This is the complete version.	I Don't Live Today CD ACL 007	Olympic Sound Studios, London, England	JHE	Mitch Mitchell / Lead Vocal
Catfish Blues	04 Feb 67	BR 1. Live performance.	Have Mercy On Me Baby CD Midnight Beat MBCD 038	Flamingo Club, London, England	JHE	

SONG TITLE	DATE	COMMENTS	RELEASE	LOCATION / VENUE	BAND	PERSONNEL
Catfish Blues	04 Feb 67	BR 1. Live performance.	Live At The Flamingo Club, London, 2-4-67 CD	Flamingo Club, London, England	JHE	
Catfish Blues	04 Sep 67	BR 2. Live performance.	Lost In Sweden CD Whoopy Cat WKP 0046 / 0047	Dans In, Tivoli Garden, Stockholm, Swede	JHE	
Catfish Blues	04 Sep 67	BR 2. Live performance.	EXP Over Sweden (CR) CD UniVibes 1002	Dans In, Grona Lund, Tivoli Garden, Stockholm, Sweden	JHE	
Catfish Blues	04 Sep 67	BR 3. Live performance.	Lost In Sweden CD Whoopy Cat WKP 0046 / 0047	Tivolis Konsertsal, Copenhagen, Denmark	JHE	
Catfish Blues	06 Oct 67	CR 1. Live BBC performance.	Guitar Hero CD Document DR 013	Top Gear, BBC Playhouse Theatre, London, England	JHE	
Catfish Blues	06 Oct 67	CR 1. Live BBC performance.	Primal Keys LP Impossible Record Works	Top Gear, BBC Playhouse Theatre, London, England	JHE	
Catfish Blues	06 Oct 67	CR 1. Live BBC performance.	Radio One (CR) CD Rykodisc RCD 20078	Top Gear, BBC Playhouse Theatre, London, England	JHE	
Catfish Blues	06 Oct 67	CR 1. Live BBC performance.	Official Bootleg Album, The CD Yellow Dog YD 051	Top Gear, BBC Playhouse Theatre, London, England	JHE	
Catfish Blues	06 Oct 67	CR 1. Live BBC performance.	Ultimate BBC Collection CD Classical CL006	Top Gear, BBC Playhouse Theatre, London, England	JHE	
Catfish Blues	06 Oct 67	CR 1. Live BBC performance.	Jimi Hendrix Vol 2: A Man Of Our Times LP Napoleon NLP 11018	Top Gear, BBC Playhouse Theatre, London, England	JHE	
Catfish Blues	06 Oct 67	CR 1. Live BBC performance.	Live In London 1967 CD Koine Records K881104	Top Gear, BBC Playhouse Theatre, London, England	JHE	
Catfish Blues	06 Oct 67	CR 1. Live BBC performance.	Live In Concert 1967 CD Living Legend LLR-CD 001	Top Gear, BBC Playhouse Theatre, London, England	JHE	
Catfish Blues	06 Oct 67	CR 1. Live BBC performance.	Broadcasts LP Trade Mark Of Quality TMQ 1841 & TMQ 71019	Top Gear, BBC Playhouse Theatre, London, England	JHE	
Catfish Blues	06 Oct 67	CR 1. Live BBC performance.	In Concert CD Starlife	Top Gear, BBC	JHE	

Song	Date	CR	Release	Venue	Performer
			ST 3612	Playhouse Theatre, London, England	
Catfish Blues	06 Oct 67	CR 1. Live BBC performance.	King And Wonder Sessions CD Oh Boy 1-9170	Top Gear, BBC Playhouse Theatre, London, England	JHE
Catfish Blues	06 Oct 67	CR 1. Live BBC performance.	Complete BBC Session And.... The CD Last Bootleg Records LBR 036 / 2	Top Gear, BBC Playhouse Theatre, London, England	JHE
Catfish Blues	06 Oct 67	CR 1. Live BBC performance.	Jimi: A Musical Legacy CD KTS BX 010	Top Gear, BBC Playhouse Theatre, London, England	JHE
Catfish Blues	06 Oct 67	CR 1. Live BBC performance.	Black Strings CD CDM G-53 258	Top Gear, BBC Playhouse Theatre, London, England	JHE
Catfish Blues	06 Oct 67	CR 1. Live BBC performance.	BBC Sessions (CR) CD MCACD 2-11742	Top Gear, BBC Playhouse Theatre, London, England	JHE
Catfish Blues	10 Nov 67	CR 2. Live television performance.	You Can't Use My Name LP Rock Folders 2, Q 9020	Hoepla TV Show, Vitus Studio, Bussom, Holland	JHE
Catfish Blues	10 Nov 67	CR 2. Live television performance.	Wild Man Of Pop Plays Vol 2, The CD Pyramid RFTCD 004	Hoepla TV Show, Vitus Studio, Bussom, Holland	JHE
Catfish Blues	10 Nov 67	CR 2. Live television performance.	51st Anniversary CD Future Disc JMH 001 / 8	Hoepla TV Show, Vitus Studio, Bussom, Holland	JHE
Catfish Blues	10 Nov 67	CR 2. Live television performance.	Jimi Hendrix: Blues (CR) CD MCA MCAD-11060	Hoepla TV Show, Vitus Studio, Bussom, Holland	JHE
Catfish Blues	10 Nov 67	CR 2. Live television performance.	Mannish Boy LP Contraband CBM 88	Hoepla TV Show, Vitus Studio, Bussom, Holland	JHE
Catfish Blues	10 Nov 67	CR 2. Live television performance.	Fire CD The Entertainers CD297	Hoepla TV Show, Vitus Studio, Bussom, Holland	JHE
Catfish Blues	10 Nov 67	CR 2. Live television performance.	Sweet Angel CD Compact Music WPOCM 0589	Hoepla TV Show, Vitus Studio, Bussom, Holland	JHE
Catfish Blues	10 Nov 67	CR 2. Live television performance.	Very Best, The CD Irec / Retro MILCD-03	Hoepla TV Show, Vitus Studio, Bussom, Holland	JHE

SONG TITLE	DATE	COMMENTS	RELEASE	LOCATION / VENUE	BAND	PERSONNEL
Catfish Blues	10 Nov 67	CR 2. Live television performance.	Experience II CD More MTT 1021	Hoepla TV Show, Vitus Studio, Bussom, Holland	JHE	
Catfish Blues	10 Nov 67	CR 2. Live television performance.	Rarities CD The Genuine Pig TGP-CD-091	Hoepla TV Show, Vitus Studio, Bussom, Holland	JHE	
Catfish Blues	10 Nov 67	CR 2. Live television performance.	Flames CD Missing In Action ACT 1	Hoepla TV Show, Vitus Studio, Bussom, Holland	JHE	
Catfish Blues	10 Nov 67	CR 2. Live television performance.	Calling Long Distance (CR) CD Univibes & Booted On Dynamite DS930055	Hoepla TV Show, Vitus Studio, Bussom, Holland	JHE	
Catfish Blues	10 Nov 67	CR 2. Live television performance.	Valley Of Neptune CD PC 28355	Hoepla TV Show, Vitus Studio, Bussom, Holland	JHE	
Catfish Blues	10 Nov 67	CR 2. Live television performance.	Anthology CD Box 9	Hoepla TV Show, Vitus Studio, Bussom, Holland	JHE	
Catfish Blues	07 Jan 68	CR 3. Live performance.	Cat's Squirrel CD CS 001 / 2	Tivolis Konsertsal, Copenhagen, Denmark	JHE	
Catfish Blues	07 Jan 68	CR 3. Live performance.	Fuckin' His Guitar For Denmark LP Polymore Or JH CO	Tivolis Konsertsal, Copenhagen, Denmark 1st Show	JHE	
Catfish Blues	07 Jan 68	CR 3. Live performance.	Jimi In Denmark (CR) CD UniVibes 1003 & Booted On Dynamite Studios	Tivolis Konsertsal, Copenhagen, Denmark 1st Show	JHE	
Catfish Blues	07 Jan 68	CR 3. Live performance.	Live In Copenhagen CD The Swingin' Pig TSP-220-2	Tivolis Konsertsal, Copenhagen, Denmark 1st Show	JHE	
Catfish Blues	08 Jan 68	BR 4. Live performance	Lost In Sweden CD Whoopy Cat WKP 0046 / 0047	Konserthuset, Stockholm, Sweden 1st Show	JHE	
Catfish Blues	29 Jan 68	CR 4. Live performance.	Live In Paris CD Swingin' Pig TSP-016	L' Olympia Theatre, Paris, France 1st Show	JHE	
Catfish Blues	29 Jan 68	CR 4. Live performance.	Stages Paris 68 (CR) CD Reprise 9 27632-2	L' Olympia Theatre, Paris, France 1st Show	JHE	

Song	Date	Take/Notes	Comments	Release	Venue	Band	Musicians
Catfish Blues	29 Jan 68	CR 4. Live performance.		Recorded Live In Europe CD Bulldog BGCD 023	L' Olympia Theatre, Paris, France 1st Show	JHE	
Catfish Blues	29 Jan 68	CR 4. Live performance.		In Europe 67 / 68 / 69 CD Vulture CD 009 / 2	L' Olympia Theatre, Paris, France 1st Show	JHE	
Catfish Blues	29 Jan 68	CR 4. Live performance.		In Concert CD Starlife ST 3612	L' Olympia Theatre, Paris, France 1st Show	JHE	
Catfish Blues	29 Jan 68	CR 4. Live performance.		Hey Joe CD Crocodile Beat CB 53039	L' Olympia Theatre, Paris, France 1st Show	JHE	
Catfish Blues	29 Jan 68	CR 4. Live performance.		Jimi Hendrix CD Flute FLCD 2008	L' Olympia Theatre, Paris, France 1st Show	JHE	
Catfish Blues	17 Feb 68	BR 5. Live performance		Remember The Alamo CD	Will Rogers Auditorium, Fort Worth, T X	JHE	
Catfish Blues	31 Aug 70	BR 5. Live performance		Come On Stockholm CD No Label	Stora Scenen, Grona Lund, Stockholm, Sweden	COL	
Catfish Blues	31 Aug 70	BR 5. Live performance		Free Concert CD Midnight Beat MBCD 013	Stora Scenen, Tivoli Garden, Stockholm, Sweden	COL	
Cherokee Mist	?? Mar 68	CR 2 mix 1. "Stereo" mix of this composing tape.		Jimi By Himself The Home Recordings (CR) BSP-VC1	New York Apartment	Solo	
Cherokee Mist	?? / ?? 68	CR 2 mix 2. Mono mix of this composing tape.		Acoustic Jams CD Sphinx SX CD 001	New York Apartment	Solo	
Cherokee Mist	?? / ?? 68	CR 2 mix 2. Mono mix of this composing tape.		1968 AD Part Two CD Whoopy Cat WKP 0013	New York Apartment	Solo	
Cherokee Mist	?? / ?? 68	CR 2 mix 2. Mono mix of this composing tape.		Black Gold CD Midnight Beat MBCD 058-062	New York Apartment	Solo	
Cherokee Mist	?? Mar 68	CR 2 mix 2. Mono mix of this composing tape.		First Rays Of The New Rising Sun CD Living Legend LLRCD 023	New York Apartment	Solo	
Cherokee Mist	02 May 68	CR1. One of the most widely booted Jimi songs. Based on Jimi's roots as being 1 / 16 Cherokee Indian. This appeared incomplete on 'Lifelines'.		Redskin' Jammin' CD JH 01 / 02	Record Plant, New York, NY	Jimi	Mitch Mitchell / Drums
Cherokee Mist	02 May 68	CR1. One of the most widely booted Jimi songs. Based on Jimi's roots as being 1 / 16 Cherokee Indian. This appeared incomplete on 'Lifelines'.		Best Of The Bootlegs CD MS 666	Record Plant, New York, NY	Jimi	Mitch Mitchell / Drums

SONG TITLE	DATE	COMMENTS	RELEASE	LOCATION / VENUE	BAND	PERSONNEL
Cherokee Mist	02 May 68	CR1. One of the most widely booted Jimi songs. Based on Jimi's roots as being 1 / 16 Cherokee Indian. This appeared incomplete on 'Lifelines'.	Mixdown Master Tapes Volume 2 CD Dandelion DL 006	Record Plant, New York, NY	Jimi	Mitch Mitchell / Drums
Cherokee Mist	02 May 68	CR1. One of the most widely booted Jimi songs. Based on Jimi's roots as being 1 / 16 Cherokee Indian. This appeared incomplete on 'Lifelines'.	Cherokee Mist CD Triangle PYCD 070	Record Plant, New York, NY	Jimi	Mitch Mitchell / Drums
Cherokee Mist	02 May 68	CR1. One of the most widely booted Jimi songs. Based on Jimi's roots as being 1 / 16 Cherokee Indian. This appeared incomplete on 'Lifelines'.	Flames CD Missing In Action ACT 1	Record Plant, New York, NY	Jimi	Mitch Mitchell / Drums
Cherokee Mist	02 May 68	CR1. One of the most widely booted Jimi songs. Based on Jimi's roots as being 1 / 16 Cherokee Indian. This appeared incomplete on 'Lifelines'.	Every Way To Paradise CD Tintangel TIBX 021 / 22 / 23 / 24	Record Plant, New York, NY	Jimi	Mitch Mitchell / Drums
Cherokee Mist	02 May 68	CR1. One of the most widely booted Jimi songs. Based on Jimi's roots as being 1 / 16 Cherokee Indian. This appeared incomplete on 'Lifelines'.	Jimi: A Musical Legacy CD KTS BX 010	Record Plant, New York, NY	Jimi	Mitch Mitchell / Drums
Cherokee Mist	02 May 68	CR1. One of the most widely booted Jimi songs. Based on Jimi's roots as being 1 / 16 Cherokee Indian. This appeared incomplete on 'Lifelines'.	Gypsy Charm CD Mum MUCD 018	Record Plant, New York, NY	Jimi	Mitch Mitchell / Drums
Cherokee Mist	02 May 68	CR1. One of the most widely booted Jimi songs. Based on Jimi's roots as being 1 / 16 Cherokee Indian. This appeared incomplete on 'Lifelines'.	Living Reels Vol 2 CD JMH 012 / 2	Record Plant, New York, NY	Jimi	Mitch Mitchell / Drums
Cherokee Mist	02 May 68	CR1. One of the most widely booted Jimi songs. Based on Jimi's roots as being 1 / 16 Cherokee Indian. This appeared incomplete on 'Lifelines'. Incomplete.	Talent And Feeling Vol 2 CD Extremely Rare EXR 22	Record Plant, New York, NY	Jimi	Mitch Mitchell / Drums
Cherokee Mist	?? ?? 68	CR 2 mix 2. Part of a medley beginning with "Voodoo Chile" and ending with "Gypsy Eyes". Mono mix of this composing tape.	1968 AD Part Two CD Whoopy Cat WKP 0013	New York Apartment	Solo	
Cherokee Mist	?? Mar 68	CR 2 mix 1. Part of a medley beginning with "Gypsy Eyes". "Stereo" mix of this composing tape.	Jimi By Himself The Home Recordings (CR) BSP-VC1	New York Apartment	Solo	
Cherokee Mist	02 May 68	CR1. One of the most widely booted Jimi songs. Based on Jimi's roots as being 1 / 16 Cherokee Indian. This appeared incomplete on 'Lifelines'.	First Rays Of The New Rising Sun CD Living Legend LLRCD 023	Record Plant, New York, NY	Jimi	Mitch Mitchell / Drums
Cherokee Mist	02 May 68	CR1. One of the most widely booted Jimi songs. Based on Jimi's roots as being 1 / 16 Cherokee Indian. This appeared incomplete on 'Lifelines'.	Electric Gypsy CD Scorpio? 40176 / 15	Record Plant, New York, NY	Jimi	Mitch Mitchell / Drums
Cherokee Mist	02 May 68	CR1. One of the most widely booted Jimi songs. Based on Jimi's roots as being 1 / 16 Cherokee Indian. This appeared incomplete on 'Lifelines'.	Record Plant Jam CD Pilot Records HJCD 69	Record Plant, New York, NY	Jimi	Mitch Mitchell / Drums
Cherokee Mist	02 May 68	CR1. One of the most widely booted Jimi songs. Based on	Ladyland In Flames LP	Record Plant, New York, NY	Jimi	Mitch Mitchell / Drums

Song	Date	Notes	Release	Location		Drums
Cherokee Mist		Jimi's roots as being 1 / 16 Cherokee Indian. This appeared twice on this bootleg.	Marshall Records JIMI 1,2,3,4	York, NY		
Cherokee Mist	02 May 68	CR1. One of the most widely booted Jimi songs. Based on Jimi's roots as being 1 / 16 Cherokee Indian. This appeared incomplete on 'Lifelines'. This is mastered twice on this bootleg.	Ladyland In Flames LP Marshall Records JIMI 1,2,3,4	Record Plant, New York, NY	Jimi	Mitch Mitchell / Drums
Cherokee Mist	02 May 68	CR1. One of the most widely booted Jimi songs. Based on Jimi's roots as being 1 / 16 Cherokee Indian. This appeared incomplete on 'Lifelines'.	Lifelines (CR) CD Reprise 9 26435-2	Record Plant, New York, NY	Jimi	Mitch Mitchell / Drums
Cherokee Mist	02 May 68	CR1. One of the most widely booted Jimi songs. Based on Jimi's roots as being 1 / 16 Cherokee Indian. This appeared incomplete on 'Lifelines'.	Unsurpassed Studio Takes CD Yellow Dog YD 050	Record Plant, New York, NY	Jimi	Mitch Mitchell / Drums
Cherokee Mist	02 May 68	CR1. One of the most widely booted Jimi songs. Based on Jimi's roots as being 1 / 16 Cherokee Indian. This appeared incomplete on 'Lifelines'.	Official Bootleg Album, The CD Yellow Dog YD 051	Record Plant, New York, NY	Jimi	Mitch Mitchell / Drums
Cherokee Mist	02 May 68	CR1. One of the most widely booted Jimi songs. Based on Jimi's roots as being 1 / 16 Cherokee Indian. This appeared incomplete on 'Lifelines'.	51st Anniversary CD Future Disc JMH 001 / 8	Record Plant, New York, NY	Jimi	Mitch Mitchell / Drums
Cherokee Mist	02 May 68	CR1. One of the most widely booted Jimi songs. Based on Jimi's roots as being 1 / 16 Cherokee Indian. This appeared incomplete on 'Lifelines'.	Diamonds In The Dust CD Midnight Beat MBCD 022 / 23	Record Plant, New York, NY	Jimi	Mitch Mitchell / Drums
Cherokee Mist	02 May 68	CR1. One of the most widely booted Jimi songs. Based on Jimi's roots as being 1 / 16 Cherokee Indian. This appeared incomplete on 'Lifelines'.	Electric Anniversary Jimi CD Midnight Beat MBCD 024	Record Plant, New York, NY	Jimi	Mitch Mitchell / Drums
Cherokee Mist / In From The Storm / Valleys Of Neptune	25 Jun 70	BR 1 mix 1. The complete medley.	Acoustic Jams CD Sphinx SX CD 001	Electric Lady Studio, New York, NY	COL	
Cherokee Mist / In From The Storm / Valleys Of Neptune	25 Jun 70	BR 1 mix 1. The complete medley. On the CD this is part of the track 'Pride Of Man'.	Multicolored Blues CD Luna LU 9317	Electric Lady Studio, New York, NY	COL	
Cherokee Mist / In From The Storm / Valleys Of Neptune (Cherokee Mist Blues)	25 Jun 70	BR 1 mix 1. The complete medley.	Completer, The CD Whoopy Cat WKP 0018 / 19	Electric Lady Studio, New York, NY	COL	
Cherokee Mist / In From The Storm / Valleys Of Neptune	25 Jun 70	BR 1 mix 2. "Valleys Of Neptune" is missing from this version.	Freak Out Jam CD GH 002	Electric Lady Studio, New York, NY	COL	
Cherokee Mist / In From The Storm / Valleys Of Neptune (Pride Of Man)	25 Jun 70	BR 1 mix 2. "Valleys Of Neptune" is missing from this version.	Diamonds In The Dust CD Midnight Beat MBCD 022 / 23	Electric Lady Studio, New York, NY	COL	
Cherokee Mist / In From The Storm / Valleys Of Neptune	25 Jun 70	BR 1 mix 2. "Valleys Of Neptune" is missing from this version.	Studio Experience CD Sodium Haze SH 099	Electric Lady Studio, New York, NY	COL	
Cherokee Mist / In From The Storm / Valleys Of Neptune (Valleys Of Neptune)	25 Jun 70	BR 1 mix 2. "Valleys Of Neptune" is missing from this version.	Electronic Church Music CD Pyramid PYCD 023	Electric Lady Studio, New York, NY	COL	

SONG TITLE	DATE	COMMENTS	RELEASE	LOCATION / VENUE	BAND	PERSONNEL
Cherokee Mist / In From The Storm / Valleys Of Neptune	25 Jun 70	BR 1 mix 2. "Valleys Of Neptune" is missing from this version.	Electric Ladyland Outtakes CD Invasion Unlimited IU9417-1	Electric Lady Studio, New York, NY	COL	
Collage	Various	A sound collage from a selection of recordings probably done by the bootleggers of this release...	51st Anniversary CD Future Disc JMH 001 / 8		Misc.	
Come Down Hard On Me Baby	15 Jul 70	CR1. This was edited together from two different versions by John Jansen for release.	Loose Ends (CR) LP Polydor 837574-2	Electric Lady Studio, New York, NY	COL	
Come Down Hard On Me Baby	15 Jul 70	CR1. This was edited together from two different versions by John Jansen for release but has the original COL line up.	Voice Of Experience CD Rhinozerous RHP 789	Electric Lady Studio, New York, NY	COL	
Come Down Hard On Me Baby	15 Jul 70	CR1. This was edited together from two different versions by John Jansen for release but has the original COL line up.	Rarities On Compact Disc CD On The Radio	Electric Lady Studio, New York, NY	COL	
Come Down Hard On Me Baby	15 Jul 70	CR 2 mix 1. The original musicians were replaced in 1974 by Alan Douglas.	Crash Landing (CR) LP Reprise MS 2204	Electric Lady Studio, New York, NY	Jimi	Crash Landing Line Up 1974
Come Down Hard On Me Baby	15 Jul 70	CR 2 mix 2. An unused mix with some additional rhythm guitar parts by Jeff Mironov..	Electric Hendrix Vol 2 CD Pyramid PYCD 031	Electric Lady Studio, New York, NY	Jimi	Crash Landing Line Up 1974
Come Down Hard On Me Baby	15 Jul 70	CR 2 mix 2. An unused mix with some additional rhythm guitar parts by Jeff Mironov..	I Don't Live Today CD ACL 007	Electric Lady Studio, New York, NY	Jimi	Crash Landing Line Up 1974
Come Down Hard On Me Baby	15 Jul 70	CR 2 mix 3. An unused mix with an extra guitar part added and an extenuated fade.	Electric Hendrix Vol 2 CD Pyramid PYCD 031	Electric Lady Studio, New York, NY	Jimi	Crash Landing Line Up 1974
Come Down Hard On Me Baby	15 Jul 70	CR 2 mix 3. An unused mix with an extra guitar part added and an extenuated fade.	Paper Airplanes CD Midnight Beat MBCD 25	Electric Lady Studio, New York, NY	Jimi	Crash Landing Line Up 1974
Come Down Hard On Me Baby	15 Jul 70	CR 2 mix 4. An odd mix featuring the isolated bass track with Jimi's guitar parts.	Paper Airplanes CD Midnight Beat MBCD 25	Electric Lady Studio, New York, NY	Jimi	Crash Landing Line Up 1974
Come On (Part One)	27 Aug 68	CR 3. An alternate take that originally turned up on a French CD single.	Rarities On Compact Disc CD On The Radio	Record Plant, New York, NY	JHE	
Come On (Part One)	27 Aug 68	CR 3. An alternate take that originally turned up on a French CD single.	Not Just A Voodoo Chile CD Pilot HJCD 071	Record Plant, New York, NY	JHE	
Come On (Part One)	27 Aug 68	BR 1. Take 8 of 14 takes. This was a breakdown. This released continues with take 9.	1968 AD CD Whoopy Cat WKP 0001	Record Plant, New York, NY	JHE	
Come On (Part One)	27 Aug 68	CR 2. Take 9 of 14 takes. CR on 'Lifelines'.	Acoustic Jams CD Sphinx SX CD 001	Record Plant, New York, NY	JHE	
Come On (Part One)	27 Aug 68	CR 2. Take 9 of 14 takes. CR on 'Lifelines'.	Lifelines (CR) CD Reprise 9 26435-2	Record Plant, New York, NY	JHE	
Come On (Part One)	27 Aug 68	CR 2. Take 9 of 14 takes. CR on 'Lifelines'. Continued from take	1968 AD CD Whoopy	Record Plant, New	JHE	

Title	Date	Notes	Cat WKP 0001	Venue (York, NY)	Artist	Personnel
Come On (Part One)	27 Aug 68	CR 2. Take 9 of 14 takes. CR on 'Lifelines'.	Voice Of Experience CD Rhinozerous RHP 789	Record Plant, New York, NY	JHE	
Come On (Part One)	27 Aug 68	CR 2. Take 9 of 14 takes. CR on 'Lifelines'.	Voodoo Blues CD Smurf	Record Plant, New York, NY	JHE	
Come On (Part One)	27 Aug 68	CR 2. Take 9 of 14 takes. CR on 'Lifelines'.	Studio Experience CD Sodium Haze SH 099	Record Plant, New York, NY	JHE	
Come On (Part One)	27 Aug 68	CR 2. Take 9 of 14 takes. CR on 'Lifelines'.	Electric Ladyland Outtakes CD Invasion Unlimited IU 9417-1	Record Plant, New York, NY	JHE	
Come On (Part One)	27 Aug 68	CR 2. Take 9 of 14 takes. CR on 'Lifelines'.	Voodoo In Ladyland CD MUM MUCD 006	Record Plant, New York, NY	JHE	
Come On (Part One)	27 Aug 68	CR 1. The last of 14 takes.	Electric Ladyland (CR) CD MCACD-11600	Record Plant, New York, NY	JHE	
Come On (Part One)	17 Jan 69	BR 2. Live performance	Burning At Frankfurt CD Midnight Beat MBCD 040	Jahrhunderthalle, Frankfurt, Germany	JHE	
Come On (Part One)	23 Jan 69	BR 3. Live performance	Up Against The Berlin Wall CD Midnight Beat MBCD 046	Sportpalast, Berlin, Germany	JHE	
Come On (Part One)	18 May 69	BR 4. Live performance	Roman Coliseum, The CD Starquake SQ 11	Madison Square Garden, New York, NY	JHE	
Come On (Part One)	31 Aug 70	BR 5. Live performance	Come On Stockholm CD No Label	Stora Scenen, Liesberg, Goteborg, Sweden	COL	
Come On (Part One)	31 Aug 70	BR 5. Live performance	Free Concert CD Midnight Beat MBCD 013	Stora Scenen, Tivoli Garden, Stockholm, Sweden	COL	
Country Blues	?? / ?? 69	BR 1. A longer portion of this apartment jam than is featured on 'Apartment Jam 70'.	Two Sides Of The Same Genius LP Amazing Kornyphone TAKRL H677	New York Apartment	Jimi	Unknown / Guitar
Country Blues	?? / ?? 69	BR 1. A short portion of this apartment jam and mastered twice on the same disc!	Apartment Jam 70 CD Spicy Essence	New York Apartment	Jimi	Unknown / Guitar

8

SONG TITLE	DATE	COMMENTS	RELEASE	LOCATION / VENUE	BAND	PERSONNEL
Country Blues	23 Jan 70	BR 2 mix 1. The most complete version of this jam / medley with the harmonica played by the mysterious 'Don' intact. The jam starts with 'Country Blues', moves on to 'Astro Man' and ends with some solo guitar improvising.	Mixdown Master Tapes Volume 3 CD Dandelion DL 007	Record Plant, New York, NY	BOG	Don ? / Harmonica
Country Blues	23 Jan 70	BR 2 mix 1. The most complete version of this jam / medley with the harmonica played by the mysterious 'Don' intact. The jam starts with 'Country Blues', moves on to 'Astro Man' and ends with some solo guitar improvising.	Cherokee Mist CD Triangle PYCD 070	Record Plant, New York, NY	BOG	Don ? / Harmonica
Country Blues	23 Jan 70	BR 2 mix 2. A slightly shorter mix than on 'Mixdown Master Tapes Vol 3' and without the harmonica.	Mannish Boy LP Contraband CBM 88	Record Plant, New York, NY	BOG	Don ? / Harmonica Mixed Out
Country Blues	23 Jan 70	BR 2 mix 2. A slightly shorter mix than on 'Mixdown Master Tapes Vol 3' and without the harmonica.	Completer, The CD Whoopy Cat WKP 0018 / 19	Record Plant, New York, NY	BOG	Don ? / Harmonica Mixed Out
Country Blues	23 Jan 70	BR 2 mix 3. The shortest mix and still without the harmonica.	51st Anniversary CD Future Disc JMH 001 / 8	Record Plant, New York, NY	BOG	Don ? / Harmonica Mixed Out
Country Blues	23 Jan 70	BR 2 mix 3. The shortest mix and still without the harmonica.	Freak Out Blues CD GH 001	Record Plant, New York, NY	BOG	Don ? / Harmonica Mixed Out
Country Blues	23 Jan 70	BR 2 mix 3. The shortest mix and still without the harmonica.	Gypsy Suns, Moons And Rainbows CD Sidewalk JHX 8868	Record Plant, New York, NY	BOG	Don ? / Harmonica Mixed Out
Country Blues	23 Jan 70	BR 2 mix 3. The shortest mix and still without the harmonica.	Midnight Shines Down CD Blue Kangaroo BK 04	Record Plant, New York, NY	BOG	Don ? / Harmonica Mixed Out
Country Blues	23 Jan 70	BR 2 mix 3. The shortest mix and still without the harmonica.	Midnight Sun CD Third Eye NK 007	Record Plant, New York, NY	BOG	Don ? / Harmonica Mixed Out
Country Blues	23 Jan 70	BR 2 mix 3. The shortest mix and still without the harmonica. Incomplete.	Drone Blues CD Great Dane GDR SAT 2	Record Plant, New York, NY	BOG	Don ? / Harmonica Mixed Out
Crash Landing	24 Apr 69	CR 1 mix 1. This had the original musicians replaced in 1974.	Crash Landing (CR) LP Reprise MS 2204	Record Plant, New York, NY	Jimi	Crash Landing Line Up 1974
Crash Landing	24 Apr 69	CR 1 mix 2. The complete and original version used as the basis for the CR with a single lead vocal. The louder vocal from the double vocal track was used.	Electric Hendrix Vol 1 CD Pyramid PYCD 030	Record Plant, New York, NY	Jimi	Unknown / Bass
Crash Landing	24 Apr 69	CR 1 mix 2. The complete and original version used as the basis for the CR with a single lead vocal. The louder vocal from the double vocal track was used.	Band Of Gypsys Vol 3	Record Plant, New York, NY	Jimi	Unknown / Bass Drums & Organ
Crash Landing	24 Apr 69	CR 1 mix 2. The complete and original version used as the basis for the CR with a single lead vocal. The louder vocal from the double vocal track was used.	Talent And Feeling Vol 2 CD Extremely Rare EXR 22	Record Plant, New York, NY	Jimi	Unknown / Bass

Song	Date	Notes	Release	Location	Producer	Personnel
Crash Landing	24 Apr 69	CR 1 mix 2. The complete and original version used as the basis for the CR with a single lead vocal. The louder vocal track was used the double vocal track was used.	Unsurpassed Studio Takes CD Yellow Dog YD 050	Record Plant, New York, NY	Jimi	Unknown / Bass
Crash Landing	24 Apr 69	CR 1 mix 2. The complete and original version used as the basis for the CR with a single lead vocal. The louder vocal track was used the double vocal track was used.	51st Anniversary CD Future Disc JMH 001 / 8	Record Plant, New York, NY	Jimi	Unknown / Bass
Crash Landing	24 Apr 69	CR 1 mix 2. The complete and original version used as the basis for the CR with a single lead vocal. The louder vocal track was used the double vocal track was used.	Paper Airplanes CD Midnight Beat MBCD 25	Record Plant, New York, NY	Jimi	Unknown / Bass
Crash Landing	24 Apr 69	CR 1 mix 2. The complete and original version used as the basis for the CR with a single lead vocal. The louder vocal track was used the double vocal track was used.	Magic Hand CD Mum MUCD 012	Record Plant, New York, NY	Jimi	Unknown / Bass
Crash Landing	24 Apr 69	CR 1 mix 2. The complete and original version used as the basis for the CR with a single lead vocal. The louder vocal track was used the double vocal track was used.	Band Of Gypsys- The Ultimate CD JMH 010 / 3	Record Plant, New York, NY	JHE	Unknown / Bass
Crash Landing	24 Apr 69	CR 1 mix 3. The complete and original version used as the basis for the CR with a double lead vocal.	Master's Masters, The CD JH-01	Record Plant, New York, NY	Jimi	Don ? / Harmonica
Crash Landing	24 Apr 69	CR 1 mix 3. The complete and original version used as the basis for the CR with a double lead vocal.	Talent And Feeling Vol 2 CD Extremely Rare EXR 22	Record Plant, New York, NY	Jimi	Unknown / Bass
Crash Landing	24 Apr 69	CR 1 mix 4. This has the drums mixed for the first part of the song and also uses an alternate vocal track.	Shine On Earth, Shine On CD Sidewalk SW 89010 / 89011	Record Plant, New York, NY	Jimi	Crash Landing Line Up 1974
Crash Landing	24 Apr 69	CR 1 mix 4. This has the drums mixed for the first part of the song and also uses an alternate vocal track.	Paper Airplanes CD Midnight Beat MBCD 25	Record Plant, New York, NY	Jimi	Crash Landing Line Up 1974
Crash Landing	24 Apr 69	CR 1 mix 4. This has the drums mixed for the first part of the song and also uses an alternate vocal track.	Multicolored Blues CD Luna LU 9317	Record Plant, New York, NY	Jimi	Crash Landing Line Up 1974
Crash Landing	24 Apr 69	CR 1 mix 4. This has the drums mixed for the first part of the song and also uses an alternate vocal track.	Midnight Shines Down CD Blue Kangaroo BK 04	Record Plant, New York, NY	Jimi	Crash Landing Line Up 1974
Crash Landing	24 Apr 69	CR 1 mix 4. This has the drums mixed for the first part of the song and also uses an alternate vocal track.	Kiss The Skies CD Mum MUCD 024	Record Plant, New York, NY	Jimi	Crash Landing Line Up 1974
Crash Landing	24 Apr 69	CR 1 mix 5. This mix highlights the bass and guitar parts and drops the vocals.	Paper Airplanes CD Midnight Beat MBCD 25	Record Plant, New York, NY	Jimi	Crash Landing Line Up 1974
Crash Landing	24 Apr 69	CR 1 mix 5. This mix highlights the bass and guitar parts and drops the vocals.	Gypsy Suns, Moons And Rainbows CD Sidewalk JHX 8868	Record Plant, New York, NY	Jimi	Crash Landing Line Up 1974
Crosstown Traffic	20 Dec 67	CR 1 mix 1 (stereo).	Red House CD The Entertainers CD294	Olympic Sound Studios, London, England	JHE	Dave Mason / Backing Vocals

SONG TITLE	DATE	COMMENTS	RELEASE	LOCATION / VENUE	BAND	PERSONNEL
Crosstown Traffic	20 Dec 67	CR 1 mix 1 (stereo).	Electric Ladyland (CR) CD MCACD-11600	Olympic Sound Studios, London, England	JHE	Dave Mason / Backing Vocals
Crosstown Traffic	20 Dec 67	CR 1 mix 1 (stereo).	The Singles Album (CR) CD Polydor 827 369-2	Olympic Sound Studios, London, England	JHE	Dave Mason / Backing Vocals
Crosstown Traffic	20 Dec 67	CR 1 mix 1 (stereo).	Smash Hits (CR) CD Reprise 2276-2	Olympic Sound Studios, London, England	JHE	Dave Mason / Backing Vocals
Crosstown Traffic	20 Dec 67	CR 1 mix 1 (stereo).	Legacy (CR) LP Polydor	Olympic Sound Studios, London, England	JHE	Dave Mason / Backing Vocals
Crosstown Traffic	20 Dec 67	CR 1 mix 2 (mono).	Single: All Along The Watchtower / Crosstown Traffic Reprise GRE 0742	Olympic Sound Studios, London, England	JHE	Dave Mason / Backing Vocals
Crosstown Traffic	20 Dec 67	CR 1 mix 3. An unused mix without the cross channel panning.	Unsurpassed Studio Takes CD Yellow Dog YD 050	Olympic Sound Studios, London, England	JHE	Dave Mason / Backing Vocals
Crosstown Traffic	20 Dec 67	CR 1 mix 3. An unused mix without the cross channel panning.	Screaming Eagle CD Pink Poodle POO 001	Olympic Sound Studios, London, England	JHE	Dave Mason / Backing Vocals
Crosstown Traffic	20 Dec 67	CR 1 mix 3. An unused mix without the cross channel panning.	Voodoo In Ladyland CD MUM MUCD 006	Olympic Sound Studios, London, England	JHE	Dave Mason / Backing Vocals
Dance	20 Dec 67	BR 1. Vocal version of this unreleased Redding / Mitchell composition.	Sotheby Auction Tapes, The CD Midnight Beat MBCD 010	Olympic Sound Studios, London, England	JHE	
Dance	20 Dec 67	BR 1. Vocal version of this unreleased Redding / Mitchell composition.	Symphony Of Experience CD Third Stone Discs TDS 24966	Olympic Sound Studios, London, England	JHE	
Dance	20 Dec 67	BR 1. Vocal version of this unreleased Redding / Mitchell composition.	Get The Experience CD Invasion Unlimited IU 9424-1	Olympic Sound Studios, London, England	JHE	
Dance	20 Dec 67	BR 1. Vocal version of this unreleased Redding / Mitchell composition.	Notes In Colours CD JHR 001 / 002	Olympic Sound Studios, London, England	JHE	
Dance (Ezy Rider Jam)	20 Dec 67	BR 1. Vocal version of this unreleased Redding / Mitchell composition.	Completer, The CD Whoopy Cat WKP 0018 / 19	Olympic Sound Studios, London, England	JHE	

Title	Date	Notes	Release	Location	Band
Dance	20 Dec 67	BR 1. Vocal version of this unreleased Redding / Mitchell composition.	Jimi: A Musical Legacy CD KTS BX 010	Olympic Sound Studios, London, England	JHE
Dance (Ezy Rider)	?? / ?? 68-69	BR 2. Vocal version of this unreleased Redding / Mitchell composition. This instrumental version is frequently mistaken for or referred to as "Ezy Rider".	Electric Hendrix Vol 1 CD Pyramid PYCD 030	Olympic Sound Studios, London, England	JHE
Dance (Ezy Rider)	?? / ?? 68-69	BR 2. Vocal version of this unreleased Redding / Mitchell composition. This instrumental version is frequently mistaken for or referred to as "Ezy Rider".	Multicolored Blues CD Luna LU 9317	Record Plant, New York, NY	BOG
Dance (Ezy Rider)	?? / ?? 68-69	BR 2. Vocal version of this unreleased Redding / Mitchell composition. This instrumental version is frequently mistaken for or referred to as "Ezy Rider".	Diamonds In The Dust CD Midnight Beat MBCD 022 / 23	Record Plant, New York, NY	BOG
Dance (Ezy Rider)	?? / ?? 68-69	BR 2. Vocal version of this unreleased Redding / Mitchell composition. This instrumental version is frequently mistaken for or referred to as "Ezy Rider".	Mixdown Master Tapes Volume 3 CD Dandelion DL 007	Olympic Sound Studios, London, England	JHE
Dance (Ezy Rider)	?? / ?? 68-69	BR 2. Vocal version of this unreleased Redding / Mitchell composition. This instrumental version is frequently mistaken for or referred to as "Ezy Rider".	Completer, The CD Whoopy Cat WKP 0018 / 19	Olympic Sound Studios, London, England	JHE
Dance (Ezy Rider)	?? / ?? 68-69	BR 2. Vocal version of this unreleased Redding / Mitchell composition. This instrumental version is frequently mistaken for or referred to as "Ezy Rider".	Gypsy Charm CD Mum MUCD 018	Olympic Sound Studios, London, England	JHE
Dance	?? / ?? 68-69	BR 2. Vocal version of this unreleased Redding / Mitchell composition. This instrumental version is frequently mistaken for or referred to as "Ezy Rider".	Atlanta CD JMH 009 / 02	Olympic Sound Studios, London, England	JHE
Dance, The	?? Aug 69	BR 1. This is a percussive composition by Juma Sultan and was rehearsed at Jimi's Shokan house prior to the Woodstock show.	Shokan Sunrise CD	Shokan House, Woodstock, NY	GSRB
Dance, The	?? Aug 69	BR 1. This is a percussive composition by Juma Sultan and was rehearsed at Jimi's Shokan house prior to the Woodstock show.	Woodstock Rehearsals CD Midnight Beat MBCD 009	Record Plant, New York, NY	COL
Dance, The	14 Aug 69	BR 2. An incomplete live performance of Juma Sultan's composition.	Shokan Sunrise CD	Tinker Street Cinema, Woodstock, NY	GSRB
Day Tripper	15 Dec 67	CR 1. Live BBC performance.	Guitar Hero CD Document DR 013	Top Gear, BBC Playhouse Theatre, London, England	JHE
Day Tripper	15 Dec 67	CR 1. Live BBC performance.	Primal Keys LP Impossible Record Works	Top Gear, BBC Playhouse Theatre, London, England	JHE
Day Tripper	15 Dec 67	CR 1. Live BBC performance.	Radio One (CR) CD Rykodisc RCD 20078	Top Gear, BBC Playhouse Theatre, London, England	JHE

SONG TITLE	DATE	COMMENTS	RELEASE	LOCATION / VENUE	BAND	PERSONNEL
Day Tripper	15 Dec 67	CR 1. Live BBC performance.	Ultimate BBC Collection CD Classical CL006	Top Gear, BBC Playhouse Theatre, London, England	JHE	
Day Tripper	15 Dec 67	Live In London 1967 CD Koine Records K881104	Live In London 1967 CD Koine Records K881104	Top Gear, BBC Playhouse Theatre, London, England	JHE	
Day Tripper	15 Dec 67	CR 1. Live BBC performance.	Live In Concert 1967 CD Living Legend LLR-CD 001	Top Gear, BBC Playhouse Theatre, London, England	JHE	
Day Tripper	15 Dec 67	CR 1. Live BBC performance.	In Concert CD Starlife ST 3612	Top Gear, BBC Playhouse Theatre, London, England	JHE	
Day Tripper	15 Dec 67	CR 1. Live BBC performance.	Complete BBC Session And..., The CD Last Bootleg Records LBR 036 / 2	Top Gear, BBC Playhouse Theatre, London, England	JHE	
Day Tripper	15 Dec 67	CR 1. Live BBC performance.	Rarities On Compact Disc CD On The Radio	Top Gear, BBC Playhouse Theatre, London, England	JHE	
Day Tripper	15 Dec 67	CR 1. Live BBC performance.	BBC Sessions (CR) CD MCACD 2-11742	Top Gear, BBC Playhouse Theatre, London, England	JHE	
Day Tripper	15 Dec 67	CR 1. Live BBC performance.	Day Tripper (CR) CD-3 Rykodisc RCD 31-008	Top Gear, BBC Playhouse Theatre, London, England	JHE	
Dear Mr. Fantasy	03 Aug 68	BR 1. A one off live performance of this song although it's reported that The Experience also played this at Winterland on 2 / 4 / 68.	Crosstown Traffic CD M25 3664	Moody Coliseum, Southern Methodist University, Dallas, TX	JHE	
Destructive Love (The Street Things)	22 Jun 69	Produced for The Buddy Miles express by Jimi.	51st Anniversary CD Future Disc JMH 001 / 8		BME	Jimi Hendrix / Producer
Destructive Love (The Sweet Things)	22 Jun 69	Produced for The Buddy Miles express by Jimi.	Two Days At Newport CD JMH 007 / 2		BME	Jimi Hendrix / Producer
Dolly Dagger	01 Jul 70	CR 1 mix 1 (stereo).	Rainbow Bridge (CR) LP Reprise K44159	Electric Lady Studio, New York, NY	COL	Ghetto Fighters / Backing Vocals, Juma Sultan / Percussion
Dolly Dagger	01 Jul 70	CR 1 mix 1 (stereo).	Rainbow Bridge & More CD	Electric Lady Studio, New York, NY	COL	Ghetto Fighters / Backing Vocals, Juma Sultan / Percussion

Song	Date	Notes	Release	Studio	Producer	Personnel
Dolly Dagger	01 Jul 70	CR 1 mix 1 (stereo).	First Rays Of The New Rising Sun (CR) CD MCACD 11599	Electric Lady Studio, New York, NY	COL	Ghetto Fighters / Backing Vocals, Juma Sultan / Percussion
Dolly Dagger	01 Jul 70	CR 1 mix 2 (mono).	Dolly Dagger Mono / Stereo Promo Single Reprise 1044	Electric Lady Studio, New York, NY	Jimi	Ghetto Fighters / Backing Vocals, Juma Sultan / Percussion
Dolly Dagger	01 Jul 70	CR 1 mix 3. An unused mix that has an alternate lead vocal track.	Studio Haze CD INA 6	Electric Lady Studio, New York, NY	COL	Ghetto Fighters / Backing Vocals, Juma Sultan / Percussion
Dolly Dagger	01 Jul 70	CR 1 mix 3. An unused mix that has an alternate lead vocal track.	Multicolored Blues CD Luna LU 9317	Electric Lady Studio, New York, NY	COL	Ghetto Fighters / Backing Vocals, Juma Sultan / Percussion
Dolly Dagger	01 Jul 70	CR 1 mix 3. An unused mix that has an alternate lead vocal track.	First Rays - The Sessions CD Whoopy Cat WKP 0002	Electric Lady Studio, New York, NY	COL	Ghetto Fighters / Backing Vocals, Juma Sultan / Percussion
Dolly Dagger	01 Jul 70	CR 1 mix 3. An unused mix that has an alternate lead vocal track.	Notes In Colours CD JHR 001 / 002	Electric Lady Studio, New York, NY	COL	Ghetto Fighters / Backing Vocals, Juma Sultan / Percussion
Dolly Dagger	01 Jul 70	CR 1 mix 3. An unused mix that has an alternate lead vocal track.	Gypsy Charm CD Mum MUCD 018	Electric Lady Studio, New York, NY	COL	Ghetto Fighters / Backing Vocals, Juma Sultan / Percussion
Dolly Dagger	01 Jul 70	CR 1 mix 3. An unused mix that has an alternate lead vocal track.	Eyes And Imagination CD Third Stone TSD 18970	Electric Lady Studio, New York, NY	COL	Ghetto Fighters / Backing Vocals, Juma Sultan / Percussion
Dolly Dagger	30 Jul 70	CR 2. Live performance.	You Can't Use My Name L P Rock Folders 2, Q 9020	Rainbow Bridge Vibratory Sound-Color Experiment, Maui, HI 2nd Show	COL	
Dolly Dagger	30 Jul 70	CR 2. Live performance.	Last American Concert Vol 2 CD The Swingin' Pig TSP-072	Rainbow Bridge Vibratory Sound-Color Experiment, Maui, HI 2nd Show	COL	
Dolly Dagger	30 Jul 70	CR 2. Live performance.	In From The Storm CD Silver Rarities SIRA 109 / 110	Rainbow Bridge Vibratory Sound-Color Experiment, Maui, HI 2nd Show	COL	
Dolly Dagger	30 Jul 70	CR 2. Live performance.	Rainbow Bridge (CR) LP Reprise K44159	Rainbow Bridge Vibratory Sound-Color Experiment, Maui, HI 2nd Show	COL	
Dolly Dagger	30 Jul 70	CR 2. Live performance.	Rainbow Bridge 2 CD JMH 003 / 2	Rainbow Bridge Vibratory Sound-Color Experiment, Maui, HI 2nd Show	COL	

SONG TITLE	DATE	COMMENTS	RELEASE	LOCATION / VENUE	BAND	PERSONNEL
Dolly Dagger	30 Aug 70	CR 3. Live performance.	Lifelines (CR) CD Reprise 9 26435-2	Isle Of Wight Festival, Isle Of Wight, England	COL	
Dolly Dagger	30 Aug 70	CR 3. Live performance.	Island Man CD Silver Rarities SIRA 39 / 40	Isle Of Wight Festival, Isle Of Wight, England	COL	
Dolly Dagger	30 Aug 70	CR 3. Live performance.	At The Isle Of Wight (CR) Laserdisc CBS / Sony CLSM 791	Isle Of Wight Festival, Isle Of Wight, England	COL	
Dolly Dagger	30 Aug 70	CR 3. Live performance.	Live! CD Black B-05	Isle Of Wight Festival, Isle Of Wight, England	COL	
Dolly Dagger	30 Aug 70	CR 3. Live performance.	Live - Isle Of Wight 70 (CR) CD Polydor 847236-2	Isle Of Wight Festival, Isle Of Wight, England	COL	
Dolly Dagger	30 Aug 70	CR 3. Live performance.	Rainbow Bridge 2 CD JMH 003 / 2	Isle Of Wight Festival, Isle Of Wight, England	COL	
Dolly Dagger	30 Aug 70	CR 3. Live performance.	Wight CD JMH 006 / 2	Isle Of Wight Festival, Isle Of Wight, England	COL	
Doriella Du Fontaine	?? Nov 69	CR 1 mix 1.	Doriella Du Fontaine CD Single Restless 7 72663-2	Record Plant, New York, NY	Jimi	Jimi / Bass, Lightnin' Rod / Vocals, Buddy Miles / Drums & Organ
Doriella Du Fontaine	?? Nov 69	CR 1 mix 2. Radio edit.	Doriella Du Fontaine CD Single Restless 7 72663-2	Record Plant, New York, NY	Jimi	
Doriella Du Fontaine	?? Nov 69	CR 1 mix 3t Instrumental	Doriella Du Fontaine CD Single Restless 7 72663-2	Record Plant, New York, NY	Jimi	
Dream	20 Dec 67	An unreleased Redding composition from an original acetate with vocals by Noel Redding.	Sotheby Auction Tapes, The CD Midnight Beat MBCD 010	Olympic Sound Studios, London, England	JHE	Noel Redding / Vocals
Dream	20 Dec 67	An unreleased Redding composition from an original acetate with vocals by Noel Redding.	Symphony Of Experience CD Third Stone Discs TDS 24966	Olympic Sound Studios, London, England	JHE	Noel Redding / Vocals
Dream	20 Dec 67	An unreleased Redding composition from an original acetate with vocals by Noel Redding.	Get The Experience CD Invasion Unlimited IU 9424-1	Olympic Sound Studios, London, England	JHE	Noel Redding / Vocals
Dream	20 Dec 67	An unreleased Redding composition from an original acetate	Notes In Colours CD	Olympic Sound	JHE	Noel Redding / Vocals

Song	Date	Notes	JHR 001 / 002	Studios	Band	Personnel
Dream		with vocals by Noel Redding.		Studios, London, England		Noel Redding / Vocals
Dream	20 Dec 67	An unreleased Redding composition from an original acetate with vocals by Noel Redding.	Completer, The CD Whoopy Cat WKP 0018 / 19	Olympic Sound Studios, London, England	JHE	Noel Redding / Vocals
Dream	20 Dec 67	An unreleased Redding composition from an original acetate with vocals by Noel Redding.	Jimi: A Musical Legacy CD KTS BX 010	Olympic Sound Studios, London, England	JHE	
Drifter's Escape	17 Jun 70	CR 1 mix 1.	Loose Ends (CR) LP Polydor 837574-2	Electric Lady Studio, New York, NY	COL	
Drifter's Escape	17 Jun 70	CR 1 mix 1.	Rarities On Compact Disc CD On The Radio	Electric Lady Studio, New York, NY	COL	
Drifter's Escape	17 Jun 70	CR 1 mix 2. Alternate mix.	Lifelines (CR) CD Reprise 9 26435-2	Electric Lady Studio, New York, NY	COL	
Drifter's Escape	17 Jun 70	CR 1 mix 2. Alternate mix.	I Don't Live Today CD ACL 007	Electric Lady Studio, New York, NY	COL	
Drifter's Escape	17 Jun 70	CR 1 mix 3. Alternate mix.	South Saturn Delta (CR) CD MCACD 11684	Electric Lady Studio, New York, NY	COL	
Drifter's Escape	17 Jun 70	CR 1 mix 4. An alternate mix with extra guitar overdubs but with the cow bell mixed out. Mastered at the right speed.	Electric Hendrix Vol 1 CD Pyramid PYCD 030	Electric Lady Studio, New York, NY	COL	
Drifter's Escape	17 Jun 70	CR 1 mix 4. An alternate mix with extra guitar overdubs but with the cow bell mixed out. Mastered at the right speed.	Freak Out Jam CD GH 002	Electric Lady Studio, New York, NY	COL	
Drifter's Escape	17 Jun 70	CR 1 mix 5. Unused mix.	Talent And Feeling Vol 2 CD Extremely Rare EXR 22	Electric Lady Studio, New York, NY	COL	
Drifter's Escape (Help Me In My Weakness)	17 Jun 70	CR 1 mix 5. Unused mix.	TTG Studios ???? CD WHOAMI WAI 015	Electric Lady Studio, New York, NY	COL	
Drifter's Escape	17 Jun 70	CR 1 mix 5. Unused mix.	Multicolored Blues CD Luna LU 9317	Electric Lady Studio, New York, NY	COL	
Drifter's Escape	17 Jun 70	CR 1 mix 5. Unused mix.	Gypsy Charm CD Mum MUCD 018	Electric Lady Studio, New York, NY	COL	
Drifter's Escape	22? Aug? 70	CR 1 mix 6. From an overdub session, possibly from 8 / 22 / 70. This mix is just two very different vocal tracks over the isolated guitar tracks.	500,000 Halos CD EXP 500,000	Electric Lady Studio, New York, NY	COL	
Drifting	25 Jun 70	CR 1 mix1.	First Rays Of The New Rising Sun (CR) CD MCACD 11599	Electric Lady Studio, New York, NY	COL	Buzzy Linhart / Vibes
Drifting	25 Jun 70	CR 1 mix1.	Cry Of Love, The (CR) CD Reprise 2034-2	Electric Lady Studio, New York, NY	COL	Buzzy Linhart / Vibes

SONG TITLE	DATE	COMMENTS	RELEASE	LOCATION / VENUE	BAND	PERSONNEL
Drifting	25 Jun 70	CR 1 mix 2. This has some additional backwards guitar over-dubs.	Voodoo Soup (CR) CD MCA 11206	Electric Lady Studio, New York, NY	COL	Buzzy Linhart / Vibes
Drifting	25 Jun 70	CR 1 mix 3. This is actually the basic track including vocals used for the CR. This is distinguished by Jimi saying at the start of the song "Let me do some sea sounds".	Acoustic Jams CD Sphinx SX CD 001	Electric Lady Studio, New York, NY	COL	
Drifting (Pride Of Man)	25 Jun 70	CR 1 mix 3. This is actually the basic track including vocals used for the CR. This is distinguished by Jimi saying at the start of the song "Let me do some sea sounds". This release has extra chat at the start.	Multicolored Blues CD Luna LU 9317	Electric Lady Studio, New York, NY	COL	
Drifting	25 Jun 70	CR 1 mix 3. This is actually the basic track including vocals used for the CR. This is distinguished by Jimi saying at the start of the song "Let me do some sea sounds".	First Rays - The Sessions CD Whoopy Cat WKP 0002	Electric Lady Studio, New York, NY	COL	
Drifting	25 Jun 70	CR 1 mix 3. This is actually the basic track including vocals used for the CR. This is distinguished by Jimi saying at the start of the song "Let me do some sea sounds".	Studio Experience CD Sodium Haze SH 099	Electric Lady Studio, New York, NY	COL	
Drifting	25 Jun 70	CR 1 mix 3. This is actually the basic track including vocals used for the CR. This is distinguished by Jimi saying at the start of the song "Let me do some sea sounds".	Notes In Colours CD JHR 001 / 002	Electric Lady Studio, New York, NY	COL	
Drifting	25 Jun 70	CR 1 mix 3. This is actually the basic track including vocals used for the CR. This is distinguished by Jimi saying at the start of the song "Let me do some sea sounds".	Gypsy Charm CD Mum MUCD 018	Electric Lady Studio, New York, NY	COL	
Drifting	25 Jun 70	BR 1. Incomplete instrumental take from the CR #1 session.	Notes In Colours CD JHR 001 / 002	Electric Lady Studio, New York, NY	COL	
Drifting	25 Jun 70	BR 2. Continuation from the previous track on 'Notes In Colour' CD without Mitch playing drums.	Notes In Colours CD JHR 001 / 002	Electric Lady Studio, New York, NY	COL	
Drifting	23 Jul 70	BR 1. This is a short solo version plus a longer instrumental version.	Multicolored Blues CD Luna LU 9317	Electric Lady Studio, New York, NY	COL	
Drifting	23 Jul 70	BR 2. This is a short solo version plus a longer instrumental version. On this release the short version appears before and after the long version.	Acoustic Jams CD Sphinx SX CD 001	Electric Lady Studio, New York, NY	COL	
Drifting	23 Jul 70	BR 2. This is a short solo version plus a longer instrumental version.	First Rays - The Sessions CD Whoopy Cat WKP 0002	Electric Lady Studio, New York, NY	COL	
Drifting	23 Jul 70	BR 2. This is a short solo version plus a longer instrumental version.	Studio Experience CD Sodium Haze SH 099	Electric Lady Studio, New York, NY	COL	
Drifting	25 Jun 70	An outfake of the CR in poor sound.	TTG Studios ???? CD WHOAMI WAI 015		COL	
Driving South	26 Dec 65	CR 4. An incomplete live version with the Curtis Knight Band.	Lifelines (CR) CD Reprise 9 26435-2	George's Club 20, Hackensack, NJ	CKB	

Song	Date	Notes	Source	Venue	Band
Driving South	06 Oct 67	CR 1 Mix 1. Complete live BBC performance.	Broadcasts LP Trade Mark Of Quality TMQ 1841 & TMQ 71019	Top Gear, BBC Playhouse Theatre, London, England	JHE
Driving South	06 Oct 67	CR 1 Mix 1. Complete live BBC performance.	BBC Sessions (CR) CD MCACD 2-11742	Top Gear, BBC Playhouse Theatre, London, England	JHE
Driving South	06 Oct 67	CR 1 mix 2. This is the edited version of the live BBC performance.	Official Bootleg Album, The CD Yellow Dog YD 051	Top Gear, BBC Playhouse Theatre, London, England	JHE
Driving South	06 Oct 67	CR 1 mix 2. This is the edited version of the live BBC performance.	Symphony Of Experience CD Third Stone Discs TDS 24966	Top Gear, BBC Playhouse Theatre, London, England	JHE
Driving South (Catfish Blues / Rolling & Tumbling)	06 Oct 67	CR 1 mix 2. This is the edited version of the live BBC performance.	King And Wonder Sessions CD Oh Boy 1-9170	Top Gear, BBC Playhouse Theatre, London, England	JHE
Driving South	06 Oct 67	CR 1 mix 2. This is the edited version of the live BBC performance.	Day Tripper (CR) CD-3 Rykodisc RCD 31-008	Top Gear, BBC Playhouse Theatre, London, England	JHE
Driving South	06 Oct 67	CR 2. This is the alternate version recorded live for the BBC that was left unbroadcast.	Radio One (CR) CD Rykodisc RCD 20078	Top Gear, BBC Playhouse Theatre, London, England	JHE
Driving South	06 Oct 67	CR 2. This is the alternate version recorded live for the BBC that was left unbroadcast.	Ultimate BBC Collection CD Classical CL006	Top Gear, BBC Playhouse Theatre, London, England	JHE
Driving South	06 Oct 67	CR 2. This is the alternate version recorded live for the BBC that was left unbroadcast.	Complete BBC Session And... The CD Last Bootleg Records LBR 036 / 2	Top Gear, BBC Playhouse Theatre, London, England	JHE
Driving South	06 Oct 67	CR 2. This is the alternate version recorded live for the BBC that was left unbroadcast.	BBC Sessions (CR) CD MCACD 2-11742	Top Gear, BBC Playhouse Theatre, London, England	JHE
Driving South	17 Oct 67	CR 3. This live BBC recording ends after Jimi breaks a string and Mitch breaks into a drum solo.	Guitar Hero CD Document DR 013	Rhythm And Blues, BBC Playhouse Theatre, London, England	JHE
Driving South	17 Oct 67	CR 3. This live BBC recording ends after Jimi breaks a string and Mitch breaks into a drum solo.	Primal Keys LP Impossible Record Works	Rhythm And Blues, BBC Playhouse Theatre, London, England	JHE

SONG TITLE	DATE	COMMENTS	RELEASE	LOCATION / VENUE	BAND	PERSONNEL
Driving South	17 Oct 67	CR 3. This live BBC recording ends after Jimi breaks a string and Mitch breaks into a drum solo.	Freak Out Jam CD GH 002	Rhythm And Blues, BBC Playhouse Theatre, London, England	JHE	
Driving South	17 Oct 67	CR 3. This live BBC recording ends after Jimi breaks a string and Mitch breaks into a drum solo.	Symphony Of Experience CD Third Stone Discs TDS 24966	Rhythm And Blues, BBC Playhouse Theatre, London, England	JHE	
Driving South	17 Oct 67	CR 3. This live BBC recording ends after Jimi breaks a string and Mitch breaks into a drum solo.	Live In London 1967 CD Koine Records K881104	Rhythm And Blues, BBC Playhouse Theatre, London, England	JHE	
Driving South	17 Oct 67	CR 3. This live BBC recording ends after Jimi breaks a string and Mitch breaks into a drum solo.	Live In Concert 1967 CD Living Legend LLR-CD 001	Rhythm And Blues, BBC Playhouse Theatre, London, England	JHE	
Driving South	17 Oct 67	CR 3. This live BBC recording ends after Jimi breaks a string and Mitch breaks into a drum solo.	Can You Please Crawl Out Your Window? LP Ruthless Rhymes Jimi1	Rhythm And Blues, BBC Playhouse Theatre, London, England	JHE	
Driving South	17 Oct 67	CR 3. This live BBC recording ends after Jimi breaks a string and Mitch breaks into a drum solo.	In Concert CD Starlife ST 3612	Rhythm And Blues, BBC Playhouse Theatre, London, England	JHE	
Driving South	17 Oct 67	CR 3. This live BBC recording ends after Jimi breaks a string and Mitch breaks into a drum solo.	Black Strings CD CDM G-53 258	Rhythm And Blues, BBC Playhouse Theatre, London, England	JHE	
Driving South	17 Oct 67	CR 3. This live BBC recording ends after Jimi breaks a string and Mitch breaks into a drum solo.	BBC Sessions (CR) CD MCACD 2-11742	Rhythm And Blues, BBC Playhouse Theatre, London, England	JHE	
Driving South	29 Jan 68	CR 5. Live performance.	Live In Paris CD Swingin' Pig TSP-016	L' Olympia Theatre, Paris, France 1st Show	JHE	
Driving South	29 Jan 68	CR 5. Live performance.	Stages Paris 68 (CR) CD Reprise 9 27632-2	L' Olympia Theatre, Paris, France 1st Show	JHE	
Driving South	29 Jan 68	CR 5. Live performance.	Recorded Live In Europe CD Bulldog BGCD 023	L' Olympia Theatre, Paris, France 1st Show	JHE	

Song	Date	Description	Release	Location	Band	Musicians
Driving South	29 Jan 68	CR 5. Live performance.	In Europe 67 / 68 / 69 CD Vulture CD 009 / 2	L' Olympia Theatre, Paris, France 1st Show	JHE	
Driving South	29 Jan 68	CR 5. Live performance.	Very Best, The CD Irec / Retro MILCD-03	L' Olympia Theatre, Paris, France 1st Show	JHE	
Driving South	29 Jan 68	CR 5. Live performance.	In Concert CD Starlife ST 3612	L' Olympia Theatre, Paris, France 1st Show	JHE	
Driving South	29 Jan 68	CR 5. Live performance.	Jimi Hendrix CD Flute FLCD 2008	L' Olympia Theatre, Paris, France 1st Show	JHE	
Driving South	29 Jan 68	CR 5. Live performance.	Anthology CD Box 9	L' Olympia Theatre, Paris, France 1st Show	JHE	
Driving South / Sgt. Peppers Lonely Heart	?? / ?? 68	BR 2. A fast paced studio jam of 'Driving South' in which Jimi apparently breaks a string. After Mitch and Noel trade off solos, Jimi tunes up in rhythm and continues until the jam breaks down. A short (40 Seconds) bit of 'Sgt. Pepper' is played.	Symphony Of Experience CD Third Stone Discs TDS 24966	Unknown	JHE	
Driving South / Sgt. Peppers Lonely Heart	?? / ?? 68	BR 2. A fast paced studio jam of 'Driving South' in which Jimi apparently breaks a string. After Mitch and Noel trade off solos, Jimi tunes up in rhythm and continues until the jam breaks down. A short (40 Seconds) bit of 'Sgt. Pepper' is played.	Best Of The Bootlegs CD MS 666	Unknown	JHE	
Driving South / Sgt. Peppers Lonely Heart	?? / ?? 68	BR 2. A fast paced studio jam of 'Driving South' in which Jimi apparently breaks a string. After Mitch and Noel trade off solos, Jimi tunes up in rhythm and continues until the jam breaks down. A short (40 Seconds) bit of 'Sgt. Pepper' is played.	Lost Experience, The, CD JHCD203	Unknown	JHE	
Driving South / Sgt. Peppers Lonely Heart	?? / ?? 68	BR 2. A fast paced studio jam of 'Driving South' in which Jimi apparently breaks a string. After Mitch and Noel trade off solos, Jimi tunes up in rhythm and continues until the jam breaks down. A short (40 Seconds) bit of 'Sgt. Pepper' is played.	Screaming Eagle CD Pink Poodle POO 001	Unknown	JHE	
Driving South / Sgt. Peppers Lonely Heart	?? / ?? 68	BR 2. A fast paced studio jam of 'Driving South' in which Jimi apparently breaks a string. After Mitch and Noel trade off solos, Jimi tunes up in rhythm and continues until the jam breaks down. A short (40 Seconds) bit of 'Sgt. Pepper' is played.	Completer, The CD Whoopy Cat WKP 0018 / 19	Unknown	JHE	
Driving South / Sgt. Peppers Lonely Heart (Listed Separately On CD)	?? / ?? 68	BR 2. A fast paced studio jam of 'Driving South' in which Jimi apparently breaks a string. After Mitch and Noel trade off solos, Jimi tunes up in rhythm and continues until the jam breaks down. A short (40 Seconds) bit of 'Sgt. Pepper' is played.	Diamonds In The Dust CD Midnight Beat MBCD 022 / 23	Unknown	JHE	
Driving South / Everything's Gonna Be Alright (Drivin' South Jam)	25 Mar 69	BR 1. Part of a jam that begins with 'Driving South' and continues with "Everything's Gonna Be Alright". Incomplete at the start and at the end.	Record Plant Jam CD Pilot Records HJCD 69	Record Plant, New York, NY	Jimi	John Mc Laughlin / Guitar, Buddy Miles / Drums, Dave Holland / Bass

SONG TITLE	DATE	COMMENTS	RELEASE	LOCATION / VENUE	BAND	PERSONNEL
Driving South / Everything's Gonna Be Alright (Coast To Coast)	25 Mar 69	BR 1. Part of a jam that begins with 'Driving South and continues with "Everything's Gonna Be Alright". Incomplete at the start and at the end.	Redskin' Jammin' CD JH 01 / 02	Record Plant, New York, NY	Jimi	John Mc Laughlin / Guitar, Buddy Miles / Drums, Dave Holland / Bass
Driving South / Everything's Gonna Be Alright (Tarnia)	25 Mar 69	BR 1. Part of a jam that begins with 'Driving South and continues with "Everything's Gonna Be Alright". Incomplete at the start and at the end.	McLaughlin Sessions, The CD HML CD 9409	Record Plant, New York, NY	Jimi	John Mc Laughlin / Guitar, Buddy Miles / Drums, Dave Holland / Bass
Driving South / Everything's Gonna Be Alright (Second Jam Session)	25 Mar 69	BR 1. A long jam that begins with 'Driving South' and continues with "Eveything's Gonna Be Alright". This is the complete jam from start to finish.	Atlanta CD JMH 009 / 02	Record Plant, New York, NY	JHE	John Mc Laughlin / Guitar, Buddy Miles / Drums, Dave Holland / Bass
Driving South / Everything's Gonna Be Alright (First Jam)	25 Mar 69	BR 1. Part of a jam that begins with 'Driving South and continues with "Everything's Gonna Be Alright". Incomplete at the start and at the end.	51st Anniversary CD Future Disc JMH 001 / 8	Record Plant, New York, NY	Jimi	John Mc Laughlin / Guitar, Buddy Miles / Drums, Dave Holland / Bass
Driving South / Everything's Gonna Be Alright	25 Mar 69	BR 1. Part of a jam that begins with 'Driving South and continues with "Everything's Gonna Be Alright". Incomplete at the start but does continue to the end.	Let's Drop Some Ludes And Vomit With Jimi CD Midnight Beat MBCD 026	Record Plant, New York, NY	Jimi	John Mc Laughlin / Guitar, Buddy Miles / Drums, Dave Holland / Bass
Driving South / Everything's Gonna Be Alright (Jimi / Jimmy Jam)	25 Mar 69	BR 1. Part of a jam that begins with 'Driving South and continues with "Everything's Gonna Be Alright". Incomplete at the start and at the end.	Jimi: A Musical Legacy CD KTS BX 010	Record Plant, New York, NY	Jimi	John Mc Laughlin / Guitar, Buddy Miles / Drums, Dave Holland / Bass
Driving South / Everything's Gonna Be Alright (Driving South Jam)	25 Mar 69	BR 1. A long jam that begins with 'Driving South' and continues with "Eveything's Gonna Be Alright". This is the complete jam from start to finish.	Every Way To Paradise CD Tintangel TIBX 021 / 22 / 23 / 24	Record Plant, New York, NY	Jimi	John Mc Laughlin / Guitar, Buddy Miles / Drums, Dave Holland / Bass
Drone Blues	24 Apr 69	CR 1. The title 'Drone Blues' is made up.	Nine To The Universe (CR) LP Reprise HS2299	Record Plant, New York, NY	Jimi	Unknown / Bass, Unknown / Drums
Drone Blues	24 Apr 69	CR 1. The title 'Drone Blues' is made up.	Message From Nine To The Universe CD Oil Well 122	Record Plant, New York, NY	Jimi	Unknown / Bass, Unknown / Drums
Drone Blues	24 Apr 69	BR 1. The complete version of the CR. The title 'Drone Blues' is made up.	Drone Blues CD Great Dane GDR SAT 2	Record Plant, New York, NY	Jimi	Unknown / Bass, Unknown / Drums
Drone Blues	24 Apr 69	BR 1. The complete version of the CR. The title 'Drone Blues' is made up.	Shine On Earth, Shine On CD Sidewalk SW 89010 / 89011	Record Plant, New York, NY	Jimi	Unknown / Bass, Unknown / Drums
Drone Blues	24 Apr 69	BR 1. The complete version of the CR. The title 'Drone Blues' is made up.	Let's Drop Some Ludes And Vomit With Jimi CD Midnight Beat MBCD 026	Record Plant, New York, NY	BOG	
Drone Blues	24 Apr 69	BR 1. The complete version of the CR. The title 'Drone Blues' is made up.	Let's Drop Some Ludes And Vomit With Jimi CD Midnight Beat MBCD 026	Record Plant, New York, NY	BOG	

Song	Date	Notes	Release	Studio	Group	Personnel
Drone Blues (Electric Indians)	24 Apr 69	BR 1. The complete version of the CR. The title 'Drone Blues' is made up.	Voodoo Blues CD Smurf	Record Plant, New York, NY	Jimi	Unknown / Bass, Unknown / Drums
Drone Blues (Doin' Germ)	24 Apr 69	BR 1. The complete version of the CR. The title 'Drone Blues' is made up.	McLaughlin Sessions, The CD HML CD 9409	Record Plant, New York, NY	Jimi	Unknown / Bass, Unknown / Drums
Drone Blues (Electric Indians)	24 Apr 69	BR 1. The complete version of the CR. The title 'Drone Blues' is made up.	Every Way To Paradise CD Tintangel TIBX 021 / 22 / 23 / 24	Record Plant, New York, NY	Jimi	Unknown / Bass, Unknown / Drums
Drone Blues (Bridge To Nowhere)	24 Apr 69	BR 1. The complete version of the CR. The title 'Drone Blues' is made up. Incomplete.	Redskin' Jammin' CD JH 01 / 02	Record Plant, New York, NY	Jimi	Unknown / Bass, Unknown / Drums
Drone Blues	24 Apr 69	BR 1. The complete version of the CR. The title 'Drone Blues' is made up. Incomplete.	Cherokee Mist CD Triangle PYCD 070	Record Plant, New York, NY	Jimi	Unknown / Bass, Unknown / Drums
Drum Solo	03 May 69	Live performance. Listed here as it's given a track listing on the CD.	Hendrix, Busted In Toronto CD Venue VE 100502	Maple Leaf Gardens, Toronto, Canada	JHE	
Earth Blues (We Don't Know What To Play)	07 May 69	BR 1. Part of a longer jam, this is loosely arranged around the basic chord progression that would become 'Earth Blues'. Incomplete	Things I Used To Do CD The Early Years 02-CD-3334	Record Plant, New York, NY	Jimi	Johnny Winter / Slide Guitar, Stephen Stills / Bass, Dallas Taylor / Drums
Earth Blues	?? Sep 69	CR 2. Not immediately recognizable but the chord progression is there for 'Earth Blues'. Another song from the mediocre sessions with Mike Ephron.	Jimi Hendrix At His Best Vol 1 (CR) LP Sagapan 6313	Shokan House, Woodstock. NY	Jimi	Mike Ephron / Keyboards, Jerry Velez & Juma Sultan / Percussion
Earth Blues	19 Dec 69	CR 1 mix 1. This is one of the songs worked on during Jimi's last studio session before his death.	Rainbow Bridge (CR) LP Reprise K44159	Record Plant, New York, NY	BOG	Juma Sultan / Percussion, The Ronnettes / Backing Vocals, Mitch Mitchell / Drums, Overdubbed On 1 / 20 / 70
Earth Blues	19 Dec 69	CR 1 mix 1. This is one of the songs worked on during Jimi's last studio session before his death.	Rainbow Bridge & More CD	Record Plant, New York, NY	BOG	Juma Sultan / Percussion, The Ronnettes / Backing Vocals, Mitch Mitchell / Drums, Overdubbed On 1 / 20 / 70
Earth Blues	19 Dec 69	CR 1 mix 1. This is one of the songs worked on during Jimi's last studio session before his death.	Jewel Box CD Home HR-5824-3	Record Plant, New York, NY	BOG	Juma Sultan / Percussion, The Ronnettes / Backing Vocals, Mitch Mitchell / Drums, Overdubbed On 1 / 20 / 70
Earth Blues	19 Dec 69	CR 1 mix 1. This is one of the songs worked on during Jimi's last studio session before his death.	First Rays Of The New Rising Sun CD Triangle PYCD 084-2	Record Plant, New York, NY	BOG	Juma Sultan / Percussion, The Ronnettes / Backing Vocals, Mitch Mitchell / Drums, Overdubbed On 1 / 20 / 70

SONG TITLE	DATE	COMMENTS	RELEASE	LOCATION / VENUE	BAND	PERSONNEL
Earth Blues	19 Dec 69	CR 1 mix 1. This is one of the songs worked on during Jimi's last studio session before his death.	Rainbow Bridge 2 CD JMH 003 / 2	Record Plant, New York, NY	BOG	Juma Sultan / Percussion, The Ronnettes / Backing Vocals, Mitch Mitchell / Drums, Overdubbed On 1 / 20 / 70
Earth Blues	19 Dec 69	CR 1 mix 2. This version has some extra guitar in the mix.	Studio Haze CD INA 6	Record Plant, New York, NY	BOG	Juma Sultan / Percussion, The Ronnettes / Backing Vocals, Mitch Mitchell / Drums, Overdubbed On 1 / 20 / 70
Earth Blues	19 Dec 69	CR 1 mix 2. This version has some extra guitar in the mix.	Multicolored Blues CD Luna LU 9317	Record Plant, New York, NY	BOG	Juma Sultan / Percussion, The Ronnettes / Backing Vocals, Mitch Mitchell / Drums, Overdubbed On 1 / 20 / 70
Earth Blues	19 Dec 69	CR 1 mix 2. This version has some extra guitar in the mix.	First Rays - The Sessions CD Whoopy Cat WKP 0002	Record Plant, New York, NY	BOG	Juma Sultan / Percussion, The Ronnettes / Backing Vocals, Mitch Mitchell / Drums, Overdubbed On 1 / 20 / 70
Earth Blues	19 Dec 69	CR 1 mix 2. This version has some extra guitar in the mix.	Notes In Colours CD JHR 001 / 002	Record Plant, New York, NY	BOG	Juma Sultan / Percussion, The Ronnettes / Backing Vocals, Mitch Mitchell / Drums, Overdubbed On 1 / 20 / 70
Earth Blues	19 Dec 69	CR 1 mix 2. This version has some extra guitar in the mix.	Gypsy Charm CD Mum MUCD 018	Record Plant, New York, NY	BOG	Juma Sultan / Percussion, The Ronnettes / Backing Vocals, Mitch Mitchell / Drums, Overdubbed On 1 / 20 / 70
Earth Blues	19 Dec 69	CR 1 mix 2. This version has some extra guitar in the mix.	Eyes And Imagination CD Third Stone TSD 18970	Record Plant, New York, NY	BOG	
Earth Blues	18-22 Dec 69	BR 2. From the rehearsals for the New York Fillmore shows.	Band Of Gypsys Rehearsals CD Whoopy Cat WKP 003	Baggies, New York, NY	BOG	
Earth Blues	18-22 Dec 69	BR 2. From the rehearsals for the New York Fillmore shows.	Gypsy Haze CD Lords Of Archive LAR 16	Baggies, New York, NY	BOG	
Earth Blues	18-22 Dec 69	BR 2. From the rehearsals for the New York Fillmore shows.	Jimi: A Musical Legacy CD KTS BX 010	Baggies, New York, NY	BOG	
Earth Blues	31 Dec 69	BR 3. Live performance	Official Bootleg Album, The CD Yellow Dog YD 051	Fillmore East, New York, NY 1st Show	BOG	

Song	Date	Notes	Description	Release	Venue	Source
Earth Blues	31 Dec 69	BR 3. Live performance		Band Of Gypsys Happy New Year, Jimi LP Cops & Robbers JTYM 01	Fillmore East, New York, NY 1st Show	BOG
Earth Blues	31 Dec 69	BR 3. Live performance		Band Of Gold CD-R Major Tom MT 087	Fillmore East, New York, NY 1st Show	BOG
Earth Blues	31 Dec 69	BR 3. Live performance		Power Of Soul CD SQ-100.275"	Fillmore East, New York, NY 1st Show	BOG
Earth Blues	01 Jan 70	BR 4. Live performance		Band Of Gold CD-R Major Tom MT 087	Fillmore East, New York, NY 1st Show	BOG
Earth Blues	01 Jan 70	BR 4. Live performance. Incomplete.		Every Way To Paradise CD Tintangel TIBX 021 / 22 / 23 / 24	Fillmore East, New York, NY 1st Show	BOG
Earth Blues	01 Jan 70	BR 5. Live performance. Incomplete.		Ladyland In Flames LP Marshall Records JIMI 1,2,3,4	Fillmore East, New York, NY 2nd Show	BOG
Earth Blues	01 Jan 70	BR 5. Live performance. Incomplete.		Voodoo Blues CD Smurf	Fillmore East, New York, NY 2nd Show	BOG
Earth Blues	01 Jan 70	BR 5. Live performance. Incomplete.		Band Of Gold CD-R Major Tom MT 087	Fillmore East, New York, NY 2nd Show	BOG
Earth Blues	01 Jan 70	BR 5. Live performance. Incomplete.		Band Of Gypsys- The Ultimate CD JMH 010 / 3	Fillmore East, New York, NY 2nd Show	BOG
Earth Blues	28 Jan 70	BR 6. Live performance.		Live At The Forum 1970 CD Whoopy Cat WKP 021 / 22	Madison Square Garden, New York, NY	BOG
Earth Blues	30 May 70	BR 7. Officially released on the videotape and laserdisc.		Berkeley Soundchecks, The CD Whoopy Cat WKP 0008	Berkeley Community Theater, Berkeley, CA	COL
Earth Vs Space	22 Jun 69	Actually a medley featuring portions of "Gypsy Eyes", "Midnight Lightning" and "Machine Gun".		It Never Takes An End CD Genuine Pig TGP-118	Newport Pop Festival, San Fernando State, Northridge, CA	NJK
Earth Vs Space	22 Jun 69	Actually a medley featuring portions of "Gypsy Eyes", "Midnight Lightning" and "Machine Gun".		Live! CD Black B-05	Newport Pop Festival, San Fernando State, Northridge, CA	NJK
Earth Vs Space	22 Jun 69	Actually a medley featuring portions of "Gypsy Eyes", "Midnight Lightning" and "Machine Gun".		Two Days At Newport CD JMH 007 / 2	Newport Pop Festival, San Fernando State, Northridge, CA	NJK

SONG TITLE	DATE	COMMENTS	RELEASE	LOCATION / VENUE	BAND	PERSONNEL
Earth Vs Space	22 Jun 69	Actually a medley featuring portions of "Gypsy Eyes", "Midnight Lightning" and "Machine Gun".	Ultimate Live Collection, The CD The Beat Goes On BGO BX 9307-4	Newport Pop Festival, San Fernando State, Northridge, CA	NJK	
Easy Blues	28 Aug 69	CR 1 mix 1. Larry Lee's guitar solo has been edited out of the original recording.	Nine To The Universe (CR) LP Reprise HS2299	Hit Factory, New York, N.Y	COL	Larry Lee / Guitar, Unknown / Tambourine
Easy Blues	28 Aug 69	CR 1 mix 1. Larry Lee's guitar solo has been edited out of the original recording.	Message From Nine To The Universe CD Oil Well 122	Hit Factory, New York, N.Y	COL	Larry Lee / Guitar, Unknown / Tambourine
Easy Blues	28 Aug 69	CR 1 mix 2. An unused mix with Larry Lee's guitar still missing.	Let's Drop Some Ludes And Vomit With Jimi CD Midnight Beat MBCD 026	Hit Factory, New York, N.Y	COL	Larry Lee / Guitar, Unknown / Tambourine
Easy Blues	28 Aug 69	CR 1 mix 2. An unused mix with Larry Lee's guitar still missing.	Mannish Boy LP Contraband CBM 88	Hit Factory, New York, N.Y	COL	Larry Lee / Guitar, Unknown / Tambourine
Easy Blues	28 Aug 69	CR 1 mix 2. An unused mix with Larry Lee's guitar still missing.	Cherokee Mist CD Triangle PYCD 070	Hit Factory, New York, N.Y	COL	Larry Lee / Guitar, Unknown / Tambourine
Easy Blues (Untitled Jam)	28 Aug 69	CR 1 mix 2. An unused mix with Larry Lee's guitar still missing.	Every Way To Paradise CD Tintangel TIBX 021 / 22 / 23 / 24	Hit Factory, New York, N.Y	COL	Larry Lee / Guitar
Easy Blues	28 Aug 69	CR 1 mix 2. An unused mix with Larry Lee's guitar still missing.	Completer, The CD Whoopy Cat WKP 0018 / 19	Hit Factory, New York, N.Y	COL	Larry Lee / Guitar, Unknown / Tambourine
Easy Blues (Rollin' Em)	28 Aug 69	CR 1 mix 2. An unused mix with Larry Lee's guitar still missing. Incomplete	Things I Used To Do CD The Early Years 02-CD-3334	Record Plant, New York, NY	Jimi	Buddy Miles / Drums
Easy Blues	28 Aug 69	CR 1 mix 2. An unused mix with Larry Lee's guitar still missing. Incomplete	51st Anniversary CD Future Disc JMH 001 / 8	Hit Factory, New York, N.Y	COL	Larry Lee / Guitar, Unknown / Tambourine
Electric Church (Hollywood Jam)	21 Oct 68	BR 1. Incomplete. This version fades in for only the last two minutes, is in poorer quality and is mastered too fast compared to the 'Mixdown Masters' release. Yet it does run slightly past the point where the 'Mixdown Masters' version fades out.	Freak Out Jam CD GH 002	T.T.G. Studios, Hollywood, CA	Jimi	Buddy Miles / Drums, Lee Michaels / Organ
Electric Church (Hear My Freedom)	21 Oct 68	BR 2. The full jam from which the intro was cut and used on the "Electric Church Red House" track.	Mixdown Master Tapes Volume 1 CD Dandelion DL 005	T.T.G. Studios, Hollywood, CA	JHE	Buddy Miles / Drums, Lee Michaels / Organ
Electric Ladyland	?? Jan 68	BR 1. An alternate version from the Sotheby's Tapes. This sounds like its from the same session as CR 2. It starts with Jimi playing solo then the band joins in.	Master's Masters, The CD JH-01	Olympic Sound Studios, London, England	Jimi	Dave Mason / Backing Vocals, Unknown / Drums

Song	Date	Notes	Source	Studio		Credits
Electric Ladyland	?? Jan 68	BR 1. An alternate version from the Sotheby's Tapes. This sounds like its from the same session as CR 2. It starts with Jimi playing solo then the band joins in.	1968 AD Part Two CD Whoopy Cat WKP 0013	Olympic Sound Studios, London, England	Jimi	Dave Mason / Backing Vocals, Unknown / Drums
Electric Ladyland	?? Jan 68	BR 1. An alternate version from the Sotheby's Tapes. This sounds like its from the same session as CR 2. It starts with solo from Jimi then the band joins in.	51st Anniversary CD Future Disc JMH 001 / 8	Olympic Sound Studios, London, England	Jimi	Dave Mason / Backing Vocals, Unknown / Drums
Electric Ladyland	?? Jan 68	BR 1. An alternate version from the Sotheby's Tapes. This sounds like its from the same session as CR 2. It starts with Jimi playing solo then the band joins in.	Midnight Shines Down CD Blue Kangaroo BK 04	Olympic Sound Studios, London, England	Jimi	Dave Mason / Backing Vocals, Unknown / Drums
Electric Ladyland	?? Jan 68	BR 1. An alternate version from the Sotheby's Tapes. This sounds like its from the same session as CR 2. It starts with Jimi playing solo then the band joins in.	Sotheby's Private Reels CD JHR 003 / 004	Olympic Sound Studios, London, England	Jimi	Dave Mason / Backing Vocals, Unknown / Drums
Electric Ladyland	?? Jan 68	BR 1. An alternate version from the Sotheby's Tapes. This sounds like its from the same session as CR 2. It starts with Jimi playing solo then the band joins in.	Sotheby's Private Reels CD JHR 003 / 004	Olympic Sound Studios, London, England	Jimi	Dave Mason / Backing Vocals, Unknown / Drums
Electric Ladyland	?? Jan 68	BR 1. An alternate version from the Sotheby's Tapes. This sounds like its from the same session as CR 2. It starts with Jimi playing solo then the band joins in.	Living Reels Vol 2 CD JMH 012 / 2	Olympic Sound Studios, London, England	Jimi	Dave Mason / Backing Vocals, Unknown / Drums
Electric Ladyland	?? Jan 68	BR 2. An alternate version from the Sotheby's Tapes. This sounds like its from the same session as CR 2. This has the whole band playing right from the start.	1968 AD Part Two CD Whoopy Cat WKP 0013	Olympic Sound Studios, London, England	Jimi	Dave Mason / Backing Vocals, Unknown / Drums
Electric Ladyland	?? Jan 68	BR 2. An alternate version from the Sotheby's Tapes. This sounds like its from the same session as CR 2. This has the whole band playing right from the start.	Sotheby Auction Tapes, The CD Midnight Beat MBCD 010	Olympic Sound Studios, London, England	Jimi	Dave Mason / Backing Vocals, Unknown / Drums
Electric Ladyland	?? Jan 68	BR 2. An alternate version from the Sotheby's Tapes. This sounds like its from the same session as CR 2. This has then whole band playing right from the start.	51st Anniversary CD Future Disc JMH 001 / 8	Olympic Sound Studios, London, England	Jimi	Dave Mason / Backing Vocals, Unknown / Drums
Electric Ladyland	?? Jan 68	BR 2. An alternate version from the Sotheby's Tapes. This sounds like its from the same session as CR 2. This has the whole band playing right from the start.	Lost Experience, The, CD JHCD203	Olympic Sound Studios, London, England	Jimi	Dave Mason / Backing Vocals, Unknown / Drums
Electric Ladyland	?? Jan 68	BR 2. An alternate version from the Sotheby's Tapes. This sounds like its from the same session as CR 2. This has the whole band playing right from the start.	Sotheby's Private Reels CD JHR 003 / 004	Olympic Sound Studios, London, England	Jimi	Dave Mason / Backing Vocals, Unknown / Drums
Electric Ladyland	?? Jan 68	BR 2. An alternate version from the Sotheby's Tapes. This sounds like its from the same session as CR 2. This has the whole band playing right from the start.	Sotheby's Private Reels CD JHR 003 / 004	Olympic Sound Studios, London, England	Jimi	Dave Mason / Backing Vocals, Unknown / Drums
Electric Ladyland	?? Jan 68	BR 2. An alternate version from the Sotheby's Tapes. This sounds like its from the same session as CR 2. This has the whole band playing right from the start.	Electric Ladyland Outtakes CD Invasion Unlimited IU 9417-1	Olympic Sound Studios, London, England	Jimi	Dave Mason / Backing Vocals, Unknown / Drums
Electric Ladyland	?? Jan 68	BR 2. An alternate version from the Sotheby's Tapes. This sounds like its from the same session as CR 2. This has the whole band playing right from the start.	Voodoo In Ladyland CD MUM MUCD 006	Olympic Sound Studios, London, England	Jimi	Dave Mason / Backing Vocals, Unknown / Drums

SONG TITLE	DATE	COMMENTS	RELEASE	LOCATION / VENUE	BAND	PERSONNEL
Electric Ladyland	?? Jan /8	CR 2.	Loose Ends (CR) LP Polydor 837574-2	Olympic Sound Studios, London, England	Jimi	Jimi Hendrix / Bass, Mitch Mitchell / Drums
Electric Ladyland	?? Jan /8	CR 2.	Rarities On Compact Disc CD On The Radio	Olympic Sound Studios, London, England	Jimi	Jimi Hendrix / Bass, Mitch Mitchell / Drums
Electric Ladyland	?? Jan /8	CR 2.	Jimi: A Musical Legacy CD KTS BX 010	Olympic Sound Studios, London, England	Jimi	Jimi Hendrix / Bass, Mitch Mitchell / Drums
Electric Ladyland	?? Jan /8	CR 2. Incomplete.	I Don't Live Today CD ACL 007	Olympic Sound Studios, London, England	Jimi	Jimi Hendrix / Bass, Mitch Mitchell / Drums
Electric Ladyland	?? May 68	CR 1.	Electric Ladyland (CR) CD MCACD-11600	Record Plant, New York, NY	Jimi	Jimi Hendrix / Bass, Mitch Mitchell / Drums
Electric Ladyland	?? May 68	CR 1.	Legacy (CR) LP Polydor	Record Plant, New York, NY	Jimi	Jimi Hendrix / Bass, Mitch Mitchell / Drums
Everything's Gonna Be Alright	?? Mar 68	CR 1.Part of a medley usually listed as 'Woke Up This Morning And Found Myself Dead' on all of the Scene Club releases.	Woke Up This Morning And Found Myself Dead (CR) LP Red Lightning 0068	Scene Club, New York, NY	Scene	
Everything's Gonna Be Alright	17 Mar 68	BR 1. Live performance. All sources fade early.	Drone Blues CD Great Dane GDR SAT 2	Cafe A Go Go, New York, NY	Cafe	
Everything's Gonna Be Alright	17 Mar 68	BR 1. Live performance. All sources fade early.	Shine On Earth, Shine On CD Sidewalk SW 89010 / 89011	Cafe A Go Go, New York, NY	Cafe	
Everything's Gonna Be Alright	17 Mar 68	BR 1. Live performance. All sources fade early.	Blues At Midnight CD Midnight Beat MBCD 037	Cafe A Go Go, New York, NY	Cafe	
Everything's Gonna Be Alright	17 Mar 68	BR 1. Live performance. All sources fade early.	A Lifetime Of Experience LP Sleepy Dragon 55 10	Cafe A Go Go, New York, NY	Cafe	
Everything's Gonna Be Alright	17 Mar 68	BR 1. Live performance. All sources fade early.	Cafe Au Go Go CD Koine 880802	Cafe A Go Go, New York, NY	Cafe	
Everything's Gonna Be Alright	17 Mar 68	BR 1. Live performance. All sources fade early.	Live USA CD Imtrat 902-001	Cafe A Go Go, New York, NY	Cafe	
Everything's Gonna Be Alright (Rock Baby)	17 Mar 68	BR 1. Live performance. All sources fade early.	Living Reels Vol 2 CD JMH 012 / 2	Cafe A Go Go, New York, NY	Cafe	
Everything's Gonna Be Alright	18-20? Oct 68	BR 2. This could be from the same sessions that produced the "Piano Roll" jams.	Ball And Chain CD Jimi 009	T.T.G. Studios?, Hollywood, CA	Jimi	Mitch Mitchell / Drums

Song	Date	Description	Release	Location	Jimi	Buddy Miles / Drums
Everything's Gonna Be Alright (Driving South)	25 Mar 69	BR 3. This is the last half of a jam that begins with "Driving South / Everything's Gonna Be Alright" (See "Driving South / Everything's Gonna Be Alright")	Diamonds In The Dust CD Midnight Beat MBCD 022 / 23	Record Plant, New York, NY		
Exp	05 May 67	CR 1 mix 1.	Axis: Bold As Love (CR) CD MCACD 11601	Olympic Sound Studios, London, England	JHE	
Exp	05 May 67	CR 1 mix 2. (mono)	Axis: Bold As Love (CR) LP Track 612 003	Olympic Sound Studios, London, England	JHE	
Exp	05 May 67	CR 1 mix 3. An unused mix from the Sotheby's Tapes.	51st Anniversary CD Future Disc JMH 001 / 8	Olympic Sound Studios, London, England	JHE	
Exp	05 May 67	CR 1 mix 3. An unused mix from the Sotheby's Tapes.	Sotheby's Private Reels CD JHR 003 / 004	Olympic Sound Studios, London, England	JHE	
Exp	05 May 67	CR 1 mix 3. An unused mix from the Sotheby's Tapes.	Jimi: A Musical Legacy CD KTS BX 010	Olympic Sound Studios, London, England	JHE	
Exp	05 May 67	CR 1 mix 3. An unused mix from the Sotheby's Tapes.	Sotheby's Reels, The CD Gold Standard TOM-800	Olympic Sound Studios, London, England	JHE	
Exp	05 May 67	CR 1 mix 3. An unused mix from the Sotheby's Tapes.	Living Reels Vol 1 CD JMH 011	Olympic Sound Studios, London, England	JHE	
Exp	08 Jan 68	CR 2. Live performance.	Live In Paris 66 / 67 CD Whoopy Cat WKP 0012	Konserthuset, Stockholm, Sweden	JHE	
Exp	08 Jan 68	CR 2. Live performance.	Lost In Sweden CD Whoopy Cat WKP 0046 / 0047	Konserthuset, Stockholm, Sweden	JHE	
Exp	08 Jan 68	CR 2. Live performance.	EXP Over Sweden (CR) CD UniVibes 1002	Konserthuset, Stockholm, Sweden 1st Show	Jimi	Mitch Mitchell / Voice Of Announcer
Express Horns Jam	22 Jun 69	Live performance of a jam with parts of "Sunshine of Your Love", "Star Spangled Banner", and "Come On".	Two Days At Newport CD JMH 007 / 2	Newport Pop Festival, San Fernando State, Northridge, CA	NJK	
Ezy Rider	?? Dec 69	BR 1. This is the first rehearsal of the song from Baggies.	Sir James Marshall LP Jester Productions JP 106	Baggies, New York, NY	BOG	
Ezy Rider	?? Dec 69	BR 1. This is the first rehearsal of the song from Baggies.	This One's For You LP Veteran Music MF-243	Baggies, New York, NY	BOG	

SONG TITLE	DATE	COMMENTS	RELEASE	LOCATION / VENUE	BAND	PERSONNEL
Ezy Rider	?? Dec 69	BR 1. This is the first rehearsal of the song from Baggies.	Band Of Gypsys Rehearsals CD Whoopy Cat WKP 003	Baggies, New York, NY	BOG	
Ezy Rider	?? Dec 69	BR 1. This is the first rehearsal of the song from Baggies.	Redskin' Jammin' CD JH 01 / 02	Baggies, New York, NY	BOG	
Ezy Rider	?? Dec 69	BR 1. This is the first rehearsal of the song from Baggies.	Talent And Feeling Vol 1 CD Extremely Rare EXR 17	Baggies, New York, NY	BOG	
Ezy Rider	?? Dec 69	BR 2. The second attempt at Baggies from a session later than BR 1.	Band Of Gypsys Vol 3	Baggies, New York, NY	BOG	
Ezy Rider	?? Dec 69	BR 2. The second attempt at Baggies from a session later than BR 1.	Band Of Gypsys Rehearsals CD Whoopy Cat WKP 003	Baggies, New York, NY	BOG	
Ezy Rider	?? Dec 69	BR 2. The second attempt at Baggies from a session later than BR 1.	Gypsy Haze CD Lords Of Archive LAR 16	Baggies, New York, NY	BOG	
Ezy Rider	?? Dec 69	BR 2. The second attempt at Baggies from a session later than BR 1.	Rainbow Bridge 2 CD JMH 003 / 2	Baggies, New York, NY	BOG	
Ezy Rider	?? Dec 69	BR 2. The second attempt at Baggies from a session later than BR 1.	Band Of Gypsys- The Ultimate CD JMH 010 / 3	Baggies, New York, NY	BOG	
Ezy Rider	?? Dec 69	BR 3. This is a rough mix of an alternate take with overdubs and can be identified by someone saying "Roger, take it away" at the beginning. This CD features a false start not on other releases.	Studio Haze CD INA 6	Record Plant, New York, NY	BOG	
Ezy Rider	?? Dec 69	BR 3. This is a rough mix of an alternate take with overdubs and can be identified by someone saying "Roger, take it away" at the beginning. This CD features a false start not on other releases.	First Rays - The Sessions CD Whoopy Cat WKP 0002	Record Plant, New York, NY	BOG	
Ezy Rider	?? Dec 69	BR 3. This is a rough mix of an alternate take with overdubs and can be identified by someone saying "Roger, take it away" at the beginning. This CD features a false start not on other releases.	Notes In Colours CD JHR 001 / 002	Record Plant, New York, NY	BOG	
Ezy Rider	?? Dec 69	BR 3. This is a rough mix of an alternate take with overdubs and can be identified by someone saying "Roger, take it away" at the beginning. This CD features a false start not on other releases.	Eyes And Imagination CD Third Stone TSD 18970	Record Plant, New York, NY	BOG	
Ezy Rider	18 Dec 69	CR 1 mix 1.	First Rays Of The New Rising Sun (CR) CD MCACD 11599	Record Plant, New York, NY	BOG	Juma Sultan / Percussion, Steve Winwood / Backing Vocals, Chris Wood / Backing Vocals

Song	Date	Take / Notes	Release	Location	Label	Musicians
Ezy Rider	18 Dec 69	CR 1 mix 1.	Cry Of Love, The (CR) CD Reprise 2034-2	Record Plant, New York, NY	BOG	Juma Sultan / Percussion / Backing Vocals, Steve Winwood / Backing Vocals, Chris Wood / Backing Vocals
Ezy Rider	18 Dec 69	CR 1 mix 2.	Voodoo Soup (CR) CD MCA 11206	Record Plant, New York, NY	BOG	Juma Sultan / Percussion / Backing Vocals, Steve Winwood / Backing Vocals, Chris Wood / Backing Vocals
Ezy Rider	18 Dec 69	CR 1 mix 3. An unused mix.	Studio Haze CD INA 6	Record Plant, New York, NY	BOG	Juma Sultan / Percussion / Backing Vocals, Steve Winwood / Backing Vocals, Chris Wood / Backing Vocals
Ezy Rider	18 Dec 69	CR 1 mix 3. An unused mix.	First Rays - The Sessions CD Whoopy Cat WKP 0002	Record Plant, New York, NY	BOG	Juma Sultan / Percussion / Backing Vocals, Steve Winwood / Backing Vocals, Chris Wood / Backing Vocals
Ezy Rider	31 Dec 69	BR 3. Live performance	Band Of Gold CD-R Major Tom MT 087	Fillmore East, New York, NY 1st Show	BOG	
Ezy Rider	31 Dec 69	BR 3. Live performance	Power Of Soul CD SQ-10	Fillmore East, New York, NY 1st Show	BOG	
Ezy Rider	31 Dec 69	BR 4. Live performance	Auld Lang Syne CD JH 100 03	Fillmore East, New York, NY 2nd Show	BOG	
Ezy Rider	31 Dec 69	BR 4. Live performance	Band Of Gypsys: Happy New Year CD Silver Shadow CD 9103	Fillmore East, New York, NY 2nd Show	BOG	
Ezy Rider	31 Dec 69	BR 4. Live performance	Fillmore Concerts, The CD Whoopy Cat WKP 0006 / 7	Fillmore East, New York, NY 2nd Show	BOG	
Ezy Rider	31 Dec 69	BR 4. Live performance	Band Of Gold CD-R Major Tom MT 087	Fillmore East, New York, NY 2nd Show	BOG	
Ezy Rider	31 Dec 69	BR 4. Live performance	Band Of Gypsys- The Ultimate CD JMH 010 / 3	Fillmore East, New York, NY 2nd Show	BOG	
Ezy Rider	25 Apr 70	BR 5. Live performance	Enjoy Jimi Hendrix LP Rubber Dubber 700-001-01	Los Angeles Forum, Los Angeles, CA	COL	
Ezy Rider	25 Apr 70	BR 5. Live performance	Portrait Of Jimi Hendrix, A LP Catalog # Varies On Dead Wax	Los Angeles Forum, Los Angeles, CA	COL	
Ezy Rider	25 Apr 70	BR 5. Live performance	Live At The Forum 1970 CD Whoopy Cat WKP 021 / 22	Los Angeles Forum, Los Angeles, CA	COL	

SONG TITLE	DATE	COMMENTS	RELEASE	LOCATION / VENUE	BAND	PERSONNEL
Ezy Rider	25 Apr 70	BR 5. Live performance. The Luna disc is from a tape source while the JHCD 528 disc is copied from vinyl.	Scuse Me While I Kiss The Sky CD Luna CD & JHCD 528	Los Angeles Forum, Los Angeles, CA	COL	
Ezy Rider	30 May 70	CR 2. Live performance.	Riots In Berkeley CD Beech Marten BM 038	Berkeley Community Theater, Berkeley, CA 1st Show	COL	
Ezy Rider	30 May 70	CR 2. Live performance.	Good Karma 2 LP Berkeley 2023	Berkeley Community Theater, Berkeley, CA 1st Show	COL	
Ezy Rider	30 May 70	CR 2. Live performance.	Band Of Gypsys Vol 2 (CR) LP Capitol SJ 12416	Berkeley Community Theater, Berkeley, CA 1st Show	COL	
Ezy Rider	30 May 70	CR 2. Live performance.	51st Anniversary CD Future Disc JMH 001 / 8	Berkeley Community Theater, Berkeley, CA 1st Show	COL	
Ezy Rider	30 May 70	CR 2. Live performance.	Midnight Magic CD Neutral Zone NZCD 89012	Berkeley Community Theater, Berkeley, CA 1st Show	COL	
Ezy Rider	30 May 70	CR 2. Live performance.	Berkeley Concert LP Audifon AF 008	Berkeley Community Theater, Berkeley, CA 1st Show	COL	
Ezy Rider	30 May 70	CR 2. Live performance.	Berkeley Concerts, The CD Whoopy Cat WKP 004 / 5	Berkeley Community Theater, Berkeley, CA 1st Show	COL	
Ezy Rider	30 May 70	CR 2. Live performance.	Jimi Plays Berkeley CD JMH 005 / 2	Berkeley Community Theater, Berkeley, CA 1st Show	COL	
Ezy Rider	30 May 70	CR 2. Live performance.	Ultimate Live Collection, The CD The Beat Goes On BGO BX 9307-4	Berkeley Community Theater, Berkeley, CA 1st Show	COL	
Ezy Rider	13 Jun 70	BR 6. Live performance	Baltimore Civic Center, June 13, 1970 CD Starquake SQ-09	Baltimore Civic Center, Baltimore, MD	COL	
Ezy Rider	17 Jul 70	BR 7. Live performance	Can You Here Me LP Hemero 01 / KERI	New York Pop-Downing Stadium, Randalls Island, NY	COL	
Ezy Rider	17 Jul 70	BR 7. Live performance	Live At Randall's Island LP Moon Tree Records PH1962	New York Pop-Downing Stadium, Randalls Island, NY	COL	
Ezy Rider	17 Jul 70	BR 7. Live performance	Live USA CD Imtrat	New York Pop-	COL	

Song	Date	BR	Release	Venue	Format
			902-001	Downing Stadium, Randalls Island, NY	
Ezy Rider	30 Jul 70	BR 8. Live performance	Maui, Hawaii LP JH 106 (Trademark Of Quality?)	Rainbow Bridge Vibratory Sound-Color Experiment, Maui, HI 2nd Show	COL
Ezy Rider	30 Jul 70	BR 8. Live performance	Last American Concert Vol 2 CD The Swingin' Pig TSP-072	Rainbow Bridge Vibratory Sound-Color Experiment, Maui, HI 2nd Show	COL
Ezy Rider	30 Jul 70	BR 8. Live performance	Last American Concert- Alive And Flowing From... LP Jupiter 444	Rainbow Bridge Vibratory Sound-Color Experiment, Maui, HI 2nd Show	COL
Ezy Rider	30 Jul 70	BR 8. Live performance	In From The Storm CD Silver Rarities SIRA 109 / 110	Rainbow Bridge Vibratory Sound-Color Experiment, Maui, HI 2nd Show	COL
Ezy Rider	30 Jul 70	BR 8. Live performance	Rainbow Bridge 2 CD JMH 003 / 2	Rainbow Bridge Vibratory Sound-Color Experiment, Maui, HI 1st Show	COL
Ezy Rider	30 Aug 70	BR 9. Live performance	Island Man CD Silver Rarities SIRA 39 / 40	Isle Of Wight Festival, Isle Of Wight, England	COL
Ezy Rider	30 Aug 70	BR 9. Live performance	Berkeley Soundchecks, The CD Whoopy Cat WKP 0008	Isle Of Wight Festival, Isle Of Wight, England	COL
Ezy Rider	30 Aug 70	BR 9. Live performance	Wight CD JMH 006 / 2	Isle Of Wight Festival, Isle Of Wight, England	COL
Ezy Rider	31 Aug 70	BR 10. Live performance	Come On Stockholm CD No Label	Stora Scenen, Grona Lund, Stockholm, Sweden	COL
Ezy Rider	31 Aug 70	BR 10. Live performance	Free Concert CD Midnight Beat MBCD 013	Stora Scenen, Tivoli Garden, Stockholm, Sweden	COL
Ezy Rider	03 Sep 70	BR 11. Live performance	Welcome To The Electric Circus Vol 2 CD Midnight Beat 018	K.B. Hallen, Copenhagen, Denmark	COL
Ezy Rider	03 Sep 70	BR 11. Live performance	Copenhagen '70 CD Whoopy Cat WKP 044 / 45	K.B. Hallen, Copenhagen, Denmark	COL

SONG TITLE	DATE	COMMENTS	RELEASE	LOCATION / VENUE	BAND	PERSONNEL
Ezy Rider	04 Sep 70	BR 12 Live performance	Back To Berlin CD Midnight Beat 049	Deutsche- Landhalle, Berlin, Germany	COL	
Ezy Rider	06 Sep 70	BR 13. Live performance	Love & Peace CD Midnight Beat MBCD 015	Love And Peace Festival, Isle Of Fehrman, Germany	COL	
Ezy Rider	06 Sep 70	BR 13. Live performance	Wink Of An Eye CD Whoopy Cat WKP 0033 / 34	Love And Peace Festival, Isle Of Fehrman, Germany	COL	
Ezy Rider Instrumental Jam (Instrumental #3)	?? / ?? / ??	BR 15. An instrumental jam loosely built around a repeating guitar riff from "Ezy Rider". Its hard to say if this precedes "Ezy Rider" or was inspired by it.	TTG Studios ???? CD WHOAMI WAI 015	Unknown But Probably A New York Studio.	Unknown	
Ezy Rider Instrumental Jam (Mushy Name)	?? / ?? / ??	BR 15. An instrumental jam loosely built around a repeating guitar riff from "Ezy Rider". Its hard to say if this precedes "Ezy Rider" or was inspired by it.	Freak Out Jam CD GH 002	Unknown But Probably A New York Studio.	Unknown	
Ezy Rider Instrumental Jam (Instrumental Jam)	?? / ?? / ??	BR 15. An instrumental jam loosely built around a repeating guitar riff from "Ezy Rider". Its hard to say if this precedes "Ezy Rider" or was inspired by it.	Electric Hendrix Vol 2 CD Pyramid PYCD 031	Unknown But Probably A New York Studio.	Unknown	
Ezy Rider Instrumental Jam	?? / ?? / ??	BR 15. An instrumental jam loosely built around a repeating guitar riff from "Ezy Rider". Its hard to say if this precedes "Ezy Rider" or was inspired by it.	1968 AD CD Whoopy Cat WKP 0001	Unknown But Probably A New York Studio.	Unknown	
Ezy Rider Instrumental Jam	?? / ?? / ??	BR 15. An instrumental jam loosely built around a repeating guitar riff from "Ezy Rider". Its hard to say if this precedes "Ezy Rider" or was inspired by it.	Electric Ladyland Outtakes CD Invasion Unlimited IU 9417-1	Unknown But Probably A New York Studio.	Unknown	
Ezy Rider Instrumental Jam	?? / ?? / ??	BR 15. An instrumental jam loosely built around a repeating guitar riff from "Ezy Rider". Its hard to say if this precedes "Ezy Rider" or was inspired by it.	Every Way To Paradise CD Tintangel TIBX 021 / 22 / 23 / 24	Unknown But Probably A New York Studio.	Unknown	
Ezy Rider Instrumental Jam (Cat Talking To Me)	?? / ?? / ??	BR 15. An instrumental jam loosely built around a repeating guitar riff from "Ezy Rider". Its hard to say if this precedes "Ezy Rider" or was inspired by it.	Voodoo In Ladyland CD MUM MUCD 006	Unknown But Probably A New York Studio.	Unknown	
Ezy Rider Jam (Astro Man Jam)	23 Jan 70	BR 14. This is a long jam that worked its way into a version of "Cherokee Mist". This is the first part only. See "Jam / Cherokee Mist" in this song index for the second part.	Eyes And Imagination CD Third Stone TSD 18970	Record Plant, New York, NY	BOG	Don ? / Harmonica
Ezy Rider Jam (Instrumental Jam)	23 Jan 70	BR 14. This is a long jam that worked its way into a version of "Cherokee Mist". This is the first part only. See "Jam / Cherokee Mist" in this song index for the second part.	Sir James Marshall LP Jester Productions JP 106	Record Plant, New York, NY	BOG	Don ? / Harmonica
Ezy Rider Jam (Heavy Rider)	23 Jan 70	BR 14. This is a long jam that worked its way into a version of "Cherokee Mist". This is the first part only. See "Jam / Cherokee Mist" in this song index for the second part.	51st Anniversary CD Future Disc JMH 001 / 8	Record Plant, New York, NY	BOG	Don ? / Harmonica
Ezy Rider Jam (Instrumental Ezy Rider)	23 Jan 70	BR 14. This is a long jam that worked its way into a version of	Multicolored Blues CD	Record Plant, New	BOG	Don ? / Harmonica

Song	Date	Notes	Release	Location	Source	Personnel
		"Cherokee Mist". This is the first part only. See "Jam / Cherokee Mist" in this song index for the second part.	Luna LU 9317	York, NY		
Ezy Rider Jam (Soul Power)	23 Jan 70	BR 14. This is a long jam that worked its way into a version of "Cherokee Mist". This is the first part only and even though the second part is also on this disc, they are separated. See "Jam / Cherokee Mist" in this song index for the second part.	Redskin Jammin' CD JH 01 / 02	Record Plant, New York, NY	BOG	Don ? / Harmonica
Ezy Rider Jam (Instrumental Jam)	23 Jan 70	BR 14. This is a long jam that worked its way into a version of "Cherokee Mist". This is the first part only. See "Jam / Cherokee Mist" in this song index for the second part.	Electric Gypsy's CD Pilot HJCD 070	Record Plant, New York, NY	BOG	Don ? / Harmonica
Ezy Rider Jam	23 Jan 70	BR 14. This is a long jam that worked its way into a version of "Cherokee Mist". This is the first part only and even though the second part is on this disc they are separated. See "Jam / Cherokee Mist" in this song index for the second part.	Sotheby's Reels, The CD Gold Standard TOM-800	Record Plant, New York, NY	BOG	Don ? / Harmonica
Ezy Rider Jam (Rehearsal Jam)	23 Jan 70	BR 14. This is a long jam that worked its way into a version of "Cherokee Mist". This is the first part only. See "Jam / Cherokee Mist" in this song index for the second part.	Jimi Plays Berkeley CD JMH 005 / 2	Record Plant, New York, NY	BOG	Don ? / Harmonica
Ezy Rider Jam / Cherokee Mist (MLK & Cherokee Mist)	23 Jan 70	BR 14. This is a long jam that worked its way into a version of "Cherokee Mist". This is the complete jam.	Mixdown Master Tapes Volume 3 CD Dandelion DL 007	Record Plant, New York, NY	BOG	Don ? / Harmonica
Ezy Rider Jam / Cherokee Mist	23 Jan 70	BR 14. This is a long jam that worked its way into a version of "Cherokee Mist". This is the complete jam.	Hear My Freedom CD Kobra KRCR 010	Record Plant, New York, NY	BOG	Don ? / Harmonica
F.H.I.T.A.	?? Mar 68	See 'Morrison's Lament'.		Scene Club, New York NY	Scene	
Fire	03 Feb 67	CR 1 mix 1 (stereo).	Are You Experienced? (CR) CD MCACD 11602	Olympic Sound Studios, London, England	JHE	
Fire	03 Feb 67	CR 1 mix 1 (stereo).	The Singles Album (CR) CD Polydor 827 369-2	Olympic Sound Studios, London, England	JHE	
Fire	03 Feb 67	CR 1 mix 1 (stereo).	Smash Hits (CR) CD Reprise 2276-2	Olympic Sound Studios, London, England	JHE	
Fire	03 Feb 67	CR 2 mix 2 (mono).	Legacy (CR) LP Polydor	Olympic Sound Studios, London, England	JHE	
Fire	03 Feb 67	CR 2 mix 2 (mono).	Are You Experienced? (CR) LP Track 612 001	Olympic Sound Studios, London, England	JHE	
Fire	03 Feb 67	CR 1 mix 3. This is the original backing track of the CR prior to vocal overdubs.	Out Of The Studio: Demos From 1967 CD BHCD 931022	Olympic Sound Studios, London, England	JHE	

SONG TITLE	DATE	COMMENTS	RELEASE	LOCATION / VENUE	BAND	PERSONNEL
Fire	03 Feb 67	CR 1 mix 3. This is the original backing track of the CR prior to vocal overdubs.	DeLane Lea And Olympic Outs CD Gold Standard CD-R	Olympic Sound Studios, London, England	JHE	
Fire	03 Feb 67	CR 1 mix 3. This is the original backing track of the CR prior to vocal overdubs.	Get The Experience CD Invasion Unlimited IU 9424-1	Olympic Sound Studios, London, England	JHE	
Fire	03 Feb 67	CR 1 mix 3. This is the original backing track of the CR prior to vocal overdubs.	Complete BBC Session And..., The CD Last Bootleg Records LBR 036 / 2	Olympic Sound Studios, London, England	JHE	
Fire	03 Feb 67	CR 1 mix 3. This is the original backing track of the CR prior to vocal overdubs.	Jimi: A Musical Legacy CD KTS BX 010	Olympic Sound Studios, London, England	JHE	
Fire	03 Feb 67	CR 1 mix 3. This is the original backing track of the CR prior to vocal overdubs.	Magic Hand CD Mum MUCD 012	Olympic Sound Studios, London, England	JHE	
Fire	03 Feb 67	CR 1 mix 3. This is the original backing track of the CR prior to vocal overdubs.	Olympic Gold Vol 1 CD Blimp 0067	Olympic Sound Studios, London, England	JHE	
Fire	03 Feb 67	BR 1. Alternate instrumental take #1 from the same session as the CR 1. Breakdown.	Olympic Gold Vol 1 CD Blimp 0067	Olympic Sound Studios, London, England	JHE	
Fire	03 Feb 67	BR 2. Alternate instrumental take #2 from the same session as the CR 1. Breakdown.	Olympic Gold Vol 1 CD Blimp 0067	Olympic Sound Studios, London, England	JHE	
Fire	03 Feb 67	BR 3. Alternate instrumental take #3 from the same session as the CR 1. Breakdown.	Olympic Gold Vol 1 CD Blimp 0067	Olympic Sound Studios, London, England	JHE	
Fire	03 Feb 67	BR 4. Alternate instrumental take #4 from the same session as the CR 1. Breakdown.	Olympic Gold Vol 1 CD Blimp 0067	Olympic Sound Studios, London, England	JHE	
Fire	03 Feb 67	BR 5. Alternate instrumental take #5 from the same session as the CR this time complete but with an odd gap in the tape after the guitar solo.	Olympic Gold Vol 1 CD Blimp 0067	Olympic Sound Studios, London, England	JHE	
Fire	18 Mar 67	BR 6. Live performance for German radio broadcast.	Legendary Star Club Tapes, The CD The Early Years 02-CD-3309	N D R Radiohouse, Studio 1, Hamburg, Germany	JHE	
Fire	18 Mar 67	BR 6. Live performance for German radio broadcast.	Can You Here Me LP Hemero 01 / KERI	N D R Radiohouse, Studio 1, Hamburg, Germany	JHE	

Song	Date	Notes	Source	Venue	Band
Fire	18 Mar 67	BR 6. Live performance for German radio broadcast.	Tomorrow...Or Just The End Of Time CD Batz 0028	N D R Radiohouse, Studio 1, Hamburg, Germany	JHE
Fire	28 Mar 67	CR 2. Live BBC performance.	Radio One (CR) CD Rykodisc RCD 20078	Saturday Club, BBC Broadcasting House, London, England	JHE
Fire	28 Mar 67	CR 2. Live BBC performance.	BBC Sessions (CR) CD MCACD 2-11742	Saturday Club, BBC Broadcasting House, London, England	JHE
Fire	28 Mar 67	CR 2. Live BBC performance.	Tomorrow...Or Just The End Of Time CD Batz 0028	Saturday Club, BBC Broadcasting House, London, England	JHE
Fire	28 Mar 67	CR 2. Live BBC performance. Incomplete.	Ultimate BBC Collection CD Classical CL006	Saturday Club, BBC Broadcasting House, London, England	JHE
Fire	28 Mar 67	CR 2. Live BBC performance. Incomplete.	Complete BBC Session And..., The CD Last Bootleg Records LBR 036 / 2	Saturday Club, BBC Broadcasting House, London, England	JHE
Fire	04 Sep 67	CR 3. Live performance.	EXP Over Sweden (CR) CD UniVibes 1002	Dans In, Grona Lund, Tivoli Garden, Stockholm, Sweden	JHE
Fire	05 Sep 67	CR 4. Live BBC performance.	Live In Stockholm 1967 CD Document DR 003	Studio 4, Radiohuset, Stockholm, Sweden	JHE
Fire	05 Sep 67	CR 4. Live BBC performance.	Wild Man Of Pop Plays Vol 1, The CD Pyramid RFTCD 003	Studio 4, Radiohuset, Stockholm, Sweden	JHE
Fire	05 Sep 67	CR 4. Live BBC performance.	Stages Stockholm 67 (CR) CD Reprise 9 27632-2	Studio 4, Radiohuset, Stockholm, Sweden	JHE
Fire	05 Sep 67	CR 4. Live BBC performance.	Recorded Live In Europe CD Bulldog BGCD 023	Studio 4, Radiohuset, Stockholm, Sweden	JHE
Fire	05 Sep 67	CR 4. Live BBC performance.	Two Sides Of The Same Genius LP Amazing Kornyphone TAKRL H677	Studio 4, Radiohuset, Stockholm, Sweden	JHE
Fire	05 Sep 67	CR 4. Live BBC performance.	Fire CD The Entertainers CD297	Studio 4, Radiohuset, Stockholm, Sweden	JHE
Fire	05 Sep 67	CR 4. Live BBC performance.	In Europe 67 / 68 / 69 CD Vulture CD 009 / 2	Studio 4, Radiohuset, Stockholm, Sweden	JHE

SONG TITLE	DATE	COMMENTS	RELEASE	LOCATION / VENUE	BAND	PERSONNEL
Fire	05 Sep 67	CR 4. Live BBC performance.	Jimi Hendrix Experience CD Rockstars In Concert 6127092	Studio 4, Radiohuset, Stockholm, Sweden	JHE	
Fire	05 Sep 67	CR 4. Live BBC performance.	Jimi Hendrix CD Flute FLCD 2008	Studio 4, Radiohuset, Stockholm, Sweden	JHE	
Fire	05 Sep 67	CR 4. Live BBC performance.	Loaded Guitar LP Starlight SL 87013	Studio 4, Radiohuset, Stockholm, Sweden	JHE	
Fire	05 Sep 67	CR 4. Live BBC performance.	Greatest Hits Live CD Chartbusters CHER 089A	Studio 4, Radiohuset, Stockholm, Sweden	JHE	
Fire	11 Sep 67	BR 7. Live performance.	Lost In Sweden CD Whoopy Cat WKP 0046 / 0047	Stora Scenen, Grona Lund, Stockholm, Sweden	JHE	
Fire	07 Jan 68	BR 8. Live performance.	Cat's Squirrel CD CS 001 / 2	Tivolis Konsertsal, Copenhagen, Denmark	JHE	
Fire	07 Jan 68	BR 8. Live performance.	Fuckin' His Guitar For Denmark LP Polymore Or JH CO	Tivolis Konsertsal, Copenhagen, Denmark	JHE	
Fire	08 Jan 68	BR 9. Live performance.	Lost In Sweden CD Whoopy Cat WKP 0046 / 0047	Konserthuset, Stockholm, Sweden	JHE	
Fire	29 Jan 68	CR 5. Live performance.	Live In Paris CD Swingin' Pig TSP-016	L' Olympia Theatre, Paris, France 2nd Show	JHE	
Fire	29 Jan 68	CR 5. Live performance.	Stages Paris 68 (CR) CD Reprise 9 27632-2	L' Olympia Theatre, Paris, France 2nd Show	JHE	
Fire	29 Jan 68	CR 5. Live performance.	Once Upon A Time CD Wall Of Sound WS CD011	L' Olympia Theatre, Paris, France 2nd Show	JHE	
Fire	29 Jan 68	CR 5. Live performance.	Recorded Live In Europe CD Bulldog BGCD 023	L' Olympia Theatre, Paris, France 2nd Show	JHE	
Fire	29 Jan 68	CR 5. Live performance.	In Europe 67 / 68 / 69 CD Vulture CD 009 / 2	L' Olympia Theatre, Paris, France 2nd Show	JHE	
Fire	29 Jan 68	CR 5. Live performance.	Live CD DV More CDDV 2401	L' Olympia Theatre, Paris, France 2nd Show	JHE	

Song	Code	Date	Release	Venue	Band
Fire	CR 5. Live performance.	29 Jan 68	In Concert CD Starlife ST 3612	L' Olympia Theatre, Paris, France 2nd Show	JHE
Fire	CR 5. Live performance.	29 Jan 68	Foxy Lady CD Alegra CD 9008	L' Olympia Theatre, Paris, France 2nd Show	JHE
Fire	BR 10. Live performance.	16 Feb 68	Biggest Square In The Building, The CD Reverb Music 1993	State Fair Music Hall, Dallas, TX	JHE
Fire	BR 10. Live performance.	16 Feb 68	Scuse Me While I Kiss The Sky CD Sonic Zoom SZ 1001	State Fair Music Hall, Dallas, TX	JHE
Fire	BR 10. Live performance.	16 Feb 68	Scuse Me While I Kiss The Sky CD Sonic Zoom SZ 1001	State Fair Music Hall, Dallas, TX	JHE
Fire	BR 11. Live performance.	17 Feb 68	Remember The Alamo CD	Will Rogers Auditorium, Fort Worth, T X	JHE
Fire	BR 12. Live performance.	25 Feb 68	Winterland Vol 2 CD Whoopy Cat WKP 00279 / 28	Civic Opera House, Chicago, IL	JHE
Fire	BR 13. Live performance.	19 Mar 68	Thanks Ottawa For The Memories CD Luna 9319	Capitol Theatre, Ottawa, Canada	JHE
Fire	BR 13. Live performance.	19 Mar 68	Canadian Club CD WPOCM 0888 D 006-2	Capitol Theatre, Ottawa, Canada	JHE
Fire	BR 13. Live performance.	19 Mar 68	Live From Ottawa LP Starlight SL 87010	Capitol Theatre, Ottawa, Canada	JHE
Fire	BR 13. Live performance.	19 Mar 68	Superconcert 1968 CD Firepower FP03	Capitol Theatre, Ottawa, Canada	JHE
Fire	BR 14. Live performance.	10 May 68	It's Only A Paper Moon CD Luna 9420	Fillmore East, New York, NY	JHE
Fire	BR 14. Live performance.	10 May 68	One Night Stand CD Hep Cat 101	Fillmore East, New York, NY	JHE
Fire	CR 6. Live performance.	18 May 68	51st Anniversary CD Future Disc JMH 001 / 8	Miami Pop Festival, Hallendale, FL 2nd Show	JHE
Fire	CR 6. Live performance.	18 May 68	1968 AD CD Whoopy Cat WKP 0001	Miami Pop Festival, Hallendale, FL 2nd Show	JHE

SONG TITLE	DATE	COMMENTS	RELEASE	LOCATION / VENUE	BAND	PERSONNEL
Fire	18 May 68	CR 6. Live performance.	Rarities CD The Genuine Pig TGP-CD-091	Miami Pop Festival, Hallendale, FL 2nd Show	JHE	
Fire	18 May 68	CR 6. Live performance.	Calling Long Distance (CR) CD Univibes & Booted On Dynamite DS930055	Miami Pop Festival, Hallendale, FL 2nd Show	JHE	
Fire	18 May 68	CR 6. Live performance.	Living Reels Vol 2 CD JMH 012 / 2	Miami Pop Festival, Hallendale, FL 2nd Show	JHE	
Fire	03 Aug 68	BR 15. Live performance.	Crosstown Traffic CD M25 3664	Moody Coliseum, Southern Methodist University, Dallas, TX	JHE	
Fire	11 Aug 68	BR 16. Live performance.	Davenport, Iowa '68 LP Creative Artistry 26K10 / 55K10	Col Ballroom, Davenport, IA	JHE	
Fire	23 Aug 68	BR 17. Live performance.	Historic Concert CD Midnight Beat MBCD 017	New York Rock Festival, Singer Bowl, Queens, NY	JHE	
Fire	14 Sep 68	BR 18. Live performance.	Live At The Hollywood Bowl LP RSR / International RSR 251	Hollywood Bowl, Los Angeles, CA	JHE	
Fire	11 Oct 68	CR 7 mix 1. Live performance with Herbie Rich's organ part mixed out.	Fire CD The Entertainers CD297	Winterland Theatre, San Francisco, CA 2nd Show	JHE	Herbie Rich / Organ (Mixed Out)
Fire	11 Oct 68	CR 7 mix 1. Live performance with Herbie Rich's organ part mixed out.	Hendrix In Words And Music CD Outlaw Records OTR 1100030	Winterland Theatre, San Francisco, CA 2nd Show	JHE	Herbie Rich / Organ (Mixed Out)
Fire	11 Oct 68	CR 7 mix 1. Live performance with Herbie Rich's organ part mixed out.	Live At Winterland (CR) CD Rykodisc RCD 20038	Winterland Theatre, San Francisco, CA 2nd Show	JHE	Herbie Rich / Organ (Mixed Out)
Fire	11 Oct 68	CR 7 mix 1. Live performance with Herbie Rich's organ part mixed out.	Ultimate Live Collection, The CD The Beat Goes On BGO BX 9307-4	Winterland Theatre, San Francisco, CA 2nd Show	JHE	Herbie Rich / Organ (Mixed Out)
Fire	11 Oct 68	CR 7 mix 2. Live performance with Herbie Rich's organ part intact.	Winterland Days, The CD Manic Depression 001	Winterland Theatre, San Francisco, CA 2nd Show	JHE	Herbie Rich / Organ
Fire	11 Oct 68	CR 7 mix 2. Live performance with Herbie Rich's organ part intact.	Winterland Vol 2 CD Whoopy Cat WKP 00279 / 28	Winterland Theatre, San Francisco, CA 2nd Show	JHE	Herbie Rich / Organ

Song	Date	Notes	CD Release	Venue	Band	Organ
Fire	11 Oct 68	CR 7 mix 2. Live performance with Herbie Rich's organ part intact.	Star Spangled Blues CD Neutral Zone NZCD 89011	Winterland Theatre, San Francisco, CA 2nd Show	JHE	Herbie Rich / Organ
Fire	12 Oct 68	CR 8. Live performance.	Concerts (CR) CD Reprise 9-22306-2	Winterland Theatre, San Francisco, CA 1st Show	JHE	
Fire	12 Oct 68	CR 8. Live performance.	Little Wing CD Oil Well RSC 036	Winterland Theatre, San Francisco, CA 1st Show	JHE	
Fire	12 Oct 68	CR 8. Live performance.	Winterland Vol 3 CD Whoopy Cat WKP 0029 / 30	Winterland Theatre, San Francisco, CA 1st Show	JHE	
Fire	09 Jan 69	BR 19. Live performance.	On The Killing Floor Swingin' Pig TSP-012-2	Konserthuset, Stockholm, Sweden 1st Show	JHE	
Fire	09 Jan 69	BR 19. Live performance.	Electronic Church Music CD Pyramid PYCD 023	Konserthuset, Stockholm, Sweden 1st Show	JHE	
Fire	09 Jan 69	BR 19. Live performance.	In Concert CD Starlife ST 3612	Konserthuset, Stockholm, Sweden 1st Show	JHE	
Fire	09 Jan 69	BR 20. Live performance.	On The Killing Floor Swingin' Pig TSP-012-2	Konserthuset, Stockholm, Sweden 2nd Show	JHE	
Fire	09 Jan 69	BR 20. Live performance.	In Europe 67 / 68 / 69 CD Vulture CD 009 / 2	Konserthuset, Stockholm, Sweden 2nd Show	JHE	
Fire	09 Jan 69	BR 20. Live performance.	Very Best, The CD Irec / Retro MILCD-03	Konserthuset, Stockholm, Sweden 2nd Show	JHE	
Fire	09 Jan 69	BR 20. Live performance.	Valley Of Neptune CD PC 28355	Konserthuset, Stockholm, Sweden 2nd Show	JHE	
Fire	09 Jan 69	BR 20. Live performance.	Anthology CD Box 9	Konserthuset, Stockholm, Sweden 2nd Show	JHE	
Fire	10 Jan 69	BR 21. Live performance.	Welcome To The Electric Circus Vol 1 CD Midnight Beat 016	Falkoner Centret, Copenhagen, Denmark 1st Show	JHE	
Fire	10 Jan 69	BR 22. Live performance.	Jimi In Denmark (CR) CD UniVibes 1003 & Booted On Dynamite Studios	Falkoner Centret, Copenhagen, Denmark 2nd Show	JHE	

SONG TITLE	DATE	COMMENTS	RELEASE	LOCATION / VENUE	BAND	PERSONNEL
Fire	10 Jan 69	BR 22. Live performance.	Live In Copenhagen CD The Swingin' Pig TSP-220-2	Falkoner Centret, Copenhagen, Denmark 2nd Show	JHE	
Fire	10 Jan 69	BR 22. Live performance.	Live In Copenhagen CD The Swingin' Pig TSP-220-2	Falkoner Centret, Copenhagen, Denmark 2nd Show	JHE	
Fire	17 Jan 69	BR 23. Live performance.	Burning At Frankfurt CD Midnight Beat MBCD 040	Jahrhunderthalle, Frankfurt, Germany	JHE	
Fire	23 Jan 69	BR 24. Live performance.	Up Against The Berlin Wall CD Midnight Beat MBCD 046	Sportpalast, Berlin, Germany	JHE	
Fire	18 Feb 69	BR 25. Live performance.	First Night At The Royal Albert Hall CD Midnight Beat MBCD 047 / 48	Royal Albert Hall, London, England	JHE	
Fire	24 Feb 69	CR 9. Live performance.	Last Experience, The (CR) CD Bescol CD 42	Royal Albert Hall, London, England	JHE	
Fire	24 Feb 69	CR 9. Live performance.	King Of Gypsies CD Rockyssimo RK 001	Royal Albert Hall, London, England	JHE	
Fire	24 Feb 69	CR 9. Live performance.	Live! CD Black B-05	Royal Albert Hall, London, England	JHE	
Fire	24 Feb 69	CR 9. Live performance.	Rarities On Compact Disc CD On The Radio	Royal Albert Hall, London, England	JHE	
Fire	24 Feb 69	CR 9. Live performance.	Royal Albert Hall CD Blimp 008 / 009 & Listen To This Eric CD JH 003 / 4	Royal Albert Hall, London, England	JHE	
Fire	24 Feb 69	CR 9. Live performance.	Stone Free CD Silver Rarities SIRA 58 / 59	Royal Albert Hall, London, England	JHE	
Fire	27 Apr 69	BR 26. Live performance.	Live At The Oakland Coliseum (CR) CD Dagger Records DBRO-11743	Oakland Coliseum, Oakland, CA	JHE	
Fire	03 May 69	BR 27. Live performance.	Hendrix, Busted In Toronto CD Venue VE 100502	Maple Leaf Gardens, Toronto, Canada	JHE	
Fire	03 May 69	BR 27. Live performance.	I Don't Live Today CD ACL 007	Maple Leaf Gardens, Toronto, Canada	JHE	

Song	Date	Notes	Release	Venue	Band
Fire	18 May 69	BR 28. Live performance.	Roman Coliseum, The CD Starquake SQ 11	Madison Square Garden, New York, N Y	JHE
Fire	18 May 69	BR 28. Live performance.	Roman Coliseum, The CD Starquake SQ 11	Madison Square Garden, New York, NY	JHE
Fire	24 May 69	CR 10. Live performance.	Stages San Diego 69 (CR) CD Reprise 9 27632-2	San Diego Sports Arena, San Diego, CA	JHE
Fire	24 May 69	CR 10. Live performance.	Midnight Magic CD Neutral Zone NZCD 89012	San Diego Sports Arena, San Diego, CA	JHE
Fire	24 May 69	CR 10. Live performance.	Don't Miss Him This Time CD Pyramid PYCD 096	San Diego Sports Arena, San Diego, CA	JHE
Fire	25 May 69	BR 29. Live performance.	Historic Concert Vol 2 CD Midnight Beat MBCD 050	Santa Clara Pop Festival, San Jose, CA	JHE
Fire	20 Jun 69	BR 29. Live performance.	More Electricity From Newport CD Luna LU 9201	Newport Pop Festival, San Fernando State, Northridge, CA	JHE
Fire	20 Jun 69	BR 29. Live performance.	A Lifetime Of Experience LP Sleepy Dragon 55 10	Newport Pop Festival, San Fernando State, Northridge, CA	JHE
Fire	20 Jun 69	BR 29. Live performance.	Two Days At Newport CD JMH 007 / 2	Newport Pop Festival, San Fernando State, Northridge, CA	JHE
Fire	29 Jun 69	BR 30. Live performance.	Wink Of An Eye CD Whoopy Cat WKP 0033 / 34	Mile High Stadium, Denver, CO	JHE
Fire	18 Aug 69	CR 11. Live performance.	Woodstock Nation CD Wild Bird 89090 1 / 2	Woodstock Music And Art Fair, Bethel, NY	GSRB
Fire	18 Aug 69	CR 11. Live performance.	At Woodstock (CR) Laserdisc BMG BVLP 86	Woodstock Music And Art Fair, Bethel, NY	GSRB
Fire	18 Aug 69	CR 11. Live performance.	Woodstock (CR) CD MCA 11063	Woodstock Music And Art Fair, Bethel, NY	GSRB

SONG TITLE	DATE	COMMENTS	RELEASE	LOCATION / VENUE	BAND	PERSONNEL
Fire	18 Aug 69	CR 11. Live performance.	Gypsy Sun And Rainbows CD Manic Depression MDCD 05 / 06	Woodstock Music And Art Fair, Bethel, NY	GSRB	
Fire	18 Aug 69	CR 11. Live performance.	Woodstock Monday, August 18 1969, 8AM CD JMH 008	Woodstock Music And Art Fair, Bethel, NY	GSRB	
Fire	18 Aug 69	CR 11. Live performance.	Ultimate Live Collection, The CD The Beat Goes On BGO BX 9307-4	Woodstock Music And Art Fair, Bethel, NY	GSRB	
Fire	31 Dec 69	BR 31. Live performance.	Auld Lang Syne CD JH 100 03	Fillmore East, New York, NY 2nd Show	BOG	
Fire	31 Dec 69	BR 31. Live performance.	Band Of Gypsys: Happy New Year CD Silver Shadow CD 9103	Fillmore East, New York, NY 2nd Show	BOG	
Fire	31 Dec 69	BR 31. Live performance.	Fillmore Concerts, The CD Whoopy Cat WKP 0006 / 7	Fillmore East, New York, NY 2nd Show	BOG	
Fire	31 Dec 69	BR 31. Live performance.	Band Of Gold CD-R Major Tom MT 087	Fillmore East, New York, NY 2nd Show	BOG	
Fire	31 Dec 69	BR 31. Live performance.	Band Of Gypsys- The Ultimate CD JMH 010 / 3	Fillmore East, New York, NY 2nd Show	BOG	
Fire	30 May 70	BR 32. Live performance.	Good Karma 1 LP Berkeley 2022	Berkeley Community Theater, Berkeley, CA 1st Show	COL	
Fire	30 May 70	BR 32. Live performance.	Berkeley Concert LP Audifon AF 008	Berkeley Community Theater, Berkeley, CA 1st Show	COL	
Fire	30 May 70	BR 32. Live performance.	Berkeley Concerts, The CD Whoopy Cat WKP 004 / 5	Berkeley Community Theater, Berkeley, CA 1st Show	COL	
Fire	30 May 70	BR 32. Live performance.	Jimi Hendrix CD Imtrat 40-90355	Berkeley Community Theater, Berkeley, CA 1st Show	COL	
Fire	30 May 70	BR 32. Live performance.	Ultimate Live Collection, The CD The Beat Goes On BGO BX 9307-4	Berkeley Community Theater, Berkeley, CA 1st Show	COL	
Fire	04 Jul 70	CR 12. Live performance.	At The Atlanta Pop	2nd International Pop	COL	

Song	Date	Notes	Title	Venue	Label
Fire			Festival (CR) Laserdisc BMG BVLP 77 (74321-10987)	Festival, Atlanta, GA	COL
Fire	04 Jul 70	CR 12. Live performance.	Stages Atlanta 70 (CR) CD Reprise 9 27632-2	2nd International Pop Festival, Atlanta, GA	COL
Fire	04 Jul 70	CR 12. Live performance.	Atlanta CD JMH 009 / 02	2nd International Pop Festival, Atlanta, GA	COL
Fire	04 Jul 70	CR 12. Live performance.	Oh, Atlanta CD Tendolar TDR-009	2nd International Pop Festival, Atlanta, GA	COL
Fire	17 Jul 70	BR 33. Live performance.	Can You Here Me Me LP Hemero 01 / KERI	New York Pop-Downing Stadium, Randalls Island, NY	COL
Fire	17 Jul 70	BR 33. Live performance.	Live At Randall's Island LP Moon Tree Records PH1962	New York Pop-Downing Stadium, Randalls Island, NY	COL
Fire	17 Jul 70	BR 33. Live performance.	Live USA CD Imtrat 902-001	New York Pop-Downing Stadium, Randalls Island, NY	COL
Fire	30 Jul 70	BR 34. Live performance.	Last American Concert Vol 1 CD The Swingin' Pig TSP-062	Rainbow Bridge Vibratory Sound-Color Experiment, Maui, HI 1st Show	COL
Fire	30 Jul 70	BR 34. Live performance.	In From The Storm CD Silver Rarities SIRA 109 / 110	Rainbow Bridge Vibratory Sound-Color Experiment, Maui, HI 1st Show	COL
Fire	30 Jul 70	BR 34. Live performance.	Rainbow Bridge 2 CD JMH 003 / 2	Rainbow Bridge Vibratory Sound-Color Experiment, Maui, HI 1st Show	COL
Fire	03 Sep 70	BR 35. Live performance.	Welcome To The Electric Circus Vol 2 CD Midnight Beat 018	K.B. Hallen, Copenhagen, Denmark	COL
Fire	03 Sep 70	BR 35. Live performance.	Copenhagen '70 CD Whoopy Cat WKP 044 / 45	K.B. Hallen, Copenhagen, Denmark	COL
Fire	03 Feb 67	Outfaked mix of the CR 1.	Sotheby's Private Reels CD JHR 003 / 004	Olympic Sound Studios, London, England	JHE
Fire		Outfaked mix of the CR 1.	Living Reels Vol 1 CD JMH 011		JHE

SONG TITLE	DATE	COMMENTS	RELEASE	LOCATION / VENUE	BAND	PERSONNEL
Flute Instrumental		From the rehearsals at Jimi's Shokan house. No Jimi Participation	Shokan Sunrise CD		No Jimi	
Foxy Lady	13 Dec 66	CR 1 mix 1. (stereo)	Are You Experienced? (CR) CD MCACD 11602	CBS Studios, London, England	JHE	
Foxy Lady	13 Dec 66	CR 1 mix 1. (stereo)	The Singles Album (CR) CD Polydor 827 369-2	CBS Studios, London, England	JHE	
Foxy Lady	13 Dec 66	CR 1 mix 1. (stereo)	Smash Hits (CR) CD Reprise 2276-2	CBS Studios, London, England	JHE	
Foxy Lady	13 Dec 66	CR1 mix 2. (mono)	Legacy (CR) LP Polydor	CBS Studios, London, England	JHE	
Foxy Lady	13 Dec 66	CR1 mix 2. (mono)	Are You Experienced? (CR) LP Track 612 001	CBS Studios, London, England	JHE	
Foxy Lady	13 Feb 67	CR 2. A live BBC performance. This is take one which breaks down and was not broadcast.	Guitar Hero CD Document DR 013	Saturday Club, BBC Broadcasting House, London, England	JHE	
Foxy Lady	13 Feb 67	CR 2. A live BBC performance. This is take one which breaks down and was not broadcast.	Ultimate BBC Collection CD Classical CL006	Saturday Club, BBC Broadcasting House, London, England	JHE	
Foxy Lady	13 Feb 67	CR 2. A live BBC performance. This is take one which breaks down and was not broadcast.	Live In Concert 1967 CD Living Legend LLR-CD 001	Saturday Club, BBC Broadcasting House, London, England	JHE	
Foxy Lady	13 Feb 67	CR 2. A live BBC performance. This is take one which breaks down and was not broadcast.	Complete BBC Session And... The CD Last Bootleg Records LBR 036 / 2	Saturday Club, BBC Broadcasting House, London, England	JHE	
Foxy Lady	13 Feb 67	CR 2. A live BBC performance. This is take one which breaks down and was not broadcast.	BBC Sessions (CR) CD MCACD 2-11742	Saturday Club, BBC Broadcasting House, London, England	JHE	
Foxy Lady	13 Feb 67	CR 3. A live BBC performance. Take two, the broadcast take.	Lifelines (CR) CD Reprise 9 26435-2	Saturday Club, BBC Broadcasting House, London, England	JHE	
Foxy Lady	13 Feb 67	CR 3. A live BBC performance. Take two, the broadcast take.	Primal Keys LP Impossible Record Works	Saturday Club, BBC Broadcasting House, London, England	JHE	
Foxy Lady	13 Feb 67	CR 3. A live BBC performance. Take two, the broadcast take.	Radio One (CR) CD Rykodisc RCD 20078	Saturday Club, BBC Broadcasting House, London, England	JHE	

Song	Date	Notes	Release	Location	Band
Foxy Lady	13 Feb 67	CR 3. A live BBC performance. Take two, the broadcast take.	Jimi Hendrix Vol 2: A Man Of Our Times LP Napoleon NLP 11018	Saturday Club, BBC Broadcasting House, London, England	JHE
Foxy Lady	13 Feb 67	CR 3. A live BBC performance. Take two, the broadcast take.	Live In London 1967 CD Koine Records K881104	Saturday Club, BBC Broadcasting House, London, England	JHE
Foxy Lady	13 Feb 67	CR 3. A live BBC performance. Take two, the broadcast take.	Broadcasts LP Trade Mark Of Quality TMQ 1841 & TMQ 71019	Saturday Club, BBC Broadcasting House, London, England	JHE
Foxy Lady	13 Feb 67	CR 3. A live BBC performance. Take two, the broadcast take.	BBC Sessions (CR) CD MCACD 2-11742	Saturday Club, BBC Broadcasting House, London, England	JHE
Foxy Lady	13 Feb 67	CR 3. A live BBC performance. Take two, the broadcast take.	Tomorrow...Or Just The End Of Time CD Batz 0028	Saturday Club, BBC Broadcasting House, London, England	JHE
Foxy Lady	18 Mar 67	BR 1. Live performance for German radio broadcast.	Legendary Star Club Tapes, The CD The Early Years 02-CD-3309	N D R Radiohouse, Studio 1, Hamburg, Germany	JHE
Foxy Lady	18 Mar 67	BR 1. Live performance for German radio broadcast.	Can You Here Me LP Hemero 01 / KERI	N D R Radiohouse, Studio 1, Hamburg, Germany	JHE
Foxy Lady	18 Mar 67	BR 1. Live performance for German radio broadcast.	Tomorrow...Or Just The End Of Time CD Batz 0028	N D R Radiohouse, Studio 1, Hamburg, Germany	JHE
Foxy Lady	24 May 67	BR 2. Live performance.	Lost In Sweden CD Whoopy Cat WKP 0046 / 0047	Stora Scenen, Grona Lund, Stockholm, Sweden	JHE
Foxy Lady	18 Jun 67	CR 4. Live performance.	Once Upon A Time CD Wall Of Sound WS CD011	Monterey International Pop Festival, Monterey, CA	JHE
Foxy Lady	18 Jun 67	CR 4. Live performance.	Monterey Pop CD Evil 006 1 / 2	Monterey International Pop Festival, Monterey, CA	JHE
Foxy Lady	18 Jun 67	CR 4. Live performance.	Valley Of Neptune CD PC 28355	Monterey International Pop Festival, Monterey, CA	JHE
Foxy Lady	18 Jun 67	CR 4. Live performance.	Jimi Plays Monterey (CR) CD Polydor 827990-2	Monterey International Pop Festival, Monterey, CA	JHE

SONG TITLE	DATE	COMMENTS	RELEASE	LOCATION / VENUE	BAND	PERSONNEL
Foxy Lady	04 Sep 67	CR 5. Live performance.	EXP Over Sweden (CR) CD UniVibes 1002	Dans In, Grona Lund, Tivoli Garden, Stockholm, Sweden	JHE	
Foxy Lady	05 Sep 67	CR 6. Live performance.	Live In Stockholm 1967 CD Document DR 003	Studio 4, Radiohuset, Stockholm, Sweden	JHE	
Foxy Lady	05 Sep 67	CR 6. Live performance.	Wild Man Of Pop Plays Vol 1, The CD Pyramid RFTCD 003	Studio 4, Radiohuset, Stockholm, Sweden	JHE	
Foxy Lady	05 Sep 67	CR 6. Live performance.	Stages Stockholm 67 (CR) CD Reprise 9 27632-2	Studio 4, Radiohuset, Stockholm, Sweden	JHE	
Foxy Lady	05 Sep 67	CR 6. Live performance.	Live At The Hollywood Bowl LP RSR / International RSR 251	Studio 4, Radiohuset, Stockholm, Sweden	JHE	
Foxy Lady	05 Sep 67	CR 6. Live performance.	Recorded Live In Europe CD Bulldog BGCD 023	Studio 4, Radiohuset, Stockholm, Sweden	JHE	
Foxy Lady	05 Sep 67	CR 6. Live performance.	Two Sides Of The Same Genius LP Amazing Kornyphone TAKRL H677	Studio 4, Radiohuset, Stockholm, Sweden	JHE	
Foxy Lady	05 Sep 67	CR 6. Live performance.	Fire CD The Entertainers CD297	Studio 4, Radiohuset, Stockholm, Sweden	JHE	
Foxy Lady	05 Sep 67	CR 6. Live performance.	In Europe 67 / 68 / 69 CD Vulture CD 009 / 2	Studio 4, Radiohuset, Stockholm, Sweden	JHE	
Foxy Lady	05 Sep 67	CR 6. Live performance.	Live CD DV More CDDV 2401	Studio 4, Radiohuset, Stockholm, Sweden	JHE	
Foxy Lady	05 Sep 67	CR 6. Live performance.	Jimi Hendrix Experience CD Rockstars In Concert 6127092	Studio 4, Radiohuset, Stockholm, Sweden	JHE	
Foxy Lady	05 Sep 67	CR 6. Live performance.	Foxy Lady CD Alegra CD 9008	Studio 4, Radiohuset, Stockholm, Sweden	JHE	
Foxy Lady	05 Sep 67	CR 6. Live performance.	Greatest Hits Live CD Chartbusters CHER 089A	Studio 4, Radiohuset, Stockholm, Sweden	JHE	
Foxy Lady	09 Oct 67	BR 3. Live performance.	Wild Man Of Pop Plays Vol 2, The CD Pyramid RFTCD 004	L' Olympia Theatre, Paris, France	JHE	

Song	Date	Notes	Release	Location	Band
Foxy Lady	09 Oct 67	BR 3. Live performance.	Live In Paris 66 / 67 CD Whoopy Cat WKP 0012	L' Olympia Theatre, Paris, France	JHE
Foxy Lady	10 Nov 67	CR 7. Live performance.	Wild Man Of Pop Plays Vol 2, The CD Pyramid RFTCD 004	Hoepla TV Show, Vitus Studio, Bussom, Holland	JHE
Foxy Lady	10 Nov 67	CR 7. Live performance.	51st Anniversary CD Future Disc JMH 001 / 8	Hoepla TV Show, Vitus Studio, Bussom, Holland	JHE
Foxy Lady	10 Nov 67	CR 7. Live performance.	Fire CD The Entertainers CD297	Vitus Studios. Bussom, Holland	JHE
Foxy Lady	10 Nov 67	CR 7. Live performance.	Sweet Angel CD Compact Music WPOCM 0589	Vitus Studios, Bussom, Holland	JHE
Foxy Lady	10 Nov 67	CR 7. Live performance.	Calling Long Distance (CR) CD Univibes & Booted On Dynamite DS930055	Vitus Studios, Bussom, Holland	JHE
Foxy Lady	10 Nov 67	CR 7. Live performance.	Magic Hand CD Mum MUCD 012	Vitus Studios, Bussom, Holland	JHE
Foxy Lady	22 Dec 67	BR 4. Live performance.	Loaded Guitar LP Starlight SL 87013	Olympic Sound Studios, London, England	JHE
Foxy Lady	08 Jan 68	BR 5. Live performance.	Lost In Sweden CD Whoopy Cat WKP 0046 / 0047	Konserthuset, Stockholm, Sweden	JHE
Foxy Lady	29 Jan 68	CR 8. Live performance.	Live In Paris CD Swingin' Pig TSP-016	L' Olympia Theatre, Paris, France 1st Show	JHE
Foxy Lady	29 Jan 68	CR 8. Live performance.	Stages Paris 68 (CR) CD Reprise 9 27632-2	L' Olympia Theatre, Paris, France 1st Show	JHE
Foxy Lady	29 Jan 68	CR 8. Live performance.	Recorded Live In Europe CD Bulldog BGCD 023	L' Olympia Theatre, Paris, France 1st Show	JHE
Foxy Lady	29 Jan 68	CR 8. Live performance.	In Europe 67 / 68 / 69 CD Vulture CD 009 / 2	L' Olympia Theatre, Paris, France 1st Show	JHE
Foxy Lady	29 Jan 68	CR 8. Live performance.	In Concert CD Starlife ST 3612	L' Olympia Theatre, Paris, France 1st Show	JHE

SONG TITLE	DATE	COMMENTS	RELEASE	LOCATION / VENUE	BAND	PERSONNEL
Foxy Lady	16 Feb 68	BR 6. Live performance.	Biggest Square In The Building, The CD Reverb Music 1993	State Fair Music Hall, Dallas, TX	JHE	
Foxy Lady	16 Feb 68	BR 6. Live performance.	Scuse Me While I Kiss The Sky CD Sonic Zoom SZ 1001	State Fair Music Hall, Dallas, TX	JHE	
Foxy Lady	16 Feb 68	BR 6. Live performance.	Scuse Me While I Kiss The Sky CD Sonic Zoom SZ 1001	State Fair Music Hall, Dallas, TX	JHE	
Foxy Lady	17 Feb 68	BR 7. Live performance.	Remember The Alamo CD	Will Rogers Auditorium, Fort Worth, T X	JHE	
Foxy Lady	25 Feb 68	BR 8. Live performance.	Winterland Vol 2 CD Whoopy Cat WKP 00279 / 28	Civic Opera House, Chicago, IL	JHE	
Foxy Lady	19 Mar 68	BR 9. Live performance.	Thanks Ottawa For The Memories CD Luna 9319	Capitol Theatre, Ottawa, Canada	JHE	
Foxy Lady	19 Mar 68	BR 9. Live performance.	Canadian Club CD WPOCM 0888 D 006-2	Capitol Theatre, Ottawa, Canada 2nd Show	JHE	
Foxy Lady	19 Mar 68	BR 9. Live performance.	Live From Ottawa LP Starlight SL 87010	Capitol Theatre, Ottawa, Canada 2nd Show	JHE	
Foxy Lady	19 Mar 68	BR 9. Live performance.	Superconcert 1968 CD Firepower FP03	Capitol Theatre, Ottawa, Canada 2nd Show	JHE	
Foxy Lady	10 May 68	BR 10. Live performance.	It's Only A Paper Moon CD Luna 9420	Fillmore East, New York, NY	JHE	
Foxy Lady	10 May 68	BR 10. Live performance.	One Night Stand CD Hep Cat 101	Fillmore East, New York, NY	JHE	
Foxy Lady	18 May 68	BR 11. Live performance.	1968 AD CD Whoopy Cat WKP 0001	Miami Pop Festival, Hallendale, FL 2nd Show	JHE	
Foxy Lady	03 Aug 68	BR 12. Live performance.	Crosstown Traffic CD M25 3664	Moody Coliseum, Southern Methodist University, Dallas, TX	JHE	
Foxy Lady	11 Aug 68	BR 13. Live performance.	Davenport, Iowa '68 LP Creative Artistry 26K10 / 55K10	Col Ballroom, Davenport, IA	JHE	

Song	Date	Track	Release	Venue	Band
Foxy Lady	23 Aug 68	BR 14. Live performance.	Historic Concert CD Midnight Beat MBCD 017	New York Rock Festival, Singer Bowl, Queens, NY	JHE
Foxy Lady	10 Oct 68	BR 15. Live performance.	Winterland Vol 1 CD Whoopy Cat WKP 025 / 26	Winterland Theatre, San Francisco, CA 1st Show	JHE
Foxy Lady	10 Oct 68	BR 15. Live performance.	Lost Winterland Tapes CD Starquake SQ 051-2	Winterland Theatre, San Francisco, CA 1st Show	JHE
Foxy Lady	11 Oct 68	BR 16. Live performance.	Winterland Days, The CD Manic Depression 001	Winterland Theatre, San Francisco, CA 2nd Show	JHE
Foxy Lady	11 Oct 68	BR 16. Live performance.	Winterland Vol 2 CD Whoopy Cat WKP 00279 / 28	Winterland Theatre, San Francisco, CA 2nd Show	JHE
Foxy Lady	11 Oct 68	BR 16. Live performance.	Broadcasts CD Luna LU 9204	Winterland Theatre, San Francisco, CA 2nd Show	JHE
Foxy Lady	11 Oct 68	BR 16. Live performance.	Star Spangled Blues CD Neutral Zone NZCD 89011	Winterland Theatre, San Francisco, CA 2nd Show	JHE
Foxy Lady	11 Oct 68	CR 9. Live performance.	Fire CD The Entertainers CD297	Winterland Theatre, San Francisco, CA 2nd Show	JHE
Foxy Lady	11 Oct 68	CR 9. Live performance.	Jimi Hendrix CD Imtrat 40-90355	Winterland Theatre, San Francisco, CA 2nd Show	JHE
Foxy Lady	11 Oct 68	CR 9. Live performance.	Live At Winterland (CR) CD Rykodisc RCD 20038	Winterland Theatre, San Francisco, CA 2nd Show	JHE
Foxy Lady	11 Oct 68	CR 9. Live performance.	Ultimate Live Collection, The CD The Beat Goes On BGO BX 9307-4	Winterland Theatre, San Francisco, C A 1st Show	JHE
Foxy Lady	12 Oct 68	BR 17. Live performance.	Winterland Vol 3 CD Whoopy Cat WKP 0029 / 30	Winterland Theatre, San Francisco, CA 1st Show	JHE
Foxy Lady	12 Oct 68	BR 17. Live performance.	Star Spangled Blues CD Neutral Zone NZCD 89011	Winterland Theatre, San Francisco, CA 1st Show	JHE
Foxy Lady	12 Oct 68	BR 18. Live performance.	Winterland Vol 3 CD Whoopy Cat WKP 0029 / 30	Winterland Theatre, San Francisco, CA 2nd Show	JHE

SONG TITLE	DATE	COMMENTS	RELEASE	LOCATION / VENUE	BAND	PERSONNEL
Foxy Lady	12 Oct 68	BR 18. Live performance.	Lost Winterland Tapes CD Starquake SQ 051-2	Winterland Theatre, San Francisco, CA 2nd Show	JHE	
Foxy Lady	08 Jan 69	BR 19. Live performance.	Cat's Squirrel CD CS 001 / 2	Loresberg Cirkus, Goteborg, Sweden 1st Show	JHE	
Foxy Lady	10 Jan 69	BR 20. Live performance.	Welcome To The Electric Circus Vol 1 CD Midnight Beat 016	Falkoner Centret, Copenhagen, Denmark 1st Show	JHE	
Foxy Lady	10 Jan 69	CR 10. Live performance.	Jimi In Denmark (CR) CD UniVibes 1003 & Booted On Dynamite Studios	Falkoner Centret, Copenhagen, Denmark 2nd Show	JHE	
Foxy Lady	10 Jan 69	CR 10. Live performance.	Live In Copenhagen CD The Swingin' Pig TSP-220-2	Falkoner Centret, Copenhagen, Denmark 2nd Show	JHE	
Foxy Lady	17 Jan 69	BR 21. Live performance.	Burning At Frankfurt CD Midnight Beat MBCD 040	Jahrhunderthalle, Frankfurt, Germany	JHE	
Foxy Lady	23 Jan 69	BR 22. Live performance.	Up Against The Berlin Wall CD Midnight Beat MBCD 046	Sportpalast, Berlin, Germany	JHE	
Foxy Lady	18 Feb 69	BR 23. Live performance.	First Night At The Royal Albert Hall CD Midnight Beat MBCD 047 / 48	Royal Albert Hall, London, England	JHE	
Foxy Lady	24 Feb 69	BR 24 mix 1. Live performance. Stereo.	Royal Albert Hall CD Blimp 008 / 009 & Listen To This Eric CD JH 003 / 4	Royal Albert Hall, London, England	JHE	
Foxy Lady	24 Feb 69	BR 24 mix 2. Live performance.	Can You Here Me LP Hemero 01 / KERI	Royal Albert Hall, London, England	JHE	
Foxy Lady	24 Feb 69	BR 24 mix 2. Live performance.	Unforgettable Experience LP RAH 2469	Royal Albert Hall, London, England	JHE	
Foxy Lady	24 Feb 69	BR 24 mix 2. Live performance.	Historic Performances CD Aquarius AQ 67-JH-080	Royal Albert Hall, London, England	JHE	
Foxy Lady	24 Feb 69	BR 24 mix 2. Live performance.	Stone Free CD Silver Rarities SIRA 58 / 59	Royal Albert Hall, London, England	JHE	
Foxy Lady	26 Apr 69	CR 11. Live performance.	Concerts (CR) CD	Los Angeles Forum,	JHE	

Song	Notes	Date	Release	Location	Band
Foxy Lady			Reprise 9-22306-2	Los Angeles, CA	JHE
Foxy Lady	CR 11. Live performance.	26 Apr 69	Electric Jimi CD Jaguarondi Records	Los Angeles Forum, Los Angeles, CA	JHE
Foxy Lady	CR 11. Live performance.	26 Apr 69	I Don't Live Today, Maybe Tomorrow CD Living Legend LRCD 030	Los Angeles Forum, Los Angeles, CA	JHE
Foxy Lady	CR 11. Live performance.	26 Apr 69	Live USA CD Imtrat 902-001	Los Angeles Forum, Los Angeles, CA	JHE
Foxy Lady	CR 11. Live performance.	26 Apr 69	Very Best, The CD Irec / Retro MILCD-03	Los Angeles Forum, Los Angeles, CA	JHE
Foxy Lady	CR 11. Live performance.	26 Apr 69	Hey Joe CD Crocodile Beat CB 53039	Los Angeles Forum, Los Angeles, CA	JHE
Foxy Lady	CR 11. Live performance.	26 Apr 69	Live! CD Black B-05	Los Angeles Forum, Los Angeles, CA	JHE
Foxy Lady	CR 11. Live performance.	26 Apr 69	Anthology CD Box 9	Los Angeles Forum, Los Angeles, CA	JHE
Foxy Lady	CR 12. Live performance.	27 Apr 69	Live At The Oakland Coliseum (CR) CD Dagger Records DBRO-11743	Oakland Coliseum, Oakland, CA	JHE
Foxy Lady	BR 25. Live performance.	03 May 69	Hendrix, Busted In Toronto CD Venue VE 100502	Maple Leaf Gardens, Toronto, Canada	JHE
Foxy Lady	BR 25. Live performance.	03 May 69	I Don't Live Today CD ACL 007	Maple Leaf Gardens, Toronto, Canada	JHE
Foxy Lady	BR 26. Live performance.	17 May 69	One Night At The Arena CD Venue VE 100501	Rhode Island Arena, Providence, RI	JHE
Foxy Lady	BR 27. Live performance.	24 May 69	Midnight Magic CD Neutral Zone NZCD 89012	San Diego Sports Arena, San Diego, CA	JHE
Foxy Lady	BR 27. Live performance.	24 May 69	Don't Miss Him This Time CD Pyramid PYCD 096	San Diego Sports Arena, San Diego, CA	JHE
Foxy Lady	BR 28. Live performance.	25 May 69	Historic Concert Vol 2 CD Midnight Beat MBCD 050	Santa Clara Pop Festival, San Jose, CA	JHE
Foxy Lady	BR 29. Live performance.	20 Jun 69	More Electricity From Newport CD Luna LU 9201	Newport Pop Festival, San Fernando State, Northridge, CA	JHE

SONG TITLE	DATE	COMMENTS	RELEASE	LOCATION / VENUE	BAND	PERSONNEL
Foxy Lady	20 Jun 69	BR 29. Live performance.	A Lifetime Of Experience LP Sleepy Dragon 55 10	Newport Pop Festival, San Fernando State, Northridge, CA	JHE	
Foxy Lady	20 Jun 69	BR 29. Live performance.	Two Days At Newport CD JMH 007 / 2	Newport Pop Festival, San Fernando State, Northridge, CA	JHE	
Foxy Lady	29 Jun 69	BR 30. Live performance..	Wink Of An Eye CD Whoopy Cat WKP 0033 / 34	Mile High Stadium, Denver, CO	JHE	
Foxy Lady	18 Aug 69	BR 31. Live performance.	Woodstock Nation CD Wild Bird 89090 1 / 2	Woodstock Music And Art Fair, Bethel, NY	GSRB	
Foxy Lady	18 Aug 69	BR 31. Live performance.	Gypsy Sun And Rainbows CD Manic Depression MDCD 05 / 06	Woodstock Music And Art Fair, Bethel, NY	GSRB	
Foxy Lady	18 Aug 69	BR 31. Live performance.	Woodstock Monday, August 18 1969, 8AM CD JMH 008	Woodstock Music And Art Fair, Bethel, NY	GSRB	
Foxy Lady	31 Dec 69	BR 32. Live performance.	Band Of Gold CD-R Major Tom MT 087	Fillmore East, New York, NY 2nd Show	BOG	
Foxy Lady	01 Jan 70	CR 13. Live performance.	Band Of Gypsys Vol 2 (CR) LP Capitol SJ 12416	Fillmore East, New York, NY 1st Show	BOG	
Foxy Lady	01 Jan 70	CR 13. Live performance.	Band Of Gold CD-R Major Tom MT 087	Fillmore East, New York, NY 1st Show	BOG	
Foxy Lady	01 Jan 70	CR 13. Live performance.	Band Of Gypsys- The Ultimate CD JMH 010 / 3	Fillmore East, New York, NY 1st Show	BOG	
Foxy Lady	25 Apr 70	BR 33. Live performance.	Enjoy Jimi Hendrix LP Rubber Dubber 700-001-01	Los Angeles Forum, Los Angeles, CA	COL	
Foxy Lady	25 Apr 70	BR 33. Live performance.	Portrait Of Jimi Hendrix, A LP Catalog # Varies On Dead Wax	Los Angeles Forum, Los Angeles, CA	COL	
Foxy Lady	25 Apr 70	BR 33. Live performance.	Live At The Forum 1970 CD Whoopy Cat WKP 021 / 22	Los Angeles Forum, Los Angeles, CA	COL	
Foxy Lady	25 Apr 70	BR 33. Live performance.	Scuse Me While I Kiss	Los Angeles Forum,	COL	

Song	Reference	Date	The Sky CD Luna CD & JHCD 528	Los Angeles, CA	
Foxy Lady	BR 34. Live performance..	30 May 70	Good Karma 1 LP Berkeley 2022	Berkeley Community Theater, Berkeley, CA 1st Show	COL
Foxy Lady	BR 34. Live performance..	30 May 70	Berkeley Concert LP Audifon AF 008	Berkeley Community Theater, Berkeley, CA 1st Show	COL
Foxy Lady	BR 34. Live performance..	30 May 70	Berkeley Concerts, The CD Whoopy Cat WKP 004 / 5	Berkeley Community Theater, Berkeley, CA 1st Show	COL
Foxy Lady	BR 34. Live performance..	30 May 70	Ultimate Live Collection, The CD The Beat Goes On BGO BX 9307-4	Berkeley Community Theater, Berkeley, CA 1st Show	COL
Foxy Lady	BR 34. Live performance.	30 May 70	Riots In Berkeley CD Beech Marten BM 038	Berkeley Community Theater, Berkeley, CA 2nd Show	COL
Foxy Lady	BR 34. Live performance.	30 May 70	Berkeley Concerts, The CD Whoopy Cat WKP 004 / 5	Berkeley Community Theater, Berkeley, CA 2nd Show	COL
Foxy Lady	BR 34. Live performance.	30 May 70	Jimi Plays Berkeley CD JMH 005 / 2	Berkeley Community Theater, Berkeley, CA 1st Show	COL
Foxy Lady	BR 35. Live performance.	13 Jun 70	Baltimore Civic Center, June 13, 1970 CD Starquake SQ-09	Baltimore Civic Center, Baltimore, MD	COL
Foxy Lady	CR 14. Live performance.	04 Jul 70	Atlanta Special CD Genuine Pig TGP 121	2nd International Pop Festival, Atlanta, GA	COL
Foxy Lady	CR 14. Live performance.	04 Jul 70	At The Atlanta Pop Festival (CR) Laserdisc BMG BVLP 77 (74321-10987)	2nd International Pop Festival, Atlanta, GA	COL
Foxy Lady	CR 14. Live performance.	04 Jul 70	Stages Atlanta 70 (CR) CD Reprise 9 27632-2	2nd International Pop Festival, Atlanta, GA	COL
Foxy Lady	CR 14. Live performance.	04 Jul 70	Oh, Atlanta CD Tendolar TDR-009	2nd International Pop Festival, Atlanta, GA	COL
Foxy Lady	CR 14. Live performance.	04 Jul 70	Atlanta CD JMH 009 / 02	2nd International Pop Festival, Atlanta, GA	COL
Foxy Lady	BR 36. Live performance.	17 Jul 70	Live At Randall's Island LP Moon Tree Records PH1962	New York Pop- Downing Stadium, Randalls Island, NY	COL

SONG TITLE	DATE	COMMENTS	RELEASE	LOCATION / VENUE	BAND	PERSONNEL
Foxy Lady	17 Jul 70	BR 36. Live performance.	Live USA CD Imtrat 902-001	New York Pop-Downing Stadium, Randalls Island, NY	COL	
Foxy Lady	30 Jul 70	BR 37. Live performance. An incomplete version of this is available officially on the 'Rainbow Bridge" video and laserdisc and also on the 'Alive On Live' laserdisc.	Last American Concert Vol 1 CD The Swingin' Pig TSP-062	Rainbow Bridge Vibratory Sound-Color Experiment, Maui, HI 1st Show	COL	
Foxy Lady	30 Jul 70	BR 37. Live performance. This laserdisc release has just Jimi's parts edited from the 'Rainbow Bridge' film which.	Alive On Live (CR) Laserdisc SHLM 2005	Rainbow Bridge Vibratory Sound-Color Experiment, Maui, HI 1st Show	COL	
Foxy Lady	30 Jul 70	BR 37. Live performance. An incomplete version of this is available officially on the 'Rainbow Bridge" video and laserdisc and also on the 'Alive On Live' laserdisc.	Last American Concert-Alive And Flowing From... LP Jupiter 444	Rainbow Bridge Vibratory Sound-Color Experiment, Maui, HI 1st Show	COL	
Foxy Lady	30 Jul 70	BR 37. Live performance. An incomplete version of this is available officially on the 'Rainbow Bridge" video and laserdisc and also on the 'Alive On Live' laserdisc.	In From The Storm CD Silver Rarities SIRA 109 / 110	Rainbow Bridge Vibratory Sound-Color Experiment, Maui, HI 1st Show	COL	
Foxy Lady	30 Jul 70	BR 37. Live performance. An incomplete version of this is available officially on the 'Rainbow Bridge" video and laserdisc and also on the 'Alive On Live' laserdisc.	Gypsy Charm CD Mum MUCD 018	Rainbow Bridge Vibratory Sound-Color Experiment, Maui, HI 1st Show	COL	
Foxy Lady	30 Jul 70	BR 37. Live performance. An incomplete version of this is available officially on the 'Rainbow Bridge" video and laserdisc and also on the 'Alive On Live' laserdisc.	Rainbow Bridge 2 CD JMH 003 / 2	Rainbow Bridge Vibratory Sound-Color Experiment, Maui, HI 1st Show	COL	
Foxy Lady	30 Aug 70	CR 15. Live performance. Incomplete.	Island Man CD Silver Rarities SIRA 39 / 40	Isle Of Wight Festival, Isle Of Wight, England	COL	
Foxy Lady	30 Aug 70	CR 15. Live performance. Incomplete.	Isle Of Wight / Atlanta Pop Festival (CR) LP Columbia G3X 3085	Isle Of Wight Festival, Isle Of Wight, England	COL	
Foxy Lady	30 Aug 70	CR 15. Live performance. Incomplete.	Wight CD JMH 006 / 2	Isle Of Wight Festival, Isle Of Wight, England	COL	
Foxy Lady	30 Aug 70	CR 15. Live performance. Incomplete.	Isle Of Wight / Atlanta Pop Festival (CR) LP Columbia G3X 3085	Isle Of Wight Festival, Isle Of Wight, England	COL	
Foxy Lady	31 Aug 70	BR 38. Live performance.	Come On Stockholm CD No Label	Stora Scenen, Liesberg, Stockholm, Sweden	COL	

Song	Date	Comment	Release	Venue	Source
Foxy Lady	31 Aug 70	BR 38. Live performance.	Free Concert CD Midnight Beat MBCD 013	Stora Scenen, Tivoli Garden, Stockholm, Sweden	COL
Foxy Lady	01 Sep 70	BR 39. Live performance.	Warm Hello Of The Sun, The CD	Stora Scenen, Liseberg Nojespark, Goteborg, Sweden	COL
Foxy Lady	03 Sep 70	BR 40. Live performance.	Copenhagen '70 CD Whoopy Cat WKP 044 / 45	K.B. Hallen, Copenhagen, Denmark	COL
Foxy Lady	04 Sep 70	BR 41. Live performance.	Back To Berlin CD Midnight Beat 049	Deutsche- Landhalle, Berlin, Germany	COL
Foxy Lady	06 Sep 70	BR 43. Live performance.	Love & Peace CD Midnight Beat MBCD 015	Love And Peace Festival, Isle Of Fehrman, Germany	COL
Foxy Lady	06 Sep 70	BR 43. Live performance.	Wink Of An Eye CD Whoopy Cat WKP 0033 / 34	Love And Peace Festival, Isle Of Fehrman, Germany	COL
Foxy Lady	13 Dec 66	Outfaked mix of CR 1.	Sotheby's Private Reels CD JHR 003 / 004	CBS Studios, London, England	JHE
Foxy Lady	13 Dec 66	Outfaked mix of CR 1.	Living Reels Vol 1 CD JMH 011	CBS Studios, London, England	JHE
Free Form Blues	?? Aug 69	BR 1. Another jam from the rehearsals from Jimi's Shokan house prior to the performance at the Woodstock Festival.	Woodstock Rehearsals CD Midnight Beat MBCD 009	Shokan House, Woodstock, NY	GSRB
Free Spirit		No Hendrix involvement.	Jimi: A Musical Legacy CD KTS BX 010		No Jimi
Freedom Jam	?? / ?? 69-70	BR 1. An eight minute composing jam probably from late 1969 that was built around some elements that would end up being the middle eight chord progression and riff for "Freedom".	Mixdown Master Tapes Volume 1 CD Dandelion DL 005	Record Plant?	GSRB?
Freedom	25 Apr 70	BR 2. Live performance.	Live At The Forum 1970 CD Whoopy Cat WKP 021 / 22	Los Angeles Forum, Los Angeles, CA	COL
Freedom	25 Apr 70	BR 2. Live performance.	Enjoy Jimi Hendrix LP Rubber Dubber 700-001-01	Los Angeles Forum, Los Angeles, CA	COL
Freedom	25 Apr 70	BR 2. Live performance. The Luna disc is from a tape source while the JHCD 528 disc is copied from vinyl.	Scuse Me While I Kiss The Sky CD Luna CD & JHCD 528	Los Angeles Forum, Los Angeles, CA	COL
Freedom	15 May 70	BR 4. The earliest studio version of this song. This can be identified as Jimi says "Thank you very much" at the end of the take.	Shine On Earth, Shine On CD Sidewalk SW 89010 / 89011	Record Plant, New York, NY	COL

SONG TITLE	DATE	COMMENTS	RELEASE	LOCATION / VENUE	BAND	PERSONNEL
Freedom	15 May 70	BR 4. The earliest studio version of this song. This can be identified as Jimi says "Thank you very much" at the end of the take.	Studio Haze CD INA 6	Record Plant, New York, NY	COL	
Freedom	15 May 70	BR 4. The earliest studio version of this song. This can be identified as Jimi says "Thank you very much" at the end of the take.	Multicolored Blues CD Luna LU 9317	Record Plant, New York, NY	COL	
Freedom	15 May 70	BR 4. The earliest studio version of this song. This can be identified as Jimi says "Thank you very much" at the end of the take.	Voice Of Experience CD Rhinozerous RHP 789	Record Plant, New York, NY	COL	
Freedom	15 May 70	BR 4. The earliest studio version of this song. This can be identified as Jimi says "Thank you very much" at the end of the take.	First Rays - The Sessions CD Whoopy Cat WKP 0002	Record Plant, New York, NY	COL	
Freedom	15 May 70	BR 4. The earliest studio version of this song. This can be identified as Jimi says "Thank you very much" at the end of the take.	Electronic Church Music CD Pyramid PYCD 023	Record Plant, New York, NY	COL	
Freedom	15 May 70	BR 4. The earliest studio version of this song. This can be identified as Jimi says "Thank you very much" at the end of the take.	Voodoo In Ladyland CD MUM MUCD 006	Record Plant, New York, NY	COL	
Freedom	15 May 70	BR 4. The earliest studio version of this song. This can be identified as Jimi says "Thank you very much" at the end of the take. Incomplete.	Kiss The Skies CD Mum MUCD 024	Record Plant, New York, NY	COL	
Freedom	15 May 70	BR 4. The earliest studio version of this song. This can be identified as Jimi says "Thank you very much" at the end of the take.	Eyes And Imagination CD Third Stone TSD 18970	Record Plant, New York, NY	COL	
Freedom	15 May 70	BR 4. The earliest studio version of this song. This can be identified as Jimi says "Thank you very much" at the end of the take.	Electric Ladyland Outtakes CD Invasion Unlimited IU9417-1	Record Plant, N Y	COL	
Freedom	30 May 70	BR 5. Live performance.	Berkeley Soundchecks, The CD Whoopy Cat WKP 0008	Berkeley Community Theater, Berkeley, CA	COL	
Freedom	30 May 70	BR 5. Live performance.	Jimi Plays Berkeley CD JMH 005 / 2	Berkeley Community Theater, Berkeley, CA Sound Check	COL	
Freedom	30 May 70	BR 6. Live performance.	Good Karma 1 LP Berkeley 2022	Berkeley Community Theater, Berkeley, CA 1st Show	COL	
Freedom	30 May 70	BR 6. Live performance.	51st Anniversary CD Future Disc JMH 001 / 8	Berkeley Community Theater, Berkeley, CA 1st Show	COL	
Freedom	30 May 70	BR 6. Live performance.	Berkeley Concert LP	Berkeley Community	COL	

Song	Date	Notes	Release	Location		Musicians
Freedom			Audifon AF 008	Theater, Berkeley, CA 1st Show		
Freedom	30 May 70	BR 6. Live performance.	Berkeley Concerts, The CD Whoopy Cat WKP 004 / 5	Berkeley Community Theater, Berkeley, CA 1st Show	COL	
Freedom	30 May 70	BR 6. Live performance.	Jimi Plays Berkeley CD JMH 005 / 2	Berkeley Community Theater, Berkeley, CA 1st Show	COL	
Freedom	13 Jun 70	BR 7. Live performance.	Baltimore Civic Center, June 13, 1970 CD Starquake SQ-09	Baltimore Civic Center, Baltimore, MD	COL	
Freedom (Instrumental # 2)	?? Jun 70	BR 8. This could be from a session on 6 / 25 / 70 or a version mentioned in "Sessions" from 6 / 15 / 70.	Studio Haze CD INA 6	Electric Lady Studio, New York, NY	COL	Juma Sultan / Percussion
Freedom	?? Jun 70	BR 8. This could be from a session on 6 / 25 / 70 or a version mentioned in "Sessions" from 6 / 15 / 70.	Multicolored Blues CD Luna LU 9317	Electric Lady Studio, New York, NY	COL	Juma Sultan / Percussion
Freedom	?? Jun 70	BR 8. This could be from a session on 6 / 25 / 70 or a version mentioned in "Sessions" from 6 / 15 / 70.	First Rays - The Sessions CD Whoopy Cat WKP 0002	Electric Lady Studio, New York, NY	COL	Juma Sultan / Percussion
Freedom	25 Jun 70	CR 1 mix 1.	First Rays Of The New Rising Sun (CR) CD MCACD 11599	Electric Lady Studio, New York, NY	COL	Juma Sultan / Percussion, Ghetto Fighters / Backing Vocals
Freedom	25 Jun 70	CR 1 mix 1.	Cry Of Love, The (CR) CD Reprise 2034-2	Electric Lady Studio, New York, NY	COL	Juma Sultan / Percussion, Ghetto Fighters / Backing Vocals
Freedom	25 Jun 70	CR 1 mix 2. A slightly alternate mix for this package.	Voodoo Soup (CR) CD MCA 11206	Electric Lady Studio, New York, NY	COL	Juma Sultan / Percussion, Ghetto Fighters / Backing Vocals
Freedom	25 Jun 70	CR 1 mix 3. This mix has some guitar overdubs and vocals not found on other mixes.	Acoustic Jams CD Sphinx SX CD 001	Electric Lady Studio, New York, NY	COL	Ghetto Fighters / Backing Vocals, Juma Sultan / Percussion
Freedom	25 Jun 70	CR 1 mix 3. This mix has some guitar overdubs and vocals not found on other mixes.	First Rays - The Sessions CD Whoopy Cat WKP 0002	Electric Lady Studio, New York, NY	COL	Juma Sultan / Percussion, Ghetto Fighters / Backing Vocals
Freedom	25 Jun 70	CR 1 mix 3. This mix has some guitar overdubs and vocals not found on other mixes.	Studio Experience CD Sodium Haze SH 099	Electric Lady Studio, New York, NY	COL	Juma Sultan / Percussion, Ghetto Fighters / Backing Vocals
Freedom	25 Jun 70	CR 1 mix 3. This mix has some guitar overdubs and vocals not found on other mixes.	Wight CD JMH 006 / 2	Electric Lady Studio, New York, NY	COL	Juma Sultan / Percussion, Ghetto Fighters / Backing Vocals

SONG TITLE	DATE	COMMENTS	RELEASE	LOCATION / VENUE	BAND	PERSONNEL
Freedom	25 Jun 70	CR 1 mix 4. This has Jimi's lead vocal moved all the way into the right channel.	51st Anniversary CD Future Disc JMH 001 / 8	Electric Lady Studio, New York, NY	COL	Juma Sultan / Percussion, Ghetto Fighters / Backing Vocals
Freedom	30 May 70	CR 1 mix 5. This is a mix done for video (Superstars in Concert - Telstar video) that adds crowd noise and echo to make it sound like a live performance.	Redskin' Jammin' CD JH 01 / 02	Berkeley Community Theater, Berkeley, CA	COL	
Freedom	04 Jul 70	BR 9. Live performance.	Atlanta CD JMH 009 / 02	2nd International Pop Festival, Atlanta, GA	COL	
Freedom	04 Jul 70	BR 9. Live performance.	Atlanta Special CD Genuine Pig TGP 121	2nd International Pop Festival, Atlanta, GA	COL	
Freedom	04 Jul 70	BR 9. Live performance.	Berkeley Soundchecks, The CD Whoopy Cat WKP 0008	2nd International Pop Festival, Atlanta, GA	COL	
Freedom	04 Jul 70	BR 9. Live performance.	Live! CD Black B-05	2nd International Pop Festival, Atlanta, GA	COL	
Freedom	04 Jul 70	BR 9. Live performance.	Oh, Atlanta CD Tendolar TDR-009	2nd International Pop Festival, Atlanta, GA	COL	
Freedom	30 Jul 70	BR 10. Live performance.	Last American Concert Vol 2 CD 'The Swingin' Pig TSP-072	Rainbow Bridge Vibratory Sound-Color Experiment, Maui, HI 2nd Show	COL	
Freedom	30 Jul 70	BR 10. Live performance.	In From The Storm CD Silver Rarities SIRA 109 / 110	Rainbow Bridge Vibratory Sound-Color Experiment, Maui, HI 2nd Show	COL	
Freedom	30 Jul 70	BR 10. Live performance.	Rainbow Bridge 2 CD JMH 003 / 2	Rainbow Bridge Vibratory Sound-Color Experiment, Maui, HI 2nd Show	COL	
Freedom	30 Jul 70	BR 10. Live performance.	Greatest Hits Live CD Chartbusters CHER 089A	Rainbow Bridge Vibratory Sound-Color Experiment, Maui, HI 2nd Show	COL	
Freedom	30 Jul 70	BR 10. Live performance.	You Can't Use My Name L P Rock Folders 2, Q 9020	Rainbow Bridge Vibratory Sound-Color Experiment, Maui, HI 2nd Show	COL	
Freedom	30 Aug 70	CR 2. Live performance.	Island Man CD Silver Rarities SIRA 39 / 40	Isle Of Wight Festival, Isle Of Wight, England	COL	

Song	Date	Notes	Release	Location	Label	Personnel
Freedom	30 Aug 70	CR 2. Live performance.	At The Isle Of Wight (CR) Laserdisc CBS / Sony CLSM 791	Isle Of Wight Festival, Isle Of Wight, England	COL	
Freedom	30 Aug 70	CR 2. Live performance.	Isle Of Wight / Atlanta Pop Festival (CR) LP Columbia G3X 3085	Isle Of Wight Festival, Isle Of Wight, England	COL	
Freedom	30 Aug 70	CR 2. Live performance.	Wight CD JMH 006 / 2	Isle Of Wight Festival, Isle Of Wight, England	COL	
Freedom	02 Sep 70	BR 11. Live performance.	Welcome To The Electric Circus Vol 2 CD Midnight Beat 018	Vejlby Risskov Hallen, Århus, Denmark	COL	
Freedom	02 Sep 70	BR 11. Live performance.	Live At The Forum 1970 CD Whoopy Cat WKP 021 / 22	Vejlby Risskov Hallen, Århus, Denmark	COL	
Freedom	02 Sep 70	BR 11. Live performance.	Jewel Box CD Home HR-5824-3	Vejlby Risskov Hallen, Århus, Denmark	COL	
Freedom	03 Sep 70	CR 3. Live performance.	Jimi In Denmark (CR) CD UniVibes 1003 & Booted On Dynamite Studios	K.B. Hallen, Copenhagen, Denmark	COL	
Freedom	03 Sep 70	CR 3. Live performance.	Live In Copenhagen CD The Swingin' Pig TSP-220-2	K.B. Hallen, Copenhagen, Denmark	COL	
Freedom	03 Sep 70	CR 3. Live performance.	Copenhagen '70 CD Whoopy Cat WKP 044 / 45	K.B. Hallen, Copenhagen, Denmark	COL	
Freedom	06 Sep 70	BR 12. Live performance.	Love & Peace CD Midnight Beat MBCD 015	Love And Peace Festival, Isle Of Fehrman, Germany	COL	
Freedom	06 Sep 70	BR 12. Live performance.	Wink Of An Eye CD Whoopy Cat WKP 0033 / 34	Love And Peace Festival, Isle Of Fehrman, Germany	COL	
Freedom		Outfaked mix of the CR 1.	TTG Studios ???? CD WHOAMI WAI 015		COL	
Freedom / Easy Rider, ... Jam (Freedom Jam)	23 Jan 70	BR 2. Incomplete. "Freedom / Ezy Rider" only. See "Diamonds In The Dust" CD for the full medley.	Freak Out Blues CD GH 001	Record Plant, New York, NY	BOG	Don ? / Harmonica
Freedom / Easy Rider, ... Jam (Highway Of Desire)	23 Jan 70	BR 2. The full Jam / medley. See "Highway Of Broken Hearts Medley" for edited versions. The full medley is "Freedom / Ezy Rider / Highway Of Broken Hearts / 7 Dollars in My Pocket / Highway Of Desire / Midnight Lightning".	Diamonds In The Dust CD Midnight Beat MBCD 022 / 23	Record Plant, New York, NY	BOG	Don ? / Harmonica

SONG TITLE	DATE	COMMENTS	RELEASE	LOCATION / VENUE	BAND	PERSONNEL
From This Day On (She's So Fine)		No Hendrix involvement.	Hendrix In Words And Music CD Outlaw Records OTR 1100030		No Jimi	
Funky Jam (Instrumental Jam)	17 Mar 68	BR 1. Live performance from this club show with a made up title.	Blues At Midnight CD Midnight Beat MBCD 037	Cafe' A Go Go, New York, NY	Cafe	
Funky Jam (part of Three Little Bears)	17 Mar 68	BR 1. Live performance from this club show with a made up title.	Shine On Earth, Shine On CD Sidewalk SW 89010 / 89011	Cafe' A Go Go, New York, NY	Cafe	
Funky Jam	17 Mar 68	BR 1. Live performance from this club show with a made up title.	Cafe Au Go Go CD Koine 880802	Cafe' A Go Go, New York, NY	Cafe	
Funky Jam	17 Mar 68	BR 1. Live performance from this club show with a made up title.	Live USA CD Imtrat 902-001	Cafe' A Go Go, New York, NY	Cafe	
Further On Up The Road	24 Jun 70	BR 1. A commonly booted unreleased track.	Drone Blues CD Great Dane GDR SAT 2	Electric Lady Studio, New York, NY	COL	
Further On Up The Road	24 Jun 70	BR 1. A commonly booted unreleased track.	Ladyland In Flames LP Marshall Records JIMI 1,2,3,4	Electric Lady Studio, New York, NY	COL	
Further On Up The Road	24 Jun 70	BR 1. A commonly booted unreleased track.	Sir James Marshall LP Jester Productions JP 106	Electric Lady Studio, New York, NY	COL	
Further On Up The Road	24 Jun 70	BR 1. A commonly booted unreleased track.	Things I Used To Do CD The Early Years 02-CD-3334	Electric Lady Studio, New York, NY	COL	
Further On Up The Road	24 Jun 70	BR 1. A commonly booted unreleased track.	51st Anniversary CD Future Disc JMH 001 / 8	Electric Lady Studio, New York, NY	COL	
Further On Up The Road	24 Jun 70	BR 1. A commonly booted unreleased track.	Gypsy Suns, Moons And Rainbows CD Sidewalk JHX 8868	Electric Lady Studio, New York, NY	COL	
Further On Up The Road	24 Jun 70	BR 1. A commonly booted unreleased track.	Voice Of Experience CD Rhinozerous RHP 789	Electric Lady Studio, New York, NY	COL	
Further On Up The Road	24 Jun 70	BR 1. A commonly booted unreleased track.	Midnight Shines Down CD Blue Kangaroo BK 04	Electric Lady Studio, New York, NY	COL	
Further On Up The Road	24 Jun 70	BR 1. A commonly booted unreleased track.	Flames CD Missing In Action ACT 1	Electric Lady Studio, New York, NY	COL	
Fuzzy Guitar Jam (Young / Hendrix Jam)	?? / ?? 69	BR 1. A long (20 minutes) jam recorded the sessions that produced "Young / Hendrix", "It's Too Bad, & "World Travelers".	500,000 Halos CD EXP 500,000	Record Plant, New York, NY	Jimi	Larry Young / Organ

Song	Date	Description	Release	Location	Jimi	Larry Young / Organ
Fuzzy Guitar Jam (Instrumental Jam)	?? / ?? 69	BR 1. A long (20 minutes) jam recorded the sessions that produced "Young / Hendrix", "It's Too Bad, & "World Travelers".				
Gangster Of Love		No Hendrix involvement.	Hendrix In Words And Music CD Outlaw Records OTR 1100030		No Jimi	
Gloomy Monday Take 1 & 2	?? Jul 67	BR 1. The first of two takes of a session where Jimi tells produced Ed Champlin that "You can't use my name" upon releasing the session tapes.	You Can't Use My Name L P Rock Folders 2, Q 9020	T.T.G. Studios, Hollywood, CA	CKB	
Gloomy Monday Take 2	?? Jul 67	BR 2. The second of two takes of a session where Jimi tells produced Ed Champlin that "You can't use my name" upon releasing the session tapes.	Flames CD Missing In Action ACT 1	Studio 76, New York, NY	CKB	
Gloria	01 May 67	CR 1. CR on the bonus 45 that came with "The Essential Jimi Hendrix' package as well as a 12" single but not yet on CD.	51st Anniversary CD Future Disc JMH 001 / 8	Record Plant, New York, NY	JHE	
Gloria	01 May 68	CR 1. CR on the bonus 45 that came with "The Essential Jimi Hendrix' package as well as a 12" single but not yet on CD.	Voice Of Experience CD Rhinozerous RHP 789	Record Plant, New York, NY	JHE	
Gloria	01 May 68	CR 1. CR on the bonus 45 that came with "The Essential Jimi Hendrix' package as well as a 12" single but not yet on CD.	Complete BBC Session And.... The CD Last Bootleg Records LBR 036 / 2	Record Plant, New York, NY	JHE	
Gloria	01 May 68	CR 1. CR on the bonus 45 that came with "The Essential Jimi Hendrix' package as well as a 12" single but not yet on CD.	Rarities On Compact Disc CD On The Radio	Record Plant, New York, NY	JHE	
Gloria	01 May 68	CR 1. CR on the bonus 45 that came with "The Essential Jimi Hendrix' package as well as a 12" single but not yet on CD.	Jimi: A Musical Legacy CD KTS BX 010	Record Plant, New York, NY	JHE	
Gloria	01 May 68	CR 1. CR on the bonus 45 that came with "The Essential Jimi Hendrix' package as well as a 12" single but not yet on CD.	The Singles Album (CR) CD Polydor 827 369-2	Record Plant, New York, NY	JHE	
God Save The Queen	30 Aug 70	CR 1. Live performance.	Island Man CD Silver Rarities SIRA 39 / 40	Isle Of Wight Festival, Isle Of Wight, England	COL	
God Save The Queen	30 Aug 70	CR 1. Live performance.	At The Isle Of Wight (CR) Laserdisc CBS / Sony CLSM 791	Isle Of Wight Festival, Isle Of Wight, England	COL	
God Save The Queen	30 Aug 70	CR 1. Live performance.	Hendrix In The West (CR) LP Polydor 2302018 A	Isle Of Wight Festival, Isle Of Wight, England	COL	
God Save The Queen	30 Aug 70	CR 1. Live performance.	Live! CD Black B-05	Isle Of Wight Festival, Isle Of Wight, England	COL	

SONG TITLE	DATE	COMMENTS	RELEASE	LOCATION / VENUE	BAND	PERSONNEL
God Save The Queen	30 Aug 70	CR 1. Live performance.	Live - Isle Of Wight '70 (CR) CD Polydor 847236-2	Isle Of Wight Festival, Isle Of Wight, England	COL	
God Save The Queen	30 Aug 70	CR 1. Live performance.	Wight CD JMH 006 / 2	Isle Of Wight Festival, Isle Of Wight, England	COL	
God Save The Queen		This is a frequently booted fake track recorded by David Henderson	Master's Masters, The CD JH-01		No Jim	
God Save The Queen		This is a frequently booted fake track recorded by David Henderson	Official Bootleg Album, The CD Yellow Dog YD 051		No Jim	
God Save The Queen		This is a frequently booted fake track recorded by David Henderson	Best Of The Bootlegs CD MS 666		No Jim	
God Save The Queen		This is a frequently booted fake track recorded by David Henderson	Notes In Colours CD JHR 001 / 002		No Jim	
God Save The Queen (Denny Boy)		This is a frequently booted fake track recorded by David Henderson	Every Way To Paradise CD Tintangel TIBX 021 / 22 / 23 / 24		No Jim	
God Save The Queen		This is a frequently booted fake track recorded by David Henderson	Every Way To Paradise CD Tintangel TIBX 021 / 22 / 23 / 24		No Jim	
God Save The Queen		This is a frequently booted fake track recorded by David Henderson	Jimi: A Musical Legacy CD KTS BX 010		No Jim	
No Jimi involvement here.		No Jimi involvement here.	Whipper CD Pilz 447400-2	Unknown	No Jim	
Goodbye Bessie Mae	?? / ?? 63	CR 1. The very rare original single. This has been pirated.	Goodbye Bessie Mae / Soul Food 45 Fairmont F-1022	Abtone, New York	Jimi	Lonnie Youngblood / Sax & Vocals
Goodbye Bessie Mae	?? / ?? 63	CR 2. An alternate mix of the rare CR single b-side.	Whipper CD Pilz 447400-2	Abtone, New York	Jimi	Lonnie Youngblood / Sax & Vocals
Goodbye Bessie Mae	?? / ?? 63	CR 2. An alternate mix of the rare CR single b-side.	Jimi: A Musical Legacy CD KTS BX 010	Abtone, New York	Jimi	Lonnie Youngblood / Sax & Vocals
Gypsy Blood (Cryin' Blue Rain)	26 Feb 69	BR 1. Another unreleased track from "The Chandler Tapes" with bass & drums overdubbed in 1988 by Noel & Mitch.	Studio Haze CD INA 6	Olympic Sound Studios, London, England	JHE	Unknown / Percussion
Gypsy Blood	26 Feb 69	BR 1. Another unreleased track from "The Chandler Tapes" with bass & drums overdubbed in 1988 by Noel & Mitch.	DeLane Lea And Olympic Outs CD Gold Standard CD-R	Olympic Sound Studios, London, England	JHE	Unknown / Percussion

Song	Date	Description	Source	Location	BOG/Solo	Notes
Gypsy Boy (New Rising Sun)	16? Feb? 70?	BR 1. The most complete version of this early studio run through. All versions have an edit after the intro.	Mixdown Master Tapes Volume 3 CD Dandelion DL 007	Record Plant, New York, NY	BOG	
Gypsy Boy (New Rising Sun)	16? Feb? 70?	BR 1. An incomplete version of this early studio run through. All versions have an edit after the intro.	51st Anniversary CD Future Disc JMH 001 / 8	Record Plant, New York, NY	BOG	
Gypsy Boy (New Rising Sun)	16? Feb? 70?	BR 1. An incomplete version of this early studio run through. All versions have an edit after the intro.	First Rays - The Sessions CD Whoopy Cat WKP 0002	Record Plant, New York, NY	BOG	
Gypsy Boy (New Rising Sun)	16? Feb? 70?	BR 1. An incomplete version of this early studio run through. All versions have an edit after the intro.	Jimi: A Musical Legacy CD KTS BX 010	Record Plant, New York, NY	BOG	
Gypsy Boy (New Rising Sun) (Hey Baby-New Rising Sun)	16? Feb? 70?	BR 1. The most complete version of this early studio run through. All versions have an edit after the intro.	Notes In Colours CD JHR 001 / 002	Record Plant, New York, NY	BOG	
Gypsy Boy (New Rising Sun) (Hey Baby-New Rising Sun)	16 Feb 70	CR 1.	Midnight Lightning (CR) LP Reprise MS 2229	Record Plant, New York, NY	BOG	Midnight Lightning Line Up 1975 - Hilda Harris, Vivian Cherry, Maeretha Stewart / Backing Vocals
Gypsy Eyes	?? Mar? 68	CR 2 mix 1. A "stereo" solo home composing demo on electric guitar that begins with "Voodoo Chile", continues with 'Cherokee Mist' and concludes with 'Gypsy Eyes'.	Jimi By Himself The Home Recordings (CR) BSP-VC1	New York Apartment	Solo	
Gypsy Eyes	?? Mar? 68	CR 2 mix 2. A mono solo home composing demo on electric guitar that begins with "Voodoo Chile", continues with 'Cherokee Mist' and concludes with 'Gypsy Eyes'.	Acoustic Jams CD Sphinx SX CD 001	New York Apartment	Solo	
Gypsy Eyes	?? Mar? 68	CR 2 mix 2. A mono solo home composing demo on electric guitar that begins with "Voodoo Chile", continues with 'Cherokee Mist' and concludes with 'Gypsy Eyes'.	1968 AD Part Two CD Whoopy Cat WKP 0013	New York Apartment	Solo	
Gypsy Eyes	?? Mar? 68	CR 2 mix 2. A mono solo home composing demo on electric guitar that begins with "Voodoo Chile", continues with 'Cherokee Mist' and concludes with 'Gypsy Eyes'. Incomplete.	Studio Experience CD Sodium Haze SH 099	New York Apartment	Solo	
Gypsy Eyes	?? Mar? 68	CR 3 mix 1. Incomplete 'stereo' mix of another solo electric guitar take from the same session as CR 2.	Jimi By Himself The Home Recordings (CR) BSP-VC1	New York Apartment	Solo	
Gypsy Eyes	?? Mar? 68	CR 3 mix 2. Complete mono mix of another solo electric guitar take from the same session as CR 2.	Acoustic Jams CD Sphinx SX CD 001	New York Apartment	Solo	
Gypsy Eyes	?? Mar? 68	CR 3 mix 2. Complete mono mix of another solo electric guitar take from the same session as CR 2.	Voodoo Blues CD Smurf	New York Apartment	Solo	
Gypsy Eyes	?? Mar? 68	CR 3 mix 2. Complete mono mix of another solo electric guitar take from the same session as CR 2.	Studio Experience CD Sodium Haze SH 099	New York Apartment	Solo	
Gypsy Eyes	?? Mar? 68	BR 3. A third complete mono take of a solo electric guitar take from the same session as CR 2.	Acoustic Jams CD Sphinx SX CD 001	New York Apartment	Solo	

SONG TITLE	DATE	COMMENTS	RELEASE	LOCATION / VENUE	BAND	PERSONNEL
Gypsy Eyes	?? Mar? 68	BR 3. A third complete mono take of a solo electric guitar take from the same session as CR 2.	Black Gold CD Midnight Beat MBCD 058-062	New York Apartment	Solo	
Gypsy Eyes	24-29 Apr 68	BR 1. The first of two outtakes from a session on either 4 / 24 Or 4 / 29.	1968 AD CD Whoopy Cat WKP 0001	Record Plant, New York, NY	Jimi	
Gypsy Eyes	24-29 Apr 68	BR 2. The second of two outtakes from a session on either 4 / 24 or 4 / 29.	1968 AD CD Whoopy Cat WKP 0001	Record Plant, New York, NY	Jimi	Mitch Mitchell / Drums
Gypsy Eyes	24-29 Apr 68	BR 2. The second of two outtakes from a session on either 4 / 24 or 4 / 29.	Electric Ladyland Outtakes CD Invasion Unlimited IU 9417-1	Record Plant, New York, NY	Jimi	Mitch Mitchell / Drums
Gypsy Eyes	24-29 Apr 68	BR 2. The second of two outtakes from a session on either 4 / 24 or 4 / 29.	Voodoo In Ladyland CD MUM MUCD 006	Record Plant, New York, NY	Jimi	Mitch Mitchell / Drums
Gypsy Eyes	01 May 68	CR 1 mix 1.	Red House CD The Entertainers CD294	Record Plant, New York, NY	Jimi	Mitch Mitchell / Drums
Gypsy Eyes	01 May 68	CR 1 mix 1.	Electric Ladyland (CR) CD MCACD-11600	Record Plant, New York, NY	Jimi	Mitch Mitchell / Drums
Gypsy Eyes	01 May 68	CR 1 mix 1.	The Singles Album (CR) CD Polydor 827 369-2	Record Plant, New York, NY	Jimi	Mitch Mitchell / Drums
Gypsy Eyes	01 May 68	CR 1 mix 1.	Legacy (CR) LP Polydor	Record Plant, New York, NY	JHE	Mitch Mitchell / Drums
Gypsy Eyes	01 May 68	CR 1 mix 2. An unused mix with more guitar overdubs and with-out a fade.	TTG Studios ???? CD WHOAMI WAI 015	Record Plant, New York, NY	Jimi	Mitch Mitchell / Drums
Gypsy Eyes	01 May 68	CR 1 mix 2. An unused mix with more guitar overdubs and with-out a fade.	51st Anniversary CD Future Disc JMH 001 / 8	Record Plant, New York, NY	Jimi	Mitch Mitchell / Drums
Gypsy Eyes	01 May 68	CR 1 mix 2. An unused mix with more guitar overdubs and with-out a fade.	1968 AD CD Whoopy Cat WKP 0001	Record Plant, New York, NY	Jimi	Mitch Mitchell / Drums
Gypsy Eyes	01 May 68	CR 1 mix 2. An unused mix with more guitar overdubs and with-out a fade.	Things I Used To Do, The CD Golden Memories GM 890738	Record Plant, New York, NY	Jimi	Mitch Mitchell / Drums
Gypsy Eyes	01 May 68	CR 1 mix 2. An unused mix with more guitar overdubs and with-out a fade.	Hey Joe CD Crocodile Beat CB 53039	Record Plant, New York, NY	Jimi	Mitch Mitchell / Drums
Gypsy Eyes	01 May 68	CR 1 mix 2. An unused mix with more guitar overdubs and with-out a fade.	Electric Ladyland Outtakes CD Invasion Unlimited IU 9417-1	Record Plant, New York, NY	Jimi	Mitch Mitchell / Drums
Gypsy Eyes	01 May 68	CR 1 mix 2. An unused mix with more guitar overdubs and with-out a fade.	Jimi: A Musical Legacy CD KTS BX 010	Record Plant, New York, NY	Jimi	Mitch Mitchell / Drums
Gypsy Eyes	01 May 68	CR 1 mix 2. An unused mix with more guitar overdubs and with-	Voodoo In Ladyland CD	Record Plant, New	Jimi	Mitch Mitchell / Drums

			MUM MUCD 006	York, NY		
Gypsy Eyes	01 May 68	CR 1 mix 2. An unused mix with more guitar overdubs and with-out a fade.	Living Reels Vol 2 CD JMH 012 / 2	Record Plant, New York, NY	Jimi	Mitch Mitchell / Drums
Gypsy Eyes	22 Jun 69	Live performance. Part of the "Earth VS Space" jam from Newport.	It Never An End CD Genuine Pig TGP-118	Newport Pop Festival, San Fernando State, Northridge, CA	NJK	
Gypsy Woman	18 Aug 69	BR 1. Live performance.	Woodstock Nation CD Wild Bird 89090 1 / 2	Woodstock Music And Art Fair, Bethel, NY	GSRB	Larry Lee / Lead Vocals
Gypsy Woman	18 Aug 69	BR 1. Live performance.	Gypsy Sun And Rainbows CD Manic Depression MDCD 05 / 06	Woodstock Music And Art Fair, Bethel, NY	GSRB	Larry Lee / Lead Vocals
Gypsy Woman	18 Aug 69	BR 1. Live performance.	Woodstock Monday, August 18 1969, 8AM CD JMH 008	Woodstock Music And Art Fair, Bethel, NY	GSRB	Larry Lee / Lead Vocals
Had To Cry Today	25 Jun 70	BR 1. A 15 second bit from the Blind Faith song performed just before the two takes of 'Drifting' on this same CD.	Notes In Colours CD JHR 001 / 002	Electric Lady Studio, New York, NY	Jimi	Billy Cox / Bass
Have Mercy	04 Feb 67	BR 1. Live performance. The only known and recorded performance of this song by The Experience.	Live In Paris 66 / 67 CD Whoopy Cat WKP 0012	Flamingo Club, London, England	JHE	
Have Mercy	04 Feb 67	BR 1. Live performance. The only known and recorded performance of this song by The Experience.	Have Mercy On Me Baby CD Midnight Beat MBCD 038	Flamingo Club, London, England	JHE	
Have Mercy	04 Feb 67	BR 1. Live performance. The only known and recorded performance of this song by The Experience.	Live At The Flamingo Club, London, 2-4-67 CD	Flamingo Club, London, England	JHE	
Hear My Freedom	21 Oct 68	BR 1. A jam from the same session as, and preceding "Electric Church Jam".	Ball And Chain CD Jimi 009	T.T.G. Studios, Hollywood, CA	Jimi	Lee Michaels / Keyboards, Buddy Miles / Drums
Hear My Freedom (Had To Cry Today)	21 Oct 68	BR 1. A jam from the same session as, and preceding "Electric Church Jam".	Black Gold CD Midnight Beat MBCD 058-062	T.T.G. Studios, Hollywood, CA	Jimi	Lee Michaels / Keyboards, Buddy Miles / Drums
Hear My Freedom	21 Oct 68	BR 1. A jam from the same session as, and preceding "Electric Church Jam".	Hear My Freedom CD Kobra KRCR 010	T.T.G. Studios, Hollywood, CA	Jimi	Lee Michaels / Keyboards, Buddy Miles / Drums
Hear My Train A Coming	15 Dec 67	CR 2 mix 1. BBC performance with the 'regular' vocal track.	Guitar Hero CD Document DR 013	Top Gear, BBC Playhouse Theatre, London, England	JHE	
Hear My Train A Coming	15 Dec 67	CR 2 mix 1. BBC performance with the 'regular' vocal track.	Primal Keys LP Impossible Record Works	Top Gear, BBC Playhouse Theatre, London, England	JHE	

SONG TITLE	DATE	COMMENTS	RELEASE	LOCATION / VENUE	BAND	PERSONNEL
Hear My Train A Coming	15 Dec 67	CR 2 mix 1. BBC performance with the 'regular' vocal track.	Radio One (CR) CD Rykodisc RCD 20078	Top Gear, BBC Playhouse Theatre, London, England	JHE	
Hear My Train A Coming	15 Dec 67	CR 2 mix 1. BBC performance with the 'regular' vocal track.	51st Anniversary CD Future Disc JMH 001 / 8	Top Gear, BBC Playhouse Theatre, London, England	JHE	
Hear My Train A Coming	15 Dec 67	CR 2 mix 1. BBC performance with the 'regular' vocal track.	Live In London 1967 CD Koine Records K881104	Top Gear, BBC Playhouse Theatre, London, England	JHE	
Hear My Train A Coming	15 Dec 67	CR 2 mix 1. BBC performance with the 'regular' vocal track.	In Concert CD Starlife ST 3612	Top Gear, BBC Playhouse Theatre, London, England	JHE	
Hear My Train A Coming	15 Dec 67	CR 2 mix 1. BBC performance with the 'regular' vocal track.	Jewel Box CD Home HR-5824-3	Top Gear, BBC Playhouse Theatre, London, England	JHE	
Hear My Train A Coming	15 Dec 67	CR 2 mix 1. BBC performance with the 'regular' vocal track.	Complete BBC Session And... The CD Last Bootleg Records LBR 036 / 2	Top Gear, BBC Playhouse Theatre, London, England	JHE	
Hear My Train A Coming	15 Dec 67	CR 2 mix 1. BBC performance with the 'regular' vocal track.	BBC Sessions (CR) CD MCACD 2-11742	Top Gear, BBC Playhouse Theatre, London, England	JHE	
Hear My Train A Coming	15 Dec 67	CR 2 mix 1. BBC performance with the 'regular' vocal track.	BBC Sessions (CR) CD MCACD 2-11742	Top Gear, BBC Playhouse Theatre, London, England	JHE	
Hear My Train A Coming	15 Dec 67	CR 2 mix 1. BBC performance with the 'regular' vocal track. Incomplete.	Valley Of Neptune CD PC 28355	Top Gear, BBC Playhouse Theatre, London, England	JHE	
Hear My Train A Coming	15 Dec 67	CR 2 mix 2. The 'alternate vocal' BBC performance. Identified by Jimi saying "A little thing for the BBC people".	Freak Out Jam CD GH 002	Top Gear, BBC Playhouse Theatre, London, England	JHE	
Hear My Train A Coming	15 Dec 67	CR 2 mix 2. The 'alternate vocal' BBC performance. Identified by Jimi saying "A little thing for the BBC people".	Symphony Of Experience CD Third Stone Discs TDS 24966	Top Gear, BBC Playhouse Theatre, London, England	JHE	
Hear My Train A Coming	15 Dec 67	CR 2 mix 2. The 'alternate vocal' BBC performance. Identified by Jimi saying "A little thing for the BBC people".	Jimi: A Musical Legacy CD KTS BX 010	Top Gear, BBC Playhouse Theatre, London, England	JHE	
Hear My Train A Coming	15 Dec 67	CR 2 mix 2. The 'alternate vocal' BBC performance. Identified by Jimi saying "A little thing for the BBC people".	Day Tripper (CR) CD-3 Rykodisc RCD 31-008	Top Gear, BBC Playhouse Theatre, London, England	JHE	

Song	Date	Notes	Release	Location	Band
Hear My Train A Coming	19 Dec 67	CR 3. A beautiful solo acoustic performance. The false start has never been booted but can be found on the video 'A Film About Jimi Hendrix'.	Wild Man Of Pop Plays Vol 2, The CD Pyramid RFTCD 004	Bruce Fleming Photo Studio, London, England	Solo
Hear My Train A Coming	19 Dec 67	CR 3. A beautiful solo acoustic performance. The false start has never been booted but can be found on the video 'A Film About Jimi Hendrix'.	Smashing Amps LP Trademark Of Quality TMQ 1813	Bruce Fleming Photo Studio, London, England	Solo
Hear My Train A Coming	19 Dec 67	CR 3. A beautiful solo acoustic performance. The false start has never been booted but can be found on the video 'A Film About Jimi Hendrix'.	Soundtrack From The Film Jimi Hendrix, The (CR) LP Reprise 2RS 6481	Bruce Fleming Photo Studio, London, England	Solo
Hear My Train A Coming	19 Dec 67	CR 3. A beautiful solo acoustic performance. The false start has never been booted but can be found on the video 'A Film About Jimi Hendrix'.	Thanks Ottawa For The Memories CD Luna 9319	Bruce Fleming Photo Studio, London, England	Solo
Hear My Train A Coming	19 Dec 67	CR 3. A beautiful solo acoustic performance. The false start has never been booted but can be found on the video 'A Film About Jimi Hendrix'.	Jimi Hendrix: Blues (CR) CD MCA MCAD-11060	Bruce Fleming Photo Studio, London, England	Solo
Hear My Train A Coming	15 Dec 67	CR 3. A beautiful solo acoustic performance. The false start has never been booted but can be found on the video 'A Film About Jimi Hendrix'.	Ultimate BBC Collection CD Classical CL006	Top Gear, BBC Playhouse Theatre, London, England	JHE
Hear My Train A Coming	19 Dec 67	CR 3. A beautiful solo acoustic performance. The false start has never been booted but can be found on the video 'A Film About Jimi Hendrix'.	Loaded Guitar LP Starlight SL 87013	Bruce Fleming Photo Studio, London, England	Solo
Hear My Train A Coming	?? Apr 68	CR 4 mix 1. 'Stereo' mix. A short version this time from the apartment tape.	Jimi By Himself The Home Recordings (CR) BSP-VC1	New York Apartment	Solo
Hear My Train A Coming	?? Apr 68	CR 4 mix 2. Mono mix. A short acoustic version this time from the apartment tape.	Acoustic Jams CD Sphinx SX CD 001	New York Apartment	Solo
Hear My Train A Coming	?? Apr 68	CR 4 mix 2. Mono mix. A short acoustic version this time from the apartment tape.	1968 AD Part Two CD Whoopy Cat WKP 0013	New York Apartment	Solo
Hear My Train A Coming	?? Apr 68	CR 4 mix 2. Mono mix. A short acoustic version this time from the apartment tape.	Black Gold CD Midnight Beat MBCD 058-062	New York Apartment	Solo
Hear My Train A Coming	18 May 68	BR 1. Live performance.	It's Only A Paper Moon CD Luna 9420	Fillmore East, New York, NY	JHE
Hear My Train A Coming	10 May 68	BR 1. Live performance.	One Night Stand CD Hep Cat 101	Fillmore East, New York, NY	JHE
Hear My Train A Coming	18 May 68	CR 5. Live performance.	51st Anniversary CD Future Disc JMH 001 / 8	Miami Pop Festival, Hallendale, FL 2nd Show	JHE
Hear My Train A Coming	18 May 68	CR 5. Live performance.	1968 AD CD Whoopy Cat WKP 0001	Miami Pop Festival, Hallendale, FL 2nd Show	JHE

SONG TITLE	DATE	COMMENTS	RELEASE	LOCATION / VENUE	BAND	PERSONNEL
Hear My Train A Coming	18 May 68	CR 5. Live performance.	Rarities CD The Genuine Pig TGP-CD-091	Miami Pop Festival, Hallendale, FL 2nd Show	JHE	
Hear My Train A Coming	18 May 68	CR 5. Live performance.	Calling Long Distance (CR) CD Univibes & Booted On Dynamite DS930055	Miami Pop Festival, Hallendale, FL 2nd Show	JHE	
Hear My Train A Coming	10 Oct 68	CR 6 mix 1. Live performance. Incomplete.	Concerts (CR) CD Reprise 9-22306-2	Winterland Theatre, San Francisco, CA 2nd Show	JHE	
Hear My Train A Coming	10 Oct 68	CR 6 mix 1. Live performance. Incomplete.	Little Wing CD Oil Well RSC 036	Winterland Theatre, San Francisco, C A 2nd Show	JHE	
Hear My Train A Coming	10 Oct 68	CR 6 mix 1. Live performance. Incomplete.	Ultimate Live Collection, The CD The Beat Goes On BGO BX 9307-4	Winterland Theatre, San Francisco, CA 2nd Show	JHE	
Hear My Train A Coming	10 Oct 68	CR 6 mix 2. Live performance this time complete.	Winterland Days, The CD Manic Depression 001	Winterland Theatre, San Francisco, CA 2nd Show	JHE	
Hear My Train A Coming	28 Nov 68	BR 2. Live performance.	Have Mercy On Me Baby CD Midnight Beat MBCD 038	Philharmonic Hall, New York, NY	JHE	
Hear My Train A Coming	28 Nov 68	BR 2. Live performance.	Live At Philharmonic Hall LP Sagittarius LTD	Philharmonic Hall, New York, NY	JHE	
Hear My Train A Coming	08 Jan 69	BR 2. Live performance.	Cat's Squirrel CD CS 001 / 2	Loresberg Cirkus, Goteborg, Sweden	JHE	
Hear My Train A Coming	18 Feb 69	CR 7. Live performance.	First Night At The Royal Albert Hall CD Midnight Beat MBCD 047 / 48Fir	Royal Albert Hall, London, England	JHE	
Hear My Train A Coming	24 Feb 69	BR 3. Live performance.	Good Vibes LP Trade Mark Of Quality TMOQ 1813	Royal Albert Hall, London, England	JHE	
Hear My Train A Coming	24 Feb 69	BR 3. Live performance. This breaks down after 5 1 / 2 minutes.	First Night At The Royal Albert Hall CD Midnight Beat MBCD 047 / 48	Royal Albert Hall, London, England Sound Check	JHE	
Hear My Train A Coming	24 Feb 69	BR 4. Live performance.	Broadcasts CD Luna LU 9204	Royal Albert Hall, London, England	JHE	
Hear My Train A Coming	24 Feb 69	BR 4. Live performance.	Unforgettable Experience LP RAH 2469	Royal Albert Hall, London, England	JHE	

Song	Date	Notes	Release	Venue	Band	Personnel
Hear My Train A Coming	24 Feb 69	BR 4. Live performance.	Royal Albert Hall CD Blimp 008 / 009	Royal Albert Hall, London, England	JHE	
Hear My Train A Coming	24 Feb 69	BR 4. Live performance.	Stone Free CD Silver Rarities SIRA 58 / 59	Royal Albert Hall, London, England	JHE	
Hear My Train A Coming	02 Apr 69	CR 1.	Midnight Lightning (CR) LP Reprise MS 2229	Olympic Sound Studios, London, England	JHE	Midnight Lightning Line Up 1975, Mitch Mitchell / Drums
Hear My Train A Coming	27 Apr 69	CR 8. Live performance.	Live At The Oakland Coliseum (CR) CD Dagger Records DBRO-11743	Oakland Coliseum, Oakland, CA	JHE	
Hear My Train A Coming	03 May 69	BR 5. Live performance.	Hendrix, Busted In Toronto CD Venue VE 100502	Maple Leaf Gardens, Toronto, Canada	JHE	
Hear My Train A Coming	03 May 69	BR 5. Live performance.	I Don't Live Today CD ACL 007	Maple Leaf Gardens, Toronto, Canada	JHE	
Hear My Train A Coming	17 May 69	BR 6. Live performance.	One Night At The Arena CD Venue VE 100501	Rhode Island Arena, Providence, RI	JHE	
Hear My Train A Coming	18 May 69	BR 7. Live performance.	Roman Coliseum, The CD Starquake SQ 11	Madison Square Garden, New York, NY	JHE	
Hear My Train A Coming	21 May 69	BR 8. Slightly incomplete, this is a fine unreleased studio performance.	500,000 Halos CD EXP 500,000	Record Plant, New York, NY	BOG	Unknown / Conga
Hear My Train A Coming	25 May 69	BR 9. Live performance.	Historic Concert Vol 2 CD Midnight Beat MBCD 050	Santa Clara Pop Festival, San Jose, CA	JHE	
Hear My Train A Coming	20 Jun 69	BR 10. Live performance.	More Electricity From Newport CD Luna LU 9201	Newport Pop Festival, San Fernando State, Northridge, CA	JHE	
Hear My Train A Coming	20 Jun 69	BR 10. Live performance.	A Lifetime Of Experience LP Sleepy Dragon 55 10	Newport Pop Festival, San Fernando State, Northridge, CA	JHE	
Hear My Train A Coming	20 Jun 69	BR 10. Live performance.	Two Days At Newport CD JMH 007 / 2	Newport Pop Festival, San Fernando State, Northridge, CA	JHE	
Hear My Train A Coming	22 Jun 69	BR 11. Live performance.	It Never Takes An End CD Genuine Pig TGP-118	Newport Pop Festival, San Fernando State, Northridge, CA	NJK	

SONG TITLE	DATE	COMMENTS	RELEASE	LOCATION / VENUE	BAND	PERSONNEL
Hear My Train A Coming	29 Jun 69	BR 12. Live performance.	Wink Of An Eye CD Whoopy Cat WKP 0033 / 34	Mile High Stadium, Denver, CO	JHE	
Hear My Train A Coming	07 Jul 69	BR 13. Live television performance.	More Electricity From Newport CD Luna LU 9201	Dick Cavett Show, ABC TV Studios, New York, NY	Jimi	Jack Rosenbaum Orchestra
Hear My Train A Coming	07 Jul 69	BR 13. Live television performance.	Loaded Guitar LP Starlight SL 87013	Dick Cavett Show, ABC TV Studios, New York, NY	Jimi	Jack Rosenbaum Orchestra
Hear My Train A Coming	07 Jul 69	BR 13. Live television performance.	Woodstock Monday, August 18 1969, 8AM CD JMH 008	Dick Cavett Show, ABC TV Studios, New York, NY	Jimi	Jack Rosenbaum Orchestra
Hear My Train A Coming	?? Aug 69	BR 14. From the rehearsals at Jimi's Shokan house shortly before the Woodstock performance. Right at the start, Jimi plays the opening riff to "Machine Gun".	Can You Here Me LP Hemero 01 / KERI	Shokan House, Woodstock, NY	GSRB	
Hear My Train A Coming	?? Aug 69	BR 14. From the rehearsals at Jimi's Shokan house shortly before the Woodstock performance. Right at the start, Jimi plays the opening riff to "Machine Gun".	Gypsy Sun And Rainbows CD Manic Depression MDCD 05 / 06	Shokan House, Woodstock, NY	GSRB	
Hear My Train A Coming	?? Aug 69	BR 14. From the rehearsals at Jimi's Shokan house shortly before the Woodstock performance. Right at the start, Jimi plays the opening riff to "Machine Gun".	Woodstock Rehearsals CD Midnight Beat MBCD 009	Shokan House, Woodstock, NY	GSRB	
Hear My Train A Coming	?? Aug 69	BR 14. From the rehearsals at Jimi's Shokan house shortly before the Woodstock performance. Right at the start, Jimi plays the opening riff to "Machine Gun".	Woodstock Monday, August 18 1969, 8AM CD JMH 008	Shokan House, Woodstock, NY	GSRB	
Hear My Train A Coming	18 Aug 69	CR 9 mix 1. Edited live performance.	Woodstock (CR) CD MCA 11063	Woodstock Music And Art Fair, Bethel, NY	GSRB	
Hear My Train A Coming	18 Aug 69	CR 9 mix 2. A slightly shorted edited live performance then CR 9 mix 1.	Woodstock Two L P (CR) Cotillion SD 2400	Woodstock Music And Art Fair, Bethel, NY	GSRB	
Hear My Train A Coming	18 Aug 69	CR 9 mix 3. The complete live performance.	Woodstock Nation CD Wild Bird 89090 1 / 2	Woodstock Music And Art Fair, Bethel, NY	GSRB	
Hear My Train A Coming	18 Aug 69	CR 9 mix 3. The complete live performance.	Gypsy Sun And Rainbows CD Manic Depression MDCD 05 / 06	Woodstock Music And Art Fair, Bethel, NY	GSRB	
Hear My Train A Coming	18 Aug 69	CR 9 mix 3. The complete live performance.	Woodstock Monday, August 18 1969, 8AM CD JMH 008	Woodstock Music And Art Fair, Bethel, NY	GSRB	

Song	Date	Notes	Release	Venue	Code
Hear My Train A Coming	18 Aug 69	CR 9 mix 3. The complete live performance.	Ultimate Live Collection, The CD The Beat Goes On BGO BX 9307-4	Woodstock Music And Art Fair, Bethel, NY	GSRB
Hear My Train A Coming	31 Dec 69	CR 10. Live performance.	Band Of Gypsys Vol 3	Fillmore East, New York, NY 1st Show	BOG
Hear My Train A Coming	31 Dec 69	CR 10. Live performance.	Band Of Gypsys Vol 2 (CR) LP Capitol SJ 12416	Fillmore East, New York, NY 1st Show	BOG
Hear My Train A Coming	31 Dec 69	CR 10. Live performance.	Gypsy Haze CD Lords Of Archive LAR 16	Fillmore East, New York, NY 1st Show	BOG
Hear My Train A Coming	31 Dec 69	CR 10. Live performance.	Fillmore Concerts, The CD Whoopy Cat WKP 0006 / 7	Fillmore East, New York, NY 1st Show	BOG
Hear My Train A Coming	31 Dec 69	CR 10. Live performance.	Band Of Gold CD-R Major Tom MT 087	Fillmore East, New York, NY 1st Show	BOG
Hear My Train A Coming	31 Dec 69	CR 10. Live performance.	Power Of Soul CD SQ-10	Fillmore East, New York, NY 1st Show	BOG
Hear My Train A Coming	31 Dec 69	CR 10. Live performance.	Ultimate Live Collection, The CD The Beat Goes On BGO BX 9307-4	Fillmore East, New York, NY 1st Show	BOG
Hear My Train A Coming	25 Apr 70	BR 15. Live performance.	Enjoy Jimi Hendrix LP Rubber Dubber 700-001-01	Los Angeles Forum, Los Angeles, CA	COL
Hear My Train A Coming	25 Apr 70	BR 15. Live performance.	Portrait Of Jimi Hendrix, A LP Catalog # Varies On Dead Wax	Los Angeles Forum, Los Angeles, CA	COL
Hear My Train A Coming	25 Apr 70	BR 15. Live performance.	Live At The Forum 1970 CD Whoopy Cat WKP 021 / 22	Los Angeles Forum, Los Angeles, CA	COL
Hear My Train A Coming	25 Apr 70	BR 15. Live performance. The Luna disc is from a tape source while the JHCD 528 disc is copied from vinyl.	Scuse Me While I Kiss The Sky CD Luna CD & JHCD 528	Los Angeles Forum, Los Angeles, CA	COL
Hear My Train A Coming	30 May 70	CR 11. Live performance	Good Karma 1 LP Berkeley 2022	Berkeley Community Theater, Berkeley, CA 1st Show	COL
Hear My Train A Coming	30 May 70	CR 11. Live performance	Jimi Plays Berkeley (CR) Warner Reprise Videotape	Berkeley Community Theater, Berkeley, CA 1st Show	COL
Hear My Train A Coming	30 May 70	CR 11. Live performance	Rainbow Bridge (CR) LP Reprise K44159	Berkeley Community Theater, Berkeley, CA 1st Show	COL

SONG TITLE	DATE	COMMENTS	RELEASE	LOCATION / VENUE	BAND	PERSONNEL
Hear My Train A Coming	30 May 70	CR 11. Live performance	Jimi Hendrix: Blues (CR) CD MCA MCAD-11060	Berkeley Community Theater, Berkeley, CA 1st Show	COL	
Hear My Train A Coming	30 May 70	CR 11. Live performance	Rainbow Bridge & More CD	Berkeley Community Theater, Berkeley, CA 1st Show	COL	
Hear My Train A Coming	30 May 70	CR 11. Live performance	Berkeley Concert LP Audifon AF 008	Berkeley Community Theater, Berkeley, CA 1st Show	COL	
Hear My Train A Coming	30 May 70	CR 11. Live performance	Berkeley Concerts, The CD Whoopy Cat WKP 004 / 5	Berkeley Community Theater, Berkeley, CA 1st Show	COL	
Hear My Train A Coming	30 May 70	CR 11. Live performance	Rainbow Bridge 2 CD JMH 003 / 2	Berkeley Community Theater, Berkeley, CA 1st Show	COL	
Hear My Train A Coming	30 May 70	CR 11. Live performance	Jimi Plays Berkeley CD JMH 005 / 2	Berkeley Community Theater, Berkeley, CA 1st Show	COL	
Hear My Train A Coming	30 May 70	CR 11. Live performance	Ultimate Live Collection, The CD The Beat Goes On BGO BX 9307-4	Berkeley Community Theater, Berkeley, CA 1st Show	COL	
Hear My Train A Coming	13 Jun 70	BR 16. Live performance.	Baltimore Civic Center, June 13, 1970 CD Starquake SQ-09	Baltimore Civic Center, Baltimore, MD	COL	
Hear My Train A Coming	04 Jul 70	CR 12. Live performance.	Stages Atlanta 70 (CR) CD Reprise 9 27632-2	2nd International Pop Festival, Atlanta, GA	COL	
Hear My Train A Coming	04 Jul 70	CR 12. Live performance.	Atlanta CD JMH 009 / 02	2nd International Pop Festival, Atlanta, GA	COL	
Hear My Train A Coming	04 Jul 70	CR 12. Live performance.	Oh, Atlanta CD Tendolar TDR-009	2nd International Pop Festival, Atlanta, GA	COL	
Hear My Train A Coming	04 Jul 70	CR 12. Live performance.	Atlanta CD JMH 009 / 02	2nd International Pop Festival, Atlanta, GA	COL	
Hear My Train A Coming	30 Jul 70	CR 13. Live performance.	Last American Concert Vol 1 CD The Swingin' Pig TSP-062	Rainbow Bridge Vibratory Sound-Color Experiment, Maui, HI 1st Show	COL	
Hear My Train A Coming	30 Jul 70	CR 13. Live performance.	Maui, Hawaii LP JH 106 (Trademark Of Quality?)	Rainbow Bridge Vibratory Sound-Color Experiment, Maui, HI 1st Show	COL	

Song	Date	Notes	Release	Location	Code	Musicians
Hear My Train A Coming	30 Jul 70	CR 13. Live performance. Incomplete. This laserdisc release has just Jimi's parts edited from the full 'Rainbow Bridge' film.	Alive On Live (CR) Laserdisc SHLM 2005	Rainbow Bridge Vibratory Sound-Color Experiment, Maui, HI 1st Show	COL	
Hear My Train A Coming	30 Jul 70	CR 13. Live performance.	Last American Concert-Alive And Flowing From....LP Jupiter 444	Rainbow Bridge Vibratory Sound-Color Experiment, Maui, HI 1st Show	COL	
Hear My Train A Coming	30 Jul 70	CR 13. Live performance.	In From The Storm CD Silver Rarities SIRA 109 / 110	Rainbow Bridge Vibratory Sound-Color Experiment, Maui, HI 1st Show	COL	
Hear My Train A Coming	30 Jul 70	CR 13. Live performance.	Rainbow Bridge (CR) LP Reprise K44159	Rainbow Bridge Vibratory Sound-Color Experiment, Maui, HI 1st Show	COL	
Hear My Train A Coming	30 Jul 70	CR 13. Live performance.	Rainbow Bridge 2 CD JMH 003 / 2	Rainbow Bridge Vibratory Sound-Color Experiment, Maui, HI 1st Show	COL	
Hear My Train A Coming	01 Sep 70	BR 17. Live performance.	Warm Hello Of The Sun, The CD	Stora Scenen, Liseberg Nojespark, Goteborg, Sweden	COL	
Heaven Has No Sorrow	26 Jun 70	BR 1. A portion of the session from this day consisting of three breakdowns and a complete take.	Mixdown Master Tapes Volume 2 CD Dandelion DL 006	Electric Lady Studio, New York, NY	Jimi	Billy Cox / Bass
Heaven Has No Sorrow (Can I Whisper In Your Ear)	26 Jun 70	BR 1. A portion of the session from this day consisting of three breakdowns and a complete take. Less complete than the Mixdown Master Tapes version.	First Rays Of The New Rising Sun CD Triangle PYCD 084-2	Electric Lady Studio, New York, NY	Jimi	Billy Cox / Bass
Heaven Has No Sorrow (Can I Whisper In Your Ear)	26 Jun 70	BR 1. This just the long take from the session tape. See Mixdown Master Tapes Vol 2 for the longest session segment.	Cherokee Mist CD Triangle PYCD 070	Electric Lady Studio, New York, NY	Jimi	Billy Cox / Bass
Heavy Jam	?? Apr? 69?	BR 1. A studio jam that starts with the guitar riff from 'Bleeding Heart'.	Best Of The Bootlegs CD MS 666	Olympic Sound Studios, London, England	JHE	
Heavy Jam	?? Apr? 69?	BR 1. A studio jam that starts with the guitar riff from 'Bleeding Heart'.	Lost Experience, The, CD JHCD203	Olympic Sound Studios, London, England	JHE	
Help Me Part 1	21 Jan 66	CR 1 lifted from the 45 A-side.	Dante's Inferno CD Pink Poodle POO 002	Atlantic Studios, New York	CKB	
Hendrix / Mc Laughlin Jam # 1 & # 2	25 Mar 69	BR 1. These are the two short jams that follow a run through of 'Driving South' and 'Everything's Gonna Be Alright'.	Atlanta CD JMH 009 / 02	Record Plant, New York, NY	Jimi	John Mc Laughlin / Guitar, Buddy Miles / Drums, Dave Holland / Bass

SONG TITLE	DATE	COMMENTS	RELEASE	LOCATION / VENUE	BAND	PERSONNEL
Hendrix / Miles Jam	14 Nov 69	BR 1. Another untitled jam from the same session that produced the "Lonely Avenue" jams. Incomplete.	Earth Tones CD Whoopy Cat WKP 041	Record Plant, New York, NY	Jimi	Buddy Miles / Drums
Hendrix / Miles Jam (Gypsy Boogie)	14 Nov 69	BR 1. Another untitled jam from the same session that produced the "Lonely Avenue" jams. Incomplete.	Band Of Gypsys- The Ultimate CD JMH 010 / 3	Record Plant, New York, NY	Jimi	Buddy Miles / Drums
Hendrix / Mitchell Apartment Jam	01 Feb 70	BR 1. A long untitled jam with Mitch Mitchell and probably recorded at Jimi's apartment in Greenwich Village.	Black Gold CD Midnight Beat MBCD 058-062	New York Apartment	Jimi	Mitch Mitchell / Drums
Hendrix / Mitchell Apartment Jam	01 Feb 70	BR 1. This is only a small portion of a long untitled jam with Mitch Mitchell and probably recorded at Jimi's apartment in Greenwich Village. A longer segment is found on "Black Gold".	Acoustic Jams CD Sphinx SX CD 001	New York Apartment	Solo	Mitch Mitchell / Drums
Hey Baby (New Rising Sun)	25 Apr 70	BR 1. Live performance.	Live At The Forum 1970 CD Whoopy Cat WKP 021 / 22	Los Angeles Forum, Los Angeles, CA	COL	
Hey Baby (New Rising Sun)	25 Apr 70	BR 1. Live performance.	Enjoy Jimi Hendrix LP Rubber Dubber 700-001-01	Los Angeles Forum, Los Angeles, CA	COL	
Hey Baby (New Rising Sun)	25 Apr 70	BR 1. Live performance. The Luna disc is from a tape source while the JHCD 528 disc is copied from vinyl.	Scuse Me While I Kiss The Sky CD Luna CD & JHCD 528	Los Angeles Forum, Los Angeles, CA	COL	
Hey Baby (New Rising Sun)	30 May 70	BR 2. Only part of the song is played during this rehearsal.	Berkeley Soundchecks, The CD Whoopy Cat WKP 0008	Berkeley Community Theater, Berkeley, CA Sound Check	COL	
Hey Baby (New Rising Sun)	30 May 70	BR 3. Live performance. This song was officially released on the 'Jimi At Berkeley' videotape and laserdisc.	Riots In Berkeley CD Beech Marten BM 038	Berkeley Community Theater, Berkeley, CA 2nd Show	COL	
Hey Baby (New Rising Sun)	30 May 70	BR 3. Live performance. This song was officially released on the 'Jimi At Berkeley' videotape and laserdisc.	Jimi Plays Berkeley (CR) Warner Reprise Videotape	Berkeley Community Theater, Berkeley, CA 2nd Show	COL	
Hey Baby (New Rising Sun)	30 May 70	BR 3. Live performance. This song was officially released on the 'Jimi At Berkeley' videotape and laserdisc.	51st Anniversary CD Future Disc JMH 001 / 8	Berkeley Community Theater, Berkeley, CA 2nd Show	COL	
Hey Baby (New Rising Sun)	30 May 70	BR 3. Live performance. This song was officially released on the 'Jimi At Berkeley' videotape and laserdisc.	Midnight Magic CD Neutral Zone NZCD 89012	Berkeley Community Theater, Berkeley, CA 2nd Show	COL	
Hey Baby (New Rising Sun)	30 May 70	BR 3. Live performance. This song was officially released on the 'Jimi At Berkeley' videotape and laserdisc.	Berkeley Concerts, The CD Whoopy Cat WKP 004 / 5	Berkeley Community Theater, Berkeley, CA 2nd Show	COL	
Hey Baby (New Rising Sun)	30 May 70	BR 3. Live performance. This song was officially released on the 'Jimi At Berkeley' videotape and laserdisc.	Jimi Plays Berkeley CD JMH 005 / 2	Berkeley Community Theater, Berkeley, CA 1st Show	COL	

Song	Date	Code	Release	Location		Musician
Hey Baby (New Rising Sun)	01 Jul 70	CR 1.	Rainbow Bridge (CR) LP Reprise K44159	Electric Lady Studio, New York, NY	COL	Juma Sultan / Percussion
Hey Baby (New Rising Sun)	01 Jul 70	CR 1.	Rainbow Bridge & More CD	Electric Lady Studio, New York, NY	COL	Juma Sultan / Percussion
Hey Baby (New Rising Sun)	01 Jul 70	CR 1.	Jewel Box CD Home HR-5824-3	Electric Lady Studio, New York, NY	COL	Juma Sultan / Percussion
Hey Baby (New Rising Sun)	01 Jul 70	CR 1.	First Rays Of The New Rising Sun (CR) CD MCACD 11599	Electric Lady Studio, New York, NY	COL	Juma Sultan / Percussion
Hey Baby (New Rising Sun)	01 Jul 70	CR 1.	Rainbow Bridge (CR) LP Reprise K44159	Electric Lady Studio, New York, NY	COL	Juma Sultan / Percussion
Hey Baby (New Rising Sun)	01 Jul 70	CR 1.	Rainbow Bridge 2 CD JMH 003 / 2	Electric Lady Studio, New York, NY	COL	Juma Sultan / Percussion
Hey Baby (New Rising Sun)	04 Jul 70	BR 4. Live performance.	Atlanta Special CD Genuine Pig TGP 121	2nd International Pop Festival, Atlanta, GA	COL	
Hey Baby (New Rising Sun)	04 Jul 70	BR 4. Live performance.	Berkeley Soundchecks, The CD Whoopy Cat WKP 0008	2nd International Pop Festival, Atlanta, GA	COL	
Hey Baby (New Rising Sun)	04 Jul 70	BR 4. Live performance.	Atlanta CD JMH 009 / 02	2nd International Pop Festival, Atlanta, GA	COL	
Hey Baby (New Rising Sun)	30 Jul 70	BR 5. Live performance.	Last American Concert Vol 1 CD The Swingin' Pig TSP-062	Rainbow Bridge Vibratory Sound-Color Experiment, Maui, HI 1st Show	COL	
Hey Baby (New Rising Sun)	30 Jul 70	BR 5. Live performance.	Maui, Hawaii LP JH 106 (Trademark Of Quality?)	Rainbow Bridge Vibratory Sound-Color Experiment, Maui, HI 1st Show	COL	
Hey Baby (New Rising Sun)	30 Jul 70	BR 5. Live performance. Incomplete.	Alive On Live (CR) Laserdisc SHLM 2005	Rainbow Bridge Vibratory Sound-Color Experiment, Maui, HI 1st Show	COL	
Hey Baby (New Rising Sun)	30 Jul 70	BR 5. Live performance. Incomplete.	In From The Storm CD Silver Rarities SIRA 109 / 110	Rainbow Bridge Vibratory Sound-Color Experiment, Maui, HI 1st Show	COL	
Hey Baby (New Rising Sun)	30 Jul 70	BR 5. Live performance. Incomplete.	Rainbow Bridge 2 CD JMH 003 / 2	Rainbow Bridge Vibratory Sound-Color Experiment, Maui, HI 1st Show	COL	

SONG TITLE	DATE	COMMENTS	RELEASE	LOCATION / VENUE	BAND	PERSONNEL
Hey Baby (New Rising Sun)	30 Jul 70	BR 6. Live performance. This is a medley which includes 'Midnight Lightning'.	You Can't Use My Name L P Rock Folders 2, Q 9020	Rainbow Bridge Vibratory Sound-Color Experiment, Maui, HI 2nd Show	COL	
Hey Baby (New Rising Sun)	30 Jul 70	BR 6. Live performance. This is a medley which includes 'Midnight Lightning'.	Last American Concert Vol 2 CD The Swingin' Pig TSP-072	Rainbow Bridge Vibratory Sound-Color Experiment, Maui, HI 2nd Show	COL	
Hey Baby (New Rising Sun)	30 Jul 70	BR 6. Live performance. This is a medley which includes 'Midnight Lightning'.	Last American Concert-Alive And Flowing From.... LP Jupiter 444	Rainbow Bridge Vibratory Sound-Color Experiment, Maui, HI 2nd Show	COL	
Hey Baby (New Rising Sun)	30 Jul 70	BR 6. Live performance. This is a medley which includes 'Midnight Lightning'.	Rainbow Bridge 2 CD JMH 003 / 2	Rainbow Bridge Vibratory Sound-Color Experiment, Maui, HI 2nd Show	COL	
Hey Baby (New Rising Sun)	30 Jul 70	BR 6. Live performance. This is a medley which includes 'Midnight Lightning'.	51st Anniversary CD Future Disc JMH 001 / 8	Rainbow Bridge Vibratory Sound-Color Experiment, Maui, HI 2nd Show	COL	
Hey Baby (New Rising Sun)	30 Jul 70	BR 6. Live performance. This is a medley which includes 'Midnight Lightning'.	In From The Storm CD Silver Rarities SIRA 109 / 110	Rainbow Bridge Vibratory Sound-Color Experiment, Maui, HI 2nd Show	COL	
Hey Baby (New Rising Sun)	30 Jul 70	BR 6. Live performance. This is a medley which includes 'Midnight Lightning'. Incomplete.	Last American Concert-Alive And Flowing From.... LP Jupiter 444	Rainbow Bridge Vibratory Sound-Color Experiment, Maui, HI 2nd Show	COL	
Hey Baby (New Rising Sun)	30 Aug 70	CR 2.	Island Man CD Silver Rarities SIRA 39 / 40	Isle Of Wight Festival, Isle Of Wight, England	COL	
Hey Baby (New Rising Sun)	30 Aug 70	CR 2.	Live - Isle Of Wight '70 (CR) CD Polydor 847236-2	Isle Of Wight Festival, Isle Of Wight, England	COL	
Hey Baby (New Rising Sun)	30 Aug 70	CR 2.	Rainbow Bridge 2 CD JMH 003 / 2	Isle Of Wight Festival, Isle Of Wight, England	COL	
Hey Baby (New Rising Sun)	30 Aug 70	CR 2.	Wight CD JMH 006 / 2	Isle Of Wight Festival, Isle Of Wight, England	COL	
Hey Baby (New Rising Sun)	31 Aug 70	BR 7. Live performance.	Come On Stockholm	Stora Scenen, Tivoli	COL	

Song	Date	Notes	CD No Label	Location	Label
Hey Baby (New Rising Sun)	31 Aug 70	BR 7. Live performance.	Free Concert CD Midnight Beat MBCD 013	Stora Scenen, Tivoli Garden, Stockholm, Sweden	COL
Hey Baby (New Rising Sun)	01 Sep 70	BR 8. Live performance.	Warm Hello Of The Sun, The CD	Stora Scenen, Liseberg Nojespark, Goteborg, Sweden	COL
Hey Baby (New Rising Sun)	02 Sep 70	BR 9. Live performance.	Welcome To The Electric Circus Vol 2 CD Midnight Beat 018	Vejlby Risskov Hallen, Arhus, Denmark	COL
Hey Baby (New Rising Sun)	02 Sep 70	BR 9. Live performance.	Live At The Forum 1970 CD Whoopy Cat WKP 021 / 22	Vejlby Risskov Hallen, Arhus, Denmark	COL
Hey Baby (New Rising Sun)	03 Sep 70	CR 3. Live performance.	51st Anniversary CD Future Disc JMH 001 / 8	K.B. Hallen, Copenhagen, Denmark	COL
Hey Baby (New Rising Sun)	03 Sep 70	CR 3. Live performance.	Welcome To The Electric Circus Vol 2 CD Midnight Beat 018	K.B. Hallen, Copenhagen, Denmark	COL
Hey Baby (New Rising Sun)	03 Sep 70	CR 3. Live performance.	Calling Long Distance (CR) CD Univibes & Booted On Dynamite DS930055	K.B. Hallen, Copenhagen, Denmark	COL
Hey Baby (New Rising Sun)	03 Sep 70	CR 3. Live performance.	Copenhagen '70 CD Whoopy Cat WKP 044 / 45	K.B. Hallen, Copenhagen, Denmark	COL
Hey Baby (New Rising Sun)	04 Sep 70	BR 10. Live performance.	Back To Berlin CD Midnight Beat 049	Deutsche- Landhalle, Berlin, Germany	COL
Hey Baby (New Rising Sun)	06 Sep 70	BR 11. Live performance.	Love & Peace CD Midnight Beat MBCD 015	Love And Peace Festival, Isle Of Fehrman, Germany	COL
Hey Baby (New Rising Sun)	06 Sep 70	BR 11. Live performance.	Wink Of An Eye CD Whoopy Cat WKP 0033 / 34	Love And Peace Festival, Isle Of Fehrman, Germany	COL
Hey Joe	18 Oct 66	BR 1. Live performance.	Live In Paris 66 / 67 CD Whoopy Cat WKP 0012	Olympic Sound Studios, London, England	JHE
Hey Joe	?? / ?? 66	BR 2.This is an earlier and rejected recording from a different session complete with some overdubs.	Olympic Gold Vol 2 CD Blimp 007	De Lane Lea, London, England	JHE
Hey Joe	23 Oct 66	BR 3. Alternate instrumental take #1 from the same session as the CR 1.	Olympic Gold Vol 2 CD Blimp 007	De Lane Lea, London, England	JHE

SONG TITLE	DATE	COMMENTS	RELEASE	LOCATION / VENUE	BAND	PERSONNEL
Hey Joe	23 Oct 66	BR 4. Alternate instrumental take #2 from the same session as the CR 1.	Olympic Gold Vol 2 CD Blimp 007	De Lane Lea, London, England	JHE	
Hey Joe	23 Oct 66	CR 1 mix 1 (stereo)	Are You Experienced? (CR) CD MCACD 11602	De Lane Lea, London, England	JHE	Barbara Moore, Gloria George, Margaret Stedder (The Breakaways) / Backing Vocals
Hey Joe	23 Oct 66	CR 1 mix 1 (stereo)	The Singles Album (CR) CD Polydor 827 369-2	De Lane Lea, London, England	JHE	Barbara Moore, Gloria George, Margaret Stedder (The Breakaways) / Backing Vocals
Hey Joe	23 Oct 66	CR 1 mix 1 (stereo)	Smash Hits (CR) CD Reprise 2276-2	De Lane Lea, London, England	JHE	Barbara Moore, Gloria George, Margaret Stedder (The Breakaways) / Backing Vocals
Hey Joe	23 Oct 66	Cr1 mix 2 (mono)	Hey Joe / Stone Free 45 Rpm Single Polydor 56139	De Lane Lea, London, England	JHE	Barbara Moore, Gloria George, Margaret Stedder (The Breakaways) / Backing Vocals
Hey Joe	23 Oct 66	CR 1 mix 3. This sounds like the mono mix remixed into fake stereo.	Legacy (CR) LP Polydor	De Lane Lea, London, England	JHE	Barbara Moore, Gloria George, Margaret Stedder (The Breakaways) / Backing Vocals
Hey Joe	23 Oct 66	CR 1 mix 4. A mono mix of the CR 1 prior to overdubs.	Olympic Gold Vol 2 CD Blimp 007	De Lane Lea, London, England	JHE	
Hey Joe	23 Oct 66	CR 1 mix 5. The CR 1 backing track with the Breakaways over-dub and an alternate lead vocal track by Jimi.	51st Anniversary CD Future Disc JMH 001 / 8	De Lane Lea, London, England	JHE	
Hey Joe	23 Oct 66	CR 1 mix 5. The CR 1 backing track with the Breakaways over-dub and an alternate lead vocal track by Jimi.	Unsurpassed Studio Takes CD Yellow Dog YD 050	De Lane Lea, London, England	JHE	
Hey Joe	23 Oct 66	CR 1 mix 5. The CR 1 backing track with the Breakaways over-dub and an alternate lead vocal track by Jimi.	Complete BBC Session And..., The CD Last Bootleg Records LBR 036 / 2	De Lane Lea, London, England	JHE	
Hey Joe	23 Oct 66	CR 1 mix 5. The CR 1 backing track with the Breakaways over-dub and an alternate lead vocal track by Jimi.	Jimi: A Musical Legacy CD KTS BX 010	De Lane Lea, London, England	JHE	
Hey Joe	23 Oct 66	CR 1 mix 5. The CR 1 backing track with the Breakaways over-dub and an alternate lead vocal track by Jimi.	Voodoo In Ladyland CD MUM MUCD 006	De Lane Lea, London, England	JHE	
Hey Joe	29 Dec 66	BR 5. BBC Television performance. Incomplete.	Dante's Inferno CD Pink Poodle POO 002	Top Of The Pops, BBC Limegrove Studio, London, England	JHE	The Breakaways / Backing Vocals

Song	Date	Notes	Release	Venue	Band
Hey Joe	13 Feb 67	CR 2. BBC performance.	Primal Keys LP Impossible Record Works	Saturday Club, BBC Broadcasting House, London, England	JHE
Hey Joe	13 Feb 67	CR 2. BBC performance.	Radio One (CR) CD Rykodisc RCD 20078	Saturday Club, BBC Broadcasting House, London, England	JHE
Hey Joe	13 Feb 67	CR 2. BBC performance.	Ultimate BBC Collection CD Classical CL006	Saturday Club, BBC Broadcasting House, London, England	JHE
Hey Joe	13 Feb 67	CR 2. BBC performance.	Broadcasts LP Trade Mark Of Quality TMQ 1841 & TMQ 71019	Saturday Club, BBC Broadcasting House, London, England	JHE
Hey Joe	13 Feb 67	CR 2. BBC performance.	Complete BBC Session And..., The CD Last Bootleg Records LBR 036 / 2	Saturday Club, BBC Broadcasting House, London, England	JHE
Hey Joe	13 Feb 67	CR 2. BBC performance.	BBC Sessions (CR) CD MCACD 2-11742	Saturday Club, BBC Broadcasting House, London, England	JHE
Hey Joe	13 Feb 67	CR 2. BBC performance.	BBC Sessions (CR) CD MCACD 2-11742	Saturday Club, BBC Broadcasting House, London, England	JHE
Hey Joe	13 Feb 67	CR 2. BBC performance.	Tomorrow...Or Just The End Of Time CD Batz 0028	Saturday Club, BBC Broadcasting House, London, England	JHE
Hey Joe	04 Feb 67	BR 6. Live performance.	Have Mercy On Me Baby CD Midnight Beat MBCD 038	Flamingo Club, London, England	JHE
Hey Joe	04 Feb 67	BR 6. Live performance.	Live At The Flamingo Club, London, 2-4-67 CD	Flamingo Club, London, England	JHE
Hey Joe	02 Mar 67	BR 7. The rehearsal for the German TV show "Beat Club". Officially released on the laser disc single "Hey Joe: Beat Club" and copied on a few bootleg videos.	Loaded Guitar LP Starlight SL 87013	Marquee Club, London, England	JHE
Hey Joe	02 Mar 67	BR 7. The rehearsal for the German TV show "Beat Club". Officially released on the laser disc single "Hey Joe: Beat Club" and copied on a few bootleg videos.	Tomorrow...Or Just The End Of Time CD Batz 0028	Marquee Club, London, England	JHE
Hey Joe	02 Mar 67	BR 8. The broadcast take for the German TV show "Beat Club".	Thanks Ottawa For The Memories CD Luna 9319	Marquee Club, London, England	JHE
Hey Joe	02 Mar 67	BR 8. The broadcast take for the German TV show "Beat Club".	Unforgettable Experience LP RAH 2469	Marquee Club, London, England	JHE

SONG TITLE	DATE	COMMENTS	RELEASE	LOCATION / VENUE	BAND	PERSONNEL
Hey Joe	18 Mar 67	BR 9. Live performance for a German radio broadcast.	Legendary Star Club Tapes, The CD The Early Years 02-CD-3309	N D R Radiohouse, Studio 1, Hamburg, Germany	JHE	
Hey Joe	18 Mar 67	BR 9. Live performance for a German radio broadcast.	Can You Here Me LP Hemero 01 / KERI	N D R Radiohouse, Studio 1, Hamburg, Germany	JHE	
Hey Joe	18 Mar 67	BR 9. Live performance for a German radio broadcast.	Tomorrow...Or Just The End Of Time CD Batz 0028	N D R Radiohouse, Studio 1, Hamburg, Germany		
Hey Joe	18 May 67	BR 10. Television performance.	Wild Man Of Pop Plays Vol 1, The CD Pyramid RFTCD 003	Beat Beat Beat TV Show, Stadhalle, Offenbach, Germany	JHE	
Hey Joe	18 May 67	BR 10. Television performance.	Sweet Angel CD Compact Music WPOCM 0589	Beat Beat Beat TV Show, Stadhalle, Offenbach, Germany	JHE	
Hey Joe	24 May 67	BR 11. Live performance.	Lost In Sweden CD Whoopy Cat WKP 0046 / 0047	Stora Scenen, Grona Lund, Stockholm, Sweden	JHE	
Hey Joe	18 Jun 67	CR 3. Live performance.	Once Upon A Time CD Wall Of Sound WS CD011	Monterey International Pop Festival, Monterey, CA	JHE	
Hey Joe	18 Jun 67	CR 3. Live performance.	Soundtrack From The Film Jimi Hendrix, The (CR) LP Reprise 2RS 6481	Monterey International Pop Festival, Monterey, CA	JHE	
Hey Joe	18 Jun 67	CR 3. Live performance.	Monterey Pop CD Evil 006 1 / 2	Monterey International Pop Festival, Monterey, CA	JHE	
Hey Joe	18 Jun 67	CR 3. Live performance.	Hey Joe CD Crocodile Beat CB 53039	Monterey International Pop Festival, Monterey, CA	JHE	
Hey Joe	18 Jun 67	CR 3. Live performance.	Jimi Plays Monterey (CR) CD Polydor 827990-2	Monterey International Pop Festival, Monterey, CA	JHE	
Hey Joe	04 Sep 67	CR 4. Live performance.	Lost In Sweden CD Whoopy Cat WKP 0046 / 0047	Dans In, Grona Lund, Tivoli Garden, Stockholm, Sweden	JHE	

Song	Date	Notes	Release	Location	Artist
Hey Joe	04 Sep 67	CR 4. Live performance.	EXP Over Sweden (CR) CD UniVibes 1002	Dans In, Grona Lund, Tivoli Garden, Stockholm, Sweden	JHE
Hey Joe	05 Sep 67	CR 5. Live performance.	Live In Stockholm 1967 CD Document DR 003	Studio 4, Radiohuset, Stockholm, Sweden	JHE
Hey Joe	05 Sep 67	CR 5. Live performance.	Wild Man Of Pop Plays Vol 1, The CD Pyramid RFTCD 003	Studio 4, Radiohuset, Stockholm, Sweden	JHE
Hey Joe	05 Sep 67	CR 5. Live performance.	Stages Stockholm 67 (CR) CD Reprise 9 27632-2	Studio 4, Radiohuset, Stockholm, Sweden	JHE
Hey Joe	05 Sep 67	CR 5. Live performance.	Live In London 1967 CD Koine Records K881104	Studio 4, Radiohuset, Stockholm, Sweden	JHE
Hey Joe	05 Sep 67	CR 5. Live performance.	Live In Concert 1967 CD Living Legend LLR-CD 001	Studio 4, Radiohuset, Stockholm, Sweden	JHE
Hey Joe	05 Sep 67	CR 5. Live performance.	Recorded Live In Europe CD Bulldog BGCD 023	Studio 4, Radiohuset, Stockholm, Sweden	JHE
Hey Joe	05 Sep 67	CR 5. Live performance.	Two Sides Of The Same Genius LP Amazing Kornyphone TAKRL H677	Studio 4, Radiohuset, Stockholm, Sweden	JHE
Hey Joe	05 Sep 67	CR 5. Live performance.	Fire CD The Entertainers CD297	Studio 4, Radiohuset, Stockholm, Sweden	JHE
Hey Joe	05 Sep 67	CR 5. Live performance.	In Europe 67 / 68 / 69 CD Vulture CD 009 / 2	Studio 4, Radiohuset, Stockholm, Sweden	JHE
Hey Joe	05 Sep 67	CR 5. Live performance.	Live CD DV More CDDV 2401	Studio 4, Radiohuset, Stockholm, Sweden	JHE
Hey Joe	05 Sep 67	CR 5. Live performance.	Jimi Hendrix Experience CD Rockstars In Concert 6127092	Studio 4, Radiohuset, Stockholm, Sweden	JHE
Hey Joe	05 Sep 67	CR 5. Live performance.	Greatest Hits Live CD Chartbusters CHER 089A	Studio 4, Radiohuset, Stockholm, Sweden	JHE
Hey Joe	11 Sep 67	BR 12. Live performance.	Lost In Sweden CD Whoopy Cat WKP 0046 / 0047	Stora Scenen, Grona Lund, Stockholm, Sweden	JHE
Hey Joe	07 Jan 68	BR 13. Live performance.	Cat's Squirrel CD CS 001 / 2	Tivolis Konsertsal, Copenhagen, Denmark	JHE

SONG TITLE	DATE	COMMENTS	RELEASE	LOCATION / VENUE	BAND	PERSONNEL
Hey Joe	07 Jan 68	BR 13. Live performance.	Fuckin' His Guitar For Denmark LP Polymore Or JH CO	Tivolis Konsertsal, Copenhagen, Denmark	JHE	
Hey Joe	16 Feb 68	BR 14. Live performance.	Biggest Square In The Building, The CD Reverb Music 1993	State Fair Music Hall, Dallas, TX	JHE	
Hey Joe	16 Feb 68	BR 14. Live performance.	Scuse Me While I Kiss The Sky CD Sonic Zoom SZ 1001	State Fair Music Hall, Dallas, TX	JHE	
Hey Joe	17 Feb 68	BR 15. Live performance.	Remember The Alamo CD	Will Rogers Auditorium, Fort Worth, T X	JHE	
Hey Joe	17 Feb 68	BR 15. Live performance.	Scuse Me While I Kiss The Sky CD Sonic Zoom SZ 1001	Will Rogers Auditorium, Fort Worth, T X	JHE	
Hey Joe	25 Feb 68	BR 16. Live performance.	Winterland Vol 2 CD Whoopy Cat WKP 00279 / 28	Civic Opera House, Chicago, IL	JHE	
Hey Joe	19 Mar 68	BR 17. Live performance.	Thanks Ottawa For The Memories CD Luna 9319	Capitol Theatre, Ottawa, Canada	JHE	
Hey Joe	19 Mar 68	BR 17. Live performance.	Canadian Club CD WPOCM 0888 D 006-2	Capitol Theatre, Ottawa, Canada	JHE	
Hey Joe	19 Mar 68	BR 17. Live performance.	Live From Ottawa LP Starlight SL 87010	Capitol Theatre, Ottawa, Canada	JHE	
Hey Joe	19 Mar 68	BR 17. Live performance.	Superconcert 1968 CD Firepower FP03	Capitol Theatre, Ottawa, Canada	JHE	
Hey Joe	10 May 68	BR 18. Live performance.	It's Only A Paper Moon CD Luna 9420	Fillmore East, New York, NY	JHE	
Hey Joe	10 May 68	BR 18. Live performance.	One Night Stand CD Hep Cat 101	Fillmore East, New York, NY	JHE	
Hey Joe	03 Aug 68	BR 19. Live performance.	Crosstown Traffic CD M25 3664	Moody Coliseum, Southern Methodist University, Dallas, TX	JHE	
Hey Joe	23 Aug 68	BR 20. Live performance.	Historic Concert CD Midnight Beat MBCD 017	New York Rock Festival, Singer Bowl, Queens, NY	JHE	
Hey Joe	14 Sep 68	BR 21. Live performance.	Live At The Hollywood Bowl LP RSR / International RSR 25	Hollywood Bowl, Los Angeles, CA	JHE	

Song	Date	Notes	Release	Venue	Lineup
Hey Joe	10 Oct 68	BR 22. Live performance.	Winterland Days, The CD Manic Depression 001	Winterland Theatre, San Francisco, CA 2nd Show	JHE
Hey Joe	10 Oct 68	BR 22. Live performance.	Winterland Vol 1 CD Whoopy Cat WKP 025 / 26	Winterland Theatre, San Francisco, CA 2nd Show	JHE
Hey Joe	10 Oct 68	BR 22. Live performance.	Jimi Hendrix CD Imtrat 40-90355	Winterland Theatre, San Francisco, CA 2nd Show	JHE
Hey Joe	10 Oct 68	BR 22. Live performance.	Ultimate Live Collection, The CD The Beat Goes On BGO BX 9307-4	Winterland Theatre, San Francisco, CA 2nd Show	JHE
Hey Joe	11 Oct 68	BR 23. Live performance.	Winterland Vol 2 CD Whoopy Cat WKP 00279 / 28	Winterland Theatre, San Francisco, CA 2nd Show	JHE
Hey Joe	11 Oct 68	BR 23. Live performance.	Broadcasts CD Luna LU 9204	Winterland Theatre, San Francisco, CA 2nd Show	JHE
Hey Joe	11 Oct 68	BR 23. Live performance.	Star Spangled Blues CD Neutral Zone NZCD 89011	Winterland Theatre, San Francisco, CA 2nd Show	JHE
Hey Joe	11 Oct 68	BR 23. Live performance.	Ultimate Live Collection, The CD The Beat Goes On BGO BX 9307-4	Winterland Theatre, San Francisco, CA 2nd Show	JHE
Hey Joe	12 Oct 68	CR 6. Live performance.	Winterland Vol 3 CD Whoopy Cat WKP 0029 / 30	Winterland Theatre, San Francisco, CA 1st Show	JHE
Hey Joe	12 Oct 68	CR 6. Live performance.	Fire CD The Entertainers CD297	Winterland Theatre, San Francisco, CA 1st Show	JHE
Hey Joe	12 Oct 68	CR 6. Live performance.	Hendrix In Words And Music CD Outlaw Records OTR 1100030	Winterland Theatre, San Francisco, CA 1st Show	JHE
Hey Joe	12 Oct 68	CR 6. Live performance.	Live At Winterland (CR) CD Rykodisc RCD 20038	Winterland Theatre, San Francisco, CA 1st Show	JHE
Hey Joe	04 Jan 69	CR 7. Television performance.	Broadcasts CD Luna LU 9204	A Happening For Lulu, BBC TV, London, England	JHE
Hey Joe	04 Jan 69	CR 7. Television performance.	Broadcasts LP Trade Mark Of Quality TMQ 1841 & TMQ 71019	A Happening For Lulu, BBC TV, London, England	JHE

SONG TITLE	DATE	COMMENTS	RELEASE	LOCATION / VENUE	BAND	PERSONNEL
Hey Joe	04 Jan 69	CR 7. Television performance.	Historic Performances CD Aquarius AQ 67-JH-080	A Happening For Lulu, BBC TV, London, England	JHE	
Hey Joe	04 Jan 69	CR 7. Television performance.	Sweet Angel CD Compact Music WPOCM 0589	A Happening For Lulu, BBC TV, London, England	JHE	
Hey Joe	04 Jan 69	CR 7. Television performance.	Jimi: A Musical Legacy CD KTS BX 010	A Happening For Lulu, BBC TV, London, England	JHE	
Hey Joe	04 Jan 69	CR 7. Television performance.	BBC Sessions (CR) CD MCACD 2-11742	A Happening For Lulu, BBC TV, London, England	JHE	
Hey Joe	04 Jan 69	CR 7. Television performance.	Loaded Guitar LP Starlight SL 87013	A Happening For Lulu, BBC TV, London, England	JHE	
Hey Joe	09 Jan 69	BR 24. Live performance.	On The Killing Floor Swingin' Pig TSP-012-2	Konserthuset, Stockholm, Sweden 1st Show	JHE	
Hey Joe	09 Jan 69	BR 24. Live performance.	Electronic Church Music CD Pyramid PYCD 023	Konserthuset, Stockholm, Sweden 1st Show	JHE	
Hey Joe	09 Jan 69	BR 24. Live performance.	In Concert CD Starlife ST 3612	Konserthuset, Stockholm, Sweden 1st Show	JHE	
Hey Joe	09 Jan 69	BR 25. Live performance.	On The Killing Floor Swingin' Pig TSP-012-2	Konserthuset, Stockholm, Sweden 2nd Show	JHE	
Hey Joe	09 Jan 69	BR 25. Live performance.	In Europe 67 / 68 / 69 CD Vulture CD 009 / 2	Konserthuset, Stockholm, Sweden 2nd Show	JHE	
Hey Joe	09 Jan 69	BR 25. Live performance.	Very Best, The CD Irec / Retro MILCD-03	Konserthuset, Stockholm, Sweden 2nd Show	JHE	
Hey Joe	09 Jan 69	BR 25. Live performance.	Foxy Lady CD Alegra CD 9008	Konserthuset, Stockholm, Sweden 2nd Show	JHE	
Hey Joe	09 Jan 69	BR 25. Live performance.	Anthology CD Box 9	Konserthuset, Stockholm, Sweden 2nd Show	JHE	
Hey Joe	09 Jan 69	BR 26. Live performance.	Burning At Frankfurt CD	Jahrhunderthalle,	JHE	

Song	Date	Notes	Release	Location	Group
Hey Joe		Up Against The Berlin Wall CD Midnight Beat MBCD 046	Midnight Beat MBCD 040	Frankfurt, Germany	
Hey Joe	23 Jan 69		Up Against The Berlin Wall CD Midnight Beat MBCD 046	Sportpalast, Berlin, Germany	JHE
Hey Joe	24 Feb 69	BR 28. Live performance.	Good Vibes LP Trade Mark Of Quality TMOQ 1813	Royal Albert Hall, London, England	JHE
Hey Joe	24 Feb 69	BR 28. Live performance.	First Night At The Royal Albert Hall CD Midnight Beat MBCD 047 / 48	Royal Albert Hall, London, England Sound Check	JHE
Hey Joe	27 Apr 69	CR 8. Live performance.	Live At The Oakland Coliseum (CR) CD Dagger Records DBRO-11743	Oakland Coliseum, Oakland, CA	JHE
Hey Joe	24 May 69	CR 9. Live performance.	Stages San Diego 69 (CR) CD Reprise 9 27632-2	San Diego Sports Arena, San Diego, CA	JHE
Hey Joe	24 May 69	CR 9. Live performance.	Midnight Magic CD Neutral Zone NZCD 89012	San Diego Sports Arena, San Diego, CA	JHE
Hey Joe	24 May 69	CR 9. Live performance.	Don't Miss Him This Time CD Pyramid PYCD 096	San Diego Sports Arena, San Diego, CA	JHE
Hey Joe	18 Aug 69	BR 29. Live performance.	Woodstock Nation CD Wild Bird 89090 1 / 2	Woodstock Music And Art Fair, Bethel, NY	GSRB
Hey Joe	18 Aug 69	BR 29. Live performance.	Gypsy Sun And Rainbows CD Manic Depression MDCD 05 / 06	Woodstock Music And Art Fair, Bethel, NY	GSRB
Hey Joe	18 Aug 69	BR 29. Live performance.	Woodstock Monday, August 18 1969, 8AM CD JMH 008	Woodstock Music And Art Fair, Bethel, NY	GSRB
Hey Joe	18 Aug 69	BR 29. Live performance.	Ultimate Live Collection, The CD The Beat Goes On BGO BX 9307-4	Woodstock Music And Art Fair, Bethel, NY	GSRB
Hey Joe	01 Jan 70	BR 30. Live performance.	Band Of Gold CD-R Major Tom MT 087	Fillmore East, New York, NY 2nd Show	BOG
Hey Joe	01 Jan 70	BR 30. Live performance.	Ultimate Live Collection, The CD The Beat Goes On BGO BX 9307-4	Fillmore East, New York, NY 2nd Show	BOG

SONG TITLE	DATE	COMMENTS	RELEASE	LOCATION / VENUE	BAND	PERSONNEL
Hey Joe	30 May 70	CR 10. Live performance.	Riots In Berkeley CD Beech Marten BM 038	Berkeley Community Theater, Berkeley, CA 2nd Show	COL	
Hey Joe	30 May 70	CR 10. Live performance.	Concerts (CR) CD Reprise 9-22306-2	Berkeley Community Theater, Berkeley, CA 2nd Show	COL	
Hey Joe	30 May 70	CR 10. Live performance.	51st Anniversary CD Future Disc JMH 001 / 8	Berkeley Community Theater, Berkeley, CA 2nd Show	COL	
Hey Joe	30 May 70	CR 10. Live performance.	Redskin' Jammin' CD JH 01 / 02	Berkeley Community Theater, Berkeley, CA 2nd Show	COL	
Hey Joe	30 May 70	CR 10. Live performance.	Midnight Magic CD Neutral Zone NZCD 89012	Berkeley Community Theater, Berkeley, CA 2nd Show	COL	
Hey Joe	30 May 70	CR 10. Live performance.	Live USA CD Imtrat 902-001	Berkeley Community Theater, Berkeley, CA 2nd Show	COL	
Hey Joe	30 May 70	CR 10. Live performance.	Valley Of Neptune CD PC 28355	Berkeley Community Theater, Berkeley, CA 2nd Show	COL	
Hey Joe	30 May 70	CR 10. Live performance.	Jimi Plays Berkeley CD JMH 005 / 2	Berkeley Community Theater, Berkeley, CA 1st Show	COL	
Hey Joe	13 Jun 70	BR 31. Live performance.	Baltimore Civic Center, June 13, 1970 CD Starquake SQ-09	Baltimore Civic Center, Baltimore, MD	COL	
Hey Joe	04 Jul 70	BR 32. Live performance. Officially released on the Atlanta video cassette and laser disc.	Atlanta Special CD Genuine Pig TGP 121	2nd International Pop Festival, Atlanta, GA	COL	
Hey Joe	04 Jul 70	BR 32. Live performance. Officially released on the Atlanta video cassette and laser disc.	At The Atlanta Pop Festival (CR) Laserdisc BMG BVLP 77 (74321-10987)	2nd International Pop Festival, Atlanta, GA	COL	
Hey Joe	04 Jul 70	BR 32. Live performance. Officially released on the Atlanta video cassette and laser disc.	Atlanta CD JMH 009 / 02	2nd International Pop Festival, Atlanta, GA	COL	
Hey Joe	04 Jul 70	BR 32. Live performance. Officially released on the Atlanta video cassette and laser disc.	Live! CD Black B-05	2nd International Pop Festival, Atlanta, GA	COL	
Hey Joe	04 Jul 70	BR 32. Live performance. Officially released on the Atlanta video cassette and laser disc.	Oh, Atlanta CD Tendolar TDR-009	2nd International Pop Festival, Atlanta, GA	COL	

Song	Date	Note	Release	Location	Type
Hey Joe	04 Jul 70	BR 32. Live performance. Officially released on the Atlanta video cassette and laser disc.	Atlanta CD JMH 009 / 02	2nd International Pop Festival, Atlanta, GA	COL
Hey Joe	30 Jul 70	BR 33. Live performance.	In From The Storm CD Silver Rarities SIRA 109 / 110	Rainbow Bridge Vibratory Sound- Color Experiment, Maui, HI 2nd Show	COL
Hey Joe	30 Aug 70	BR 34. Live performance.	Berkeley Soundchecks, The CD Whoopy Cat WKP 0008	Isle Of Wight Festival, Isle Of Wight, England	COL
Hey Joe	30 Aug 70	BR 34. Live performance.	Wight CD JMH 006 / 2	Isle Of Wight Festival, Isle Of Wight, England	COL
Hey Joe	01 Sep 70	BR 35. Live performance.	Warm Hello Of The Sun, The CD	Stora Scenen, Liseberg Nojespark, Goteborg, Sweden	COL
Hey Joe	30 Aug 70	BR 36. Live performance.	Welcome To The Electric Circus Vol 2 CD Midnight Beat 018	K.B. Hallen, Copenhagen, Denmark	COL
Hey Joe	30 Aug 70	BR 36. Live performance.	Copenhagen '70 CD Whoopy Cat WKP 044 / 45	K.B. Hallen, Copenhagen, Denmark	COL
Hey Joe	04 Sep 70	BR 37. Live performance.	Back To Berlin CD Midnight Beat 049	Deutsche- Landhalle, Berlin, Germany	COL
Hey Joe	06 Sep 70	BR 38. Live performance.	Love & Peace CD Midnight Beat MBCD 015	Love And Peace Festival, Isle Of Fehrman, Germany	COL
Hey Joe	06 Sep 70	BR 38. Live performance.	Wink Of An Eye CD Whoopy Cat WKP 0033 / 34	Love And Peace Festival, Isle Of Fehrman, Germany	COL
Hey Joe	23 Oct 66	Outtake mix of CR 1 Mix 1	Symphony Of Experience CD Third Stone Discs TDS 24966	De Lane Lea, London, England	Fake
Hey Joe	23 Oct 66	Outtake mix of CR 1 Mix 1	Get The Experience CD Invasion Unlimited IU 9424-1	De Lane Lea, London, England	Fake
Hey Joe	23 Oct 66	Outtake mix of CR 1 Mix 1	Living Reels Vol 1 CD JMH 011	De Lane Lea, London, England	Fake
Highway Chile	03 Apr 67	CR 1. This is a mono recording and no stereo version has turned up yet.	War Heroes (CR) CD Polydor 847-2622	Olympic Sound Studios, London, England	JHE

SONG TITLE	DATE	COMMENTS	RELEASE	LOCATION / VENUE	BAND	PERSONNEL	
Highway Chile	03 Apr 67	CR 1. This is a mono recording and no stereo version has turned up yet.	Smash Hits (CR) CD Reprise 2276-2	Olympic Sound Studios, London, England	JHE		
Highway Chile	03 Apr 67	CR 1. This is a mono recording and no stereo version has turned up yet.	Jimi Hendrix Vol 2: A Man Of Our Times LP Napoleon NLP 11018	Olympic Sound Studios, London, England	JHE		
Highway Chile	03 Apr 67	CR 1. This is a mono recording and no stereo version has turned up yet.	Are You Experienced? (CR) CD MCACD 11602	Olympic Sound Studios, London, England	JHE		
Highway Chile	03 Apr 67	CR 1. This is a mono recording and no stereo version has turned up yet.	Smash Hits (CR) CD Reprise 2276-2	Olympic Sound Studios, London, England	JHE		
Highway Chile	03 Apr 67	CR 1. This is a mono recording and no stereo version has turned up yet.	Legacy (CR) LP Polydor	Olympic Sound Studios, London, England	JHE		
Highway Chile	03 Apr 67	CR 1. This is a mono recording and no stereo version has turned up yet.	The Singles Album (CR) CD Polydor 827 369-2	Olympic Sound Studios, London, England	JHE		
Highway Of Broken Hearts Medley	23 Jan 70	BR 1. This is part of a longer medley that begins with "Ezy Rider". This starts at the beginning of "Highway Of Broken Hearts". Timings and edits vary from source to source. See "Diamonds In The Dust" CD for the full medley.	Electric Hendrix Vol 2 CD Pyramid PYCD 0310.475"	Record Plant, New York, NY	BOG	Don ? / Harmonica	
Highway Of Broken Hearts Medley (Highway Of Broken Dreams)	23 Jan 70	BR 1. This is part of a longer medley that begins with "Ezy Rider". This starts at the beginning of "Highway Of Broken Hearts". Timings and edits vary from source to source. See "Diamonds In The Dust" CD for the full medley.	Message From Nine To The Universe CD Oil Well 122	Record Plant, New York, NY	BOG	Don ? / Harmonica	
Highway Of Broken Hearts Medley	23 Jan 70	BR 1. This is part of a longer medley that begins with "Ezy Rider". This starts at the beginning of "Highway Of Broken Hearts". Timings and edits vary from source to source. See "Diamonds In The Dust" CD for the full medley.	Talent And Feeling Vol 2 CD Extremely Rare EXR 22	Record Plant, New York, NY	BOG	Don ? / Harmonica	
Highway Of Broken Hearts Medley (First Jam)	23 Jan 70	BR 1. This is part of a longer medley that begins with "Ezy Rider". This starts at the beginning of "Highway Of Broken Hearts". Timings and edits vary from source to source. See "Diamonds In The Dust" CD for the full medley.	51st Anniversary CD Future Disc JMH 001 / 8	Record Plant, New York, NY	BOG	Don ? / Harmonica	
Highway Of Broken Hearts Medley (There Goes Ezy Rider / Seven Dollars In My Pocket)	23 Jan 70	BR 1. This is part of a longer medley that begins with "Ezy Rider". This starts at the beginning of "Highway Of Broken Hearts". Timings and edits vary from source to source. See "Diamonds In The Dust" CD for the full medley.	51st Anniversary CD Future Disc JMH 001 / 8	Record Plant, New York, NY	BOG	Don ? / Harmonica	
Highway Of Broken Hearts Medley	23 Jan 70	BR 1. This is part of a longer medley that begins with "Ezy Rider". This starts at the beginning of "Highway Of Broken Hearts". Timings and edits vary from source to source. See "Diamonds In The Dust" CD for the full medley.	First Rays Of The New Rising Sun CD Triangle PYCD 084-2	Record Plant, New York, NY	BOG	Don ? / Harmonica	

Song	Date	Notes	CD	Location		Musicians
Highway Of Broken Hearts Medley (Rider Blues)+A1693	23 Jan 70	BR 1. This is part of a longer medley that begins with "Ezy Rider". This starts at the beginning of "Highway Of Broken Hearts". Timings and edits vary from source to source. See "Diamonds In The Dust" CD for the full medley.	51st Anniversary CD Future Disc JMH 001 / 8	Record Plant, New York, NY	BOG	Don ? / Harmonica
Highway Of Broken Hearts Medley	23 Jan 70	BR 1. This is part of a longer medley that begins with "Ezy Rider". This starts at the beginning of "Highway Of Broken Hearts". Timings and edits vary from source to source. See "Diamonds In The Dust" CD for the full medley.	Every Way To Paradise CD Tintangel TIBX 021 / 22 / 23 / 24	Record Plant, New York, NY	BOG	Don ? / Harmonica
Highway Of Broken Hearts Medley (Freedom / Ezy Rider...Jam)	23 Jan 70	BR 1. This is part of a longer medley that begins with "Ezy Rider". This starts at the beginning of "Highway Of Broken Hearts". Timings and edits vary from source to source. See "Diamonds In The Dust" CD for the full medley.	I Don't Live Today CD ACL 007	Record Plant, New York, NY	BOG	Don ? / Harmonica
Highway Of Broken Hearts Medley (Freedom / Ezy Rider...Jam)	23 Jan 70	BR 1. This is part of a longer medley that begins with "Ezy Rider". This starts at the beginning of "Highway Of Broken Hearts". Timings and edits vary from source to source. See "Diamonds In The Dust" CD for the full medley.	Kiss The Skies CD Mum MUCD 024	Record Plant, New York, NY	BOG	Don ? / Harmonica
Highway Of Broken Hearts Medley (Freedom / Ezy Rider...Jam)	23 Jan 70	BR 1. This is part of a longer medley that begins with "Ezy Rider". This starts at the beginning of "Highway Of Broken Hearts". Timings and edits vary from source to source. See "Diamonds In The Dust" CD for the full medley.	Master's Masters, The CD JH-01	Record Plant, New York, NY	BOG	Don ? / Harmonica
Highway Of Broken Hearts Medley (Freedom / Ezy Rider...Jam)	23 Jan 70	BR 1. This is part of a longer medley that begins with "Ezy Rider". This starts at the beginning of "Highway Of Broken Hearts". Timings and edits vary from source to source. See "Diamonds In The Dust" CD for the full medley.	Completer, The CD Whoopy Cat WKP 0018 / 19	Record Plant, New York, NY	BOG	Don ? / Harmonica
Hollywood Jam (Instrumental Jam)	?? / ?? 68-69	BR 1. Incomplete. All version fade in at the start. Each boot gives this a different made up title so we settled on 'Hollywood Jam' to be consistent.	Talent And Feeling Vol 2 CD Extremely Rare EXR 22	Unknown	Jimi	Unknown / Other Musicians
Hollywood Jam (Devil's Jam)	?? / ?? 68-69	BR 1. Incomplete. All version fade in at the start. Each boot gives this a different made up title so we settled on 'Hollywood Jam' to be consistent.	51st Anniversary CD Future Disc JMH 001 / 8	Unknown	Jimi	Unknown / Other Musicians
Hollywood Jam (Instrumental Jam)	?? / ?? 68-69	BR 1. Incomplete. All version fade in at the start. Each boot gives this a different made up title so we settled on 'Hollywood Jam' to be consistent.	Let's Drop Some Ludes And Vomit With Jimi CD Midnight Beat MBCD 026	Unknown	Jimi	Unknown / Other Musicians
Hollywood Jam (Winter Blues)	?? / ?? 68-69	BR 1. Incomplete. All version fade in at the start. Each boot gives this a different made up title so we settled on 'Hollywood Jam' to be consistent.	Multicolored Blues CD Luna LU 9317	Unknown	Unknown Jimi	Unknown / Other Musicians
Home Acoustic Jam	FAKE	No Jimi involvement on this track.	Every Way To Paradise CD Tintangel TIBX 021 / 22 / 23 / 24		Fake	
Honeybed	23 Dec 69	BR 1. This is a session for an unreleased Hendrix composition. Take 1,2 &4 are breakdowns. Take 3 is the most complete.	Ball And Chain CD Jimi 009	Record Plant, New York, NY	BOG	

SONG TITLE	DATE	COMMENTS	RELEASE	LOCATION / VENUE	BAND	PERSONNEL
Honeybed	23 Dec 69	BR 1. This is a session for an unreleased Hendrix composition. Take 1,2 &4 are breakdowns. Take 3 is the most complete.	Black Gold CD Midnight Beat MBCD 058-062	Record Plant, New York, NY	BOG	
Hoochie Coochie Man	17 Jan 67	CR 1. BBC performance.	Jewel Box CD Home HR-5824-3	BBC Playhouse Theatre, London, England	JHE	Alexis Korner / Slide Guitar
Hoochie Coochie Man	17 Oct 67	CR 1. BBC performance.	Lifelines (CR) CD Reprise 9 26435-2	BBC Playhouse Theatre, London, England	JHE	Alexis Korner / Slide Guitar
Hoochie Coochie Man	17 Oct 67	CR 1. BBC performance.	Guitar Hero CD Document DR 013	BBC Playhouse Theatre, London, England	JHE	Alexis Korner / Slide Guitar
Hoochie Coochie Man	17 Oct 67	CR 1. BBC performance.	Primal Keys LP Impossible Record Works	BBC Playhouse Theatre, London, England	JHE	Alexis Korner / Slide Guitar
Hoochie Coochie Man	17 Oct 67	CR 1. BBC performance.	Radio One (CR) CD Rykodisc RCD 20078	BBC Playhouse Theatre, London, England	JHE	Alexis Korner / Slide Guitar
Hoochie Coochie Man	17 Oct 67	CR 1. BBC performance.	Live In London 1967 CD Koine Records K881104	BBC Playhouse Theatre, London, England	JHE	Alexis Korner / Slide Guitar
Hoochie Coochie Man	17 Oct 67	CR 1. BBC performance.	Live In Concert 1967 CD Living Legend LLR-CD 001	BBC Playhouse Theatre, London, England	JHE	Alexis Korner / Slide Guitar
Hoochie Coochie Man	17 Oct 67	CR 1. BBC performance.	In Concert CD Starlife ST 3612	BBC Playhouse Theatre, London, England	JHE	Alexis Korner / Slide Guitar
Hoochie Coochie Man	17 Oct 67	CR 1. BBC performance.	Complete BBC Session And.... The CD Last Bootleg Records LBR 036 / 2	BBC Playhouse Theatre, London, England	JHE	Alexis Korner / Slide Guitar
Hoochie Coochie Man	17 Oct 67	CR 1. BBC performance.	BBC Sessions (CR) CD MCACD 2-11742	BBC Playhouse Theatre, London, England	JHE	Alexis Korner / Slide Guitar
Hoochie Coochie Man	?? / ?? 68?	BR 1. Live performance.	Broadcasts CD Luna LU 9204	Unknown	Jimi	Unknown / Backing Band
Hoochie Coochie Man	?? Dec 69	CR 2.	Band Of Gypsys Vol 3	Record Plant Or Baggies, NY, NY	BOG	
Hoochie Coochie Man	?? Dec 69	CR 2.	Loose Ends (CR) LP Polydor 837574-2	Record Plant Or Baggies, NY, NY	BOG	

Song	Date	Notes	Release	Location	BOG
Hoochie Coochie Man	?? Dec 69	CR 2.	Band Of Gypsys- The Ultimate CD JMH 010 3	Record Plant, New York, NY	BOG
Hound Dog	06 Oct 67	CR 1. BBC performance.	Guitar Hero CD Document DR 013	Top Gear, BBC Playhouse Theatre, London, England	JHE
Hound Dog	06 Oct 67	CR 1. BBC performance.	Primal Keys LP Impossible Record Works	Top Gear, BBC Playhouse Theatre, London, England	JHE
Hound Dog	06 Oct 67	CR 1. BBC performance.	Radio One (CR) CD Rykodisc RCD 20078	Top Gear, BBC Playhouse Theatre, London, England	JHE
Hound Dog	06 Oct 67	CR 1. BBC performance.	Official Bootleg Album, The CD Yellow Dog YD 051	Top Gear, BBC Playhouse Theatre, London, England	JHE
Hound Dog	06 Oct 67	CR 1. BBC performance.	Ultimate BBC Collection CD Classical CL006	Top Gear, BBC Playhouse Theatre, London, England	JHE
Hound Dog	06 Oct 67	CR 1. BBC performance.	Jimi Hendrix Vol 2: A Man Of Our Times LP Napoleon NLP 11018	Top Gear, BBC Playhouse Theatre, London, England	JHE
Hound Dog	06 Oct 67	CR 1. BBC performance.	Live In London 1967 CD Koine Records K881104	Top Gear, BBC Playhouse Theatre, London, England	JHE
Hound Dog	06 Oct 67	CR 1. BBC performance.	Live In Concert 1967 CD Living Legend LLR-CD 001	Top Gear, BBC Playhouse Theatre, London, England	JHE
Hound Dog	06 Oct 67	CR 1. BBC performance.	Broadcasts LP Trade Mark Of Quality TMQ 1841 & TMQ 71019	Top Gear, BBC Playhouse Theatre, London, England	JHE
Hound Dog	06 Oct 67	CR 1. BBC performance.	In Concert CD Starlife ST 3612	Top Gear, BBC Playhouse Theatre, London, England	JHE
Hound Dog	06 Oct 67	CR 1. BBC performance.	King And Wonder Sessions CD Oh Boy 1-9170	Top Gear, BBC Playhouse Theatre, London, England	JHE
Hound Dog	06 Oct 67	CR 1. BBC performance.	Complete BBC Session And..., The CD Last Bootleg Records LBR 036 / 2	Top Gear, BBC Playhouse Theatre, London, England	JHE
Hound Dog	06 Oct 67	CR 1. BBC performance.	Rarities On Compact Disc CD On The Radio	Top Gear, BBC Playhouse Theatre, London, England	JHE

SONG TITLE	DATE	COMMENTS	RELEASE	LOCATION / VENUE	BAND	PERSONNEL
Hound Dog	06 Oct 67	CR 1. BBC performance.	BBC Sessions (CR) CD MCACD 2-11742	Top Gear, BBC Playhouse Theatre, London, England	JHE	
Hound Dog	24? Feb 69	BR 1. A short impromptu jam recorded at Jimi's London flat and used in the unreleased film from The Royal Albert Hall.	Thanks Ottawa For The Memories CD Luna 9319	New York Apartment	JHE	
Hound Dog	24? Feb 69	BR 1. A short impromptu jam recorded at Jimi's London flat and used in the unreleased film from The Royal Albert Hall.	Freak Out Jam CD GH 002	New York Apartment	JHE	
Hound Dog	24? Feb 69	BR 1. A short impromptu jam recorded at Jimi's London flat and used in the unreleased film from The Royal Albert Hall.	Complete BBC Session And.... The CD Last Bootleg Records LBR 036 / 2	New York Apartment	JHE	
Hound Dog	24 Feb 69	BR 2. Live performance from the soundcheck. Three short bits and a full take #1.	Live USA CD Imtrat 902-001	Royal Albert Hall, London, England Sound Check	JHE	
Hound Dog	24 Feb 69	BR 2. Live performance from the soundcheck. Three short bits and a full take #1 plus take #2.	Good Vibes LP Trade Mark Of Quality TMOQ 1813	Royal Albert Hall, London, England Sound Check	JHE	
Hound Dog	24 Feb 69	BR 2. Live performance from the soundcheck. Three short bits and a full take #1 plus take #2.	First Night At The Royal Albert Hall CD Midnight Beat MBCD 047 / 48	Royal Albert Hall, London, England Sound Check	JHE	
Hound Dog		No Jimi involvement on this track.	Jimi: A Musical Legacy CD KTS BX 010		No Jimi	
House Burning Down	01 May 68	CR 1 mix 1.	Red House CD The Entertainers CD294	Record Plant, New York, NY	Jimi	
House Burning Down	01 May 68	CR 1 mix 1.	Electric Ladyland (CR) CD MCACD-11600	Record Plant, New York, NY	Jimi	Jimi Hendrix / Bass, Mitch Mitchell / Drums
House Burning Down	01 May 68	CR 1 mix 2. An unused mix of CR 1.	1968 AD CD Whoopy Cat WKP 0001	Record Plant, New York, NY	Jimi	Jimi Hendrix / Bass, Mitch Mitchell / Drums
House Burning Down	01 May 68	CR 1 mix 2. An unused mix of CR 1.	Electric Ladyland Outtakes CD Invasion Unlimited IU 9417-1	Record Plant, New York, NY	Jimi	
House Burning Down	01 May 68	CR 1 mix 2. An unused mix of CR 1.	Voodoo In Ladyland CD MUM MUCD 006	Record Plant, New York, NY	Jimi	
House Burning Down	01 May 68	CR 1 mix 3. A second unused mix of the CR 1 from an acetate. This has some reverb added to the lead guitar solo.	Electric Gypsy CD Scorpio? 40176 / 15	Record Plant, New York, NY	Jimi	Jimi Hendrix / Bass, Mitch Mitchell / Drums

Title	Date	Notes	CD / Catalog	Studio / Location	Performer	Jimi Hendrix / Bass, Mitch Mitchell / Drums
House Burning Down	01 May 68	CR 1 mix 3. A second unused mix of the CR 1 from an acetate. This has some reverb added to the lead guitar solo.	1968 AD CD Whoopy Cat WKP 0001	Record Plant, New York, NY	Jimi	Little Richard / Vocals & Piano, Don Covay / Organ
House Of The Rising Sun		No Jimi involvement on this track.	Jimi: A Musical Legacy CD KTS BX 010		No Jimi	
How Would You Feel	15? Oct 65	CR 1. Stereo mix of the commercial 45 release that was originally in mono.	Jimi: A Musical Legacy CD KTS BX 010	Studio 76, New York, NY	CKB	
How Would You Feel	15? Oct 65	CR 1. Stereo mix of the commercial 45 release that was originally in mono.	51st Anniversary CD Future Disc JMH 001 / 8	Studio 76, New York, NY	CKB	
I Can't Find It Without You	?? Mar 70 ?	This is a recording by the group "Love" for the unreleased 'Black Beauty' album. Jimi's involvement is highly unlikely.	Midnight Sun CD Third Eye NK 007	Olympic Sound Studios, London, England	Love	
I Can't Turn You Loose	No Jimi	This doesn't sound like there's any Jimi involvement at all unless some future info documents otherwise.	Olympic Gold Vol 2 CD Blimp 007	Olympic Sound Studios, London, England	No Jimi	
I Don't Know What You Got (But It's Got Me)	?? Nov 65	CR 1. Parts I & II from the rare commercial single.	Rarities CD The Genuine Pig TGP-CD-091	Unknown	Jimi	
I Don't Live Today	20 Feb 67	CR 1 mix 1 (stereo)	Are You Experienced? (CR) CD MCACD 11602	De Lane Lea, London, England	JHE	
I Don't Live Today	20 Feb 67	CR 1 mix 2 (mono)	Are You Experienced? (CR) LP Track 612 001	De Lane Lea, London, England	JHE	
I Don't Live Today	20 Feb 67	CR 1 mix 4. An unused mix of CR 1 featuring a double lead vocal.	Out Of The Studio: Demos From 1967 CD BHCD 931022	De Lane Lea, London, England	JHE	
I Don't Live Today	20 Feb 67	CR 1 mix 3. This is the CR 1 basic track prior to vocals and overdubs.	DeLane Lea And Olympic Outs CD Gold Standard CD-R	De Lane Lea, London, England	JHE	
I Don't Live Today	20 Feb 67	CR 1 mix 4. An unused mix of CR 1 featuring a double lead vocal.	DeLane Lea And Olympic Outs CD Gold Standard CD-R	De Lane Lea, London, England	JHE	
I Don't Live Today	20 Feb 67	CR 1 mix 3. This is the CR 1 basic track prior to vocals and overdubs.	Get The Experience CD Invasion Unlimited IU 9424-1	De Lane Lea, London, England	JHE	
I Don't Live Today	20 Feb 67	CR 1 mix 3. This is the CR 1 basic track prior to vocals and overdubs.	Complete BBC Session And.... The CD Last Bootleg Records LBR 036 / 2	De Lane Lea, London, England	JHE	
I Don't Live Today	20 Feb 67	CR 1 mix 3. This is the CR 1 basic track prior to vocals and overdubs.	I Don't Live Today CD ACL 007	De Lane Lea, London, England	JHE	

SONG TITLE	DATE	COMMENTS	RELEASE	LOCATION / VENUE	BAND	PERSONNEL
I Don't Live Today	20 Feb 67	CR 1 mix 3. This is the CR 1 basic track prior to vocals and overdubs.	Gypsy Charm CD Mum MUCD 018	De Lane Lea, London, England	JHE	
I Don't Live Today	20 Feb 67	CR 1 mix 3. This is the CR 1 basic track prior to vocals and overdubs.	Olympic Gold Vol 1 CD Blimp 0067	De Lane Lea, London, England	JHE	
I Don't Live Today	20 Feb 67	CR 1 mix 3. This is the CR 1 basic track prior to vocals and overdubs.	Out Of The Studio: Demos From 1967 CD BHCD 931022	De Lane Lea, London, England	JHE	
I Don't Live Today	20 Feb 67	CR 1 mix 4. An unused mix of CR 1 featuring a double lead vocal.	I Don't Live Today CD ACL 007	De Lane Lea, London, England	JHE	
I Don't Live Today	20 Feb 67	CR 1 mix 4. An unused mix of CR 1 featuring a double lead vocal.	Gypsy Charm CD Mum MUCD 018	De Lane Lea, London, England	JHE	
I Don't Live Today	20 Feb 67	CR 1 mix 4. An unused mix of CR 1 featuring a double lead vocal.	Olympic Gold Vol 1 CD Blimp 0067	De Lane Lea, London, England	JHE	
I Don't Live Today	20 Feb 67	CR 1 mix 4. An unused mix of CR 1 featuring a double lead vocal.	Get The Experience CD Invasion Unlimited IU 9424-1	De Lane Lea, London, England	JHE	
I Don't Live Today	20 Feb 67	BR 1. An instrumental alternate take #1 from the same session as the CR 1.	DeLane Lea And Olympic Outs CD Gold Standard CD-R	De Lane Lea, London, England	JHE	
I Don't Live Today	20 Feb 67	BR 1. An instrumental alternate take #1 from the same session as the CR 1.	Complete BBC Session And.... The CD Last Bootleg Records LBR 036 / 2	De Lane Lea, London, England	JHE	
I Don't Live Today	20 Feb 67	BR 1. An instrumental alternate take #1 from the same session as the CR 1.	Jimi: A Musical Legacy CD KTS BX 010	De Lane Lea, London, England	JHE	
I Don't Live Today	20 Feb 67	BR 1. An instrumental alternate take #1 from the same session as the CR 1.	Kiss The Skies CD Mum MUCD 024	De Lane Lea, London, England	JHE	
I Don't Live Today	20 Feb 67	BR 1. An instrumental alternate take #1 from the same session as the CR 1.	Olympic Gold Vol 1 CD Blimp 0067	De Lane Lea, London, England	JHE	
I Don't Live Today	20 Feb 67	BR 1. An instrumental alternate take #1 from the same session as the CR 1.	Out Of The Studio: Demos From 1967 CD BHCD 931022	De Lane Lea, London, England	JHE	
I Don't Live Today	20 Feb 67	BR 2. An instrumental alternate take #2 from the same session as the CR 1.	DeLane Lea And Olympic Outs CD Gold Standard CD-R	De Lane Lea, London, England	JHE	
I Don't Live Today	20 Feb 67	BR 2. An instrumental alternate take #2 from the same session as the CR 1.	Complete BBC Session And.... The CD Last Bootleg Records LBR 036 / 2	De Lane Lea, London, England	JHE	

Song		Notes	Date	Release	Location	Band
I Don't Live Today		BR 2. An instrumental alternate take #2 from the same session as the CR 1.	20 Feb 67	Jimi: A Musical Legacy CD KTS BX 010	De Lane Lea, London, England	JHE
I Don't Live Today		BR 2. An instrumental alternate take #2 from the same session as the CR 1.	20 Feb 67	Olympic Gold Vol 1 CD Blimp 0067	De Lane Lea, London, England	JHE
I Don't Live Today		BR 2. An instrumental alternate take #2 from the same session as the CR 1.	20 Feb 67	Out Of The Studio: Demos From 1967 CD BHCD 931022	De Lane Lea, London, England	JHE
I Don't Live Today		BR 3. An instrumental alternate take #3 from the same session as the CR 1.	20 Feb 67	DeLane Lea And Olympic Outs CD Gold Standard CD-R	De Lane Lea, London, England	JHE
I Don't Live Today		BR 3. An instrumental alternate take #3 from the same session as the CR 1.	20 Feb 67	Complete BBC Session And.... The CD Last Bootleg Records LBR 036 / 2	De Lane Lea, London, England	JHE
I Don't Live Today		BR 3. An instrumental alternate take #3 from the same session as the CR 1.	20 Feb 67	I Don't Live Today CD ACL 007	De Lane Lea, London, England	JHE
I Don't Live Today		BR 3. An instrumental alternate take #3 from the same session as the CR 1.	20 Feb 67	Kiss The Skies CD Mum MUCD 024	De Lane Lea, London, England	JHE
I Don't Live Today		BR 3. An instrumental alternate take #3 from the same session as the CR 1.	20 Feb 67	Olympic Gold Vol 1 CD Blimp 0067	De Lane Lea, London, England	JHE
I Don't Live Today		BR 3. An instrumental alternate take #3 from the same session as the CR 1.	20 Feb 67	Out Of The Studio: Demos From 1967 CD BHCD 931022	De Lane Lea, London, England	JHE
I Don't Live Today		BR 3. An instrumental alternate take #3 from the same session as the CR 1.	20 Feb 67	Get The Experience CD Invasion Unlimited IU 9424-1	De Lane Lea, London, England	JHE
I Don't Live Today		CR 2. BBC performance.	05 Sep 67	Live In Stockholm 1967 CD Document DR 003	De Lane Lea, London, England	JHE
I Don't Live Today		CR 2. BBC performance.	05 Sep 67	Wild Man Of Pop Plays Vol 1, The CD Pyramid RFTCD 003	Studio 4, Radiohuset, Stockholm, Sweden	JHE
I Don't Live Today		CR 2. BBC performance.	05 Sep 67	Stages Stockholm 67 (CR) CD Reprise 9 27632-2	Studio 4, Radiohuset, Stockholm, Sweden	JHE
I Don't Live Today		CR 2. BBC performance.	05 Sep 67	Recorded Live In Europe CD Bulldog BGCD 023	Studio 4, Radiohuset, Stockholm, Sweden	JHE
I Don't Live Today		CR 2. BBC performance.	05 Sep 67	Two Sides Of The Same Genius LP Amazing Kornyphone TAKRL H677	Studio 4, Radiohuset, Stockholm, Sweden	JHE

SONG TITLE	DATE	COMMENTS	RELEASE	LOCATION / VENUE	BAND	PERSONNEL
I Don't Live Today	05 Sep 67	CR 2. BBC performance.	Fire CD The Entertainers CD297	Studio 4, Radiohuset, Stockholm, Sweden	JHE	
I Don't Live Today	05 Sep 67	CR 2. BBC performance.	In Europe 67 / 88 / 69 CD Vulture CD 009 / 2	Studio 4, Radiohuset, Stockholm, Sweden	JHE	
I Don't Live Today	05 Sep 67	CR 2. BBC performance.	Loaded Guitar LP Starlight SL 87013	Studio 4, Radiohuset, Stockholm, Sweden	JHE	
I Don't Live Today	05 Sep 67	CR 2. BBC performance.	Greatest Hits Live CD Chartbusters CHER 089A	Studio 4, Radiohuset, Stockholm, Sweden	JHE	
I Don't Live Today	25 Feb 68	BR 4. Live performance.	Winterland Vol 2 CD Whoopy Cat WKP 00279 / 28	Civic Opera House, Chicago, IL	JHE	
I Don't Live Today	03 Aug 68	BR 5. Live performance.	Crosstown Traffic CD M25 3664	Moody Coliseum, Southern Methodist University, Dallas, TX	JHE	
I Don't Live Today	11 Aug 68	BR 6. Live performance.	Davenport, Iowa '68 LP Creative Artistry 26K10 / 55K10	Col Ballroom, Davenport, IA	JHE	
I Don't Live Today	23 Aug 68	BR 7. Live performance.	Historic Concert CD Midnight Beat MBCD 017	New York Rock Festival, Singer Bowl, Queens, NY	JHE	
I Don't Live Today	14 Sep 68	BR 8. Live performance.	Live At The Hollywood Bowl LP RSR / International RSR 251	Hollywood Bowl, Los Angeles, CA	JHE	
I Don't Live Today	28 Nov 68	BR 9. Live performance.	Have Mercy On Me Baby CD Midnight Beat MBCD 038	Philharmonic Hall, New York, NY	JHE	
I Don't Live Today	28 Nov 68	BR 9. Live performance.	Live At Philharmonic Hall LP Sagittarius LTD	Philharmonic Hall, New York, NY	JHE	
I Don't Live Today	08 Jan 68	BR 10. Live performance.	Live In Paris 66 / 67 CD Whoopy Cat WKP 0012	Loresberg Cirkus, Goteborg, Sweden 2nd Show	JHE	
I Don't Live Today	08 Jan 69	BR 10. Live performance.	Cat's Squirrel CD CS 001 / 2	Loresberg Cirkus, Goteborg, Sweden 2nd Show	JHE	
I Don't Live Today	08 Jan 69	BR 10. Live performance.	Cat's Squirrel CD CS 001 / 2	Loresberg Cirkus, Goteborg, Sweden 2nd Show	JHE	
I Don't Live Today	08 Jan 69	BR 10. Live performance.	EXP Over Sweden (CR)	Loresberg Cirkus,	JHE	

Song	Date	BR Note	CD UniVibes 1002	Location	
I Don't Live Today	09 Jan 69	BR 11. Live performance.	On The Killing Floor Swingin' Pig TSP-012-2	Konserthuset, Stockholm, Sweden 2nd Show	JHE
I Don't Live Today	09 Jan 69	BR 11. Live performance.	Legendary Star Club Tapes, The CD The Early Years 02-CD-3309	Konserthuset, Stockholm, Sweden 2nd Show	JHE
I Don't Live Today	09 Jan 69	BR 11. Live performance.	In Europe 67 / 68 / 69 CD Vulture CD 009 / 2	Konserthuset, Stockholm, Sweden 2nd Show	JHE
I Don't Live Today	10 Jan 69	BR 12. Live performance.	Welcome To The Electric Circus Vol 1 CD Midnight Beat 016	Falkoner Centret, Copenhagen, Denmark 1st Show	JHE
I Don't Live Today	17 Jan 69	BR 13. Live performance.	Burning At Frankfurt CD Midnight Beat MBCD 040	Jahrhunderthalle, Frankfurt, Germany	JHE
I Don't Live Today	24 Feb 69	BR 14. Live performance.	Historic Performances CD Aquarius AQ 67-JH-080	Royal Albert Hall, London, England	JHE
I Don't Live Today	24 Feb 69	BR 14. Live performance. Stereo.	Royal Albert Hall CD Blimp 008 / 009 & Listen To This Eric CD JH 003 / 4	Royal Albert Hall, London, England	JHE
I Don't Live Today	24 Feb 69	BR 14. Live performance.	Stone Free CD Silver Rarities SIRA 58 / 59	Royal Albert Hall, London, England	JHE
I Don't Live Today	26 Apr 69	BR 15. This was released incomplete on the 'Lifelines' package.	Electric Jimi CD Jaguarondi Records	Los Angeles Forum, Los Angeles, CA	JHE
I Don't Live Today	26 Apr 69	BR 15. This was released incomplete on the 'Lifelines' package.	I Don't Live Today, Maybe Tomorrow CD Living Legend LRCD 030	Los Angeles Forum, Los Angeles, CA	JHE
I Don't Live Today	26 Apr 69	BR 15. This was released incomplete on the 'Lifelines' package.	Live USA CD Imtrat 902-001	Los Angeles Forum, Los Angeles, CA	JHE
I Don't Live Today	26 Apr 69	BR 15. This was released incomplete on the 'Lifelines' package.	Anthology CD Box 9	Los Angeles Forum, Los Angeles, CA	JHE
I Don't Live Today	26 Apr 69	BR 15. This was released incomplete on the 'Lifelines' package.	Unforgettable Experience LP RAH 2469	Los Angeles Forum, Los Angeles, CA	JHE
I Don't Live Today	17 May 69	BR 16. Live performance.	One Night At The Arena CD Venue VE 100501	Rhode Island Arena, Providence, RI	JHE

SONG TITLE	DATE	COMMENTS	RELEASE	LOCATION / VENUE	BAND	PERSONNEL
I Don't Live Today	18 May 69	BR 17. Live performance.	Roman Coliseum, The CD Starquake SQ 11	Madison Square Garden, New York, NY	JHE	
I Don't Live Today	24 May 69	CR 3. Live performance.	Stages San Diego 69 (CR) CD Reprise 9 27632-2	San Diego Sports Arena, San Diego, CA	JHE	
I Don't Live Today	24 May 69	CR 3. Live performance.	Concerts (CR) CD Reprise 9-22306-2	San Diego Sports Arena, San Diego, CA	JHE	
I Don't Live Today	24 May 69	CR 3. Live performance.	Midnight Magic CD Neutral Zone NZCD 89012	San Diego Sports Arena, San Diego, CA	JHE	
I Don't Live Today	24 May 69	CR 3. Live performance.	Don't Miss Him This Time CD Pyramid PYCD 096	San Diego Sports Arena, San Diego, CA	JHE	
I Don't Live Today	25 May 69	BR 18. Live performance.	It's Only A Paper Moon CD Luna 9420	Santa Clara Pop Festival, San Jose, CA	JHE	
I Don't Live Today	25 May 69	BR 18. Live performance.	Historic Concert Vol 2 CD Midnight Beat MBCD 050	Santa Clara Pop Festival, San Jose, CA	JHE	
I Don't Live Today	30 May 70	CR 4. Live performance. Officially released on a CD titled "Live Forever".	Riots In Berkeley CD Beech Marten BM 038	Berkeley Community Theater, Berkeley, CA 2nd Show	COL	
I Don't Live Today	30 May 70	CR 4. Live performance. Officially released on a CD titled "Live Forever".	Jimi Plays Berkeley (CR) Warner Reprise Videotape	Berkeley Community Theater, Berkeley, CA 2nd Show	COL	
I Don't Live Today	30 May 70	CR 4. Live performance. Officially released on a CD titled "Live Forever".	Redskin' Jammin' CD JH 01 / 02	Berkeley Community Theater, Berkeley, CA 2nd Show	COL	
I Don't Live Today	30 May 70	CR 4. Live performance. Officially released on a CD titled "Live Forever".	Berkeley Concerts, The CD Whoopy Cat WKP 004 / 5	Berkeley Community Theater, Berkeley, CA 2nd Show	COL	
I Don't Live Today	30 May 70	CR 4. Live performance. Officially released on a CD titled "Live Forever".	Jimi Plays Berkeley CD JMH 005 / 2	Berkeley Community Theater, Berkeley, CA 1st Show	COL	
I Don't Live Today		Outtake of CR 1 mix 1.	Sotheby's Private Reels CD JHR 003 / 004		Fake	
I Don't Live Today	Fake	Outtake of CR 1 mix 1.	Living Reels Vol 1 CD JMH 011		Fake	

Song	Date	Notes	Release	Location	Source	Personnel
I'm A Man	?? Dec 65	CR 1. Live performance. Commercially released on several packages of Curtis Knight material.	Jimi: A Musical Legacy CD KTS BX 010	George's Club 20, Hackensack, NJ	CKB	
I'm A Man	?? Dec 65	CR 1. Live performance. Commercially released on several packages of Curtis Knight material. Incomplete.	TTG Studios ???? CD WHOAMI WAI 015	George's Club 20, Hackensack, NJ	CKB	
I'm A Man (Mannish Boy)	?? Dec 65	CR 1. Live performance. Commercially released on several packages of Curtis Knight material.	First Rays Of The New Rising Sun CD Living Legend LLRCD 023	George's Club 20, Hackensack, NJ	CKB	
I'm Gonna Leave This Town / Everything's Gonna Be Alright	?? Mar 68	CR 1.Live performance.	Woke Up This Morning And Found Myself Dead CR (CD) RLCD 0068	Scene Club, New York, NY	Scene	
I'm Gonna Leave This Town / Everything's Gonna Be Alright (In The Morning)	?? Mar 68	CR 1.Live performance.	High Live And Dirty (CR) LP Nutmeg NUT 1001	Scene Club, New York, NY	Scene	
I'm Gonna Leave This Town / Everything's Gonna Be Alright (Woke Up This Morning...)	?? Mar 68	CR 1.Live performance.	In Concert CD Starlife ST 3612	Scene Club, New York, NY	Scene	
If Six Was Nine	04 May 67	CR 1 mix 1 (stereo).	Axis: Bold As Love (CR) CD MCACD 11601	Olympic Sound Studios, London, England	JHE	
If Six Was Nine	04 May 67	CR 1 mix 1 (stereo).	Sotheby's Reels, The CD Gold Standard TOM-800	De Lane Lea, London, England	JHE	
If Six Was Nine	04 May 67	Cr1 mix 2 (mono).	Axis: Bold As Love LP (CR) Track 612 003	De Lane Lea, London, England	JHE	
If Six Was Nine	?? Aug 69	BR 1. A rehearsal from Jimi's Shokan house that comes right after a rehearsal of 'Beginnings".	Woodstock Rehearsals CD Midnight Beat MBCD 009	New York Apartment	GSRB	
In From The Storm	22 Jul 70	CR 1 mix 1.	First Rays Of The New Rising Sun (CR) CD MCACD 11599	Electric Lady Studio, New York, NY	COL	
In From The Storm	22 Jul 70	CR 1 mix 1.	Cry Of Love, The (CR) CD Reprise 2034-2	Electric Lady Studio, New York, NY	COL	
In From The Storm	22 Jul 70	CR 1 mix 2.	Voodoo Soup (CR) CD MCA 11206	Electric Lady Studio, New York, NY	COL	
In From The Storm	22 Jul 70	CR 1 mix 3. An unused mix.	51st Anniversary CD Future Disc JMH 001 / 8	Electric Lady Studio, New York, NY	COL	
In From The Storm	30 Jul 70	BR 1. Live performance.	Last American Concert Vol 1 CD The Swingin' Pig TSP-062	Rainbow Bridge Vibratory Sound-Color Experiment, Maui, HI 1st Show	COL	Emmeretta Marks / Backing Vocals

SONG TITLE	DATE	COMMENTS	RELEASE	LOCATION / VENUE	BAND	PERSONNEL
In From The Storm	30 Jul 70	BR 1. Live performance.	Last American Concert- Alive And Flowing From... LP Jupiter 444	Rainbow Bridge Vibratory Sound- Color Experiment, Maui, HI 1st Show	COL	
In From The Storm	30 Jul 70	BR 1. Live performance.	In From The Storm CD Silver Rarities SIRA 109 / 110	Rainbow Bridge Vibratory Sound- Color Experiment, Maui, HI 1st Show	COL	
In From The Storm	30 Jul 70	BR 1. Live performance.	Rainbow Bridge 2 CD JMH 003 / 2	Rainbow Bridge Vibratory Sound- Color Experiment, Maui, HI 1st Show	COL	
In From The Storm	30 Aug 70	CR 2.	Island Man CD Silver Rarities SIRA 39 / 40	Isle Of Wight Festival, Isle Of Wight, England	COL	
In From The Storm	30 Aug 70	CR 2.	At The Isle Of Wight (CR) Laserdisc CBS / Sony CLSM 791	Isle Of Wight Festival, Isle Of Wight, England	COL	
In From The Storm	30 Aug 70	CR 2.	Isle Of Wight / Atlanta Pop Festival (CR) LP Columbia G3X 3085	Isle Of Wight Festival, Isle Of Wight, England	COL	
In From The Storm	30 Aug 70	CR 2.	Soundtrack From The Film Jimi Hendrix, The (CR) LP Reprise 2RS 6481	Isle Of Wight Festival, Isle Of Wight, England	COL	
In From The Storm	30 Aug 70	CR 2.	Live - Isle Of Wight '70 (CR) CD Polydor 847236-2	Isle Of Wight Festival, Isle Of Wight, England	COL	
In From The Storm	30 Aug 70	CR 2.	Wight CD JMH 006 / 2	Isle Of Wight Festival, Isle Of Wight, England	COL	
In From The Storm	31 Aug 70	BR 2. Live performance.	Come On Stockholm CD No Label	Stora Scenen, Tivoli Garden, Stockholm, Sweden	COL	
In From The Storm	31 Aug 70	BR 2. Live performance.	Free Concert CD Midnight Beat MBCD 013	Stora Scenen, Tivoli Garden, Stockholm, Sweden	COL	
In From The Storm	01 Sep 70	BR 3. Live performance.	Warm Hello Of The Sun, The CD	Stora Scenen, Tivoli Garden, Stockholm, Sweden	COL	
In From The Storm	03 Sep 70	BR 4. Live performance.	Welcome To Th	K.B. Hallen,	COL	

Title	Date	Comment	Release	Location	Code	Musician
In From The Storm			Electric Circus Vol 2 CD Midnight Beat 018	Copenhagen, Denmark	COL	
In From The Storm	03 Sep 70	BR 4. Live performance.	Live In Copenhagen CD The Swingin' Pig TSP-220-2	K.B. Hallen, Copenhagen. Denmark	COL	
In From The Storm	03 Sep 70	BR 4. Live performance.	Copenhagen '70 CD Whoopy Cat WKP 044 / 45	K.B. Hallen, Copenhagen, Denmark		
Instrumental Improvisation	?? / ?? 70	CR 1. Another hard to pin down instrumental studio jam with just bass and guitar.	Ladyland In Flames LP Marshall Records JIMI 1,2,3,4	Electric Lady Studio, New York, NY	Jimi	Billy Cox / Bass
Instrumental Improvisation (Electric Lady Jam)	?? / ?? 70	CR 1. Another hard to pin down instrumental studio jam with just bass and guitar.	Rarities CD The Genuine Pig TGP-CD-091	Electric Lady Studio, New York, NY	Jimi	Billy Cox / Bass
Instrumental Improvisation (Hendrix / Cox Jam)	?? / ?? 70	CR 1. Another hard to pin down instrumental studio jam with just bass and guitar.	Calling Long Distance (CR) CD Univibes & Booted On Dynamite DS930055	Electric Lady Studio, New York, NY	Jimi	Billy Cox / Bass
Instrumental Improvisation (Untitled Guitar Improvisation)	?? / ?? 70	CR 1. Another hard to pin down instrumental studio jam with just bass and guitar.	Cherokee Mist CD Triangle PYCD 070	Electric Lady Studio, New York, NY	Jimi	Billy Cox / Bass
Instrumental Solo (Villanova Junction)	18 Aug 69	Live performance. Listed here as it is given a track listing on the CD.	Woodstock Nation CD Wild Bird 89090 1 / 2	Woodstock Music And Art Fair, Bethel, NY	GSRB	
Instrumental Solo	25 Apr 70	Live performance. Listed here as it is given a track listing on the CD.	Live At The Forum 1970 CD Whoopy Cat WKP 021 / 22	Los Angeles Forum, Los Angeles, CA	COL	
Intro By Jimi	?? / ?? 70?	A short bit from a interview by Jimi.	Freak Out Jam CD GH 002		Jimi	
Intro Riffs	24 May 69	CR Live performance. Listed here as it is given a track listing on the CD.	Stages San Diego 69 (CR) CD Reprise 9 27632-2	Sports Arena, San Diego, CA	JHE	
Introduction By Alexis Korner	19 Dec 67	Introduction By Alexis Korner prior to Jimi's performance of 'Hear My Train A Coming'.	Loaded Guitar LP Starlight SL 87013	Bruce Fleming Photo Studio, London, England	Jimi	
Introduction By B. B. King	?? Apr 68	Live performance.	51st Anniversary CD Future Disc JMH 001 / 8	Generation Club, New York, NY	GEN	
Introduction By B. B. King	?? Apr 68	Live performance.	King's Jam, The CD Klondyke KR 26	Generation Club, New York, NY	GEN	
Introduction By B. B. King	?? Apr 68	Live performance.	Historic Performances CD Aquarius AQ 67-JH-080	Generation Club, New York, NY	GEN	

SONG TITLE	DATE	COMMENTS	RELEASE	LOCATION / VENUE	BAND	PERSONNEL
Introduction By B. B. King	?? Apr 68	Live performance.	51st Anniversary CD Future Disc JMH 001 / 8	Generation Club, New York, NY	GEN	
Introduction By Jimi	?? / ?? 67?	From a US Army Transcription disc broadcast on 10 / 30 / 67.	Freak Out Blues CD GH 001	Unknown	Jimi	
It's A Beautiful Day	30 Jul 70	There's no Jimi involvement on this song. It's listed here as it opens this release.	Rainbow Bridge 2 CD JMH 003 / 2	Rainbow Bridge Vibratory Sound-Color Experiment, Maui, HI 1st Show	No Jimi	
It's My Own Fault	?? Apr 68	BR 1. Live performance.	Historic Performances CD Aquarius AQ 67-JH-080	Generation Club, New York, NY	GEN	
It's My Own Fault	?? Apr 68	BR 1. Live performance.	King's Jam, The CD Klondyke KR 26	Generation Club, New York, NY	GEN	
It's Too Bad	11 Feb 69	BR 1. From the same sessions that produced "Young / Hendrix", "World Travelers", and "Fuzzy Guitar Jam".	Ladyland In Flames LP Marshall Records JIMI 1,2,3,4	Record Plant, New York, NY	Jimi	Lee Michaels / Keyboards, Buddy Miles / Drums
It's Too Bad	11 Feb 69	BR 1. From the same sessions that produced "Young / Hendrix", "World Travelers", and "Fuzzy Guitar Jam".	Freak Out Jam CD GH 002	Record Plant, New York, NY	Jimi	Lee Michaels / Keyboards, Buddy Miles / Drums
It's Too Bad	11 Feb 69	BR 1. From the same sessions that produced "Young / Hendrix", "World Travelers", and "Fuzzy Guitar Jam".	Electric Anniversary Jimi CD Midnight Beat MBCD 024	Record Plant, New York, NY	Jimi	Lee Michaels / Keyboards, Buddy Miles / Drums
It's Too Bad	11 Feb 69	BR 1. From the same sessions that produced "Young / Hendrix", "World Travelers", and "Fuzzy Guitar Jam".	Redskin' Jammin' CD JH 01 / 02	Record Plant, New York, NY	Jimi	Lee Michaels / Keyboards, Buddy Miles / Drums
It's Too Bad	11 Feb 69	BR 1. From the same sessions that produced "Young / Hendrix", "World Travelers", and "Fuzzy Guitar Jam".	Flames CD Missing In Action ACT 1	Record Plant, New York, NY	Jimi	Lee Michaels / Keyboards, Buddy Miles / Drums
It's Too Bad (My Brothers Dead)	11 Feb 69	BR 1. From the same sessions that produced "Young / Hendrix", "World Travelers", and "Fuzzy Guitar Jam". Incomplete.	McLaughlin Sessions, The CD HML CD 9409	Record Plant, New York, NY	Jimi	Lee Michaels / Keyboards, Buddy Miles / Drums
It's Too Bad (Voodoo Blues)	11 Feb 69	BR 1. From the same sessions that produced "Young / Hendrix", "World Travelers", and "Fuzzy Guitar Jam". Incomplete.	Voodoo Blues CD Smurf	Record Plant, New York, NY	Jimi	Lee Michaels / Keyboards, Buddy Miles / Drums
It's Too Bad (Voodoo Blues)	11 Feb 69	BR 1. From the same sessions that produced "Young / Hendrix", "World Travelers", and "Fuzzy Guitar Jam".	Every Way To Paradise CD Tintangel TIBX 021 / 22 / 23 / 24	Record Plant, New York, NY	Jimi	Lee Michaels / Keyboards, Buddy Miles / Drums
Izabella	29 Aug 69	BR 1-6. This is reels three and four with 3 takes each. Takes 1 & 2 on both reels are breakdowns. Take 3 on both reels are complete. Reel 4 take 3 continues with a run through of 'Machine Gun'.	First Rays Of The New Rising Sun CD Triangle PYCD 084-2	Hit Factory, New York, N Y	GSRB	

Song	Date	Description	Release	Studio	Code	Musicians
Izabella	29 Aug 69	BR 1-6. This is reels three and four with 3 takes each. Takes 1 & 2 on both reels are breakdowns, Take 3 on both reels are complete. Reel 4 take 3 continues with a run through of 'Machine Gun'.	Things I Used To Do, The CD Golden Memories GM 890738	Hit Factory, New York, NY	GSRB	
Izabella	29 Aug 69	BR 3. Just reel three take 3 from the session.	Magic Hand CD Mum MUCD 012	Hit Factory, New York, NY	GSRB	
Izabella	29 Aug 69	BR 3-6. Just takes 3-6 from the session. Stops before the run through of "Machine Gun".	Band Of Gypsys Vol 3	Hit Factory, New York, N Y	GSRB	
Izabella	29 Aug 69	BR 4-6. This disc has only the reel 4 part of the Izabella session and continues into the run through of 'Machine Gun'.	Completer, The CD Whoopy Cat WKP 0018 / 19	Hit Factory, New York, N Y	GSRB	
Izabella	29 Aug 69	BR 7. this is the take from this days session chosen for a working master. Overdubs would be recorded but the result was rejected and the song re-recorded on 11 / 21.	Black Gold CD Midnight Beat MBCD 058-062	Hit Factory, New York, NY	GSRB	
Izabella	21 Nov 69	CR 1 mix 1. The 'B' side of the rare withdrawn 'Stepping Stone' single.	Rainbow Bridge & More CD	Record Plant, New York, NY	BOG	
Izabella	21 Nov 69	CR 1 mix 1. The 'B' side of the rare withdrawn 'Stepping Stone' single.	Electric Gypsy's CD Pilot HJCD 070	Record Plant, New York, NY	BOG	
Izabella	21 Nov 69	CR 1 mix 1. The 'B' side of the rare withdrawn 'Stepping Stone' single.	Rarities On Compact Disc CD On The Radio	Record Plant, New York, NY	BOG	
Izabella	21 Nov 69	CR 1 mix 2. Re-mixed and with a different guitar solo overdub.	War Heroes (CR) CD Polydor 847-2622	Record Plant, New York, NY	BOG	
Izabella	21 Nov 69	CR 1 mix 2. Re-mixed and with a different guitar solo overdub.	First Rays Of The New Rising Sun (CR) CD MCACD 11599	Record Plant, New York, NY	BOG	
Izabella	21 Nov 69	CR 1 mix 3. Unused mix #1 of the CR 1.	Studio Haze CD INA 6	Record Plant, New York, NY	BOG	
Izabella	21 Nov 69	CR 1 mix 3. Unused mix #1 of the CR 1.	Gypsy Suns, Moons And Rainbows CD Sidewalk JHX 8868	Record Plant, New York, NY	BOG	
Izabella	21 Nov 69	CR 1 mix 3. Unused mix #1 of the CR 1.	Midnight Shines Down CD Blue Kangaroo BK 04	Record Plant, New York, NY	BOG	
Izabella	21 Nov 69	CR 1 mix 3. Unused mix #1 of the CR 1.	Notes In Colours CD JHR 001 / 002	Record Plant, New York, NY	BOG	
Izabella	21 Nov 69	CR 1 mix 4. Unused mix #2 of the CR 1 backing track.	First Rays - The Sessions CD Whoopy Cat WKP 0002	Record Plant, New York, NY	BOG	
Izabella	15 Jun 70	BR 7. A false start and complete take from this session.	Earth Tones CD Whoopy Cat WKP 041	Electric Lady Studio, New York, NY	Jimi	Steve Winwood / Piano, Dave Palmer / Drums

SONG TITLE	DATE	COMMENTS	RELEASE	LOCATION / VENUE	BAND	PERSONNEL
Izabella	15 Jun 70	BR 7. A false start and complete take from this session.	Black Gold CD Midnight Beat MBCD 058-062	Electric Lady Studio, New York, NY	Jimi	Steve Winwood / Piano, Dave Palmer / Drums
Izabella	15 Jun 70	BR 7. The complete take only from this session.	Hear My Freedom CD Kobra KRCR 010	Electric Lady Studio, New York, NY	Jimi	Steve Winwood / Piano, Dave Palmer / Drums
Izabella	?? Aug 69	BR 8. Take #1 from the rehearsals at Jimi's Shokan House.	Shokan Sunrise CD	Shokan House, Woodstock, NY	GSRB	
Izabella	?? Aug 69	BR 9. Take #2 from the rehearsals at Jimi's Shokan House.	Woodstock Rehearsals CD Midnight Beat MBCD 009	Shokan House, Woodstock, NY	GSRB	
Izabella	18 Aug 69	CR 2 mix 1. Live performance.	Woodstock Nation CD Wild Bird 89090 1 / 2	Woodstock Music And Art Fair, Bethel, NY	GSRB	
Izabella	18 Aug 69	CR 2 mix 1. Live performance.	At Woodstock (CR) Laserdisc BMG BVLP 86	Woodstock Music And Art Fair, Bethel, NY	GSRB	
Izabella	18 Aug 69	CR 2 mix 1. Live performance.	Woodstock (CR) CD MCA 11063	Woodstock Music And Art Fair, Bethel, NY	GSRB	
Izabella	18 Aug 69	CR 2 mix 1. Live performance.	Gypsy Sun And Rainbows CD Manic Depression MDCD 05 / 06	Woodstock Music And Art Fair, Bethel, NY	GSRB	
Izabella	18 Aug 69	CR 2 mix 1. Live performance.	Woodstock Monday, August 18 1969, 8AM CD JMH 008	Woodstock Music And Art Fair, Bethel, NY	GSRB	
Izabella	18 Aug 69	CR 2 mix 1. Live performance.	Ultimate Live Collection, The CD The Beat Goes On BGO BX 9307-4	Woodstock Music And Art Fair, Bethel, NY	GSRB	
Izabella	18 Aug 69	CR 2 mix 2. Live performance. Incomplete as it has Jimi's 1st guitar solo edited out.	Experience II CD More MTT 1021	Woodstock Music And Art Fair, Bethel, NY	GSRB	
Izabella	18 Aug 69	CR 2 mix 2. Live performance. Incomplete as it has Jimi's 1st guitar solo edited out.	Woodstock Two L P (CR) Cotillion SD 2400	Woodstock Music And Art Fair, Bethel, NY	GSRB	
Izabella	09 Sep 69	BR 11. Live performance on the Dick Cavett TV Show.	Loaded Guitar LP Starlight SL 87013	Dick Cavett Show, ABC TV Studios, New York, NY	COL	Juma Sultan / Percussion
Izabella	09 Sep 69	BR 11. Live performance on the Dick Cavett TV Show.	Woodstock Monday, August 18 1969, 8AM CD JMH 008	ABC TV Studios, New York NY	COL	Juma Sultan / Percussion

Title	Date	Notes	Release	Location	Label	Musicians
Izabella	31 Dec 69	BR 12. Live performance.	Band Of Gold CD-R Major Tom MT 087	Fillmore East, New York, NY 1st Show	BOG	
Izabella	31 Dec 69	BR 12. Live performance.	Power Of Soul CD SQ-10	Fillmore East, New York, NY 1st Show	BOG	
Jam #2	?? / ?? 69	BR 1. A jam with an unknown guitarist probably at one of Jimi's homes or apartments sometime in 1969 and found only on this release and the even more obscure vinyl release 'Apartment Jams'. This is the track title on the CD.	Apartment Jam 70 CD Spicy Essence	New York Apartment	Jimi	Unknown / Guitar
Jam #3	?? / ?? 69	BR 2. Another jam with an unknown guitarist probably at one of Jimi's homes or apartments sometime in 1969 and found only on this release and the even more obscure vinyl release 'Apartment Jams'. This is the track title on the CD.	Apartment Jam 70 CD Spicy Essence	New York Apartment	Jimi	Unknown / Guitar
Jam #4	?? / ?? 69	BR 3. A third jam with an unknown guitarist probably at one of Jimi's homes or apartments sometime in 1969 and found only on this release and the even more obscure vinyl release 'Apartment Jams'. This is the track title on the CD.	Apartment Jam 70 CD Spicy Essence	New York Apartment	Jimi	Unknown / Guitar
Jam 292	14 May 70	CR1. Part of a longer jam. Another part was released as "Jelly 292" on the "Blues" CD.	Loose Ends (CR) LP Polydor 837574-2	Record Plant, New York, NY	COL	Unknown / Trumpet (Mixed Out), Sharon Lane / Piano
Jam H290	?? May 69	CR 1. Made up name (taken from the tape box) of a jam from about the same time as the "Jam 292" & "Jelly 292" session.	I Don't Live Today CD ACL 007	Record Plant, New York, NY	Jimi	Stephen Stills / Bass, Dallas Taylor / Drums
Jam H290 (Midnight Lightning Rap)	?? May 69	CR 1. Made up name (taken from the tape box) of a jam from about the same time as the "Jam 292" & "Jelly 292" session.	Freak Out Jam CD GH 002	Record Plant, New York, NY	Jimi	Stephen Stills / Bass, Dallas Taylor / Drums
Jam Thing (Jam)	15 Jun 70	BR 1. One of the jams with members of Traffic. Incomplete. See also "Session Thing".	Midnight Sun CD Third Eye NK 007	Electric Lady Studio, New York, NY	Jimi	Dave Mason / Backing Vocals, Chris Wood / Sax, Dave Palmer / Drums
Jam Thing (Traffic Jam & Hey Baby (New Rising Sun))	15 Jun 70	BR 1. One of the jams with members of Traffic. Incomplete. See also "Session Thing".	51st Anniversary CD Future Disc JMH 001 / 8	Electric Lady Studio, New York, NY	Jimi	Dave Mason / Backing Vocals, Chris Wood / Sax, Dave Palmer / Drums
Jam Thing (Traffic Jam)	15 Jun 70	BR 1. One of the jams with members of Traffic. See also "Session Thing".	Drone Blues CD Great Dane GDR SAT 2	Electric Lady Studio, New York, NY	Jimi	Dave Mason / Backing Vocals, Chris Wood / Sax, Dave Palmer / Drums
Jam Thing (Traffic Jam)	15 Jun 70	BR 1. One of the jams with members of Traffic. See also "Session Thing".	A Session- Jimi Hendrix And Traffic CD Oh Boy 1-9027	Electric Lady Studio, New York, NY	Jimi	Dave Mason / Backing Vocals, Chris Wood / Sax, Dave Palmer / Drums
Jam Thing (Traffic Jam)	15 Jun 70	BR 1. One of the jams with members of Traffic. See also "Session Thing".	Jimi: A Musical Legacy CD KTS BX 010	Electric Lady Studio, New York, NY	Jimi	Dave Mason / Backing Vocals, Chris Wood / Sax, Dave Palmer / Drums
Jam With Horns And Piano (Bolero)	?? / ?? 69-70	BR 1 mix 2. Another elusive studio jam. This is an alternate stereo version.	Freak Out Jam CD GH 002	Unknown	Jimi	Unknown / Other Musicians

SONG TITLE	DATE	COMMENTS	RELEASE	LOCATION / VENUE	BAND	PERSONNEL
Jam With Horns And Piano (Jam With Trumpet And Piano)	?? / ?? 69-70	BR 1 mix 1. Another elusive studio jam. Mono version.	Talent And Feeling Vol 1 CD Extremely Rare EXR 17	Unknown	Jimi	Unknown / Other Musicians
Jam With Horns And Piano (Jam- Horns And Piano)	?? / ?? 69-70	BR 1 mix 1. Another elusive studio jam. Mono version.	This One's For You LP Veteran Music MF-243	Unknown	Jimi	Unknown / Other Musicians
Jam / Cherokee Mist	23 Jan 70	BR 1. See "Ezy Rider / Jam". This the second portion of that jam and even though the first part (Ezy Rider Jam listed as Soul Power)is on this disc they are separated. The full jam is found only on "Diamonds In The Dust".	Redskin' Jammin' CD JH 01 / 02	Record Plant, New York, NY	BOG	Don ? / Harmonica
Jam / Cherokee Mist	23 Jan 70	BR 1. See "Ezy Rider / Jam". This the second portion of that jam. The full jam is found only on "Diamonds In The Dust".	Jimi: A Musical Legacy CD KTS BX 010	Record Plant, New York, NY	BOG	Don ? / Harmonica
Jam / Cherokee Mist	23 Jan 70	BR 1. See "Ezy Rider / Jam". This the second portion of that jam and even though the first part is on this disc they are separated.The full jam is found only on "Diamonds In The Dust".	Sotheby's Reels, The CD Gold Standard TOM-800	Record Plant, New York, NY	JHE	Don ? / Harmonica
Jam / Cherokee Mist (Captain Coconut & Cherokee Mist Jam)	23 Jan 70	BR 1. See "Ezy Rider / Jam". This the second portion of that jam. The full jam is found only on "Diamonds In The Dust".	51st Anniversary CD Future Disc JMH 001 / 8	Record Plant, New York, NY	BOG	Don ? / Harmonica
Jam / Cherokee Mist (Captain Coconut I I / Cherokee Mist)	23 Jan 70	BR 1. See "Ezy Rider / Jam". This the second portion of that jam. The full jam is found only on "Diamonds In The Dust".	51st Anniversary CD Future Disc JMH 001 / 8	Record Plant, New York, NY	BOG	Don ? / Harmonica
Jam / Cherokee Mist (Captain Coconut)	23 Jan 70	BR 1. See "Ezy Rider / Jam". This the second portion of that jam. The full jam is found only on "Diamonds In The Dust".	Electric Hendrix Vol 1 CD Pyramid PYCD 030	Record Plant, New York, NY	BOG	Don ? / Harmonica
Jam / Cherokee Mist (Captain Coconut)	23 Jan 70	BR 1. See "Ezy Rider / Jam". This the second portion of that jam. The full jam is found only on "Diamonds In The Dust".	Sir James Marshall LP Jester Productions JP 106	Record Plant, New York, NY	BOG	Don ? / Harmonica
Jam / Cherokee Mist (Captain Coconut)	23 Jan 70	BR 1. See "Ezy Rider / Jam". This the second portion of that jam. The full jam is found only on "Diamonds In The Dust".	Talent And Feeling Vol 2 CD Extremely Rare EXR 22	Record Plant, New York, NY	BOG	Don ? / Harmonica
Jam / Cherokee Mist (Captain Coconut)	23 Jan 70	BR 1. See "Ezy Rider / Jam". This the second portion of that jam. The full jam is found only on "Diamonds In The Dust".	Paper Airplanes CD Midnight Beat MBCD 25	Record Plant, New York, NY	BOG	Don ? / Harmonica
Jam / Cherokee Mist (MLK / Cherokee Mist)	23 Jan 70	BR 1. See "Ezy Rider / Jam". This the second portion of that jam. The full jam is found only on "Diamonds In The Dust".	Eyes And Imagination CD Third Stone TSD 18970	Record Plant, New York, NY	JHE	Don ? / Harmonica
Jam / Cherokee Mist (M.L.K.)	23 Jan 70	BR 1. See "Ezy Rider / Jam". This the second portion of that jam. The full jam is found only on "Diamonds In The Dust".	Every Way To Paradise CD Tintangel TIBX 021 / 22 / 23 / 24	Record Plant, New York, NY	BOG	Don ? / Harmonica
Jam / Cherokee Mist (MLK Captain Coconut)	23 Jan 70	BR 1. See "Ezy Rider / Jam". This the second portion of that jam. The full jam is found only on "Diamonds In The Dust".	Not Just A Voodoo Chile CD Pilot HJCD 071	Record Plant, New York, NY	BOG	Don ? / Harmonica

Song	Date	Notes	Release	Location	JHE	Stevie Wonder / Drums
Jammin' (Ain't Too Proud To Beg)	06 Oct 67	CR 1. See "Ain't Too Proud To Beg". This is the jam performed prior to the song.	BBC Sessions (CR) CD MCACD 2-11742	Top Gear, BBC Playhouse Theatre, London, England	JHE	
Jazz Jam (Hey Baby (New Rising Sun))		No Jimi involvement.	51st Anniversary CD Future Disc JMH 001 / 8		Fake	
Jazz Jimi Jazz	?? Jan 68	BR 1. A widely booted jam from the "Sotheby's Tapes".	Rainbow Bridge & More CD	Olympic Sound Studios, London, England	Jimi	Dave Mason / Backing Vocals, Unknown / Drums
Jazz Jimi Jazz	?? Jan 68	BR 1. A widely booted jam from the "Sotheby's Tapes".	Lost Experience, The, CD JHCD203	Olympic Sound Studios, London, England	Jimi	Dave Mason / Backing Vocals, Unknown / Drums
Jazz Jimi Jazz	?? Jan 68	BR 1. A widely booted jam from the "Sotheby's Tapes". Incomplete.	Master's Masters, The CD JH-01	Olympic Sound Studios, London, England	Jimi	Dave Mason / Backing Vocals, Unknown / Drums
Jazz Jimi Jazz	?? Jan 68	BR 1. A widely booted jam from the "Sotheby's Tapes". Incomplete.	Notes In Colours CD JHR 001 / 002	Olympic Sound Studios, London, England	Jimi	Dave Mason / Backing Vocals, Unknown / Drums
Jazz Jimi Jazz (Calling All Devils Children)	?? Jan 68	BR 1. A widely booted jam from the "Sotheby's Tapes".	Sotheby's Private Reels CD JHR 003 / 004	Olympic Sound Studios, London, England	Jimi	Dave Mason / Backing Vocals, Unknown / Drums
Jazz Jimi Jazz (Instrumental Jam)	?? Jan 68	BR 1. A widely booted jam from the "Sotheby's Tapes".	Screaming Eagle CD Pink Poodle POO 001	Olympic Sound Studios, London, England	Jimi	Dave Mason / Backing Vocals, Unknown / Drums
Jazz Jimi Jazz (Jam #1)	?? Jan 68	BR 1. A widely booted jam from the "Sotheby's Tapes".	Living Reels Vol 1 CD JMH 011	Olympic Sound Studios, London, England	JHE	Dave Mason / Backing Vocals, Unknown / Drums
Jazz Jimi Jazz (Jam #2)	?? Jan 68	BR 1. A widely booted jam from the "Sotheby's Tapes".	Living Reels Vol 1 CD JMH 011	Olympic Sound Studios, London, England	JHE	Dave Mason / Backing Vocals, Unknown / Drums
Jazz Jimi Jazz (Jam #3)	?? Jan 68	BR 1. A widely booted jam from the "Sotheby's Tapes".	Sotheby's Private Reels CD JHR 003 / 004	Olympic Sound Studios, London, England	Jimi	Dave Mason / Backing Vocals, Unknown / Drums
Jazz Jimi Jazz (Love Jam)	?? Jan 68	BR 1. A widely booted jam from the "Sotheby's Tapes".	51st Anniversary CD Future Disc JMH 001 / 8	Olympic Sound Studios, London, England	Jimi	Dave Mason / Backing Vocals, Unknown / Drums
Jazz Jimi Jazz (Untitled Instrumental Jam)	?? Jan 68	BR 1. A widely booted jam from the "Sotheby's Tapes".	Mixdown Master Tapes Volume 2 CD Dandelion DL 006	Olympic Sound Studios, London, England	Jimi	Dave Mason / Backing Vocals, Unknown / Drums
Jelly 292	14 May 69	CR 1. Part of a longer jam. Another part was released as "Jam 292" on "Loose Ends".	Jimi Hendrix: Blues (CR) CD MCACD 11060	Record Plant, New York, NY	COL	Unknown / Trumpet (Mixed Out), Sharon Lane / Piano

SONG TITLE	DATE	COMMENTS	RELEASE	LOCATION / VENUE	BAND	PERSONNEL
Jimi / Jimmy Jam	25 Mar 69	CR 1 mix 1.	Nine To The Universe (CR) LP Reprise HS2299	Record Plant, New York, NY	Jimi	Mitch Mitchell / Drums, Roland Robinson / Bass
Jimi / Jimmy Jam	25 Mar 69	CR 1 mix 1.	Message From Nine To The Universe CD Oil Well 122	Record Plant, New York, NY	Jimi	Mitch Mitchell / Drums, Roland Robinson / Bass
Jimi / Jimmy Jam	25 Mar 69	CR 1 mix 2. The longer version from which the CR was edited. "Redskin Jammin'" has the longest version to date.	Every Way To Paradise CD Tintangel TIBX 021 / 22 / 23 / 24	Record Plant, New York, NY	Jimi	Mitch Mitchell / Drums, Roland Robinson / Bass
Jimi / Jimmy Jam	25 Mar 69	CR 1 mix 2. The longer version from which the CR was edited. "Redskin Jammin'" has the longest version to date.	Record Plant Jam CD Pilot Records HJCD 69	Record Plant, New York, NY	Jimi	Mitch Mitchell / Drums, Roland Robinson / Bass
Jimi / Jimmy Jam (Redskin Jammin')	25 Mar 69	CR 1 mix 2. The longer version from which the CR was edited. "Redskin Jammin'" has the longest version to date.	Redskin' Jammin' CD JH 01 / 02	Record Plant, New York, NY	Jimi	Mitch Mitchell / Drums, Roland Robinson / Bass
Jimi / Jimmy Jam (Uncommon Ground)	25 Mar 69	CR 1 mix 2. The longer version from which the CR was edited. "Redskin Jammin'" has the longest version to date.	McLaughlin Sessions, The CD HML CD 9409	Record Plant, New York, NY	Jimi	Mitch Mitchell / Drums, Roland Robinson / Bass
Johnny B Goode	30 May 70	CR 1. Live performance.	Red House CD The Entertainers CD294	Berkeley Community Theater, Berkeley, CA 1st Show	COL	
Johnny B. Goode	30 May 70	CR 1. Live performance.	Good Karma 1 LP Berkeley 2022	Berkeley Community Theater, Berkeley, CA 1st Show	COL	
Johnny B. Goode	30 May 70	CR 1. Live performance.	Jimi Plays Berkeley (CR) Warner Reprise Videotape	Berkeley Community Theater, Berkeley, CA 1st Show	COL	
Johnny B. Goode	30 May 70	CR 1. Live performance.	Hendrix In Words And Music CD Outlaw Records OTR 1100030	Berkeley Community Theater, Berkeley, CA 1st Show	COL	
Johnny B. Goode	30 May 70	CR 1. Live performance.	Soundtrack From The Film Jimi Hendrix, The (CR) LP Reprise 2RS 6481	Berkeley Community Theater, Berkeley, CA 1st Show	COL	
Johnny B. Goode	30 May 70	CR 1. Live performance.	Berkeley Concert LP Audifon AF 008	Berkeley Community Theater, Berkeley, CA 1st Show	COL	
Johnny B. Goode	30 May 70	CR 1. Live performance.	Jewel Box CD Home HR-5824-3	Berkeley Community Theater, Berkeley, CA 1st Show	COL	
Johnny B. Goode	30 May 70	CR 1. Live performance.	Berkeley Concerts, The CD Whoopy Cat WKP 004 / 5	Berkeley Community Theater, Berkeley, CA 1st Show	COL	

Song	Date	Notes	Release	Location	Label	Musicians
Johnny B. Goode	30 May 70	CR 1. Live performance.	The Singles Album (CR) CD Polydor 827 369-2	Berkeley Community Theater, Berkeley, CA 1st Show	COL	
Johnny B. Goode	30 May 70	CR 1. Live performance.	Jimi Plays Berkeley CD JMH 005 / 2	Berkeley Community Theater, Berkeley, CA 1st Show	COL	
Johnny B. Goode	30 May 70	CR 1. Live performance.	Ultimate Live Collection, The CD The Beat Goes On BGO BX 9307-4	Berkeley Community Theater, Berkeley, CA 1st Show	COL	
Johnny B. Goode	30 May 70	CR 1. Live performance.	Johnny B. Goode (CR) CD Capitol 430218-2	Berkeley Community Theater, Berkeley, CA 1st Show	COL	
Jungle (Jam / Beginning)	14? Nov 69	BR 1. Another jam with Buddy Miles with a made up name and from the same session as the 'Lonely Avenue' jams.	Completer, The CD Whoopy Cat WKP 0018 / 19	Record Plant, New York, NY	Jimi	Buddy Miles / Drums
Jungle (I'm A Man)	14? Nov 69	BR 1. Another jam with Buddy Miles with a made up name and from the same session as the 'Lonely Avenue' jams.	This One's For You LP Veteran Music MF-243	Record Plant, New York, NY	Jimi	Buddy Miles / Drums
Jungle (I'm A Man - Instrumental)	14? Nov 69	BR 1. Another jam with Buddy Miles with a made up name and from the same session as the 'Lonely Avenue' jams.	Let's Drop Some Ludes And Vomit With Jimi CD Midnight Beat MBCD 026	Record Plant, New York, NY	Jimi	Buddy Miles / Drums
Jungle Jam / Beginning	04 Sep 69	BR 1. A studio run through of 'Beginning' that starts out with drums and percussion only for a few minutes until the rest of the band joins in. Incomplete.	Master's Masters, The CD JH-01	Hit Factory, New York, NY	GSRB	
Jungle Jam / Beginning	04 Sep 69	BR 1. A studio run through of 'Beginning' that starts out with drums and percussion only for a few minutes until the rest of the band joins in. Incomplete.	Every Way To Paradise CD Tintangel TIBX 021 / 22 / 23 / 24	Hit Factory, New York, NY	GSRB	
Jungle Jam / Beginning	04 Sep 69	BR 1. A studio run through of 'Beginning' that starts out with drums and percussion only for a few minutes until the rest of the band joins in.	Diamonds In The Dust CD Midnight Beat MBCD 022 / 23	Hit Factory, New York, NY	GSRB	
Jungle Jam / Beginning	04 Sep 69	BR 1. A studio run through of 'Beginning' that starts out with drums and percussion only for a few minutes until the rest of the band joins in.	Electric Anniversary Jimi CD Midnight Beat MBCD 024	Hit Factory, New York, NY	GSRB	
Jungle Jam / Beginning	04 Sep 69	BR 1. A studio run through of 'Beginning' that starts out with drums and percussion only for a few minutes until the rest of the band joins in.	Best Of The Bootlegs CD MS 666	Hit Factory, New York, NY	GSRB	
Jungle Jam / Beginning	04 Sep 69	BR 1. A studio run through of 'Beginning' that starts out with drums and percussion only for a few minutes until the rest of the band joins in.	Eyes And Imagination CD Third Stone TSD 18970	Hit Factory, New York, NY	GSRB	
Killing Floor	18 Oct 66	BR 1. Live performance. Incomplete.	Live In Paris 66 / 67 CD Whoopy Cat WKP 0012	Olympic Sound Studios, London, England	JHE	

SONG TITLE	DATE	COMMENTS	RELEASE	LOCATION / VENUE	BAND	PERSONNEL
Killing Floor	04 Feb 67	BR 2. Live performance.	Have Mercy On Me Baby CD Midnight Beat MBCD 038	Flamingo Club, London, England	JHE	
Killing Floor	04 Feb 67	BR 2. Live performance.	Live At The Flamingo Club, London, 2-4-67 CD	Flamingo Club, London, England	JHE	
Killing Floor	28 Mar 67	CR 1. BBC performance.	Radio One (CR) CD Rykodisc RCD 20078	Saturday Club, BBC Broadcasting House, London, England	JHE	
Killing Floor	28 Mar 67	CR 1. BBC performance.	Ultimate BBC Collection CD Classical CL006	Saturday Club, BBC Broadcasting House, London, England	JHE	
Killing Floor	28 Mar 67	CR 1. BBC performance.	Live In London 1967 CD Koine Records K881104	Saturday Club, BBC Broadcasting House, London, England	JHE	
Killing Floor	28 Mar 67	CR 1. BBC performance.	In Concert CD Starlife ST 3612	Saturday Club, BBC Broadcasting House, London, England	JHE	
Killing Floor	28 Mar 67	CR 1. BBC performance.	Complete BBC Session And.... The CD Last Bootleg Records LBR 036 / 2	Saturday Club, BBC Broadcasting House, London, England	JHE	
Killing Floor	28 Mar 67	CR 1. BBC performance.	BBC Sessions (CR) CD MCACD 2-11742	Saturday Club, BBC Broadcasting House, London, England	JHE	
Killing Floor	28 Mar 67	CR 1. BBC performance.	Tomorrow...Or Just The End Of Time CD Batz 0028	Saturday Club, BBC Broadcasting House, London, England	JHE	
Killing Floor	18 Jun 67	CR 2 . Live performance.	Monterey Pop CD Evil 006 1 / 2	Monterey International Pop Festival, Monterey, CA	JHE	
Killing Floor	18 Jun 67	CR 2 . Live performance.	Jimi Hendrix Experience CD Rockstars In Concert 6127092	Monterey International Pop Festival, Monterey, CA	JHE	
Killing Floor	18 Jun 67	CR 2 . Live performance.	Valley Of Neptune CD PC 28355	Monterey International Pop Festival, Monterey, CA	JHE	
Killing Floor	18 Jun 67	CR 2 . Live performance.	Jimi Plays Monterey	Monterey Interna-	JHE	

Song	Date	Rating		Release	Venue	Band
Killing Floor	04 Sep 67	CR 3. Live performance		EXP Over Sweden (CR) CD UniVibes 1002	tional Pop Festival, Monterey, CA / Dans In, Grona Lund, Tivoli Garden, Stockholm, Sweden	JHE
Killing Floor	29 Jan 68	CR 4. Live performance.		Live In Paris CD Swingin' Pig TSP-016	L' Olympia Theatre, Paris, France	JHE
Killing Floor	29 Jan 68	CR 4. Live performance.		Stages Paris 68 (CR) CD Reprise 9 27632-2	L' Olympia Theatre, Paris, France 2nd Show	JHE
Killing Floor	29 Jan 68	CR 4. Live performance.		Recorded Live In Europe CD Bulldog BGCD 023	L' Olympia Theatre, Paris, France 2nd Show	JHE
Killing Floor	19 Mar 68	BR 3. Live performance.		Thanks Ottawa For The Memories CD Luna 9319	Capitol Theatre, Ottawa, Canada	JHE
Killing Floor	19 Mar 68	BR 3. Live performance.		Canadian Club CD WPOCM 0888 D 006-2	Capitol Theatre, Ottawa, Canada	JHE
Killing Floor	19 Mar 68	BR 3. Live performance.		Live From Ottawa LP Starlight SL 87010	Capitol Theatre, Ottawa, Canada	JHE
Killing Floor	19 Mar 68	BR 3. Live performance.		Superconcert 1968 CD Firepower FP03	Capitol Theatre, Ottawa, Canada	JHE
Killing Floor	10 Oct 68	CR 5. Live performance.		Winterland Vol 1 CD Whoopy Cat WKP 025 / 26	Winterland Theatre, San Francisco, CA 2nd Show	JHE
Killing Floor	10 Oct 68	CR 5. Live performance.		Fire CD The Entertainers CD297	Winterland Theatre, San Francisco, CA 2nd Show	JHE
Killing Floor	10 Oct 68	CR 5. Live performance.		Hendrix In Words And Music CD Outlaw Records OTR 1100030	Winterland Theatre, San Francisco, CA 2nd Show	JHE
Killing Floor	10 Oct 68	CR 5. Live performance.		Live At Winterland (CR) CD Rykodisc RCD 20038	Winterland Theatre, San Francisco, CA 2nd Show	JHE
Killing Floor	10 Oct 68	CR 5. Live performance.		Ultimate Live Collection, The CD The Beat Goes On BGO BX 9307-4	Winterland Theatre, San Francisco, CA 2nd Show	JHE
Killing Floor	09 Jan 69	BR 4. Live performance.		On The Killing Floor Swingin' Pig TSP-012-2	Konserthuset, Stockholm, Sweden 1st Show	JHE

SONG TITLE	DATE	COMMENTS	RELEASE	LOCATION / VENUE	BAND	PERSONNEL
Killing Floor	09 Jan 69	BR 4. Live performance.	Electronic Church Music CD Pyramid PYCD 023	Konserthuset, Stockholm, Sweden 1st Show	JHE	
Killing Floor	09 Jan 69	BR 4. Live performance.	In Europe 67 / 68 / 69 CD Vulture CD 009 / 2	Konserthuset, Stockholm, Sweden 1st Show	JHE	
Killing Floor	09 Jan 69	BR 4. Live performance.	Very Best, The CD Irec / Retro MILCD-03	Konserthuset, Stockholm, Sweden 1st Show	JHE	
Killing Floor	09 Jan 69	BR 4. Live performance.	Live CD DV More CDDV 2401	Konserthuset, Stockholm, Sweden 1st Show	JHE	
Killing Floor	09 Jan 69	BR 4. Live performance.	In Concert CD Starlife ST 3612	Konserthuset, Stockholm, Sweden 1st Show	JHE	
Killing Floor	09 Jan 69	BR 4. Live performance.	Foxy Lady CD Alegra CD 9008	Konserthuset, Stockholm, Sweden 1st Show	JHE	
Killing Floor	09 Jan 69	BR 4. Live performance.	Anthology CD Box 9	Konserthuset, Stockholm, Sweden 1st Show	JHE	
Killing Floor	01 Sep 70	BR 5. Live performance.	Warm Hello Of The Sun, The CD	Stora Scenen, Liseberg Nojespark, Goteborg, Sweden	COL	
Killing Floor	06 Sep 70	BR 5. Live performance.	Love & Peace CD Midnight Beat MBCD 015	Love And Peace Festival, Isle Of Fehrman, Germany	COL	
Killing Floor	06 Sep 70	BR 5. Live performance.	Wink Of An Eye CD Whoopy Cat WKP 0033 / 34	Love And Peace Festival, Isle Of Fehrman, Germany	COL	
Killing Floor	06 Sep 70	BR 5. Live performance.	Jimi: A Musical Legacy CD KTS BX 010	Love And Peace Festival, Isle Of Fehrman, Germany	COL	
La Pouppee Qui Fait Non (No No No No)	29 Mar 67	BR 1. A unique and unreleased song.	Out Of The Studio: Demos From 1967 CD BHCD 931022	De Lane Lea? London, England	JHE	
La Pouppee Qui Fait Non (No No No No)	29 Mar 67	BR 1. A unique and unreleased song.	DeLane Lea And Olympic Outs CD Gold Standard CD-R	De Lane Lea? London, England	JHE	
La Pouppee Qui Fait Non (No No No No)	29 Mar 67	BR 1. A unique and unreleased song.	Get The Experience CD	De Lane Lea?	JHE	

Song	Date	Notes	Invasion Unlimited IU 9424-1	Location		Personnel
La Pouppee Qui Fait Non (No No No No)	29 Mar 67	BR 1. A unique and unreleased song.	Complete BBC Session And.... The CD Last Bootleg Records LBR 036 / 2	De Lane Lea? London, England	JHE	
La Pouppee Qui Fait Non (No No No No)	29 Mar 67	BR 1. A unique and unreleased song.	I Don't Live Today CD ACL 007	De Lane Lea? London, England	JHE	
La Pouppee Qui Fait Non (No No No No)	29 Mar 67	BR 1. A unique and unreleased song.	Gypsy Charm CD Mum MUCD 018	De Lane Lea? London, England	JHE	
La Pouppee Qui Fait Non (No No No No)	29 Mar 67	BR 1. A unique and unreleased song.	Olympic Gold Vol 1 CD Blimp 0067	De Lane Lea? London, England	JHE	
Larry Young Instrumental Jam	?? / ?? 69	BR 1. An untitled jam recorded (presumably) at the same session as "Young / Hendrix", "It's Too Bad", & "World Travelers".	Screaming Eagle CD Pink Poodle POO 001	Record Plant, New York, NY	Jimi	Larry Young / Organ
Last Thursday Morning	?? / ?? 68-69	BR 1. An instrumental jam with the Experience. Part of it was officially released on "Lifelines".	Multicolored Blues CD Luna LU 9317	Unknown	JHE	
Lawdy Miss Clawdy	?? / ?? 64	This was released on 'Lifelines' and seeing as how Jimi has nothing to do with this recording, one wonders why it was included.	Lifelines (CR) CD Reprise 9 26435-2	Unknown	No Jimi	
Lee Michaels Untitled Jam (Electric Church Jam)	21 Oct 68	BR 1. The studio jam that precedes "Hear My Freedom".	Ball And Chain CD Jimi 009	T.T.G. Studios, Hollywood, CA	JHE	Lee Michaels / Keyboards, Buddy Miles / Drums
Lee Michaels Untitled Jam (Had To Cry Today)	21 Oct 68	BR 1. The studio jam that precedes "Hear My Freedom".	Black Gold CD Midnight Beat MBCD 058-062	T.T.G. Studios, Hollywood, CA	JHE	Lee Michaels / Keyboards, Buddy Miles / Drums
Like A Rolling Stone	04 Feb 67	BR 1. Live performance.	Have Mercy On Me Baby CD Midnight Beat MBCD 038	Flamingo Club, London, England	JHE	
Like A Rolling Stone	04 Feb 67	BR 1. Live performance.	Live At The Flamingo Club, London, 2-4-67 CD	Flamingo Club, London, England	JHE	
Like A Rolling Stone	18 Jun 67	CR 1. Live performance.	Soundtrack From The Film Jimi Hendrix, The (CR) LP Reprise 2RS 6481	Monterey International Pop Festival, Monterey, CA	JHE	
Like A Rolling Stone	18 Jun 67	CR 1. Live performance.	Monterey Pop CD Evil 006 1 / 2	Monterey International Pop Festival, Monterey, CA	JHE	
Like A Rolling Stone	18 Jun 67	CR 1. Live performance.	Experience II CD More MTT 1021	Monterey International Pop Festival, Monterey, CA	JHE	

SONG TITLE	DATE	COMMENTS	RELEASE	LOCATION / VENUE	BAND	PERSONNEL
Like A Rolling Stone	18 Jun 67	CR 1. Live performance.	Hey Joe CD Crocodile Beat CB 53039	Monterey International Pop Festival, Monterey, CA	JHE	
Like A Rolling Stone	18 Jun 67	CR 1. Live performance.	Valley Of Neptune CD PC 28355	Monterey International Pop Festival, Monterey, CA	JHE	
Like A Rolling Stone	18 Jun 67	CR 1. Live performance.	Jimi Plays Monterey (CR) CD Polydor 827990-2	Monterey International Pop Festival, Monterey, CA	JHE	
Like A Rolling Stone	25 Feb 68	BR 2. Live performance.	Winterland Vol 2 CD Whoopy Cat WKP 00279 / 28	Civic Opera House, Chicago, IL	JHE	
Like A Rolling Stone	?? Apr 68	CR 2. Live performance. Incomplete.	Lifelines (CR) CD Reprise 9 26435-2	Generation Club, New York, NY	GEN	
Like A Rolling Stone	?? Apr 68	CR 2. Live performance. Incomplete.	Broadcasts CD Luna LU 9204	Generation Club, New York, NY	GEN	
Like A Rolling Stone	?? Apr 68	CR 2. Live performance.	Sweet Angel CD Compact Music WPOCM 0589	Generation Club, New York, NY	GEN	
Like A Rolling Stone	?? Apr 68	CR 2. Live performance.	King And Wonder Sessions CD Oh Boy 1-9170	Generation Club, New York, NY	GEN	
Like A Rolling Stone	?? Apr 68	CR 2. Live performance.	King's Jam, The CD Klondyke KR 26	Generation Club, New York, NY	GEN	
Like A Rolling Stone	?? Apr 68	CR 2. Live performance.	Jimi: A Musical Legacy CD KTS BX 010	Generation Club, New York, NY	GEN	
Like A Rolling Stone	?? Apr 68	CR 2. Live performance.	Greatest Hits Live CD Chartbusters CHER 089A	Generation Club, New York, NY	GEN	
Like A Rolling Stone	?? Apr 68	CR 2. Live performance. Incomplete.	First Rays Of The New Rising Sun CD Living Legend LLRCD 023	Generation Club, New York, NY	GEN	
Like A Rolling Stone	?? Apr 68	CR 2. Live performance. Incomplete.	Voice Of Experience CD Rhinozerous RHP 789	Generation Club, New York, NY	GEN	
Like A Rolling Stone	?? Apr 68	CR 2. Live performance. Incomplete.	Rainbow Bridge & More CD	Generation Club, New York, NY	GEN	

Song	Date	Take	Release	Venue	GEN	
Like A Rolling Stone	?? Apr 68	CR 2. Live performance. Incomplete.	Voodoo In Ladyland CD MUM MUCD 006	Generation Club, New York, NY	GEN	
Like A Rolling Stone	23 Aug 68	BR 3. Live performance.	Historic Concert CD Midnight Beat MBCD 017	New York Rock Festival, Singer Bowl, Queens, NY	JHE	
Like A Rolling Stone	10 Oct 68	BR 4. Live performance.	Winterland Vol 1 CD Whoopy Cat WKP 025 / 26	Winterland Theatre, San Francisco, CA 1st Show	JHE	
Like A Rolling Stone	10 Oct 68	BR 4. Live performance.	Lost Winterland Tapes CD Starquake SQ 051-2	Winterland Theatre, San Francisco, CA 1st Show	JHE	
Like A Rolling Stone	11 Oct 68	CR 3. Live Performance	Little Wing CD Oil Well RSC 036	Winterland Theatre, San Francisco, CA 2nd Show	JHE	
Like A Rolling Stone	11 Oct 68	CR 3. Live Performance	Winterland Vol 2 CD Whoopy Cat WKP 00279 / 28	Winterland Theatre, San Francisco, CA 2nd Show	JHE	
Like A Rolling Stone	11 Oct 68	CR 3. Live Performance	Star Spangled Blues CD Neutral Zone NZCD 89011	Winterland Theatre, San Francisco, CA 2nd Show	JHE	
Like A Rolling Stone	11 Oct 68	CR 3. Live Performance	Ultimate Live Collection, The CD The Beat Goes On BGO BX 9307-4	Winterland Theatre, San Francisco, CA 1st Show	JHE	
Like A Rolling Stone	11 Oct 68	CR 3. Live Performance	Live At Winterland +3 (CR) CD-3 Rykodisc 20038 / +3	Winterland Theatre, San Francisco, CA 2nd Show	JHE	Herbie Rich / Organ
Like A Rolling Stone	12 Oct 68	BR 5. Live performance.	Winterland Days, The CD Manic Depression 001	Winterland Theatre, San Francisco, CA 1st Show	JHE	
Like A Rolling Stone	12 Oct 68	BR 5. Live performance.	Winterland Vol 3 CD Whoopy Cat WKP 0029 / 30	Winterland Theatre, San Francisco, CA 1st Show	JHE	
Like A Rolling Stone	12 Oct 68	BR 5. Live performance.	Rarities CD The Genuine Pig TGP-CD-091	Winterland Theatre, San Francisco, CA 1st Show	JHE	
Like A Rolling Stone	12 Oct 68	BR 5. Live performance.	Jimi Hendrix CD Imtrat 40-90355	Winterland Theatre, San Francisco, CA 1st Show	JHE	
Like A Rolling Stone	20 Jun 68	BR 6. Live performance.	More Electricity From Newport CD Luna LU 9201	Newport Pop Festival, San Fernando State, Northridge, CA	JHE	

SONG TITLE	DATE	COMMENTS	RELEASE	LOCATION / VENUE	BAND	PERSONNEL
Like A Rolling Stone	20 Jun 68	BR 6. Live performance.	A Lifetime Of Experience LP Sleepy Dragon 55 10	Newport Pop Festival, San Fernando State, Northridge, CA	JHE	
Like A Rolling Stone	20 Jun 69	BR 6. Live performance.	Two Days At Newport CD JMH 007 / 2	Newport Pop Festival, San Fernando State, Northridge, CA	JHE	
Lil Dog O Mine	26 Jun 70	BR 1. A short impromptu rendition prior to a version of 'Valleys Of Neptune'.	Diamonds In The Dust CD Midnight Beat MBCD 022 / 23	Record Plant, New York, NY	Jimi	Billy Cox / Bass
Little Drummer Boy	?? Dec 69	BR 1. This just "The Little Drummer Boy" part of the medley re-edited and with the choir overdub added.	Sir James Marshall LP Jester Productions JP 106	Baggies, New York, NY	BOG	Female Choir Overdub
Little Drummer Boy	?? Dec 69	BR 1. This just "The Little Drummer Boy" part of the medley re-edited and with the choir overdub added.	Redskin' Jammin' CD JH 01 / 02	Baggies, New York, NY	BOG	Female Choir Overdub
Little Drummer Boy	?? Dec 69	BR 1. This just "The Little Drummer Boy" part of the medley re-edited and with the choir overdub added.	Gypsy Haze CD Lords Of Archive LAR 16	Baggies, New York, NY	BOG	Female Choir Overdub
Little Drummer Boy	?? Dec 69	BR 1. This just "The Little Drummer Boy" part of the medley re-edited and with the choir overdub added.	Cherokee Mist CD Triangle PYCD 070	Baggies, New York, NY	BOG	Female Choir Overdub
Little Drummer Boy	?? Dec 69	BR 1. This just "The Little Drummer Boy" part of the medley re-edited and with the choir overdub added.	Talent And Feeling Vol 1 CD Extremely Rare EXR 17	Baggies, New York, NY	BOG	Female Choir Overdub
Little Drummer Boy	?? Dec 69	BR 1. This just "The Little Drummer Boy" part of the medley re-edited and with the choir overdub added.	Every Way To Paradise CD Tintangel TIBX 021 / 22 / 23 / 24	Baggies, New York, NY	BOG	Female Choir Overdub
Little Drummer Boy	?? Dec 69	BR 1. This just "The Little Drummer Boy" part of the medley re-edited and with the choir overdub added. Incomplete.	Gypsy Charm CD Mum MUCD 018	Baggies, New York, NY	BOG	Female Choir Overdub
Little Drummer Boy / Silent Night / Auld Lang Syne	?? Dec 69	CR 1. A direct copy of the CR 12" single released in 1979.	Band Of Gypsys Vol 3	Baggies, New York, NY	BOG	
Little Drummer Boy / Silent Night / Auld Lang Syne	?? Dec 69	CR 1. A direct copy of the CR 12" single released in 1979.	This One's For You LP Veteran Music MF-243	Baggies, New York, NY	BOG	
Little Drummer Boy / Silent Night / Auld Lang Syne	?? Dec 69	CR 1. A direct copy of the CR 12" single released in 1979.	Electric Anniversary Jimi CD Midnight Beat MBCD 024	Baggies, New York, NY	BOG	
Little Drummer Boy / Silent Night / Auld Lang Syne	?? Dec 69	CR 1. A direct copy of the CR 12" single released in 1979.	Can You Please Crawl Out Your Window? LP Ruthless Rhymes Jimi1	Baggies, New York, NY	BOG	
Little Drummer Boy / Silent Night / Auld Lang Syne	?? Dec 69	CR 1. A direct copy of the CR 12" single released in 1979.	Rainbow Bridge & More	Baggies, New York, NY	BOG	

Lang Syne

Song	Date	Note	CD	Location (NY)	Label
Little Drummer Boy / Silent Night / Auld Lang Syne	?? Dec 69	CR 1. A direct copy of the CR 12" single released in 1979.	Rarities On Compact Disc CD On The Radio	Baggies, New York, NY	BOG
Little Drummer Boy / Silent Night / Auld Lang Syne	?? Dec 69	CR 1. A direct copy of the CR 12" single released in 1979.	Jimi: A Musical Legacy CD KTS BX 010	Baggies, New York, NY	BOG
Little Drummer Boy / Silent Night / Auld Lang Syne	?? Dec 69	CR 1. A direct copy of the CR 12" single released in 1979. Incomplete.	Flames CD Missing In Action ACT 1	Baggies, New York, NY	BOG
Little Drummer Boy / Silent Night / Auld Lang Syne	?? Dec 69	CR 1. A direct copy of the CR 12" single released in 1979. Incomplete.	Band Of Gypsys- The Ultimate CD JMH 010 / 3	Baggies, New York, NY	BOG
Little Miss Lover	01 Oct 67	CR 1 mix 1 (stereo).	Axis: Bold As Love (CR) CD MCACD 11601	Olympic Sound Studios, London, England	JHE
Little Miss Lover	01 Oct 67	CR 1 mix 2 (mono).	Axis: Bold As Love (CR) LP Track 612-003	Olympic Sound Studios, London, England	JHE
Little Miss Lover	01 Oct 67	CR 2. An Outtake from the CR 1 session.	Sotheby Auction Tapes, The CD Midnight Beat MBCD 010	Olympic Sound Studios, London, England	JHE
Little Miss Lover	01 Oct 67	CR 2. An Outtake from the CR 1 session.	51st Anniversary CD Future Disc JMH 001 / 8	Olympic Sound Studios, London, England	JHE
Little Miss Lover	01 Oct 67	CR 2. An Outtake from the CR 1 session.	Rarities CD The Genuine Pig TGP-CD-091	Olympic Sound Studios, London, England	JHE
Little Miss Lover	01 Oct 67	CR 2. An Outtake from the CR 1 session.	Notes In Colours CD JHR 001 / 002	Olympic Sound Studios, London, England	JHE
Little Miss Lover	01 Oct 67	CR 2. An Outtake from the CR 1 session.	Completer, The CD Whoopy Cat WKP 0018 / 19	Olympic Sound Studios, London, England	JHE
Little Miss Lover	01 Oct 67	CR 2. An Outtake from the CR 1 session.	Calling Long Distance (CR) CD Univibes & Booted On Dynamite DS930055	Olympic Sound Studios, London, England	JHE
Little Miss Lover	01 Oct 67	CR 2. An Outtake from the CR 1 session.	Sotheby's Reels, The CD Gold Standard TOM-800	Olympic Sound Studios, London, England	JHE
Little Miss Lover	06 Oct 67	CR 3. BBC performance.	Guitar Hero CD Document DR 013	Top Gear, BBC Playhouse Theatre, London, England	JHE

SONG TITLE	DATE	COMMENTS	RELEASE	LOCATION / VENUE	BAND	PERSONNEL
Little Miss Lover	06 Oct 67	CR 3. BBC performance.	Primal Keys LP Impossible Record Works	Top Gear, BBC Playhouse Theatre, London, England	JHE	
Little Miss Lover	06 Oct 67	CR 3. BBC performance.	Sotheby Auction Tapes, The CD Midnight Beat MBCD 010	Top Gear, BBC Playhouse Theatre, London, England	JHE	
Little Miss Lover	06 Oct 67	CR 3. BBC performance.	Symphony Of Experience CD Third Stone Discs TDS 24966	Top Gear, BBC Playhouse Theatre, London, England	JHE	
Little Miss Lover	06 Oct 67	CR 3. BBC performance.	Ultimate BBC Collection CD Classical CL006	Top Gear, BBC Playhouse Theatre, London, England	JHE	
Little Miss Lover	06 Oct 67	CR 3. BBC performance.	Jimi Hendrix Vol 2: A Man Of Our Times LP Napoleon NLP 11018	Top Gear, BBC Playhouse Theatre, London, England	JHE	
Little Miss Lover	06 Oct 67	CR 3. BBC performance.	Live In London 1967 CD Koine Records K881104	Top Gear, BBC Playhouse Theatre, London, England	JHE	
Little Miss Lover	06 Oct 67	CR 3. BBC performance.	Live In Concert 1967 CD Living Legend LLR-CD 001	Top Gear, BBC Playhouse Theatre, London, England	JHE	
Little Miss Lover	06 Oct 67	CR 3. BBC performance.	Broadcasts LP Trade Mark Of Quality TMQ 1841 & TMQ 71019	Top Gear, BBC Playhouse Theatre, London, England	JHE	
Little Miss Lover	06 Oct 67	CR 3. BBC performance.	In Europe 67 / 68 / 69 CD Vulture CD 009 / 2	Top Gear, BBC Playhouse Theatre, London, England	JHE	
Little Miss Lover	06 Oct 67	CR 3. BBC performance.	Very Best, The CD Irec / Retro MILCD-03	Top Gear, BBC Playhouse Theatre, London, England	JHE	
Little Miss Lover	06 Oct 67	CR 3. BBC performance.	In Concert CD Starlife ST 3612	Top Gear, BBC Playhouse Theatre, London, England	JHE	
Little Miss Lover	06 Oct 67	CR 3. BBC performance.	King And Wonder Sessions CD Oh Boy 1-9170	Top Gear, BBC Playhouse Theatre, London, England	JHE	
Little Miss Lover	06 Oct 67	CR 3. BBC performance.	Complete BBC Session And.... The CD Last Bootleg Records LBR 036 / 2	Top Gear, BBC Playhouse Theatre, London, England	JHE	

Song	Date	Notes	Release	Venue	Band	Musicians
Little Miss Lover	06 Oct 67	CR 3. BBC performance.	Jimi Hendrix CD Flute FLCD 2008	Top Gear, BBC Playhouse Theatre, London, England	JHE	
Little Miss Lover	06 Oct 67	CR 3. BBC performance.	BBC Sessions (CR) CD MCACD 2-11742	Top Gear, BBC Playhouse Theatre, London, England	JHE	
Little Miss Lover	06 Oct 67	CR 3. BBC performance.	Anthology CD Box 9	Top Gear, BBC Playhouse Theatre, London, England	JHE	
Little Miss Lover	03 May 69	BR 1. Live performance.	Hendrix, Busted In Toronto CD Venue VE 100502	Maple Leaf Gardens, Toronto, Canada	JHE	
Little Miss Lover	03 May 69	BR 1. Live performance.	I Don't Live Today CD ACL 007	Maple Leaf Gardens, Toronto, Canada	JHE	
Little Miss Strange (Instrumental)	13 Mar 68	BR 1. Alternate instrumental version from the CR 1 session.	You Can't Use My Name L P Rock Folders 2, Q 9020	Sound Center, New York, NY	Jimi	Noel Redding / Guitar, Jimi Hendrix? / Bass, Jimmy Mayes? / Drums
Little Miss Strange	13 Mar 68	BR 1. Alternate instrumental version from the CR 1 session.	Ladyland In Flames LP Marshall Records JIMI 1,2,3,4	Sound Center, New York, NY	Jimi	Noel Redding / Guitar, Jimi Hendrix? / Bass, Jimmy Mayes? / Drums
Little Miss Strange	13 Mar 68	BR 1. Alternate instrumental version from the CR 1 session.	1968 AD Part Two CD Whoopy Cat WKP 0013	Sound Center, New York, NY	Jimi	Noel Redding / Guitar, Jimi Hendrix? / Bass, Jimmy Mayes? / Drums
Little Miss Strange (Instrumental #2)	13 Mar 68	BR 1. Alternate instrumental version from the CR 1 session.	TTG Studios ???? CD WHOAMI WAI 015	Sound Center, New York, NY	Jimi	Noel Redding / Guitar, Jimi Hendrix? / Bass, Jimmy Mayes? / Drums
Little Miss Strange	20 Apr 68	CR 1 mix 1.	Electric Ladyland (CR) CD MCACD-11600	Record Plant, New York, NY	JHE	
Little Miss Strange	20 Apr 68	CR 1 mix 2. An unused mix of the CR 1.	Acoustic Jams CD Sphinx SX CD 001	Record Plant, New York, NY	JHE	
Little One	?? / ?? 67-68	BR 1. Version #1.	Sotheby Auction Tapes, The CD Midnight Beat MBCD 010	Olympic Sound Studios, London, England	Jimi	Mitch Mitchell / Drums, Unknown / Bass, Sitar, Rhythm Guitar
Little One	?? / ?? 67-68	BR 1. Version #1.	Symphony Of Experience CD Third Stone Discs TDS 24966	Olympic Sound Studios, London, England	Jimi	Mitch Mitchell / Drums, Unknown / Bass, Sitar, Rhythm Guitar
Little One	?? / ?? 67-68	BR 1. Version #1.	Voice Of Experience CD Rhinozerous RHP 789	Olympic Sound Studios, London, England	Jimi	Mitch Mitchell / Drums, Unknown / Bass, Sitar, Rhythm Guitar
Little One	?? / ?? 67-68	BR 1. Version #1.	Lost Experience, The, CD JHCD203	Olympic Sound Studios, London, England	Jimi	Mitch Mitchell / Drums, Unknown / Bass, Sitar, Rhythm Guitar

SONG TITLE	DATE	COMMENTS	RELEASE	LOCATION / VENUE	BAND	PERSONNEL
Little One (Instrumental #1)	?? / ?? 67-68	BR 1. Version #1.	Sotheby's Private Reels CD JHR 003 / 004	Olympic Sound Studios, London, England	Jimi	Mitch Mitchell / Drums, Unknown / Bass, Sitar, Rhythm Guitar
Little One (Instrumental #2)	?? / ?? 67-68	BR 1. Version #1. Repeated on the same disc.	Sotheby's Private Reels CD JHR 003 / 004	Olympic Sound Studios, London, England	Jimi	Mitch Mitchell / Drums, Unknown / Bass, Sitar, Rhythm Guitar
Little One	?? / ?? 67-68	BR 1. Version #1.	Notes In Colours CD JHR 001 / 002	Olympic Sound Studios, London, England	Jimi	Mitch Mitchell / Drums, Unknown / Bass, Sitar, Rhythm Guitar
Little One	?? / ?? 67-68	BR 1. Version #1.	Every Way To Paradise CD Tintangel TIBX 021 / 22 / 23 / 24	Olympic Sound Studios, London, England	Jimi	Mitch Mitchell / Drums, Unknown / Bass, Sitar, Rhythm Guitar
Little One	?? / ?? 67-68	BR 2. Version #2.	Sotheby Auction Tapes, The CD Midnight Beat MBCD 010	Olympic Sound Studios, London, England	Jimi	Mitch Mitchell / Drums, Unknown / Bass, Sitar, Rhythm Guitar
Little One	?? / ?? 67-68	BR 2. Version #2.	Symphony Of Experience CD Third Stone Discs TDS 24966	Olympic Sound Studios, London, England	Jimi	Mitch Mitchell / Drums, Unknown / Bass, Sitar, Rhythm Guitar
Little One	?? / ?? 67-68	BR 2. Version #2.	Voice Of Experience CD Rhinozerous RHP 789	Olympic Sound Studios, London, England	Jimi	Mitch Mitchell / Drums, Unknown / Bass, Sitar, Rhythm Guitar
Little One	?? / ?? 67-68	BR 2. Version #2.	Lost Experience, The, CD JHCD203	Olympic Sound Studios, London, England	Jimi	Mitch Mitchell / Drums, Unknown / Bass, Sitar, Rhythm Guitar
Little One (Instrumental # 3)	?? / ?? 67-68	BR 2. Version #2.	Sotheby's Private Reels CD JHR 003 / 004	Olympic Sound Studios, London, England	Jimi	Mitch Mitchell / Drums, Unknown / Bass, Sitar, Rhythm Guitar
Little One (Instrumental # 4)	?? / ?? 67-68	BR 2. Version #2. Repeated on the same disc.	Sotheby's Private Reels CD JHR 003 / 004	Olympic Sound Studios, London, England	Jimi	Mitch Mitchell / Drums, Unknown / Bass, Sitar, Rhythm Guitar
Little One	?? / ?? 67-68	BR 2. Version #2.	Notes In Colours CD JHR 001 / 002	Olympic Sound Studios, London, England	Jimi	Mitch Mitchell / Drums, Unknown / Bass, Sitar, Rhythm Guitar
Little One	?? / ?? 67-68	BR 2. Version #2.	Every Way To Paradise CD Tintangel TIBX 021 / 22 / 23 / 24	Olympic Sound Studios, London, England	Jimi	Mitch Mitchell / Drums, Unknown / Bass, Sitar, Rhythm Guitar
Little One	?? / ?? 67-68	BR 2. Version #2.	Jimi: A Musical Legacy CD KTS BX 010	Olympic Sound Studios, London, England	Jimi	Mitch Mitchell / Drums, Unknown / Bass, Sitar, Rhythm Guitar
Little One (Sitar Song)+A2147	?? / ?? 67-68	BR 2. Version #2.	Living Reels Vol 1 CD	Olympic Sound	Jimi	Mitch Mitchell / Drums,

Song	Date	Notes	Release	Location	Artist	Musicians
Little One (Mushy Name)	?? / ?? 67-68	BR 3. Version #3. From the "Chandler tape".	JMH 011	Studios, London, England	Jimi	Unknown / Bass, Sitar, Rhythm Guitar
Little One	?? / ?? 67-68	BR 3. Version #3. From the "Chandler tape".	Studio Haze CD INA 6	Olympic Sound Studios, London, England	Jimi	Mitch Mitchell / Drums, Unknown / Bass, Sitar, Rhythm Guitar Noel Redding / Bass Overdub
Little One (Ain't Nothin' Wrong With That)	?? / ?? 67-68	BR 3. Version #3. From the "Chandler tape".	DeLane Lea And Olympic Outs CD Gold Standard CD-R	Olympic Sound Studios, London, England	Jimi	Mitch Mitchell / Drums, Unknown / Bass, Sitar, Rhythm Guitar Noel Redding / Bass Overdub
Little One (Ain't Nothin' Wrong With That)	?? / ?? 67-68	BR 3. Version #3. From the "Chandler tape".	Electric Ladyland Outtakes CD Invasion Unlimited IU 9417-1	Olympic Sound Studios, London, England	Jimi	Mitch Mitchell / Drums, Unknown / Bass, Sitar, Rhythm Guitar Noel Redding / Bass Overdub
Little One (Ain't Nothin' Wrong With That)	?? / ?? 67-68	BR 3. Version #3. From the "Chandler tape".	Voodoo In Ladyland CD MUM MUCD 006	Olympic Sound Studios, London, England	Jimi	Mitch Mitchell / Drums, Unknown / Bass, Sitar, Rhythm Guitar Noel Redding / Bass Overdub
Little Wing	25 Oct 67	CR 1 mix 1 (stereo).	First Rays Of The New Rising Sun CD Living Legend LLRCD 023	Olympic Sound Studios, London, England	JHE	
Little Wing	25 Oct 67	CR 1 mix 1 (stereo).	Black Strings CD CDM G-53 258	Olympic Sound Studios, London, England	JHE	
Little Wing	25 Oct 67	CR 1 mix 1 (stereo).	Axis: Bold As Love (CR) CD MCACD 11601	Olympic Sound Studios, London, England	JHE	
Little Wing	25 Oct 67	CR 1 mix 1 (stereo).	The Singles Album (CR) CD Polydor 827 369-2	Olympic Sound Studios, London, England	JHE	
Little Wing	25 Oct 67	CR 1 mix 2 (mono).	Axis: Bold As Love (CR) LP Track 612-003	Olympic Sound Studios, London, England	JHE	
Little Wing	08 Jan 68	CR 2. Live performance.	Live In Paris 66 / 67 CD Whoopy Cat WKP 0012	Konserthuset, Stockholm, Sweden 1st Show	JHE	
Little Wing	08 Jan 68	CR 2. Live performance.	Lost In Sweden CD Whoopy Cat WKP 0046 / 0047	Konserthuset, Stockholm, Sweden 1st Show	JHE	
Little Wing	08 Jan 68	CR 2. Live performance.	EXP Over Sweden (CR) CD UniVibes 1002	Konserthuset, Stockholm, Sweden 1st Show	JHE	

SONG TITLE	DATE	COMMENTS	RELEASE	LOCATION / VENUE	BAND	PERSONNEL
Little Wing	29 Jan 68	CR 3. L Live performance.	Live In Paris CD Swingin' Pig TSP-016	L' Olympia Theatre, Paris, France 2nd Show	JHE	
Little Wing	29 Jan 68	CR 3. L Live performance.	Stages Paris 68 (CR) CD Reprise 9 27632-2	L' Olympia Theatre, Paris, France 2nd Show	JHE	
Little Wing	29 Jan 68	CR 3. L Live performance.	Once Upon A Time CD Wall Of Sound WS CD011	L' Olympia Theatre, Paris, France 2nd Show	JHE	
Little Wing	29 Jan 68	CR 3. L Live performance.	Official Bootleg Album, The CD Yellow Dog YD 051	L' Olympia Theatre, Paris, France 2nd Show	JHE	
Little Wing	29 Jan 68	CR 3. L Live performance.	In Europe 67 / 68 / 69 CD Vulture CD 009 / 2	L' Olympia Theatre, Paris, France 2nd Show	JHE	
Little Wing	29 Jan 68	CR 3. L Live performance.	Very Best, The CD Irec / Retro MILCD-03	L' Olympia Theatre, Paris, France 2nd Show	JHE	
Little Wing	29 Jan 68	CR 3. L Live performance.	Live CD DV More CDDV 2401	L' Olympia Theatre, Paris, France 2nd Show	JHE	
Little Wing	29 Jan 68	CR 3. L Live performance.	Jimi Hendrix Experience CD Rockstars In Concert 6127092	L' Olympia Theatre, Paris, France 2nd Show	JHE	
Little Wing	29 Jan 68	CR 3. L Live performance.	In Concert CD Starlife ST 3612	L' Olympia Theatre, Paris, France 2nd Show	JHE	
Little Wing	29 Jan 68	CR 3. L Live performance.	Magic Hand CD Mum MUCD 012	L' Olympia Theatre, Paris, France 2nd Show	JHE	
Little Wing	29 Jan 68	CR 3. L Live performance.	Foxy Lady CD Alegra CD 9008	L' Olympia Theatre, Paris, France 2nd Show	JHE	
Little Wing	29 Jan 68	CR 3. L Live performance.	Anthology CD Box 9	L' Olympia Theatre, Paris, France 2nd Show	JHE	
Little Wing	17 Mar 68	BR 1. Live performance.	Shine On Earth, Shine On CD Sidewalk SW 89010 / 89011	Cafe' A Go Go, New York, NY	Cafe	
Little Wing	17 Mar 68	BR 1. Live performance.	Shine On Earth, Shine	Cafe' A Go Go, New	Cafe	

Song	Date	Note	On CD Sidewalk SW 89010 / 89011	Location	Band
Little Wing	17 Mar 68	BR 1. Live performance.	Blues At Midnight CD Midnight Beat MBCD 037	Cafe' A Go Go, New York, NY	Cafe
Little Wing (Jamming Wing)	17 Mar 68	BR 1. Live performance.	Cafe Au Go Go CD Koine 880802	Cafe' A Go Go, New York, NY	Cafe
Little Wing	17 Mar 68	BR 1. Live performance.	Living Reels Vol 2 CD JMH 012 / 2	Cafe' A Go Go, New York, NY	Cafe
Little Wing	14 Sep 68	BR 1. Live performance.	Live At The Hollywood Bowl LP RSR / International RSR 251	Hollywood Bowl, Los Angeles, CA	JHE
Little Wing	12 Oct 68	CR 4. Live performance.	Winterland Days, The CD Manic Depression 001	Winterland Theatre, San Francisco, CA 2nd Show	JHE
Little Wing	12 Oct 68	Concerts (CR) CD Reprise 9-22306-2	Concerts (CR) CD Reprise 9-22306-2	Winterland Theatre, San Francisco, CA 2nd Show	JHE
Little Wing	12 Oct 68	CR 4. Live performance.	Little Wing CD Oil Well RSC 036	Winterland Theatre, San Francisco, CA 2nd Show	JHE
Little Wing	12 Oct 68	CR 4. Live performance.	Winterland Vol 3 CD Whoopy Cat WKP 0029 / 30	Winterland Theatre, San Francisco, CA 2nd Show	JHE
Little Wing	12 Oct 68	CR 4. Live performance.	Jimi Hendrix CD Imtrat 40-90355	Winterland Theatre, San Francisco, CA 2nd Show	JHE
Little Wing	12 Oct 68	CR 4. Live performance.	Ultimate Live Collection, The CD The Beat Goes On BGO BX 9307-4	Winterland Theatre, San Francisco, CA 2nd Show	JHE
Little Wing	12 Oct 68	CR 4. Live performance.	Lost Winterland Tapes CD Starquake SQ 051-2	Winterland Theatre, San Francisco, CA 2nd Show	JHE
Little Wing	17 Jan 69	BR 2. Live performance.	Burning At Frankfurt CD Midnight Beat MBCD 040	Jahrhunderthalle, Frankfurt, Germany	JHE
Little Wing	17 Jan 69	BR 2. Live performance.	Fire CD The Entertainers CD297	Jahrhunderthalle, Frankfurt, Germany	JHE
Little Wing (Little Ivey)	24 Feb 69	CR 5. Live performance.	Last Experience, The (CR) CD Bescol CD 42	Royal Albert Hall, London, England	JHE

SONG TITLE	DATE	COMMENTS	RELEASE	LOCATION / VENUE	BAND	PERSONNEL
Little Wing	24 Feb 69	CR 5. Live performance.	Hendrix In The West (CR) LP Polydor 2302018 A	Royal Albert Hall, London, England	JHE	
Little Wing	24 Feb 69	CR 5. Live performance.	51st Anniversary CD Future Disc JMH 001/8	Royal Albert Hall, London, England	JHE	
Little Wing	24 Feb 69	CR 5. Live performance.	Live! CD Black B-05	Royal Albert Hall, London, England	JHE	
Little Wing	24 Feb 69	CR 5. Live performance.	Hendrix In Words And Music CD Outlaw Records OTR 1100030	Royal Albert Hall, London, England	JHE	
Little Wing	24 Feb 69	CR 5. Live performance.	Royal Albert Hall CD Blimp 008 / 009 & Listen To This Eric CD JH 003 / 4	Royal Albert Hall, London, England	JHE	
Little Wing	24 Feb 69	CR 5. Live performance.	Stone Free CD Silver Rarities SIRA 58 / 59	Royal Albert Hall, London, England	JHE	
Little Wing	24 Feb 69	CR 5. Live performance.	Greatest Hits Live CD Chartbusters CHER 089A	Royal Albert Hall, London, England	JHE	
Little Wing	25 Oct 67	Outfaked mix of CR 1 mix 1.	Sotheby's Reels, The CD Gold Standard TOM-800	Olympic Sound Studios, London, England	JHE	
Little Wing	25 Oct 67	Outfaked mix of CR 1 mix 1.	Living Reels Vol 1 CD JMH 011	Olympic Sound Studios, London, England	JHE	
Lonely Avenue Jam Part 1	14 Nov 69	BR 1 mix 1. The longest available version even though it fades early.	Diamonds In The Dust CD Midnight Beat MBCD 022 / 23	Record Plant, New York, NY	Jimi	Buddy Miles / Drums
Lonely Avenue Jam Part 1 (Jimi And Mitch Jam)	14 Nov 69	BR 1 mix 1. Incomplete. Only about five and a half minutes appear on this release.	Living Reels Vol 2 CD JMH 012 / 2	Record Plant, New York, NY	Jimi	Buddy Miles / Drums
Lonely Avenue Jam Part 1 (Guitar Thing)	14 Nov 69	BR 1 mix 2. A remixed five minute edit of Version #1 dropping the drums so there's only guitar.	A Session- Jimi Hendrix And Traffic CD Oh Boy 1-9027	Record Plant, New York, NY	Jimi	Buddy Miles / Drums
Lonely Avenue Jam Part 1 (Electric Ladyland)	14 Nov 69	BR 1 mix 2. A remixed five minute edit of Version #1 dropping the drums so there's only guitar.	Ladyland In Flames LP Marshall Records JIMI 1,2,3,4	Record Plant, New York, NY	Jimi	Buddy Miles / Drums
Lonely Avenue Jam Part 1 (Untitled Guitar Improvisation)	14 Nov 69	BR 1 mix 2. A remixed five minute edit of Version #1 dropping the drums so there's only guitar. This track is duplicated on this disc.	Ladyland In Flames LP Marshall Records JIMI 1,2,3,4	Record Plant, New York, NY	Jimi	Buddy Miles / Drums

Title	Date	Notes	Release	Location	Artist	Personnel
Lonely Avenue Jam Part 1 (Untitled Guitar Improvisation)	14 Nov 69	BR 1 mix 2. A remixed five minute edit of Version #1 dropping the drums so there's only guitar.	I Don't Live Today CD ACL 007	Record Plant, New York, NY	Jimi	Buddy Miles / Drums
Lonely Avenue Jam Part 1 (Electric Ladyland)	14 Nov 69	BR 1 mix 3. An edited and remixed section out of the "Lonely Avenue Part 1" jam.	Flames CD Missing In Action ACT 1	Record Plant, New York, NY	Jimi	Buddy Miles / Drums
Lonely Avenue Jam Part 1 (Gypsy Boy)	14 Nov 69	BR 1 mix 2. A remixed five minute edit of Version #1 dropping the drums so there's only guitar. Incomplete.	Atlanta CD JMH 009 / 02	Record Plant, New York, NY	Jimi	Buddy Miles / Drums
Lonely Avenue Jam Part 2	14 Nov 69	BR 1. This is the complete recording.	Diamonds In The Dust CD Midnight Beat MBCD 022 / 23	Record Plant, New York, NY	Jimi	Buddy Miles / Drums
Lonely Avenue Jam Part 2	14 Nov 69	BR 1. Incomplete	Freak Out Blues CD GH 001	Record Plant, New York, NY	Jimi	Buddy Miles / Drums
Lonely Avenue Jam Part 2 (Gypsy Sunset)	14 Nov 69	BR 1. Incomplete	Electric Gypsy's CD Pilot HJCD 070	Record Plant, New York, NY	Jimi	Buddy Miles / Drums
Lonely Avenue Jam Part 2 (Gypsy Sunset)	14 Nov 69	BR 1. Incomplete	Every Way To Paradise CD Tintangel TIBX 021 / 22 / 23 / 24	Record Plant, New York, NY	Jimi	
Long Hot Summer Night	?? Mar? 68	BR 1 from this mono acoustic home composing session.	Acoustic Jams CD Sphinx SX CD 001	New York Apartment	Solo	
Long Hot Summer Night	?? Mar? 68	BR 1 from this mono acoustic home composing session.	1968 AD Part Two CD Whoopy Cat WKP 0013	New York Apartment	Solo	
Long Hot Summer Night	?? Mar? 68	BR 1 from this mono acoustic home composing session.	Voodoo Blues CD Smurf	New York Apartment	Solo	
Long Hot Summer Night	?? Mar? 68	BR 1 from this mono acoustic home composing session.	Black Gold CD Midnight Beat MBCD 058-062	New York Apartment	Solo	
Long Hot Summer Night	?? Mar? 68	BR 2 from this mono acoustic home composing session.	Acoustic Jams CD Sphinx SX CD 001	New York Apartment	Solo	
Long Hot Summer Night	?? Mar? 68	BR 2 from this mono acoustic home composing session.	Voodoo Blues CD Smurf	New York Apartment	Solo	
Long Hot Summer Night	?? Mar? 68	BR 2 from this mono acoustic home composing session.	Black Gold CD Midnight Beat MBCD 058-062	New York Apartment	Solo	
Long Hot Summer Night	?? Mar? 68	BR 2 from this mono acoustic home composing session.	1968 AD Part Two CD Whoopy Cat WKP 0013	New York Apartment	JHE	
Long Hot Summer Night	?? Mar? 68	BR 2 from this mono acoustic home composing session. Incomplete.	Studio Experience CD Sodium Haze SH 099	New York Apartment	Solo	
Long Hot Summer Night	22 Apr 68	CR 1.	Electric Ladyland (CR) CD MCACD-11600	Record Plant, New York, NY	Jimi	Al Kooper / Keyboards
Long Hot Summer Night	22 Apr 68	CR 1.	The Singles Album (CR) CD Polydor 827 369-2	Record Plant, New York, NY	Jimi	Al Kooper / Keyboards

SONG TITLE	DATE	COMMENTS	RELEASE	LOCATION / VENUE	BAND	PERSONNEL
Look Over Yonder	04 May 67	CR 1. First released commercially on the 'Lifelines' box set.	First Rays Of The New Rising Sun CD Living Legend LLRCD 023	Olympic Sound Studios, London, England	JHE	
Look Over Yonder	04 May 67	CR 1. First released commercially on the 'Lifelines' box set.	Electric Gypsy CD Scorpio? 40176 / 15	Olympic Sound Studios, London, England	JHE	
Look Over Yonder	04 May 67	CR 1. First released commercially on the 'Lifelines' box set.	Master's Masters, The CD JH-01	Olympic Sound Studios, London, England	JHE	
Look Over Yonder	04 May 67	CR 1. First released commercially on the 'Lifelines' box set.	Acoustic Jams CD Sphinx SX CD 001	Olympic Sound Studios, London, England	JHE	
Look Over Yonder	04 May 67	CR 1. First released commercially on the 'Lifelines' box set.	Ladyland In Flames LP Marshall Records JIMI 1,2,3,4	Olympic Sound Studios, London, England	JHE	
Look Over Yonder	04 May 67	CR 1. First released commercially on the 'Lifelines' box set.	Lifelines (CR) CD Reprise 9 26435-2	Olympic Sound Studios, London, England	JHE	
Look Over Yonder	04 May 67	CR 1. First released commercially on the 'Lifelines' box set.	Studio Haze CD INA 6	Olympic Sound Studios, London, England	JHE	
Look Over Yonder	04 May 67	CR 1. First released commercially on the 'Lifelines' box set.	Official Bootleg Album, The CD Yellow Dog YD 051	Olympic Sound Studios, London, England	JHE	
Look Over Yonder	04 May 67	CR 1. First released commercially on the 'Lifelines' box set.	First Rays Of The New Rising Sun CD Triangle PYCD 084-2	Olympic Sound Studios, London, England	JHE	
Look Over Yonder	04 May 67	CR 1. First released commercially on the 'Lifelines' box set.	Best Of The Bootlegs CD MS 666	Olympic Sound Studios, London, England	JHE	
Look Over Yonder	04 May 67	CR 1. First released commercially on the 'Lifelines' box set.	Voodoo Blues CD Smurf	Olympic Sound Studios, London, England	JHE	
Look Over Yonder	04 May 67	CR 1. First released commercially on the 'Lifelines' box set.	Studio Experience CD Sodium Haze SH 099	Olympic Sound Studios, London, England	JHE	
Look Over Yonder	04 May 67	CR 1. First released commercially on the 'Lifelines' box set.	DeLane Lea And Olympic Outs CD Gold Standard CD-R	Olympic Sound Studios, London, England	JHE	
Look Over Yonder	04 May 67	CR 1. First released commercially on the 'Lifelines' box set.	Every Way To Paradise	Olympic Sound	JHE	

Title	Date	Notes	Release	Location	Source
Look Over Yonder	04 May 67	CR 1. First released commercially on the 'Lifelines' box set.	CD Tintangel TIBX 021 / 22 / 23 / 24	Studios, London, England	JHE
Look Over Yonder	04 May 67	CR 1. First released commercially on the 'Lifelines' box set.	Complete BBC Session And.... The CD Last Bootleg Records LBR 036 / 2	Olympic Sound Studios, London, England	JHE
Look Over Yonder	22 Oct 68	CR 2.	Living Reels Vol 2 CD JMH 012 / 2	Olympic Sound Studios, London, England	JHE
Look Over Yonder	22 Oct 68	CR 2.	Rainbow Bridge (CR) LP Reprise K44159	T.T.G. Studios, Hollywood, CA	JHE
Look Over Yonder	22 Oct 68	CR 2.	Rainbow Bridge & More CD	T.T.G. Studios, Hollywood, CA	JHE
Look Over Yonder	22 Oct 68	CR 2.	Gypsy Charm CD Mum MUCD 018	T.T.G. Studios, Hollywood, CA	JHE
Look Over Yonder	22 Oct 68	CR 2.	South Saturn Delta (CR) CD MCACD 11684	T.T.G. Studios, Hollywood, CA	JHE
Look Over Yonder	22 Oct 68	CR 2.	Rainbow Bridge (CR) LP Reprise K44159	T.T.G. Studios, Hollywood, CA	JHE
Lord I Sing The Blues (Cryin' Blue Rain)	06 Sep 69	BR 1 mix 1. An unreleased song from the rejected "Multicolored Blues" project. This is the longest version.	Diamonds In The Dust CD Midnight Beat MBCD 022 / 23	Hit Factory, New York, NY	GSRB
Lord I Sing The Blues (Me And You Blues)	06 Sep 69	BR 1 mix 1. An unreleased song from the rejected "Multicolored Blues" project. This is the longest version.	Mixdown Master Tapes Volume 3 CD Dandelion DL 007	Hit Factory, New York, NY	GSRB
Lord I Sing The Blues	06 Sep 69	BR 1 mix 1. An unreleased song from the rejected "Multicolored Blues" project. This is the longest version.	Completer, The CD Whoopy Cat WKP 0018 / 19	Hit Factory, New York, NY	GSRB
Lord I Sing The Blues	06 Sep 69	BR 1 mix 2. An unreleased song from the rejected "Multicolored Blues" project. This fades in later than mix #1 and has an edit.	First Rays Of The New Rising Sun CD Triangle PYCD 084-2	Hit Factory, New York, NY	GSRB
Lord I Sing The Blues	06 Sep 69	BR 1 mix 2. An unreleased song from the rejected "Multicolored Blues" project. This fades in later than mix #1 and has an edit.	In From The Storm CD Silver Rarities SIRA 109 / 110	Hit Factory, New York, NY	GSRB
Lord I Sing The Blues (Me And You Blues)	06 Sep 69	BR 1 mix 3. An unreleased song from the rejected "Multicolored Blues" project. This continues directly into "Lover Man"	Electric Hendrix Vol 1 CD Pyramid PYCD 030	Hit Factory, New York, NY	GSRB
Lord I Sing The Blues Instrumental)	06 Sep 69	BR 1 mix 3. An unreleased song from the rejected "Multicolored Blues" project. This continues directly into "Lover Man"	TTG Studios ???? CD WHOAMI WAI 015	Hit Factory, New York, NY	GSRB

SONG TITLE	DATE	COMMENTS	RELEASE	LOCATION / VENUE	BAND	PERSONNEL
Lord I Sing The Blues	06 Sep 69	BR 1 mix 3. An unreleased song from the rejected "Multicolored Blues" project. "Lover Man" follows after an edit.	Talent And Feeling Vol 1 CD Extremely Rare EXR 17	Hit Factory, New York, NY	GSRB	
Lord I Sing The Blues	06 Sep 69	BR 1 mix 3. An unreleased song from the rejected "Multicolored Blues" project. This continues directly into "Lover Man"	Paper Airplanes CD Midnight Beat MBCD 25	Hit Factory, New York, NY	GSRB	
Lord I Sing The Blues	06 Sep 69	BR 1 mix 4. An unreleased song from the rejected "Multicolored Blues" project. A strange edit that repeats a verse.	Mannish Boy LP Contraband CBM 88	Hit Factory, New York, NY	GSRB	
Lord I Sing The Blues	06 Sep 69	BR 1 mix 4. An unreleased song from the rejected "Multicolored Blues" project. A strange edit that repeats a verse. This fades early making it incomplete.	Gypsy Suns, Moons And Rainbows CD Sidewalk JHX 8868	Hit Factory, New York, NY	GSRB	
Lord I Sing The Blues	06 Sep 69	BR 1 mix 4. An unreleased song from the rejected "Multicolored Blues" project. A strange edit that repeats a verse. This fades early making it incomplete.	Jimi: A Musical Legacy CD KTS BX 010	Hit Factory, New York, NY	GSRB	
Lord I Sing The Blues	06 Sep 69	BR 1 mix 4. An unreleased song from the rejected "Multicolored Blues" project. A strange edit that repeats a verse. This fades early making it incomplete.	Atlanta CD JMH 009 / 02	Hit Factory, New York, NY	GSRB	
Lord I Sing The Blues	06 Sep 69	BR 1 mix 4. An unreleased song from the rejected "Multicolored Blues" project. A strange edit that repeats a verse. This fades early making it incomplete.	Drone Blues CD Great Dane GDR SAT 2	Hit Factory, New York, NY	GSRB	
Lord I Sing The Blues (Cryin' Blue Rain)	06 Sep 69	BR 1 mix 4. An unreleased song from the rejected "Multicolored Blues" project. A strange edit that repeats a verse. This fades early making it incomplete.	51st Anniversary CD Future Disc JMH 001 / 8	Hit Factory, New York, NY	GSRB	
Lord I Sing The Blues	06 Sep 69	BR 1 mix 5. An unreleased song from the rejected "Multicolored Blues" project. We'll call this mix #5 though it's actually an edit of mix #4 making this the shortest mix. Incomplete.	Midnight Shines Down CD Blue Kangaroo BK 04	Hit Factory, New York, NY	GSRB	
Love Or Confusion	24 Nov 66	CR 1 mix 1 (stereo).	Are You Experienced? (CR) CD MCACD 11602	Olympic Sound Studios, London, England	JHE	
Love Or Confusion	24 Nov 66	CR 1 mix 2 (mono).	Legacy (CR) LP Polydor	Olympic Sound Studios, London, England	JHE	
Love Or Confusion	24 Nov 66	CR 1 mix 2 (mono).	Are You Experienced? (CR) LP Track 612 001	Olympic Sound Studios, London, England	JHE	
Love Or Confusion	13 Feb 67	CR 2. BBC performance.	Radio One (CR) CD Rykodisc RCD 20078	Saturday Club, BBC Broadcasting House, London, England	JHE	

Song	Date	Notes	Release	Venue	Band
Love Or Confusion	13 Feb 67	CR 2. BBC performance.	51st Anniversary CD Future Disc JMH 001 / 8	Saturday Club, BBC Broadcasting House, London, England	JHE
Love Or Confusion	13 Feb 67	CR 2. BBC performance.	Ultimate BBC Collection CD Classical CL006	Saturday Club, BBC Broadcasting House, London, England	JHE
Love Or Confusion	13 Feb 67	CR 2. BBC performance.	Live In London 1967 CD Koïne Records K881104	Saturday Club, BBC Broadcasting House, London, England	JHE
Love Or Confusion	13 Feb 67	CR 2. BBC performance.	Broadcasts LP Trade Mark Of Quality TMQ 1841 & TMQ 71019	Saturday Club, BBC Broadcasting House, London, England	JHE
Love Or Confusion	13 Feb 67	CR 2. BBC performance.	Jewel Box CD Home HR-5824-3	Saturday Club, BBC Broadcasting House, London, England	JHE
Love Or Confusion	13 Feb 67	CR 2. BBC performance.	Complete BBC Session And.... The CD Last Bootleg Records LBR 036 / 2	Saturday Club, BBC Broadcasting House, London, England	JHE
Love Or Confusion	13 Feb 67	CR 2. BBC performance.	Jimi: A Musical Legacy CD KTS BX 010	Saturday Club, BBC Broadcasting House, London, England	JHE
Love Or Confusion	13 Feb 67	CR 2. BBC performance.	BBC Sessions (CR) CD MCACD 2-11742	Saturday Club, BBC Broadcasting House, London, England	JHE
Love Or Confusion	13 Feb 67	CR 2. BBC performance.	Tomorrow...Or Just The End Of Time CD Batz 0028	Saturday Club, BBC Broadcasting House, London, England	JHE
Lover Man	10 May 68	BR 1. Live performance.	It's Only A Paper Moon CD Luna 9420	Fillmore East, New York, NY	JHE
Lover Man	10 May 68	BR 1. Live performance.	One Night Stand CD Hep Cat 101	Fillmore East, New York, NY	JHE
Lover Man	11 Aug 68	BR 2. Live performance.	Davenport, Iowa '68 LP Creative Artistry 26K10 / 55K10	Col Ballroom, Davenport, IA	JHE
Lover Man	10 Oct 68	BR 3. Live performance.	Winterland Vol 1 CD Whoopy Cat WKP 025 / 26	Winterland Theatre, San Francisco, CA 2nd Show	JHE
Lover Man	10 Oct 68	BR 3. Live performance.	Lost Winterland Tapes CD Starquake SQ 051-2	Winterland Theatre, San Francisco, CA 2nd Show	JHE

The Song Index

SONG TITLE	DATE	COMMENTS	RELEASE	LOCATION / VENUE	BAND	PERSONNEL
Lover Man	11 Oct 68	BR 4. Live performance.	Winterland Vol 2 CD Whoopy Cat WKP 00279 / 28	Winterland Theatre, San Francisco, CA 2nd Show	JHE	Herbie Rich / Organ
Lover Man	11 Oct 68	BR 4. Live performance.	Star Spangled Blues CD Neutral Zone NZCD 89011	Winterland Theatre, San Francisco, CA 2nd Show	JHE	Herbie Rich / Organ
Lover Man	11 Oct 68	BR 4. Live performance.	Ultimate Live Collection, The CD The Beat Goes On BGO BX 9307-4	Winterland Theatre, San Francisco, CA 2nd Show	JHE	Herbie Rich / Organ
Lover Man	12 Oct 68	BR 5. Live performance.	Winterland Days, The CD Manic Depression 001	Winterland Theatre, San Francisco, CA 1st Show	JHE	
Lover Man	12 Oct 68	BR 5. Live performance.	Winterland Vol 3 CD Whoopy Cat WKP 0029 / 30	Winterland Theatre, San Francisco, CA 1st Show	JHE	
Lover Man	29 Oct 68	BR 6. Take 3 from the session that produced the CR 1.	Talent And Feeling Vol 1 CD Extremely Rare EXR 17	T.T.G. Studios, Hollywood, CA	JHE	
Lover Man	29 Oct 68	BR 7. Take 4 from the session. Even though this is the "raw" take that produced the CR 1, the CR runs longer.	This One's For You LP Veteran Music MF-243	T.T.G. Studios, Hollywood, CA	JHE	
Lover Man	29 Oct 68	BR 7. Take 4 from the session. Even though this is the "raw" take that produced the CR 1, the CR runs longer.	Talent And Feeling Vol 2 CD Extremely Rare EXR 22	T.T.G. Studios, Hollywood, CA	JHE	
Lover Man	29 Oct 68	BR 7. Take 4 from the session. Even though this is the "raw" take that produced the CR 1, the CR runs longer. Incomplete.	Unsurpassed Studio Takes CD Yellow Dog YD 050	T.T.G. Studios, Hollywood, CA	JHE	
Lover Man	29 Oct 68	BR 7. Take 4 from the session. Even though this is the "raw" take that produced the CR 1, the CR runs longer. Incomplete.	51st Anniversary CD Future Disc JMH 001 / 8	T.T.G. Studios, Hollywood, CA	JHE	
Lover Man	29 Oct 68	BR 7. Take 4 from the session. Even though this is the "raw" take that produced the CR 1, the CR runs longer. Incomplete.	Redskin' Jammin' CD JH 01 / 02	T.T.G. Studios, Hollywood, CA	JHE	
Lover Man	29 Oct 68	BR 7. Take 4 from the session. Even though this is the "raw" take that produced the CR 1, the CR runs longer.	First Rays - The Sessions CD Whoopy Cat WKP 0002	T.T.G. Studios, Hollywood, CA	JHE	
Lover Man	29 Oct 68	BR 7. Take 4 from the session. Even though this is the "raw" take that produced the CR 1, the CR runs longer.	Talent And Feeling Vol 1 CD Extremely Rare EXR 17	T.T.G. Studios, Hollywood, CA	JHE	
Lover Man	29 Oct 68	BR 7. Take 4 from the session. Even though this is the "raw" take that produced the CR 1, the CR runs longer. Incomplete.	Magic Hand CD Mum MUCD 012	T.T.G. Studios, Hollywood, CA	JHE	

Song	Date	Notes	Release	Location	Band	Personnel
Lover Man	29 Oct 68	BR 7. Take 4 from the session. Even though this is the "raw" take that produced the CR 1, the CR runs longer. Incomplete.	Wight CD JMH 006 / 2	T.T.G. Studios, Hollywood, CA	JHE	
Lover Man	29 Oct 68	CR 1. An edit of takes 1 and 4.	South Saturn Delta (CR) CD MCACD 11684	T.T.G. Studios, Hollywood, CA	JHE	
Lover Man	16 Feb 69	BR 8. An instrumental version and taken from the "Chandler Tapes".	Electric Gypsy CD Scorpio? 40176 / 15	Olympic Sound Studios, London, England	JHE	
Lover Man	16 Feb 69	BR 8. An instrumental version and taken from the "Chandler Tapes".	Studio Haze CD INA 6	Olympic Sound Studios, London, England	JHE	
Lover Man	16 Feb 69	BR 8. An instrumental version and taken from the "Chandler Tapes".	DeLane Lea And Olympic Outs CD Gold Standard CD-R	Olympic Sound Studios, London, England	JHE	
Lover Man	16 Feb 69	BR 8. An instrumental version and taken from the "Chandler Tapes".	Eyes And Imagination CD Third Stone TSD 18970	Olympic Sound Studios, London, England	JHE	
Lover Man	24 Feb 69	BR 9 mix 1 (stereo). Live performance.	Royal Albert Hall CD Blimp 008 / 009 & Listen To This Eric CD JH 003 / 4	Royal Albert Hall, London, England	JHE	
Lover Man	24 Feb 69	BR 9 mix 2. Live performance.	Stone Free CD Silver Rarities SIRA 58 / 59	Royal Albert Hall, London, England	JHE	
Lover Man	17 May 69	BR 10. Live performance.	One Night At The Arena CD Venue VE 100501	Rhode Island Arena, Providence, RI	JHE	
Lover Man	18 May 69	BR 11. Live performance.	Roman Coliseum, The CD Starquake SQ 11	Madison Square Garden, New York, NY	JHE	
Lover Man	10 Jul 69	BR 12-13. The Tonight Show hosted by Flip Wilson. Take 1 where Jimi blows his amp! Continues with take 2.	Dante's Inferno CD Pink Poodle POO 002	NBC TV, The Tonight Show, New York, NY	Jimi	Billy Cox / Bass, Ed Shaughnessy / Drums
Lover Man	10 Jul 69	BR 12-13. The Tonight Show hosted by Flip Wilson. Take 1 where Jimi blows his amp! Continues with take 2.	Live At Philharmonic Hall LP Sagittarius LTD	The Tonight Show W / Flip Wilson, New York, NY	Jimi	Billy Cox / Bass, Ed Shaughnessy / Drums
Lover Man	?? Aug 69	BR 14. The first of two rehearsals from Jimi's Shokan house.	Gypsy Sun And Rainbows CD Manic Depression MDCD 05 / 06	Shokan House, Woodstock, NY	GSRB	
Lover Man	?? Aug 69	BR 14. The first of two rehearsals from Jimi's Shokan house.	Woodstock Monday, August 18 1969, 8AM CD JMH 008	Shokan House, Woodstock, NY	GSRB	

SONG TITLE	DATE	COMMENTS	RELEASE	LOCATION / VENUE	BAND	PERSONNEL
Lover Man	?? Aug 69	BR 14. The first of two rehearsals from Jimi's Shokan house.	Woodstock Rehearsals CD Midnight Beat MBCD 009	Shokan House, Woodstock, NY	GSRB	
Lover Man	?? Aug 69	BR 15. The second of two rehearsals from Jimi's Shokan house.	Gypsy Sun And Rainbows CD Manic Depression MDCD 05 / 06	Shokan House, Woodstock, NY	GSRB	
Lover Man	?? Aug 69	BR 15. The second of two rehearsals from Jimi's Shokan house.	Woodstock Monday, August 18 1969, 8AM CD JMH 008	Shokan House, Woodstock, NY	GSRB	
Lover Man	18 Aug 69	BR 16. Live performance.	Woodstock Nation CD Wild Bird 89090 1 / 2	Woodstock Music And Art Fair, Bethel, NY	GSRB	
Lover Man	18 Aug 69	BR 16. Live performance.	Gypsy Sun And Rainbows CD Manic Depression MDCD 05 / 06	Woodstock Music And Art Fair, Bethel, NY	GSRB	
Lover Man	18 Aug 69	BR 16. Live performance.	Woodstock Monday, August 18 1969, 8AM CD JMH 008	Woodstock Music And Art Fair, Bethel, NY	GSRB	
Lover Man (Rock Me Baby)	06 Sep 69	BR 17 mix 1. This version is the one that the band goes into right after "Lord I Sing The Blues".	Electric Hendrix Vol 1 CD Pyramid PYCD 030	Hit Factory, New York, NY	GSRB	
Lover Man	06 Sep 69	BR 17 mix 1. This version is the one that the band goes into right after "Lord I Sing The Blues".	This One's For You LP Veteran Music MF-243	Hit Factory, New York, NY	GSRB	
Lover Man	06 Sep 69	BR 17 mix 1. This version is the one that the band goes into right after "Lord I Sing The Blues".	TTG Studios ???? CD WHOAMI WAI 015	Hit Factory, New York, NY	GSRB	
Lover Man	06 Sep 69	BR 17 mix 1. This version is the one that the band goes into right after "Lord I Sing The Blues".	Talent And Feeling Vol 1 CD Extremely Rare EXR 17	Hit Factory, New York, NY	GSRB	
Lover Man	06 Sep 69	BR 17 mix 1. This version is the one that the band goes into right after "Lord I Sing The Blues".	Paper Airplanes CD Midnight Beat MBCD 25	Hit Factory, New York, NY	GSRB	
Lover Man	06 Sep 69	BR 18 mix 2. An unused mix of this version. This CD has a goofy intro by Jimi edited on from another source. Incomplete.	Message From Nine To The Universe CD Oil Well 122	T.T.G. Studios, Hollywood, CA	JHE	
Lover Man	06 Sep 69	BR 18 mix 2. An unused mix of this version. Incomplete and in poor quality.	In From The Storm CD Silver Rarities SIRA 109 / 110	Hit Factory, New York, NY	COL	
Lover Man	06 Sep 69	BR 18 mix 2. An unused mix of this version. Incomplete.	I Don't Live Today CD ACL 007	Hit Factory, New York, NY	GSRB	

Song	Date	Notes	Release	Location	Label
Lover Man	?? Dec 69	BR 19. Rehearsal #1 from this session at Baggies. Preceded by a false start.	Band Of Gypsys Vol 3	Baggies, New York, NY	BOG
Lover Man	?? Dec 69	BR 19. Rehearsal #1 from this session at Baggies. Preceded by a false start.	Band Of Gypsys Rehearsals CD Whoopy Cat WKP 003	Baggies, New York, NY	BOG
Lover Man	?? Dec 69	BR 19. Rehearsal #1 from this session at Baggies. Preceded by a false start.	Gypsy Haze CD Lords Of Archive LAR 16	Baggies, New York, NY	BOG
Lover Man	?? Dec 69	BR 19. Rehearsal #1 from this session at Baggies. Preceded by a false start.	Band Of Gypsys- The Ultimate CD JMH 010 / 3	Baggies, New York, NY	BOG
Lover Man	?? Dec 69	BR 20. Rehearsal #2 from this session at Baggies.	Gypsy Haze CD Lords Of Archive LAR 16	Baggies, New York, NY	BOG
Lover Man	31 Dec 69	BR 21. Live performance.	Band Of Gypsys Vol 3	Fillmore East, New York, NY 1st Show	BOG
Lover Man	31 Dec 69	BR 21. Live performance.	Band Of Gypsys Happy New Year, Jimi LP Cops & Robbers JTYM 01	Fillmore East, New York, NY 1st Show	BOG
Lover Man	31 Dec 69	BR 21. Live performance.	Gypsy Haze CD Lords Of Archive LAR 16	Fillmore East, New York, NY 1st Show	BOG
Lover Man	31 Dec 69	BR 21. Live performance.	Fillmore Concerts, The CD Whoopy Cat WKP 0006 / 7	Fillmore East, New York, NY 1st Show	BOG
Lover Man	31 Dec 69	BR 21. Live performance.	Band Of Gold CD-R Major Tom MT 087	Fillmore East, New York, NY 1st Show	BOG
Lover Man	31 Dec 69	BR 21. Live performance.	Power Of Soul CD SQ-10	Fillmore East, New York, NY 1st Show	BOG
Lover Man	31 Dec 69	BR 21. Live performance.	Ultimate Live Collection, The CD The Beat Goes On BGO BX 9307-4	Fillmore East, New York, NY 1st Show	BOG
Lover Man (Getting Your Brothers Shoes Together)	25 Apr 70	BR 22. Live performance.	Enjoy Jimi Hendrix LP Rubber Dubber 700-001-01	Los Angeles Forum, Los Angeles, CA	COL
Lover Man	25 Apr 70	BR 22. Live performance.	Portrait Of Jimi Hendrix, A LP Catalog # Varies On Dead Wax	Los Angeles Forum, Los Angeles, CA	COL
Lover Man	25 Apr 70	BR 22. Live performance.	Live At The Forum 1970 CD Whoopy Cat WKP 021 / 22	Los Angeles Forum, Los Angeles, CA	COL
Lover Man	25 Apr 70	BR 22. Live performance. The Luna disc is from a tape source while the JHCD 528 disc is copied from vinyl.	Scuse Me While I Kiss The Sky CD Luna CD & JHCD 528	Los Angeles Forum, Los Angeles, CA	COL

SONG TITLE	DATE	COMMENTS	RELEASE	LOCATION / VENUE	BAND	PERSONNEL
Lover Man	15 May 70	BR 23. This track continues from the version of "Freedom" recorded on the same date.	Studio Haze CD INA 6	Record Plant, New York, NY	COL	
Lover Man	15 May 70	BR 23. This track continues from the version of "Freedom" recorded on the same date.	Multicolored Blues CD Luna LU 9317	Record Plant, New York, NY	COL	
Lover Man	30 May 70	CR 2. Live performance.	Riots In Berkeley CD Beech Marten BM 038	Berkeley Community Theater, Berkeley, CA 2nd Show	COL	
Lover Man	30 May 70	CR 2. Live performance.	Jimi Plays Berkeley (CR) Warner Reprise Videotape	Berkeley Community Theater, Berkeley, CA 2nd Show	COL	
Lover Man	30 May 70	CR 2. Live performance.	Hendrix In The West (CR) LP Polydor 2302018 A	Berkeley Community Theater, Berkeley, CA 2nd Show	COL	
Lover Man	30 May 70	CR 2. Live performance.	Midnight Magic CD Neutral Zone NZCD 89012	Berkeley Community Theater, Berkeley, CA 2nd Show	COL	
Lover Man	30 May 70	CR 2. Live performance.	Fire CD The Entertainers CD297	Berkeley Community Theater, Berkeley, CA 2nd Show	COL	
Lover Man	30 May 70	CR 2. Live performance.	Berkeley Concerts, The CD Whoopy Cat WKP 004 / 5	Berkeley Community Theater, Berkeley, CA 2nd Show	COL	
Lover Man	30 May 70	CR 2. Live performance.	Jimi Plays Berkeley CD JMH 005 / 2	Berkeley Community Theater, Berkeley, CA 1st Show	COL	
Lover Man	13 Jun 70	BR 24. Live performance.	Baltimore Civic Center, June 13, 1970 CD Starquake SQ-09	Baltimore Civic Center, Baltimore, MD	COL	
Lover Man	04 Jul 70	CR 3. Live performance.	Stages Atlanta 70 (CR) CD Reprise 9 27632-2	2nd International Pop Festival, Atlanta, GA	COL	
Lover Man	04 Jul 70	CR 3. Live performance.	Atlanta CD JMH 009 / 02	2nd International Pop Festival, Atlanta, GA	COL	
Lover Man	04 Jul 70	CR 3. Live performance.	Oh, Atlanta CD Tendolar TDR-009	2nd International Pop Festival, Atlanta, GA	COL	
Lover Man	04 Jul 70	CR 3. Live performance.	Atlanta CD JMH 009 / 02	2nd International Pop Festival, Atlanta, GA	COL	
Lover Man	17 Jul 70	BR 25. Live performance.	Can You Here Me LP Hemero 01 / KERI	New York Pop-Downing Stadium, Randalls Island, NY	COL	

Song	Date	Notes	Release	Location	Label
Lover Man	17 Jul 70	BR 25. Live performance.	Live At Randall's Island LP Moon Tree Records PH1962	New York Pop-Downing Stadium, Randalls Island, NY	COL
Lover Man	17 Jul 70	BR 25. Live performance.	Live USA CD Imtrat 902-001	New York Pop-Downing Stadium, Randalls Island, NY	COL
Lover Man	30 Jul 70	BR 26. Live performance.	Last American Concert Vol 1 CD The Swingin' Pig TSP-062	Rainbow Bridge Vibratory Sound-Color Experiment, Maui, HI 1st Show	COL
Lover Man	30 Jul 70	BR 26. Live performance.	In From The Storm CD Silver Rarities SIRA 109 / 110	Rainbow Bridge Vibratory Sound-Color Experiment, Maui, HI 1st Show	COL
Lover Man	30 Jul 70	BR 26. Live performance.	Rainbow Bridge 2 CD JMH 003 / 2	Rainbow Bridge Vibratory Sound-Color Experiment, Maui, HI 1st Show	COL
Lover Man	30 Aug 70	CR 4. Live performance.	Island Man CD Silver Rarities SIRA 39 / 40	Isle Of Wight Festival, Isle Of Wight, England	COL
Lover Man	30 Aug 70	CR 4. Live performance.	Isle Of Wight / Atlanta Pop Festival (CR) LP Columbia G3X 3085	Isle Of Wight Festival, Isle Of Wight, England	COL
Lover Man	30 Aug 70	CR 4. Live performance.	Live - Isle Of Wight '70 (CR) CD Polydor 847236-2	Isle Of Wight Festival, Isle Of Wight, England	COL
Lover Man	30 Aug 70	CR 4. Live performance.	Wight CD JMH 006 / 2	Isle Of Wight Festival, Isle Of Wight, England	COL
Lover Man	31 Aug 70	CR 4. Live performance.	Come On Stockholm CD No Label	Stora Scenen, Grona Lund, Stockholm, Sweden	COL
Lover Man	31 Aug 70	BR 26. Live performance.	Free Concert CD Midnight Beat MBCD 013	Stora Scenen, Tivoli Garden, Stockholm, Sweden	COL
Machine Gun	22 Jun 69	BR 4. Live performance.	It Never Takes An End CD Genuine Pig TGP-118	Newport Pop Festival, San Fernando State, Northridge, CA	NJK
Machine Gun	29 Aug 69	BR 1. A very early version recorded at the same session as and following the 6 takes of "Izabella" found on other releases.	Band Of Gypsys Vol 3	Hit Factory, New York, NY	GSRB

SONG TITLE	DATE	COMMENTS	RELEASE	LOCATION / VENUE	BAND	PERSONNEL
Machine Gun	29 Aug 69	BR 1. A very early version recorded at the same session as and following the 6 takes of "Izabella" also found on this release.	First Rays Of The New Rising Sun CD Triangle PYCD 084-2	Hit Factory, New York, N Y	GSRB	
Machine Gun	29 Aug 69	BR 1. A very early version recorded at the same session as and following the 6 takes of "Izabella" also found on this release.	Completer, The CD Whoopy Cat WKP 0018 / 19	Hit Factory, New York, N Y	GSRB	
Machine Gun	29 Aug 69	BR 1. A very early version recorded at the same session as and following the 6 takes of "Izabella" found on other releases.	I Don't Live Today CD ACL 007	Hit Factory, New York, NY	GSRB	
Machine Gun	29 Aug 69	BR 1. A very early version recorded at the same session as and following the 6 takes of "Izabella" found on other releases.	Magic Hand CD Mum MUCD 012	Hit Factory, New York, NY	GSRB	
Machine Gun	29 Aug 69	BR 2. A second take from this session.	Mixdown Master Tapes Volume 1 CD Dandelion DL 005	Hit Factory, New York, N Y	GSRB	
Machine Gun	29 Aug 69	BR 3. A composite of takes recorded this day and compiled for possible release at some time. This features the lyrics from 'Izabella' at the start. Incomplete.	Sir James Marshall LP Jester Productions JP 106	Hit Factory, New York, N Y	GSRB	
Machine Gun (Bury Me Body)	29 Aug 69	BR 3. A composite of takes recorded this day and compiled for possible release at some time. This features the lyrics from 'Izabella' at the start. Incomplete.	Things I Used To Do CD The Early Years 02-CD-3334	Hit Factory, New York, N Y	GSRB	
Machine Gun	29 Aug 69	BR 3. A composite of takes recorded this day and compiled for possible release at some time. This features the lyrics from 'Izabella' at the start. Incomplete.	51st Anniversary CD Future Disc JMH 001 / 8	Hit Factory, New York, N Y	GSRB	
Machine Gun	29 Aug 69	BR 3. A composite of takes recorded this day and compiled for possible release at some time. This features the lyrics from 'Izabella' at the start. Incomplete.	Gypsy Suns, Moons And Rainbows CD Sidewalk JHX 8868	Hit Factory, New York, N Y	GSRB	
Machine Gun	29 Aug 69	BR 3. A composite of takes recorded this day and compiled for possible release at some time. This features the lyrics from 'Izabella' at the start. Incomplete.	Midnight Shines Down CD Blue Kangaroo BK 04	Hit Factory, New York, N Y	GSRB	
Machine Gun	29 Aug 69	BR 3. A composite of takes recorded this day and compiled for possible release at some time. This features the lyrics from 'Izabella' at the start. Incomplete.	Completer, The CD Whoopy Cat WKP 0018 / 19	Hit Factory, New York, N Y	GSRB	
Machine Gun	29 Aug 69	CR 3.	Midnight Lightning (CR) LP Reprise MS 2229	Hit Factory, New York, N Y	GSRB	Midnight Lightning Line Up 1975
Machine Gun	09 Sep 69	BR 5. Live performance on the Dick Cavett TV Show.	Loaded Guitar LP Starlight SL 87013	Dick Cavett Show, ABC TV Studios, New York, NY	COL	Juma Sultan / Percussion
Machine Gun	09 Sep 69	BR 6. Live performance.	Woodstock Monday, August 18 1969, 8AM CD JMH 008	Dick Cavett Show, ABC TV Studios, New York, NY	COL	Juma Sultan / Percussion

Song	Date	Notes	Release	Venue	
Machine Gun	31 Dec 69	BR 7. Live performance.	Band Of Gypsys Happy New Year, Jimi LP Cops & Robbers JTYM 01	Fillmore East, New York, NY 2nd Show	BOG
Machine Gun	31 Dec 69	BR 7. Live performance.	Band Of Gold CD-R Major Tom MT 087	Fillmore East, New York, NY 1st Show	BOG
Machine Gun	31 Dec 69	BR 7. Live performance.	Power Of Soul CD SQ-10	Fillmore East, New York, NY 1st Show	BOG
Machine Gun	31 Dec 69	CR 1. Live performance. Incomplete.	First Rays Of The New Rising Sun CD Living Legend LLRCD 023	Fillmore East, New York, NY 2nd Show	BOG
Machine Gun	31 Dec 69	CR 1. Live performance.	Band Of Gypsys Vol 3	Fillmore East, New York, NY 1st Show	BOG
Machine Gun	31 Dec 69	CR 1. Live performance. Incomplete.	Lifelines (CR) CD Reprise 9 26435-2	Fillmore East, New York, NY	BOG
Machine Gun	31 Dec 69	CR 1. Live performance.	Auld Lang Syne CD JH 100 03	Fillmore East, New York, NY 2nd Show	BOG
Machine Gun	31 Dec 69	CR 1. Live performance.	Band Of Gypsys: Happy New Year CD Silver Shadow CD 9103	Fillmore East, New York, NY 2nd Show	BOG
Machine Gun	31 Dec 69	CR 1. Live performance.	Fillmore Concerts, The CD Whoopy Cat WKP 0006 / 7	Fillmore East, New York, NY 1st Show	BOG
Machine Gun	31 Dec 69	CR 2. Live performance.	Fillmore Concerts, The CD Whoopy Cat WKP 0006 / 7	Fillmore East, New York, NY 2nd Show	BOG
Machine Gun	31 Dec 69	CR 1. Live performance.	Band Of Gold CD-R Major Tom MT 087	Fillmore East, New York, NY 2nd Show	BOG
Machine Gun	31 Dec 69	CR 1. Live performance.	Band Of Gypsys- The Ultimate CD JMH 010 / 3	Fillmore East, New York, NY 2nd Show	BOG
Machine Gun	01 Jan 70	CR 2. Live performance.	Band Of Gypsys (CR) CD Capitol 72434-93446-2-4	Fillmore East, New York, NY 1st Show	BOG
Machine Gun	01 Jan 70	CR 2. Live performance.	Soundtrack From The Film Jimi Hendrix, The (CR) LP Reprise 2RS 6481	Fillmore East, New York, NY 1st Show	BOG
Machine Gun	01 Jan 70	CR 2. Live performance.	Band Of Gold CD-R Major Tom MT 087	Fillmore East, New York, NY 1st Show	BOG
Machine Gun	01 Jan 70	BR 7. Live performance.	Band Of Gold CD-R Major Tom MT 087	Fillmore East, New York, NY 2nd Show	BOG

SONG TITLE	DATE	COMMENTS	RELEASE	LOCATION / VENUE	BAND	PERSONNEL
Machine Gun	01 Jan 70	BR 7. Live performance.	Band Of Gypsys- The Ultimate CD JMH 010 / 3	Fillmore East, New York, NY 2nd Show	BOG	
Machine Gun	25 Apr 70	BR 8. Live performance.	Enjoy Jimi Hendrix LP Rubber Dubber 700-001-01	Los Angeles Forum, Los Angeles, CA	COL	
Machine Gun	25 Apr 70	BR 8. Live performance.	Portrait Of Jimi Hendrix, A LP Catalog # Varies On Dead Wax	Los Angeles Forum, Los Angeles, CA	COL	
Machine Gun	25 Apr 70	BR 8. Live performance.	Live At The Forum 1970 CD Whoopy Cat WKP 021 / 22	Los Angeles Forum, Los Angeles, CA	COL	
Machine Gun	25 Apr 70	BR 8. Live performance. The Luna disc is from a tape source while the JHCD 528 disc is copied from vinyl.	Scuse Me While I Kiss The Sky CD Luna CD & JHCD 528	Los Angeles Forum, Los Angeles, CA	COL	
Machine Gun	30 May 70	BR 9. Live performance.	Atlanta Special CD Genuine Pig TGP 121	Winterland Theatre, San Francisco, CA 2nd Show	COL	
Machine Gun	30 May 70	BR 9. Live performance.	Jimi Plays Berkeley (CR) Warner Reprise Videotape	Berkeley Community Theater, Berkeley, CA	COL	
Machine Gun	30 May 70	BR 9. Live performance.	Berkeley Soundchecks, The CD The Whoopy Cat WKP 0008	Berkeley Community Theater, Berkeley, CA	COL	
Machine Gun	30 May 70	BR 9. Live performance.	Jimi Plays Berkeley CD JMH 005 / 2	Berkeley Community Theater, Berkeley, CA Sound Check	COL	
Machine Gun	30 May 70	CR 4. Live performance.	Good Karma 1 LP Berkeley 2022	Berkeley Community Theater, Berkeley, CA 1st Show	COL	
Machine Gun	30 May 70	CR 4. Live performance.	Berkeley Concert LP Audifon AF 008	Berkeley Community Theater, Berkeley, CA 1st Show	COL	
Machine Gun	30 May 70	CR 4. Live performance.	Berkeley Concerts, The CD Whoopy Cat WKP 004 / 5	Berkeley Community Theater, Berkeley, CA 1st Show	COL	
Machine Gun	30 May 70	CR 4. Live performance.	Ultimate Live Collection, The CD The Beat Goes On BGO BX 9307-4	Berkeley Community Theater, Berkeley, CA 1st Show	COL	
Machine Gun	30 May 70	CR 4. Live performance.	Johnny B. Goode (CR)	Berkeley Community	COL	

Song	Date	Notes	CD Release	Venue	Format
			CD Capitol 430218-2	Theater, Berkeley, CA 1st Show	
Machine Gun	30 May 70	BR 10. Live performance.	Riots In Berkeley CD Beech Marten BM 038	Berkeley Community Theater, Berkeley, CA 2nd Show	COL
Machine Gun	30 May 70	BR 10. Live performance.	Berkeley Concerts, The CD Whoopy Cat WKP 004 / 5	Berkeley Community Theater, Berkeley, CA 2nd Show	COL
Machine Gun	30 May 70	BR 10. Live performance.	Jimi Plays Berkeley CD JMH 005 / 2	Berkeley Community Theater, Berkeley, CA 1st Show	COL
Machine Gun	13 Jun 70	BR 11. Live performance.	Baltimore Civic Center, June 13, 1970 CD Starquake SQ-09	Baltimore Civic Center, Baltimore, MD	COL
Machine Gun	30 Aug 70	CR 5 mix 1. Live performance. This is an edited version of the full performance.	Live - Isle Of Wight '70 (CR) CD Polydor 847236-2	Isle Of Wight Festival, Isle Of Wight, England	COL
Machine Gun	30 Aug 70	CR 5mix 2. Live performance. Incomplete.	Island Man CD Silver Rarities SIRA 39 / 40	Isle Of Wight Festival, Isle Of Wight, England	COL
Machine Gun	30 Aug 70	CR 5 mix 2. Live performance. Complete but missing the intro.	Wight CD JMH 006 / 2	Isle Of Wight Festival, Isle Of Wight, England	COL
Machine Gun	30 Aug 70	CR 5 mix 3. This is an edited version of the full performance. Officially released on the "Jimi Hendrix At The Isle Of Wight" video and laserdisc. Copied onto CD.	At The Isle Of Wight (CR) Laserdisc CBS / Sony CLSM 791	Isle Of Wight Festival, Isle Of Wight, England	COL
Machine Gun	30 Aug 70	CR 5 mix 3. This is an edited version of the full performance. Officially released on the "Jimi Hendrix At The Isle Of Wight" video and laserdisc. Copied onto CD.	51st Anniversary CD Future Disc JMH 001 / 8	Isle Of Wight Festival, Isle Of Wight, England	COL
Machine Gun	30 Aug 70	CR 5 mix 3. This is an edited version of the full performance. Officially released on the "Jimi Hendrix At The Isle Of Wight" video and laserdisc. Copied onto CD.	Valley Of Neptune CD PC 28355	Isle Of Wight Festival, Isle Of Wight, England	JHE
Machine Gun	31 Aug 70	BR 12. Live performance.	Come On Stockholm CD No Label	Stora Scenen, Liesberg, Stockholm, Sweden	COL
Machine Gun	31 Aug 70	BR 12. Live performance.	Free Concert CD Midnight Beat MBCD 013	Stora Scenen, Tivoli Garden, Stockholm, Sweden	COL
Machine Gun	03 Sep 70	BR 13. Live performance.	Copenhagen '70 CD Whoopy Cat WKP 044 / 45	K.B. Hallen, Copenhagen, Denmark	COL

SONG TITLE	DATE	COMMENTS	RELEASE	LOCATION / VENUE	BAND	PERSONNEL
Machine Gun	04 Sep 70	BR 14. Live performance.	Back To Berlin CD Midnight Beat 049	Deutsche- Landhalle, Berlin, Germany	COL	
Manic Depression	23 Feb 67	CR 1 mix 1 (stereo)	Are You Experienced? (CR) CD MCACD 11602	De Lane Lea, London, England	JHE	
Manic Depression	23 Feb 67	CR 1 mix 1 (stereo)	The Singles Album (CR) CD Polydor 827 369-2	De Lane Lea, London, England	JHE	
Manic Depression	23 Feb 67	CR 1 mix 1 (stereo)	Smash Hits (CR) CD Reprise 2276-2	De Lane Lea, London, England	JHE	
Manic Depression	23 Feb 67	Cr 1 mix 2 (mono).	Legacy (CR) LP Polydor	De Lane Lea, London, England	JHE	
Manic Depression	23 Feb 67	Cr 1 mix 2 (mono).	Are You Experienced? (CR) LP Track 612 001	De Lane Lea, London, England	JHE	
Manic Depression	23 Feb 67	CR 1 mix 3. Unused mix of the CR 1. Mono.	Olympic Gold Vol 2 CD Blimp 007	De Lane Lea, London, England	JHE	
Manic Depression	23 Feb 67	BR 1. Alternate take to the CR #1. Includes a false start.	Olympic Gold Vol 2 CD Blimp 007	De Lane Lea, London, England	JHE	
Manic Depression	25 Feb 68	BR 2. Live performance.	Winterland Vol 2 CD Whoopy Cat WKP 00279 / 28	Civic Opera House, Chicago, IL	JHE	
Manic Depression	17 Apr 67	CR 2. BBC performance.	BBC Sessions (CR) CD MCACD 2-11742	Late Nite Line Up, B B C T V, London, England	JHE	
Manic Depression	12 Oct 68	CR 3. Live performance.	First Rays Of The New Rising Sun CD Living Legend LLRCD 023	Winterland Theatre, San Francisco, CA 2nd Show	JHE	
Manic Depression	12 Oct 68	CR 3. Live performance.	Lifelines (CR) CD Reprise 9 26435-2	Winterland Theatre, San Francisco, CA 2nd Show	JHE	
Manic Depression	12 Oct 68	CR 3. Live performance.	Winterland Vol 3 CD Whoopy Cat WKP 0029 / 30	Winterland Theatre, San Francisco, CA 2nd Show	JHE	
Manic Depression	12 Oct 68	CR 3. Live performance.	Can You Here Me LP Hemero 01 / KERI	Winterland Theatre, San Francisco, CA 2nd Show	JHE	
Manic Depression	12 Oct 68	CR 3. Live performance.	Fire CD The Entertainers CD297	Winterland Theatre, San Francisco, CA 2nd Show	JHE	

Song	Date	Notes	Release	Venue	Artist	Personnel
Manic Depression	12 Oct 68	CR 3. Live performance.	Hendrix In Words And Music CD Outlaw Records OTR 1100030	Winterland Theatre, San Francisco, CA 2nd Show	JHE	
Manic Depression	12 Oct 68	CR 3. Live performance.	Live At Winterland (CR) CD Rykodisc RCD 20038	Winterland Theatre, San Francisco, CA 2nd Show	JHE	
Manic Depression	12 Oct 68	CR 3. Live performance.	Greatest Hits Live CD Chartbusters CHER 089A	Winterland Theatre, San Francisco, CA 2nd Show	JHE	
Manic Depression	12 Oct 68	CR 3. Live performance.	Lost Winterland Tapes CD Starquake SQ 051-2	Winterland Theatre, San Francisco, CA 2nd Show	JHE	
Manic Depression	12 Oct 68	CR 3. Live performance. Incomplete.	Black Strings CD CDM G-53 258	Winterland Theatre, San Francisco, CA 2nd Show	JHE	
Mannish Boy (I'm A Man / Mannish Boy)	22 Apr 69	BR 1-2. Frequently confused with "I'm A Man". This is both the first and second group of takes including many false starts.	Earth Tones CD Whoopy Cat WKP 041	Record Plant, New York, NY	Jimi	Devon Wilson / Tambourine, Billy Cox / Bass?, Unknown / Drums
Mannish Boy	22 Apr 69	BR 1-2. Frequently confused with "I'm A Man". This is both the first and second group of takes including many false starts.	Black Gold CD Midnight Beat MBCD 058-062	Record Plant, New York, NY	Jimi	Devon Wilson / Tambourine, Billy Cox / Bass?, Unknown / Drums
Mannish Boy	22 Apr 69	BR 2. Frequently confused with "I'm A Man". The second group of takes including many false starts.	Electric Gypsy's CD Pilot HJCD 070	Record Plant, New York, NY	Jimi	Devon Wilson / Tambourine, Billy Cox / Bass?, Unknown / Drums
Mannish Boy (I'm A Man)	22 Apr 69	BR 2. Just one of the many takes from the second group of takes recorded this day. See "Black Gold" or "Earth Tones" for a more complete session tape segment.	Band Of Gypsys- The Ultimate CD JMH 010 / 3	Record Plant, New York, NY	Jimi	Devon Wilson / Tambourine, Billy Cox / Bass?, Unknown / Drums
Mannish Boy	22 Apr 69	BR 2. Just one of the many takes from the second group of takes recorded this day. See "Black Gold" or "Earth Tones" for a more complete session tape segment.	Mannish Boy LP Contraband CBM 88	Record Plant, New York, NY	Jimi	Devon Wilson / Tambourine, Billy Cox / Bass?, Unknown / Drums
Mannish Boy	22 Apr 69	BR 2. Just one of the many takes from the second group of takes recorded this day. See "Black Gold" or "Earth Tones" for a more complete session tape segment.	Band Of Gypsys- The Ultimate CD JMH 010 / 3	Record Plant, New York, NY	Jimi	Devon Wilson / Tambourine, Billy Cox / Bass?, Unknown / Drums
Mannish Boy	22 Apr 69	CR 1. A composite of several takes recorded this day. See "Black Gold" or "Earth Tones" for a more complete session tape segment	Jimi Hendrix: Blues (CR) CD MCA MCAD-11060	Record Plant, New York, NY	Jimi	Devon Wilson / Tambourine, Billy Cox / Bass?, Unknown / Drums
Marshall Attack Jam (Instrumental)	?? Oct 68	BR 1. Another studio jam with a made up name (taken from the 'Sotheby's Reels' bootleg) All releases call it something different.	51st Anniversary CD Future Disc JMH 001 / 8	T.T.G. Studios, Hollywood, CA	JHE	
Marshall Attack Jam (Midnight Sun)	?? Oct 68	BR 1. Another studio jam with a made up name (taken from the 'Sotheby's Reels' bootleg) All releases call it something different.	Redskin' Jammin' CD JH 01 / 02	T.T.G. Studios, Hollywood, CA	JHE	

SONG TITLE	DATE	COMMENTS	RELEASE	LOCATION / VENUE	BAND	PERSONNEL
Marshall Attack Jam (Instrumental)	?? Oct 68	BR 1. Another studio jam with a made up name (taken from the 'Sotheby's Reels' bootleg) All releases call it something different.	Mannish Boy LP Contraband CBM 88	T.T.G. Studios, Hollywood, CA	JHE	
Marshall Attack Jam (TTG Instrumental / Experience Jam 2)	?? Oct 68	BR 1. Another studio jam with a made up name (taken from the 'Sotheby's Reels' bootleg) All releases call it something different.	Lost Experience, The, CD JHCD203	T.T.G. Studios, Hollywood, CA	JHE	
Marshall Attack Jam	?? Oct 68	BR 1. Another studio jam with a made up name (taken from the 'Sotheby's Reels' bootleg) All releases call it something different.	Sotheby's Reels, The CD Gold Standard TOM-800	T.T.G. Studios, Hollywood, CA	JHE	
Master James & Co.	10 Jan 69	Interview with the JHE by Niels Olaf Gudme.	Jimi In Denmark (CR) CD UniVibes 1003 & Booted On Dynamite Studios	Falkoner Centret, Copenhagen, Denmark	Jimi	
Mastermind	18 Aug 69	BR 1. Live performance.	Woodstock Nation CD Wild Bird 89090 1 / 2	Woodstock Music And Art Fair, Bethel, NY	GSRB	
Mastermind	18 Aug 69	BR 1. Live performance.	Gypsy Sun And Rainbows CD Manic Depression MDCD 05 / 06	Woodstock Music And Art Fair, Bethel, NY	GSRB	
Mastermind	18 Aug 69	BR 1. Live performance.	Woodstock Monday, August 18 1969, 8AM CD JMH 008	Woodstock Music And Art Fair, Bethel, NY	GSRB	
May This Be Love	03 Apr 67	CR 1 mix 1 (stereo)	Are You Experienced? (CR) CD MCACD 11602	Olympic Sound Studios, London, England	JHE	
May This Be Love	03 Apr 67	CR 1 mix 2 (mono).	Are You Experienced? (CR) LP Track 612 001	Olympic Sound Studios, London, England	JHE	
May This Be Love	03 Apr 67	CR 1 mix 3 (mono). An alternate mono mix copied from the rare official release on the French 45 (Barklay 061389). This is a much easier way to find this longer running mix.	Sotheby Auction Tapes, The CD Midnight Beat MBCD 010	Olympic Sound Studios, London, England	JHE	
May This Be Love	03 Apr 67	Outtaked mix of CR 1 mix 1.	Sotheby's Private Reels CD JHR 003 / 004	Olympic Sound Studios, London, England	Fake	
Message From Nine To The Universe (Nine To The Universe)	22 May 69	CR 1. See other entries of this title for a longer version. During this jam Jimi touches on the themes from "Message To Love" and "Earth Blues".	Nine To The Universe (CR) LP Reprise HS2299	Record Plant, New York, NY	BOG	Devon Wilson / Vocals
Message From Nine To The Universe	22 May 69	CR 1. See other entries of this title for a longer version. During this jam Jimi touches on the themes from "Message To Love" and "Earth Blues".	Message From Nine To The Universe CD Oil Well 122	Record Plant, New York, NY	BOG	Devon Wilson / Vocals

Song	Date	Notes	Release	Location	Source	Personnel
Message From Nine To The Universe (Earth Blues / Message To Love)	22 May 69	BR 1. The full version of this song (with a made up title) that was edited for release.	Dante's Inferno CD Pink Poodle POO 002	Record Plant, New York, NY	BOG	Devon Wilson / Vocals
Message From Nine To The Universe	22 May 69	BR 1. The full version of this song (with a made up title) that was edited for release.	Mixdown Master Tapes Volume 1 CD Dandelion DL 005	Record Plant, New York, NY	BOG	Devon Wilson / Vocals
Message From Nine To The Universe	22 May 69	BR 1. This is an incomplete version of the unedited track. See "Dante's Inferno" or "Mixdown Master Tapes Vol 1" for the full version.	Ladyland In Flames LP Marshall Records JIMI 1,2,3,4	Record Plant, New York, NY	BOG	Devon Wilson / Vocals
Message From Nine To The Universe	22 May 69	BR 1. This is an incomplete version of the unedited track. See "Dante's Inferno" or "Mixdown Master Tapes Vol 1" for the full version.	Electric Anniversary Jimi CD Midnight Beat MBCD 024	Record Plant, New York, NY	BOG	Devon Wilson / Vocals
Message From Nine To The Universe (Strato Strut)	22 May 69	BR 1. This is an incomplete version of the unedited track. See "Dante's Inferno" or "Mixdown Master Tapes Vol 1" for the full version.	Flames CD Missing In Action ACT 1	Record Plant, New York, NY	BOG	Devon Wilson / Vocals
Message From Nine To The Universe (Tribute To Donna)	22 May 69	BR 1. This is an incomplete version of the unedited track. See "Dante's Inferno" or "Mixdown Master Tapes Vol 1" for the full version.	McLaughlin Sessions, The CD HML CD 9409	Record Plant, New York, NY	BOG	Devon Wilson / Vocals
Message To Love	18 Feb 69	BR 1. Live performance. This is a medley with "Spanish Castle Magic" and some jamming based on the main riff and chord progression of "Message To Love".	First Night At The Royal Albert Hall CD Midnight Beat MBCD 047 / 48	Royal Albert Hall, London, England	JHE	
Message To Love	15 Mar 69	BR 2. A short jam loosely built around what would become "Message To Love".	Freak Out Jam CD GH 002	Mercury Sound Studios, New York, NY	Jimi	Buddy Miles Express
Message To Love	25 May 69	BR 3. Live performance.	Historic Concert Vol 2 CD Midnight Beat MBCD 050	Santa Clara Pop Festival, San Jose, CA	JHE	
Message To Love	?? Aug 69	BR 4. Live performance.	Woodstock Rehearsals CD Midnight Beat MBCD 009	Shokan House, Woodstock, NY	GSRB	
Message To Love	?? Aug 69	BR 4. Live performance.	Shokan Sunrise CD	Shokan House, Woodstock, NY	GSRB	
Message To Love	18 Aug 69	BR 5. Live performance. Complete for the first time anywhere.	500,000 Halos CD EXP 500,000	Woodstock Music And Art Fair, Bethel, NY	GSRB	
Message To Love	18 Aug 69	BR 5. Live performance. Incomplete. Probably copied from the officially released video that had a partial version of this track.	51st Anniversary CD Future Disc JMH 001 / 8	Woodstock Music And Art Fair, Bethel, NY	GSRB	
Message To Love	18 Aug 69	BR 5. Live performance. Incomplete. Probably copied from the officially released video that had a partial version of this track.	Jimi: A Musical Legacy CD KTS BX 010	Woodstock Music And Art Fair, Bethel, NY	GSRB	

SONG TITLE	DATE	COMMENTS	RELEASE	LOCATION / VENUE	BAND	PERSONNEL
Message To Love	18 Aug 69	BR 5. Live performance. Incomplete. Probably copied from the officially released video that had a partial version of this track.	Woodstock Monday, August 18 1969, 8AM CD JMH 008	Woodstock Music And Art Fair, Bethel, NY	GSRB	
Message To Love	18 Aug 69	BR 5. Live performance. Incomplete. Probably copied from the officially released video that had a partial version of this track.	Ultimate Live Collection, The CD The Beat Goes On BGO BX 9307-4	Woodstock Music And Art Fair, Bethel, NY	GSRB	
Message To Love	28 Aug 69	CR 5.	South Saturn Delta (CR) CD MCACD 11684	Hit Factory, New York, N Y	GSRB	
Message To Love	28 Aug 69	BR 6. An alternate take from the same session that produced the CR 5.	Ball And Chain CD Jimi 009	Hit Factory, New York, N Y	GSRB	
Message To Love	19 Dec 69	CR 2.	Crash Landing (CR) LP Reprise MS 2204	Record Plant, New York, NY	BOG	Jimmy Maeulin / Percussion
Message To Love	19 Dec 69	BR 7. This is the original version of the take used for CR 1.	Talent And Feeling Vol 2 CD Extremely Rare EXR 22	Record Plant, New York, NY	BOG	
Message To Love	19 Dec 69	BR 7. This is the original version of the take used for CR 1.	Shine On Earth, Shine On CD Sidewalk SW 89010 / 89011	Record Plant, New York, NY	BOG	Juma Sultan / Percussion
Message To Love	19 Dec 69	BR 7. This is the original version of the take used for CR 1.	First Rays - The Sessions CD Whoopy Cat WKP 0002	Record Plant, New York, NY	BOG	Juma Sultan / Percussion
Message To Love	19 Dec 69	BR 7. This is the original version of the take used for CR 1.	Wight CD JMH 006 / 2	Record Plant, New York, NY	BOG	Juma Sultan / Percussion
Message To Love	19 Dec 69	CR 4 mix 1.	Voodoo Soup (CR) CD MCA 11206	Record Plant, New York, NY	BOG	Jimmy Maeulin / Percussion - 1974
Message To Love	19 Dec 69	CR 4 mix 2. Unused mix of the CR 4.	Paper Airplanes CD Midnight Beat MBCD 25	Record Plant, New York, NY	BOG	Jimmy Maeulin / Percussion - 1974
Message To Love	19 Dec 69	CR 4 mix 2. Unused mix of the CR 4.	Multicolored Blues CD Luna LU 9317	Record Plant, New York, NY	BOG	Jimmy Maeulin / Percussion - 1974
Message To Love	19 Dec 69	CR 4 mix 2. Unused mix of the CR 4.	Gypsy Suns, Moons And Rainbows CD Sidewalk JHX 8868	Record Plant, New York, NY	BOG	Jimmy Maeulin / Percussion - 1974
Message To Love	19 Dec 69	CR 4 mix 2. Unused mix of the CR 4.	Midnight Shines Down CD Blue Kangaroo BK 04	Record Plant, New York, NY	BOG	Jimmy Maeulin / Percussion - 1974
Message To Love	?? Dec 69	BR 8. Version #1 from the BOG rehearsals at Baggies prior to the legendary Fillmore shows. Includes 2 false starts	Band Of Gypsys Rehearsals CD Whoopy Cat WKP 003	Baggies, New York, NY	BOG	

Song	Date	Description	Source	Location		Notes
Message To Love	?? Dec 69	BR 9. Version #2 from the BOG rehearsals at Baggies prior to the legendary Fillmore shows.	Unsurpassed Studio Takes CD Yellow Dog YD 050	Baggies, New York, NY		BOG
Message To Love	?? Dec 69	BR 10. Version #3 from the BOG rehearsals at Baggies prior to the legendary Fillmore shows.	Sir James Marshall LP Jester Productions JP 106	Baggies, New York, NY		BOG
Message To Love	?? Dec 69	BR 10. Version #3 from the BOG rehearsals at Baggies prior to the legendary Fillmore shows.	This One's For You LP Veteran Music MF-243	Baggies, New York, NY		BOG
Message To Love	?? Dec 69	BR 10. Version #3 from the BOG rehearsals at Baggies prior to the legendary Fillmore shows.	Band Of Gypsys Rehearsals CD Whoopy Cat WKP 003	Baggies, New York, NY		BOG
Message To Love	?? Dec 69	BR 10. Version #3 from the BOG rehearsals at Baggies prior to the legendary Fillmore shows.	Redskin' Jammin' CD JH 01 / 02	Baggies, New York, NY		BOG
Message To Love	?? Dec 69	BR 10. Version #3 from the BOG rehearsals at Baggies prior to the legendary Fillmore shows.	Talent And Feeling Vol 1 CD Extremely Rare EXR 17	Baggies, New York, NY		BOG
Message To Love	?? Dec 69	BR 11. Version #4 from the legendary Fillmore shows. The end features Jimi and Billy and / or Buddy laughing along with some tongue in cheek verbalizations. This precedes a take of 'Ezy Rider'.	Band Of Gypsys Vol 3	Baggies, New York, NY		BOG
Message To Love	?? Dec 69	BR 11. Version #4 from the BOG rehearsals at Baggies prior to the legendary Fillmore shows. The end features Jimi and Billy and / or Buddy laughing along with some tongue in cheek verbalizations. This precedes a take of 'Ezy Rider'.	Band Of Gypsys Rehearsals CD Whoopy Cat WKP 003	Baggies, New York, NY		BOG
Message To Love	?? Dec 69	BR 11. Version #4 from the BOG rehearsals at Baggies prior to the legendary Fillmore shows. The end features Jimi and Billy and / or Buddy laughing along with some tongue in cheek verbalizations. This precedes a take of 'Ezy Rider'.	Gypsy Haze CD Lords Of Archive LAR 16	Baggies, New York, NY		BOG
Message To Love	?? Dec 69	BR 11. Version #4 from the BOG rehearsals at Baggies prior to the legendary Fillmore shows. The end features Jimi and Billy and / or Buddy laughing along with some tongue in cheek verbalizations. This precedes a take of 'Ezy Rider'.	Rainbow Bridge 2 CD JMH 003 / 2	Baggies, New York, NY		BOG
Message To Love	?? Dec 69	BR 11. Version #4 from the BOG rehearsals at Baggies prior to the legendary Fillmore shows. The end features Jimi and Billy and / or Buddy laughing along with some tongue in cheek verbalizations. This precedes a take of 'Ezy Rider'.	Band Of Gypsys- The Ultimate CD JMH 010 / 3	Baggies, New York, NY		BOG
Message To Love	?? Dec 69	BR 12. An incomplete take following several attempts at 'Who Knows'.	Band Of Gypsys- The Ultimate CD JMH 010 / 3	Baggies, New York, NY		BOG
Message To Love	?? Dec 69	BR 12-13. An incomplete take and a complete take following several attempts at 'Who Knows'. Version #5 from the BOG rehearsals at Baggies prior to the legendary Fillmore shows.	Things I Used To Do, The CD Golden Memories GM 890738	Baggies, New York, NY		BOG

SONG TITLE	DATE	COMMENTS	RELEASE	LOCATION / VENUE	BAND	PERSONNEL
Message To Love	?? Dec 69	BR 12-13. An incomplete take and a complete take following several attempts at 'Who Knows'. Version #5 from the BOG rehearsals at Baggies prior to the legendary Fillmore shows.	Notes In Colours CD JHR 001 / 002	Baggies, New York, NY	BOG	
Message To Love	?? Dec 69	BR 13. A complete take (minus the incomplete take) following several attempts at 'Who Knows'. Version #5 from the BOG rehearsals at Baggies prior to the legendary Fillmore shows.	Band Of Gypsys Vol 3	Baggies, New York, NY	BOG	
Message To Love	31 Dec 69	CR12. Live performance.	Auld Lang Syne CD JH 100 03	Fillmore East, New York, NY 2nd Show	BOG	
Message To Love	31 Dec 69	CR12. Live performance.	Shine On Earth, Shine On CD Sidewalk SW 89010 / 89011	Fillmore East, New York, NY 2nd Show	BOG	
Message To Love	31 Dec 69	CR12. Live performance.	Fillmore Concerts, The CD Whoopy Cat WKP 0006 / 7	Fillmore East, New York, NY 2nd Show	BOG	
Message To Love	31 Dec 69	CR12. Live performance.	Band Of Gold CD-R Major Tom MT 087	Fillmore East, New York, NY 2nd Show	BOG	
Message To Love	31 Dec 69	CR12. Live performance.	Band Of Gypsys- The Ultimate CD JMH 010 / 3	Fillmore East, New York, NY 2nd Show	BOG	
Message To Love	01 Jan 70	CR 1.	Band Of Gypsys (CR) CD Capitol 72434-93446-2-4	Fillmore East, New York, NY 2nd Show	BOG	
Message To Love	01 Jan 70	CR 1.	Legacy (CR) LP Polydor	Fillmore East, New York, NY 2nd Show	BOG	
Message To Love	01 Jan 70	CR 1.	Band Of Gold CD-R Major Tom MT 087	Fillmore East, New York, NY 2nd Show	BOG	
Message To Love	25 Apr 70	BR 13. Live performance.	Enjoy Jimi Hendrix LP Rubber Dubber 700-001-01	Los Angeles Forum, Los Angeles, CA	COL	
Message To Love	25 Apr 70	BR 13. Live performance.	Portrait Of Jimi Hendrix, A LP Catalog # Varies On Dead Wax	Los Angeles Forum, Los Angeles, CA	COL	
Message To Love	25 Apr 70	BR 13. Live performance.	Live At The Forum 1970 CD Whoopy Cat WKP 021 / 22	Los Angeles Forum, Los Angeles, CA	COL	
Message To Love	25 Apr 70	BR 13. Live performance. The Luna disc is from a tape source while the JHCD 528 disc is copied from vinyl.	Scuse Me While I Kiss The Sky CD Luna CD & JHCD 528	Los Angeles Forum, Los Angeles, CA	COL	
Message To Love	30 May 70	BR 14. Live performance.	Berkeley Soundchecks,	Berkeley Community	COL	

Song	Date	BR	Release	Venue	COL
Message To Love			The CD Whoopy Cat WKP 0008	Theater, Berkeley, CA Sound Check	COL
Message To Love	30 May 70	BR 14. Live performance.	Jimi Plays Berkeley CD JMH 005 / 2	Berkeley Community Theater, Berkeley, CA Sound Check	COL
Message To Love	30 May 70	BR 15. Live performance.	Good Karma 2 LP Berkeley 2023	Berkeley Community Theater, Berkeley, CA 1st Show	COL
Message To Love	30 May 70	BR 15. Live performance.	Berkeley Concert LP Audifon AF 008	Berkeley Community Theater, Berkeley, CA 1st Show	COL
Message To Love	30 May 70	BR 15. Live performance.	Berkeley Concerts, The CD Whoopy Cat WKP 004 / 5	Berkeley Community Theater, Berkeley, CA 1st Show	COL
Message To Love	30 May 70	BR 15. Live performance.	Ultimate Live Collection, The CD The Beat Goes On BGO BX 9307-4	Berkeley Community Theater, Berkeley, CA 1st Show	COL
Message To Love	30 May 70	BR 15. Live performance.	Atlanta Special CD Genuine Pig TGP 121	Berkeley Community Theater, Berkeley, CA Sound Check	COL
Message To Love	13 Jun 70	BR 16. Live performance.	Baltimore Civic Center, June 13, 1970 CD Starquake SQ-09	Baltimore Civic Center, Baltimore, MD	COL
Message To Love	04 Jul 70	BR 17. Live performance.	Berkeley Soundchecks, The CD Whoopy Cat WKP 0008	2nd International Pop Festival, Atlanta, GA	COL
Message To Love	04 Jul 70	BR 17. Live performance.	Atlanta CD JMH 009 / 02	2nd International Pop Festival, Atlanta, GA	COL
Message To Love	04 Jul 70	BR 17. Live performance.	Oh, Atlanta CD Tendolar TDR-009	2nd International Pop Festival, Atlanta, GA	COL
Message To Love	04 Jul 70	BR 17. Live performance.	Atlanta CD JMH 009 / 02	2nd International Pop Festival, Atlanta, GA	COL
Message To Love	17 Jul 70	BR 18. Live performance.	Can You Here Me LP Hemero 01 / KERI	New York Pop- Downing Stadium, Randalls Island, NY	COL
Message To Love	17 Jul 70	BR 18. Live performance.	Live At Randall's Island LP Moon Tree Records PH1962	New York Pop- Downing Stadium, Randalls Island, NY	COL
Message To Love	17 Jul 70	BR 18. Live performance.	Live USA CD Imtrat 902-001	New York Pop- Downing Stadium, Randalls Island, NY	COL

SONG TITLE	DATE	COMMENTS	RELEASE	LOCATION / VENUE	BAND	PERSONNEL
Message To Love	30 Jul 70	BR 19. Live performance.	Last American Concert Vol 1 CD 'The Swingin' Pig TSP-062	Rainbow Bridge Vibratory Sound-Color Experiment, Maui, HI 1st Show	COL	
Message To Love	30 Jul 70	BR 19. Live performance.	In From The Storm CD Silver Rarities SIRA 109 / 110	Rainbow Bridge Vibratory Sound-Color Experiment, Maui, HI 1st Show	COL	
Message To Love	30 Jul 70	BR 19. Live performance.	Rainbow Bridge 2 CD JMH 003 / 2	Rainbow Bridge Vibratory Sound-Color Experiment, Maui, HI 1st Show	COL	
Message To Love	30 Aug 70	CR 3.	Island Man CD Silver Rarities SIRA 39 / 40	Isle Of Wight Festival, Isle Of Wight, England	COL	
Message To Love	30 Aug 70	CR 3.	At The Isle Of Wight (CR) Laserdisc CBS / Sony CLSM 791	Isle Of Wight Festival, Isle Of Wight, England	COL	
Message To Love (Power To Love)	30 Aug 70	CR 3.	Isle Of Wight / Atlanta Pop Festival (CR) LP Columbia G3X 3085	Isle Of Wight Festival, Isle Of Wight, England	GSRB	
Message To Love	30 Aug 70	CR 3.	Live - Isle Of Wight '70 (CR) CD Polydor 847236-2	Isle Of Wight Festival, Isle Of Wight, England	COL	
Message To Love	30 Aug 70	CR 3.	Wight CD JMH 006 / 2	Isle Of Wight Festival, Isle Of Wight, England	COL	
Message To Love	31 Aug 70	BR 20. Live performance.	Come On Stockholm CD No Label	Stora Scenen, Liesberg, Stockholm, Sweden	COL	
Message To Love	31 Aug 70	BR 20. Live performance.	Free Concert CD Midnight Beat MBCD 013	Stora Scenen, Tivoli Garden, Stockholm, Sweden	COL	
Message To Love	01 Sep 70	BR 21. Live performance.	Warm Hello Of The Sun, The CD	Stora Scenen, Liseberg Nojespark, Goteborg, Sweden	COL	
Message To Love	02 Sep 70	BR 22. Live performance.	Welcome To The Electric Circus Vol 2 CD Midnight Beat 018	Vejlby Risskov Hallen, Arhus, Denmark	COL	
Message To Love	02 Sep 70	BR 22. Live performance.	Live At The Forum 1970 CD Whoopy Cat WKP	Vejlby Risskov Hallen, Arhus,	COL	

Song	Date	Notes	021 / 22	Denmark	Source	
Message To Love	03 Sep 70	BR 23. Live performance.	Copenhagen 70 CD Whoopy Cat WKP 044 / 45	K.B. Hallen, Copenhagen, Denmark	COL	
Message To Love	04 Sep 70	BR 24. Live performance.	Back To Berlin CD Midnight Beat 049	Deutsche- Landhalle, Berlin, Germany	COL	
Message To Love	06 Sep 70	BR 25. Live performance.	Love & Peace CD Midnight Beat MBCD 015	Love And Peace Festival, Isle Of Fehrman, Germany	COL	
Message To Love	06 Sep 70	BR 25. Live performance.	Wink Of An Eye CD Whoopy Cat WKP 0033 / 34	Love And Peace Festival, Isle Of Fehrman, Germany	COL	
Messenger	?? Oct 68	An instrumental track of an unreleased song. Unknown if this is really the song "Messenger".	Ball And Chain CD Jimi 009	T.T.G. Studios?, Hollywood, CA	JHE	Lee Michaels / Piano?
Midnight	01 Apr 69	CR 2 mix 1.	Voodoo Soup (CR) CD MCA 11206	Olmstead Studios, London, England	JHE	
Midnight (Trashman)	01 Apr 69	CR 2 mix 2.	War Heroes (CR) CD Polydor 847-2622	Olmstead Studios, London, England	JHE	
Midnight	01 Apr 69	CR 2 mix 2.	Jewel Box CD Home HR-5824-3	Olmstead Studios, London, England	JHE	
Midnight	01 Apr 69	CR 2 mix 2.	South Saturn Delta (CR) CD MCACD 11684	Olympic Sound Studios, London, England	JHE	
Midnight (Trashman)	04 Apr 69	04 Apr 69	Midnight Lightning (CR) LP Reprise MS 2229	Olmstead Studios, London, England	Jimi	Midnight Lightning Line Up 1975
Midnight	01 Apr 69	This is performed by a group called "Rainbow Bridge".	Electric Hendrix Vol 1 CD Pyramid PYCD 030	Olmstead Studios, London, England	Fake	
Midnight	01 Apr 69	This is performed by a group called "Rainbow Bridge".	Master's Masters, The CD JH-01	Olmstead Studios, London, England	Fake	
Midnight	01 Apr 69	This is performed by a group called "Rainbow Bridge".	Every Way To Paradise CD Tintangel TIBX 021 / 22 / 23 / 24	Olmstead Studios, London, England	Fake	
Midnight Lightning	14 Feb 69	BR 1. A very early run through by Jimi in the studio. Repeated twice on this release!	Ladyland In Flames LP Marshall Records JIMI 1,2,3,4	Olympic Sound Studios, London, England	Solo	
Midnight Lightning	14 Feb 69	BR 1. A very early run through by Jimi in the studio. Repeated twice on this release!	Ladyland In Flames LP Marshall Records JIMI 1,2,3,4	Olympic Sound Studios, London, England	Solo	

SONG TITLE	DATE	COMMENTS	RELEASE	LOCATION / VENUE	BAND	PERSONNEL
Midnight Lightning	14 Feb 69	BR 1. A very early run through by Jimi in the studio.	Things I Used To Do CD The Early Years 02-CD-3334	Olympic Sound Studios, London, England	Solo	
Midnight Lightning	14 Feb 69	BR 1. A very early run through by Jimi in the studio.	51st Anniversary CD Future Disc JMH 001 / 8	Olympic Sound Studios, London, England	Solo	
Midnight Lightning	14 Feb 69	BR 1. A very early run through by Jimi in the studio.	Freak Out Blues CD GH 001	Olympic Sound Studios, London, England	Solo	
Midnight Lightning	14 Feb 69	BR 1. A very early run through by Jimi in the studio.	Flames CD Missing In Action ACT 1	Olympic Sound Studios, London, England	Solo	
Midnight Lightning	17 Apr 69	BR 2. A long jam that touches on enough of the elements of "Midnight Lightning" to justify inclusion here. The original tape box called this 'Jam with Harmonica-Chorus Left / Chorus Right'.	Message From Nine To The Universe CD Oil Well 122	Record Plant, New York, NY	Jimi	Paul Caruso / Harmonica, Devon Wilson / Vocals
Midnight Lightning (Keep On Groovin')	17 Apr 69	BR 2. A long jam that touches on enough of the elements of "Midnight Lightning" to justify inclusion here. The original tape box called this 'Jam with Harmonica-Chorus Left / Chorus Right'.	In From The Storm CD Silver Rarities SIRA 109 / 110	In From The Storm CD Silver Rarities SIRA 109 / 110	GSRB	
Midnight Lightning (Keep On Groovin')	17 Apr 69	BR 2. A long jam that touches on enough of the elements of "Midnight Lightning" to justify inclusion here. The original tape box called this 'Jam with Harmonica-Chorus Left / Chorus Right'.	In From The Storm CD Silver Rarities SIRA 109 / 110	Record Plant, New York, NY	Jimi	Paul Caruso / Harmonica, Devon Wilson / Vocals
Midnight Lightning (Keep On Groovin')	17 Apr 69	BR 2. A long jam that touches on enough of the elements of "Midnight Lightning" to justify inclusion here. The original tape box called this 'Jam with Harmonica-Chorus Left / Chorus Right'.	I Don't Live Today CD ACL 007	Record Plant, New York, NY	Jimi	Paul Caruso / Harmonica, Devon Wilson / Vocals
Midnight Lightning (Keep On Movin')	17 Apr 69	BR 2. A long jam that touches on enough of the elements of "Midnight Lightning" to justify inclusion here. The original tape box called this 'Jam with Harmonica-Chorus Left / Chorus Right'.	Two Days At Newport CD JMH 007 / 2	Record Plant, New York, NY	JHE	Paul Caruso / Harmonica, Devon Wilson / Vocals
Midnight Lightning (Keep On Movin')	17 Apr 69	BR 2. A long jam that touches on enough of the elements of "Midnight Lightning" to justify inclusion here. The original tape box called this 'Jam with Harmonica-Chorus Left / Chorus Right'. Incomplete.	Band Of Gypsys Vol 3	Record Plant, New York, NY	Jimi	Paul Caruso / Harmonica, Devon Wilson / Vocals
Midnight Lightning (Lower Alcatraz)	14 May 69	BR 3. A studio run through where Jimi Makes a reference to the working title of "Lower Alcatraz" as "L.A. without the words or the bullshit".	51st Anniversary CD Future Disc JMH 001 / 8	Record Plant, New York, NY	COL	
Midnight Lightning (Lower Alcatraz)	14 May 69	BR 3. A studio run through where Jimi Makes a reference to the working title of "Lower Alcatraz" as "L.A. without the words or the bullshit".	First Rays Of The New Rising Sun CD Triangle PYCD 084-2	Record Plant, New York, NY	COL	

Title	Date	Notes	Release	Location	Label	Musicians
Midnight Lightning (Alcatraz)	14 May 69	BR 3. A studio run through where Jimi Makes a reference to the working title of "Lower Alcatraz" as "L.A. without the words or the bullshit!".	Mixdown Master Tapes Volume 3 CD Dandelion DL 007	Record Plant, New York, NY	COL	
Midnight Lightning (LA Without The Words)	14 May 69	BR 3. A studio run through where Jimi Makes a reference to the working title of "Lower Alcatraz" as "L.A. without the words or the bullshit!".	Talent And Feeling Vol 1 CD Extremely Rare EXR 17	Record Plant, New York, NY	COL	
Midnight Lightning (Lower Alcatraz)	14 May 69	BR 3. A studio run through where Jimi Makes a reference to the working title of "Lower Alcatraz" as "L.A. without the words or the bullshit!".	Completer, The CD Whoopy Cat WKP 0018 / 19	Record Plant, New York, NY	COL	
Midnight Lightning	14 May 69	BR 3. A studio run through where Jimi Makes a reference to the working title of "Lower Alcatraz" as "L.A. without the words or the bullshit!".	I Don't Live Today CD ACL 007	Record Plant, New York, NY	COL	
Midnight Lightning (Alcatraz)	14 May 69	BR 3. A studio run through where Jimi Makes a reference to the working title of "Lower Alcatraz" as "L.A. without the words or the bullshit!".	Jimi: A Musical Legacy CD KTS BX 010	Record Plant, New York, NY	COL	
Midnight Lightning	14 Jul 70	CR 1 mix 1.	Midnight Lightning (CR) LP Reprise MS 2229	Electric Lady Studio, New York, NY	Jimi	Midnight Lightning Line Up 1975
Midnight Lightning	14 Jul 70	CR 1 mix 2. This is the original version of CR 1 with the original musicians intact.	Sir James Marshall LP Jester Productions JP 106	Electric Lady Studio, New York, NY	COL	Juma Sultan / Percussion
Midnight Lightning	14 Jul 70	CR 1 mix 2. This is the original version of CR 1 with the original musicians intact.	This One's For You LP Veteran Music MF-243	Electric Lady Studio, New York, NY	COL	Juma Sultan / Percussion
Midnight Lightning	14 Jul 70	CR 1 mix 2. This is the original version of CR 1 with the original musicians intact.	Things I Used To Do CD The Early Years 02-CD-3334	Electric Lady Studio, New York, NY	COL	Juma Sultan / Percussion
Midnight Lightning	14 Jul 70	CR 1 mix 2. This is the original version of CR 1 with the original musicians intact.	51st Anniversary CD Future Disc JMH 001 / 8	Electric Lady Studio, New York, NY	COL	Juma Sultan / Percussion
Midnight Lightning	14 Jul 70	CR 1 mix 2. This is the original version of CR 1 with the original musicians intact.	Freak Out Jam CD GH 002	Electric Lady Studio, New York, NY	COL	Juma Sultan / Percussion
Midnight Lightning	14 Jul 70	CR 1 mix 2. This is the original version of CR 1 with the original musicians intact.	First Rays Of The New Rising Sun CD Triangle PYCD 084-2	Electric Lady Studio, New York, NY	COL	Juma Sultan / Percussion
Midnight Lightning	14 Jul 70	CR 1 mix 2. This is the original version of CR 1 with the original musicians intact.	Gypsy Suns, Moons And Rainbows CD Sidewalk JHX 8868	Electric Lady Studio, New York, NY	COL	Juma Sultan / Percussion
Midnight Lightning	14 Jul 70	CR 1 mix 2. This is the original version of CR 1 with the original musicians intact.	Midnight Shines Down CD Blue Kangaroo BK 04	Electric Lady Studio, New York, NY	COL	Juma Sultan / Percussion
Midnight Lightning (Midnight)	14 Jul 70	BR 4. This is a version that opens a session for "Bolero" (track 10 on the disc). See that entry.	Black Gold CD Midnight Beat MBCD 058-062	Electric Lady Studio, New York, NY	COL	Juma Sultan / Percussion

SONG TITLE	DATE	COMMENTS	RELEASE	LOCATION / VENUE	BAND	PERSONNEL
Midnight Lightning	30 May 70	BR5. Live performance. There is enough of the song performed here to justify this listing.	Berkeley Soundchecks, The CD Whoopy Cat WKP 0008	Berkeley Community Theater, Berkeley, CA	COL	
Midnight Lightning	30 Aug 70	CR 2. Live performance. This is the only real stand alone version of "Midnight Lightning" recorded live, however the theme was often incorporated into other songs for a brief couple of lines.	Island Man CD Silver Rarities SIRA 39 / 40	Isle Of Wight Festival, Isle Of Wight, England	COL	
Midnight Lightning	30 Aug 70	CR 2. Live performance. This is the only real stand alone version of "Midnight Lightning" recorded live, however the theme was often incorporated into other songs for a brief couple of lines.	Isle Of Wight (CR) LP Polydor 2302-016	Isle Of Wight Festival, Isle Of Wight, England	COL	
Midnight Lightning	30 Aug 70	CR 2. Live performance. This is the only real stand alone version of "Midnight Lightning" recorded live, however the theme was often incorporated into other songs for a brief couple of lines.	Wight CD JMH 006 / 2	Isle Of Wight Festival, Isle Of Wight, England	COL	
Midnight Lightning	30 Aug 70	CR 2. Live performance. This is the only stand alone version of "Midnight Lightning" recorded live however, the theme was often incorporated into other songs for a brief couple of lines. This is an edit of the complete recording.	Isle Of Wight / Atlanta Pop Festival (CR) LP Columbia G3X 3085	Isle Of Wight Festival, Isle Of Wight, England	COL	
Midnight Lightning	23 Mar 70	CR #3.	South Saturn Delta (CR) CD MCACD 11684	Record Plant, New York, NY	Solo	
Midnight Sun		This is a recording by the group "Love" for the unreleased 'Black Beauty' album. Jimi's involvement is highly unlikely.	Electric Gypsy CD Scorpio? 40176 / 15		Love	
Midnight Sun		This is a recording by the group "Love" for the unreleased 'Black Beauty' album. Jimi's involvement is highly unlikely.	Midnight Sun CD Third Eye NK 007	Olympic Sound Studios, London, England	Love	
Mockingbird	05 Jun 68	BR 1. A one off TV performance from the "It Must Be Dusty" show.	Screaming Eagle CD Pink Poodle POO 001	It Must Be Dusty T V Show, Elstree Studios, Borehamwood, UK	JHE	Dusty Springfield
Moon Turn The Tides...Gently Gently Away	22 Apr 68	CR See "1983...A Merman I Should Turn To Be".	Electric Ladyland (CR) CD MCACD-11600	Record Plant, New York, NY	Jimi	Jimi Hendrix / Percussion, Jimi Hendrix / Bass, Mitch Mitchell / Drums, Chris Wood / Flute
Moon Turn The Tides...Gently Gently Away	?? Apr 68	From Jimi's solo composing tape. Mono. Included with most all of the releases with the "1983...A Merman I Should Turn To Be" tape. Refer to those releases.	Black Gold CD Midnight Beat MBCD 058-062	New York Apartment	Jimi	Jimi Hendrix / Percussion, Jimi Hendrix / Bass, Mitch Mitchell / Drums, Chris Wood / Flute
Moonlight Jam		No Jimi involvement on this recording.	51st Anniversary CD Future Disc JMH 001/8		Fake	

Title	Date	Notes	Release	Location	Artist	Personnel
Morrison's Lament	?? Mar 68	CR 1. Live performance medley including 'Tomorrow Never Knows', 'Uranus Rock' (aka F.H.I.T.A.), 'Outside Woman Blues' and 'Sunshine Of Your Love'.	Woke Up This Morning And Found Myself Dead CR (CD) RLCD 0068	Scene Club, New York, NY	Scene	
Morrison's Lament (No! No!)	?? Mar 68	CR 1. Live performance medley including 'Tomorrow Never Knows', 'Uranus Rock' (aka F.H.I.T.A.), 'Outside Woman Blues' and 'Sunshine Of Your Love'.	High Live And Dirty (CR) LP Nutmeg NUT 1001	Scene Club, New York, NY	Scene	
Morrison's Lament	?? Mar 68	CR 1. Live performance medley including 'Tomorrow Never Knows', 'Uranus Rock' (aka F.H.I.T.A.), 'Outside Woman Blues' and 'Sunshine Of Your Love'.	In Concert CD Starlife ST 3612	Scene Club, New York, NY	Scene	
Morrison's Lament	?? Mar 68	CR 1. Live performance medley including 'Tomorrow Never Knows', 'Uranus Rock' (aka F.H.I.T.A.), 'Outside Woman Blues' and 'Sunshine Of Your Love'.	Jimi: A Musical Legacy CD KTS BX 010	Scene Club, New York, NY	Scene	
Morrison's Lament (F.H.I.T.A.)	?? Mar 68	CR 1. Live performance medley including 'Tomorrow Never Knows', 'Uranus Rock' (aka F.H.I.T.A.), 'Outside Woman Blues' and 'Sunshine Of Your Love'.	High Live And Dirty (CR) LP Nutmeg NUT 1001	Scene Club, New York, NY	Scene	
Mother Earth	17 Sep 70	BR 1. Live performance. An audience tape of Jimi's last performance before his death.	Can You Please Crawl Out Your Window? LP Ruthless Rhymes Jimi1	Ronnie Scotts Club, London, England	Jimi	Eric Burden & War
My Diary	?? Mar 64	CR 1. Copied from the extremely rare original 45.	51st Anniversary CD Future Disc JMH 001 / 8	Unknown	Jimi	Rosa Lee Brooks / Vocals, Arthur Lee / Backing Vocals, Big Francis / Drums, Alvin ? / Bass
My Diary	?? Mar 64	CR 1. Copied from the extremely rare original 45.	Rarities CD The Genuine Pig TGP-CD-091	Unknown	Jimi	Rosa Lee Brooks / Vocals, Arthur Lee / Backing Vocals, Big Francis / Drums, Alvin ? / Bass
My Diary	?? Mar 64	CR 1. Copied from the extremely rare original 45.	Rarities On Compact Disc CD On The Radio	Unknown	Jimi	Rosa Lee Brooks / Vocals, Arthur Lee / Backing Vocals, Big Francis / Drums, Alvin ? / Bass
My Diary	?? Mar 64	CR 1. Copied from the extremely rare original 45.	Jimi: A Musical Legacy CD KTS BX 010	Unknown	Jimi	Rosa Lee Brooks / Vocals, Arthur Lee / Backing Vocals, Big Francis / Drums, Alvin ? / Bass
My Friend	18 Mar 68	CR 1 mix 1.	First Rays Of The New Rising Sun (CR) CD MCACD 11599	Sound Center, New York, NY	Jimi	Stephen Stills / Piano, Paul Caruso / Harmonica, Ken Pine / 12 String Guitar, Jimmy Mayes / Drums

SONG TITLE	DATE	COMMENTS	RELEASE	LOCATION / VENUE	BAND	PERSONNEL
My Friend	18 Mar 68	CR 1 mix 1.	Cry Of Love, The (CR) CD Reprise 2034-2	Sound Center, New York, NY	Jimi	Stephen Stills / Piano, Paul Caruso / Harmonica, Ken Pine / 12 String Guitar, Jimmy Mayes / Drums
My Friend	18 Mar 68	CR 1 mix 2. Unused mix of the CR.	Multicolored Blues CD Luna LU 9317	Sound Center, New York, NY	Jimi	
My Friend	18 Mar 68	CR 1 mix 2. Unused mix of the CR.	Kiss The Skies CD Mum MUCD 024	Sound Center, New York, NY	Jimi	
My Friend	18 Mar 68	CR 1 mix 2. Unused mix of the CR.	Atlanta CD JMH 009 / 02	Sound Center, New York, NY	Jimi	
My Friend	18 Mar 68	CR 1 mix 2. Unused mix of the CR.	Living Reels Vol 2 CD JMH 012 / 2	Sound Center, New York, NY	Jimi	
My Friend (Calling All Devils Children)	18 Mar 68	CR 1 mix 2. Unused mix of the CR.	TTG Studios ???? CD WHOAMI WAI 015	Sound Center, New York, NY	Jimi	
New Rising Sun	23 Oct 68	CR 1. A portion of this was used in the composite CR "Captain Coconut" released on the "Crash Landing" L.P.	Voodoo Soup (CR) CD MCA 11206	Record Plant, New York, NY	Solo	
Night Bird Flying	16 Jun 70	CR 1 mix 1.	First Rays Of The New Rising Sun (CR) CD MCACD 11599	Electric Lady Studio, New York, NY	COL	Juma Sultan / Percussion
Night Bird Flying	16 Jun 70	CR 1 mix 1.	The Singles Album (CR) CD Polydor 827 369-2	Electric Lady Studio, New York, NY	COL	Juma Sultan / Percussion
Night Bird Flying	16 Jun 70	CR 1 mix 1.	Cry Of Love, The (CR) CD Reprise 2034-2	Electric Lady Studio, New York, NY	COL	Juma Sultan / Percussion
Night Bird Flying	16 Jun 70	CR 1 mix 2. An alternate mix of CR 1.	Lifelines (CR) CD Reprise 9 26435-2	Electric Lady Studio, New York, NY	COL	Juma Sultan / Percussion
Night Bird Flying	16 Jun 70	CR 1 mix 3. A second alternate mix of CR 1.	Voodoo Soup (CR) CD MCA 11206	Electric Lady Studio, New York, NY	COL	Juma Sultan / Percussion
Night Bird Flying (Drone Blues)	?? / ?? 69-70	BR 2. An unreleased instrumental version with a guitar over-dub.	Let's Drop Some Ludes And Vomit With Jimi CD Midnight Beat MBCD 026	Record Plant?	COL	Juma Sultan / Percussion
Night Bird Flying (Midnight Blues Jam)	?? / ?? 69-70	BR 2. An unreleased instrumental version with a guitar over-dub.	Atlanta CD JMH 009 / 02	Record Plant?	COL	Juma Sultan / Percussion
Night Bird Flying / Ships Passing In The Night (Night Messenger)	?? Apr 69	BR 1. A solo electric guitar composing demo highlighted by lyrics from "Ships Passing In The Night".	Multicolored Blues CD Luna LU 9317	Record Plant?	Solo	
Night Bird Flying / Ships Passing In The Night	?? / ?? 69-70	BR 1. A solo composing demo highlighted by lyrics from "Ships Passing In The Night". Incomplete.	Talent And Feeling Vol 1 CD Extremely Rare EXR 17	Record Plant?	Solo	

Song	Date	Notes	Source	Location	Group	Extra
Night Bird Flying / Ships Passing In The Night	?? / ?? 69-70	BR 1. A solo composing demo highlighted by lyrics from "Ships Passing In The Night". Incomplete.	Completer, The CD Whoopy Cat WKP 0018 / 19		Solo	
Night Bird Flying / Ships Passing In The Night (Ships Passing In The Night)	?? / ?? 69-70	BR 1. A solo composing demo highlighted by lyrics from "Ships Passing In The Night".	First Rays Of The New Rising Sun CD Triangle PYCD 084-2		Solo	Midnight Lightning Line Up 1975
Once I Had A Woman	23 Jan 70	CR 1 mix 1. Recorded as a jam, this version has had all of the original musicians except Jimi replaced.	Midnight Lightning (CR) LP Reprise MS 2229	Record Plant, New York, NY	BOG	Don ? / Harmonica
Once I Had A Woman	23 Jan 70	CR 1 mix 2. This version still has the original line up and is the longest running of all versions.	Jimi Hendrix: Blues (CR) CD MCA MCAD-11060	Record Plant, New York, NY	BOG	Don ? / Harmonica
Once I Had A Woman	23 Jan 70	CR 1 mix 3. Unused mix that has a verse intact that was cut from the CR 1 mix 1 but overall runs shorter.	Drone Blues CD Great Dane GDR SAT 2	Record Plant, New York, NY	BOG	Don ? / Harmonica
Once I Had A Woman	23 Jan 70	CR 1 mix 3. Unused mix that has a verse intact that was cut from the CR 1 mix 1 but overall runs shorter.	Shine On Earth, Shine On CD Sidewalk SW 89010 / 89011	Record Plant, New York, NY	BOG	Don ? / Harmonica
Once I Had A Woman	23 Jan 70	CR 1 mix 3. Unused mix that has a verse intact that was cut from the CR 1 mix 1 but overall runs shorter.	Sir James Marshall LP Jester Productions JP 106	Record Plant, New York, NY	BOG	Don ? / Harmonica
Once I Had A Woman	23 Jan 70	CR 1 mix 3. Unused mix that has a verse intact that was cut from the CR 1 mix 1 but overall runs shorter.	51st Anniversary CD Future Disc JMH 001 / 8	Record Plant, New York, NY	BOG	Don ? / Harmonica
Once I Had A Woman	23 Jan 70	CR 1 mix 3. Unused mix that has a verse intact that was cut from the CR 1 mix 1 but overall runs shorter.	Freak Out Blues CD GH 001	Record Plant, New York, NY	BOG	Don ? / Harmonica
Once I Had A Woman	23 Jan 70	CR 1 mix 3. Unused mix that has a verse intact that was cut from the CR 1 mix 1 but overall runs shorter.	Eyes And Imagination CD Third Stone TSD 18970	Record Plant, New York, NY	BOG	Don ? / Harmonica
Once I Had A Woman	23 Jan 70	CR 1 mix 3. Unused mix that has a verse intact that was cut from the CR 1 mix 1 but overall runs shorter. Incomplete.	Electric Hendrix Vol 2 CD Pyramid PYCD 031	Record Plant, New York, NY	BOG	Don ? / Harmonica
One Rainy Wish	03 Oct 67	CR 1 mix 1 (stereo).	Axis: Bold As Love (CR) CD MCACD 11601	Olympic Sound Studios, London, England	JHE	
One Rainy Wish	03 Oct 67	CR 1 mix 2 (mono).	Axis: Bold As Love LP (CR) Track 612-003	Olympic Sound Studios, London, England	JHE	
One Rainy Wish	03 Oct 67	CR 1 mix 3. An alternate stereo mix.	Axis: Bold As Love LP (CR) Backtrack 2407-011	Olympic Sound Studios, London, England	JHE	
One Rainy Wish	03 Oct 67	CR 1 mix 4. Another alternate stereo mix that plays slightly longer and has some different overdubs.	First Rays Of The New Rising Sun CD Living Legend LLRCD 023	Olympic Sound Studios, London, England	JHE	

SONG TITLE	DATE	COMMENTS	RELEASE	LOCATION / VENUE	BAND	PERSONNEL
One Rainy Wish	03 Oct 67	CR 1 mix 4. Another alternate stereo mix that plays slightly longer and has some different overdubs.	Lifelines (CR) CD Reprise 9 26435-2	Olympic Sound Studios, London, England	JHE	
One Rainy Wish	03 Oct 67	CR 1 mix 4. Another alternate stereo mix that plays slightly longer and has some different overdubs.	Voice Of Experience CD Rhinozerous RHP 789	Olympic Sound Studios, London, England	JHE	
One Rainy Wish	03 Oct 67	CR 1 mix 4. Another alternate stereo mix that plays slightly longer and has some different overdubs.	Voodoo Blues CD Smurf	Olympic Sound Studios, London, England	JHE	
One Rainy Wish	03 Oct 67	CR 1 mix 4. Another alternate stereo mix that plays slightly longer and has some different overdubs. Incomplete.	Black Strings CD CDM G-53 258	Olympic Sound Studios, London, England	JHE	
One Rainy Wish	03 Oct 67	CR 1 mix 5. An unused mix of the CR 1.	Sotheby Auction Tapes, The CD Midnight Beat MBCD 010	Olympic Sound Studios, London, England	JHE	
One Rainy Wish	03 Oct 67	CR 1 mix 5. An unused mix of the CR 1.	Sotheby's Private Reels CD JHR 003 / 004	Olympic Sound Studios, London, England	JHE	
One Rainy Wish	03 Oct 67	CR 1 mix 5. An unused mix of the CR 1.	Sotheby's Private Reels CD JHR 003 / 004	Olympic Sound Studios, London, England	JHE	
One Rainy Wish	03 Oct 67	CR 1 mix 5. An unused mix of the CR 1.	Get The Experience CD Invasion Unlimited IU 9424-1	Olympic Sound Studios, London, England	JHE	
One Rainy Wish	03 Oct 67	CR 1 mix 5. An unused mix of the CR 1.	Notes In Colours CD JHR 001 / 002	Olympic Sound Studios, London, England	Jimi	
One Rainy Wish	03 Oct 67	CR 1 mix 5. An unused mix of the CR 1.	I Don't Live Today CD ACL 007	Olympic Sound Studios, London, England	JHE	
One Rainy Wish	03 Oct 67	CR 1 mix 5. An unused mix of the CR 1.	Sotheby's Reels, The CD Gold Standard TOM-800	Olympic Sound Studios, London, England	JHE	
One Rainy Wish	03 Oct 67	CR 1 mix 5. An unused mix of the CR 1.	Living Reels Vol 1 CD JMH 011	Olympic Sound Studios, London, England	JHE	
Only You		This is a recording by the group "Love" for the unreleased 'Black Beauty' album. Jimi's involvement is highly unlikely.	Midnight Sun CD Third Eye NK 007	Olympic Sound Studios, London, England	Love	
Pali Gap	01 Jul 70	CR 1 mix 1. This was recorded at the same session for 'Dolly	Rainbow Bridge (CR)	Electric Lady Studio,	COL	Juma Sultan / Percussion

Title	Date	Notes	Release	Location	Band	Musicians
Pali Gap		Dagger' and though Jimi did some overdubs he had no plans for release. The title was made up by Mike Jeffrey, Jimi's manager when it was prepared for inclusion on the CR of 'Rainbow Bridge'.	LP Reprise K44159	New York, NY		Juma Sultan / Percussion
Pali Gap	01 Jul 70	CR 1 mix 1. This was recorded at the same session for 'Dolly Dagger' and though Jimi did some overdubs he had no plans for release. The title was made up by Mike Jeffrey, Jimi's manager when it was prepared for inclusion on the CR of 'Rainbow Bridge'.	Rainbow Bridge & More CD	Electric Lady Studio, New York, NY	COL	Juma Sultan / Percussion
Pali Gap	01 Jul 70	CR 1 mix 1. This was recorded at the same session for 'Dolly Dagger' and though Jimi did some overdubs he had no plans for release. The title was made up by Mike Jeffrey, Jimi's manager when it was prepared for inclusion on the CR of 'Rainbow Bridge'.	Jewel Box CD Home HR-5824-3	Electric Lady Studio, New York, NY	COL	Juma Sultan / Percussion
Pali Gap	01 Jul 70	CR 1 mix 1. This was recorded at the same session for 'Dolly Dagger' and though Jimi did some overdubs he had no plans for release. The title was made up by Mike Jeffrey, Jimi's manager when it was prepared for inclusion on the CR of 'Rainbow Bridge'.	South Saturn Delta (CR) CD MCACD 11684	Electric Lady Studio, New York, NY	COL	Juma Sultan / Percussion
Pali Gap	01 Jul 70	CR 1 mix 1. This was recorded at the same session for 'Dolly Dagger' and though Jimi did some overdubs he had no plans for release. The title was made up by Mike Jeffrey, Jimi's manager when it was prepared for inclusion on the CR of 'Rainbow Bridge'.	Rainbow Bridge (CR) LP Reprise K44159	Electric Lady Studio, New York, NY	COL	Juma Sultan / Percussion
Pali Gap	01 Jul 70	CR 1 mix 2. The title 'Pali Gap' was coined by Mike Jeffrey, Jimi's manager.	Voodoo Soup (CR) CD MCA 11206	Electric Lady Studio, New York, NY	COL	Juma Sultan / Percussion
Peace In Mississippi	24 Oct 68	CR 1 mix 1.This has had all the original musicians replaced.	Crash Landing (CR) LP Reprise MS 2204	T.T.G. Studios, Hollywood, CA	Jimi	Crash Landing Line Up 1974
Peace In Mississippi	24 Oct 68	CR 1 mix2. This has the original studio line up intact but is edited.	Voodoo Soup (CR) CD MCA 11206	T.T.G. Studios, Hollywood, CA	JHE	
Peace In Mississippi	24 Oct 68	CR 1 mix 3. The unedited recording used for all subsequent mixes.	Electric Hendrix Vol 1 CD Pyramid PYCD 030	T.T.G. Studios, Hollywood, CA	JHE	
Peace In Mississippi	24 Oct 68	CR 1 mix 3. The unedited recording used for all subsequent mixes.	Sir James Marshall LP Jester Productions JP 106	T.T.G. Studios, Hollywood, CA	JHE	
Peace In Mississippi	24 Oct 68	CR 1 mix 3. The unedited recording used for all subsequent mixes.	This One's For You LP Veteran Music MF-243	T.T.G. Studios, Hollywood, CA	JHE	
Peace In Mississippi	24 Oct 68	CR 1 mix 3. The unedited recording used for all subsequent mixes.	Redskin' Jammin' CD JH 01 / 02	T.T.G. Studios, Hollywood, CA	JHE	
Peace In Mississippi	24 Oct 68	CR 1 mix 3. The unedited recording used for all subsequent mixes.	Talent And Feeling Vol 1 CD Extremely Rare EXR 17	T.T.G. Studios, Hollywood, CA	JHE	

SONG TITLE	DATE	COMMENTS	RELEASE	LOCATION / VENUE	BAND	PERSONNEL
Peace In Mississippi	24 Oct 68	CR 1 mix 3. The unedited recording used for all subsequent mixes.	Talent And Feeling Vol 1 CD Extremely Rare EXR 17	T.T.G. Studios, Hollywood, CA	JHE	
Peace In Mississippi	24 Oct 68	CR 1 mix 3. The unedited recording used for all subsequent mixes.	Completer, The CD Whoopy Cat WKP 0018 / 19	T.T.G. Studios, Hollywood, CA	JHE	
Peace In Mississippi	24 Oct 68	CR 1 mix 3. The unedited recording used for all subsequent mixes.	Paper Airplanes CD Midnight Beat MBCD 25	T.T.G. Studios, Hollywood, CA	JHE	
Peace In Mississippi	24 Oct 68	CR 1 mix 3. The unedited recording used for all subsequent mixes. Incomplete.	Redskin' Jammin' CD JH 01 / 02	T.T.G. Studios, Hollywood, CA	JHE	
Peace In Mississippi	24 Oct 68	CR 1 mix 3. The unedited recording used for all subsequent mixes. Incomplete.	Living Reels Vol 2 CD JMH 012 / 2	T.T.G. Studios, Hollywood, CA	JHE	
Peace In Mississippi	24 Oct 68	CR 1 mix 4. Unused mix of CR 1 mix 3 featuring only drums, lead guitar, and bass.	Shine On Earth, Shine On CD Sidewalk SW 89010 / 89011	T.T.G. Studios, Hollywood, CA	Jimi	Crash Landing Line Up 1974
Peace In Mississippi	24 Oct 68	CR 1 mix 4. Unused mix of CR 1 mix 3 featuring only drums, lead guitar, and bass.	Paper Airplanes CD Midnight Beat MBCD 25	T.T.G. Studios, Hollywood, CA	Jimi	Crash Landing Line Up 1974
Peace In Mississippi	24 Oct 68	CR 1 mix 5. Unused mix of CR 1 mix 1 with guitar and bass only.	Paper Airplanes CD Midnight Beat MBCD 25	T.T.G. Studios, Hollywood, CA	Jimi	Crash Landing Line Up 1974
Peace In Mississippi	24 Oct 68	CR 1 mix 6. Unused mix of the CR 1 mix 3 with Jeff Mirnonov's rhythm guitar part mixed up front.	Electric Hendrix Vol 2 CD Pyramid PYCD 031	T.T.G. Studios, Hollywood, CA	Jimi	Crash Landing Line Up 1974
Peace In Mississippi	24 Oct 68	CR 1 mix 6. Unused mix of the CR 1 mix 3 with Jeff Mirnonov's rhythm guitar part mixed up front.	Living Reels Vol 2 CD JMH 012 / 2	T.T.G. Studios, Hollywood, CA	Jimi	Crash Landing Line Up 1974
Peace In Mississippi	24 Oct 68	CR 1 mix 7. Unused mix of the CR mix 3 with reverb added.	Ladyland In Flames LP Marshall Records JIMI 1,2,3,4	T.T.G. Studios, Hollywood, CA	Jimi	Crash Landing Line Up 1974
Peace In Mississippi	24 Oct 68	CR 1 mix 7. Unused mix of the CR mix 3 with reverb added.	51st Anniversary CD Future Disc JMH 001 / 8	T.T.G. Studios, Hollywood, CA	Jimi	Crash Landing Line Up 1974
Peace In Mississippi	24 Oct 68	CR 1 mix 7. Unused mix of the CR mix 3 with reverb added.	Flames CD Missing In Action ACT 1	T.T.G. Studios, Hollywood, CA	Jimi	Crash Landing Line Up 1974
Peter Gunn Catastrophe	15 May 70	CR 1.	War Heroes (CR) CD Polydor 847-2622	Record Plant, New York, NY	COL	
Piano Roll 1,2,3 (Jimi Jams With Piano)	?? Oct 68	BR 1. Three jams with an unknown pianist (possibly Lee Michaels) at an unknown studio (possibly T.T.G.) on an unknown date (possibly October of 1968).	Ball And Chain CD Jimi 009	T.T.G. Studios?, Hollywood, CA	JHE	Lee Michaels? / Piano
Playing Over James Brown	?? / ?? ??	A guitar player (that may or may not be Jimi) playing to a recording (that may or may not be James Brown). I guess this goes into the "maybe" column.	Living Reels Vol 1 CD JMH 011	New York Apartment	Jimi?	

Song	Date	Notes	Release	Location		Musicians
Power Of Soul	22 Jun 69	BR 1. Live performance. Part of a medley that's track 3 on the CD.	It Never Takes An End CD Genuine Pig TGP-118	Newport Pop Festival, San Fernando State, Northridge, CA	NJK	
Power Of Soul	24 Sep 69	BR 2-4. Three short instrumental jams that represent the first studio attempts at "Power Of Soul".	Copenhagen '70 CD Whoopy Cat WKP 044 / 45	Record Plant, New York, NY	Jimi	Buddy Miles / Drums
Power Of Soul (Paper Airplanes)	21 Nov 69	BR 5. This session is the second in the studio incarnation of 'Power Of Soul'. This is a long segment with numerous break-downs and false starts with a couple of longer run throughs.	Earth Tones CD Whoopy Cat WKP 041	Record Plant, New York, NY	Jimi	Buddy Miles / Drums
Power Of Soul (Paper Airplanes)	21 Nov 69	BR 5. This session is the second in the studio incarnation of 'Power Of Soul'. This is a long segment with numerous break-downs and false starts with a couple of longer run throughs.	Black Gold CD Midnight Beat MBCD 058-062	Record Plant, New York, NY	Jimi	Buddy Miles / Drums
Power Of Soul	?? Dec 69	BR 6. This is missing the false start and has just the full take from the rehearsals at Baggies for the Fillmore shows.	Band Of Gypsys Vol 3	Baggies, New York, NY	BOG	
Power Of Soul	?? Dec 69	BR 6. This is missing the false start anc has just the full take from the rehearsals at Baggies for the Fillmore shows.	Band Of Gypsys Rehearsals CD Whoopy Cat WKP 003	Baggies, New York, NY	BOG	
Power Of Soul	?? Dec 69	BR 6. A false start and full take from the rehearsals at Baggies for the Fillmore shows.	Gypsy Haze CD Lords Of Archive LAR 16	Baggies, New York, NY	BOG	
Power Of Soul	?? Dec 69	BR 6. A false start and full take from the rehearsals at Baggies for the Fillmore shows.	Band Of Gypsys- The Ultimate CD JMH 010 / 3	Baggies, New York, NY	BOG	
Power Of Soul	31 Dec 69	BR 7. Live performance.	Band Of Gypsys Vol 3	Fillmore East, New York, NY 1st Show	BOG	
Power Of Soul	31 Dec 69	BR 7. Live performance.	Band Of Gypsys Happy New Year, Jimi LP Cops & Robbers JTYM 01	Fillmore East, New York, NY 1st Show	BOG	
Power Of Soul	31 Dec 69	BR 7. Live performance.	Gypsy Haze CD Lords Of Archive LAR 16	Fillmore East, New York, NY 1st Show	BOG	
Power Of Soul	31 Dec 69	BR 7. Live performance.	Fillmore Concerts, The CD Whoopy Cat WKP 0006 / 7	Fillmore East, New York, NY 1st Show	BOG	
Power Of Soul	31 Dec 69	BR 7. Live performance.	Band Of Gold CD-R Major Tom MT 087	Fillmore East, New York, NY 1st Show	BOG	
Power Of Soul	31 Dec 69	BR 7. Live performance.	Power Of Soul CD SQ-10	Fillmore East, New York, NY 1st Show	BOG	
Power Of Soul	31 Dec 69	BR 7. Live performance.	Ultimate Live Collection, The CD The Beat Goes On BGO BX 9307-4	Fillmore East, New York, NY 1st Show	BOG	

The Song Index

SONG TITLE	DATE	COMMENTS	RELEASE	LOCATION / VENUE	BAND	PERSONNEL
Power Of Soul	31 Dec 69	BR 8. Live performance.	Auld Lang Syne CD JH 100 03	Fillmore East, New York, NY 2nd Show	BOG	
Power Of Soul	31 Dec 69	BR 8. Live performance.	Band Of Gypsys: Happy New Year CD Silver Shadow CD 9103	Fillmore East, New York, NY 2nd Show	BOG	
Power Of Soul	31 Dec 69	BR 8. Live performance.	Fillmore Concerts, The CD Whoopy Cat WKP 0006 / 7	Fillmore East, New York, NY 2nd Show	BOG	
Power Of Soul	31 Dec 69	BR 8. Live performance.	Band Of Gold CD-R Major Tom MT 087	Fillmore East, New York, NY 2nd Show	BOG	
Power Of Soul	31 Dec 69	BR 8. Live performance.	Band Of Gypsys- The Ultimate CD JMH 010 / 3	Fillmore East, New York, NY 2nd Show	BOG	
Power Of Soul	01 Jan 70	BR 9. Live performance.	Band Of Gold CD-R Major Tom MT 087	Fillmore East, New York, NY 1st Show	BOG	
Power Of Soul	01 Jan 70	BR 9. Live performance.	Band Of Gypsys- The Ultimate CD JMH 010 / 3	Fillmore East, New York, NY 2nd Show	BOG	
Power Of Soul (Power To Love)	01 Jan 70	CR 1. Live performance.	Band Of Gypsys (CR) CD Capitol 72434-93446-2-4	Fillmore East, New York, NY 2nd Show	BOG	
Power Of Soul	01 Jan 70	CR 1. Live performance.	Legacy (CR) LP Polydor	Fillmore East, New York, NY 2nd Show	BOG	
Power Of Soul	01 Jan 70	CR 1. Live performance.	Band Of Gold CD-R Major Tom MT 087	Fillmore East, New York, NY 2nd Show	BOG	
Power Of Soul Money)	?? / ?? 70	BR 10. A jam from Jimi's apartment with an unknown guitarist from early in 1970, possibly before the January 16 session.	Acoustic Jams CD Sphinx SX CD 001	New York Apartment	Jimi	Unknown Guitarist
Power Of Soul (Tajami Boogie)	?? / ?? / 70	BR 10. A jam from Jimi's apartment with an unknown guitarist from early in 1970, possibly before the January 16 session.	Two Sides Of The Same Genius LP Amazing Kornyphone TAKRL H677	New York Apartment	Jimi	Unknown Guitarist
Power Of Soul	16 Jan 70	BR 11. The third of the 'Power Of Soul' development sessions. There is one complete take after several false starts and a breakdown. This is a longer segment than on 'Copenhagen '70' on Whoopy Cat.	Ball And Chain CD Jimi 009	Record Plant, New York, NY	BOG	
Power Of Soul	16 Jan 70	BR 11. The third of the 'Power Of Soul' development sessions. There is one complete take after several false starts and a breakdown. This a less complete segment than on 'Ball And Chain' and fades out early	Copenhagen '70 CD Whoopy Cat WKP 044 / 45	Record Plant, New York, NY	BOG	

Song	Date	Notes	Release	Location	Band	Jimmy Maeulin / Percussion
Power Of Soul	21 Jan 70	CR 2 mix 1.	Crash Landing (CR) LP Reprise MS 2204	Record Plant, New York, NY	BOG	
Power Of Soul	21 Jan 70	CR 2 mix 2. This is the basic and unaltered recording that was used for the CR 1.	Electric Hendrix Vol 1 CD Pyramid PYCD 030	Record Plant, New York, NY	BOG	
Power Of Soul	21 Jan 70	CR 2 mix 2. This is the basic and unaltered recording that was used for the CR 1.	Talent And Feeling Vol 2 CD Extremely Rare EXR 22	Record Plant, New York, NY	BOG	
Power Of Soul	21 Jan 70	CR 2 mix 2. This is the basic and unaltered recording that was used for the CR 1.	Paper Airplanes CD Midnight Beat MBCD 25	Record Plant, New York, NY	BOG	
Power Of Soul	21 Jan 70	CR 2 mix 2. This is the basic and unaltered recording that was used for the CR 1.	First Rays - The Sessions CD Whoopy Cat WKP 0002	Record Plant, New York, NY	BOG	
Power Of Soul	21 Jan 70	CR 3. Almost the full unadulterated version used for CR #1.	South Saturn Delta (CR) CD MCACD 11684	Record Plant, New York, NY	BOG	Crash Landing Line Up 1974
Power Of Soul	30 May 70	BR 12. Live performance at the soundcheck. Not a full run through.	Berkeley Soundchecks, The CD Whoopy Cat WKP 0008	Berkeley Community Theater, Berkeley, CA	COL	
Power Of Soul	30 May 70	BR 12. Live performance at the soundcheck. Not a full run through.	Jimi Plays Berkeley CD JMH 005 / 2	Berkeley Community Theater, Berkeley, CA Sound Check	COL	
Purple Haze	11 Jan 67	CR 1 mix 1 (stereo)	Are You Experienced? (CR) CD MCACD 11602	Olympic Sound Studios, London, England	JHE	
Purple Haze	11 Jan 67	CR 1 mix 1 (stereo)	The Singles Album (CR) CD Polydor 827 369-2	Olympic Sound Studios, London, England	JHE	
Purple Haze	11 Jan 67	CR 1 mix 1 (stereo)	Smash Hits (CR) CD Reprise 2276-2	Olympic Sound Studios, London, England	JHE	
Purple Haze	11 Jan 67	CR 1 mix 2 (mono)	Purple Haze / 51st Anniversary (CR) Single Track 604 001	Olympic Sound Studios, London, England	JHE	
Purple Haze	11 Jan 67	CR 1 mix 3. Alternate mix that sounds like mono mixed into fake stereo.	Legacy (CR) LP Polydor	Olympic Sound Studios, London, England	JHE	
Purple Haze	11 Jan 67	CR 1 mix 5. An unused mono mix with the vocals mixed forward.	Out Of The Studio: Demos From 1967 CD BHCD 931022	De Lane Lea, London, England	JHE	
Purple Haze	11 Jan 67	CR 1 mix 4. A double lead vocal track is featured in this unused mono mix.	Symphony Of Experience CD Third Stone Discs TDS 24966	De Lane Lea, London, England	JHE	

SONG TITLE	DATE	COMMENTS	RELEASE	LOCATION / VENUE	BAND	PERSONNEL
Purple Haze	11 Jan 67	CR 1 mix 5. An unused mono mix with the vocals mixed forward.	DeLane Lea And Olympic Outs CD Gold Standard CD-R	De Lane Lea, London, England	JHE	
Purple Haze	11 Jan 67	CR 1 mix 5. An unused mono mix with the vocals mixed forward.	Get The Experience CD Invasion Unlimited IU 9424-1	De Lane Lea, London, England	JHE	
Purple Haze	11 Jan 67	CR 1 mix 5. An unused mono mix with the vocals mixed forward.	Complete BBC Session And..., The CD Last Bootleg Records LBR 036 / 2	De Lane Lea, London, England	JHE	
Purple Haze	11 Jan 67	CR 1 mix 5. An unused mono mix with the vocals mixed forward.	Jimi: A Musical Legacy CD KTS BX 010	De Lane Lea, London, England	JHE	
Purple Haze	11 Jan 67	CR 1 mix 4. A double lead vocal track is featured in this unused mono mix.	Jimi: A Musical Legacy CD KTS BX 010	De Lane Lea, London, England	JHE	
Purple Haze	11 Jan 67	CR 1 mix 5. An unused mono mix with the vocals mixed forward.	Magic Hand CD Mum MUCD 012	De Lane Lea, London, England	JHE	
Purple Haze	11 Jan 67	CR 1 mix 5. An unused mono mix with the vocals mixed forward.	Olympic Gold Vol 1 CD Blimp 0067	De Lane Lea, London, England	JHE	
Purple Haze	02 Mar 67	BR 1. Live incomplete rehearsal for the "Beat Club" TV show. Officially available on the videocassette "25 Years Of The Marquee Club" and booted on this CD.	Loaded Guitar LP Starlight SL 87013	Marquis Club, London, England	JHE	
Purple Haze	02 Mar 67	BR 1. Live incomplete rehearsal for the "Beat Club" TV show. Officially available on the videocassette "25 Years Of The Marquee Club" and booted on this CD.	Thanks Ottawa For The Memories CD Luna 9319	Marquis Club, London, England	JHE	
Purple Haze	02 Mar 67	BR 1. Live incomplete rehearsal for the "Beat Club" TV show. Officially available on the videocassette "25 Years Of The Marquee Club" and booted on this CD.	Unforgettable Experience LP RAH 2469	Marquis Club, London, England	JHE	
Purple Haze	02 Mar 67	BR 1. Live incomplete rehearsal for the "Beat Club" TV show. Officially available on the videocassette "25 Years Of The Marquee Club" and booted on this CD.	Tomorrow...Or Just The End Of Time CD Batz 0028	Marquis Club, London, England	JHE	
Purple Haze	28 Mar 67	CR 2. Performance on BBC radio.	Radio One (CR) CD Rykodisc RCD 20078	Top Of The Pops, BBC Limegrove Studio, London, England	JHE	
Purple Haze	28 Mar 67	CR 2. Performance on BBC radio.	Ultimate BBC Collection CD Classical CL006	Top Of The Pops, BBC Limegrove Studio, London, England	JHE	
Purple Haze	28 Mar 67	CR 2. Performance on BBC radio.	Live In London 1967 CD Koine Records	Top Of The Pops, BBC Limegrove	JHE	

Song	Date	Notes	Release	Location	Artist
			K881104	Studio, London, England	
Purple Haze	28 Mar 67	CR 2. Performance on BBC radio.	In Concert CD Starlife ST 3612	Top Of The Pops, BBC Limegrove Studio, London, England	JHE
Purple Haze	28 Mar 67	CR 2. Performance on BBC radio.	Complete BBC Session And..., The CD Last Bootleg Records LBR 036 / 2	Top Of The Pops, BBC Limegrove Studio, London, England	JHE
Purple Haze	28 Mar 67	CR 2. Performance on BBC radio.	BBC Sessions (CR) CD MCACD 2-11742	Top Of The Pops, BBC Limegrove Studio, London, England	JHE
Purple Haze	28 Mar 67	CR 2. Performance on BBC radio.	Tomorrow...Or Just The End Of Time CD Batz 0028	Top Of The Pops, BBC Limegrove Studio, London, England	JHE
Purple Haze	18 Mar 67	BR 3. Live performance for a German radio broadcast.	Legendary Star Club Tapes, The CD The Early Years 02-CD-3309	N D R Radiohouse, Studio 1, Hamburg, Germany	JHE
Purple Haze	18 Mar 67	BR 3. Live performance for a German radio broadcast.	Can You Here Me Me LP Hemero 01 / KERI	N D R Radiohouse, Studio 1, Hamburg, Germany	JHE
Purple Haze	18 Mar 67	BR 3. Live performance for a German radio broadcast.	Tomorrow...Or Just The End Of Time CD Batz 0028	N D R Radiohouse, Studio 1, Hamburg, Germany	JHE
Purple Haze	30 Mar 67	BR 4. From BBC TV, this is a studio backing track with the vocals sung live.	Loaded Guitar LP Starlight SL 87013	Top Of The Pops, BBC Limegrove Studio, London, England	JHE
Purple Haze	18 May 67	BR 5. Live performance.	Wild Man Of Pop Plays Vol 1, The CD Pyramid RFTCD 003	Beat Beat Beat TV Show, Stadhalle, Offenbach, Germany	JHE
Purple Haze	18 May 67	BR 5. Live performance.	Sweet Angel CD Compact Music WPOCM 0589	Beat Beat Beat TV Show, Stadhalle, Offenbach, Germany	JHE
Purple Haze	24 May 67	BR 6. Live performance from Swedish TV.	Wild Man Of Pop Plays Vol 1, The CD Pyramid RFTCD 003	Popside TV Show, Stockholm, Sweden	JHE
Purple Haze	24 May 67	BR 7. Live performance.	Lost In Sweden CD Whoopy Cat WKP 0046 / 0047	Stora Scenen, Grona Lund, Stockholm, Sweden	JHE

SONG TITLE	DATE	COMMENTS	RELEASE	LOCATION / VENUE	BAND	PERSONNEL
Purple Haze	18 Jun 67	CR 3. Live performance.	Monterey Pop CD Evil 006 1 / 2	Monterey International Pop Festival, Monterey, CA	JHE	
Purple Haze	18 Jun 67	CR 3. Live performance.	Valley Of Neptune CD PC 28355	Monterey International Pop Festival, Monterey, CA	JHE	
Purple Haze	18 Jun 67	CR 3. Live performance.	Jimi Plays Monterey (CR) CD Polydor 827990-2	Monterey International Pop Festival, Monterey, CA	JHE	
Purple Haze	18 Jun 67	CR 3. Live performance.	Various Artists - Monterey Pop '67 CD Evil 2004 & Black Panther 042	Monterey International Pop Festival, Monterey, CA	JHE	
Purple Haze	04 Sep 67	BR 8. Live performance.	Lost In Sweden CD Whoopy Cat WKP 0046 / 0047	Stora Scenen, Grona Lund, Stockholm, Sweden	JHE	
Purple Haze	04 Sep 67	CR 4. Live performance.	EXP Over Sweden (CR) CD UniVibes 1002	Dans In, Grona Lund, Tivoli Garden, Stockholm, Sweden	JHE	
Purple Haze	05 Sep 67	CR 5. Live performance.	Live In Stockholm 1967 CD Document DR 003	Studio 4, Radiohuset, Stockholm, Sweden	JHE	
Purple Haze	05 Sep 67	CR 5. Live performance.	Wild Man Of Pop Plays Vol 1, The CD Pyramid RFTCD 003	Studio 4, Radiohuset, Stockholm, Sweden	JHE	
Purple Haze	05 Sep 67	CR 5. Live performance.	Stages Stockholm 67 (CR) CD Reprise 9 27632-2	Studio 4, Radiohuset, Stockholm, Sweden	JHE	
Purple Haze	05 Sep 67	CR 5. Live performance.	Recorded Live In Europe CD Bulldog BGCD 023	Studio 4, Radiohuset, Stockholm, Sweden	JHE	
Purple Haze	05 Sep 67	CR 5. Live performance.	Two Sides Of The Same Genius LP Amazing Kornyphone TAKRL H677	Studio 4, Radiohuset, Stockholm, Sweden	JHE	
Purple Haze	05 Sep 67	CR 5. Live performance.	Fire CD The Entertainers CD297	Studio 4, Radiohuset, Stockholm, Sweden	JHE	
Purple Haze	05 Sep 67	CR 5. Live performance.	In Europe 67 / 68 / 69	Studio 4, Radiohuset,	JHE	

Song	Date	Notes	Release	Venue	Band
Purple Haze	05 Sep 67	CR 5. Live performance.	Jimi Hendrix Experience CD Rockstars In Concert 6127092	Studio 4, Radiohuset, Stockholm, Sweden	JHE
Purple Haze	05 Sep 67	CR 5. Live performance.	Greatest Hits Live CD Chartbusters CHER 089A	Studio 4, Radiohuset, Stockholm, Sweden	JHE
Purple Haze	11 Sep 67	BR 9. Live performance.	Lost In Sweden CD Whoopy Cat WKP 0046 / 0047	Stora Scenen, Grona Lund, Stockholm, Sweden	JHE
Purple Haze	09 Oct 67	BR 10. Live performance.	Wild Man Of Pop Plays Vol 2, The CD Pyramid RFTCD 004	L' Olympia Theatre, Paris, France	JHE
Purple Haze	09 Oct 67	BR 10. Live performance.	Live In Paris 66 / 67 CD Whoopy Cat WKP 0012	L' Olympia Theatre, Paris, France	JHE
Purple Haze	10 Nov 67	BR 11. Live performance from Dutch TV.	Wild Man Of Pop Plays Vol 2, The CD Pyramid RFTCD 004	Hoepla TV Show, Vitus Studio, Bussom, Holland	JHE
Purple Haze	10 Nov 67	BR 11. Live performance from Dutch TV.	Fire CD The Entertainers CD297	Hoepla TV Show, Vitus Studio, Bussom, Holland	JHE
Purple Haze	10 Nov 67	BR 11. Live performance from Dutch TV.	Sweet Angel CD Compact Music WPOCM 0589	Hoepla TV Show, Vitus Studio, Bussom, Holland	JHE
Purple Haze	10 Nov 67	BR 11. Live performance from Dutch TV.	Gypsy Charm CD Mum MUCD 018	Hoepla TV Show, Vitus Studio, Bussom, Holland	JHE
Purple Haze	25 Nov 67	BR 12. Live performance. Officially released on the videocassette "Experience" and "On The Road: The Ultimate Experience Live".	Wild Man Of Pop Plays Vol 2, The CD Pyramid RFTCD 004	Blackpool Opera House, Lancashire, England	JHE
Purple Haze	25 Nov 67	BR 12. Live performance. Officially released on the videocassette "Experience" and "On The Road: The Ultimate Experience Live".	Smashing Amps LP Trademark Of Quality TMQ 1813	Blackpool Opera House, Lancashire, England	JHE
Purple Haze	25 Nov 67	BR 12. Live performance. Officially released on the videocassette "Experience" and "On The Road: The Ultimate Experience Live".	Livel CD Black B-05	Blackpool Opera House, Lancashire, England	JHE
Purple Haze	07 Jan 68	BR 13. Live performance.	Cat's Squirrel CD CS 001 / 2	Tivolis Konsertsal, Copenhagen, Denmark	JHE

SONG TITLE	DATE	COMMENTS	RELEASE	LOCATION / VENUE	BAND	PERSONNEL
Purple Haze	07 Jan 68	BR 13. Live performance.	Fuckin' His Guitar For Denmark LP Polymore Or JH CO	Tivolis Konsertsal, Copenhagen, Denmark	JHE	
Purple Haze	07 Jan 68	BR 14. Live performance.	Lost In Sweden CD Whoopy Cat WKP 0046 / 0047	Tivolis Konsertsal, Copenhagen, Denmark	JHE	
Purple Haze	29 Jan 68	CR 6. Live performance	Live In Paris CD Swingin' Pig TSP-016	L' Olympia Theatre, Paris, France 2nd Show	JHE	
Purple Haze	29 Jan 68	CR 6. Live performance	Stages Paris 68 (CR) CD Reprise 9 27632-2	L' Olympia Theatre, Paris, France 2nd Show	JHE	
Purple Haze	29 Jan 68	CR 6. Live performance	Once Upon A Time CD Wall Of Sound WS CD011	L' Olympia Theatre, Paris, France 2nd Show	JHE	
Purple Haze	29 Jan 68	CR 6. Live performance	In Europe 67 / 68 / 69 CD Vulture CD 009 / 2	L' Olympia Theatre, Paris, France 2nd Show	JHE	
Purple Haze	29 Jan 68	CR 6. Live performance	In Concert CD Starlife ST 3612	L' Olympia Theatre, Paris, France 2nd Show	JHE	
Purple Haze	16 Feb 68	BR 15. Live performance.	Biggest Square In The Building, The CD Reverb Music 1993	State Fair Music Hall, Dallas, TX	JHE	
Purple Haze	16 Feb 68	BR 15. Live performance.	Scuse Me While I Kiss The Sky CD Sonic Zoom SZ 1001	State Fair Music Hall, Dallas, TX	JHE	
Purple Haze	16 Feb 68	BR 15. Live performance.	Scuse Me While I Kiss The Sky CD Sonic Zoom SZ 1001	State Fair Music Hall, Dallas, TX	JHE	
Purple Haze	17 Feb 68	BR 16. Live performance.	Remember The Alamo CD	Will Rogers Auditorium, Fort Worth, T X	JHE	
Purple Haze	17 Feb 68	BR 16. Live performance.	Scuse Me While I Kiss The Sky CD Sonic Zoom SZ 1001	Will Rogers Auditorium, Fort Worth, T X	JHE	
Purple Haze	17 Feb 68	BR 16. Live performance.	Scuse Me While I Kiss The Sky CD Sonic Zoom SZ 1001	Will Rogers Auditorium, Fort Worth, T X	JHE	
Purple Haze	25 Feb 68	BR 17. Live performance.	Winterland Vol 2 CD	Civic Opera House,	JHE	

Song	Date	Notes	Whoopy Cat WKP 00279 / 28	Chicago, IL	JHE
Purple Haze	15 Mar 68	BR 18. Live performance.	Broadcasts CD Luna LU 9204	Atwood Hall, Clark University, Worcester, MA	JHE
Purple Haze	15 Mar 68	BR 18. Live performance.	Jimi Hendrix Vol 2: A Man Of Our Times LP Napoleon NLP 11018	Atwood Hall, Clark University, Worcester, MA	JHE
Purple Haze	15 Mar 68	BR 18. Live performance.	Broadcasts LP Trade Mark Of Quality TMQ 1841 & TMQ 71019	Atwood Hall, Clark University, Worcester, MA	JHE
Purple Haze	19 Mar 68	CR 7. Live performance.	51st Anniversary CD Future Disc JMH 001 / 8	Capitol Theatre, Ottawa, Canada 2nd Show	JHE
Purple Haze	19 Mar 68	CR 7. Live performance.	Thanks Ottawa For The Memories CD Luna 9319	Capitol Theatre, Ottawa, Canada 2nd Show	JHE
Purple Haze	19 Mar 68	CR 7. Live performance.	Canadian Club CD WPOCM 0888 D 006-2	Capitol Theatre, Ottawa, Canada 2nd Show	JHE
Purple Haze	19 Mar 68	CR 7. Live performance.	Live From Ottawa LP Starlight SL 87010	Capitol Theatre, Ottawa, Canada 2nd Show	JHE
Purple Haze	19 Mar 68	CR 7. Live performance.	Calling Long Distance (CR) CD Univibes & Booted On Dynamite DS930055	Capitol Theatre, Ottawa, Canada 2nd Show	JHE
Purple Haze	19 Mar 68	CR 7. Live performance.	Superconcert 1968 CD Firepower FP03	Capitol Theatre, Ottawa, Canada 2nd Show	JHE
Purple Haze	10 May 68	BR 19. Live performance.	It's Only A Paper Moon CD Luna 9420	Fillmore East, New York, NY	JHE
Purple Haze	10 May 68	BR 19. Live performance.	One Night Stand CD Hep Cat 101	Fillmore East, New York, NY	JHE
Purple Haze	18 May 68	BR 20. Live performance.	1968 AD CD Whoopy Cat WKP 0001	Miami Pop Festival, Hallendale, FL 2nd Show	JHE
Purple Haze	03 Aug 68	BR 21. Live performance.	Crosstown Traffic CD M25 3664	Moody Coliseum, Southern Methodist University, Dallas, TX	JHE

SONG TITLE	DATE	COMMENTS	RELEASE	LOCATION / VENUE	BAND	PERSONNEL
Purple Haze	23 Aug 68	BR 22. Live performance.	Historic Concert CD Midnight Beat MBCD 017	New York Rock Festival, Singer Bowl, Queens, NY	JHE	
Purple Haze	14 Sep 68	BR 23. Live performance.	Live At The Hollywood Bowl LP RSR / International RSR 251	Hollywood Bowl, Los Angeles, CA	JHE	
Purple Haze	10 Oct 68	BR 24. Live performance.	Winterland Vol 1 CD Whoopy Cat WKP 025 / 26	Winterland Theatre, San Francisco, CA 1st Show	JHE	
Purple Haze	10 Oct 68	BR 24. Live performance.	Lost Winterland Tapes CD Starquake SQ 051-2	Winterland Theatre, San Francisco, C A 1st Show	JHE	
Purple Haze	10 Oct 68	BR 25. Live performance.	Winterland Days, The CD Manic Depression 001	Winterland Theatre, San Francisco, CA 2nd Show	JHE	
Purple Haze	10 Oct 68	BR 25. Live performance.	Winterland Vol 1 CD Whoopy Cat WKP 025 / 26	Winterland Theatre, San Francisco, CA 2nd Show	JHE	
Purple Haze	10 Oct 68	BR 25. Live performance.	Jimi Hendrix CD Imtrat 40-90355	Winterland Theatre, San Francisco, CA 2nd Show	JHE	
Purple Haze	11 Oct 68	BR 26. Live performance.	Winterland Vol 2 CD Whoopy Cat WKP 00279 / 28	Winterland Theatre, San Francisco, CA 2nd Show	JHE	
Purple Haze	11 Oct 68	BR 26. Live performance.	Star Spangled Blues CD Neutral Zone NZCD 89011	Winterland Theatre, San Francisco, CA 2nd Show	JHE	
Purple Haze	12 Oct 68	CR 8. Live performance.	Winterland Vol 3 CD Whoopy Cat WKP 0029 / 30	Winterland Theatre, San Francisco, CA 1st Show	JHE	
Purple Haze	12 Oct 68	CR 8. Live performance.	Fire CD The Entertainers CD297	Winterland Theatre, San Francisco, CA 1st Show	JHE	
Purple Haze	12 Oct 68	CR 8. Live performance.	Hendrix In Words And Music CD Outlaw Records OTR 1100030	Winterland Theatre, San Francisco, CA 1st Show	JHE	
Purple Haze	12 Oct 68	CR 8. Live performance.	Live At Winterland (CR) CD Rykodisc RCD 20038	Winterland Theatre, San Francisco, CA 1st Show	JHE	
Purple Haze	12 Oct 68	BR 27. Live performance.	Winterland Vol 3 CD	Winterland Theatre,	JHE	

Song	Date	Notes	Release	Location	Format
Purple Haze			Whoopy Cat WKP 0029 / 30	San Francisco, CA 2nd Show	
Purple Haze	12 Oct 68	BR 27. Live performance.	Ultimate Live Collection, The CD The Beat Goes On BGO BX 9307-4	Winterland Theatre, San Francisco, CA 2nd Show	JHE
Purple Haze	12 Oct 68	BR 27. Live performance.	Lost Winterland Tapes CD Starquake SQ 051-2	Winterland Theatre, San Francisco, CA 2nd Show	JHE
Purple Haze	08 Jan 69	BR 28. Live performance.	Cat's Squirrel CD CS 001 / 2	Loresberg Cirkus, Goteborg, Sweden 2nd Show	JHE
Purple Haze	09 Jan 69	BR 29. Live performance.	On The Killing Floor Swingin' Pig TSP-012-2	Konserthuset, Stockholm, Sweden 2nd Show	JHE
Purple Haze	09 Jan 69	BR 29. Live performance.	In Europe 67 / 68 / 69 CD Vulture CD 009 / 2	Konserthuset, Stockholm, Sweden 2nd Show	JHE
Purple Haze	09 Jan 69	BR 29. Live performance.	Live CD DV More CDDV 2401	Konserthuset, Stockholm, Sweden 2nd Show	JHE
Purple Haze	09 Jan 69	BR 29. Live performance.	Foxy Lady CD Alegra CD 9008	Konserthuset, Stockholm, Sweden 2nd Show	JHE
Purple Haze	10 Jan 68	BR 30. Live performance.	Welcome To The Electric Circus Vol 1 CD Midnight Beat 016	Falkoner Centret, Copenhagen, Denmark 1st Show	JHE
Purple Haze	17 Jan 69	BR 31. Live performance.	Burning At Frankfurt CD Midnight Beat MBCD 040	Jahrhunderthalle, Frankfurt, Germany	JHE
Purple Haze	23 Jan 69	BR 32. Live performance.	Up Against The Berlin Wall CD Midnight Beat MBCD 046	Sportpalast, Berlin, Germany	JHE
Purple Haze	18 Feb 69	BR 33. Live performance.	First Night At The Royal Albert Hall CD Midnight Beat MBCD 047 / 48	Royal Albert Hall, London, England	JHE
Purple Haze	24 Feb 69	CR 9. Live Performance.	Last Experience, The (CR) CD Bescol CD 42	Royal Albert Hall, London, England	JHE
Purple Haze	24 Feb 69	CR 9. Live Performance.	king Of Gypsies CD Rockyssimo RK 001	Royal Albert Hall, London, England	JHE
Purple Haze	24 Feb 69	CR 9. Live Performance.	Hendrix In Words And Music CD Outlaw Records OTR 1100030	Royal Albert Hall, London, England	JHE

SONG TITLE	DATE	COMMENTS	RELEASE	LOCATION / VENUE	BAND	PERSONNEL
Purple Haze	24 Feb 69	CR 9. Live Performance.	Royal Albert Hall CD Blimp 008 / 009 & Listen To This Eric CD JH 003 / 4	Royal Albert Hall, London, England	JHE	
Purple Haze	24 Feb 69	Stone Free CD Silver Rarities SIRA 58 / 59	Stone Free CD Silver Rarities SIRA 58 / 59	Royal Albert Hall, London, England	JHE	
Purple Haze	26 Apr 69	BR 34. Live performance.	Electric Jimi CD Jaguarondi Records	Los Angeles Forum, Los Angeles, CA	JHE	
Purple Haze	26 Apr 69	BR 34. Live performance.	I Don't Live Today, Maybe Tomorrow CD Living Legend LRCD 030	Los Angeles Forum, Los Angeles, CA	JHE	
Purple Haze	26 Apr 69	BR 34. Live performance.	Very Best, The CD Irec / Retro MILCD-03	Los Angeles Forum, Los Angeles, CA	JHE	
Purple Haze	26 Apr 69	BR 34. Live performance.	Hey Joe CD Crocodile Beat CB 53039	Los Angeles Forum, Los Angeles, CA	JHE	
Purple Haze	26 Apr 69	BR 34. Live performance.	Jimi Hendrix CD Flute FLCD 2008	Los Angeles Forum, Los Angeles, CA	JHE	
Purple Haze	26 Apr 69	BR 34. Live performance.	Anthology CD Box 9	Los Angeles Forum, Los Angeles, CA	JHE	
Purple Haze	27 Apr 69	CR 10. Live performance.	Live At The Oakland Coliseum (CR) CD Dagger Records DBRO-11743	Oakland Coliseum, Oakland, CA	JHE	
Purple Haze	03 May 69	BR 35. Live performance.	Hendrix, Busted In Toronto CD Venue VE 100502	Maple Leaf Gardens, Toronto, Canada	JHE	
Purple Haze	03 May 69	BR 35. Live performance.	I Don't Live Today CD ACL 007	Maple Leaf Gardens, Toronto, Canada	JHE	
Purple Haze	17 May 69	BR 36. Live performance.	One Night At The Arena CD Venue VE 100501	Rhode Island Arena, Providence, RI	JHE	
Purple Haze	24 May 69	CR 11. Live performance.	Stages San Diego 69 (CR) CD Reprise 9 27632-2	San Diego Sports Arena, San Diego, CA	JHE	
Purple Haze	24 May 69	CR 11. Live performance.	Midnight Magic CD Neutral Zone NZCD 89012	San Diego Sports Arena, San Diego, CA	JHE	
Purple Haze	24 May 69	CR 11. Live performance.	Don't Miss Him This Time CD Pyramid PYCD 096	San Diego Sports Arena, San Diego, CA	JHE	

Song	Date	Notes	Release	Venue	Band
Purple Haze	25 May 69	BR 37. Live performance.	Historic Concert Vol 2 CD Midnight Beat MBCD 050	Santa Clara Pop Festival, San Jose, CA	JHE
Purple Haze	20 Jun 69	BR 38. Live performance.	More Electricity From Newport CD Luna LU 9201	Newport Pop Festival, San Fernando State, Northridge, CA	JHE
Purple Haze	20 Jun 69	BR 38. Live performance.	A Lifetime Of Experience LP Sleepy Dragon 55 10	Newport Pop Festival, San Fernando State, Northridge, CA	JHE
Purple Haze	20 Jun 69	BR 38. Live performance.	Two Days At Newport CD JMH 007 / 2	Newport Pop Festival, San Fernando State, Northridge, CA	JHE
Purple Haze	20 Jun 69	BR 39. Live performance.	Wink Of An Eye CD Whoopy Cat WKP 0033 / 34	Mile High Stadium, Denver, CO	JHE
Purple Haze	18 Aug 69	CR 12. Live performance.	Woodstock Nation CD Wild Bird 89090 1 / 2	Woodstock Music And Art Fair, Bethel, NY	GSRB
Purple Haze	18 Aug 69	CR 12. Live performance.	At Woodstock (CR) Laserdisc BMG BVLP 86	Woodstock Music And Art Fair, Bethel, NY	GSRB
Purple Haze	18 Aug 69	CR 12. Live performance.	Woodstock (CR) CD MCA 11063	Woodstock Music And Art Fair, Bethel, NY	GSRB
Purple Haze	18 Aug 69	CR 12. Live performance.	Gypsy Sun And Rainbows CD Manic Depression MDCD 05 / 06	Woodstock Music And Art Fair, Bethel, NY	GSRB
Purple Haze	18 Aug 69	CR 12. Live performance.	Woodstock Monday, August 18 1969, 8AM CD JMH 008	Woodstock Music And Art Fair, Bethel, NY	GSRB
Purple Haze	18 Aug 69	CR 12. Live performance.	Ultimate Live Collection, The CD The Beat Goes On BGO BX 9307-4	Woodstock Music And Art Fair, Bethel, NY	GSRB
Purple Haze	31 Dec 69	BR 40. Live performance.	Band Of Gold CD-R Major Tom MT 087	Fillmore East, New York, NY 2nd Show	BOG
Purple Haze	01 Jan 70	BR 41. Live performance.	Band Of Gold CD-R Major Tom MT 087	Fillmore East, New York, NY 2nd Show	BOG

SONG TITLE	DATE	COMMENTS	RELEASE	LOCATION / VENUE	BAND	PERSONNEL
Purple Haze	01 Jan 70	BR 41. Live performance.	Ultimate Live Collection, The CD The Beat Goes On BGO BX 9307-4	Fillmore East, New York, NY 2nd Show	BOG	
Purple Haze	25 Apr 70	BR 42. Live performance.	Enjoy Jimi Hendrix LP Rubber Dubber 700-001-01	Los Angeles Forum, Los Angeles, CA	COL	
Purple Haze	25 Apr 70	BR 42. Live performance.	Portrait Of Jimi Hendrix, A LP Catalog # Varies On Dead Wax	Los Angeles Forum, Los Angeles, CA	COL	
Purple Haze	25 Apr 70	BR 42. Live performance.	Live At The Forum 1970 CD Whoopy Cat WKP 021 / 22	Los Angeles Forum, Los Angeles, CA	COL	
Purple Haze	25 Apr 70	BR 42. Live performance. The Luna disc is from a tape source while the JHCD 528 disc is copied from vinyl.	Scuse Me While I Kiss The Sky CD Luna CD & JHCD 528	Los Angeles Forum, Los Angeles, CA	COL	
Purple Haze	30 May 70	CR 13. Live performance.	Good Karma 2 LP Berkeley 2023	Berkeley Community Theater, Berkeley, CA 1st Show	COL	
Purple Haze	30 May 70	CR 13. Live performance.	Jimi Plays Berkeley (CR) Warner Reprise Videotape	Berkeley Community Theater, Berkeley, CA 1st Show	COL	
Purple Haze	30 May 70	CR 13. Live performance.	Soundtrack From The Film Jimi Hendrix, The (CR) LP Reprise 2RS 6481	Berkeley Community Theater, Berkeley, CA 1st Show	COL	
Purple Haze	30 May 70	CR 13. Live performance.	Riots In Berkeley CD Beech Marten BM 038	Berkeley Community Theater, Berkeley, CA 2nd Show	COL	
Purple Haze	30 May 70	CR 13. Live performance.	Berkeley Concerts, The CD Whoopy Cat WKP 004 / 5	Berkeley Community Theater, Berkeley, CA 2nd Show	COL	
Purple Haze	30 May 70	CR 13. Live performance.	Jimi Plays Berkeley CD JMH 005 / 2	Berkeley Community Theater, Berkeley, CA 1st Show	COL	
Purple Haze	13 Jun 70	BR 43. Live performance.	Baltimore Civic Center, June 13, 1970 CD Starquake SQ-09	Baltimore Civic Center, Baltimore, MD	COL	
Purple Haze	04 Jul 70	CR 14. Live performance.	Atlanta Special CD Genuine Pig TGP 121	2nd International Pop Festival, Atlanta, GA	COL	
Purple Haze	04 Jul 70	CR 14. Live performance.	At The Atlanta Pop	2nd International Pop	COL	

Song	Date	Notes	Festival (CR) Laserdisc BMG BVLP 77 (74321-10987)	Venue	COL
Purple Haze	04 Jul 70	CR 14. Live performance.	Stages Atlanta 70 (CR) CD Reprise 9 27632-2	2nd International Pop Festival, Atlanta, GA	COL
Purple Haze	04 Jul 70	CR 14. Live performance.	Atlanta CD JMH 009 / 02	2nd International Pop Festival, Atlanta, GA	COL
Purple Haze	04 Jul 70	CR 14. Live performance.	Oh, Atlanta CD Tendolar TDR-009	2nd International Pop Festival, Atlanta, GA	COL
Purple Haze	04 Jul 70	CR 14. Live performance.	Atlanta CD JMH 009 / 02	2nd International Pop Festival, Atlanta, GA	COL
Purple Haze	04 Jul 70	BR 44. Live performance.	Electric Gypsy CD Scorpio? 40176 / 15	2nd International Pop Festival, Atlanta, GA	COL
Purple Haze	17 Jul 70	BR 44. Live performance.	Can You Here Me LP Hemero 01 / KERI	New York Pop- Downing Stadium, Randalls Island, NY	COL
Purple Haze	17 Jul 70	BR 44. Live performance.	Live At Randall's Island LP Moon Tree Records PH1962	New York Pop- Downing Stadium, Randalls Island, NY	COL
Purple Haze	17 Jul 70	BR 44. Live performance.	Live USA CD Imtrat 902-001	New York Pop- Downing Stadium, Randalls Island, NY	COL
Purple Haze	30 Jul 70	BR 44. Only part of this was officially released on the 'Rainbow Bridge' and 'Alive On Live' videos.	Last American Concert Vol 1 CD The Swingin' Pig TSP-062	Rainbow Bridge Vibratory Sound-Color Experiment, Maui, HI 1st Show	COL
Purple Haze	30 Jul 70	BR 44. Live performance. Incomplete. This laserdisc release has just Jimi's parts edited from the full 'Rainbow Bridge' film.	Alive On Live (CR) Laserdisc SHLM 2005	Rainbow Bridge Vibratory Sound-Color Experiment, Maui, HI 1st Show	COL
Purple Haze	30 Jul 70	BR 44. Only part of this was officially released on the 'Rainbow Bridge' and 'Alive On Live' videos.	Last American Concert- Alive And Flowing From... LP Jupiter 444	Rainbow Bridge Vibratory Sound-Color Experiment, Maui, HI 1st Show	COL
Purple Haze	30 Jul 70	BR 44. Only part of this was officially released on the 'Rainbow Bridge' and 'Alive On Live' videos.	In From The Storm CD Silver Rarities SIRA 109 / 110	Rainbow Bridge Vibratory Sound-Color Experiment, Maui, HI 1st Show	COL
Purple Haze	30 Jul 70	BR 44. Only part of this was officially released on the 'Rainbow Bridge' and 'Alive On Live' videos.	Kiss The Skies CD Mum MUCD 024	Rainbow Bridge Vibratory Sound-Color Experiment, Maui, HI 1st Show	COL

SONG TITLE	DATE	COMMENTS	RELEASE	LOCATION / VENUE	BAND	PERSONNEL
Purple Haze	30 Jul 70	BR 44. Only part of this was officially released on the 'Rainbow Bridge' and 'Alive On Live' videos.	Rainbow Bridge 2 CD JMH 003 / 2	Rainbow Bridge Vibratory Sound-Color Experiment, Maui, HI 1st Show	COL	
Purple Haze	30 Aug 70	BR 44. Only part of this was officially released on the 'Rainbow Bridge' and 'Alive On Live' videos.	Island Man CD Silver Rarities SIRA 39 / 40	Isle Of Wight Festival, Isle Of Wight, England	COL	
Purple Haze	30 Aug 70	BR 44. Only part of this was officially released on the 'Rainbow Bridge' and 'Alive On Live' videos.	Berkeley Soundchecks, The CD Whoopy Cat WKP 0008	Isle Of Wight Festival, Isle Of Wight, England	COL	
Purple Haze	30 Aug 70	BR 44. Only part of this was officially released on the 'Rainbow Bridge' and 'Alive On Live' videos.	Wight CD JMH 006 / 2	Isle Of Wight Festival, Isle Of Wight, England	COL	
Purple Haze	31 Aug 70	BR 45. Live performance.	Come On Stockholm CD No Label	Stora Scenen, Liesberg, Stockholm, Sweden	COL	
Purple Haze	31 Aug 70	BR 45. Live performance.	Free Concert CD Midnight Beat MBCD 013	Stora Scenen, Tivoli Garden, Stockholm, Sweden	COL	
Purple Haze	01 Sep 70	BR 46. Live performance.	Warm Hello Of The Sun, The CD	Stora Scenen, Liseberg Nojespark, Goteborg, Sweden	COL	
Purple Haze	03 Sep 70	BR 47. Live performance.	Welcome To The Electric Circus Vol 2 CD Midnight Beat 018	K.B. Hallen, Copenhagen, Denmark	COL	
Purple Haze	03 Sep 70	BR 47. Live performance.	Live In Copenhagen CD The Swingin' Pig TSP-220-2	K.B. Hallen, Copenhagen, Denmark	COL	
Purple Haze	03 Sep 70	BR 47. Live performance.	Copenhagen '70 CD Whoopy Cat WKP 044 / 45	K.B. Hallen, Copenhagen, Denmark	COL	
Purple Haze	04 Sep 70	BR 48. Live performance.	Back To Berlin CD Midnight Beat 049	Deutsche- Landhalle, Berlin, Germany	COL	
Purple Haze	06 Sep 70	BR 49. Live performance.	Love & Peace CD Midnight Beat MBCD 015	Love And Peace Festival, Isle Of Fehrman, Germany	COL	
Purple Haze	06 Sep 70	BR 49. Live performance.	Wink Of An Eye CD Whoopy Cat WKP 0033 / 34	Love And Peace Festival, Isle Of Fehrman, Germany	COL	
Radio One Theme	15 Dec 67	CR 1. Live BBC performance.	Guitar Hero CD	Top Gear, BBC	JHE	

Song	Date	Notes	Release (Document DR 013)	Location	Artist	Personnel
Radio One Theme	15 Dec 67	CR 1. Live BBC performance.	Primal Keys LP Impossible Record Works	Top Gear, BBC Playhouse Theatre, London, England	JHE	
Radio One Theme	15 Dec 67	CR 1. Live BBC performance.	Radio One (CR) CD Rykodisc RCD 20078	Top Gear, BBC Playhouse Theatre, London, England	JHE	
Radio One Theme	15 Dec 67	CR 1. Live BBC performance.	Radio One (CR) CD Rykodisc RCD 20078	Top Gear, BBC Playhouse Theatre, London, England	JHE	
Radio One Theme	15 Dec 67	CR 1. Live BBC performance.	Live In London 1967 CD Koine Records K881104	Top Gear, BBC Playhouse Theatre, London, England	JHE	
Radio One Theme	15 Dec 67	CR 1. Live BBC performance.	In Concert CD Starlife ST 3612	Top Gear, BBC Playhouse Theatre, London, England	JHE	
Radio One Theme	15 Dec 67	CR 1. Live BBC performance.	Complete BBC Session And..., The CD Last Bootleg Records LBR 036 / 2	Top Gear, BBC Playhouse Theatre, London, England	JHE	
Radio One Theme	15 Dec 67	CR 1. Live BBC performance.	BBC Sessions (CR) CD MCACD 2-11742	Top Gear, BBC Playhouse Theatre, London, England	JHE	
Rainy Day Dream Away / Still Raining Still Dreaming	10 Jun 68	CR 1 mix 1. This was recorded as one track then split into two separate tracks for the album.	Electric Ladyland (CR) CD MCACD-11600	Record Plant, New York, NY	Jimi	Buddy Miles / Drums, Mike Finnegan / Organ, Freddie Smith / Sax, Larry Faucette / Percussion
Rainy Day Dream Away / Still Raining Still Dreaming	10 Jun 68	CR 1 mix 2. Unused mix #1 of the CR. This is the complete performance prior to the editing for the album.	Black Gold CD Midnight Beat MBCD 058-062	Record Plant, New York, NY	Jimi	Buddy Miles / Drums, Mike Finnegan / Organ, Freddie Smith / Sax, Larry Faucette / Percussion
Rainy Day Dream Away / Still Raining Still Dreaming	10 Jun 68	CR 1 mix 2. Unused mix #1 of the CR. This is the complete performance prior to the editing for the album. This release sounds a bit slow to me.	Hear My Freedom CD Kobra KRCR 010	Record Plant, New York, NY	Jimi	Buddy Miles / Drums, Mike Finnegan / Organ, Freddie Smith / Sax, Larry Faucette / Percussion
Rainy Day Dream Away / Still Raining Still Dreaming	10 Jun 68	CR 1 mix 3. Unused mix of the complete track without the split although the first two minutes are missing. This mix has some additional guitar overdubs not present on the final mix.	Screaming Eagle CD Pink Poodle POO 001	Record Plant, New York, NY	Jimi	Buddy Miles / Drums, Mike Finnegan / Organ, Freddie Smith / Sax, Larry Faucette / Percussion

SONG TITLE	DATE	COMMENTS	RELEASE	LOCATION / VENUE	BAND	PERSONNEL
Rainy Day Outtake #1 (Rainy Day:Dream Away Take 1)	10 Jun 68	BR 1. Two short bits of outtakes from the session.	Black Gold CD Midnight Beat MBCD 058-062	Record Plant, New York, NY	Jimi	Buddy Miles / Drums, Mike Finnegan / Organ, Freddie Smith / Sax, Larry Faucette / Percussion
Rainy Day Outtake #2 (Rainy Day Tryout)	10 Jun 68	BR 2. Two additional and different pieces of outtakes from the session.	Freak Out Blues CD GH 001	Record Plant, New York, NY	Jimi	Buddy Miles / Drums, Mike Finnegan / Organ, Freddie Smith / Sax, Larry Faucette / Percussion
Rainy Day Outtake #2 (Rainy Day)	10 Jun 68	BR 2. Two additional and different pieces of outtakes from the session.	Mixdown Master Tapes Volume 2 CD Dandelion DL 006	Record Plant, New York, NY	Jimi	Buddy Miles / Drums, Mike Finnegan / Organ, Freddie Smith / Sax, Larry Faucette / Percussion
Rainy Day Outtake #2 (Rainy Day, Dream Away)	10 Jun 68	BR 2. Two additional and different pieces of outtakes from the session.	1968 AD Part Two CD Whoopy Cat WKP 0013	Record Plant, New York, NY	Jimi	Buddy Miles / Drums, Mike Finnegan / Organ, Freddie Smith / Sax, Larry Faucette / Percussion
Rainy Day Outtake #3 (Rainy Day:Dream Away Take 2)	10 Jun 68	BR 3. This is another 2 minutes of jamming from the session.	Black Gold CD Midnight Beat MBCD 058-062	Record Plant, New York, NY	Jimi	Buddy Miles / Drums, Mike Finnegan / Organ, Freddie Smith / Sax, Larry Faucette / Percussion
Rainy Day Shuffle	10 Jun 68	CR 1 mix 1. A very jazzy jam / rehearsal Outtake from the session that showcases Mike Finnegan's organ playing. Incomplete as this is only a portion of the bootlegged versions.	Lifelines (CR) CD Reprise 9 26435-2	Record Plant, New York, NY	Jimi	Buddy Miles / Drums, Mike Finnegan / Organ, Freddie Smith / Sax, Larry Faucette / Percussion
Rainy Day Shuffle	10 Jun 68	CR 1 mix 2. A very jazzy jam / rehearsal Outtake from the session that showcases Mike Finnegan's organ playing for about 5 minutes.	Lost Experience, The, CD JHCD203	Record Plant, New York, NY	Jimi	Buddy Miles / Drums, Mike Finnegan / Organ, Freddie Smith / Sax, Larry Faucette / Percussion
Rainy Day Shuffle (Organ / Jazz Solo / Let The Sun Take A Holiday)	10 Jun 68	CR 1 mix 2. A very jazzy jam / rehearsal Outtake from the session that showcases Mike Finnegan's organ playing. CR 1 mix 3 of 'Rainy Day Dream Away / Still Raining Still Dreaming' is tacked onto the end of this version.	TTG Studios ???? CD WHOAMI WAI 015	Record Plant, New York, NY	Jimi	Buddy Miles / Drums, Mike Finnegan / Organ, Freddie Smith / Sax, Larry Faucette / Percussion
Rainy Day Shuffle (Rainy Day Jam)	10 Jun 68	CR 1 mix 2. A very jazzy jam / rehearsal Outtake from the session that showcases Mike Finnegan's organ playing for about 5 minutes.	Living Reels Vol 2 CD JMH 012 / 2	Record Plant, New York, NY	Jimi	Buddy Miles / Drums, Mike Finnegan / Organ, Freddie Smith / Sax, Larry Faucette / Percussion
Rainy Day Shuffle (Rainy Day Super Jam)	10 Jun 68	CR 1 mix 2. A very jazzy jam / rehearsal Outtake from the session that showcases Mike Finnegan's organ playing for about 5 minutes.	51st Anniversary CD Future Disc JMH 001 / 8	Record Plant, New York, NY	Jimi	Buddy Miles / Drums, Mike Finnegan / Organ, Freddie Smith / Sax, Larry Faucette / Percussion
Rainy Day Shuffle / Rainy Day Dream Away	10 Jun 68	CR 1 mix 2. A very jazzy jam / rehearsal Outtake from the session that showcases Mike Finnegan's organ playing. CR 1 mix	I Don't Live Today CD ACL 007	Record Plant, New York, NY	Jimi	Buddy Miles / Drums, Mike Finnegan / Organ, Freddie

Title	Date	Notes	Release	Studio	Artist	Personnel
Rainy Day Shuffle / Rainy Day Dream Away		3 of 'Rainy Day Dream Away / Still Raining Still Dreaming' is tacked onto the end of this version.				Smith / Sax, Larry Faucette / Percussion
Rainy Day Shuffle / Rainy Day Dream Away	10 Jun 68	CR 1 mix 2. A very jazzy jam / rehearsal Outtake from the session that showcases Mike Finnegan's organ playing. CR 1 mix 3 of 'Rainy Day Dream Away / Still Raining Still Dreaming' is tacked onto the end of this version.	1968 AD CD Whoopy Cat WKP 0001	Record Plant, New York, NY	Jimi	Buddy Miles / Drums, Mike Finnegan / Organ, Larry Faucette / Percussion
Rainy Day Shuffle / Rainy Day Dream Away (Rainy Day Dream Away)	10 Jun 68	CR 1 mix 2. A very jazzy jam / rehearsal Outtake from the session that showcases Mike Finnegan's organ playing. CR 1 mix 3 of 'Rainy Day Dream Away / Still Raining Still Dreaming' is tacked onto the end of this version.	Mixdown Master Tapes Volume 2 CD Dandelion DL 006	Record Plant, New York, NY	Jimi	Buddy Miles / Drums, Mike Finnegan / Organ, Freddie Smith / Sax, Larry Faucette / Percussion
Red House	13 Dec 66	CR 1 mix 1 (stereo)	Jimi Hendrix: Blues (CR) CD MCA MCAD-11060	CBS Studios, London, England	JHE	
Red House	13 Dec 66	CR 1 mix 1 (stereo)	Legacy (CR) LP Polydor	CBS Studios, London, England	JHE	
Red House	13 Dec 66	CR 1 mix 1 (stereo)	Are You Experienced? (CR) CD Polydor 825 416-2	CBS Studios, London, England	JHE	
Red House	13 Dec 66	CR 1 mix 2 (mono). The first press mono LP release has some of Chas Chandler's chat at the end that's not found elsewhere.	Are You Experienced (CR) LP Track 612 001	CBS Studios, London, England	JHE	
Red House	13 Dec 66	CR 1 mix 3. Unused mono mix of CR 1.	Olympic Gold Vol 2 CD Blimp 007	CBS Studios, London, England	JHE	
Red House	29 Mar 67	BR 1. Take 1 which breaks down from the session that produced CR 2.	Magic Hand CD Mum MUCD 012	De Lane Lea, London, England	JHE	
Red House	29 Mar 67	BR 1-3. Takes 1-3 from the session that produced CR 2 all of which are breakdowns.	Gypsy Charm CD Mum MUCD 018	De Lane Lea, London, England	JHE	
Red House	29 Mar 67	BR 1-4. Takes 1-4 from the session that produced CR 2. The first three takes breakdown. Take 4 produced the master for CR 2.	Out Of The Studio: Demos From 1967 CD BHCD 931022	De Lane Lea, London, England	JHE	
Red House	29 Mar 67	BR 1-4. Takes 1-4 from the session that produced CR 2. The first three takes breakdown. Take 4 produced the master for CR 2.	DeLane Lea And Olympic Outs CD Gold Standard CD-R	De Lane Lea, London, England	JHE	
Red House	29 Mar 67	BR 1-4. Takes 1-4 from the session that produced CR 2. The first three takes breakdown. Take 4 produced the master for CR 2.	Get The Experience CD Invasion Unlimited IU 9424-1	De Lane Lea, London, England	JHE	
Red House	29 Mar 67	BR 1-4. Takes 1-4 from the session that produced CR 2. The first three takes breakdown. Take 4 produced the master for CR 2.	Complete BBC Session And..., The CD Last Bootleg Records LBR 036 / 2	De Lane Lea, London, England	JHE	
Red House	29 Mar 67	BR 1-4. Takes 1-4 from the session that produced CR 2. The first three takes breakdown. Take 4 produced the master for CR 2.	Jimi: A Musical Legacy CD KTS BX 010	De Lane Lea, London, England	JHE	

SONG TITLE	DATE	COMMENTS	RELEASE	LOCATION / VENUE	BAND	PERSONNEL
Red House	29 Mar 67	BR 1-4. Takes 1-4 from the session that produced CR 2. The first three takes breakdown. Take 4 produced the master for CR 2.	Olympic Gold Vol 1 CD Blimp 0067	De Lane Lea, London, England	JHE	
Red House	29 Mar 67	CR 2. Take 4 from the session.	Smash Hits (CR) CD Reprise 2276-2	De Lane Lea, London, England	JHE	
Red House	29 Mar 67	CR 2. Take 4 from the session.	Are You Experienced? (CR) CD MCACD 11602	CBS Studios, London, England	JHE	
Red House	09 Oct 67	BR 5. Live performance.	Wild Man Of Pop Plays Vol 2, The CD Pyramid RFTCD 004	L' Olympia Theatre, Paris, France	JHE	
Red House	09 Oct 67	BR 5. Live performance.	Live In Paris 66 / 67 CD Whoopy Cat WKP 0012	L' Olympia Theatre, Paris, France	JHE	
Red House	29 Jan 68	CR 4. Live performance.	Live In Paris CD Swingin' Pig TSP-016	L' Olympia Theatre, Paris, France 1st Show	JHE	
Red House	29 Jan 68	CR 4. Live performance.	Stages Paris 68 (CR) CD Reprise 9 27632-2	L' Olympia Theatre, Paris, France 1st Show	JHE	
Red House	29 Jan 68	CR 4. Live performance.	Recorded Live In Europe CD Bulldog BGCD 023	L' Olympia Theatre, Paris, France 1st Show	JHE	
Red House	29 Jan 68	CR 4. Live performance.	In Europe 67 / 68 / 69 CD Vulture CD 009 / 2	L' Olympia Theatre, Paris, France 1st Show	JHE	
Red House	29 Jan 68	CR 4. Live performance.	Live CD DV More CDDV 2401	L' Olympia Theatre, Paris, France 1st Show	JHE	
Red House	29 Jan 68	CR 4. Live performance.	Jimi Hendrix Experience CD Rockstars In Concert 6127092	L' Olympia Theatre, Paris, France 1st Show	JHE	
Red House	29 Jan 68	CR 4. Live performance.	In Concert CD Starlife ST 3612	L' Olympia Theatre, Paris, France 1st Show	JHE	
Red House	29 Jan 68	CR 4. Live performance.	Foxy Lady CD Alegra CD 9008	L' Olympia Theatre, Paris, France 1st Show	JHE	
Red House	29 Jan 68	CR 4. Live performance. Incomplete.	Lifelines (CR) CD Reprise 9 26435-2	L' Olympia Theatre, Paris, France 1st Show	JHE	

Song	Date	Notes	Release	Venue	Band
Red House	16 Feb 68	BR 6. Live performance.	Biggest Square In The Building, The CD Reverb Music 1993	State Fair Music Hall, Dallas, TX	JHE
Red House	?? Mar 68	CR 5. Live performance.	In Concert CD Starlife ST 3612	Scene Club, New York, NY	Scene
Red House	?? Mar 68	CR 5. Live performance.	Hendrix In Words And Music CD Outlaw Records OTR 1100030	Scene Club, New York, NY	Scene
Red House	?? Mar 68	CR 5. Live performance.	Jimi Hendrix CD Flute FLCD 2008	Scene Club, New York, NY	Scene
Red House	?? Mar 68	CR 5. Live performance.	Woke Up This Morning And Found Myself Dead CR (CD) RLCD 0068	Scene Club, New York, NY	Scene
Red House (Jimi's Blues)	?? Mar 68	CR 5. Live performance.	High Live And Dirty (CR) LP Nutmeg NUT 1001	Scene Club, New York, NY	Scene
Red House	19 Mar 68	BR 7. Live performance.	Once Upon A Time CD Wall Of Sound WS CD011	Capitol Theatre, Ottawa, Canada	JHE
Red House	19 Mar 68	BR 7. Live performance.	Thanks Ottawa For The Memories CD Luna 9319	Capitol Theatre, Ottawa, Canada	JHE
Red House	19 Mar 68	BR 7. Live performance.	Canadian Club CD WPOCM 0888 D 006-2	Capitol Theatre, Ottawa, Canada	JHE
Red House	19 Mar 68	BR 7. Live performance.	Live From Ottawa LP Starlight SL 87010	Capitol Theatre, Ottawa, Canada	JHE
Red House	19 Mar 68	BR 7. Live performance.	Superconcert 1968 CD Firepower FP03	Capitol Theatre, Ottawa, Canada	JHE
Red House	10 May 68	BR 8. Live performance.	It's Only A Paper Moon CD Luna 9420	Fillmore East, New York, NY	JHE
Red House	10 May 68	BR 8. Live performance.	One Night Stand CD Hep Cat 101	Fillmore East, New York, NY	JHE
Red House	03 Aug 68	BR 9. Live performance.	Crosstown Traffic CD M25 3664	Moody Coliseum, Southern Methodist University, Dallas, TX	JHE
Red House	11 Aug 68	BR 10. Live performance.	Davenport, Iowa '68 LP Creative Artistry 26K10 / 55K10	Col Ballroom, Davenport, IA	JHE
Red House	23 Aug 68	BR 11. Live performance.	Historic Concert CD Midnight Beat MBCD 017	New York Rock Festival, Singer Bowl, Queens, NY	JHE

SONG TITLE	DATE	COMMENTS	RELEASE	LOCATION / VENUE	BAND	PERSONNEL
Red House	23 Aug 68	BR 11. Live performance.	Historic Concert CD Midnight Beat MBCD 017	New York Rock Festival, Singer Bowl, Queens, NY	JHE	
Red House	14 Sep 68	BR 12. Live performance.	Live At The Hollywood Bowl LP RSR / International RSR 251	Hollywood Bowl, Los Angeles, CA	JHE	
Red House	10 Oct 68	CR 6. Live performance.	First Rays Of The New Rising Sun CD Triangle PYCD 084-2	Winterland Theatre, San Francisco, CA 1st Show	JHE	
Red House	10 Oct 68	CR 6. Live performance.	Winterland Days, The CD Manic Depression 001	Winterland Theatre, San Francisco, CA 1st Show	JHE	
Red House	10 Oct 68	CR 6. Live performance.	Jimi Hendrix CD Imtrat 40-90355	Winterland Theatre, San Francisco, CA 1st Show	JHE	
Red House	10 Oct 68	CR 6. Live performance.	Red House: Variations On A Theme CD Hal Leonard HL00660040	Winterland Theatre, San Francisco, CA 1st Show	JHE	
Red House	11 Oct 68	CR 7. Live performance.	Winterland Vol 1 CD Whoopy Cat WKP 025 / 26	Winterland Theatre, San Francisco, CA 1st Show	JHE	
Red House	11 Oct 68	CR 7. Live performance.	Winterland Vol 2 CD Whoopy Cat WKP 00279 / 28	Winterland Theatre, San Francisco, CA 1st Show	JHE	
Red House	11 Oct 68	CR 7. Live performance.	Live At Winterland (CR) CD Rykodisc RCD 20038	Winterland Theatre, San Francisco, CA 1st Show	JHE	
Red House	11 Oct 68	CR 7. Live performance.	Living Reels Vol 2 CD JMH 012 / 2	Winterland Theatre, San Francisco, CA 1st Show	JHE	
Red House	12 Oct 68	BR 13. Live performance.	Winterland Vol 3 CD Whoopy Cat WKP 0029 / 30	Winterland Theatre, San Francisco, CA 2nd Show	JHE	
Red House	12 Oct 68	BR 13. Live performance.	Lost Winterland Tapes CD Starquake SQ 051-2	Winterland Theatre, San Francisco, CA 2nd Show	JHE	
Red House (Electric Church Red House)	29 Oct 68	CR 3 mix 1. The slightly less complete composite version as some of the intro is missing. The intro was edited on from "Electric Church" recorded on 10 / 21 / 68.	Jimi Hendrix: Blues (CR) CD MCA MCAD-11060	T.T.G. Studios, Hollywood, CA	JHE	
Red House	29 Oct 68	CR 3 mix 2. The complete composite version. The intro was	Electric Gypsy CD	T.T.G. Studios,	JHE	Lee Michaels / Organ,

Song	Notes	Date	Release	Location	Lineup	Personnel
Red House (Electric Church Jam)	edited on from "Electric Church" recorded on 10/21/68.		Scorpio? 40176/15	Hollywood, CA		Buddy Miles / Additional Drums
Red House	CR 3 mix 2. The complete composite version. The intro was edited on from "Electric Church" recorded on 10/21/68.	29 Oct 68	Master's Masters, The CD JH-01	T.T.G. Studios, Hollywood, CA	JHE	Lee Michaels / Organ, Buddy Miles / Additional Drums
Red House	CR 3 mix 2. The complete composite version. The intro was edited on from "Electric Church" recorded on 10/21/68.	29 Oct 68	Official Bootleg Album, The CD Yellow Dog YD 051	T.T.G. Studios, Hollywood, CA	JHE	Lee Michaels / Organ, Buddy Miles / Additional Drums
Red House	CR 3 mix 2. The complete composite version. The intro was edited on from "Electric Church" recorded on 10/21/68.	29 Oct 68	51st Anniversary CD Future Disc JMH 001/8	T.T.G. Studios, Hollywood, CA	JHE	Lee Michaels / Organ, Buddy Miles / Additional Drums
Red House	CR 3 mix 2. The complete composite version. The intro was edited on from "Electric Church" recorded on 10/21/68.	29 Oct 68	51st Anniversary CD Future Disc JMH 001/8	T.T.G. Studios, Hollywood, CA	JHE	Lee Michaels / Organ, Buddy Miles / Additional Drums
Red House	CR 3 mix 2. The complete composite version. The intro was edited on from "Electric Church" recorded on 10/21/68.	29 Oct 68	Freak Out Blues CD GH 001	T.T.G. Studios, Hollywood, CA	JHE	Lee Michaels / Organ, Buddy Miles / Additional Drums
Red House	CR 3 mix 2. The complete composite version. The intro was edited on from "Electric Church" recorded on 10/21/68.	29 Oct 68	Best Of The Bootlegs CD MS 666	T.T.G. Studios, Hollywood, CA	JHE	Lee Michaels / Organ, Buddy Miles / Additional Drums
Red House	CR 3 mix 2. The complete composite version. The intro was edited on from "Electric Church" recorded on 10/21/68.	29 Oct 68	King Of Gypsies CD Rockyssimo RK 001	T.T.G. Studios, Hollywood, CA	JHE	Lee Michaels / Organ, Buddy Miles / Additional Drums
Red House	CR 3 mix 2. The complete composite version. The intro was edited on from "Electric Church" recorded on 10/21/68.	29 Oct 68	Red House: Variations On A Theme CD Hal Leonard HL00660040	T.T.G. Studios, Hollywood, CA	JHE	Lee Michaels / Organ, Buddy Miles / Additional Drums
Red House	BR 14. Live performance. One of Jimi's longest performances of this song.	02 Nov 68	Dante's Inferno CD Pink Poodle POO 002	Minneapolis Auditorium, Minneapolis, MN	JHE	
Red House	BR 15. Live performance.	08 Jan 69	Cat's Squirrel CD CS 001/2	Loresberg Cirkus, Goteborg, Sweden	JHE	
Red House	BR 16. Live performance.	09 Jan 69	On The Killing Floor Swingin' Pig TSP-012-2	Konserthuset, Stockholm, Sweden 1st Show	JHE	
Red House	BR 16. Live performance.	09 Jan 69	Electronic Church Music CD Pyramid PYCD 023	Konserthuset, Stockholm, Sweden	JHE	
Red House	BR 16. Live performance.	09 Jan 69	In Concert CD Starlife ST 3612	Konserthuset, Stockholm, Sweden	JHE	
Red House	BR 17. Live performance.	09 Jan 69	On The Killing Floor Swingin' Pig TSP-012-2	Konserthuset, Stockholm, Sweden 2nd Show	JHE	

SONG TITLE	DATE	COMMENTS	RELEASE	LOCATION / VENUE	BAND	PERSONNEL
Red House	09 Jan 69	BR 17. Live performance.	In Europe 67 / 68 / 69 CD Vulture CD 009 / 2	Konserthuset, Stockholm, Sweden	JHE	
Red House	10 Jan 69	BR 19. Live performance.	Welcome To The Electric Circus Vol 1 CD Midnight Beat 016	Falkoner Centret, Copenhagen, Denmark 1st Show	JHE	
Red House	17 Jan 69	BR 20. Live performance.	Burning At Frankfurt CD Midnight Beat MBCD 040	Jahrhunderthalle, Frankfurt, Germany	JHE	
Red House	23 Jan 69	BR 21. Live performance.	Up Against The Berlin Wall CD Midnight Beat MBCD 046	Sportpalast, Berlin, Germany	JHE	
Red House	18 Feb 69	BR 22. Live performance.	First Night At The Royal Albert Hall CD Midnight Beat MBCD 047 / 48	Royal Albert Hall, London, England	JHE	
Red House	24 Feb 69	CR 8. Live performance.	Broadcasts CD Luna LU 9204	Royal Albert Hall, London, England	JHE	
Red House	24 Feb 69	CR 8. Live performance.	Unforgettable Experience LP RAH 2469	Royal Albert Hall, London, England	JHE	
Red House	24 Feb 69	CR 8. Live performance.	Historic Performances CD Aquarius AQ 67-JH-080	Royal Albert Hall, London, England	JHE	
Red House	24 Feb 69	CR 8. Live performance.	Royal Albert Hall CD Blimp 008 / 009	Royal Albert Hall, London, England	JHE	
Red House	24 Feb 69	CR 8. Live performance.	Stone Free CD Silver Rarities SIRA 58 / 59	Royal Albert Hall, London, England	JHE	
Red House	24 Feb 69	CR 8. Live performance.	Red House: Variations On A Theme CD Hal Leonard HL00660040	Royal Albert Hall, London, England	JHE	
Red House	26 Apr 69	CR 9. Live performance.	Electric Jimi CD Jaguarondi Records	Los Angeles Forum, Los Angeles, CA	JHE	
Red House	26 Apr 69	CR 9. Live performance.	I Don't Live Today, Maybe Tomorrow CD Living Legend LRCD 030	Los Angeles Forum, Los Angeles, CA	JHE	
Red House	26 Apr 69	CR 9. Live performance.	Live USA CD Imtrat 902-001	Los Angeles Forum, Los Angeles, CA	JHE	
Red House	26 Apr 69	CR 9. Live performance.	Hey Joe CD Crocodile Beat CB 53039	Los Angeles Forum, Los Angeles, CA	JHE	

Song	Date	Notes	Release	Venue	Band
Red House	26 Apr 69	CR 9. Live performance.	Anthology CD Box 9	Los Angeles Forum, Los Angeles, CA	JHE
Red House	26 Apr 69	CR 9. Live performance.	Red House: Variations On A Theme CD Hal Leonard HL00660040	Los Angeles Forum, Los Angeles, CA	JHE
Red House	27 Apr 69	CR 10. Live performance.	Live At The Oakland Coliseum (CR) CD Dagger Records DBRO-11743	Oakland Coliseum, Oakland, CA	JHE
Red House	03 May 69	BR 22. Live performance.	Hendrix, Busted In Toronto CD Venue VE 100502	Maple Leaf Gardens, Toronto, Canada	JHE
Red House	03 May 68	BR 22. Live performance.	I Don't Live Today CD ACL 007	Maple Leaf Gardens, Toronto, Canada	JHE
Red House	17 May 69	BR 23. Live performance.	One Night At The Arena CD Venue VE 100501	Rhode Island Arena, Providence, RI	JHE
Red House	18 May 69	BR 24. Live performance.	Roman Coliseum, The CD Starquake SQ 11	Madison Square Garden, New York, NY	JHE
Red House	24 May 69	CR 11. Live performance.	Stages San Diego 69 (CR) CD Reprise 9 27632-2	San Diego Sports Arena, San Diego, CA	JHE
Red House	24 May 69	CR 11. Live performance.	Hendrix In The West (CR) LP Polydor 2302018 A	San Diego Sports Arena, San Diego, CA	JHE
Red House	24 May 69	CR 11. Live performance.	Red House CD The Entertainers CD294	San Diego Sports Arena, San Diego, CA	JHE
Red House	24 May 69	CR 11. Live performance.	Don't Miss Him This Time CD Pyramid PYCD 096	San Diego Sports Arena, San Diego, CA	JHE
Red House	25 May 69	BR 25. Live performance.	Historic Concert Vol 2 CD Midnight Beat MBCD 050	Santa Clara Pop Festival, San Jose, CA	JHE
Red House	20 Jun 69	BR 26. Live performance.	More Electricity From Newport CD Luna LU 9201	Newport Pop Festival, San Fernando State, Northridge, CA	JHE
Red House	20 Jun 69	BR 26. Live performance.	A Lifetime Of Experience LP Sleepy Dragon 55 10	Newport Pop Festival, San Fernando State, Northridge, CA	JHE

SONG TITLE	DATE	COMMENTS	RELEASE	LOCATION / VENUE	BAND	PERSONNEL
Red House	20 Jun 69	BR 26. Live performance.	Two Days At Newport CD JMH 007 / 2	Newport Pop Festival, San Fernando State, Northridge, CA	JHE	
Red House	22 Jun 69	BR 27. Live performance.	It Never Takes An End CD Genuine Pig TGP-118	Newport Pop Festival, San Fernando State, Northridge, CA	NJK	
Red House	29 Jun 69	BR 28. Live performance.	Wink Of An Eye CD Whoopy Cat WKP 0033 / 34	Mile High Stadium, Denver, CO	JHE	
Red House	18 Aug 69	CR 12 mix 2. Complete live performance.	Woodstock Nation CD Wild Bird 89090 1 / 2	Woodstock Music And Art Fair, Bethel, NY	GSRB	
Red House	18 Aug 69	CR 12 mix 2. Complete live performance.	At Woodstock (CR) Laserdisc BMG BVLP 86	Woodstock Music And Art Fair, Bethel, NY	GSRB	
Red House	18 Aug 69	CR 12 mix 2. Complete live performance.	Gypsy Sun And Rainbows CD Manic Depression MDCD 05 / 06	Woodstock Music And Art Fair, Bethel, NY	GSRB	
Red House	18 Aug 69	CR 12 mix 2. Complete live performance.	Woodstock Monday, August 18 1969, 8AM CD JMH 008	Woodstock Music And Art Fair, Bethel, NY	GSRB	
Red House	18 Aug 69	CR 12 mix 2. Complete live performance.	Ultimate Live Collection, The CD The Beat Goes On BGO BX 9307-4	Woodstock Music And Art Fair, Bethel, NY	GSRB	
Red House	18 Aug 69	CR 12 mix 1. Edited live performance.	Woodstock (CR) CD MCA 11063	Woodstock Music And Art Fair, Bethel, NY	GSRB	
Red House	18 Aug 69	CR 12 mix 1. Edited live performance.	51st Anniversary CD Future Disc JMH 001 / 8	Woodstock Music And Art Fair, Bethel, NY	GSRB	
Red House	30 May 70	CR 13. Live performance.	Good Karma 2 LP Berkeley 2023	Berkeley Community Theater, Berkeley, CA 1st Show	COL	
Red House	30 May 70	CR 13. Live performance.	51st Anniversary CD Future Disc JMH 001 / 8	Berkeley Community Theater, Berkeley, CA 1st Show	COL	
Red House	30 May 70	CR 13. Live performance.	Berkeley Concert LP Audifon AF 008	Berkeley Community Theater, Berkeley,	COL	

Song	Date	Notes	Release	Venue	Format
Red House	30 May 70	CR 13. Live performance.	Berkeley Concerts, The CD Whoopy Cat WKP 004 / 5	Berkeley Community Theater, Berkeley, CA 1st Show	COL
Red House	30 May 70	CR 13. Live performance.	Valley Of Neptune CD PC 28355	Berkeley Community Theater, Berkeley, CA 1st Show	COL
Red House	30 May 70	CR 13. Live performance.	Jimi Plays Berkeley CD JMH 005 / 2	Berkeley Community Theater, Berkeley, CA 1st Show	COL
Red House	30 May 70	CR 13. Live performance.	Ultimate Live Collection, The CD The Beat Goes On BGO BX 9307-4	Berkeley Community Theater, Berkeley, CA 1st Show	COL
Red House	30 May 70	CR 13. Live performance.	Red House: Variations On A Theme CD Hal Leonard HL00660040	Berkeley Community Theater, Berkeley, CA 1st Show	COL
Red House	13 Jun 70	BR 29. Live performance.	Live At The Forum 1970 CD Whoopy Cat WKP 021 / 22	Baltimore Civic Center, Baltimore, MD	COL
Red House	13 Jun 70	BR 29. Live performance.	Baltimore Civic Center, June 13, 1970 CD Starquake SQ-09	Baltimore Civic Center, Baltimore, MD	COL
Red House	04 Jul 70	BR 30. Live performance. Officially released on the video tape and laserdisc.	At The Atlanta Pop Festival (CR) Laserdisc BMG BVLP 77 (74321-10987)	2nd International Pop Festival, Atlanta, GA	COL
Red House	04 Jul 70	BR 30. Live performance. Officially released on the video tape and laserdisc.	Atlanta CD JMH 009 / 02	2nd International Pop Festival, Atlanta, GA	COL
Red House	04 Jul 70	BR 30. Live performance. Officially released on the video tape and laserdisc.	Oh, Atlanta CD Tendolar TDR-009	2nd International Pop Festival, Atlanta, GA	COL
Red House	04 Jul 70	BR 30. Live performance. Officially released on the video tape and laserdisc.	Atlanta CD JMH 009 / 02	2nd International Pop Festival, Atlanta, GA	COL
Red House	17 Jul 70	CR 14 mix 1. Live performance.	Concerts (CR) CD Reprise 9-22306-2	New York Pop-Downing Stadium, Randalls Island, NY	COL
Red House	17 Jul 70	CR 14 mix 1. Live performance.	Can You Here Me LP Hemero 01 / KERI	New York Pop-Downing Stadium, Randalls Island, NY	COL
Red House	17 Jul 70	CR 14 mix 2. Live performance.	Broadcasts CD Luna LU 9204	New York Pop-Downing Stadium, Randalls Island, NY	COL

SONG TITLE	DATE	COMMENTS	RELEASE	LOCATION / VENUE	BAND	PERSONNEL
Red House	17 Jul 70	CR 14 mix 2. Live performance.	Red House: Variations On A Theme CD Hal Leonard HL00660040	New York Pop-Downing Stadium, Randalls Island, NY	COL	
Red House	30 Jul 70	BR 31. Live performance.	Maui, Hawaii LP JH 106 (Trademark Of Quality?)	Rainbow Bridge Vibratory Sound-Color Experiment, Maui, HI 2nd Show	COL	
Red House	30 Jul 70	BR 31. Live performance.	Last American Concert Vol 2 CD The Swingin' Pig TSP-072	Rainbow Bridge Vibratory Sound-Color Experiment, Maui, HI 2nd Show	COL	
Red House	30 Jul 70	BR 31. Live performance.	Last American Concert-Alive And Flowing From.... LP Jupiter 444	Rainbow Bridge Vibratory Sound-Color Experiment, Maui, HI 2nd Show	COL	
Red House	30 Jul 70	BR 31. Live performance.	In From The Storm CD Silver Rarities SIRA 109 / 110	Rainbow Bridge Vibratory Sound-Color Experiment, Maui, HI 2nd Show	COL	
Red House	30 Jul 70	BR 31. Live performance.	Rainbow Bridge 2 CD JMH 003 / 2	Rainbow Bridge Vibratory Sound-Color Experiment, Maui, HI 2nd Show	COL	
Red House	30 Aug 70	CR 15. Live performance.	Island Man CD Silver Rarities SIRA 39 / 40	Isle Of Wight Festival, Isle Of Wight, England	COL	
Red House	30 Aug 70	CR 15. Live performance.	At The Isle Of Wight (CR) Laserdisc CBS / Sony CLSM 791	Isle Of Wight Festival, Isle Of Wight, England	COL	
Red House	30 Aug 70	CR 15. Live performance.	Soundtrack From The Film Jimi Hendrix, The (CR) LP Reprise 2RS 6481	Isle Of Wight Festival, Isle Of Wight, England	COL	
Red House	30 Aug 70	CR 15. Live performance.	Live - Isle Of Wight '70 (CR) CD Polydor 847236-2	Isle Of Wight Festival, Isle Of Wight, England	COL	
Red House	30 Aug 70	CR 15. Live performance.	Wight CD JMH 006 / 2	Isle Of Wight Festival, Isle Of Wight, England	COL	
Red House	31 Aug 70	BR 32. Live performance.	Come On Stockholm CD No Label	Stora Scenen, Liesberg, Goteborg, Sweden	COL	

Song	Date	Take/Notes	Release	Location	Source						
Red House	01 Sep 70	BR 33. Live performance.	Warm Hello Of The Sun, The CD	Stora Scenen, Liseberg Nojespark, Goteborg, Sweden	COL						
Red House	03 Sep 70	CR 16. Live performance.	Welcome To The Electric Circus Vol 2 CD Midnight Beat 018	K.B. Hallen, Copenhagen, Denmark	COL						
Red House	03 Sep 70	CR 16. Live performance.	Calling Long Distance (CR) CD Univibes & Booted On Dynamite DS930055	K.B. Hallen, Copenhagen, Denmark	COL						
Red House	03 Sep 70	CR 16. Live performance.	Live In Copenhagen CD The Swingin' Pig TSP-220-2	K.B. Hallen, Copenhagen, Denmark	COL						
Red House	03 Sep 70	CR 16. Live performance.	Copenhagen 70 CD Whoopy Cat WKP 044 / 45	K.B. Hallen, Copenhagen, Denmark	COL						
Red House	04 Sep 70	BR 34. Live performance.	Back To Berlin CD Midnight Beat 049	Deutsche- Landhalle, Berlin, Germany	COL						
Red House	06 Sep 70	BR 35. Live performance.	Love & Peace CD Midnight Beat MBCD 015	Love And Peace Festival, Isle Of Fehrman, Germany	COL						
Red House	06 Sep 70	BR 35. Live performance.	Wink Of An Eye CD Whoopy Cat WKP 0033 / 34	Love And Peace Festival, Isle Of Fehrman, Germany	COL						
Remember	08 Feb 67	BR 1-5. Five instrumental takes from the session that produced the CR 1 master. All are breakdowns except the last take which is complete.	Olympic Gold Vol 2 CD Blimp 007	De Lane Lea, London, England	JHE						
Remember	08 Feb 67	CR 1 mix 1 (stereo).	Smash Hits (CR) CD Reprise 2276-2	De Lane Lea, London, England	JHE						
Remember	08 Feb 67	CR 1 mix 1 (stereo).	Are You Experienced? (CR) CD MCACD 11602	De Lane Lea, London, England	JHE						
Remember	08 Feb 67	CR 1 mix 1 (stereo).	The Singles Album (CR) CD Polydor 827 369-2	De Lane Lea, London, England	JHE						
Remember	08 Feb 67	CR 1 mix 1 (stereo).	Smash Hits (CR) CD Reprise 2276-2	De Lane Lea, London, England	JHE						
Remember	08 Feb 67	CR 1 mix 2 (mono).	Are You Experienced? (CR) LP Track 612 001	De Lane Lea, London, England	JHE						
Remember	08 Feb 67	CR 1 mix 3. Unused mix of the CR 1 mix 2. Preceded by a false start.	Olympic Gold Vol 2 CD Blimp 007	De Lane Lea, London, England	JHE						

SONG TITLE	DATE	COMMENTS	RELEASE	LOCATION / VENUE	BAND	PERSONNEL
Rock And Roll Band	05 Jan 69	This is a guest appearance by Jimi with the group Eire Apparent. Jimi plays guitar.	51st Anniversary CD Future Disc JMH 001 / 8	Polydor Studios, London, England	Jimi	Eire Apparent
Rock And Roll Band	05 Jan 69	This is a guest appearance by Jimi with the group Eire Apparent. Jimi plays guitar.	Jewel Box CD Home HR-5824-3	Polydor Studios, London, England	Jimi	Eire Apparent
Rock And Roll Jam	04 Apr 69	BR 1. A short impromptu instrumental jam built on a standard rock 'n' roll arrangement.	Midnight Shines Down CD Blue Kangaroo BK 04	Olympic Sound Studios, London, England	JHE	
Rock And Roll Jam	04 Apr 69	BR 1. A short impromptu instrumental jam built on a standard rock 'n' roll arrangement.	Living Reels Vol 2 CD JMH 012 / 2	Olympic Sound Studios, London, England	JHE	
Rock And Roll Jam (Instrumental #4)	04 Apr 69	BR 1. A short impromptu instrumental jam built on a standard rock 'n' roll arrangement.	TTG Studios ???? CD WHOAMI WAI 015	Olympic Sound Studios, London, England	JHE	
Rock And Roll Jam (Instrumental Jam)	04 Apr 69	BR 1. A short impromptu instrumental jam built on a standard rock 'n' roll arrangement.	Gypsy Suns, Moons And Rainbows CD Sidewalk JHX 8868	Olympic Sound Studios, London, England	JHE	
Rock Me Baby	04 Feb 67	BR 1. Live performance of an early concert favorite. No studio recordings have surfaced.	Have Mercy On Me Baby CD Midnight Beat MBCD 038	Flamingo Club, London, England	JHE	
Rock Me Baby	04 Feb 67	BR 1. Live performance of an early concert favorite. No studio recordings have surfaced.	Live At The Flamingo Club, London, 2-4-67 CD	Flamingo Club, London, England	JHE	
Rock Me Baby	24 May 67	BR 2. Live performance of an early concert favorite. No studio recordings have surfaced.	Lost In Sweden CD Whoopy Cat WKP 0046 / 0047	Stora Scenen, Grona Lund, Stockholm, Sweden	JHE	
Rock Me Baby	18 Jun 67	CR 1. Live performance of an early concert favorite. No studio recordings have surfaced.	Lifelines (CR) CD Reprise 9 26435-2	Monterey International Pop Festival, Monterey, CA	JHE	
Rock Me Baby	18 Jun 67	CR 1. Live performance of an early concert favorite. No studio recordings have surfaced.	Soundtrack From The Film Jimi Hendrix, The (CR) LP Reprise 2RS 6481	Monterey International Pop Festival, Monterey, CA	JHE	
Rock Me Baby	18 Jun 67	CR 1. Live performance of an early concert favorite. No studio recordings have surfaced.	Monterey Pop CD Evil 006 1 / 2	Monterey International Pop Festival, Monterey, CA	JHE	
Rock Me Baby	18 Jun 67	CR 1. Live performance of an early concert favorite. No studio recordings have surfaced.	Experience II CD More MTT 1021	Monterey International Pop Festival, Monterey, CA	JHE	

Song	Date	Notes	Release	Location		
				CA		
Rock Me Baby	18 Jun 67	CR 1. Live performance of an early concert favorite. No studio recordings have surfaced.	Jimi Plays Monterey (CR) CD Polydor 827990-2	Monterey International Pop Festival, Monterey, CA	JHE	
Rock Me Baby	04 Sep 67	BR 3. Live performance of an early concert favorite. No studio recordings have surfaced.	Lost In Sweden CD Whoopy Cat WKP 0046 / 0047	Stora Scenen, Grona Lund, Stockholm, Sweden	JHE	
Rock Me Baby	09 Oct 67	BR 4. Live performance of an early concert favorite. No studio recordings have surfaced.	Wild Man Of Pop Plays Vol 2, The CD Pyramid RFTCD 004	L' Olympia Theatre, Paris, France	JHE	
Rock Me Baby	09 Oct 67	BR 4. Live performance of an early concert favorite. No studio recordings have surfaced.	Live In Paris 66 / 67 CD Whoopy Cat WKP 0012	L' Olympia Theatre, Paris, France	JHE	
Rock Me Baby	03 Aug 68	BR 5. Live performance of an early concert favorite. No studio recordings have surfaced.	Crosstown Traffic CD M25 3664	Moody Coliseum, Southern Methodist University, Dallas, TX	JHE	
Room Full Of Mirrors	24 Feb 69	CR 2 mix 1. Live performance.	Last Experience, The (CR) CD Bescol CD 42	Royal Albert Hall, London, England	JHE	Chris Wood / Flute, Rocky Dziddzournou / Bongos
Room Full Of Mirrors	24 Feb 69	CR 2 mix 1. Live performance.	Smashing Amps LP Trademark Of Quality TMQ 1813	Royal Albert Hall, London, England	JHE	Chris Wood / Flute, Rocky Dziddzournou / Bongos
Room Full Of Mirrors	24 Feb 69	CR 2 mix 1. Live performance.	Rhinozerous RHP 789	Royal Albert Hall, London, England	JHE	Chris Wood / Flute, Rocky Dziddzournou / Bongos
Room Full Of Mirrors	24 Feb 69	CR 2 mix 1. Live performance.	King Of Gypsies CD Rockyssimo RK 001	Royal Albert Hall, London, England	JHE	Chris Wood / Flute, Rocky Dziddzournou / Bongos
Room Full Of Mirrors	24 Feb 69	CR 2 mix 1. Live performance.	Stone Free CD Silver Rarities SIRA 58 / 59	Royal Albert Hall, London, England	JHE	Chris Wood / Flute, Rocky Dziddzournou / Bongos
Room Full Of Mirrors	24 Feb 69	CR 2 mix 1. Live performance.	Anthology CD Box 9	Royal Albert Hall, London, England	JHE	Chris Wood / Flute, Rocky Dziddzournou / Bongos
Room Full Of Mirrors	24 Feb 69	CR 2 mix 1. Live performance.	Voice Of Experience CD Rhinozerous RHP 789	Royal Albert Hall, London, England	JHE	Chris Wood / Flute, Rocky Dziddzournou / Bongos
Room Full Of Mirrors	24 Feb 69	CR 2 mix 2. Live performance. A second but incomplete version of the same song is on this same disc!	Last Experience, The (CR) CD Bescol CD 42	Royal Albert Hall, London, England	JHE	Chris Wood / Flute, Rocky Dziddzournou / Bongos
Room Full Of Mirrors	24 Feb 69	CR 2 mix 2. Live performance. Incomplete.	Jimi Hendrix CD Flute FLCD 2008	Royal Albert Hall, London, England	JHE	Chris Wood / Flute, Rocky Dziddzournou / Bongos
Room Full Of Mirrors	24 Feb 69	CR 2 mix 3. Live performance. Stereo.	Royal Albert Hall CD Blimp 008 / 009 & Listen To This Eric CD JH 003 / 4	Royal Albert Hall, London, England	JHE	Chris Wood / Flute, Rocky Dziddzournou / Bongos

SONG TITLE	DATE	COMMENTS	RELEASE	LOCATION / VENUE	BAND	PERSONNEL
Room Full Of Mirrors	26 Feb 69	BR 1. An early studio version with overdubs added in 1988 by Noel & Mitch. Part of the Chandler tapes.	Studio Haze CD INA 6	Olympic Sound Studios, London, England	JHE	Noel Redding / Bass & Mitch Mitchell / Drum Overdubs In 1988
Room Full Of Mirrors	26 Feb 69	BR 1. An early studio version with overdubs added in 1988 by Noel & Mitch. Part of the Chandler tapes.	DeLane Lea And Olympic Outs CD Gold Standard CD-R	Olympic Sound Studios, London, England	JHE	Noel Redding / Bass & Mitch Mitchell / Drum Overdubs In 1988
Room Full Of Mirrors	26 Feb 69	BR 1. An early studio version with overdubs added in 1988 by Noel & Mitch. Part of the Chandler tapes.	Electric Ladyland Outtakes CD Invasion Unlimited IU 9417-1	Olympic Sound Studios, London, England	JHE	Noel Redding / Bass & Mitch Mitchell / Drum Overdubs In 1988
Room Full Of Mirrors	26 Feb 69	BR 1. An early studio version with overdubs added in 1988 by Noel & Mitch. Part of the Chandler tapes.	I Don't Live Today CD ACL 007	Olympic Sound Studios, London, England	JHE	Noel Redding / Bass & Mitch Mitchell / Drum Overdubs In 1988
Room Full Of Mirrors	26 Feb 69	BR 1. An early studio version with overdubs added in 1988 by Noel & Mitch. Part of the Chandler tapes.	Jimi: A Musical Legacy CD KTS BX 010	Olympic Sound Studios, London, England	JHE	Noel Redding / Bass & Mitch Mitchell / Drum Overdubs In 1988
Room Full Of Mirrors	26 Feb 69	BR 1. An early studio version with overdubs added in 1988 by Noel & Mitch. Part of the Chandler tapes.	Voodoo In Ladyland CD MUM MUCD 006	Olympic Sound Studios, London, England	JHE	Noel Redding / Bass & Mitch Mitchell / Drum Overdubs In 1988
Room Full Of Mirrors	03 May 69	BR 2. Live performance. The beginning of a medley that continued with 'Crash Landing', 'Midnight Lightning', & 'Gypsy Eyes'.	Hendrix, Busted In Toronto CD Venue VE 100502	Maple Leaf Gardens, Toronto, Canada	JHE	
Room Full Of Mirrors	03 May 69	BR 2. Live performance. The beginning of a medley that continued with 'Crash Landing', 'Midnight Lightning', & 'Gypsy Eyes'.	I Don't Live Today CD ACL 007	Maple Leaf Gardens, Toronto, Canada	JHE	
Room Full Of Mirrors	25 May 69	BR 3. Live performance. Part of a medley.	Historic Concert Vol 2 CD Midnight Beat MBCD 050	Santa Clara Pop Festival, San Jose, CA	JHE	
Room Full Of Mirrors	17 Nov 69	CR 1 mix 1.	Rainbow Bridge (CR) LP Reprise K44159	Record Plant, New York, NY	BOG	Ghetto Fighters / Backing Vocals
Room Full Of Mirrors	17 Nov 69	CR 1 mix 1.	Rainbow Bridge & More CD	Record Plant, New York, NY	BOG	Ghetto Fighters / Backing Vocals
Room Full Of Mirrors	17 Nov 69	CR 1 mix 1.	First Rays Of The New Rising Sun (CR) CD MCACD 11599	Record Plant, New York, NY	BOG	Ghetto Fighters / Backing Vocals
Room Full Of Mirrors	17 Nov 69	CR 1 mix 1.	Rainbow Bridge (CR) LP Reprise K44159	Record Plant, New York, NY	BOG	Ghetto Fighters / Backing Vocals
Room Full Of Mirrors	17 Nov 69	CR 1 mix 1.	Rainbow Bridge 2 CD JMH 003 / 2	Record Plant, New York, NY	BOG	Ghetto Fighters / Backing Vocals
Room Full Of Mirrors	17 Nov 69	CR 1 mix 2. Alternate mix.	Electric Hendrix Vol 1 CD Pyramid PYCD 030	Record Plant, New York, NY	BOG	Ghetto Fighters / Backing Vocals

Title	Date	Notes	Release	Location	Producer	Personnel
Room Full Of Mirrors	17 Nov 69	CR 1 mix 2. Alternate mix.	Lifelines (CR) CD Reprise 9 26435-2	Record Plant, New York, NY	BOG	Ghetto Fighters / Backing Vocals
Room Full Of Mirrors	17 Nov 69	CR 1 mix 2. Alternate mix.	Multicolored Blues CD Luna LU 9317	Record Plant, New York, NY	BOG	Ghetto Fighters / Backing Vocals
Room Full Of Mirrors	17 Nov 69	CR 1 mix 2. Alternate mix.	First Rays - The Sessions CD Whoopy Cat WKP 0002	Record Plant, New York, NY	BOG	Ghetto Fighters / Backing Vocals
Room Full Of Mirrors	17 Nov 69	CR 1 mix 2. Alternate mix.	Voodoo Blues CD Smurf	Record Plant, New York, NY	BOG	Ghetto Fighters / Backing Vocals
Room Full Of Mirrors	17 Nov 69	CR 1 mix 2. Alternate mix.	Every Way To Paradise CD Tintangel TIBX 021 / 22 / 23 / 24	Record Plant, New York, NY	BOG	Ghetto Fighters / Backing Vocals
Room Full Of Mirrors	17 Nov 69	CR 1 mix 2. Alternate mix.	Voodoo In Ladyland CD MUM MUCD 006	Record Plant, New York, NY	BOG	Ghetto Fighters / Backing Vocals
Room Full Of Mirrors	17 Nov 69	CR 1 mix 4. Unused mix.	Studio Haze CD INA 6	Record Plant, New York, NY	BOG	Ghetto Fighters / Backing Vocals
Room Full Of Mirrors	17 Nov 69	CR 1 mix 4. Unused mix.	Notes In Colours CD JHR 001 / 002	Record Plant, New York, NY	BOG	Ghetto Fighters / Backing Vocals
Room Full Of Mirrors	17 Nov 69	CR 1 mix 4. Unused mix.	Eyes And Imagination CD Third Stone TSD 18970	Record Plant, New York, NY	BOG	Ghetto Fighters / Backing Vocals
Room Full Of Mirrors	17 Nov 69	CR 1 mix 3.	Voodoo Soup (CR) CD MCA 11206	Record Plant, New York, NY	BOG	Ghetto Fighters / Backing Vocals, Bruce Gary / New Drums
Room Full Of Mirrors (Afternoon Blues Jam)	?? / Nov-Dec 69	BR 1. A jam with an unknown guitarist probably at one of Jimi's homes or apartments sometime in 1969. This is part of the track "Afternoon Blues Jam".	Two Sides Of The Same Genius LP Amazing Kornyphone TAKRL H677	New York Apartment	Jimi	Unknown / 2nd Guitar
Room Full Of Mirrors	?? / Nov-Dec 69	BR 1. A jam with an unknown guitarist probably at one of Jimi's homes or apartments sometime in 1969. This is continued from "Jam 2" on this release.	Apartment Jam 70 CD Spicy Essence	New York Apartment	Jimi	Unknown / 2nd Guitar
Room Full Of Mirrors	25 Apr 70	BR 4. Live performance. The beginning of a medley that segues through 'Hey Baby', 'Villanova Junction' and 'Freedom'.	Enjoy Jimi Hendrix LP Rubber Dubber 700-001-01	Los Angeles Forum, Los Angeles, CA	COL	
Room Full Of Mirrors	25 Apr 70	BR 4. Live performance. The beginning of a medley that segues through 'Hey Baby', 'Villanova Junction' and 'Freedom'.	Portrait Of Jimi Hendrix, A LP Catalog # Varies On Dead Wax	Los Angeles Forum, Los Angeles, CA	COL	
Room Full Of Mirrors	25 Apr 70	BR 4. Live performance. The beginning of a medley that segues through 'Hey Baby', 'Villanova Junction' and 'Freedom'.	Live At The Forum 1970 CD Whoopy Cat WKP 021 / 22	Los Angeles Forum, Los Angeles, CA	COL	

SONG TITLE	DATE	COMMENTS	RELEASE	LOCATION / VENUE	BAND	PERSONNEL
Room Full Of Mirrors	25 Apr 70	BR 4. Live performance. The beginning of a medley that segues through 'Hey Baby', 'Villanova Junction' and 'Freedom'. The Luna disc is from a tape source while the JHCD 528 disc is copied from vinyl.	Scuse Me While I Kiss The Sky CD Luna CD & JHCD 528	Los Angeles Forum, Los Angeles, CA	COL	
Room Full Of Mirrors	30 May 70	BR 6. Live performance.	Berkeley Soundchecks, The CD Whoopy Cat WKP 0008	Berkeley Community Theater, Berkeley, CA	COL	
Room Full Of Mirrors	30 May 70	BR 6. Live performance.	Jimi Plays Berkeley CD JMH 005 / 2	Berkeley Community Theater, Berkeley, CA Sound Check	COL	
Room Full Of Mirrors	13 Jun 70	BR 5. Live performance.	Baltimore Civic Center, June 13, 1970 CD Starquake SQ-09	Baltimore Civic Center, Baltimore, MD	COL	
Room Full Of Mirrors	04 Jul 70	CR 3. Live performance.	Stages Atlanta 70 (CR) CD Reprise 9 27632-2	2nd International Pop Festival, Atlanta, GA	COL	
Room Full Of Mirrors	04 Jul 70	CR 3. Live performance.	Atlanta CD JMH 009 / 02	2nd International Pop Festival, Atlanta, GA	COL	
Room Full Of Mirrors	04 Jul 70	CR 3. Live performance.	Oh, Atlanta CD Tendolar TDR-009	2nd International Pop Festival, Atlanta, GA	COL	
Room Full Of Mirrors	31 Aug 70	BR 7. Live performance.	Come On Stockholm CD No Label	Stora Scenen, Liesberg, Goteborg, Sweden	COL	
Room Full Of Mirrors	31 Aug 70	BR 7. Live performance.	Free Concert CD Midnight Beat MBCD 013	Stora Scenen, Tivoli Garden, Stockholm, Sweden	COL	
Room Full Of Mirrors	01 Sep 70	BR 7. Live performance.	Warm Hello Of The Sun, The CD	Stora Scenen, Liseberg Nojespark, Goteborg, Sweden	COL	
Room Full Of Mirrors	06 Sep 70	BR 7. Live performance.	Love & Peace CD Midnight Beat MBCD 015	Love And Peace Festival, Isle Of Fehrman, Germany	COL	
Room Full Of Mirrors	06 Sep 70	BR 7. Live performance.	Wink Of An Eye CD Whoopy Cat WKP 0033 / 34	Love And Peace Festival, Isle Of Fehrman, Germany	COL	
Room Full Of Mirrors Poetry Reading	?? / ?? / ??	A weird recording of Jimi reciting poetry (or is just a stream of consciousness?) to pre recorded music .	Black Gold CD Midnight Beat MBCD 058-062	Record Plant?	Jimi	
San Francisco Bay Blues	Fake	Not Jimi.	51st Anniversary CD Future Disc JMH 001 / 8		Fake	

Song	Date	Notes	Release	Location	Artist	Musicians
See Myself In You	?? Mar 70 ?	This is a recording by the group "Love" for the unreleased 'Black Beauty' album. Jimi's involvement is highly unlikely.	Midnight Sun CD Third Eye NK 007	Olympic Sound Studios, London, England	Love	
Send My Love To Linda	16 Jan 70	BR 1-3. Incomplete take #1- #3 from a composing tape.	First Rays Of The New Rising Sun CD Triangle PYCD 084-2	Record Plant, New York, NY	Solo	
Send My Love To Linda	16 Jan 70	BR 1-3. Incomplete take #1- #3 from a composing tape.	Diamonds In The Dust CD Midnight Beat MBCD 022 / 23	Record Plant, New York, NY	Solo	
Send My Love To Linda	16 Jan 70	BR 2. Incomplete take #2 from a composing tape.	Acoustic Jams CD Sphinx SX CD 001	Record Plant, New York, NY	Solo	
Send My Love To Linda	16 Jan 70	BR 2. Incomplete take #2 from a composing tape.	Lifelines (CR) CD Reprise 9 26435-2	Record Plant, New York, NY	Solo	
Send My Love To Linda	16 Jan 70	BR 2. Incomplete take #2 from a composing tape.	Get The Experience CD Invasion Unlimited IU 9424-1	Record Plant, New York, NY	Solo	
Send My Love To Linda	16 Jan 70	BR 2. Incomplete take #2 from a composing tape.	Black Strings CD CDM G-53 258	Record Plant, New York, NY	Solo	
Send My Love To Linda	16 Jan 70	BR 2. Incomplete take #2 from a composing tape. This appears to be an outtake.	Studio Experience CD Sodium Haze SH 099	Record Plant, New York, NY	Solo	
Send My Love To Linda / Live And Let Live	13-16 / May 69	BR 1. Part 1 of a composing jam in the studio that includes a false start and a longer take.	Electric Anniversary Jimi CD Midnight Beat MBCD 024	Record Plant, New York, NY	Jimi	Stephen Stills / Bass, Dallas Taylor / Drums
Send My Love To Linda / Live And Let Live	13-16 / May 69	BR 1. Part 1 of a composing jam in the studio that includes a false start and a longer take.	Copenhagen '70 CD Whoopy Cat WKP 044 / 45	Record Plant, New York, NY	Jimi	Stephen Stills / Bass, Dallas Taylor / Drums
Send My Love To Linda / Live And Let Live	13-16 / May 69	BR 2. Part 2 of a composing jam in the studio. One long take preceded by two breakdowns.	Black Gold CD Midnight Beat MBCD 058-062	Record Plant, New York, NY	Jimi	Stephen Stills / Bass, Dallas Taylor / Drums
Send My Love To Linda / Live And Let Live	13-16 / May 69	BR 2. Part 2 of a composing jam in the studio. One long take preceded by two breakdowns.	Hear My Freedom CD Kobra KRCR 010	Record Plant, New York, NY	Jimi	Stephen Stills / Bass, Dallas Taylor / Drums
Sergeant Pepper's Lonely Hearts Club Band	04 Sep 67	BR 1. Live performance.	Lost In Sweden CD Whoopy Cat WKP 0046 / 0047	Stora Scenen, Grona Lund, Stockholm, Sweden	JHE	
Sergeant Pepper's Lonely Hearts Club Band	05 Sep 67	CR 1. Live performance.	Live In Stockholm 1967 CD Document DR 003	Studio 4, Radiohuset, Stockholm, Sweden	JHE	
Sergeant Pepper's Lonely Hearts Club Band	05 Sep 67	CR 1. Live performance.	Wild Man Of Pop Plays Vol 1, The CD Pyramid RFTCD 003	Studio 4, Radiohuset, Stockholm, Sweden	JHE	
Sergeant Pepper's Lonely Hearts Club Band	05 Sep 67	CR 1. Live performance.	Stages Stockholm 67 (CR) CD Reprise 9 27632-2	Studio 4, Radiohuset, Stockholm, Sweden	JHE	

SONG TITLE	DATE	COMMENTS	RELEASE	LOCATION / VENUE	BAND	PERSONNEL
Sergeant Pepper's Lonely Hearts Club Band	05 Sep 67	CR 1. Live performance.	Official Bootleg Album, The CD Yellow Dog YD 051	Studio 4, Radiohuset, Stockholm, Sweden	JHE	
Sergeant Pepper's Lonely Hearts Club Band	05 Sep 67	CR 1. Live performance.	Recorded Live In Europe CD Bulldog BGCD 023	Studio 4, Radiohuset, Stockholm, Sweden	JHE	
Sergeant Pepper's Lonely Hearts Club Band	05 Sep 67	CR 1. Live performance.	Two Sides Of The Same Genius LP Amazing Kornyphone TAKRL H677	Studio 4, Radiohuset, Stockholm, Sweden	JHE	
Sergeant Pepper's Lonely Hearts Club Band	05 Sep 67	CR 1. Live performance.	Fire CD The Entertainers CD297	Studio 4, Radiohuset, Stockholm, Sweden	JHE	
Sergeant Pepper's Lonely Hearts Club Band	05 Sep 67	CR 1. Live performance.	In Europe 67 / 68 / 69 CD Vulture CD 009 / 2	Studio 4, Radiohuset, Stockholm, Sweden	JHE	
Sergeant Pepper's Lonely Hearts Club Band	05 Sep 67	CR 1. Live performance.	Very Best, The CD Irec / Retro MILCD-03	Studio 4, Radiohuset, Stockholm, Sweden	JHE	
Sergeant Pepper's Lonely Hearts Club Band	05 Sep 67	CR 1. Live performance.	Live CD DV More CDDV 2401	Studio 4, Radiohuset, Stockholm, Sweden	JHE	
Sergeant Pepper's Lonely Hearts Club Band	05 Sep 67	CR 1. Live performance.	Hey Joe CD Crocodile Beat CB 53039	Studio 4, Radiohuset, Stockholm, Sweden	JHE	
Sergeant Pepper's Lonely Hearts Club Band	05 Sep 67	CR 1. Live performance.	Complete BBC Session And..., The CD Last Bootleg Records LBR 036 / 2	Studio 4, Radiohuset, Stockholm, Sweden	JHE	
Sergeant Pepper's Lonely Hearts Club Band	05 Sep 67	CR 1. Live performance.	Jimi: A Musical Legacy CD KTS BX 010	Studio 4, Radiohuset, Stockholm, Sweden	JHE	
Sergeant Pepper's Lonely Hearts Club Band	05 Sep 67	CR 1. Live performance.	Foxy Lady CD Alegra CD 9008	Studio 4, Radiohuset, Stockholm, Sweden	JHE	
Sergeant Pepper's Lonely Hearts Club Band	05 Sep 67	CR 1. Live performance.	Greatest Hits Live CD Chartbusters CHER 089A	Studio 4, Radiohuset, Stockholm, Sweden	JHE	
Sergeant Pepper's Lonely Hearts Club Band	05 Sep 67	CR 1. Live performance.	Anthology CD Box 9	Studio 4, Radiohuset, Stockholm, Sweden	JHE	
Sergeant Pepper's Lonely Hearts Club Band	22 Dec 67	BR 2. Live performance. Officially released (although edited) on the 'Jimi Hendrix Live At Monterey' video tape and laserdisc.	Loaded Guitar LP Starlight SL 87013	Olympic Sound Studios, London, England	JHE	
Sergeant Pepper's Lonely Hearts Club Band	22 Dec 67	BR 2. Live performance. Officially released (although edited) on the 'Jimi Hendrix Live At Monterey' video tape and laserdisc.	Various Artists - Monterey Pop '67 CD Evil 2004 & Black Panther 042	Olympic Sound Studios, London, England	JHE	

Song	Date	Notes	Release	Venue	Artist	Personnel
Sergeant Pepper's Lonely Hearts Club Band	07 Jan 69	BR 3. Live performance.	Cat's Squirrel CD CS 001 / 2	Tivolis Konsertsal, Copenhagen, Denmark	JHE	
Sergeant Pepper's Lonely Hearts Club Band	07 Jan 69	BR 3. Live performance.	Live At The Hollywood Bowl LP RSR / International RSR 251	Tivolis Konsertsal, Copenhagen, Denmark 1st Show	JHE	
Sergeant Pepper's Lonely Hearts Club Band	07 Jan 69	BR 3. Live performance.	Fuckin' His Guitar For Denmark LP Polymore Or JH CO	Tivolis Konsertsal, Copenhagen, Denmark 1st Show	JHE	
Sergeant Pepper's Lonely Hearts Club Band	08 Jan 69	BR 4. Live performance.	Lost In Sweden CD Whoopy Cat WKP 0046 / 0047	Konserthuset, Stockholm, Sweden 1st Show	JHE	
Sergeant Pepper's Lonely Hearts Club Band	17 Feb 68	BR 5. Live performance.	Remember The Alamo CD	Will Rogers Auditorium, Fort Worth, TX	JHE	
Sergeant Pepper's Lonely Hearts Club Band	25 Feb 68	BR 6. Live performance.	Winterland Vol 2 CD Whoopy Cat WKP 00279 / 28	Civic Opera House, Chicago, IL	JHE	
Sergeant Pepper's Lonely Hearts Club Band	30 Aug 70	CR 2. Live performance.	Island Man CD Silver Rarities SIRA 39 / 40	Isle Of Wight Festival, Isle Of Wight, England	COL	
Sergeant Pepper's Lonely Hearts Club Band	30 Aug 70	CR 2. Live performance.	At The Isle Of Wight (CR) Laserdisc CBS / Sony CLSM 791	Isle Of Wight Festival, Isle Of Wight, England	COL	
Sergeant Pepper's Lonely Hearts Club Band	30 Aug 70	CR 2. Live performance.	Hendrix In The West (CR) LP Polydor 2302018 A	Isle Of Wight Festival, Isle Of Wight, England	COL	
Sergeant Pepper's Lonely Hearts Club Band	30 Aug 70	CR 2. Live performance.	Live! CD Black B-05	Isle Of Wight Festival, Isle Of Wight, England	COL	
Sergeant Pepper's Lonely Hearts Club Band	30 Aug 70	CR 2. Live performance.	Rarities On Compact Disc CD On The Radio	Isle Of Wight Festival, Isle Of Wight, England	COL	
Sergeant Pepper's Lonely Hearts Club Band	30 Aug 70	CR 2. Live performance.	Greatest Hits Live CD Chartbusters CHER 089A	Isle Of Wight Festival, Isle Of Wight, England	COL	
Sergeant Pepper's Lonely Hearts Club Band	30 Aug 70	CR 2. Live performance.	Wight CD JMH 006 / 2	Isle Of Wight Festival, Isle Of Wight, England	COL	
Session Thing	15 Jun 70	BR 1. A very long (35 minute!) jam with members of the group Traffic. See "Jam Thing".	A Session- Jimi Hendrix And Traffic CD Oh Boy 1-9027	Electric Lady Studio, New York, NY	Jimi	Steve Winwood / Keyboards, Dave Palmer / Drums, Chris Wood / Flute, Unknown / Bass

SONG TITLE	DATE	COMMENTS	RELEASE	LOCATION / VENUE	BAND	PERSONNEL
Session Thing	15 Jun 70	BR 1. A very long (35 minute!) jam with members of the group Traffic. See "Jam Thing". Incomplete.	Not Just A Voodoo Chile CD Pilot HJCD 071	Electric Lady Studio, New York, NY	Jimi	Steve Winwood / Keyboards, Dave Palmer / Drums, Chris Wood / Flute, Unknown / Bass
Session Thing (Valleys Of Neptune)	15 Jun 70	BR 1. A very long (35 minute!) jam with members of the group Traffic. See "Jam Thing".	Every Way To Paradise CD Tintangel TIBX 021 / 22 / 23 / 24	Electric Lady Studio, New York, NY	Jimi	Steve Winwood / Keyboards, Dave Palmer / Drums, Chris Wood / Flute, Unknown / Bass
Shame Shame Shame	15 Feb 69	BR 1. An unreleased song that surfaced on the Chandler Tapes.	Electric Gypsy CD Scorpio? 40176 / 15	Olympic Sound Studios, London, England	JHE	Noel Redding / Bass In 1988
Shame Shame Shame	15 Feb 69	BR 1. An unreleased song that surfaced on the Chandler Tapes.	Studio Haze CD INA 6	Olympic Sound Studios, London, England	JHE	Noel Redding / Bass In 1988
Shame, Shame, Shame	15 Feb 69	BR 1. An unreleased song that surfaced on the Chandler Tapes.	DeLane Lea And Olympic Outs CD Gold Standard CD-R	Olympic Sound Studios, London, England	JHE	Noel Redding / Bass In 1988
Shame, Shame, Shame	15 Feb 69	BR 1. An unreleased song that surfaced on the Chandler Tapes.	Every Way To Paradise CD Tintangel TIBX 021 / 22 / 23 / 24	Olympic Sound Studios, London, England	JHE	Noel Redding / Bass In 1988
Shame, Shame, Shame	15 Feb 69	BR 1. An unreleased song that surfaced on the Chandler Tapes.	Jimi: A Musical Legacy CD KTS BX 010	Olympic Sound Studios, London, England	JHE	Noel Redding / Bass In 1988
She's So Fine	04 May 67	CR 1 mix 1 (stereo)	Axis: Bold As Love (CR) CD MCACD 11601	Olympic Sound Studios, London, England	JHE	Noel Redding / Lead Vocal
She's So Fine	04 May 67	CR 1 mix 2 (mono)	Axis: Bold As Love (CR) LP Track 612-003	Olympic Sound Studios, London, England	JHE	Noel Redding / Lead Vocal
She's So Fine	04 May 67	CR 1 mix 3 (stereo) The lead guitar is mixed differently in the stereo imaging.	Axis: Bold As Love (CR) LP Backtrack 11	Olympic Sound Studios, London, England	JHE	Noel Redding / Lead Vocal
She's So Fine	04 May 67	CR 1 mix 4. Unused mix with an alternate vocal by Noel.	Sotheby Auction Tapes, The CD Midnight Beat MBCD 010	Olympic Sound Studios, London, England	JHE	Noel Redding / Lead Vocal
She's So Fine	04 May 67	CR 1 mix 4. Unused mix with an alternate vocal by Noel.	51st Anniversary CD Future Disc JMH 001 / 8	Olympic Sound Studios, London, England	JHE	Noel Redding / Lead Vocal
She's So Fine	04 May 67	CR 1 mix 4. Unused mix with an alternate vocal by Noel.	Symphony Of Experience CD Third Stone Discs TDS 24966	Olympic Sound Studios, London, England	JHE	Noel Redding / Lead Vocal

Song	Date	Notes	Release	Location	Source	Personnel
She's So Fine	04 May 67	CR 1 mix 4. Unused mix with an alternate vocal by Noel.	Sotheby's Private Reels CD JHR 003 / 004	Olympic Sound Studios, London, England	JHE	Noel Redding / Lead Vocal
She's So Fine	04 May 67	CR 1 mix 4. Unused mix with an alternate vocal by Noel.	Get The Experience CD Invasion Unlimited IU 9424-1	Olympic Sound Studios, London, England	JHE	Noel Redding / Lead Vocal
She's So Fine	04 May 67	CR 1 mix 4. Unused mix with an alternate vocal by Noel.	Completer, The CD Whoopy Cat WKP 0018 / 19	Olympic Sound Studios, London, England	JHE	Noel Redding / Lead Vocal
She's So Fine	04 May 67		Jimi: A Musical Legacy CD KTS BX 010	Olympic Sound Studios, London, England	JHE	Noel Redding / Lead Vocal
She's So Fine	04 May 67	CR 1 mix 4. Unused mix with an alternate vocal by Noel.	Sotheby's Reels, The CD Gold Standard TOM-800	Olympic Sound Studios, London, England	JHE	Noel Redding / Lead Vocal
She's So Fine	04 May 67	CR 1 mix 4. Unused mix with an alternate vocal by Noel.	Living Reels Vol 1 CD JMH 011	Olympic Sound Studios, London, England	JHE	Noel Redding / Lead Vocal
She's So Fine	04 May 67	Not Jimi	King Of Gypsies CD Rockyssimo RK 001	Olympic Sound Studios, London, England	Fake	Noel Redding / Lead Vocal
Ships Passing In The Night	14 Apr 69	BR 1. A studio run through of an unreleased song with some unknown musicians.	Diamonds In The Dust CD Midnight Beat MBCD 022 / 23	Record Plant, New York, NY	Jimi	Unknown / Piano, Unknown / Trumpet
Ships Passing In The Night	14 Apr 69	BR 1. A studio run through of an unreleased song with some unknown musicians.	I Don't Live Today CD ACL 007	Record Plant, New York, NY	Jimi	Unknown / Piano, Unknown / Trumpet
Ships Passing In The Night	14 Apr 69	BR 1. A studio run through of an unreleased song with some unknown musicians.	Jimi: A Musical Legacy CD KTS BX 010	Record Plant, New York, NY	Jimi	Unknown / Piano, Unknown / Trumpet
Ships Passing In The Night	14 Apr 69	BR 1. A studio run through of an unreleased song with some unknown musicians.	First Rays Of The New Rising Sun CD Triangle PYCD 084-2	Record Plant, New York, NY	Jimi	Unknown / Piano, Unknown / Trumpet
Ships Passing In The Night	14 Apr 69	BR 1. A studio run through of an unreleased song with some unknown musicians.	Cherokee Mist CD Triangle PYCD 070	Record Plant, New York, NY	Jimi	Unknown / Piano, Unknown / Trumpet
Ships Passing In The Night (Alcatraz)	14 Apr 69	BR 1. A studio run through of an unreleased song with some unknown musicians.	Kiss The Skies CD Mum MUCD 024	Record Plant, New York, NY	Jimi	Unknown / Piano, Unknown / Trumpet
Shokan Jam # 1 (Instrumental Jam 3)	?? Aug 69	BR 1. One of the instrumental jams recorded at Jimi's house in Shokan prior to the Woodstock show.	Woodstock Rehearsals CD Midnight Beat MBCD 009	Shokan House, Woodstock, NY	GSRB	
Shokan Jam # 1 (Instrumental)	?? Aug 69	BR 1. One of the instrumental jams re-corded at Jimi's house in Shokan prior to the Woodstock show.	Shokan Sunrise CD	Shokan House, Woodstock, NY	GSRB	

SONG TITLE	DATE	COMMENTS	RELEASE	LOCATION / VENUE	BAND	PERSONNEL
Shokan Jam # 2	?? Aug 69	BR 2. A second instrumental jam recorded at Jimi's house in Shokan prior to the Woodstock show.	Woodstock Rehearsals CD Midnight Beat MBCD 009	Shokan House, Woodstock, NY	GSRB	
Shokan Jam # 2 (Shokan Sunrise)	?? Aug 69	BR 2. A second instrumental jam recorded at Jimi's house in Shokan prior to the Woodstock show.	Shokan Sunrise CD	Shokan House, Woodstock, NY	GSRB	
Shotgun	?? / ?? 65	BR 1. Live TV performance.	Screaming Eagle CD Pink Poodle POO 001	Unknown	Jimi	The Breakaways / Backing Vocals
Skin		This is a recording by the group "Love" for the unreleased 'Black Beauty' album. Jimi's involvement is highly unlikely.	Midnight Sun CD Third Eye NK 007	Olympic Sound Studios, London, England	Love	
Slow Walking Talk	25 Oct 68	CR 1. This is Jimi playing bass guitar for a Robert Wyatt recording.	51st Anniversary CD Future Disc JMH 001 / 8	T.T.G. Studios, Hollywood, CA	Jimi	Jimi Hendrix / Bass, Robert Wyatt / Keyboards, Drums & Vocals
Slow Walking Talk	25 Oct 68	CR 1. This is Jimi playing bass guitar for a Robert Wyatt recording.	Calling Long Distance (CR) CD Unvibes & Booted On Dynamite DS930055	T.T.G. Studios, Hollywood, CA	Jimi	Jimi Hendrix / Bass, Robert Wyatt / Keyboards, Drums & Vocals
Solo Acoustic		No Jimi.	Not Just A Voodoo Chile CD Pilot HJCD 071		Fake	
Something You Got	26 Dec 65	CR 1. Live performance commercially released on the LP 'Mr. Pitiful' on the Astan label.	King Of Gypsies CD Rockyssimo RK 001	George's Club 20, Hackensack, NJ	CKB	
Somewhere	13 Mar 68	CR 1 mix 1. This has had the original musicians replaced.	Crash Landing (CR) LP Reprise MS 2204	Sound Center, New York, NY	Jimi	Crash Landing Line Up 1974
Somewhere (Somewhere Over The Rainbow)	13 Mar 68	CR 1 mix 2. The unadulterated version of the recording with the original band line up.	Talent And Feeling Vol 2 CD Extremely Rare EXR 22	Sound Center, New York, NY	Jimi	Mitch Mitchell / Drums, Jimi Or Stephen Stills / Bass
Somewhere	13 Mar 68	CR 1 mix 2. The unadulterated version of the recording with the original band line up.	Unsurpassed Studio Takes CD Yellow Dog YD 050	Sound Center, New York, NY	Jimi	Mitch Mitchell / Drums, Jimi Or Stephen Stills / Bass
Somewhere	13 Mar 68	CR 1 mix 2. The unadulterated version of the recording with the original band line up.	Gypsy Charm CD Mum MUCD 018	Sound Center, New York, NY	Jimi	Mitch Mitchell / Drums, Jimi Or Stephen Stills / Bass
Somewhere	13 Mar 68	CR 1 mix 2. The unadulterated version of the recording with the original band line up.	Sotheby's Reels, The CD Gold Standard TOM-800	Sound Center, New York, NY	Jimi	Mitch Mitchell / Drums, Jimi Or Stephen Stills / Bass
Somewhere	13 Mar 68	CR 1 mix 2. The unadulterated version of the recording with the original band line up.	Living Reels Vol 2 CD JMH 012 / 2	Sound Center, New York, NY	Jimi	Mitch Mitchell / Drums, Jimi Or Stephen Stills / Bass
Somewhere	13 Mar 68	CR 1 mix 3. This version has the original band line up but with reverb added to the mix.	Ladyland In Flames LP Marshall Records JIMI 1,2,3,4	Sound Center, New York, NY	Jimi	Mitch Mitchell / Drums, Jimi Or Stephen Stills / Bass

Song	Date	Notes	Source	Location	Performer	Musicians
Somewhere	13 Mar 68	CR 1 mix 3. This version has the original band line up but with reverb added to the mix.	1968 AD Part Two CD Whoopy Cat WKP 0013	Sound Center, New York, NY	Jimi	Mitch Mitchell / Drums, Jimi Or Stephen Stills / Bass
Somewhere (I See Fingers)	13 Mar 68	CR 1 mix 3. This version has the original band line up but with reverb added to the mix.	TTG Studios ???? CD WHOAMI WAI 015	Sound Center, New York, NY	Jimi	Mitch Mitchell / Drums, Jimi Or Stephen Stills / Bass
Somewhere	13 Mar 68	CR 1 mix 3. This version has the original band line up but with reverb added to the mix.	51st Anniversary CD Future Disc JMH 001 / 8	Sound Center, New York, NY	Jimi	Mitch Mitchell / Drums, Jimi Or Stephen Stills / Bass
Somewhere	13 Mar 68	CR 1 mix 3. This version has the original band line up but with reverb added to the mix. This is mastered twice on this release.	51st Anniversary CD Future Disc JMH 001 / 8	Sound Center, New York, NY	Jimi	Mitch Mitchell / Drums, Jimi Or Stephen Stills / Bass
Somewhere	13 Mar 68	CR 1 mix 3. This version has the original band line up but with reverb added to the mix.	Flames CD Missing In Action ACT 1	Sound Center, New York, NY	Jimi	Mitch Mitchell / Drums, Jimi Or Stephen Stills / Bass
Somewhere	13 Mar 68	CR 1 mix 3. This version has the original band line up but with reverb added to the mix.	Jimi: A Musical Legacy CD KTS BX 010	Sound Center, New York, NY	Jimi	Mitch Mitchell / Drums, Jimi Or Stephen Stills / Bass
Somewhere	13 Mar 68	CR 1 mix 3. This version has the original band line up but with reverb added to the mix.	Living Reels Vol 2 CD JMH 012 / 2	Sound Center, New York, NY	Jimi	Mitch Mitchell / Drums, Jimi Or Stephen Stills / Bass
Somewhere	13 Mar 68	CR 1 mix 4. Unused mix of the CR's isolated guitar and bass tracks.	Paper Airplanes CD Midnight Beat MBCD 25	Sound Center, New York, NY	Jimi	Crash Landing Line Up 1974
Somewhere (Somewhere Over The Rainbow)	13 Mar 68	CR 1 mix 5. Unused mix of the CR's isolated guitar track only.	Electric Hendrix Vol 2 CD Pyramid PYCD 031	Sound Center, New York, NY	Jimi	Mitch Mitchell / Drums, Jimi Or Stephen Stills / Bass
Somewhere	13 Mar 68	CR 1 mix 5. Unused mix of the CR's isolated guitar track only.	Paper Airplanes CD Midnight Beat MBCD 25	Sound Center, New York, NY	Jimi	
Somewhere (Where Some)	13 Mar 68	CR 1 mix 5. Unused mix of the CR's isolated guitar track only.	Every Way To Paradise CD Tintangel TIBX 021 / 22 / 23 / 24	Sound Center, New York, NY	Jimi	
Soul Food (That's What I Like)	?? / ?? 63	CR 1. Copied from the 45 with Lonnie Youngblood.	Whipper CD Pilz 447400-2	Unknown	Jimi	Lonnie Youngblood / Sax
Soul Food (That's What I Like)	?? / ?? 63	CR 1. Copied from the 45 with Lonnie Youngblood.	Jimi: A Musical Legacy CD KTS BX 010	Unknown	Jimi	Lonnie Youngblood / Sax
South Saturn Delta	?? Apr 68	BR 1. From a home composing tape.	Acoustic Jams CD Sphinx SX CD 001	New York Apartment	Solo	
South Saturn Delta	?? Apr 68	BR 1. From a home composing tape.	Black Gold CD Midnight Beat MBCD 058-062	New York Apartment	Solo	
South Saturn Delta	?? Jan? 68?	CR 1 mix 1.	Lifelines (CR) CD Reprise 9 26435-2	Olympic Sound Studios, London, England	Jimi	Dave Mason / Backing Vocals, Unknown / Drums
South Saturn Delta	?? Jan? 68?	CR 1 mix 2. This is the original version of the CR 1 mix 1 prior to overdubs.	Sotheby Auction Tapes, The CD Midnight Beat MBCD 010	Olympic Sound Studios, London, England	Jimi	Dave Mason / Backing Vocals, Unknown / Drums

SONG TITLE	DATE	COMMENTS	RELEASE	LOCATION / VENUE	BAND	PERSONNEL
South Saturn Delta (Jazzy Jamming)	?? Jan? 68?	CR 1 mix 2. This is the original version of the CR 1 mix 1 prior to overdubs.	51st Anniversary CD Future Disc JMH 001 / 8	Olympic Sound Studios, London, England	Jimi	Dave Mason / Backing Vocals, Unknown / Drums
South Saturn Delta (Jam #1)	?? Jan? 68?	CR 1 mix 2. This is the original version of the CR 1 mix 1 prior to overdubs.	Sotheby's Private Reels CD JHR 003 / 004	Olympic Sound Studios, London, England	Jimi	Dave Mason / Backing Vocals, Unknown / Drums
South Saturn Delta (Jam #2)	?? Jan? 68?	CR 1 mix 2. This is the original version of the CR 1 mix 1 prior to overdubs and mastered twice on this disc.	Sotheby's Private Reels CD JHR 003 / 004	Olympic Sound Studios, London, England	Jimi	Dave Mason / Backing Vocals, Unknown / Drums
South Saturn Delta	?? Jan? 68?	CR 1 mix 2. This is the original version of the CR 1 mix 1 prior to overdubs.	Living Reels Vol 1 CD JMH 011	Olympic Sound Studios, London, England	Jimi	Dave Mason / Backing Vocals, Unknown / Drums
South Saturn Delta	?? Jan? 68?	CR 1 mix 1 with part of CR 1 mix 2 edited onto the end.	I Don't Live Today CD ACL 007	Olympic Sound Studios, London, England	Jimi	Dave Mason / Backing Vocals, Unknown / Drums
South Saturn Delta	?? Jan? 68?	CR 2.	South Saturn Delta (CR) CD MCACD 11684	Record Plant, New York, NY	Jimi	Jimi Hendrix / Bass, Mitch Mitchell / Drums, Larry Faucette / Percussion, Unknown / Horns
Spanish Castle Magic	27 Oct 67	BR 1. An instrumental take from the same session that produced the CR 1.	Sotheby Auction Tapes, The CD Midnight Beat MBCD 010	Olympic Sound Studios, London, England	JHE	
Spanish Castle Magic	27 Oct 67	BR 1. An instrumental take from the same session that produced the CR 1.	Symphony Of Experience CD Third Stone Discs TDS 24966	Olympic Sound Studios, London, England	JHE	
Spanish Castle Magic	27 Oct 67	BR 1. An instrumental take from the same session that produced the CR 1.	Lost Experience, The, CD JHCD203	Olympic Sound Studios, London, England	JHE	
Spanish Castle Magic	27 Oct 67	BR 1. An instrumental take from the same session that produced the CR 1.	Sotheby's Private Reels CD JHR 003 / 004	Olympic Sound Studios, London, England	JHE	
Spanish Castle Magic	27 Oct 67	BR 1. An instrumental take from the same session that produced the CR 1. This is mastered twice and repeated on this release.	Sotheby's Private Reels CD JHR 003 / 004	Olympic Sound Studios, London, England	JHE	
Spanish Castle Magic	27 Oct 67	BR 1. An instrumental take from the same session that produced the CR 1.	Get The Experience CD Invasion Unlimited IU 9424-1	Olympic Sound Studios, London, England	JHE	
Spanish Castle Magic	27 Oct 67	BR 1. An instrumental take from the same session that produced the CR 1.	Notes In Colours CD JHR 001 / 002	Olympic Sound Studios, London, England	JHE	

Title	Date	Notes	Release	Location		
Spanish Castle Magic	27 Oct 67	BR 1. An instrumental take from the same session that produced the CR 1.	Sotheby's Reels, The CD Gold Standard TOM-800	Olympic Sound Studios, London, England	JHE	
Spanish Castle Magic	27 Oct 67	BR 1. An instrumental take from the same session that produced the CR 1.	Living Reels Vol 1 CD JMH 011	Olympic Sound Studios, London, England	JHE	
Spanish Castle Magic	27 Oct 67	CR 1 mix 1 (stereo).	Axis: Bold As Love (CR) CD MCACD 11601	Olympic Sound Studios, London, England	JHE	
Spanish Castle Magic	27 Oct 67	CR 1 mix 1 (stereo).	Legacy (CR) LP Polydor	Olympic Sound Studios, London, England	JHE	
Spanish Castle Magic	27 Oct 67	CR 1 mix 2 (mono).	Axis: Bold As Love (CR) LP Track 612-003	Olympic Sound Studios, London, England	JHE	
Spanish Castle Magic	27 Oct 67	CR 1 mix 2. An unused mix of the CR 1.	Notes In Colours CD JHR 001 / 002	Olympic Sound Studios, London, England	JHE	
Spanish Castle Magic	15 Dec 67	CR 2. BBC performance.	Guitar Hero CD Document DR 013	Top Gear, BBC Playhouse Theatre, London, England	JHE	
Spanish Castle Magic	15 Dec 67	CR 2. BBC performance.	Primal Keys LP Impossible Record Works	Top Gear, BBC Playhouse Theatre, London, England	JHE	
Spanish Castle Magic	15 Dec 67	CR 2. BBC performance.	Radio One (CR) CD Rykodisc RCD 20078	Top Gear, BBC Playhouse Theatre, London, England	JHE	
Spanish Castle Magic	15 Dec 67	CR 2. BBC performance.	51st Anniversary CD Future Disc JMH 001 / 8	Top Gear, BBC Playhouse Theatre, London, England	JHE	
Spanish Castle Magic	15 Dec 67	CR 2. BBC performance.	Ultimate BBC Collection CD Classical CL006	Top Gear, BBC Playhouse Theatre, London, England	JHE	
Spanish Castle Magic	15 Dec 67	CR 2. BBC performance.	Live In London 1967 CD Koine Records K881104	Top Gear, BBC Playhouse Theatre, London, England	JHE	
Spanish Castle Magic	15 Dec 67	CR 2. BBC performance.	Live In Concert 1967 CD Living Legend LLR-CD 001	Top Gear, BBC Playhouse Theatre, London, England	JHE	
Spanish Castle Magic	15 Dec 67	CR 2. BBC performance.	In Concert CD Starlife ST 3612	Top Gear, BBC Playhouse Theatre, London, England	JHE	

SONG TITLE	DATE	COMMENTS	RELEASE	LOCATION / VENUE	BAND	PERSONNEL
Spanish Castle Magic	15 Dec 67	CR 2. BBC performance.	Jewel Box CD Home HR-5824-3	Top Gear, BBC Playhouse Theatre, London, England	JHE	
Spanish Castle Magic	15 Dec 67	CR 2. BBC performance.	Complete BBC Session And... The CD Last Bootleg Records LBR 036 / 2	Top Gear, BBC Playhouse Theatre, London, England	JHE	
Spanish Castle Magic	15 Dec 67	CR 2. BBC performance.	BBC Sessions (CR) CD MCACD 2-11742	Top Gear, BBC Playhouse Theatre, London, England	JHE	
Spanish Castle Magic	07 Jan 68	BR 2. Live performance.	Cat's Squirrel CD CS 001 / 2	Tivolis Konsertsal, Copenhagen, Denmark	JHE	
Spanish Castle Magic	07 Jan 68	BR 2. Live performance.	Fuckin' His Guitar For Denmark LP Polymore Or JH CO	Tivolis Konsertsal, Copenhagen, Denmark	JHE	
Spanish Castle Magic	08 Jan 68	BR 3. Live performance.	Lost In Sweden CD Whoopy Cat WKP 0046 / 0047	Konserthuset, Stockholm, Sweden	JHE	
Spanish Castle Magic	16 Feb 68	BR 4. Live performance.	Biggest Square In The Building, The CD Reverb Music 1993	State Fair Music Hall, Dallas, TX	JHE	
Spanish Castle Magic	16 Feb 68	BR 4. Live performance.	Scuse Me While I Kiss The Sky CD Sonic Zoom SZ 1001	State Fair Music Hall, Dallas, TX	JHE	
Spanish Castle Magic	16 Feb 68	BR 4. Live performance.	Scuse Me While I Kiss The Sky CD Sonic Zoom SZ 1001	State Fair Music Hall, Dallas, TX	JHE	
Spanish Castle Magic	19 Mar 68	BR 5. Live performance.	Thanks Ottawa For The Memories CD Luna 9319	Capitol Theatre, Ottawa, Canada	JHE	
Spanish Castle Magic	19 Mar 68	BR 5. Live performance.	Canadian Club CD WPOCM 0888 D 006-2	Capitol Theatre, Ottawa, Canada	JHE	
Spanish Castle Magic	19 Mar 68	BR 5. Live performance.	Live From Ottawa LP Starlight SL 87010	Capitol Theatre, Ottawa, Canada	JHE	
Spanish Castle Magic	19 Mar 68	BR 5. Live performance.	Superconcert 1968 CD Firepower FP03	Capitol Theatre, Ottawa, Canada	JHE	
Spanish Castle Magic	12 Oct 68	CR 3. Live performance.	Winterland Days, The CD Manic Depression 001	Winterland Theatre, San Francisco, CA 2nd Show	JHE	

Song	Date	Reference	Release	Venue	Type
Spanish Castle Magic	12 Oct 68	CR 3. Live performance.	51st Anniversary CD Future Disc JMH 001 / 8	Winterland Theatre, San Francisco, CA 2nd Show	JHE
Spanish Castle Magic	12 Oct 68	CR 3. Live performance.	Winterland Vol 2 CD Whoopy Cat WKP 00279 / 28	Winterland Theatre, San Francisco, CA 2nd Show	JHE
Spanish Castle Magic	12 Oct 68	CR 3. Live performance.	Rarities CD The Genuine Pig TGP-CD-091	Winterland Theatre, San Francisco, CA 2nd Show	JHE
Spanish Castle Magic	12 Oct 68	CR 3. Live performance.	Calling Long Distance (CR) CD Univibes & Booted On Dynamite DS930055	Winterland Theatre, San Francisco, CA 2nd Show	JHE
Spanish Castle Magic	12 Oct 68	CR 3. Live performance.	Jimi: A Musical Legacy CD KTS BX 010	Winterland Theatre, San Francisco, CA 2nd Show	JHE
Spanish Castle Magic	12 Oct 68	CR 4. Live performance.	Winterland Vol 3 CD Whoopy Cat WKP 0029 / 30	Winterland Theatre, San Francisco, CA 2nd Show	JHE
Spanish Castle Magic	12 Oct 68	CR 4. Live performance.	Live At Winterland (CR) CD Rykodisc RCD 20038	Winterland Theatre, San Francisco, CA 2nd Show	JHE
Spanish Castle Magic	12 Oct 68	CR 4. Live performance.	Lost Winterland Tapes CD Starquake SQ 051-2	Winterland Theatre, San Francisco, CA 2nd Show	JHE
Spanish Castle Magic	28 Nov 68	BR 6. Live performance.	Have Mercy On Me Baby CD Midnight Beat MBCD 038	Philharmonic Hall, New York, NY	JHE
Spanish Castle Magic	28 Nov 68	BR 6. Live performance.	Live At Philharmonic Hall LP Sagittarius LTD	Philharmonic Hall, New York, NY	JHE
Spanish Castle Magic	08 Jan 69	BR 7. Live performance.	Cat's Squirrel CD CS 001 / 2	Loresberg Cirkus, Goteborg, Sweden	JHE
Spanish Castle Magic	09 Jan 69	BR 8. Live performance.	On The Killing Floor Swingin' Pig TSP-012-2	Konserthuset, Stockholm, Sweden 1st Show	JHE
Spanish Castle Magic	09 Jan 69	BR 8. Live performance.	Can You Here Me Me LP Hemero 01 / KERI	Konserthuset, Stockholm, Sweden 1st Show	JHE
Spanish Castle Magic	09 Jan 69	BR 8. Live performance.	Electronic Church Music CD Pyramid PYCD 023	Konserthuset, Stockholm, Sweden 1st Show	JHE

SONG TITLE	DATE	COMMENTS	RELEASE	LOCATION / VENUE	BAND	PERSONNEL
Spanish Castle Magic	09 Jan 69	BR 8. Live performance.	In Concert CD Starlife ST 3612	Konserthuset, Stockholm, Sweden 1st Show	JHE	
Spanish Castle Magic	09 Jan 69	BR 9. Live performance.	On The Killing Floor Swingin' Pig TSP-012-2	Konserthuset, Stockholm, Sweden 2nd Show	JHE	
Spanish Castle Magic	09 Jan 69	BR 9. Live performance.	Legendary Star Club Tapes, The CD The Early Years 02-CD-3309	Konserthuset, Stockholm, Sweden 2nd Show	JHE	
Spanish Castle Magic	09 Jan 69	BR 9. Live performance.	In Europe 67 / 68 / 69 CD Vulture CD 009 / 2	Konserthuset, Stockholm, Sweden 2nd Show	JHE	
Spanish Castle Magic	09 Jan 69	BR 9. Live performance.	Jimi Hendrix Experience CD Rockstars In Concert 6127092	Konserthuset, Stockholm, Sweden 2nd Show	JHE	
Spanish Castle Magic	09 Jan 69	BR 9. Live performance.	Experience II CD More MTT 1021	Konserthuset, Stockholm, Sweden 2nd Show	JHE	
Spanish Castle Magic	10 Jan 69	BR 10. Live performance.	Welcome To The Electric Circus Vol 1 CD Midnight Beat 016	Falkoner Centret, Copenhagen, Denmark 1st Show	JHE	
Spanish Castle Magic	10 Jan 69	BR 11. Live performance.	Jimi In Denmark (CR) CD UniVibes 1003 & Booted On Dynamite Studios	Falkoner Centret, Copenhagen, Denmark 2nd Show	JHE	
Spanish Castle Magic	10 Jan 69	BR 11. Live performance.	Jimi In Denmark (CR) CD UniVibes 1003 & Booted On Dynamite Studios	Falkoner Centret, Copenhagen, Denmark	JHE	
Spanish Castle Magic	10 Jan 69	BR 11. Live performance.	Live In Copenhagen CD The Swingin' Pig TSP-220-2	Falkoner Centret, Copenhagen, Denmark	JHE	
Spanish Castle Magic	23 Jan 69	BR 12. Live performance.	Up Against The Berlin Wall CD Midnight Beat MBCD 046	Sportpalast, Berlin, Germany	JHE	
Spanish Castle Magic	18 Feb 69	BR 13. Live performance.	First Night At The Royal Albert Hall CD Midnight Beat MBCD 047 / 48	Royal Albert Hall, London, England	JHE	
Spanish Castle Magic	26 Apr 69	BR 14. Live performance.	Electric Jimi CD Jaguarondi Records	Los Angeles Forum, Los Angeles, CA	JHE	

Song	Date	Notes	Release	Venue	Source
Spanish Castle Magic	26 Apr 69	BR 14. Live performance.	I Don't Live Today, Maybe Tomorrow CD Living Legend LRCD 030	Los Angeles Forum, Los Angeles, CA	JHE
Spanish Castle Magic	26 Apr 69	BR 14. Live performance.	Live USA CD Imtrat 902-001	Los Angeles Forum, Los Angeles, CA	JHE
Spanish Castle Magic	26 Apr 69	BR 14. Live performance.	Very Best, The CD Irec / Retro MILCD-03	Los Angeles Forum, Los Angeles, CA	JHE
Spanish Castle Magic	26 Apr 69	BR 14. Live performance.	Jimi Hendrix CD Flute FLCD 2008	Los Angeles Forum, Los Angeles, CA	JHE
Spanish Castle Magic	26 Apr 69	BR 14. Live performance.	Anthology CD Box 9	Los Angeles Forum, Los Angeles, CA	JHE
Spanish Castle Magic	27 Apr 69	CR 7. Live performance.	Live At The Oakland Coliseum (CR) CD Dagger Records DBRO-11743	Oakland Coliseum, Oakland, CA	JHE
Spanish Castle Magic	03 May 69	BR 15. Live performance. Part of a medley that also includes with 'Little Miss Lover' and '3rd Stone From The Sun'.	Hendrix, Busted In Toronto CD Venue VE 100502	Maple Leaf Gardens, Toronto, Canada	JHE
Spanish Castle Magic	03 May 69	BR 15. Live performance. Part of a medley that also includes with 'Little Miss Lover' and '3rd Stone From The Sun'.	I Don't Live Today CD ACL 007	Maple Leaf Gardens, Toronto, Canada	JHE
Spanish Castle Magic	17 May 69	BR 16. Live performance. Part of a medley with 'Sunshine Of Your Love'.	One Night At The Arena CD Venue VE 100501	Rhode Island Arena, Providence, RI	JHE
Spanish Castle Magic	18 May 69	BR 17. Live performance.	Wink Of An Eye CD Whoopy Cat WKP 0033 / 34	Madison Square Garden, New York, NY	JHE
Spanish Castle Magic	18 May 69	BR 17. Live performance.	Roman Coliseum, The CD Starquake SQ 11	Madison Square Garden, New York, NY	JHE
Spanish Castle Magic	24 May 69	CR 5. Live performance.	Stages San Diego 69 (CR) CD Reprise 9 27632-2	San Diego Sports Arena, San Diego, CA	JHE
Spanish Castle Magic	24 May 69	CR 5. Live performance.	Midnight Magic CD Neutral Zone NZCD 89012	San Diego Sports Arena, San Diego, CA	JHE
Spanish Castle Magic	24 May 69	CR 5. Live performance.	Don't Miss Him This Time CD Pyramid PYCD 096	San Diego Sports Arena, San Diego, CA	JHE
Spanish Castle Magic	24 May 69	CR 5. Live performance.	Atlanta CD JMH 009 / 02	2nd International Pop Festival, Atlanta, GA	COL

SONG TITLE	DATE	COMMENTS	RELEASE	LOCATION / VENUE	BAND	PERSONNEL
Spanish Castle Magic	25 May 69	BR 18. Live performance.	Historic Concert Vol 2 CD Midnight Beat MBCD 050	Santa Clara Pop Festival, San Jose, CA	JHE	
Spanish Castle Magic	29 Jun 69	BR 19. Live performance.	Wink Of An Eye CD Whoopy Cat WKP 0033 / 34	Mile High Stadium, Denver, CO	JHE	
Spanish Castle Magic	?? Aug 69	BR 20. Live performance.	Woodstock Rehearsals CD Midnight Beat MBCD 009	Shokan House, Woodstock, NY	GSRB	
Spanish Castle Magic	14 Aug 69	BR 20. Live performance.	Gypsy Sun And Rainbows CD Manic Depression MDCD 05 / 06	Shokan House, Woodstock, NY	GSRB	
Spanish Castle Magic	14 Aug 69	BR 20. Live performance.	Woodstock Monday, August 18 1969, 8AM CD JMH 008	Shokan House, Woodstock, NY	GSRB	
Spanish Castle Magic	18 Aug 69	BR 21. Live performance.	Woodstock Nation CD Wild Bird 89090 1 / 2	Woodstock Music And Art Fair, Bethel, NY	GSRB	
Spanish Castle Magic	18 Aug 69	BR 21. Live performance.	Gypsy Sun And Rainbows CD Manic Depression MDCD 05 / 06	Woodstock Music And Art Fair, Bethel, NY	GSRB	
Spanish Castle Magic	18 Aug 69	BR 21. Live performance.	Woodstock Monday, August 18 1969, 8AM CD JMH 008	Woodstock Music And Art Fair, Bethel, NY	GSRB	
Spanish Castle Magic	25 Apr 70	BR 22. Live performance.	Enjoy Jimi Hendrix LP Rubber Dubber 700-001-01	Los Angeles Forum, Los Angeles, CA	COL	
Spanish Castle Magic	25 Apr 70	BR 22. Live performance.	Portrait Of Jimi Hendrix, A LP Catalog # Varies On Dead Wax	Los Angeles Forum, Los Angeles, CA	COL	
Spanish Castle Magic	25 Apr 70	BR 22. Live performance.	Live At The Forum 1970 CD Whoopy Cat WKP 021 / 22	Los Angeles Forum, Los Angeles, CA	COL	
Spanish Castle Magic	25 Apr 70	BR 22. Live performance. The Luna disc is from a tape source while the JHCD 528 disc is copied from vinyl.	Scuse Me While I Kiss The Sky CD Luna CD & JHCD 528	Los Angeles Forum, Los Angeles, CA	COL	
Spanish Castle Magic	04 Jul 70	CR 7. Live performance.	At The Atlanta Pop Festival (CR) Laserdisc BMG BVLP 77 (74321-109871)	2nd International Pop Festival, Atlanta, GA	COL	

Song	Date	Performance	Release	Venue	COL
Spanish Castle Magic	04 Jul 70	CR 7. Live performance.	Stages Atlanta 1970 (CR) CD Reprise 9 27632-2	2nd International Pop Festival, Atlanta, GA	COL
Spanish Castle Magic	04 Jul 70	CR 7. Live performance.	Atlanta CD JMH 009 / 02	2nd International Pop Festival, Atlanta, GA	COL
Spanish Castle Magic	04 Jul 70	CR 7. Live performance.	Oh, Atlanta CD Tendolar TDR-009	2nd International Pop Festival, Atlanta, GA	COL
Spanish Castle Magic	30 Jul 70	BR 23. Live performance.	In From The Storm CD Silver Rarities SIRA 109 / 110	Rainbow Bridge Vibratory Sound-Color Experiment, Maui, HI 1st Show	COL
Spanish Castle Magic	30 Jul 70	BR 23. Live performance.	Rainbow Bridge 2 CD JMH 003 / 2	Rainbow Bridge Vibratory Sound-Color Experiment, Maui, HI 1st Show	COL
Spanish Castle Magic	30 Aug 70	BR 24. Live performance. Officially available on the video and laserdisc.	Island Man CD Silver Rarities SIRA 39 / 40	Isle Of Wight Festival, Isle Of Wight, England	COL
Spanish Castle Magic	30 Aug 70	BR 24. Live performance. Officially available on the video and laserdisc.	At The Isle Of Wight (CR) Laserdisc CBS / Sony CLSM 791	Isle Of Wight Festival, Isle Of Wight, England	COL
Spanish Castle Magic	30 Aug 70	BR 24. Live performance. Officially available on the video and laserdisc.	Live! CD Black B-05	Isle Of Wight Festival, Isle Of Wight, England	COL
Spanish Castle Magic	30 Aug 70	BR 24. Live performance. Officially available on the video and laserdisc.	Wight CD JMH 006 / 2	Isle Of Wight Festival, Isle Of Wight, England	COL
Spanish Castle Magic	01 Sep 70	BR 25. Live performance.	Warm Hello Of The Sun, The CD	Stora Scenen, Liseberg Nojespark, Goteborg, Sweden	COL
Spanish Castle Magic	03 Sep 70	BR 26. Live performance.	Copenhagen '70 CD Whoopy Cat WKP 044 / 45	K.B. Hallen, Copenhagen, Denmark	COL
Spanish Castle Magic	04 Sep 70	BR 27. Live performance.	Back To Berlin CD Midnight Beat 049	Deutsche- Landhalle, Berlin, Germany	COL
Spanish Castle Magic	06 Sep 70	BR 28. Live performance.	Love & Peace CD Midnight Beat MBCD 015	Love And Peace Festival, Isle Of Fehrman, Germany	COL
Spanish Castle Magic	06 Sep 70	BR 28. Live performance.	Wink Of An Eye CD Whoopy Cat WKP 0033 / 34	Love And Peace Festival, Isle Of Fehrman, Germany	COL

SONG TITLE	DATE	COMMENTS	RELEASE	LOCATION / VENUE	BAND	PERSONNEL
Star Spangled Banner	23 Aug 68	BR 1. Live performance.	Historic Concert CD Midnight Beat MBCD 017	New York Rock Festival, Singer Bowl, Queens, NY	JHE	
Star Spangled Banner	14 Sep 68	BR 2. Live performance.	Live At The Hollywood Bowl LP RSR / International RSR 251	Hollywood Bowl, Los Angeles, CA	JHE	
Star Spangled Banner (This Is America)	10 Oct 68	BR 3. Live performance.	Winterland Vol 1 CD Whoopy Cat WKP 025 / 26	Winterland Theatre, San Francisco, CA 1st Show	JHE	
Star Spangled Banner	10 Oct 68	BR 3. Live performance.	Lost Winterland Tapes CD Starquake SQ 051-2	Winterland Theatre, San Francisco, CA 1st Show	JHE	
Star Spangled Banner	10 Oct 68	BR 4. Live performance.	Winterland Days, The CD Manic Depression 001	Winterland Theatre, San Francisco, CA 2nd Show	JHE	
Star Spangled Banner (This Is America)	10 Oct 68	BR 4. Live performance.	Winterland Vol 1 CD Whoopy Cat WKP 025 / 26	Winterland Theatre, San Francisco, CA 2nd Show	JHE	
Star Spangled Banner	10 Oct 68	BR 4. Live performance.	Jimi Hendrix CD Imtrat 40-90355	Winterland Theatre, San Francisco, CA 2nd Show	JHE	
Star Spangled Banner (This Is America)	12 Oct 68	BR 5. Live performance.	Winterland Vol 3 CD Whoopy Cat 0029 / 30	Winterland Theatre, San Francisco, CA 2nd Show	JHE	
Star Spangled Banner (This Is America)	12 Oct 68	BR 5. Live performance.	Ultimate Live Collection, The CD The Beat Goes On BGO BX 9307-4	Winterland Theatre, San Francisco, CA 2nd Show	JHE	
Star Spangled Banner	12 Oct 68	BR 5. Live performance.	Lost Winterland Tapes CD Starquake SQ 051-2	Winterland Theatre, San Francisco, CA 2nd Show	JHE	
Star Spangled Banner	08 Jan 69	BR 6. Live performance.	Cat's Squirrel CD CS 001 / 2	Winterland Theatre, San Francisco, CA 2nd Show	JHE	
Star Spangled Banner	09 Jan 69	BR 7. Live performance.	On The Killing Floor Swingin' Pig TSP-012-2	Winterland Theatre, San Francisco, CA 2nd Show	JHE	
Star Spangled Banner	09 Jan 69	BR 7. Live performance.	In Europe 67 / 68 / 69 CD Vulture CD 009 / 2	Winterland Theatre, San Francisco, CA 2nd Show	JHE	
Star Spangled Banner	09 Jan 69	BR 7. Live performance.	Live CD DV More	Winterland Theatre,	JHE	

Song	Date	Notes	Release	Location	Artist
Star Spangled Banner	09 Jan 69	BR 7. Live performance.	Jimi Hendrix Experience CD Rockstars In Concert 6127092	Winterland Theatre, San Francisco, CA 2nd Show	JHE
Star Spangled Banner	09 Jan 69	BR 7. Live performance.	Foxy Lady CD Alegra CD 9008	Winterland Theatre, San Francisco, CA 2nd Show	JHE
Star Spangled Banner	10 Jan 69	BR 8. Live performance.	Welcome To The Electric Circus Vol 1 CD Midnight Beat 016	Winterland Theatre, San Francisco, CA 2nd Show	JHE
Star Spangled Banner	18 Feb 69	BR 9. Live performance.	First Night At The Royal Albert Hall CD Midnight Beat MBCD 047 / 48	Winterland Theatre, San Francisco, CA 2nd Show	JHE
Star Spangled Banner (Smashing The Amps)	24 Feb 69	CR 2. Live performance. Part of a medley. Incomplete.	Last Experience, The (CR) CD Bescol CD 42	Winterland Theatre, San Francisco, CA 2nd Show	COL
Star Spangled Banner	24 Feb 69	CR 2. Live performance. Part of a medley. Incomplete.	Smashing Amps LP Trademark Of Quality TMQ 1813	Winterland Theatre, San Francisco, CA 2nd Show	JHE
Star Spangled Banner	24 Feb 69	CR 2. Live performance. Part of a medley. Incomplete.	King Of Gypsies CD Rockyssimo RK 001	Winterland Theatre, San Francisco, CA 2nd Show	COL
Star Spangled Banner	24 Feb 69	CR 2. Live performance. Part of a medley. Incomplete.	Stone Free CD Silver Rarities SIRA 58 / 59	Winterland Theatre, San Francisco, CA 2nd Show	JHE
Star Spangled Banner	24 Feb 69	CR 2. Live performance. Part of a medley. The complete version of "Star Spangled Banner that's at the end of 'Wild Thing'. Stereo.	Royal Albert Hall CD Blimp 008 / 009 & Listen To This Eric CD JH 003 / 4	Winterland Theatre, San Francisco, CA 2nd Show	JHE
Star Spangled Banner	18 Mar 69	CR 1 mix 1. Jimi's solo studio rendition of this concert favorite done during his first session at a 16 track facility.	Rainbow Bridge (CR) LP Reprise K44159	Winterland Theatre, San Francisco, CA 2nd Show	Solo
Star Spangled Banner	18 Mar 69	CR 1 mix 1. Jimi's solo studio rendition of this concert favorite done during his first session at a 16 track facility.	Rainbow Bridge & More CD	Winterland Theatre, San Francisco, CA 2nd Show	Solo
Star Spangled Banner	18 Mar 69	CR 1 mix 1. Jimi's solo studio rendition of this concert favorite done during his first session at a 16 track facility.	Rainbow Bridge (CR) LP Reprise K44159	Winterland Theatre, San Francisco, CA 2nd Show	Solo

SONG TITLE	DATE	COMMENTS	RELEASE	LOCATION / VENUE	BAND	PERSONNEL
Star Spangled Banner	18 Mar 69	CR 1 mix 2. Unused mix of the CR 1. Jimi's solo studio rendition of this concert favorite done during his first session at a 16 track facility.	Mixdown Master Tapes Volume 1 CD Dandelion DL 005	Winterland Theatre, San Francisco, CA 2nd Show	Solo	
Star Spangled Banner	26 Apr 69	CR 3. Live performance.	Electric Jimi CD Jaguarondi Records	Winterland Theatre, San Francisco, CA 2nd Show	JHE	
Star Spangled Banner	26 Apr 69	CR 3. Live performance.	I Don't Live Today, Maybe Tomorrow CD Living Legend LRCD 030	Winterland Theatre, San Francisco, CA 2nd Show	JHE	
Star Spangled Banner	26 Apr 69	CR 3. Live performance.	Very Best, The CD Irec / Retro MILCD-03	Winterland Theatre, San Francisco, CA 2nd Show	JHE	
Star Spangled Banner	26 Apr 69	CR 3. Live performance.	Anthology CD Box 9	Winterland Theatre, San Francisco, CA 2nd Show	JHE	
Star Spangled Banner	26 Apr 69	CR 3. Live performance.	Lifelines (CR) CD Reprise 9 26435-2	Winterland Theatre, San Francisco, CA 2nd Show	JHE	
Star Spangled Banner	27 Apr 69	CR 4. Live performance.	Live At The Oakland Coliseum (CR) CD Dagger Records DBRO-11743	Winterland Theatre, San Francisco, CA 2nd Show	JHE	
Star Spangled Banner	17 May 69	BR 10. From the complete and unedited show, this segues from 'Purple Haze'.	One Night At The Arena CD Venue VE 100501	Winterland Theatre, San Francisco, CA 2nd Show	JHE	
Star Spangled Banner	24 May 69	CR 5. Live performance. Part of a medley.	Don't Miss Him This Time CD Pyramid PYCD 096	Winterland Theatre, San Francisco, CA 2nd Show	JHE	
Star Spangled Banner	22 Jun 69	BR 11. Live performance. Part of a medley.	It Never Takes An End CD Genuine Pig TGP-118	Winterland Theatre, San Francisco, CA 2nd Show	NJK	
Star Spangled Banner	29 Jun 69	BR 12. Live performance.	Wink Of An Eye CD Whoopy Cat WKP 0033 / 34	Winterland Theatre, San Francisco, CA 2nd Show	JHE	
Star Spangled Banner	18 Aug 69	CR 6. Live performance. Part of a medley.	Woodstock Nation CD Wild Bird 89090 1 / 2	Winterland Theatre, San Francisco, CA 2nd Show	GSRB	
Star Spangled Banner	18 Aug 69	CR 6. Live performance. Part of a medley.	At Woodstock (CR) Laserdisc BMG BVLP 86	Winterland Theatre, San Francisco, CA 2nd Show	GSRB	

Song	Date	Notes	Release	Venue	Label
Star Spangled Banner	18 Aug 69	CR 6. Live performance. Part of a medley.	Soundtrack From The Film Jimi Hendrix, The (CR) LP Reprise 2RS 6481	Winterland Theatre, San Francisco, CA 2nd Show	GSRB
Star Spangled Banner	18 Aug 69	CR 6. Live performance. Part of a medley.	Woodstock (CR) CD MCA 11063	Winterland Theatre, San Francisco, CA 2nd Show	GSRB
Star Spangled Banner	18 Aug 69	CR 6. Live performance. Part of a medley.	Gypsy Sun And Rainbows CD Manic Depression MDCD 05 / 06	Winterland Theatre, San Francisco, CA 2nd Show	GSRB
Star Spangled Banner	18 Aug 69	CR 6. Live performance. Part of a medley.	Woodstock Monday, August 18 1969, 8AM CD JMH 008	Winterland Theatre, San Francisco, CA 2nd Show	GSRB
Star Spangled Banner	18 Aug 69	CR 6. Live performance. Part of a medley.	Ultimate Live Collection, The CD The Beat Goes On BGO BX 9307-4	Winterland Theatre, San Francisco, CA 2nd Show	GSRB
Star Spangled Banner	25 Apr 70	BR 13. Live performance.	Enjoy Jimi Hendrix LP Rubber Dubber 700-001-01	Winterland Theatre, San Francisco, CA 2nd Show	COL
Star Spangled Banner	25 Apr 70	BR 13. Live performance.	Portrait Of Jimi Hendrix, A LP Catalog # Varies On Dead Wax	Winterland Theatre, San Francisco, CA 2nd Show	COL
Star Spangled Banner	25 Apr 70	BR 13. Live performance.	Live At The Forum 1970 CD Whoopy Cat WKP 021 / 22	Winterland Theatre, San Francisco, CA 2nd Show	COL
Star Spangled Banner	25 Apr 70	BR 13. Live performance. The Luna disc is from a tape source while the JHCD 528 disc is copied from vinyl.	Scuse Me While I Kiss The Sky CD Luna CD & JHCD 528	Winterland Theatre, San Francisco, CA 2nd Show	COL
Star Spangled Banner	30 May 70	BR 14. Live performance. This was available officially but incomplete on the video and laserdisc Jimi Plays Berkeley.	Good Karma 2 LP Berkeley 2023	Winterland Theatre, San Francisco, CA 2nd Show	COL
Star Spangled Banner	30 May 70	BR 14. Live performance. This was available officially but incomplete on the video and laserdisc Jimi Plays Berkeley.	Jimi Plays Berkeley (CR) Warner Reprise Videotape	Winterland Theatre, San Francisco, CA 2nd Show	COL
Star Spangled Banner	30 May 70	BR 15. Live performance.	Riots In Berkeley CD Beech Marten BM 038	Winterland Theatre, San Francisco, CA 2nd Show	COL
Star Spangled Banner	30 May 70	BR 15. Live performance.	Berkeley Concerts, The CD Whoopy Cat WKP 004 / 5	Winterland Theatre, San Francisco, CA 2nd Show	COL

SONG TITLE	DATE	COMMENTS	RELEASE	LOCATION / VENUE	BAND	PERSONNEL
Star Spangled Banner	30 May 70	BR 15. Live performance.	Jimi Plays Berkeley CD JMH 005 / 2	Winterland Theatre, San Francisco, CA 2nd Show	COL	
Star Spangled Banner	13 Jun 70	BR 17. Live performance.	Baltimore Civic Center, June 13, 1970 CD Starquake SQ-09	Winterland Theatre, San Francisco, CA 2nd Show	COL	
Star Spangled Banner	04 Jul 70	CR 7. Live performance.	Atlanta Special CD Genuine Pig TGP 121	Winterland Theatre, San Francisco, CA 2nd Show	COL	
Star Spangled Banner	04 Jul 70	CR 7. Live performance.	At The Atlanta Pop Festival (CR) Laserdisc BMG BVLP 77 (74321-10987)	Winterland Theatre, San Francisco, CA 2nd Show	COL	
Star Spangled Banner	04 Jul 70	CR 7. Live performance.	Stages Atlanta 70 (CR) CD Reprise 9 27632-2	Winterland Theatre, San Francisco, CA 2nd Show	COL	
Star Spangled Banner	04 Jul 70	CR 7. Live performance.	Atlanta CD JMH 009 / 02	Winterland Theatre, San Francisco, CA 2nd Show	COL	
Star Spangled Banner	04 Jul 70	CR 7. Live performance.	Oh, Atlanta CD Tendolar TDR-009	Winterland Theatre, San Francisco, CA 2nd Show	COL	
Star Spangled Banner	04 Jul 70	CR 7. Live performance.	Atlanta CD JMH 009 / 02	Winterland Theatre, San Francisco, CA 2nd Show	COL	
Star Spangled Banner	04 Jul 70	CR 7. Live performance.	Johnny B. Goode (CR) CD Capitol 430218-2	Winterland Theatre, San Francisco, CA 2nd Show	COL	
Star Spangled Banner	17 Jul 70	BR 17. Live performance.	Can You Here Me LP Hemero 01 / KERI	Winterland Theatre, San Francisco, CA 2nd Show	COL	
Star Spangled Banner	17 Jul 70	BR 17. Live performance.	Live At Randall's Island LP Moon Tree Records PH1962	Winterland Theatre, San Francisco, CA 2nd Show	COL	
Star Spangled Banner	17 Jul 70	BR 17. Live performance.	Live USA CD Imtrat 902-001	Winterland Theatre, San Francisco, CA 2nd Show	COL	
Star Spangled Banner	17 Jul 70	BR 17. Live performance.	Greatest Hits Live CD Chartbusters CHER 089A	Winterland Theatre, San Francisco, CA 2nd Show	COL	

Song	Date	Notes	Release	Location	COL	Personnel
Star Spangled Banner	31 Aug 70	BR 18. Live performance.	Come On Stockholm	Winterland Theatre, San Francisco, CA 2nd Show		
Star Spangled Banner		No Jimi	Star Spangled Blues CD Neutral Zone NZCD 89011		Fake	
Stay Away	?? Mar? 70 ?	This is a recording by the group "Love" for the unreleased 'Black Beauty' album. Jimi's involvement is highly unlikely.	Midnight Sun CD Third Eye NK 007	Olympic Sound Studios, London, England	Love	
Stepping Stone (She Went To Bed With My Guitar)	?? Aug? 69	One of the few recognizable songs from the mediocre sessions with Mike Ephron.	Jimi Hendrix At His Best Vol 1 (CR) LP Sagapan 6313	Shokan House, Woodstock. NY	Jimi	Mike Ephron / Keyboards, Jerry Velez & Juma Sultan / Percussion
Stepping Stone	?? Sep? 69	BR 1. A long studio jam with elements that ultimately evolved into "Stepping Stone".	Electric Hendrix Vol 2 CD Pyramid PYCD 031	Hit Factory, New York, NY	GSRB	
Stepping Stone	?? Sep? 69	BR 1. A long studio jam with elements that ultimately evolved into "Stepping Stone".	Let's Drop Some Ludes And Vomit With Jimi CD Midnight Beat MBCD 026	Hit Factory, New York, NY	GSRB	
Stepping Stone (I'm A Man So I'm Trying To Be)	?? Sep? 69	BR 1. A long studio jam with elements that ultimately evolved into "Stepping Stone".	First Rays Of The New Rising Sun CD Triangle PYCD 084-2	Hit Factory, New York, NY	GSRB	
Stepping Stone (I'm A Man)	?? Sep? 69	BR 1. A long studio jam with elements that ultimately evolved into "Stepping Stone". Incomplete.	Kiss The Skies CD Mum MUCD 024	Hit Factory, New York, NY	GSRB	
Stepping Stone (Trying To Be)	15 Sep 69	BR 2. A second studio jam in the evolution of "Stepping Stone". Billy Cox does not appear to be present on this recording.	Message From Nine To The Universe CD Oil Well 122	Hit Factory, New York, NY	GSRB	Juma Sultan / Percussion, Unknown / Drums
Stepping Stone (Trying To Be)	15 Sep 69	BR 2. A second studio jam in the evolution of "Stepping Stone". Billy Cox does not appear to be present on this recording.	Talent And Feeling Vol 2 CD Extremely Rare EXR 22	Record Plant, New York, NY	GSRB	Juma Sultan / Percussion, Unknown / Drums
Stepping Stone (Trying To Be In Love)	15 Sep 69	BR 2. A second studio jam in the evolution of "Stepping Stone". Billy Cox does not appear to be present on this recording.	Unsurpassed Studio Takes CD Yellow Dog YD 050	Record Plant, New York, NY	GSRB	Juma Sultan / Percussion, Unknown / Drums
Stepping Stone (#7 Man)	15 Sep 69	BR 2. A second studio jam in the evolution of "Stepping Stone". Billy Cox does not appear to be present on this recording.	51st Anniversary CD Future Disc JMH 001 / 8	Record Plant, New York, NY	GSRB	Juma Sultan / Percussion, Unknown / Drums
Stepping Stone (I'm A Man So I'm Trying To Be)	15 Sep 69	BR 2. A second studio jam in the evolution of "Stepping Stone". Billy Cox does not appear to be present on this recording.	First Rays Of The New Rising Sun CD Triangle PYCD 084-2	Record Plant, New York, NY	GSRB	Juma Sultan / Percussion, Unknown / Drums
Stepping Stone (Trying To Be / Earth Blues)	15 Sep 69	BR 2. A second studio jam in the evolution of "Stepping Stone". Billy Cox does not appear to be present on this recording.	I Don't Live Today CD ACL 007	Record Plant, New York, NY	GSRB	Juma Sultan / Percussion, Unknown / Drums

SONG TITLE	DATE	COMMENTS	RELEASE	LOCATION / VENUE	BAND	PERSONNEL
Stepping Stone (Trying To Be)	15 Sep 69	BR 2. A second studio jam in the evolution of "Stepping Stone". Billy Cox does not appear to be present on this recording.	Magic Hand CD Mum MUCD 012	Record Plant, New York, NY	GSRB	Juma Sultan / Percussion, Unknown / Drums
Stepping Stone (Trying To Be Jam)	15 Sep 69	BR 2. A second studio jam in the evolution of "Stepping Stone". Billy Cox does not appear to be present on this recording.	Wight CD JMH 006 / 2	Record Plant, New York, NY	GSRB	Juma Sultan / Percussion, Unknown / Drums
Stepping Stone (I'm A Man)	15 Sep 69	BR 2. A second studio jam in the evolution of "Stepping Stone". Billy Cox does not appear to be present on this recording. Incomplete.	Kiss The Skies CD Mum MUCD 024	Record Plant, New York, NY	GSRB	Juma Sultan / Percussion, Unknown / Drums
Stepping Stone	31 Dec 69	BR 3. Live performance.	Auld Lang Syne CD JH 100 03	Fillmore East, New York, NY 2nd Show	BOG	
Stepping Stone	31 Dec 69	BR 3. Live performance.	Band Of Gypsys: Happy New Year CD Silver Shadow CD 9103	Fillmore East, New York, NY 2nd Show	BOG	
Stepping Stone	31 Dec 69	BR 3. Live performance.	Fillmore Concerts, The CD Whoopy Cat WKP 0006 / 7	Fillmore East, New York, NY 2nd Show	BOG	
Stepping Stone	31 Dec 69	BR 3. Live performance.	Band Of Gold CD-R Major Tom MT 087	Fillmore East, New York, NY 2nd Show	BOG	
Stepping Stone	31 Dec 69	BR 3. Live performance.	Band Of Gypsys- The Ultimate CD JMH 010 / 3	Fillmore East, New York, NY 2nd Show	BOG	
Stepping Stone (Trying To Be)	01 Jan 70	BR 4. Live performance.	Shine On Earth, Shine On CD Sidewalk SW 89010 / 89011	Fillmore East, New York, NY 1st Show	BOG	
Stepping Stone	01 Jan 70	BR 4. Live performance.	Band Of Gold CD-R Major Tom MT 087	Fillmore East, New York, NY 1st Show	BOG	
Stepping Stone	01 Jan 70	BR 4. Live performance.	Band Of Gypsys- The Ultimate CD JMH 010 / 3	Fillmore East, New York, NY 1st Show	BOG	
Stepping Stone	07 Jan 70	CR 1 mix 1. Copied from the very rare single that was withdrawn immediately after release.	Band Of Gypsys Vol 3	Record Plant, New York, NY	BOG	Mitch Mitchell / Drums
Stepping Stone	07 Jan 70	CR 1 mix 1. Copied from the very rare single that was withdrawn immediately after release.	51st Anniversary CD Future Disc JMH 001 / 8	Record Plant, New York, NY	BOG	Mitch Mitchell / Drums
Stepping Stone	07 Jan 70	CR 1 mix 1. Copied from the very rare single that was withdrawn immediately after release.	Rainbow Bridge & More CD	Record Plant, New York, NY	BOG	Mitch Mitchell / Drums
Stepping Stone	07 Jan 70	CR 1 mix 1. Copied from the very rare single that was withdrawn immediately after release.	Electric Gypsy's CD Pilot HJCD 070	Record Plant, New York, NY	BOG	Mitch Mitchell / Drums
Stepping Stone	07 Jan 70	CR 1 mix 1. Copied from the very rare single that was with-	Rarities On Compact	Record Plant, New	BOG	Mitch Mitchell / Drums

Song	Date	Notes	Disc CD On The Radio	Location		Musicians
Stepping Stone		drawn immediately after release.		York, NY		
Stepping Stone	07 Jan 70	CR 1 mix 1. Copied from the very rare single that was withdrawn immediately after release.	Rainbow Bridge 2 CD JMH 003 / 2	Record Plant, New York, NY	BOG	Mitch Mitchell / Drums
Stepping Stone	07 Jan 70	CR 1 mix 2. Alternate mix of CR 1 copied from the Warner Bros. sampler LP 'Loony Toons & Merrie Melodies'.	Band Of Gypsys Vol 3	Record Plant, New York, NY	BOG	Mitch Mitchell / Drums
Stepping Stone	07 Jan 70	CR 1 mix 3. Another re-mix of CR 1.	War Heroes (CR) CD Polydor 847-2622	Record Plant, New York, NY	BOG	Mitch Mitchell / Drums
Stepping Stone	07 Jan 70	CR 1 mix 3. Another re-mix of CR 1.	First Rays Of The New Rising Sun (CR) CD MCACD 11599	Record Plant, New York, NY	BOG	Mitch Mitchell / Drums
Stepping Stone	07 Jan 70	CR 1 mix 4. An alternate mix of CR #1 but with Bruce Gary's drum overdub.	Voodoo Soup (CR) CD MCA 11206	Record Plant, New York, NY	BOG	Bruce Gary / Drums Added
Stepping Stone	07 Jan 70	CR 1 mix 5. Unused mix of the CR 1.	Multicolored Blues CD Luna LU 9317	Record Plant, New York, NY	BOG	Mitch Mitchell / Drums
Stepping Stone	07 Jan 70	CR 1 mix 5. Unused mix of the CR 1.	Cherokee Mist CD Triangle PYCD 070	Record Plant, New York, NY	BOG	Mitch Mitchell / Drums
Stepping Stone	07 Jan 70	CR 1 mix 5. Unused mix of the CR 1.	I Don't Live Today CD ACL 007	Record Plant, New York, NY	BOG	Mitch Mitchell / Drums
Stepping Stone	07 Jan 70	CR 1 mix 5. Unused mix of the CR 1.	Gypsy Charm CD Mum MUCD 018	Record Plant, New York, NY	BOG	Mitch Mitchell / Drums
Still Raining Still Dreaming	10 Jun 68	CR See "Rainy Day Dream Away".	Electric Ladyland (CR) CD MCACD-11600	Record Plant, New York, NY	Jimi	Buddy Miles / Drums, Mike Finnegan / Organ, Freddie Smith / Sax, Larry Faucette / Percussion
Still Raining, Still Dreaming	10 Jun 68	CR See "Rainy Day Dream Away".	Red House CD The Entertainers CD294	Record Plant, New York, NY	Jimi	Buddy Miles / Drums, Mike Finnegan / Organ, Freddie Smith / Sax, Larry Faucette / Percussion
Still Raining, Still Dreaming	10 Jun 68	CR See "Rainy Day Dream Away".	Legacy (CR) LP Polydor	Record Plant, New York, NY	Jimi	Buddy Miles / Drums, Mike Finnegan / Organ, Freddie Smith / Sax, Larry Faucette / Percussion
Stone Free	02 Nov 66	CR 1 mix 1 (stereo).	Smash Hits (CR) CD Reprise 2276-2	De Lane Lea, London, England	JHE	
Stone Free	02 Nov 66	CR 1 mix 1 (stereo)	Are You Experienced? (CR) CD MCACD 11602	De Lane Lea, London, England	JHE	
Stone Free	02 Nov 66	CR 1 mix 1 (stereo)	The Singles Album (CR) CD Polydor 827 369-2	De Lane Lea, London, England	JHE	

SONG TITLE	DATE	COMMENTS	RELEASE	LOCATION / VENUE	BAND	PERSONNEL
Stone Free	02 Nov 66	CR 1 mix 2 (mono).	Legacy (CR) LP Polydor	De Lane Lea, London, England	JHE	
Stone Free	04 Feb 67	BR 1. Live performance.	Have Mercy On Me Baby CD Midnight Beat MBCD 038	Flamingo Club, London, England	JHE	
Stone Free	04 Feb 67	BR 1. Live performance.	Live At The Flamingo Club, London, 2-4-67 CD	Flamingo Club, London, England	JHE	
Stone Free	13 Feb 67	CR 3. BBC performance.	Guitar Hero CD Document DR 013	Saturday Club, BBC Broadcasting House, London, England	JHE	
Stone Free	13 Feb 67	CR 3. BBC performance.	Primal Keys LP Impossible Record Works	Saturday Club, BBC Broadcasting House, London, England	JHE	
Stone Free	13 Feb 67	CR 3. BBC performance.	Radio One (CR) CD Rykodisc RCD 20078	Saturday Club, BBC Broadcasting House, London, England	JHE	
Stone Free	13 Feb 67	CR 3. BBC performance.	Ultimate BBC Collection CD Classical CL006	Saturday Club, BBC Broadcasting House, London, England	JHE	
Stone Free	13 Feb 67	CR 3. BBC performance.	Jimi Hendrix Vol 2: A Man Of Our Times LP Napoleon NLP 11018	Saturday Club, BBC Broadcasting House, London, England	JHE	
Stone Free	13 Feb 67	CR 3. BBC performance.	Live In London 1967 CD Koine Records K881104	Saturday Club, BBC Broadcasting House, London, England	JHE	
Stone Free	13 Feb 67	CR 3. BBC performance.	Live In Concert 1967 CD Living Legend LLR-CD 001	Saturday Club, BBC Broadcasting House, London, England	Jimi	
Stone Free	13 Feb 67	CR 3. BBC performance.	Broadcasts LP Trade Mark Of Quality TMQ 1841	Saturday Club, BBC Broadcasting House, London, England	JHE	
Stone Free	13 Feb 67	CR 3. BBC performance.	In Concert CD Starlife ST 3612	Saturday Club, BBC Broadcasting House, London, England	JHE	
Stone Free	13 Feb 67	CR 3. BBC performance.	Complete BBC Session And.... The CD Last Bootleg Records LBR 036 / 2	Saturday Club, BBC Broadcasting House, London, England	JHE	
Stone Free	13 Feb 67	CR 3. BBC performance.	Black Strings CD CDM	Saturday Club, BBC	JHE	

Song	Date	Notes	Release	Location	Artist	Personnel
Stone Free	13 Feb 67	CR 3. BBC performance.	BBC Sessions (CR) CD MCACD 2-11742	Saturday Club, BBC Broadcasting House, London, England	JHE	
Stone Free	13 Feb 67	CR 3. BBC performance.	Tomorrow...Or Just The End Of Time CD Batz 0028	Saturday Club, BBC Broadcasting House, London, England	JHE	
Stone Free	18 Mar 67	BR 2. Live performance for a German radio broadcast.	Legendary Star Club Tapes, The CD The Early Years 02-CD-3309	N D R Radiohouse, Studio 1, Hamburg, Germany	JHE	
Stone Free	18 Mar 67	BR 2. Live performance for a German radio broadcast.	Can You Here Me LP Hemero 01 / KERI	N D R Radiohouse, Studio 1, Hamburg, Germany	JHE	
Stone Free	18 Mar 67	BR 2. Live performance for a German radio broadcast.	Tomorrow...Or Just The End Of Time CD Batz 0028	N D R Radiohouse, Studio 1, Hamburg, Germany	JHE	
Stone Free	07-09 Apr 69	CR 2 mix 1. This has had the original musicians replaced.	Crash Landing (CR) LP Reprise MS 2204	Record Plant, New York, NY	Jimi	Crash Landing Line Up 1974 - R Chapman / Backing Vocal - A Fairweather-Low / Backing Vocal - J Maeulin / Percussion
Stone Free	07-09 Apr 69	CR 2 mix 2. Unused mix of the CR 2. This has an additional guitar overdub.	Shine On Earth, Shine On CD Sidewalk SW 89010 / 89011	Record Plant, New York, NY	Jimi	Crash Landing Line Up 1974 - R Chapman / Backing Vocal - A Fairweather-Low / Backing Vocal - J Maeulin / Percussion
Stone Free	07-09 Apr 69	CR 2 mix 2. Unused mix of the CR 2. This has an additional guitar overdub.	Electric Hendrix Vol 1 CD Pyramid PYCD 030	Record Plant, New York, NY	Jimi	Crash Landing Line Up 1974 - R Chapman / Backing Vocal - A Fairweather-Low / Backing Vocal - J Maeulin / Percussion
Stone Free	07-09 Apr 69	CR 2 mix 2. Unused mix of the CR 2. This has an additional guitar overdub.	Paper Airplanes CD Midnight Beat MBCD 25	Record Plant, New York, NY	Jimi	Crash Landing Line Up 1974 - R Chapman / Backing Vocal - A Fairweather-Low / Backing Vocal - J Maeulin / Percussion

SONG TITLE	DATE	COMMENTS	RELEASE	LOCATION / VENUE	BAND	PERSONNEL
Stone Free	07-09 Apr 69	CR 2 mix 2. Unused mix of the CR 2. This has an additional guitar overdub.	Gypsy Suns, Moons And Rainbows CD Sidewalk JHX 8868	Record Plant, New York, NY	Jimi	Crash Landing Line Up 1974 - R Chapman / Backing Vocal - A Fairweather-Low / Backing Vocal - J Maeulin / Percussion
Stone Free	07-09 Apr 69	CR 2 mix 2. Unused mix of the CR 2. This has an additional guitar overdub.	Midnight Shines Down CD Blue Kangaroo BK 04	Record Plant, New York, NY	Jimi	Crash Landing Line Up 1974 - R Chapman / Backing Vocal - A Fairweather-Low / Backing Vocal - J Maeulin / Percussion
Stone Free	18 May 67	BR 3. Live performance from German TV.	Wild Man Of Pop Plays Vol 1, The CD Pyramid RFTCD 003	Beat Beat Beat TV Show, Stadhalle, Offenbach, Germany	JHE	
Stone Free	18 May 67	BR 3. Live performance from German TV.	Sweet Angel CD Compact Music WPOCM 0589	Beat Beat Beat TV Show, Stadhalle, Offenbach, Germany	JHE	
Stone Free	05 Jun 68	BR 4. Live performance.	Screaming Eagle CD Pink Poodle POO 001	It Must Be Dusty T V Show, Elstree Studios, Borehamwood, UK	JHE	
Stone Free	24 Feb 69	CR 4 mix 2. Live performance. Stereo	Royal Albert Hall CD Blimp 008 / 009 & Listen To This Eric CD JH 003 / 4	Royal Albert Hall, London, England	JHE	
Stone Free	24 Feb 69	CR 4 mix 2. Live performance. Stereo	Stone Free CD Silver Rarities SIRA 58 / 59	Royal Albert Hall, London, England	JHE	
Stone Free	24 Feb 69	CR 4 mix 1. Live performance with the drum solo edited out.	Concerts (CR) CD Reprise 9-22306-2	Royal Albert Hall, London, England	JHE	
Stone Free	20 Jun 69	BR 5. Live performance.	More Electricity From Newport CD Luna LU 9201	Newport Pop Festival, San Fernando State, Northridge, CA	NJK	
Stone Free	20 Jun 69	BR 5. Live performance.	A Lifetime Of Experience LP Sleepy Dragon 55 10	Newport Pop Festival, San Fernando State, Northridge, CA	NJK	
Stone Free	20 Jun 69	BR 5. Live performance.	Two Days At Newport CD JMH 007 / 2	Newport Pop Festival, San Fernando State, Northridge, CA	JHE	

Song	Date	Notes	Release	Venue	Label
Stone Free	31 Dec 69	BR 6. Live performance. Part of a medley.	Auld Lang Syne CD JH 100 03	Fillmore East, New York, NY 2nd Show	BOG
Stone Free	31 Dec 69	BR 6. Live performance. Part of a medley.	Band Of Gypsys: Happy New Year CD Silver Shadow CD 9103	Fillmore East, New York, NY 2nd Show	BOG
Stone Free	31 Dec 69	BR 6. Live performance. Part of a medley.	Fillmore Concerts, The CD Whoopy Cat WKP 0006 / 7	Fillmore East, New York, NY 2nd Show	BOG
Stone Free	31 Dec 69	BR 6. Live performance. Part of a medley.	Band Of Gold CD-R Major Tom MT 087	Fillmore East, New York, NY 2nd Show	BOG
Stone Free	31 Dec 69	BR 6. Live performance. Part of a medley.	Band Of Gypsys- The Ultimate CD JMH 010 / 3	Fillmore East, New York, NY 2nd Show	BOG
Stone Free	01 Jan 70	BR 10. Live performance.	500,000 Halos CD EXP 500,000	Fillmore East, New York, NY 2nd Show	BOG
Stone Free	01 Jan 70	BR 8. Live performance.	Band Of Gold CD-R Major Tom MT 087	Fillmore East, New York, NY 2nd Show	BOG
Stone Free	30 May 70	CR 5. Live performance.	Riots In Berkeley CD Beech Marten BM 038	Berkeley Community Theater, Berkeley, CA 2nd Show	COL
Stone Free	30 May 70	CR 5. Live performance.	Band Of Gypsys Vol 2 (CR) LP Capitol SJ 12416	Berkeley Community Theater, Berkeley, CA 2nd Show	COL
Stone Free	30 May 70	CR 5. Live performance.	51st Anniversary CD Future Disc JMH 001 / 8	Berkeley Community Theater, Berkeley, CA 2nd Show	COL
Stone Free	30 May 70	CR 5. Live performance.	Redskin' Jammin' CD JH 01 / 02	Berkeley Community Theater, Berkeley, CA 2nd Show	COL
Stone Free	30 May 70	CR 5. Live performance.	Berkeley Concerts, The CD Whoopy Cat WKP 004 / 5	Berkeley Community Theater, Berkeley, CA 2nd Show	COL
Stone Free	30 May 70	CR 5. Live performance.	Jimi Plays Berkeley CD JMH 005 / 2	Berkeley Community Theater, Berkeley, CA 1st Show	COL
Stone Free	07 Apr 70	CR 6. Live performance.	You Can't Use My Name LP Rock Folders 2, Q 9020	Rainbow Bridge Vibratory Sound-Color Experiment, Maui, HI 2nd Show	COL

SONG TITLE	DATE	COMMENTS	RELEASE	LOCATION / VENUE	BAND	PERSONNEL
Stone Free	04 Jul 70	CR 6. Live performance.	Atlanta Special CD Genuine Pig TGP 121	2nd International Pop Festival, Atlanta, GA	COL	
Stone Free	04 Jul 70	CR 6. Live performance.	At The Atlanta Pop Festival (CR) Laserdisc BMG BVLP 77 (74321-10987)	2nd International Pop Festival, Atlanta, GA	COL	
Stone Free	04 Jul 70	CR 6. Live performance.	Stages Atlanta 70 (CR) CD Reprise 9 27632-2	2nd International Pop Festival, Atlanta, GA	COL	
Stone Free	04 Jul 70	CR 6. Live performance.	Atlanta CD JMH 009 / 02	2nd International Pop Festival, Atlanta, GA	COL	
Stone Free	04 Jul 70	CR 6. Live performance.	Oh, Atlanta CD Tendolar TDR-009	2nd International Pop Festival, Atlanta, GA	COL	
Stone Free	04 Jul 70	CR 6. Live performance.	Oh, Atlanta CD Tendolar TDR-009	2nd International Pop Festival, Atlanta, GA	COL	
Stone Free	04 Jul 70	CR 6. Live performance.	Atlanta CD JMH 009 / 02	2nd International Pop Festival, Atlanta, GA	COL	
Stone Free	17 Jul 70	BR 7. Live performance.	Can You Here Me LP Hemero 01 / KERI	New York Pop-Downing Stadium, Randalls Island, NY	COL	
Stone Free	17 Jul 70	BR 7. Live performance.	Live At Randall's Island LP Moon Tree Records PH1962	New York Pop-Downing Stadium, Randalls Island, NY	COL	
Stone Free	17 Jul 70	BR 7. Live performance.	Live USA CD Imtrat 902-001	New York Pop-Downing Stadium, Randalls Island, NY	COL	
Stone Free	17 Jul 70	BR 7. Live performance.	Greatest Hits Live CD Chartbusters CHER 089A	New York Pop-Downing Stadium, Randalls Island, NY	COL	
Stone Free	30 Jul 70	BR 7. Live performance.	In From The Storm CD Silver Rarities SIRA 109 / 110	Rainbow Bridge Vibratory Sound-Color Experiment, Maui, HI 2nd Show	COL	
Stone Free	03 Sep 70	BR 9. Live performance.	Copenhagen '70 CD Whoopy Cat WKP 044 / 45	K.B. Hallen, Copenhagen, Denmark	COL	
Stop	31 Dec 69	BR 1. Live performance.	51st Anniversary CD Future Disc JMH 001 / 8	Fillmore East, New York, NY 1st Show	BOG	
Stop	31 Dec 69	BR 1. Live performance.	Band Of Gold CD-R Major Tom MT 087	Fillmore East, New York, NY 1st Show	BOG	

Song	Date	Source	Release	Venue	Code
Stop	31 Dec 69	BR 1. Live performance.	Power Of Soul CD SQ-10	Fillmore East, New York, NY 1st Show	BOG
Stop	31 Dec 69	BR 2. Live performance.	Auld Lang Syne CD JH 100 03	Fillmore East, New York, NY 2nd Show	BOG
Stop	31 Dec 69	BR 2. Live performance.	Fillmore Concerts, The CD Whoopy Cat WKP 0006 / 7	Fillmore East, New York, NY 2nd Show	BOG
Stop	31 Dec 69	BR 2. Live performance.	Band Of Gold CD-R Major Tom MT 087	Fillmore East, New York, NY 2nd Show	BOG
Stop	31 Dec 69	BR 2. Live performance.	Band Of Gypsys- The Ultimate CD JMH 010 / 3	Fillmore East, New York, NY 2nd Show	BOG
Stop	01 Jan 70	CR 1. Live performance.	Band Of Gypsys Vol 2 (CR) LP Capitol SJ 12416	Fillmore East, New York, NY 1st Show	BOG
Stop	01 Jan 70	CR 1. Live performance.	Jewel Box CD Home HR-5824-3	Fillmore East, New York, NY 1st Show	BOG
Stop	01 Jan 70	CR 1. Live performance.	Valley Of Neptune CD PC 28355	Fillmore East, New York, NY 1st Show	BOG
Stop	01 Jan 70	CR 1. Live performance.	Band Of Gold CD-R Major Tom MT 087	Fillmore East, New York, NY 1st Show	BOG
Stormy Monday	17 Mar 68	BR 1. Live performance.	Blues At Midnight CD Midnight Beat MBCD 037	Cafe' A Go Go, New York, NY	Cafe
Stormy Monday	17 Mar 68	BR 1. Live performance.	A Lifetime Of Experience LP Sleepy Dragon 55 10	Cafe' A Go Go, New York, NY	Cafe
Stormy Monday(Monday Jam)	17 Mar 68	BR 1. Live performance.	Cafe Au Go Go CD Koine 880802	Cafe' A Go Go, New York, NY	Cafe
Straight Ahead (Pass It On)	30 May 70	BR 1. Live performance.	Riots In Berkeley CD Beech Marten BM 038	Berkeley Community Theater, Berkeley, CA 2nd Show	COL
Straight Ahead (Pass It On)	30 May 70	BR 1. Live performance.	51st Anniversary CD Future Disc JMH 001 / 8	Berkeley Community Theater, Berkeley, CA 2nd Show	COL
Straight Ahead	30 May 70	BR 1. Live performance.	Mannish Boy LP Contraband CBM 88	Berkeley Community Theater, Berkeley, CA 2nd Show	COL

SONG TITLE	DATE	COMMENTS	RELEASE	LOCATION / VENUE	BAND	PERSONNEL
Straight Ahead	30 May 70	BR 1. Live performance.	Berkeley Concerts, The CD Whoopy Cat WKP 004 / 5	Berkeley Community Theater, Berkeley, CA 1st Show	COL	
Straight Ahead (Pass It On)	30 May 70	BR 1. Live performance.	Jimi Plays Berkeley CD JMH 005 / 2	Berkeley Community Theater, Berkeley, CA 1st Show	COL	
Straight Ahead	13 Jun 70	BR 2. Live performance.	Live At The Forum 1970 CD Whoopy Cat WKP 021 / 22	Baltimore Civic Center, Baltimore, MD	COL	
Straight Ahead (Pass It On)	13 Jun 70	BR 2. Live performance.	Baltimore Civic Center, June 13, 1970 CD Starquake SQ-09	Baltimore Civic Center, Baltimore, MD	COL	
Straight Ahead	17 Jun 70	CR 1 mix 1.	First Rays Of The New Rising Sun (CR) CD MCACD 11599	Electric Lady Studio, New York, NY	COL	
Straight Ahead	17 Jun 70	CR 1 mix 1.	Cry Of Love, The (CR) CD Reprise 2034-2	Electric Lady Studio, New York, NY	COL	
Straight Ahead	17 Jun 70	CR 1 mix 2. Unused mix of the CR 1. Incomplete.	Multicolored Blues CD Luna LU 9317	Electric Lady Studio, New York, NY	COL	
Straight Ahead	17 Jun 70	CR 1 mix 2. Unused mix of the CR 1. Incomplete.	Completer, The CD Whoopy Cat WKP 0018 / 19	Electric Lady Studio, New York, NY	COL	
Straight Ahead	17 Jun 70	CR 1 mix 2. Unused mix of the CR 1. Incomplete.	Kiss The Skies CD Mum MUCD 024	Electric Lady Studio, New York, NY	COL	
Straight Ahead	04 Jul 70	CR 2. Live performance.	Atlanta Special CD Genuine Pig TGP 121	2nd International Pop Festival, Atlanta, GA	COL	
Straight Ahead	04 Jul 70	CR 2. Live performance.	At The Atlanta Pop Festival (CR) Laserdisc BMG BVLP 77 (74321-10987)	2nd International Pop Festival, Atlanta, GA	COL	
Straight Ahead	04 Jul 70	CR 2. Live performance.	Stages Atlanta 70 (CR) CD Reprise 9 27632-2	2nd International Pop Festival, Atlanta, GA	COL	
Straight Ahead	04 Jul 70	CR 2. Live performance.	Atlanta CD JMH 009 / 02	2nd International Pop Festival, Atlanta, GA	COL	
Straight Ahead	01 Sep 70	BR 3. Live performance.	Warm Hello Of The Sun, The CD	Stora Scenen, Liseberg Nojespark, Goteborg, Sweden	COL	
Straight Ahead	04 Sep 70	BR 4. Live performance.	Back To Berlin CD Midnight Beat 049	Deutsche- Landhalle, Berlin, Germany	COL	

Title	Date	Notes	Release	Location	Group	Extra
Strange Things	?? / ?? 65	With Curtis Knight.	Jimi: A Musical Legacy CD KTS BX 010	Studio 76, New York, NY	CKB	
Strato Strut (Funky Blues Jam)	?? / ?? 69-70	BR 1. Another short studio jam with a made up title.	Freak Out Blues CD GH 001	Record Plant, New York, NY	BOG	
Strato Strut (Sky Jam)	?? / ?? 69-70	BR 1. Another short studio jam with a made up title. Incomplete.	Redskin' Jammin' CD JH 01 / 02	Record Plant, New York, NY	BOG	
Studio Catastrophe	14 May 70	BR 1. A short impromptu bit from the studio.	51st Anniversary CD Future Disc JMH 001 / 8	Record Plant, New York, NY	JHE	
Studio Catastrophe	14 May 70	BR 1. A short impromptu bit from the studio. This is not listed on the disc but comes after 'Red House'.	Freak Out Blues CD GH 001	Electric Lady Studio, New York, NY	Jimi	
Suey	?? / ?? 65	CR 1. Copied from the rare single with Jayne Mansfield.	Screaming Eagle CD Pink Poodle POO 001	Dimensional Sound Studios, New York, NY	Jimi	Jayne Mansfield / Vocals
Sundance, The	?? Aug? 69	BR 2. Live performance.	Woodstock Rehearsals CD Midnight Beat MBCD 009	Shokan House, Woodstock, NY	GSRB	
Sundance, The	?? Aug? 69	BR 1. From the rehearsals at Jimi's Shokan house just before the performance at Woodstock.	Shokan Sunrise CD	Shokan House, Woodstock, NY	GSRB	
Sunshine Of Your Love	26 Feb 69	BR 1. The only studio version recorded, this is from the Chandler tapes.	Studio Haze CD INA 6	Olympic Sound Studios, London, England	JHE	
Sunshine Of Your Love	26 Feb 69	BR 1. The only studio version recorded, this is from the Chandler tapes.	DeLane Lea And Olympic Outs CD Gold Standard CD-R	Olympic Sound Studios, London, England	JHE	
Sunshine Of Your Love	26 Feb 69	BR 1. The only studio version recorded, this is from the Chandler tapes.	I Don't Live Today CD ACL 007	Olympic Sound Studios, London, England	JHE	
Sunshine Of Your Love	26 Feb 69	BR 1. The only studio version recorded, this is from the Chandler tapes.	Gypsy Charm CD Mum MUCD 018	Olympic Sound Studios, London, England	JHE	
Sunshine Of Your Love	?? Mar? 68	Live performance. Only a small part of the "Morrison's Lament" medley. This is on all releases of the Scene Club Show.	Jimi Hendrix CD Flute FLCD 2008	Scene Club, New York, N Y	JHE	
Sunshine Of Your Love	10 May 68	BR 2. Live performance.	It's Only A Paper Moon CD Luna 9420	Fillmore East, New York, NY	JHE	
Sunshine Of Your Love	10 May 68	BR 2. Live performance.	One Night Stand CD Hep Cat 101	Fillmore East, New York, NY	JHE	

SONG TITLE	DATE	COMMENTS	RELEASE	LOCATION / VENUE	BAND	PERSONNEL
Sunshine Of Your Love	10 Oct 68	CR 1. Live performance.	Winterland Days, The CD Manic Depression 001	Winterland Theatre, San Francisco, CA 2nd Show	JHE	
Sunshine Of Your Love	10 Oct 68	CR 1. Live performance.	Winterland Vol 1 CD Whoopy Cat WKP 025 / 26	Winterland Theatre, San Francisco, CA 2nd Show	JHE	
Sunshine Of Your Love	10 Oct 68	CR 1. Live performance.	Jimi Hendrix CD Imtrat 40-90355	Winterland Theatre, San Francisco, CA 2nd Show	JHE	
Sunshine Of Your Love	10 Oct 68	CR 1. Live performance.	Live At Winterland (CR) CD Rykodisc RCD 20038	Winterland Theatre, San Francisco, CA 2nd Show	JHE	
Sunshine Of Your Love	12 Oct 68	CR 1. Live performance.	Winterland Vol 3 CD Whoopy Cat WKP 0029 / 30	Winterland Theatre, San Francisco, CA 2nd Show	JHE	
Sunshine Of Your Love	12 Oct 68	CR 1. Live performance.	Fire CD The Entertainers CD297	Winterland Theatre, San Francisco, CA 2nd Show	JHE	
Sunshine Of Your Love	12 Oct 68	CR 1. Live performance.	Lost Winterland Tapes CD Starquake SQ 051-2	Winterland Theatre, San Francisco, CA 2nd Show	JHE	
Sunshine Of Your Love	04 Jan 69	CR 2. Live performance from BBC TV.	Jimi Hendrix Vol 2: A Man Of Our Times LP Napoleon NLP 11018	A Happening For Lulu, BBC TV, London, England	JHE	
Sunshine Of Your Love	04 Jan 69	CR 2. Live performance from BBC TV.	Broadcasts LP Trade Mark Of Quality TMQ 1841 & TMQ 71019	A Happening For Lulu, BBC TV, London, England	JHE	
Sunshine Of Your Love	04 Jan 69	CR 2. Live performance from BBC TV.	Historic Performances CD Aquarius AQ 67-JH-080	A Happening For Lulu, BBC TV, London, England	JHE	
Sunshine Of Your Love	04 Jan 69	CR 2. Live performance from BBC TV.	Sweet Angel CD Compact Music WPOCM 0589	A Happening For Lulu, BBC TV, London, England	JHE	
Sunshine Of Your Love	04 Jan 69	CR 2. Live performance from BBC TV.	Rarities On Compact Disc CD On The Radio	A Happening For Lulu, BBC TV, London, England	JHE	
Sunshine Of Your Love	04 Jan 69	CR 2. Live performance from BBC TV.	Jimi: A Musical Legacy CD KTS BX 010	A Happening For Lulu, BBC TV, London, England	JHE	
Sunshine Of Your Love	04 Jan 69	CR 2. Live performance from BBC TV.	BBC Sessions (CR) CD	A Happening For	JHE	

Song	Date	Notes	Release	Venue	Band
Sunshine Of Your Love	04 Jan 69	CR 2. Live performance from BBC TV.	Loaded Guitar LP Starlight SL 87013	A Happening For LuLu, BBC TV, London, England	JHE
Sunshine Of Your Love	04 Jan 69	CR 2. Live performance from BBC TV. Incomplete.	Broadcasts CD Luna LU 9204	A Happening For LuLu, BBC TV, London, England	JHE
Sunshine Of Your Love	08 Jan 69	BR 3. Live performance.	Cat's Squirrel CD CS 001 / 2	Loresberg Cirkus, Goteborg, Sweden	JHE
Sunshine Of Your Love	09 Jan 69	BR 4. Live performance.	On The Killing Floor Swingin' Pig TSP-012-2	Konserthuset, Stockholm, Sweden 1st Show	JHE
Sunshine Of Your Love	09 Jan 69	BR 4. Live performance.	Live In Stockholm 1967 CD Document DR 003	Konserthuset, Stockholm, Sweden 1st Show	JHE
Sunshine Of Your Love	09 Jan 69	BR 4. Live performance.	Electronic Church Music CD Pyramid PYCD 023	Konserthuset, Stockholm, Sweden 1st Show	JHE
Sunshine Of Your Love	09 Jan 69	BR 4. Live performance.	In Concert CD Starlife ST 3612	Konserthuset, Stockholm, Sweden 1st Show	JHE
Sunshine Of Your Love	09 Jan 69	BR 5. Live performance.	On The Killing Floor Swingin' Pig TSP-012-2	Konserthuset, Stockholm, Sweden 2nd Show	JHE
Sunshine Of Your Love	09 Jan 69	BR 5. Live performance.	Live At The Hollywood Bowl LP RSR / International RSR 251	Konserthuset, Stockholm, Sweden 2nd Show	JHE
Sunshine Of Your Love	09 Jan 69	BR 5. Live performance.	In Europe 67 / 68 / 69 CD Vulture CD 009 / 2	Konserthuset, Stockholm, Sweden 2nd Show	JHE
Sunshine Of Your Love	09 Jan 69	BR 5. Live performance. Incomplete.	Legendary Star Club Tapes, The CD The Early Years 02-CD-3309	Konserthuset, Stockholm, Sweden 2nd Show	JHE
Sunshine Of Your Love	10 Jan 69	BR 6. Live performance.	Welcome To The Electric Circus Vol 1 CD Midnight Beat 016	Falkoner Centret, Copenhagen, Denmark 1st Show	JHE
Sunshine Of Your Love	17 Jan 69	BR 7. Live performance.	Burning At Frankfurt CD Midnight Beat MBCD 040	Jahrhunderthalle, Frankfurt, Germany	JHE

SONG TITLE	DATE	COMMENTS	RELEASE	LOCATION / VENUE	BAND	PERSONNEL
Sunshine Of Your Love	23 Jan 69	BR 8. Live performance.	Up Against The Berlin Wall CD Midnight Beat MBCD 046	Sportpalast, Berlin, Germany	JHE	
Sunshine Of Your Love	18 Feb 69	BR 9. Live performance.	First Night At The Royal Albert Hall CD Midnight Beat MBCD 047 / 48	Royal Albert Hall, London, England	JHE	
Sunshine Of Your Love	24 Feb 69	CR 3. Live performance.	Last Experience, The (CR) CD Bescol CD 42	Royal Albert Hall, London, England	JHE	
Sunshine Of Your Love	24 Feb 69	CR 3. Live performance.	Smashing Amps LP Trademark Of Quality TMQ 1813	Royal Albert Hall, London, England	JHE	
Sunshine Of Your Love	24 Feb 69	CR 3. Live performance.	king Of Gypsies CD Rockyssimo RK 001	Royal Albert Hall, London, England	JHE	
Sunshine Of Your Love	24 Feb 69	CR 3. Live performance.	Hendrix In Words And Music CD Outlaw Records OTR 1100030	Royal Albert Hall, London, England	JHE	
Sunshine Of Your Love	24 Feb 69	CR 3. Live performance. Stereo	Royal Albert Hall CD Blimp 008 / 009 & Listen To This Eric CD JH 003 / 4	Royal Albert Hall, London, England	JHE	
Sunshine Of Your Love	24 Feb 69	CR 3. Live performance.	Stone Free CD Silver Rarities SIRA 58 / 59	Royal Albert Hall, London, England	JHE	
Sunshine Of Your Love	26 Apr 69	BR 10. Live performance. A very short edit appeared on 'Lifelines'.	Electric Jimi CD Jaguarondi Records	Los Angeles Forum, Los Angeles, CA	JHE	
Sunshine Of Your Love	26 Apr 69	BR 10. Live performance. A very short edit appeared on 'Lifelines'.	I Don't Live Today, Maybe Tomorrow CD Living Legend LRCD 030	Los Angeles Forum, Los Angeles, CA	JHE	
Sunshine Of Your Love	26 Apr 69	BR 10. Live performance. A very short edit appeared on 'Lifelines'.	Very Best, The CD Irec / Retro MILCD-03	Los Angeles Forum, Los Angeles, CA	JHE	
Sunshine Of Your Love	26 Apr 69	BR 10. Live performance. A very short edit appeared on 'Lifelines'.	Live CD DV More CDDV 2401	Los Angeles Forum, Los Angeles, CA	JHE	
Sunshine Of Your Love	26 Apr 69	BR 10. Live performance. A very short edit appeared on 'Lifelines'.	Hey Joe CD Crocodile Beat CB 53039	Los Angeles Forum, Los Angeles, CA	JHE	
Sunshine Of Your Love	26 Apr 69	BR 10. Live performance. A very short edit appeared on 'Lifelines'.	Foxy Lady CD Alegra CD 9008	Los Angeles Forum, Los Angeles, CA	JHE	
Sunshine Of Your Love	26 Apr 69	BR 10. Live performance. A very short edit appeared on 'Lifelines'.	Anthology CD Box 9	Los Angeles Forum, Los Angeles, CA	JHE	
Sunshine Of Your Love	26 Apr 69	BR 10. Live performance. Incomplete. A very short edit	Valley Of Neptune CD	Los Angeles Forum,	JHE	

Song	Date	appeared on 'Lifelines'.	PC 28355	Los Angeles, CA	
Sunshine Of Your Love	27 Apr 69	CR 4. Live performance.	Live At The Oakland Coliseum (CR) CD Dagger Records DBRO-11743	Oakland Coliseum, Oakland, CA	JHE
Sunshine Of Your Love	17 May 69	BR 11. Live performance. Part of a medley	One Night At The Arena CD Venue VE 100501	Rhode Island Arena, Providence, RI	JHE
Sunshine Of Your Love	24 May 69	CR 5. Live performance. Part of a medley CR on the 'Stages' set where it's listed as "Spanish Castle Magic / Sunshine Of Your Love'.	Don't Miss Him This Time CD Pyramid PYCD 096	San Diego Sports Arena, San Diego, CA	JHE
Sunshine Of Your Love	25 May 69	CR 5. Live performance. Part of a medley CR on the 'Stages' set where it's listed as "Spanish Castle Magic / Sunshine Of Your Love'.	Historic Concert Vol 2 CD Midnight Beat MBCD 050	Santa Clara Pop Festival, San Jose, CA	JHE
Sunshine Of Your Love	20 Jun 69	CR 5. Live performance. Part of a medley CR on the 'Stages' set where it's listed as "Spanish Castle Magic / Sunshine Of Your Love'.	More Electricity From Newport CD Luna LU 9201	San Diego Sports Arena, San Diego, CA	JHE
Sunshine Of Your Love	20 Jun 69	CR 5. Live performance. Part of a medley CR on the 'Stages' set where it's listed as "Spanish Castle Magic / Sunshine Of Your Love'.	A Lifetime Of Experience LP Sleepy Dragon 55 10	Newport Pop Festival, San Fernando State, Northridge, CA	JHE
Sunshine Of Your Love	20 Jun 69	CR 5. Live performance. Part of a medley CR on the 'Stages' set where it's listed as "Spanish Castle Magic / Sunshine Of Your Love'.	Two Days At Newport CD JMH 007 / 2	Newport Pop Festival, San Fernando State, Northridge, CA	JHE
Sunshine Of Your Love	22 Jun 69	CR 5. Live performance. Part of a medley CR on the 'Stages' set where it's listed as "Spanish Castle Magic / Sunshine Of Your Love'.	It Never Takes An End CD Genuine Pig TGP-118	Newport Pop Festival, San Fernando State, Northridge, CA	NJK
Sunshine Of Your Love	31 Dec 69	BR 13. Live performance.	Band Of Gypsys: Happy New Year CD Silver Shadow CD 9103	Fillmore East, New York, NY 2nd Show	BOG
Sunshine Of Your Love	04 Sep 70	BR 14. Live performance.	Back To Berlin CD Midnight Beat 049	Deutsche-Landhalle, Berlin, Germany	COL
Suspicious		No Jimi	Whipper CD Pilz 447400-2	Unknown	Fake
Suspicious		No Jimi	king Of Gypsies CD Rockyssimo RK 001	Unknown	Fake
Swing Jimi Jam (Instrumental Jam)	17 Mar 68	BR 1. Live performance with a made up name for an otherwise untitled jam.	Cafe Au Go Go CD Koine 880802	Cafe' A Go Go, New York, NY	Cafe
Swing Jimi Jam (Tomorrow Never Knows)	17 Mar 68	BR 1. Live performance with a made up name for an otherwise untitled jam.	Shine On Earth, Shine On CD Sidewalk SW 89010 / 89011	Cafe' A Go Go, New York, NY	Cafe

SONG TITLE	DATE	COMMENTS	RELEASE	LOCATION / VENUE	BAND	PERSONNEL
Takin' Care Of Business	04 May 67	BR 1. An unreleased from the Chandler Tape.	Studio Haze CD INA 6	Olympic Sound Studios, London, England	JHE	Unknown / Brass In 1988, Noel Redding / Bass In 1988, Mitch Mitchell / Drums In 1988
Takin' Care Of Business	04 May 67	BR 1. An unreleased from the Chandler Tape.	DeLane Lea And Olympic Outs CD Gold Standard CD-R	Olympic Sound Studios, London, England	JHE	Unknown / Brass In 1988, Noel Redding / Bass In 1988, Mitch Mitchell / Drums In 1988
Takin' Care Of Business	04 May 67	BR 1. An unreleased from the Chandler Tape.	Electric Ladyland Outtakes CD Invasion Unlimited IU 9417-1	Olympic Sound Studios, London, England	JHE	Unknown / Brass In 1988, Noel Redding / Bass In 1988, Mitch Mitchell / Drums In 1988
Takin' Care Of Business	04 May 67	BR 1. An unreleased from the Chandler Tape.	I Don't Live Today CD ACL 007	Olympic Sound Studios, London, England	JHE	Unknown / Brass In 1988, Noel Redding / Bass In 1988, Mitch Mitchell / Drums In 1988
Takin' Care Of Business	04 May 67	BR 1. An unreleased from the Chandler Tape.	Voodoo In Ladyland CD MUM MUCD 006	Olympic Sound Studios, London, England	JHE	Unknown / Brass In 1988, Noel Redding / Bass In 1988, Mitch Mitchell / Drums In 1988
Tax Free	26 Jan 68	CR 1 mix 1.	War Heroes (CR) CD Polydor 847-2622	Olympic Sound Studios, London, England	JHE	
Tax Free	26 Jan 68	CR 1 mix 1.	South Saturn Delta (CR) CD MCACD 11684	Olympic Sound Studios, London, England	JHE	
Tax Free	26 Jan 68	CR 1 mix 2. Unused mix for the CR 1.	TTG Studios ???? CD WHOAMI WAI 015	Olympic Sound Studios, London, England	JHE	
Tax Free (Midnight)	26 Jan 68	CR 1 mix 2. Unused mix for the CR 1.	Multicolored Blues CD Luna LU 9317	Olympic Sound Studios, London, England	JHE	
Tax Free	26 Jan 68	CR 1 mix 2. Unused mix for the CR 1.	1968 AD CD Whoopy Cat WKP 0001	Olympic Sound Studios, London, England	JHE	
Tax Free	26 Jan 68	CR 1 mix 2. Unused mix for the CR 1.	Voodoo In Ladyland CD MUM MUCD 006	Olympic Sound Studios, London, England	JHE	
Tax Free	26 Jan 68	CR 1 mix 2. Unused mix for the CR 1.	Living Reels Vol 2 CD JMH 012 / 2	Olympic Sound Studios, London, England	JHE	

Song		Date	Notes	Release	Venue	Band
Tax Free		16 Feb 68	BR 1. Live performance.	Biggest Square In The Building, The CD Reverb Music 1993	State Fair Music Hall, Dallas, TX	JHE
Tax Free		16 Feb 68	BR 1. Live performance.	Scuse Me While I Kiss The Sky CD Sonic Zoom SZ 1001	State Fair Music Hall, Dallas, TX	JHE
Tax Free		16 Feb 68	BR 1. Live performance.	Scuse Me While I Kiss The Sky CD Sonic Zoom SZ 1001	State Fair Music Hall, Dallas, TX	JHE
Tax Free		19 Mar 68	BR 2. Live performance.	Once Upon A Time CD Wall Of Sound WS CD011	Capitol Theatre, Ottawa, Canada 2nd Show	JHE
Tax Free		19 Mar 68	BR 2. Live performance.	Thanks Ottawa For The Memories CD Luna 9319	Capitol Theatre, Ottawa, Canada 2nd Show	JHE
Tax Free		19 Mar 68	BR 2. Live performance.	Live From Ottawa LP Starlight SL 87010	Capitol Theatre, Ottawa, Canada 2nd Show	JHE
Tax Free		19 Mar 68	BR 2. Live performance.	Superconcert 1968 CD Firepower FP03	Capitol Theatre, Ottawa, Canada 2nd Show	JHE
Tax Free		10 Oct 68	BR 3. Live performance.	Winterland Vol 1 CD Whoopy Cat WKP 025 / 26	Winterland Theatre, San Francisco, CA 2nd Show	JHE
Tax Free		10 Oct 68	BR 3. Live performance.	Lost Winterland Tapes CD Starquake SQ 051-2	Winterland Theatre, San Francisco, CA 2nd Show	JHE
Tax Free		11 Oct 68	CR 2 mix 2. Live performance.	Winterland Vol 2 CD Whoopy Cat WKP 00279 / 28	Winterland Theatre, San Francisco, CA 2nd Show	JHE
Tax Free (Foxey Lady Instrumental Version)		11 Oct 68	CR 2 mix 2. Live performance.	Live USA CD Imtrat 902-001	Winterland Theatre, San Francisco, CA 2nd Show	JHE
Tax Free		11 Oct 68	CR 2 mix 1. Live performance. Edited for CR.	Fire CD The Entertainers CD297	Winterland Theatre, San Francisco, CA 2nd Show	JHE
Tax Free		11 Oct 68	CR 2 mix 1. Live performance. Edited for CR.	Live At Winterland (CR) CD Rykodisc RCD 20038	Winterland Theatre, San Francisco, CA 2nd Show	JHE
Tax Free		11 Oct 68	BR 4. Live performance.	Winterland Days, The CD Manic Depression 001	Winterland Theatre, San Francisco, CA 1st Show	JHE

SONG TITLE	DATE	COMMENTS	RELEASE	LOCATION / VENUE	BAND	PERSONNEL
Tax Free	11 Oct 68	BR 4. Live performance.	Winterland Vol 3 CD Whoopy Cat WKP 0029 / 30	Winterland Theatre, San Francisco, CA 1st Show	JHE	
Tax Free	10 Jan 69	CR 3. Live performance.	Welcome To The Electric Circus Vol 1 CD Midnight Beat 016	Falkoner Centret, Copenhagen, Denmark 1st Show	JHE	
Tax Free	10 Jan 69	CR 3. Live performance.	Jimi In Denmark (CR) CD UniVibes 1003 & Booted On Dynamite Studios	Falkoner Centret, Copenhagen, Denmark 1st Show	JHE	
Tax Free	10 Jan 69	CR 3. Live performance.	Live In Copenhagen CD The Swingin' Pig TSP-220-2	Falkoner Centret, Copenhagen, Denmark 1st Show	JHE	
Tax Free	18 Feb 69	BR 5. Live performance.	First Night At The Royal Albert Hall CD Midnight Beat MBCD 047 / 48	Royal Albert Hall, London, England	JHE	
Tax Free	26 Apr 69	CR 6. Live performance. An edited version (with 4 minutes cut out) appeared on 'Lifelines'.	51st Anniversary CD Future Disc JMH 001 / 8	Los Angeles Forum, Los Angeles, CA	JHE	
Tax Free	26 Apr 69	CR 6. Live performance. An edited version (with 4 minutes cut out) appeared on 'Lifelines'.	Electric Jimi CD Jaguarondi Records	Los Angeles Forum, Los Angeles, CA	JHE	
Tax Free	26 Apr 69	CR 6. Live performance. An edited version (with 4 minutes cut out) appeared on 'Lifelines'.	I Don't Live Today, Maybe Tomorrow CD Living Legend LRCD 030	Los Angeles Forum, Los Angeles, CA	JHE	
Tax Free	26 Apr 69	CR 6. Live performance. An edited version (with 4 minutes cut out) appeared on 'Lifelines'.	Live USA CD Imtrat 902-001	Los Angeles Forum, Los Angeles, CA	JHE	
Tax Free	26 Apr 69	CR 6. Live performance. An edited version (with 4 minutes cut out) appeared on 'Lifelines'.	Very Best, The CD Irec / Retro MILCD-03	Los Angeles Forum, Los Angeles, CA	JHE	
Tax Free	26 Apr 69	CR 6. Live performance. An edited version (with 4 minutes cut out) appeared on 'Lifelines'.	Experience II CD More MTT 1021	Los Angeles Forum, Los Angeles, CA	JHE	
Tax Free	26 Apr 69	CR 6. Live performance. An edited version (with 4 minutes cut out) appeared on 'Lifelines'.	Anthology CD Box 9	Los Angeles Forum, Los Angeles, CA	JHE	
Tax Free	29 Jun 69	BR 6. Live performance.	Wink Of An Eye CD Whoopy Cat WKP 0033 / 34	Mile High Stadium, Denver, CO	JHE	
Testify	?? Mar 64	CR 1. Live performance.	Lifelines (CR) CD Reprise 9 26435-2	Unknown	Jimi	Isley Brothers / Band
Testify	?? Mar 64	CR 1. Live performance. Incomplete.	Jimi: A Musical Legacy CD KTS BX 010	Unknown	Jimi	Isley Brothers / Band

Title	Date	Notes	Release	Location	
The Queen (America The Beautiful)	No Jimi	No Jimi. This is 'God Save The Queen' by David Henderson.	Electric Gypsy CD Scorpio? 40176 / 15		Fake
The Queen (Denny Boy)		No Jimi. This is 'God Save The Queen' by David Henderson.	Cherokee Mist CD Triangle PYCD 070		Fake
The Stars That Play With Laughing Sams Dice	28 Jun 67	BR 1. This is an instrumental version from a Mayfair studios mono acetate.	Electric Gypsy CD Scorpio? 40176 / 15	Houston Studios, Los Angeles, CA	JHE
The Stars That Play With Laughing Sams Dice	28 Jun 67	BR 1. This is an instrumental version from a Mayfair studios mono acetate.	Jimi: A Musical Legacy CD KTS BX 010	Houston Studios, Los Angeles, CA	JHE
The Stars That Play With Laughing Sams Dice	19 Jul 67	CR 1 mix 2 (mono).	Rarities On Compact Disc CD On The Radio	Mayfair Studios, New York, NY	JHE
The Stars That Play With Laughing Sams Dice	19 Jul 67	CR 1 mix 2 (mono).	The Singles Album (CR) CD Polydor 827 369-2	Mayfair Studios, New York, NY	JHE
The Stars That Play With Laughing Sams Dice	19 Jul 67	CR 1 mix 2 (mono).	Legacy (CR) LP Polydor	Mayfair Studios, New York, NY	JHE
The Stars That Play With Laughing Sams Dice	19 Jul 67	CR 1 mix 1 (stereo)	Electric Gypsy CD Scorpio? 40176 / 15	Mayfair Studios, New York, NY	JHE
The Stars That Play With Laughing Sams Dice	19 Jul 67	CR 1 mix 1 (stereo)	Loose Ends (CR) LP Polydor 837574-2	Mayfair Studios, New York, NY	JHE
The Stars That Play With Laughing Sams Dice	19 Jul 67	CR 1 mix 1 (stereo)	South Saturn Delta (CR) CD MCACD 11684	Mayfair Studios, New York, NY	JHE
The Stars That Play With Laughing Sams Dice	19 Jul 67	CR 1 mix 3. Unused mix of the CR.	Dante's Inferno CD Pink Poodle POO 002	Mayfair Studios, New York, NY	JHE
The Stars That Play With Laughing Sams Dice	19 Jul 67	CR 1 mix 3. Unused mix of the CR.	Mixdown Master Tapes Volume 1 CD Dandelion DL 005	Mayfair Studios, New York, NY	JHE
The Stars That Play With Laughing Sams Dice	19 Jul 67	CR 1 mix 3. Unused mix of the CR.	Get The Experience CD Invasion Unlimited IU 9424-1	Mayfair Studios, New York, NY	JHE
The Stars That Play With Laughing Sams Dice	19 Jul 67	CR 1 mix 3. Unused mix of the CR.	Completer, The CD Whoopy Cat WKP 0018 / 19	Mayfair Studios, New York, NY	JHE
Them Changes	?? Dec 69	BR 1. From the rehearsal for the New Years Fillmore shows. This disc has a breakdown performance prior to the full take.	Gypsy Haze CD Lords Of Archive LAR 16	Baggies, New York, NY	BOG
Them Changes	?? Dec 69	BR 1. From the rehearsal for the New Years Fillmore shows. This disc has a breakdown performance prior to the full take.	Band Of Gypsys Vol 3	Baggies, New York, NY	BOG

SONG TITLE	DATE	COMMENTS	RELEASE	LOCATION / VENUE	BAND	PERSONNEL
Them Changes	?? Dec 69	BR 1. From the rehearsal for the New Years Fillmore shows. This disc has a breakdown performance prior to the full take.	Band Of Gypsys Rehearsals CD Whoopy Cat WKP 003	Record Plant Or Baggies, NY, NY	BOG	
Them Changes	?? Dec 69	BR 1. From the rehearsal for the New Years Fillmore shows. This disc has a breakdown performance prior to the full take.	Band Of Gypsys- The Ultimate CD JMH 010 / 3	Baggies, New York, NY	BOG	
Them Changes	31 Dec 69	BR 2. Live performance.	Band Of Gypsys Vol 3	Fillmore East, New York, NY 1st Show	BOG	
Them Changes	31 Dec 69	BR 2. Live performance.	Gypsy Haze CD Lords Of Archive LAR 16	Fillmore East, New York, NY 1st Show	BOG	
Them Changes	31 Dec 69	BR 2. Live performance.	Fillmore Concerts, The CD Whoopy Cat WKP 0006 / 7	Fillmore East, New York, NY 1st Show	BOG	
Them Changes	31 Dec 69	BR 2. Live performance.	Band Of Gold CD-R Major Tom MT 087	Fillmore East, New York, NY 1st Show	BOG	
Them Changes	31 Dec 69	BR 2. Live performance.	Power Of Soul CD SQ-10	Fillmore East, New York, NY 1st Show	BOG	
Them Changes	31 Dec 69	BR 2. Live performance.	Ultimate Live Collection, The CD The Beat Goes On BGO BX 9307-4	Fillmore East, New York, NY 1st Show	BOG	
Them Changes	31 Dec 69	BR 3. Live performance.	Auld Lang Syne CD JH 100 03	Fillmore East, New York, NY 2nd Show	BOG	
Them Changes	31 Dec 69	BR 3. Live performance.	Band Of Gypsys: Happy New Year CD Silver Shadow CD 9103	Fillmore East, New York, NY 2nd Show	BOG	
Them Changes	31 Dec 69	BR 3. Live performance.	Fillmore Concerts, The CD Whoopy Cat WKP 0006 / 7	Fillmore East, New York, NY 2nd Show	BOG	
Them Changes	31 Dec 69	BR 3. Live performance.	Band Of Gold CD-R Major Tom MT 087	Fillmore East, New York, NY 2nd Show	BOG	
Them Changes	31 Dec 69	BR 3. Live performance.	Band Of Gypsys- The Ultimate CD JMH 010 / 3	Fillmore East, New York, NY 2nd Show	BOG	
Them Changes	01 Jan 70	BR 4. Live performance.	Band Of Gold CD-R Major Tom MT 087	Fillmore East, New York, NY 1st Show	BOG	
Them Changes	01 Jan 70	CR 1. Live performance.	Band Of Gypsys (CR) CD Capitol 72434-93446-2-4	Fillmore East, New York, NY 2nd Show	BOG	

Title	Date	Notes	Release	Location	Musician	Personnel
Them Changes	01 Jan 70	CR 1. Live performance.	Band Of Gold CD-R Major Tom MT 087	Fillmore East, New York, NY 2nd Show	BOG	
Them Changes	01 Jan 70	CR 1. Live performance.		Fillmore East, New York, NY 2nd Show	BOG	
Things I Used To Do	07 May 69	BR 1-3 & CR 1 mix 2. This session consisted of 4 takes. It begins with some guitar tuning, then a breakdown, a longer take, another breakdown and finally a complete take.	Freak Out Jam CD GH 002	Record Plant, New York, NY	Jimi	Johnny Winter / Slide Guitar, Stephen Stills / Bass, Dallas Taylor / Drums
Things I Used To Do	07 May 69	CR 1 mix 2. Take 4 only.	First Rays Of The New Rising Sun CD Living Legend LLRCD 023	Record Plant, New York, NY	Jimi	Johnny Winter / Slide Guitar, Stephen Stills / Bass, Dallas Taylor / Drums
Things I Used To Do	07 May 69	CR 1 mix 2. Take 4 only.	Sir James Marshall LP Jester Productions JP 106	Record Plant, New York, NY	Jimi	Johnny Winter / Slide Guitar, Stephen Stills / Bass, Dallas Taylor / Drums
Things I Used To Do	07 May 69	CR 1 mix 2. Take 4 only.	This One's For You LP Veteran Music MF-243	Record Plant, New York, NY	Jimi	Johnny Winter / Slide Guitar, Stephen Stills / Bass, Dallas Taylor / Drums
Things I Used To Do (Jam Part 2)	07 May 69	CR 1 mix 2. Take 4 only without the three breakdowns.	Things I Used To Do CD The Early Years 02-CD-3334	Record Plant, New York, NY	Jimi	Johnny Winter / Slide Guitar, Stephen Stills / Bass, Dallas Taylor / Drums
Things I Used To Do	07 May 69	CR 1 mix 2. Take 4 only.	51st Anniversary CD Future Disc JMH 001 / 8	Record Plant, New York, NY	Jimi	Johnny Winter / Slide Guitar, Stephen Stills / Bass, Dallas Taylor / Drums
Things I Used To Do	07 May 69	CR 1 mix 2. Take 4 only.	Things I Used To Do, The CD Golden Memories GM 890738	Record Plant, New York, NY	Jimi	Johnny Winter / Slide Guitar, Stephen Stills / Bass, Dallas Taylor / Drums
Things I Used To Do	07 May 69	CR 1 mix 2. Take 4 only.	Talent And Feeling Vol 1 CD Extremely Rare EXR 17	Record Plant, New York, NY	Jimi	Johnny Winter / Slide Guitar, Stephen Stills / Bass, Dallas Taylor / Drums
Things I Used To Do	07 May 69	CR 1 mix 2. Take 4 only.	Every Way To Paradise CD Tintangel TIBX 021 / 22 / 23 / 24	Record Plant, New York, NY	Jimi	Johnny Winter / Slide Guitar, Stephen Stills / Bass, Dallas Taylor / Drums
Things I Used To Do	07 May 69	CR 1 mix 2. Take 4 only.	Midnight Sun CD Third Eye NK 007	Record Plant, New York, NY	Jimi	Johnny Winter / Slide Guitar, Stephen Stills / Bass, Dallas Taylor / Drums
Things I Used To Do	07 May 69	CR 1 mix 1.	Lifelines (CR) CD Reprise 9 26435-2	Record Plant, New York, NY	Jimi	Johnny Winter / Slide Guitar, Stephen Stills / Bass, Dallas Taylor / Drums
Things I Used To Do	07 May 69	CR 1 mix 1.	Black Strings CD CDM G-53 258	Record Plant, New York, NY	Jimi	Johnny Winter / Slide Guitar, Stephen Stills / Bass, Dallas Taylor / Drums

SONG TITLE	DATE	COMMENTS	RELEASE	LOCATION / VENUE	BAND	PERSONNEL
Things I Used To Do	22 Jun 69	BR 4. Live performance. Incomplete	It Never Takes An End CD Genuine Pig TGP-118	Newport Pop Festival, San Fernando State, Northridge, CA	NJK	
Things I Used To Do	22 Jun 69	BR 4. Live performance. Incomplete	Two Days At Newport CD JMH 007 / 2	Newport Pop Festival, San Fernando State, Northridge, CA	NJK	
Third Stone From The Sun	11 Jan 67	CR 1 mix 1 (stereo)	Are You Experienced? (CR) CD MCACD 11602	De Lane Lea, London, England	JHE	
Third Stone From The Sun	11 Jan 67	CR 1 mix 1 (stereo)	The Singles Album (CR) CD Polydor 827 369-2	De Lane Lea, London, England	JHE	
Third Stone From The Sun	11 Jan 67	CR 1 mix 2 (mono)	Are You Experienced? (CR) LP Track 612 001	De Lane Lea, London, England	JHE	
Third Stone From The Sun	03 May 67	BR 1. Live performance from a medley. Jimi touches on this song only briefly but I chose to include it here because it was the only time he ever did on stage.	Hendrix, Busted In Toronto CD Venue VE 100502	Maple Leaf Gardens, Toronto, Canada	JHE	
Third Stone From The Sun / Villanova Junction	15 Jun 70	BR 1. A collection of loose jams from the newly constructed Electric Lady studio spliced together. I don't hear much that resembles "3rd Stone..." but there is a bit of "Villanova Junction" here. From the same session as "Session Thing" and "Jam Thing".	Black Gold CD Midnight Beat MBCD 058-062	Electric Lady Studio, New York, NY	Jimi	Steve Winwood / Electric Piano, Dave Palmer / Some Drums, Unknown / Bass
Three Little Bears	?? / ?? 68	BR 1. From one of Jimi's home composing tape.	Acoustic Jams CD Sphinx SX CD 001	New York Apartment	Solo	
Three Little Bears	?? / ?? 68	BR 1. From one of Jimi's home composing tape.	Black Gold CD Midnight Beat MBCD 058-062	New York Apartment	Solo	
Three Little Bears	17 Mar 68	BR 2. Live performance.	Shine On Earth, Shine On CD Sidewalk SW 89010 / 89011	Cafe' A Go Go, New York, NY	Cafe	
Three Little Bears	17 Mar 68	BR 2. Live performance.	Blues At Midnight CD Midnight Beat MBCD 037	Cafe' A Go Go, New York, NY	Cafe	
Three Little Bears	17 Mar 68	BR 2. Live performance.	Blues At Midnight CD Midnight Beat MBCD 037	Cafe' A Go Go, New York, NY	Cafe	
Three Little Bears (Jimi Jam)	17 Mar 68	BR 2. Live performance.	Cafe Au Go Go CD Koine 880802	Cafe' A Go Go, New York, NY	Cafe	
Three Little Bears	17 Mar 68	BR 2. Live performance.	Every Way To Paradise	Cafe' A Go Go, New York, NY	Cafe	

Song	Date	Notes	Release	Location		Musician
Three Little Bears	02 May 68	CR 1 mix 1. The European pressings included Jimi's remarks "Oh fuck me, fuck me". The US releases mixed this out for our protection.	War Heroes (CR) LP Polydor 2302 020	Record Plant, New York, NY	Jimi	Mitch Mitchell / Drums
Three Little Bears	02 May 68	CR 1 mix 2. The US pressing with Jimi's offensive remarks mixed out.	War Heroes (CR) CD Polydor 847-2622	Record Plant, New York, NY	Jimi	Mitch Mitchell / Drums
Three Little Bears	02 May 68	CR 1 mix 3. Unused mix of the CR 1 mix 1 that plays longer.	TTG Studios ???? CD WHOAMI WAI 015	Record Plant, New York, NY	Jimi	Mitch Mitchell / Drums
Three Little Bears	02 May 68	CR 1 mix 3. Unused mix of the CR 1 mix 1 that plays longer.	Multicolored Blues CD Luna LU 9317	Record Plant, New York, NY	Jimi	Mitch Mitchell / Drums
Three Little Bears	02 May 68	CR 1 mix 3. Unused mix of the CR 1 mix 1 that plays longer.	1968 AD CD Whoopy Cat WKP 0001	Record Plant, New York, NY	Jimi	Mitch Mitchell / Drums
Three Little Bears	02 May 68	CR 1 mix 3. Unused mix of the CR 1 mix 1 that plays longer.	Things I Used To Do, The CD Golden Memories GM 890738	Record Plant, New York, NY	Jimi	Mitch Mitchell / Drums
Three Little Bears	02 May 68	CR 1 mix 3. Unused mix of the CR 1 mix 1 that plays longer.	Jimi: A Musical Legacy CD KTS BX 010	Record Plant, New York, NY	Jimi	Mitch Mitchell / Drums
Three Little Bears	02 May 68	CR 1 mix 3. Unused mix of the CR 1 mix 1 that plays longer.	Kiss The Skies CD Mum MUCD 024	Record Plant, New York, NY	Jimi	Mitch Mitchell / Drums
Three Little Bears	02 May 68	CR 1 mix 3. Unused mix of the CR 1 mix 1 that plays longer.	Living Reels Vol 2 CD JMH 012 / 2	Record Plant, New York, NY	Jimi	Mitch Mitchell / Drums
Three Little Bears	02 May 68	Cr 1 mix 4. The complete and unedited long version of the CR. A version of "South Saturn Delta" is played during the long jam part.	Unsurpassed Studio Takes CD Yellow Dog YD 050	Record Plant, New York, NY	Jimi	Mitch Mitchell / Drums
Three Little Bears	02 May 68	Cr 1 mix 4. The complete and unedited long version of the CR. A version of "South Saturn Delta" is played during the long jam part.	Mixdown Master Tapes Volume 2 CD Dandelion DL 006	Record Plant, New York, NY	Jimi	Mitch Mitchell / Drums
Three Little Bears	02 May 68	Cr 1 mix 5. The complete and unedited long version of the CR from the vocal booth so Jimi's vocal track is emphasized.	Ball And Chain CD Jimi 009	Record Plant, New York, NY	Jimi	Mitch Mitchell / Drums
Three Little Bears	02 May 68	Cr 1 mix 5. The complete and unedited long version of the CR from the vocal booth so Jimi's vocal track is emphasized.	Mixdown Master Tapes Volume 3 CD Dandelion DL 007	Record Plant, New York, NY	Jimi	Mitch Mitchell / Drums
Tobacco Road	17 Sep 70	BR. Live performance. An audience tape of Jimi's last performance ever.	Can You Please Crawl Out Your Window? LP Ruthless Rhymes Jimi1	Ronnie Scotts Club, London, England	Jimi	Eric Burden & War
Tomorrow Never Knows / Uranus Rock	?? Mar? 68	Part of the long "Morrison's Lament" medley. Many of the other Scene Club releases also list these titles.	Jimi: A Musical Legacy CD KTS BX 010	Scene Club, New York, NY	Scene	

Note at top of release column: CD Tintangel TIBX 021 / 22 / 23 / 24 — York, NY

SONG TITLE	DATE	COMMENTS	RELEASE	LOCATION / VENUE	BAND	PERSONNEL
Train Kept A Rollin'	22 Jun 69	BR 1. Live performance. Part of a medley.	It Never Takes An End CD Genuine Pig TGP-118	Newport Pop Festival, San Fernando State, Northridge, CA	NJK	
Tune Up Song	29 Jan 68	CR Live performance. Actually this is just a bit of rock and roll guitar riff during the tune up preceding "The Wind Cries Mary" from this show.	Stages Paris 68 (CR) CD Reprise 9 27632-2	L' Olympia Theatre, Paris, France	JHE	
Tune Up Song (Spanish Castle Magic)	29 Jan 68	CR Live performance. Actually this is just a bit of rock and roll guitar riff during the tune up preceding "The Wind Cries Mary" from this show.	Official Bootleg Album, The CD Yellow Dog YD 051	L' Olympia Theatre, Paris, France	JHE	
Two Guitars Jam		No Jimi	51st Anniversary CD Future Disc JMH 001 / 8		Fake	
Up From The Skies	29 Oct 67	Cr 1 mix 1 (stereo)	Axis: Bold As Love (CR) CD MCACD 11601	Olympic Sound Studios, London, England	JHE	
Up From The Skies	29 Oct 67	CR1 mix 2 (mono)	Axis: Bold As Love (CR) LP Track 612 003	Olympic Sound Studios, London, England	JHE	
Up From The Skies	29 Oct 67	CR 1 mix 3. An alternate stereo mix without the guitar solo moving from left to right channels. Also the vocal track is mixed to the center.	Axis: Bold As Love (CR) LP Backtrack 11	Olympic Sound Studios, London, England	JHE	
Up From The Skies	29 Oct 67	CR 1 mix 4. Unused mix of the CR from the Sotheby's Tape.	Sotheby Auction Tapes, The CD Midnight Beat MBCD 010	Olympic Sound Studios, London, England	JHE	
Up From The Skies	29 Oct 67	CR 1 mix 4. Unused mix of the CR from the Sotheby's Tape.	51st Anniversary CD Future Disc JMH 001 / 8	Olympic Sound Studios, London, England	JHE	
Up From The Skies	29 Oct 67	CR 1 mix 4. Unused mix of the CR from the Sotheby's Tape.	Sotheby's Private Reels CD JHR 003 / 004	Olympic Sound Studios, London, England	JHE	
Up From The Skies	29 Oct 67	CR 1 mix 4. Unused mix of the CR from the Sotheby's Tape.	Notes In Colours CD JHR 001 / 002	Olympic Sound Studios, London, England	JHE	
Up From The Skies	29 Oct 67	CR 1 mix 4. Unused mix of the CR from the Sotheby's Tape.	Jimi: A Musical Legacy CD KTS BX 010	Olympic Sound Studios, London, England	JHE	
Up From The Skies	29 Oct 67	CR 1 mix 4. Unused mix of the CR from the Sotheby's Tape.	Sotheby's Reels, The CD Gold Standard TOM-800	Olympic Sound Studios, London, England	JHE	

Title	Date	Notes	Release	Location	Band	Personnel
Up From The Skies	29 Oct 67	CR 1 mix 4. Unused mix of the CR from the Sotheby's Tape.	Living Reels Vol 1 CD JMH 011	Olympic Sound Studios, London, England	JHE	
Up From The Skies	08 Jan 68	Cr 2. The only live performance of this song.	Live In Paris 66 / 67 CD Whoopy Cat WKP 0012	Konserthuset, Stockholm, Sweden 1st Show	JHE	
Up From The Skies	08 Jan 68	Cr 2. The only live performance of this song.	Lost In Sweden CD Whoopy Cat WKP 0046 / 0047	Konserthuset, Stockholm, Sweden 1st Show	JHE	
Up From The Skies	08 Jan 68	Cr 2. The only live performance of this song.	EXP Over Sweden (CR) CD UniVibes 1002	Konserthuset, Stockholm, Sweden 1st Show	JHE	
Utee	?? Mar? 64	CR 1. Copied from the single.	51st Anniversary CD Future Disc JMH 001 / 8	Unknown	Jimi	Rosa Lee Brooks / Vocals, Arthur Lee / Backing Vocals, Big Francis / Drums, Alvin ? / Bass
Utee	?? Mar? 64	CR 1. Copied from the single.	Rarities CD The Genuine Pig TGP-CD-091	Unknown	Jimi	Rosa Lee Brooks / Vocals, Arthur Lee / Backing Vocals, Big Francis / Drums, Alvin ? / Bass
Utee	?? Mar? 64	CR 1. Copied from the single.	Rarities On Compact Disc CD On The Radio	Unknown	Jimi	Rosa Lee Brooks / Vocals, Arthur Lee / Backing Vocals, Big Francis / Drums, Alvin ? / Bass
Utee	?? Mar? 64	CR 1. Copied from the single.	Jimi: A Musical Legacy CD KTS BX 010	Unknown	Jimi	Rosa Lee Brooks / Vocals, Arthur Lee / Backing Vocals, Big Francis / Drums, Alvin ? / Bass
Valleys Of Neptune (part of Instrumental Jams)	?? / May 69	BR 1. A very early and short attempt.	Electric Anniversary Jimi CD Midnight Beat MBCD 024	Record Plant, New York, NY	Jimi	Stephen Stills / Bass, Dallas Taylor / Drums
Valleys Of Neptune (Cactus)	06 Sep 69	BR 2. Another studio run-through of this song.	Record Plant Jam CD Pilot Records HJCD 69	Hit Factory, New York, NY	GSRB	
Valleys Of Neptune (Lonely Avenue)	06 Sep 69	BR 2. Another studio run-through of this song.	Ladyland In Flames LP Marshall Records JIMI 1,2,3,4	Hit Factory, New York, NY	GSRB	
Valleys Of Neptune (Valleys Of Neptune Jam)	06 Sep 69	BR 2. Another studio run-through of this song.	Electric Anniversary Jimi CD Midnight Beat MBCD 024	Hit Factory, New York, NY	GSRB	
Valleys Of Neptune (Jimi / Jimmy Jam)	06 Sep 69	BR 2. Another studio run-through of this song. This CD has extra studio chat at the start and finish.	Mixdown Master Tapes Volume 3 CD Dandelion DL 007	Hit Factory, New York, NY	GSRB	

SONG TITLE	DATE	COMMENTS	RELEASE	LOCATION / VENUE	BAND	PERSONNEL
Valleys Of Neptune	06 Sep 69	BR 2. Another studio run-through of this song.	Flames CD Missing In Action ACT 1	Hit Factory, New York, NY	GSRB	
Valleys Of Neptune (You Wouldn't Understand)	06 Sep 69	BR 2. Another studio run-through of this song. Incomplete.	McLaughlin Sessions, The CD HML CD 9409	Hit Factory, New York, NY	GSRB	
Valleys Of Neptune (Cactus)	06 Sep 69	BR 2. Another studio run-through of this song. Incomplete.	Every Way To Paradise CD Tintangel TIBX 021 / 22 / 23 / 24	Hit Factory, New York, NY	GSRB	
Valleys Of Neptune	23 Sep 69	CR 1 mix 1. As included on the 'Lifelines' release, this is heavily edited and is further marred by some voice over.	Electric Hendrix Vol 1 CD Pyramid PYCD 030	Hit Factory, New York, NY	COL	Juma Sultan / Percussion
Valleys Of Neptune	23 Sep 69	CR 1 mix 1. As included on the 'Lifelines' release, this is heavily edited and is further marred by some voice over.	Lifelines (CR) CD Reprise 9 26435-2	Hit Factory, New York, NY	COL	Juma Sultan / Percussion
Valleys Of Neptune	23 Sep 69	CR 1 mix 2. This is the complete version used for the CR.	51st Anniversary CD Future Disc JMH 001 / 8	Hit Factory, New York, NY	COL	Juma Sultan / Percussion
Valleys Of Neptune	23 Sep 69	CR 1 mix 3. A second unused mix of the complete version of the CR with the bass mixed out.	Mixdown Master Tapes Volume 2 CD Dandelion DL 006	Hit Factory, New York, NY	COL	Juma Sultan / Percussion
Valleys Of Neptune	23 Sep 69	CR 1 mix 3. A second unused mix of the complete version of the CR with the bass mixed out.	Cherokee Mist CD Triangle PYCD 070	Hit Factory, New York, NY	COL	Juma Sultan / Percussion
Valleys Of Neptune	23 Sep 69	CR 1 mix 3. A second unused mix of the complete version of the CR with the bass mixed out.	Electric Gypsy's CD Pilot HJCD 070	Hit Factory, New York, NY	COL	Juma Sultan / Percussion
Valleys Of Neptune	23 Sep 69	CR 1 mix 3. A second unused mix of the complete version of the CR with the bass mixed out.	First Rays - The Sessions CD Whoopy Cat WKP 0002	Hit Factory, New York, NY	COL	Juma Sultan / Percussion
Valleys Of Neptune	23 Sep 69	CR 1 mix 3. A second unused mix of the complete version of the CR with the bass mixed out.	Electric Ladyland Outtakes CD Invasion Unlimited IU 9417-1	Hit Factory, New York, NY	COL	Juma Sultan / Percussion
Valleys Of Neptune	23 Sep 69	CR 1 mix 3. A second unused mix of the complete version of the CR with the bass mixed out.	Every Way To Paradise CD Tintangel TIBX 021 / 22 / 23 / 24	Hit Factory, New York, NY	COL	Juma Sultan / Percussion
Valleys Of Neptune	23 Sep 69	CR 1 mix 3. A second unused mix of the complete version of the CR with the bass mixed out.	I Don't Live Today CD ACL 007	Hit Factory, New York, NY	COL	Juma Sultan / Percussion
Valleys Of Neptune	23 Sep 69	CR 1 mix 3. A second unused mix of the complete version of the CR with the bass mixed out.	Gypsy Charm CD Mum MUCD 018	Hit Factory, New York, NY	COL	Juma Sultan / Percussion
Valleys Of Neptune (Unknown Instrumental #1)	15 May 70	BR 3. An instrumental version from this date.	Studio Haze CD INA 6	Electric Lady Studio, New York, NY	COL	
Valleys Of Neptune (Slow Time Blues)	15 May 70	BR 3. An instrumental version from this date.	Multicolored Blues CD Luna LU 9317	Electric Lady Studio, New York, NY	COL	

Title	Date	Notes	Release	Location	Label	Personnel
Valleys Of Neptune	15 May 70	BR 3. An instrumental version from this date.	Eyes And Imagination CD Third Stone TSD 18970	Electric Lady Studio, New York, NY	COL	
Valleys Of Neptune	26 Jun 70	BR 4. This is from a session tape with several false starts and breakdowns ending in a complete take.	First Rays Of The New Rising Sun CD Triangle PYCD 084-2	Electric Lady Studio, New York, NY	Jimi	Billy Cox / Bass
Valleys Of Neptune (Lil Dog O Mine / Valleys Of Neptune)	26 Jun 70	BR 4. This is from a session tape with several false starts and breakdowns ending in a complete take.	Diamonds In The Dust CD Midnight Beat MBCD 022 / 23	Electric Lady Studio, New York, NY	Jimi	Billy Cox / Bass
Valleys Of Neptune	26 Jun 70	BR 4. This is from a session tape with several false starts and breakdowns ending in a complete take that fades early here.	Mixdown Master Tapes Volume 2 CD Dandelion DL 006	Electric Lady Studio, New York, NY	Jimi	Billy Cox / Bass
Valleys Of Neptune	25 Jun 70	BR 5 mix 1. The complete medley that begins with "Cherokee Mist" and "In From The Storm". See 'Cherokee Mist / In From The Storm / Valleys Of Neptune" for other CD's with the full medley.	Multicolored Blues CD Luna LU 9317	Electric Lady Studio, New York, NY	COL	
Valleys Of Neptune	25 Jun 70	BR 5 mix 2. Incomplete. This just the "Valleys Of Neptune" part edited from a longer medley. See the "Multicolored Blues" CD for the full medley.	First Rays Of The New Rising Sun CD Triangle PYCD 084-2	Electric Lady Studio, New York, NY	COL	
Valleys Of Neptune	25 Jun 70	BR 5 mix 2. Incomplete. This just the "Valleys Of Neptune" part edited from a longer medley. See the "Multicolored Blues" CD for the full medley.	Acoustic Jams CD Sphinx SX CD 001	Electric Lady Studio, New York, NY	COL	
Villanova Junction (Maui Sunset)	?? Aug 69	BR 1. This is about12 minutes of jamming from Jimi's Shokan House. At about the 9 minute mark 'Villanova Junction' appears and plays to the end so we'll drop this under that title for convenience.	Multicolored Blues CD Luna LU 9317	Shokan House, Woodstock, NY	GSRB	
Villanova Junction	?? Aug 69	CR 2. A long rambling workout at Jimi's house in Shokan from the mediocre sessions with Mike Ephron.	Jimi Hendrix At His Best Vol 1 (CR) LP Sagapan 6313	Shokan House, Woodstock, NY	Jimi	Mike Ephron / Keyboards, Juma Sultan & Jerry Velez / Percussion
Villanova Junction	18 Aug 69	CR 2. Live performance.	At Woodstock (CR) Laserdisc BMG BVLP 86	Woodstock Music And Art Fair, Bethel, NY	COL	
Villanova Junction	18 Aug 69	CR 2. Live performance.	Woodstock (CR) CD MCA 11063	Woodstock Music And Art Fair, Bethel, NY	GSRB	
Villanova Junction	18 Aug 69	CR 2. Live performance.	Gypsy Sun And Rainbows CD Manic Depression MDCD 05 / 06	Woodstock Music And Art Fair, Bethel, NY	GSRB	
Villanova Junction	18 Aug 69	CR 2. Live performance.	Woodstock Monday, August 18 1969, 8AM CD JMH 008	Woodstock Music And Art Fair, Bethel, NY	GSRB	

SONG TITLE	DATE	COMMENTS	RELEASE	LOCATION / VENUE	BAND	PERSONNEL
Villanova Junction	18 Aug 69	CR 2. Live performance.	Ultimate Live Collection, The CD The Beat Goes On BGO BX 9307-4	Woodstock Music And Art Fair, Bethel, NY	GSRB	
Villanova Junction	23 Jan 70	BR 6. This studio version was considered for inclusion on the official "Jimi Hendrix: Blues" CD.	500,000 Halos CD EXP 500,000	Record Plant, New York, NY	BOG	
Villanova Junction	23 Jan 70	BR 6. This studio version was considered for inclusion on the official "Jimi Hendrix: Blues" CD.	Mixdown Master Tapes Volume 3 CD Dandelion DL 007	Record Plant, New York, NY	BOG	
Villanova Junction	25 Apr 70	BR 3. Live performance.	Enjoy Jimi Hendrix LP Rubber Dubber 700-001-01	Los Angeles Forum, Los Angeles, CA	COL	
Villanova Junction	25 Apr 70	BR 3. Live performance. The Luna disc is from a tape source while the JHCD 528 disc is copied from vinyl.	Scuse Me While I Kiss The Sky CD Luna CD & JHCD 528	Los Angeles Forum, Los Angeles, CA	COL	
Villanova Junction	30 May 70	BR 4. Live performance. A medley including 'Midnight Lightning'.	Berkeley Soundchecks, The CD Whoopy Cat WKP 0008	Berkeley Community Theater, Berkeley, CA Sound Check	COL	
Villanova Junction	30 Jul 70	BR 5. Live performance.	Maui, Hawaii LP JH 106 (Trademark Of Quality?)	Berkeley Community Theater, Berkeley, CA 2nd Show	COL	
Villanova Junction	30 Jul 70	BR 5. Live performance.	Last American Concert Vol 2 CD The Swingin' Pig TSP-072	Rainbow Bridge Vibratory Sound-Color Experiment, Maui, HI 2nd Show	COL	
Villanova Junction	30 Jul 70	BR 5. Live performance.	In From The Storm CD Silver Rarities SIRA 109 / 110	Rainbow Bridge Vibratory Sound-Color Experiment, Maui, HI 2nd Show	COL	
Villanova Junction	30 Jul 70	BR 5. Live performance.	Rainbow Bridge 2 CD JMH 003 / 2	Rainbow Bridge Vibratory Sound-Color Experiment, Maui, HI 2nd Show	COL	
Villanova Junction / Ships Passing		No Jimi involvement on this track	Diamonds In The Dust CD Midnight Beat MBCD 022 / 23		Fake	
Voice In The Wind		No Jimi involvement on this track	Whisper CD Pilz 447400-2		No Jimi	
Voice In The Wind		No Jimi involvement on this track	Hendrix In Words And Music CD Outlaw Records OTR 1100030		No Jimi	

Voices		No Jimi involvement on this track	Whipper CD Pilz 447400-2	Unknown	No Jimi	
Voodoo Chile	?? Mar 68	CR 2 mix 1. The stereo mix from this home composing tape.	Jimi By Himself The Home Recordings (CR) BSP-VC1	New York Apartment	Solo	
Voodoo Chile	?? Mar 68	CR 2 mix 2. The mono mix from this home composing tape. Incomplete.	Acoustic Jams CD Sphinx SX CD 001	New York Apartment	Solo	
Voodoo Chile	?? Mar 68	CR 2 mix 2. The mono mix from this home composing tape. Incomplete.	1968 AD Part Two CD Whoopy Cat WKP 0013	New York Apartment	Solo	Jack Casady / Bass, Mitch Mitchell / Drums, Steve Winwood / Organ
Voodoo Chile	?? Mar 68	CR 2 mix 2. The mono mix from this home composing tape. Incomplete.	Voodoo Blues CD Smurf	New York Apartment	Solo	
Voodoo Chile	?? Mar 68	CR 2 mix 2. The mono mix from this home composing tape. Incomplete.	Jimi: A Musical Legacy CD KTS BX 010	Record Plant, New York, NY	JHE	
Voodoo Chile	?? Mar 68	CR 2 mix 2. The mono mix from this home composing tape. Incomplete.	Black Gold CD Midnight Beat MBCD 058-062	New York Apartment	Solo	
Voodoo Chile	02 May 68	BR 1-5 & CR 1 mix 2. The first 5 takes from the session. The last version is an unused mix of the CR 1.	Experience The Voodoo Sessions CD No Label	Record Plant, New York, NY	Jimi	Jack Casady / Bass, Mitch Mitchell / Drums, Steve Winwood / Organ
Voodoo Chile	02 May 68	BR 2,4,5 & CR 1 mix 2. This release has takes 2,4 & 5 plus an unused mix of CR 1.	Living Reels Vol 2 CD JMH 012 / 2	Record Plant, New York, NY	Jimi	Jack Casady / Bass, Mitch Mitchell / Drums, Steve Winwood / Organ
Voodoo Chile	02 May 68	BR 2. Only part of take 2 from the session.	1968 AD Part Two CD Whoopy Cat WKP 0013	Record Plant, New York, NY	Jimi	Jack Casady / Bass, Mitch Mitchell / Drums, Steve Winwood / Organ
Voodoo Chile	02 May 68	BR 2-4 & CR 1 mix 2. This release has part of take 2, takes 3 & 4 and finishes with an unused mix of the CR 1.	Black Gold CD Midnight Beat MBCD 058-062	Record Plant, New York, NY	Jimi	Jack Casady / Bass, Mitch Mitchell / Drums, Steve Winwood / Organ
Voodoo Chile	02 May 68	BR 3-4 & CR 1 mix 2. This release has takes 3 & 4 and finishes with an unused mix of the CR 1.	51st Anniversary CD Future Disc JMH 001 / 8	Record Plant, New York, NY	Jimi	Jack Casady / Bass, Mitch Mitchell / Drums, Steve Winwood / Organ
Voodoo Chile	02 May 68	CR 1 mix 1.	1968 AD Part Two CD Whoopy Cat 0013	Record Plant, New York, NY	Jimi	Jack Casady / Bass, Mitch Mitchell / Drums, Steve Winwood / Organ
Voodoo Chile	02 May 68	CR 1 mix 1.	Red House CD The Entertainers CD294	Record Plant, New York, NY	Jimi	Jack Casady / Bass, Mitch Mitchell / Drums, Steve Winwood / Organ
Voodoo Chile	02 May 68	CR 1 mix 1.	Electric Ladyland (CR) CD MCACD-11600	Record Plant, New York, NY	Jimi	Jack Casady / Bass, Mitch Mitchell / Drums, Steve Winwood / Organ

SONG TITLE	DATE	COMMENTS	RELEASE	LOCATION / VENUE	BAND	PERSONNEL
Voodoo Chile	02 May 68	CR 1 mix 3. A second unused mix of the CR 1.	First Rays Of The New Rising Sun CD Living Legend LLRCD 023	Record Plant, New York, NY	Jimi	Jack Casady / Bass, Mitch Mitchell / Drums, Steve Winwood / Organ
Voodoo Chile	02 May 68	BR 6. A weird edit of takes 4 and 2.	Freak Out Blues CD GH 001	Record Plant, New York, NY	Jimi	Jack Casady / Bass, Mitch Mitchell / Drums, Steve Winwood / Organ
Voodoo Chile (Voodoo Chile Blues)	02 May 68	CR 3. An edit of three of the sessions takes.	Jimi Hendrix: Blues (CR) CD MCA MCAD-11060	Record Plant, New York, NY	Jimi	Jack Casady / Bass, Mitch Mitchell / Drums, Steve Winwood / Organ
Voodoo Chile (Slight Return)	03 May 68	BR 1-3 & 5-20. All of the takes for this classic track with the exception of what should be take 4. Take 16 should be identified as CR 2 mix 2 as its the raw take for the "Lifelines" mix. Take 20 should be CR 1 mix for the CR 1.	Experience The Voodoo Sessions CD No Label	Record Plant, New York, NY	JHE	
Voodoo Chile (Slight Return)	03 May 68	BR 1-3 & 5-20. All of the takes for this classic track with the exception of what should be take 4. Take 16 should be identified as CR 2 mix 2 as its the raw take for the "Lifelines" mix. Take 20 should be CR 1 mix 3, again the raw mix for the CR 1.	Black Gold CD Midnight Beat MBCD 058-062	Record Plant, New York, NY	JHE	
Voodoo Chile (Slight Return)	03 May 68	BR 10-12. Two false starts and one longer take from the session.	Hear My Freedom CD Kobra KRCR 010	Record Plant, New York, NY	JHE	
Voodoo Chile (Slight Return)	03 May 68	CR 1 mix 1. (stereo)	Red House CD The Entertainers CD294	Record Plant, New York, NY	JHE	
Voodoo Chile (Slight Return)	03 May 68	CR 1 mix 1. (stereo)	Electric Ladyland (CR) CD MCACD-11600	Record Plant, New York, NY	JHE	
Voodoo Chile (Slight Return)	03 May 68	CR 1 mix 1. (stereo)	The Singles Album (CR) CD Polydor 827 369-2	Record Plant, New York, NY	JHE	
Voodoo Chile (Slight Return)	03 May 68	CR 1 mix 2. (mono)	Voodoo Chile (Slight Return) EP. CR Polydor 2121011A (Australia)	Record Plant, New York, NY	JHE	
Voodoo Chile (Slight Return)	03 May 68	CR 2 mix 1. This is take 16 (even though 'Lifelines' indicates take 8) from the session.	Lifelines (CR) CD Reprise 9 26435-2	Record Plant, New York, NY	JHE	
Voodoo Chile (Slight Return)	03 May 68	CR 2 mix 1. This is take 16 (even though 'Lifelines' indicates take 8) from the session.	Voodoo Blues CD Smurf	Record Plant, New York, NY	JHE	
Voodoo Chile (Slight Return)	03 May 68	CR 2 mix 1. This is take 16 (even though 'Lifelines' indicates take 8) from the session.	Studio Experience CD Sodium Haze SH 099	Record Plant, New York, NY	JHE	
Voodoo Chile (Slight Return)	03 May 68	CR 2 mix 1. This is take 16 (even though 'Lifelines' indicates take 8) from the session.	Jewel Box CD Home HR-5824-3	Record Plant, New York, NY	JHE	
Voodoo Chile (Slight Return)	03 May 68	CR 2 mix 1. This is take 16 (even though 'Lifelines' indicates take 8) from the session.	Electric Ladyland Outtakes CD Invasion Unlimited IU 9417-1	Record Plant, New York, NY	JHE	

Song	Date	Notes	Release	Location	
Voodoo Chile (Slight Return)	03 May 68	CR 2 mix 1. This is take 16 (even though 'Lifelines' indicates take 8) from the session.	Voodoo In Ladyland CD MUM MUCD 006	Record Plant, New York, NY	JHE
Voodoo Chile (Slight Return)	05 Jun 68	BR 21. Live performance from a TV broadcast.	Screaming Eagle CD Pink Poodle POO 001	It Must Be Dusty TV Show, Elstree Studios, Borehamwood, UK	JHE
Voodoo Chile (Slight Return)	14 Sep 68	BR 22. Live performance.	Live At The Hollywood Bowl LP RSR / International RSR 251	Hollywood Bowl, Los Angeles, CA	JHE
Voodoo Chile (Slight Return)	10 Oct 68	CR 3. Live performance.	Winterland Days, The CD Manic Depression 001	Winterland Theatre, San Francisco, CA 1st Show	JHE
Voodoo Chile (Slight Return)	10 Oct 68	CR 3. Live performance.	Concerts (CR) CD Reprise 9-22306-2	Winterland Theatre, San Francisco, CA 1st Show	JHE
Voodoo Chile (Slight Return)	10 Oct 68	CR 3. Live performance.	Winterland Vol 1 CD Whoopy Cat WKP 025 / 26	Winterland Theatre, San Francisco, CA 1st Show	JHE
Voodoo Chile (Slight Return)	10 Oct 68	CR 3. Live performance.	Jimi Hendrix CD Imtrat 40-90355	Winterland Theatre, San Francisco, C A 1st Show	JHE
Voodoo Chile (Slight Return)	10 Oct 68	CR 3. Live performance.	Little Wing CD Oil Well RSC 036	Winterland Theatre, San Francisco, CA 1st Show	JHE
Voodoo Chile (Slight Return)	10 Oct 68	CR 3. Live performance.	Winterland Vol 2 CD Whoopy Cat WKP 00279 / 28	Winterland Theatre, San Francisco, CA 1st Show	JHE
Voodoo Chile (Slight Return)	10 Oct 68	CR 3. Live performance.	Living Reels Vol 2 CD JMH 012 / 2	Winterland Theatre, San Francisco, CA 1st Show	JHE
Voodoo Chile (Slight Return)	11 Oct 68	CR 3. Live performance.	Live At Winterland +3 (CR) CD-3 Rykodisc 20038 / +3	Winterland Theatre, San Francisco, CA 1st Show	JHE
Voodoo Chile (Slight Return)	12 Oct 68	BR 23. Live performance.	Winterland Vol 3 CD Whoopy Cat WKP 0029 / 30	Winterland Theatre, San Francisco, CA 2nd Show	JHE
Voodoo Chile (Slight Return)	12 Oct 68	BR 23. Live performance.	Lost Winterland Tapes CD Starquake SQ 051-2	Winterland Theatre, San Francisco, CA 2nd Show	JHE
Voodoo Chile (Slight Return)	04 Jan 69	CR 4. Live performance for BBC TV.	Broadcasts CD Luna LU 9204	A Happening For Lulu, BBC TV, London, England	JHE

SONG TITLE	DATE	COMMENTS	RELEASE	LOCATION / VENUE	BAND	PERSONNEL
Voodoo Chile (Slight Return)	04 Jan 69	CR 4. Live performance for BBC TV.	Broadcasts LP Trade Mark Of Quality TMQ 1841 & TMQ 71019	A Happening For Lulu, BBC TV, London, England	JHE	
Voodoo Chile (Slight Return)	04 Jan 69	CR 4. Live performance for BBC TV.	Historic Performances CD Aquarius AQ 67-JH-080	A Happening For Lulu, BBC TV, London, England	JHE	
Voodoo Chile (Slight Return)	04 Jan 69	CR 4. Live performance for BBC TV.	Sweet Angel CD Compact Music WPOCM 0589	A Happening For Lulu, BBC TV, London, England	JHE	
Voodoo Chile (Slight Return)	04 Jan 69	CR 4. Live performance for BBC TV.	Jimi: A Musical Legacy CD KTS BX 010	A Happening For Lulu, BBC TV, London, England	JHE	
Voodoo Chile (Slight Return)	04 Jan 69	CR 4. Live performance for BBC TV.	BBC Sessions (CR) CD MCACD 2-11742	A Happening For Lulu, BBC TV, London, England	JHE	
Voodoo Chile (Slight Return)	08 Jan 69	BR 24. Live performance.	Cat's Squirrel CD CS 001 / 2	Loresberg Cirkus, Goteborg, Sweden	JHE	
Voodoo Chile (Slight Return)	09 Jan 69	BR 25. Live performance.	On The Killing Floor Swingin' Pig TSP-012-2	Konserthuset, Stockholm, Sweden 1st Show	JHE	
Voodoo Chile (Slight Return)	09 Jan 69	BR 26. Live performance.	On The Killing Floor Swingin' Pig TSP-012-2	Konserthuset, Stockholm, Sweden 2nd Show	JHE	
Voodoo Chile (Slight Return)	09 Jan 69	BR 26. Live performance.	Live In Stockholm 1967 CD Document DR 003	Konserthuset, Stockholm, Sweden 2nd Show	JHE	
Voodoo Chile (Slight Return)	09 Jan 69	BR 26. Live performance.	Live In Concert 1967 CD Living Legend LLR-CD 001	Konserthuset, Stockholm, Sweden 2nd Show	JHE	
Voodoo Chile (Slight Return)	09 Jan 69	BR 26. Live performance.	Legendary Star Club Tapes, The CD The Early Years 02-CD-3309	Konserthuset, Stockholm, Sweden 2nd Show	JHE	
Voodoo Chile (Slight Return)	09 Jan 69	BR 26. Live performance.	In Europe 67 / 68 / 69 CD Vulture CD 009 / 2	Konserthuset, Stockholm, Sweden 2nd Show	JHE	
Voodoo Chile (Slight Return)	09 Jan 69	BR 26. Live performance.	Live CD DV More CDDV 2401	Konserthuset, Stockholm, Sweden 2nd Show	JHE	
Voodoo Chile (Slight Return)	09 Jan 69	BR 26. Live performance.	Jimi Hendrix Experience CD Rockstars In Concert 6127092	Konserthuset, Stockholm, Sweden 2nd Show	JHE	

Song	Date	Notes	Release	Location	
Voodoo Chile (Slight Return)	09 Jan 69	BR 26. Live performance. Incomplete.	Foxy Lady CD Alegra CD 9008	Konserthuset, Stockholm, Sweden 2nd Show	JHE
Voodoo Chile (Slight Return)	10 Jan 69	BR 27. Live performance.	Jimi In Denmark (CR) CD UniVibes 1003 & Booted On Dynamite Studios	Falkoner Centret, Copenhagen, Denmark 2nd Show	JHE
Voodoo Chile (Slight Return)	10 Jan 69	BR 27. Live performance.	Live In Copenhagen CD The Swingin' Pig TSP-220-2	Falkoner Centret, Copenhagen, Denmark 2nd Show	JHE
Voodoo Chile (Slight Return)	18 Feb 69	BR 28. Live performance.	First Night At The Royal Albert Hall CD Midnight Beat MBCD 047 / 48	Royal Albert Hall, London, England	JHE
Voodoo Chile (Slight Return)	24 Feb 69	BR 29 & 30. Live performance from the afternoon soundcheck. There is a short version and then a longer one later on the disc.	Good Vibes LP Trade Mark Of Quality TMOQ 1813	Royal Albert Hall, London, England Sound Check	JHE
Voodoo Chile (Slight Return)	24 Feb 69	BR 29 & 30. Live performance from the afternoon soundcheck. There is a short version and then a longer one later on the disc.	First Night At The Royal Albert Hall CD Midnight Beat MBCD 047 / 48	Royal Albert Hall, London, England Sound Check	JHE
Voodoo Chile (Slight Return)	24 Feb 69	CR 5 mix 1. Live performance.	Last Experience, The (CR) CD Besocl CD 42	Royal Albert Hall, London, England	JHE
Voodoo Chile (Slight Return)	24 Feb 69	CR 5 mix 2. Live performance. Stereo.	Hendrix In The West (CR) LP Polydor 2302018 A	Royal Albert Hall, London, England	JHE
Voodoo Chile (Slight Return)	24 Feb 69	CR 5 mix 1. Live performance.	King Of Gypsies CD Rockyssimo RK 001	Royal Albert Hall, London, England	JHE
Voodoo Chile (Slight Return)	24 Feb 69	CR 5 mix 2. Live performance. Stereo.	Royal Albert Hall CD Blimp 008 / 009 & Listen To This Eric CD JH 003 / 4	Royal Albert Hall, London, England	JHE
Voodoo Chile (Slight Return)	24 Feb 69	CR 5 mix 1. Live performance.	Stone Free CD Silver Rarities SIRA 58 / 59	Royal Albert Hall, London, England	JHE
Voodoo Chile (Slight Return)	26 Apr 69	BR 31. Live performance.	Electric Jimi CD Jaguarondi Records	Los Angeles Forum, Los Angeles, CA	JHE
Voodoo Chile (Slight Return)	26 Apr 69	BR 31. Live performance.	I Don't Live Today, Maybe Tomorrow CD Living Legend LRCD 030	Los Angeles Forum, Los Angeles, CA	JHE
Voodoo Chile (Slight Return)	26 Apr 69	BR 31. Live performance.	Very Best, The CD Irec / Retro MILCD-03	Los Angeles Forum, Los Angeles, CA	JHE
Voodoo Chile (Slight Return)	26 Apr 69	BR 31. Live performance.	Hey Joe CD Crocodile Beat CB 53039	Los Angeles Forum, Los Angeles, CA	JHE

SONG TITLE	DATE	COMMENTS	RELEASE	LOCATION / VENUE	BAND	PERSONNEL
Voodoo Chile (Slight Return)	26 Apr 69	BR 31. Live performance.	Anthology CD Box 9	Los Angeles Forum, Los Angeles, CA	JHE	Jack Casady / Bass, Mitch Mitchell / Drums, Steve Winwood / Organ
Voodoo Chile (Slight Return)	27 Apr 69	CR 6. Live performance.	Live At The Oakland Coliseum (CR) CD Dagger Records DBRO-11743	Oakland Coliseum, Oakland, CA	JHE	
Voodoo Chile (Slight Return)	03 May 69	BR 32. Live performance.	Hendrix, Busted In Toronto CD Venue VE 100502	Maple Leaf Gardens, Toronto, Canada	JHE	
Voodoo Chile (Slight Return)	03 May 69	BR 33. Live performance.	I Don't Live Today CD ACL 007	Maple Leaf Gardens, Toronto, Canada	JHE	
Voodoo Chile (Slight Return)	17 May 69	BR 34. Live performance.	One Night At The Arena CD Venue VE 100501	Rhode Island Arena, Providence, RI	JHE	
Voodoo Chile (Slight Return)	18 May 69	BR 35. Live performance.	Roman Coliseum, The CD Starquake SQ 11	Madison Square Garden, New York, NY	JHE	
Voodoo Chile (Slight Return)	24 May 69	CR 7. Live performance.	Stages San Diego 69 (CR) CD Reprise 9 27632-2	Sports Arena, San Diego, CA	JHE	
Voodoo Chile (Slight Return)	24 May 69	CR 7. Live performance.	Midnight Magic CD Neutral Zone NZCD 89012	Sports Arena, San Diego, CA	JHE	
Voodoo Chile (Slight Return)	25 May 69	BR 36. Live performance.	Historic Concert Vol 2 CD Midnight Beat MBCD 050	Santa Clara Pop Festival, San Jose, CA	JHE	
Voodoo Chile (Slight Return)	20 Jun 69	BR 37. Live performance.	More Electricity From Newport CD Luna LU 9201	Newport Pop Festival, San Fernando State, Northridge, CA	JHE	
Voodoo Chile (Slight Return)	20 Jun 69	BR 37. Live performance.	A Lifetime Of Experience LP Sleepy Dragon 55 10	Newport Pop Festival, San Fernando State, Northridge, CA	JHE	
Voodoo Chile (Slight Return)	20 Jun 69	BR 37. Live performance.	Two Days At Newport CD JMH 007 / 2	Newport Pop Festival, San Fernando State, Northridge, CA	JHE	
Voodoo Chile (Slight Return)	22 Jun 69	BR 38. Live performance.	It Never Takes An End CD Genuine Pig TGP-118	Newport Pop Festival, San Fernando State, Northridge, CA	NJK	

Song	Date	Notes	Release	Venue	Code
Voodoo Chile (Slight Return)	18 Aug 69	CR 8 mix 1. Live performance. Incomplete.	Woodstock (CR) CD MCA 11063	Woodstock Music And Art Fair, Bethel, NY	GSRB
Voodoo Chile (Slight Return)	18 Aug 69	CR 8 mix 2. Live performance.	Woodstock Nation CD Wild Bird 89090 1 / 2	Woodstock Music And Art Fair, Bethel, NY	GSRB
Voodoo Chile (Slight Return)	18 Aug 69	CR 8 mix 2. Live performance.	At Woodstock (CR) Laserdisc BMG BVLP 86	Woodstock Music And Art Fair, Bethel, NY	GSRB
Voodoo Chile (Slight Return)	18 Aug 69	CR 8 mix 2. Live performance.	Gypsy Sun And Rainbows CD Manic Depression MDCD 05 / 06	Woodstock Music And Art Fair, Bethel, NY	GSRB
Voodoo Chile (Slight Return)	18 Aug 69	CR 8 mix 2. Live performance.	Woodstock Monday, August 18 1969, 8AM CD JMH 008	Woodstock Music And Art Fair, Bethel, NY	GSRB
Voodoo Chile (Slight Return)	18 Aug 69	CR 8 mix 2. Live performance.	Ultimate Live Collection, The CD The Beat Goes On BGO BX 9307-4	Woodstock Music And Art Fair, Bethel, NY	GSRB
Voodoo Chile (Slight Return)	31 Dec 69	BR 39. Live performance.	Band Of Gold CD-R Major Tom MT 087	Fillmore East, New York, NY 2nd Show	BOG
Voodoo Chile (Slight Return)	01 Jan 70	BR 40. Live performance.	Band Of Gold CD-R Major Tom MT 087	Fillmore East, New York, NY 2nd Show	BOG
Voodoo Chile (Slight Return)	01 Jan 70	BR 40. Live performance.	Band Of Gypsys- The Ultimate CD JMH 010 / 3	Fillmore East, New York, NY 2nd Show	BOG
Voodoo Chile (Slight Return)	25 Apr 70	BR 41. Live performance.	Enjoy Jimi Hendrix LP Rubber Dubber 700-001-01	Los Angeles Forum, Los Angeles, CA	COL
Voodoo Chile (Slight Return)	25 Apr 70	BR 41. Live performance.	Portrait Of Jimi Hendrix, A LP Catalog # Varies On Dead Wax	Los Angeles Forum, Los Angeles, CA	COL
Voodoo Chile (Slight Return)	25 Apr 70	BR 41. Live performance.	Live At The Forum 1970 CD Whoopy Cat WKP 021 / 22	Los Angeles Forum, Los Angeles, CA	COL
Voodoo Chile (Slight Return)	25 Apr 70	BR 41. Live performance. The Luna disc is from a tape source while the JHCD 528 disc is copied from vinyl.	Scuse Me While I Kiss The Sky CD Luna CD & JHCD 528	Los Angeles Forum, Los Angeles, CA	COL
Voodoo Chile (Slight Return)	30 May 70	BR 42. Live performance.	Good Karma 2 LP Berkeley 2023	Berkeley Community Theater, Berkeley, CA 1st Show	COL

SONG TITLE	DATE	COMMENTS	RELEASE	LOCATION / VENUE	BAND	PERSONNEL
Voodoo Chile (Slight Return)	30 May 70	BR 42. Live performance.	Berkeley Concert LP Audifon AF 008	Berkeley Community Theater, Berkeley, CA 1st Show	COL	
Voodoo Chile (Slight Return)	30 May 70	BR 42. Live performance.	Berkeley Concerts, The CD Whoopy Cat WKP 004 / 5	Berkeley Community Theater, Berkeley, CA 1st Show	COL	
Voodoo Chile (Slight Return)	30 May 70	BR 42. Live performance.	Ultimate Live Collection, The CD The Beat Goes On BGO BX 9307-4	Berkeley Community Theater, Berkeley, CA 1st Show	COL	
Voodoo Chile (Slight Return)	30 May 70	BR 43. Live performance.	Riots In Berkeley CD Beech Marten BM 038	Berkeley Community Theater, Berkeley, CA 2nd Show	COL	
Voodoo Chile (Slight Return)	30 May 70	BR 43. Live performance.	Jimi Plays Berkeley (CR) Warner Reprise Videotape	Berkeley Community Theater, Berkeley, CA 2nd Show	COL	
Voodoo Chile (Slight Return)	30 May 70	BR 43. Live performance.	Berkeley Concerts, The CD Whoopy Cat WKP 004 / 5	Berkeley Community Theater, Berkeley, CA 2nd Show	COL	
Voodoo Chile (Slight Return)	30 May 70	BR 43. Live performance.	Jimi Plays Berkeley CD JMH 005 / 2	Berkeley Community Theater, Berkeley, CA 2nd Show	COL	
Voodoo Chile (Slight Return)	13 Jun 70	BR 44. Live performance.	Baltimore Civic Center, June 13, 1970 CD Starquake SQ-09	BBC Playhouse Theatre, London, England	COL	
Voodoo Chile (Slight Return)	04 Jul 70	CR 9. Live performance.	Atlanta Special CD Genuine Pig TGP 121	2nd International Pop Festival, Atlanta, GA	COL	
Voodoo Chile (Slight Return)	04 Jul 70	CR 9. Live performance.	At The Atlanta Pop Festival (CR) Laserdisc BMG BVLP 77 (74321-10987)	2nd International Pop Festival, Atlanta, GA	COL	
Voodoo Chile (Slight Return)	04 Jul 70	CR 9. Live performance.	Stages Atlanta 70 (CR) CD Reprise 9 27632-2	2nd International Pop Festival, Atlanta, GA	COL	
Voodoo Chile (Slight Return)	04 Jul 70	CR 9. Live performance.	Band Of Gypsys Vol 2 (CR) LP Capitol SJ 12416	2nd International Pop Festival, Atlanta, GA	COL	
Voodoo Chile (Slight Return)	04 Jul 70	CR 9. Live performance.	Atlanta CD JMH 009 / 02	2nd International Pop Festival, Atlanta, GA	COL	
Voodoo Chile (Slight Return)	04 Jul 70	CR 9. Live performance.	Live! CD Black B-05	2nd International Pop Festival, Atlanta, GA	COL	

Song	Date	Notes	Release	Venue	
Voodoo Chile (Slight Return)	04 Jul 70	CR 9. Live performance.	Oh, Atlanta CD Tendolar TDR-009	2nd International Pop Festival, Atlanta, GA	COL
Voodoo Chile (Slight Return)	04 Jul 70	CR 9. Live performance.	Atlanta CD JMH 009 / 02	2nd International Pop Festival, Atlanta, GA	COL
Voodoo Chile (Slight Return)	04 Jul 70	CR 9. Live performance. Incomplete.	Johnny B. Goode (CR) CD Capitol 430218-2	2nd International Pop Festival, Atlanta, GA	COL
Voodoo Chile (Slight Return)	17 Jul 70	BR 45. Live performance.	Electric Gypsy CD Scorpio? 40176 / 15	New York Pop-Downing Stadium, Randalls Island, NY	COL
Voodoo Chile (Slight Return)	17 Jul 70	BR 45. Live performance.	Can You Here Me LP Hemero 01 / KERI	New York Pop-Downing Stadium, Randalls Island, NY	COL
Voodoo Chile (Slight Return)	17 Jul 70	BR 45. Live performance.	Live At Randall's Island LP Moon Tree Records PH1962	New York Pop-Downing Stadium, Randalls Island, NY	COL
Voodoo Chile (Slight Return)	17 Jul 70	BR 45. Live performance.	Live USA CD Imtrat 902-001	New York Pop-Downing Stadium, Randalls Island, NY	COL
Voodoo Chile (Slight Return)	17 Jul 70	BR 45. Live performance.	Greatest Hits Live CD Chartbusters CHER 089A	New York Pop-Downing Stadium, Randalls Island, NY	COL
Voodoo Chile (Slight Return)	30 Jul 70	BR 46. Live performance.	Last American Concert Vol 1 CD The Swingin' Pig TSP-062	Rainbow Bridge Vibratory Sound-Color Experiment, Maui, HI 1st Show	COL
Voodoo Chile (Slight Return)	30 Jul 70	BR46. Live performance. Incomplete. This laserdisc release has just Jimi's parts edited from the full 'Rainbow Bridge' film.	Alive On Live (CR) Laserdisc SHLM 2005	Rainbow Bridge Vibratory Sound-Color Experiment, Maui, HI 1st Show	COL
Voodoo Chile (Slight Return)	30 Jul 70	BR 46. Live performance.	Last American Concert-Alive And Flowing From.... LP Jupiter 444	Rainbow Bridge Vibratory Sound-Color Experiment, Maui, HI 1st Show	COL
Voodoo Chile (Slight Return)	30 Jul 70	BR 46. Live performance.	In From The Storm CD Silver Rarities SIRA 109 / 110	Rainbow Bridge Vibratory Sound-Color Experiment, Maui, HI 1st Show	COL
Voodoo Chile (Slight Return)	30 Jul 70	BR 46. Live performance.	Rainbow Bridge 2 CD JMH 003 / 2	Rainbow Bridge Vibratory Sound-Color Experiment, Maui, HI 1st Show	COL

SONG TITLE	DATE	COMMENTS	RELEASE	LOCATION / VENUE	BAND	PERSONNEL
Voodoo Chile (Slight Return)	30 Aug 70	CR 10. Live performance.	Island Man CD Silver Rarities SIRA 39 / 40	Isle Of Wight Festival, Isle Of Wight, England	COL	
Voodoo Chile (Slight Return)	30 Aug 70	CR 10. Live performance.	At The Isle Of Wight (CR) Laserdisc CBS / Sony CLSM 791	Isle Of Wight Festival, Isle Of Wight, England	COL	
Voodoo Chile (Slight Return)	30 Aug 70	CR 10. Live performance.	51st Anniversary CD Future Disc JMH 001 / 8	Isle Of Wight Festival, Isle Of Wight, England	COL	
Voodoo Chile (Slight Return)	30 Aug 70	CR 10. Live performance.	Valley Of Neptune CD PC 28355	Isle Of Wight Festival, Isle Of Wight, England	COL	
Voodoo Chile (Slight Return)	30 Aug 70	CR 10. Live performance.	Live - Isle Of Wight '70 (CR) CD Polydor 847236-2	Isle Of Wight Festival, Isle Of Wight, England	COL	
Voodoo Chile (Slight Return)	30 Aug 70	CR 10. Live performance.	Wight CD JMH 006 / 2	Isle Of Wight Festival, Isle Of Wight, England	COL	
Voodoo Chile (Slight Return)	31 Aug 70	BR 47. Live performance.	Come On Stockholm CD No Label	Stora Scenen, Liesberg, Stockholm, Sweden	COL	
Voodoo Chile (Slight Return)	31 Aug 70	BR 47. Live performance.	Free Concert CD Midnight Beat MBCD 013	Stora Scenen, Tivoli Garden, Stockholm, Sweden	COL	
Voodoo Chile (Slight Return)	01 Sep 70	BR 48. Live performance.	Warm Hello Of The Sun, The CD	Stora Scenen, Liseberg Nojespark, Goteborg, Sweden	COL	
Voodoo Chile (Slight Return)	03 Sep 70	BR 49. Live performance. Part of a medley.	Welcome To The Electric Circus Vol 2 CD Midnight Beat 018	K.B. Hallen, Copenhagen, Denmark	COL	
Voodoo Chile (Slight Return)	03 Sep 70	BR 49. Live performance. Part of a medley.	Live In Copenhagen CD The Swingin' Pig TSP-220-2	K.B. Hallen, Copenhagen, Denmark	COL	
Voodoo Chile (Slight Return)	03 Sep 70	BR 49. Live performance. Part of a medley.	Copenhagen 70 CD Whoopy Cat WKP 044 / 45	K.B. Hallen, Copenhagen, Denmark	COL	
Voodoo Chile (Slight Return)	06 Sep 70	BR 50. Live performance.	Love & Peace CD Midnight Beat MBCD 015	Love And Peace Festival, Isle Of Fehrman, Germany	COL	
Voodoo Chile (Slight Return)	06 Sep 70	BR 50. Live performance.	Wink Of An Eye CD	Love And Peace	COL	

Title	Date	Notes	Release	Location	Band
Voodoo Chile (Slight Return)	06 Sep 70	BR 50. Live performance.	Whoopy Cat WKP 0033 / 34	Festival, Isle Of Fehrman, Germany	COL
Wait Until Tomorrow			Jimi: A Musical Legacy CD KTS BX 010	Love And Peace Festival, Isle Of Fehrman, Germany	JHE
Wait Until Tomorrow	26 Oct 67	CR 1 mix 1 (stereo).	Axis: Bold As Love (CR) CD MCACD 11601	Olympic Sound Studios, London, England	JHE
Wait Until Tomorrow	26 Oct 67	CR 1 mix 1 (stereo).	Legacy (CR) LP Polydor	Olympic Sound Studios, London, England	JHE
Wait Until Tomorrow	26 Oct 67	CR 1 mix 2 (mono).	Axis: Bold As Love (CR) LP Track 612 003	Olympic Sound Studios, London, England	JHE
Wait Until Tomorrow	26 Oct 67	CR 1 mix 3. Unused mix of the CR 1.	Sotheby Auction Tapes, The CD Midnight Beat MBCD 010	Olympic Sound Studios, London, England	JHE
Wait Until Tomorrow	26 Oct 67	CR 1 mix 3. Unused mix of the CR 1.	Sotheby's Private Reels CD JHR 003 / 004	Olympic Sound Studios, London, England	JHE
Wait Until Tomorrow	26 Oct 67	CR 1 mix 3. Unused mix of the CR 1.	Sotheby's Private Reels CD JHR 003 / 004	Olympic Sound Studios, London, England	JHE
Wait Until Tomorrow	26 Oct 67	CR 1 mix 3. Unused mix of the CR 1.	Get The Experience CD Invasion Unlimited IU 9424-1	Olympic Sound Studios, London, England	JHE
Wait Until Tomorrow	26 Oct 67	CR 1 mix 3. Unused mix of the CR 1.	Complete BBC Session And..., The CD Last Bootleg Records LBR 036 / 2	Olympic Sound Studios, London, England	JHE
Wait Until Tomorrow	26 Oct 67	CR 1 mix 3. Unused mix of the CR 1.	Sotheby's Reels, The CD Gold Standard TOM-800	Olympic Sound Studios, London, England	JHE
Wait Until Tomorrow	26 Oct 67	CR 1 mix 3. Unused mix of the CR 1.	Living Reels Vol 1 CD JMH 011	Olympic Sound Studios, London, England	JHE
Wait Until Tomorrow	15 Dec 67	CR 3. BBC performance.	Guitar Hero CD Document DR 013	Top Gear, BBC Playhouse Theatre, London, England	JHE
Wait Until Tomorrow	15 Dec 67	CR 3. BBC performance.	Primal Keys LP Impossible Record Works	Top Gear, BBC Playhouse Theatre, London, England	JHE

SONG TITLE	DATE	COMMENTS	RELEASE	LOCATION / VENUE	BAND	PERSONNEL
Wait Until Tomorrow	15 Dec 67	CR 3. BBC performance.	Radio One (CR) CD Rykodisc RCD 20078	Top Gear, BBC Playhouse Theatre, London, England	JHE	
Wait Until Tomorrow	15 Dec 67	CR 3. BBC performance.	Official Bootleg Album, The CD Yellow Dog YD 051	Top Gear, BBC Playhouse Theatre, London, England	JHE	
Wait Until Tomorrow	15 Dec 67	CR 3. BBC performance.	Ultimate BBC Collection CD Classical CL006	Top Gear, BBC Playhouse Theatre, London, England	JHE	
Wait Until Tomorrow	15 Dec 67	CR 3. BBC performance.	Live In London 1967 CD Koine Records K881104	Top Gear, BBC Playhouse Theatre, London, England	JHE	
Wait Until Tomorrow	15 Dec 67	CR 3. BBC performance.	Live In Concert 1967 CD Living Legend LLR-CD 001	Top Gear, BBC Playhouse Theatre, London, England	JHE	
Wait Until Tomorrow	15 Dec 67	CR 3. BBC performance.	In Concert CD Starlife ST 3612	Top Gear, BBC Playhouse Theatre, London, England	JHE	
Wait Until Tomorrow	15 Dec 67	CR 3. BBC performance.	Lost Experience, The, CD JHCD203	Top Gear, BBC Playhouse Theatre, London, England	JHE	
Wait Until Tomorrow	15 Dec 67	CR 3. BBC performance.	BBC Sessions (CR) CD MCACD 2-11742	Top Gear, BBC Playhouse Theatre, London, England	JHE	
Wait Until Tomorrow	15 Dec 67	CR 3. BBC performance. Incomplete.	Black Strings CD CDM G-53 258	Top Gear, BBC Playhouse Theatre, London, England	JHE	
Wait Until Tomorrow		No Jimi involvement	Symphony Of Experience CD Third Stone Discs TDS 24966		Fake	
Wait Until Tomorrow		No Jimi involvement	Get The Experience CD Invasion Unlimited IU 9424-1		Fake	
Walk Right In / Always See Your Face	?? Mar 70 ?	This is a recording by the group "Love" for the unreleased 'Black Beauty' album. Jimi's involvement is highly unlikely.	Midnight Sun CD Third Eye NK 007	Olympic Sound Studios, London, England	Love	
We Gotta Live Together	22 Jun 69	BR 1. Live performance.	It Never Takes An End CD Genuine Pig TGP-118	Newport Pop Festival, San Fernando State, Northridge, CA	NJK	

Song	Date	Notes	Release	Location	
We Gotta Live Together	01 Jan 70	CR 1 mix 1. Live performance. Edited to 5 1 / 2 minutes from 16 3 / 4!	Band Of Gypsys (CR) CD Capitol 72434-93446-2-4	Fillmore East, New York, NY 2nd Show	BOG
We Gotta Live Together	01 Jan 70	CR 1 mix 1. Live performance. Edited to 5 1 / 2 minutes from 16 3 / 4!	Band Of Gold CD-R Major Tom MT 087	Fillmore East, New York, NY 2nd Show	BOG
We Gotta Live Together	01 Jan 70	CR 1 mix 2. Live performance. Complete.	Band Of Gypsys- The Ultimate CD JMH 010 / 3	Fillmore East, New York, NY 2nd Show	BOG
Whipper		No Jimi involvement	Whipper CD Pilz 447400-2	Unknown	No Jimi
Who Knows	?? Dec 69	BR 1. A final complete take preceded by a number of false starts and breakdowns.	Band Of Gypsys Rehearsals CD Whoopy Cat WKP 003	Baggies, New York, NY	BOG
Who Knows	?? Dec 69	BR 1. A final complete take preceded by a number of false starts and breakdowns.	Things I Used To Do, The CD Golden Memories GM 890738	Baggies, New York, NY	BOG
Who Knows	?? Dec 69	BR 1. A final complete take preceded by a number of false starts and breakdowns. This release continues with 2 versions of "Message To Love".	Notes In Colours CD JHR 001 / 002	Baggies, New York, NY	BOG
Who Knows	?? Dec 69	BR 1. This is only the complete take from this session.	Band Of Gypsys Vol 3	Baggies, New York, NY	BOG
Who Knows	?? Dec 69	BR 1. This is only the complete take from this session.	Band Of Gypsys- The Ultimate CD JMH 010 / 3	Baggies, New York, NY	BOG
Who Knows	31 Dec 69	BR 2. Live performance.	Auld Lang Syne CD JH 100 03	Fillmore East, New York, NY 2nd Show	BOG
Who Knows	31 Dec 69	BR 2. Live performance.	Band Of Gypsys: Happy New Year CD Silver Shadow CD 9103	Fillmore East, New York, NY 2nd Show	BOG
Who Knows	31 Dec 69	BR 2. Live performance.	Fillmore Concerts, The CD Whoopy Cat WKP 0006 / 7	Fillmore East, New York, NY 2nd Show	BOG
Who Knows	31 Dec 69	BR 2. Live performance.	Band Of Gold CD-R Major Tom MT 087	Fillmore East, New York, NY 2nd Show	BOG
Who Knows	31 Dec 69	BR 2. Live performance.	Band Of Gypsys- The Ultimate CD JMH 010 / 3	Fillmore East, New York, NY 2nd Show	BOG
Who Knows	01 Jan 70	CR 1. Live Performance.	Band Of Gypsys (CR) CD Capitol 72434-2-4	Fillmore East, New York, NY 1st Show	BOG

SONG TITLE	DATE	COMMENTS	RELEASE	LOCATION / VENUE	BAND	PERSONNEL
Who Knows	01 Jan 70	CR 1. Live Performance.	Band Of Gold CD-R Major Tom MT 087	Fillmore East, New York, NY 1st Show	BOG	
Who Knows	01 Jan 70	CR 1. Live Performance.	Band Of Gypsys- The Ultimate CD JMH 010 / 3	Fillmore East, New York, NY 1st Show	BOG	
Who Knows	01 Jan 70	BR 3. Live performance. From the ill fated Madison Square Garden show, the BOG's final night as a band.	Live At The Forum 1970 CD Whoopy Cat WKP 021 / 22	Madison Square Garden, New York, NY	BOG	
Whole Lotta Shakin'		No Jimi involvement	Jimi: A Musical Legacy CD KTS BX 010		No Jimi	
Wild Thing	04 Feb 67	BR 1. Live performance.	Have Mercy On Me Baby CD Midnight Beat MBCD 038	Flamingo Club, London, England	JHE	
Wild Thing	04 Feb 67	BR 1. Live performance.	Live At The Flamingo Club, London, 2-4-67 CD	Flamingo Club, London, England	JHE	
Wild Thing	24 May 67	BR 2. Live performance.	Lost In Sweden CD Whoopy Cat WKP 0046 / 0047	Stora Scenen, Grona Lund, Stockholm, Sweden	JHE	
Wild Thing	18 Jun 67	CR 1. Live performance.	Once Upon A Time CD Wall Of Sound WS CD011	Monterey International Pop Festival, Monterey, CA	JHE	
Wild Thing	18 Jun 67	CR 1. Live performance.	Soundtrack From The Film Jimi Hendrix, The (CR) LP Reprise 2RS 6481	Monterey International Pop Festival, Monterey, CA	JHE	
Wild Thing	18 Jun 67	CR 1. Live performance.	Monterey Pop CD Evil 006 1 / 2	Monterey International Pop Festival, Monterey, CA	JHE	
Wild Thing	18 Jun 67	CR 1. Live performance.	Jimi Hendrix Experience CD Rockstars In Concert 6127092	Monterey International Pop Festival, Monterey, CA	JHE	
Wild Thing	18 Jun 67	CR 1. Live performance.	Experience II CD More MTT 1021	Monterey International Pop Festival, Monterey, CA	JHE	
Wild Thing	18 Jun 67	CR 1. Live performance.	Hey Joe CD Crocodile Beat CB 53039	Monterey International Pop	JHE	

Song	Date	Notes	Release	Venue	Band
Wild Thing	18 Jun 67	CR 1. Live performance.	Jimi Plays Monterey (CR) CD Polydor 827990-2	Monterey International Pop Festival, Monterey, CA	JHE
Wild Thing	18 Jun 67	CR 1. Live performance. Incomplete.	Ultimate BBC Collection CD Classical CL006	Monterey International Pop Festival, Monterey, CA	JHE
Wild Thing	18 Jun 67	CR 1. Live performance. Incomplete.	Complete BBC Session And..., The CD Last Bootleg Records LBR 036 / 2	Monterey International Pop Festival, Monterey, CA	JHE
Wild Thing	09 Oct 67	BR 3. Live performance.	Wild Man Of Pop Plays Vol 2, The CD Pyramid RFTCD 004	L' Olympia Theatre, Paris, France	JHE
Wild Thing	09 Oct 67	BR 3. Live performance.	Live In Paris 66 / 67 CD Whoopy Cat WKP 0012	L' Olympia Theatre, Paris, France	JHE
Wild Thing	09 Oct 67	BR 3. Live performance. Incomplete.	Redskin' Jammin' CD JH 01 / 02	L' Olympia Theatre, Paris, France	JHE
Wild Thing	25 Nov 67	BR 4. Live performance.	Wild Man Of Pop Plays Vol 2, The CD Pyramid RFTCD 004	Blackpool Opera House, Lancashire, England	JHE
Wild Thing	25 Nov 67	BR 4. Live performance.	Smashing Amps LP Trademark Of Quality TMQ 1813	Blackpool Opera House, Lancashire, England	JHE
Wild Thing	07 Jan 68	BR 5. Live performance.	Cat's Squirrel CD CS 001 / 2	Tivolis Konsertsal, Copenhagen, Denmark	JHE
Wild Thing	07 Jan 68	BR 5. Live performance.	Fuckin' His Guitar For Denmark LP Polymore Or JH CO	Tivolis Konsertsal, Copenhagen, Denmark	JHE
Wild Thing	16 Feb 68	BR 6. Live performance.	Biggest Square In The Building, The CD Reverb Music 1993	State Fair Music Hall, Dallas, TX	JHE
Wild Thing	16 Feb 68	BR 6. Live performance.	Scuse Me While I Kiss The Sky CD Sonic Zoom SZ 1001	State Fair Music Hall, Dallas, TX	JHE
Wild Thing	16 Feb 68	BR 6. Live performance.	Scuse Me While I Kiss The Sky CD Sonic Zoom SZ 1001	State Fair Music Hall, Dallas, TX	JHE

SONG TITLE	DATE	COMMENTS	RELEASE	LOCATION / VENUE	BAND	PERSONNEL
Wild Thing	17 Feb 68	BR 7. Live performance.	Remember The Alamo CD	Will Rogers Auditorium, Fort Worth, T X	JHE	
Wild Thing	17 Feb 68	BR 7. Live performance.	Superconcert 1968 CD Firepower FP03	Will Rogers Auditorium, Fort Worth, T X	JHE	
Wild Thing	17 Feb 68	BR 7. Live performance. Incomplete.	Scuse Me While I Kiss The Sky CD Sonic Zoom SZ 1001	Will Rogers Auditorium, Fort Worth, T X	JHE	
Wild Thing	17 Feb 68	BR 7. Live performance. Incomplete.	Scuse Me While I Kiss The Sky CD Sonic Zoom SZ 1001	Will Rogers Auditorium, Fort Worth, T X	JHE	
Wild Thing	15 Mar 68	BR 8. Live performance.	Broadcasts CD Luna LU 9204	Atwood Hall, Clark University, Worcester, MA	JHE	
Wild Thing	15 Mar 68	BR 8. Live performance.	Broadcasts LP Trade Mark Of Quality TMQ 1841 & TMQ 71019	Atwood Hall, Clark University, Worcester, MA	JHE	
Wild Thing	15 Mar 68	BR 8. Live performance.	Live USA CD Imtrat 902-001	Atwood Hall, Clark University, Worcester, MA	JHE	
Wild Thing	15 Mar 68	BR 8. Live performance.	Jimi: A Musical Legacy CD KTS BX 010	Atwood Hall, Clark University, Worcester, MA	JHE	
Wild Thing	15 Mar 68	BR 8. Live performance.	Greatest Hits Live CD Chartbusters CHER 089A	Atwood Hall, Clark University, Worcester, MA	JHE	
Wild Thing	03 Aug 68	BR 9. Live performance.	Crosstown Traffic CD M25 3664	Moody Coliseum, Southern Methodist University, Dallas, TX	JHE	
Wild Thing	23 Aug 68	BR 10. Live performance.	Historic Concert CD Midnight Beat MBCD 017	New York Rock Festival, Singer Bowl, Queens, NY	JHE	
Wild Thing	12 Oct 68	CR 2. Live performance.	Concerts (CR) CD Reprise 9-22306-2	Winterland Theatre, San Francisco, CA 1st Show	JHE	
Wild Thing	12 Oct 68	CR 2. Live performance.	Little Wing CD Oil Well RSC 036	Winterland Theatre, San Francisco, CA 1st Show	JHE	
Wild Thing	12 Oct 68	CR 2. Live performance.	Winterland Vol 3 CD	Winterland Theatre,	JHE	

Song	Date	Notes	Source	Venue	Band
			Whoopy Cat WKP 0029 / 30	San Francisco, CA 1st Show	
Wild Thing	12 Oct 68	CR 2. Live performance.	Fire CD The Entertainers CD297	Winterland Theatre, San Francisco, CA 1st Show	JHE
Wild Thing	12 Oct 68	CR 2. Live performance.	Hendrix In Words And Music CD Outlaw Records OTR 1100030	Winterland Theatre, San Francisco, CA 1st Show	JHE
Wild Thing	12 Oct 68	CR 2. Live performance.	Live At Winterland (CR) CD Rykodisc RCD 20038	Winterland Theatre, San Francisco, CA 1st Show	JHE
Wild Thing	24 Feb 69	CR 3 mix 1. Live performance. Incomplete.	Last Experience, The (CR) CD Bescol CD 42	Royal Albert Hall, London, England	JHE
Wild Thing	24 Feb 69	CR 3 mix 1. Live performance. Incomplete.	Very Best, The CD Irec / Retro MILCD-03	Royal Albert Hall, London, England	JHE
Wild Thing	24 Feb 69	CR 3 mix 1. Live performance. Incomplete.	king Of Gypsies CD Rockyssimo RK 001	Royal Albert Hall, London, England	JHE
Wild Thing	24 Feb 69	CR 3 mix 1. Live performance. Incomplete.	Hendrix In Words And Music CD Outlaw Records OTR 1100030	Royal Albert Hall, London, England	JHE
Wild Thing	24 Feb 69	CR 3 mix 1. Live performance. Incomplete.	Jimi Hendrix CD Flute FLCD 2008	Royal Albert Hall, London, England	JHE
Wild Thing	24 Feb 69	CR 3 mix 1. Live performance. Incomplete.	Anthology CD Box 9	Royal Albert Hall, London, England	JHE
Wild Thing	24 Feb 69	CR 3 mix 2. Live performance. Complete. Stereo.	Royal Albert Hall CD Blimp 008 / 009 & Listen To This Eric CD JH 003 / 4	Royal Albert Hall, London, England	JHE
Wild Thing	24 Feb 69	CR 3 mix 3. Live performance. Complete but mono.	Stone Free CD Silver Rarities SIRA 58 / 59	Royal Albert Hall, London, England	JHE
Wild Thing	01 Jan 70	BR 11. Live performance.	Band Of Gold CD-R Major Tom MT 087	Fillmore East, New York, NY 2nd Show	BOG
Wild Thing	01 Jan 70	BR 11. Live performance.	Ultimate Live Collection, The CD The Beat Goes On BGO BX 9307-4	Fillmore East, New York, NY 2nd Show	BOG
Win Your Love		No Jimi involvement	Hendrix In Words And Music CD Outlaw Records OTR 1100030		No Jimi
Wind Cries Mary (The)	11 Jan 67	CR 1 mix 2 (mono)	Legacy (CR) LP Polydor	De Lane Lea, London, England	JHE

SONG TITLE	DATE	COMMENTS	RELEASE	LOCATION / VENUE	BAND	PERSONNEL
Wind Cries Mary (The)	11 Jan 67	CR 1 mix 1 (stereo)	Are You Experienced? (CR) CD MCACD 11602	De Lane Lea, London, England	JHE	
Wind Cries Mary (The)	11 Jan 67	CR 1 mix 1 (stereo)	The Singles Album (CR) CD Polydor 827 369-2	De Lane Lea, London, England	JHE	
Wind Cries Mary (The)	11 Jan 67	CR 1 mix 1 (stereo)	Smash Hits (CR) CD Reprise 2276-2	De Lane Lea, London, England	JHE	
Wind Cries Mary (The)	11 Jan 67	CR 1 mix 1 (stereo) Incomplete.	Ultimate BBC Collection CD Classical CL006	De Lane Lea, London, England	JHE	
Wind Cries Mary (The)	11 Jan 67	CR 1 mix 1 (stereo) Incomplete.	Complete BBC Session And..., The CD Last Bootleg Records LBR 036 / 2	De Lane Lea, London, England	JHE	
Wind Cries Mary (The)	15 Jan 67	BR 1. Instrumental version from a second session which was 4 days after the 1st session according to Mitch Mitchell.	Out Of The Studio: Demos From 1967 CD BHCD 931022	De Lane Lea, London, England	JHE	
Wind Cries Mary (The)	15 Jan 67	BR 1. Instrumental version from a second session which was 4 days after the 1st session according to Mitch Mitchell.	DeLane Lea And Olympic Outs CD Gold Standard CD-R	De Lane Lea, London, England	JHE	
Wind Cries Mary (The)	15 Jan 67	BR 1. Instrumental version from a second session which was 4 days after the 1st session according to Mitch Mitchell.	Get The Experience CD Invasion Unlimited IU 9424-1	De Lane Lea, London, England	JHE	
Wind Cries Mary (The)	15 Jan 67	BR 1. Instrumental version from a second session which was 4 days after the 1st session according to Mitch Mitchell.	Complete BBC Session And..., The CD Last Bootleg Records LBR 036 / 2	De Lane Lea, London, England	JHE	
Wind Cries Mary (The)	15 Jan 67	BR 1. Instrumental version from a second session which was 4 days after the 1st session according to Mitch Mitchell.	I Don't Live Today CD ACL 007	De Lane Lea, London, England	JHE	
Wind Cries Mary (The)	15 Jan 67	BR 1. Instrumental version from a second session which was 4 days after the 1st session according to Mitch Mitchell.	Jimi: A Musical Legacy CD KTS BX 010	De Lane Lea, London, England	JHE	
Wind Cries Mary (The)	15 Jan 67	BR 1. Instrumental version from a second session which was 4 days after the 1st session according to Mitch Mitchell.	Magic Hand CD Mum MUCD 012	De Lane Lea, London, England	JHE	
Wind Cries Mary (The)	15 Jan 67	BR 1. Instrumental version from a second session which was 4 days after the 1st session according to Mitch Mitchell.	Olympic Gold Vol 1 CD Blimp 0067	De Lane Lea, London, England	JHE	
Wind Cries Mary (The)	24 May 67	BR 2. Live performance from Swedish TV.	Wild Man Of Pop Plays Vol 1, The CD Pyramid RFTCD 003	Popside TV Show, Stockholm, Sweden	JHE	
Wind Cries Mary (The)	24 May 67	BR 2. Live performance from Swedish TV.	Unforgettable	Popside TV Show,	JHE	

Song	Date		Experience LP RAH 2469	Stockholm, Sweden	
Wind Cries Mary (The)	18 Jun 67	CR 2. Live performance.	Monterey Pop CD Evil 006 1 / 2	Monterey International Pop Festival, Monterey, CA	JHE
Wind Cries Mary (The)	18 Jun 67	CR 2. Live performance.	Live! CD Black B-05	Monterey International Pop Festival, Monterey, CA	JHE
Wind Cries Mary (The)	18 Jun 67	CR 2. Live performance.	Valley Of Neptune CD PC 28355	Monterey International Pop Festival, Monterey, CA	JHE
Wind Cries Mary (The)	18 Jun 67	CR 2. Live performance.	Jimi Plays Monterey (CR) CD Polydor 827990-2	Monterey International Pop Festival, Monterey, CA	JHE
Wind Cries Mary (The)	18 Jun 67	CR 2. Live performance.	Various Artists - Monterey Pop '67 CD Evil 2004 & Black Panther 042	Monterey International Pop Festival, Monterey, CA	JHE
Wind Cries Mary (The)	04 Sep 67	BR 3. Live performance.	EXP Over Sweden (CR) CD UniVibes 1002	Dans In, Grona Lund, Tivoli Garden, Stockholm, Sweden	JHE
Wind Cries Mary (The)	05 Sep 67	CR 3. Live performance.	Live In Stockholm 1967 CD Document DR 003	Studio 4, Radiohuset, Stockholm, Sweden	JHE
Wind Cries Mary (The)	05 Sep 67	CR 3. Live performance.	Wild Man Of Pop Plays Vol 1, The CD Pyramid RFTCD 003	Studio 4, Radiohuset, Stockholm, Sweden	JHE
Wind Cries Mary (The)	05 Sep 67	CR 3. Live performance.	Stages Stockholm 67 (CR) CD Reprise 9 27632-2	Studio 4, Radiohuset, Stockholm, Sweden	JHE
Wind Cries Mary (The)	05 Sep 67	CR 3. Live performance.	Live At The Hollywood Bowl LP RSR / International RSR 251	Studio 4, Radiohuset, Stockholm, Sweden	JHE
Wind Cries Mary (The)	05 Sep 67	CR 3. Live performance.	Recorded Live In Europe CD Bulldog BGCD 023	Studio 4, Radiohuset, Stockholm, Sweden	JHE
Wind Cries Mary (The)	05 Sep 67	CR 3. Live performance.	Two Sides Of The Same Genius LP Amazing Kornyphone TAKRL H677	Konserthuset, Stockholm, Sweden	JHE

SONG TITLE	DATE	COMMENTS	RELEASE	LOCATION / VENUE	BAND	PERSONNEL
Wind Cries Mary (The)	05 Sep 67	CR 3. Live performance.	Fire CD The Entertainers CD297	Konserthuset, Stockholm, Sweden	JHE	
Wind Cries Mary (The)	05 Sep 67	CR 3. Live performance.	In Europe 67 / 68 / 69 CD Vulture CD 009 / 2	Konserthuset, Stockholm, Sweden	JHE	
Wind Cries Mary (The)	05 Sep 67	CR 3. Live performance.	Live CD DV More CDDV 2401	Konserthuset, Stockholm, Sweden	JHE	
Wind Cries Mary (The)	05 Sep 67	CR 3. Live performance.	Jimi Hendrix Experience CD Rockstars In Concert 6127092	Konserthuset, Stockholm, Sweden	JHE	
Wind Cries Mary (The)	05 Sep 67	CR 3. Live performance.	Foxy Lady CD Alegra CD 9008	Konserthuset, Stockholm, Sweden	JHE	
Wind Cries Mary (The)	05 Sep 67	CR 3. Live performance.	Loaded Guitar LP Starlight SL 87013	Konserthuset, Stockholm, Sweden	JHE	
Wind Cries Mary (The)	05 Sep 67	CR 3. Live performance.	Greatest Hits Live CD Chartbusters CHER 089A	Konserthuset, Stockholm, Sweden	JHE	
Wind Cries Mary (The)	09 Oct 67	BR 4. Live performance.	Wild Man Of Pop Plays Vol 2, The CD Pyramid RFTCD 004	L' Olympia Theatre, Paris, France	JHE	
Wind Cries Mary (The)	07 Jan 68	BR 5. Live performance.	Live In Paris 66 / 67 CD Whoopy Cat WKP 0012	Tivolis Konsertsal, Copenhagen, Denmark	JHE	
Wind Cries Mary (The)	07 Jan 68	BR 5. Live performance.	Cat's Squirrel CD CS 001 / 2	Tivolis Konsertsal, Copenhagen, Denmark	JHE	
Wind Cries Mary (The)	07 Jan 68	BR 5. Live performance.	Fuckin' His Guitar For Denmark LP Polymore Or JH CO	Tivolis Konsertsal, Copenhagen, Denmark	JHE	
Wind Cries Mary (The)	08 Jan 68	BR 6. Live performance.	Lost In Sweden CD Whoopy Cat WKP 0046 / 0047	Konserthuset, Stockholm, Sweden	JHE	
Wind Cries Mary (The)	29 Jan 68	CR 4. Live performance.	Live In Paris CD Swingin' Pig TSP-016	L' Olympia Theatre, Paris, France	JHE	
Wind Cries Mary (The)	29 Jan 68	CR 4. Live performance.	Stages Paris 68 (CR) CD Reprise 9 27632-2	L' Olympia Theatre, Paris, France 2nd Show	JHE	
Wind Cries Mary (The)	29 Jan 68	CR 4. Live performance.	Once Upon A Time CD Wall Of Sound WS CD011	L' Olympia Theatre, Paris, France 2nd Show	JHE	

Title	Date	CR/BR	Release	Comment	Location	Artist	Musicians
Wind Cries Mary (The)	29 Jan 68	CR 4. Live performance.	Official Bootleg Album, The CD Yellow Dog YD 051		L' Olympia Theatre, Paris, France 2nd Show	JHE	
Wind Cries Mary (The)	29 Jan 68	CR 4. Live performance.	Recorded Live In Europe CD Bulldog BGCD 023		L' Olympia Theatre, Paris, France 2nd Show	JHE	
Wind Cries Mary (The)	29 Jan 68	CR 4. Live performance.	In Europe 67 / 68 / 69 CD Vulture CD 009 / 2		L' Olympia Theatre, Paris, France 2nd Show	JHE	
Wind Cries Mary (The)	29 Jan 68	CR 4. Live performance.	Very Best, The CD Irec / Retro MILCD-03		L' Olympia Theatre, Paris, France 2nd Show	JHE	
Wind Cries Mary (The)	29 Jan 68	CR 4. Live performance.	Anthology CD Box 9		L' Olympia Theatre, Paris, France 2nd Show	JHE	
Wind Cries Mary (The)	16 Feb 68	BR 7. Live performance.	Biggest Square In The Building, The CD Reverb Music 1993		State Fair Music Hall, Dallas, TX	JHE	
Wind Cries Mary (The)	16 Feb 68	BR 7. Live performance.	Scuse Me While I Kiss The Sky CD Sonic Zoom SZ 1001		State Fair Music Hall, Dallas, TX	JHE	
Wind Cries Mary (The)	17 Feb 68	BR 8. Live performance.	Remember The Alamo CD		Will Rogers Auditorium, Fort Worth, T X	JHE	
Wind Cries Mary (The)	25 Feb 68	BR 9. Live performance.	Winterland Vol 2 CD Whoopy Cat WKP 00279 / 28		Civic Opera House, Chicago, IL	JHE	
Woodstock	?? / ?? / ??	BR 1.	Screaming Eagle CD Pink Poodle POO 001	The jury is still out as to whether Jimi is even on this or not. Some claim that Jimi plays bass on this.	Unknown	Jimi	Buddy Miles / Drums, Stephen Stills / Keyboards, John Sebastian / Guitar
Woodstock Improvisation	18 Aug 69	CR	At Woodstock (CR) Laserdisc BMG BVLP 86	Not listed on most Woodstock releases, this is a bit of improvising between "Purple Haze" and "Villanova Junction". It was listed on the CR. That's why it's listed here.	Woodstock Music And Art Fair, Bethel, NY	GSRB	
Woodstock Improvisation	18 Aug 69	CR	Woodstock (CR) CD MCA 11063	Not listed on most Woodstock releases, this is a bit of improvising between "Purple Haze" and "Villanova Junction". It was listed on the CR. That's why it's listed here.	Woodstock Music And Art Fair, Bethel, NY	GSRB	
World Traveler	11 Feb 69	BR 1. Recorded at the same time as "Young / Hendrix", "Fuzzy Guitar" and "It's Too Bad".	Electric Anniversary Jimi CD Midnight Beat MBCD 024		Record Plant, New York, NY	Jimi	Lee Michaels / Keyboards, Buddy Miles / Drums
World Traveler	11 Feb 69	BR 1. Recorded at the same time as "Young / Hendrix", "Fuzzy Guitar" and "It's Too Bad".	Ladyland In Flames LP Marshall Records JIMI 1,2,3,4		Record Plant, New York, NY	Jimi	Lee Michaels / Keyboards, Buddy Miles / Drums

SONG TITLE	DATE	COMMENTS	RELEASE	LOCATION / VENUE	BAND	PERSONNEL
World Traveler	11 Feb 69	BR 1. Recorded at the same time as "Young / Hendrix", "Fuzzy Guitar" and "It's Too Bad".	Freak Out Jam CD GH 002	Record Plant, New York, NY	Jimi	Lee Michaels / Keyboards, Buddy Miles / Drums
World Traveler	11 Feb 69	BR 1. Recorded at the same time as "Young / Hendrix", "Fuzzy Guitar" and "It's Too Bad".	Flames CD Missing In Action ACT 1	Record Plant, New York, NY	Jimi	Lee Michaels / Keyboards, Buddy Miles / Drums
World Traveler	11 Feb 69	BR 1. Recorded at the same time as "Young / Hendrix", "Fuzzy Guitar" and "It's Too Bad".	McLaughlin Sessions, The CD HML CD 9409	Record Plant, New York, NY	Jimi	Lee Michaels / Keyboards, Buddy Miles / Drums
World Traveler (Bad Feelings)	11 Feb 69	BR 1. Recorded at the same time as "Young / Hendrix", "Fuzzy Guitar" and "It's Too Bad".	Redskin' Jammin' CD JH 01 / 02	Record Plant, New York, NY	Jimi	Lee Michaels / Keyboards, Buddy Miles / Drums
You Can't Use My Name	?? Jul 67	The studio chat with Ed Chalpin where Jimi tells him that "You can't use my name" on the session recordings that he was con- tractually obligated to do.	You Can't Use My Name L P Rock Folders 2, Q 9020	Dimensional Sound Studios, New York, NY	Cks	
You Got Me Floating	03 Oct 67	CR 1 mix 1 (stereo)	Axis: Bold As Love (CR) CD MCACD 11601	Olympic Sound Studios, London, England	JHE	Trevor Burton / Backing Vocals, Graham Nash / Backing Vocals
You Got Me Floating	03 Oct 67	CR 1 mix 2. (mono)	Axis: Bold As Love (CR) LP Track 612 003	Olympic Sound Studios, London, England	JHE	Trevor Burton / Backing Vocals, Graham Nash / Backing Vocals
You Got Me Floating	03 Oct 67	CR 1 mix 3. An alternate mix of CR 1 Mix 1 with some of the backwards guitar overdub left out.	Axis: Bold As Love (CR) LP Backtrack 11	Olympic Sound Studios, London, England	JHE	Trevor Burton / Backing Vocals, Graham Nash / Backing Vocals
You Got Me Floating	03 Oct 67	CR 1 mix 4. Unused mix of the CR 1 mix 1.	Sotheby's Reels, The CD Gold Standard TOM-800	Olympic Sound Studios, London, England	JHE	Trevor Burton / Backing Vocals, Graham Nash / Backing Vocals
You Got Me Floating	03 Oct 67	CR 1 mix 4. Unused mix of the CR 1 mix 1. Incomplete	Get The Experience CD Invasion Unlimited IU 9424-1	Olympic Sound Studios, London, England	JHE	Trevor Burton / Backing Vocals, Graham Nash / Backing Vocals
You Make Me Feel	?? Aug 69	BR 1. Part of what appears to be a longer session from Jimi's Shokan House.	Dante's Inferno CD Pink Poodle POO 002	Shokan House, Woodstock, NY	GSRB	
You Make Me Feel	?? Aug 69	BR 1. Part of what appears to be a longer session from Jimi's Shokan House.	Electric Anniversary Jimi CD Midnight Beat MBCD 024	Hit Factory, New York, NY	GSRB	
Young / Hendrix	14 May 69	CR 1 mix 1.	Nine To The Universe (CR) LP Reprise HS2299	Record Plant, New York, NY	Jimi	Billy Cox / Bass, Larry Young / Keyboards
Young / Hendrix	14 May 69	CR 1 mix 1.	Message From Nine To The Universe CD Oil Well 122	Record Plant, New York, NY	Jimi	Billy Cox / Bass, Larry Young / Keyboards
Young / Hendrix	14 May 69	CR 1 mix 2. The long take which the CR was edited from. This is the longest available version.	Dante's Inferno CD Pink Poodle POO 002	Record Plant, New York, NY	Jimi	Billy Cox / Bass, Larry Young / Keyboards

Young / Hendrix (Live At The Burwood)	14 May 69	CR 1 mix 2. The long take which the CR was edited from. Incomplete.	McLaughlin Sessions, The CD HML CD 9409	Record Plant, New York, NY	Jimi	Billy Cox / Bass, Larry Young / Keyboards
Young / Hendrix (Tarot Mistress)	14 May 69	CR 1 mix 2. The long take which the CR was edited from. Yes, this is repeated on the same disc and yes, it's still incomplete.	McLaughlin Sessions, The CD HML CD 9409	Record Plant, New York, NY	Jimi	Billy Cox / Bass, Larry Young / Keyboards

END OF SONG INDEX

About The Authors

I was schooled by radio and records.
My teachers were common sense and imagination.
Jimi: Berlin 1969

About the Authors

Belmo

Belmo (aka: Scott F. Belmer) has loved the music of Jimi Hendrix ever since he heard the album 'Are You Experienced?' in 1967. For Belmo, Jimi Hendrix was the "Psychedelic Shaman" who took him places he had never gone before. Thereafter, Belmo searched out every new Hendrix release (official and unofficial) he could find. His quest continues to this day. *And he never heard surf music again!*

Belmo has written several books in his spare time: THE MYSTIC WARRIOR (1991) , THE BLACK HOLE HANDBOOK (1981), BLACK MARKET BEATLES (with co-author Jim Berkenstadt) (1995), THE BEATLES: NOT FOR SALE (1997), and THE MAKING OF THE BEATLES' SERGEANT PEPPER (1996). He is also the editor and publisher of the Beatles bootleg newsletter BELMO'S BEATLEG NEWS and editor of THE OFFICIAL ADRIAN BELEW NEWSLETTER. Belmo is a 1974 graduate of South Dakota State University, Brookings, South Dakota. Formerly a 15-year resident of Alaska, he now lives in Northern Kentucky with his wife and three cats.

Steve Loveless

Steve Loveless was first introduced to the sounds of Jimi in 1967 by his older brother with the release of the 'Are You Experienced?' LP. His love and appreciation for guitar-based rock music grew, but Jimi's music always held a special place. Steve bought his first bootleg music in his college days at Northern Michigan University in Michigan's upper peninsula in 1976, and a whole new world was opened up. After graduating in 1978 with a BFA, Steve's collection of records and tapes (and now CDs) has grown and expanded to the status of a small radio station. Steve is a contributing editor of BELMO'S BEATLEG NEWS and is active in his local arts community. He currently lives in Northern Michigan with his wife, two dogs and two cats.

I hear music in my head all the time. Sometimes it makes by brain throb
and the room starts to turn. I feel I'm going mad.
With this music we will paint pictures of earth and space
so that the listener can be taken somewhere.
Jimi: London 1968

References & Recommended Reading
Reference Books

HOT WACKS BOOK XV and Supplements 1 to 4
Author: Bob Walker
Distributed by The Hot Wacks Press
Bob Walker: Editor / Publisher of HOT WACKS BOOTLEG DISCOGRAPHIES & LED ZEPPELIN LIVE
Distributor of THE BEATLES: NOT FOR SALE by Belmo
Box 544
Owen Sound, Ontario
N4K 5R1 Canada
Fax: 519-376-9781
E-mail: hotwacks@log.on.ca
Web-site: http://www.bootlegs.com

THE GREAT WHITE WONDERS: A HISTORY OF ROCK BOOTLEGS
Author: Clinton Heylin
Penguin Books (1994)

FROM THE BENJAMIN FRANKLIN STUDIOS
Authors: Gary Geldeart and Steve Rodham
Distributed by Jimpress (1998)
108 Warrington Road,
Penketh, Warrington,
Cheshire
WA5 2JZ England

THE INNER WORLD OF JIMI HENDRIX
Author: Monika Dannemann
St. Martin's Press (1995)
JIMI HENDRIX: SESSIONS
Author: John McDermott with Billy Cox and Eddie Kramer
Little, Brown and Company (1995)

JIMI HENDRIX: THE MAN, THE MUSIC, THE MEMORABILIA
Authors: Caesar Glebbeek & Douglas J. Noble
Thunder's Mouth Press (1996)

JIMI HENDRIX: INSIDE THE EXPERIENCE
Author: Mitch Mitchell with John Platt
St. Martin's Press (1990)

JIMI HENDRIX: A VISUAL DOCUMENTARY-HIS LIVE, LOVES AND MUSIC

Author: Tony Brown
Omnibus Press (1992)

BOLD AS LOVE
Author: Frank Moriarty
Metro Books (1996)

JIMI HENDRIX: ELECTRIC GYPSY
Authors: Harry Shapiro & Caesar Glebbeek
St. Martin's Press (1997)

ARE YOU EXPERIENCED
Author: Noel Redding with Carol Appleby
Fourth Estate (1990)

JIMI HENDRIX: IN HIS OWN WORDS
Author: Tony Brown
Omnibus Press (1994)

JIMI HENDRIX: VOODOO CHILD OF THE AQUARIAN AGE
Author: David Henderson
Doubleday (1978)

THE COMPLETE GUIDE TO THE MUSIC OF JIMI HENDRIX
Author: John Robertson
Omnibus Press (1995)

* **Please Note:** If you wish to contact the authors, you may address your correspondence to: Belmo Publishing, P.O. Box 17163, Ft. Mitchell, KY 41017, USA.

If you would like a personal response, please send a large S.A.S.E. to the above address. For corrections or additions to this book, please send documentation. Also, a cassette tape of the music would also be nice so that we may hear it for ourselves.

Recommended Periodicals

JIMPRESS
108 Warrington Road
Penketh, Warrington
Cheshire
WA5 2Jz England

UNIVIBES
Coppeen, Enniskeane
County Cork
Republic Of Ireland

RELIX MAGAZINE
P.O. Box 94
Brooklyn, NY 11229

GUITAR PLAYER
411 Borel Ave. #100
San Mateo, CA 94402

MOJO
Mappin House
4 Winsley Street
London W1N 7AR
England

GUITAR WORLD
1115 Broadway
New York, NY 10010

MUSICIAN
1515 Broadway
New York, NY 10036

ICE: THE CD NEWS AUTHORITY
P.O. Box 3043
Santa Monica, CA 90408

EXPERIENCE HENDRIX
P.O. Box 4459
Seattle, WA 98104